Early Modern Women's Writing and Sor Juana Inés de la Cruz

Early Modern Women's Writing and Sor Juana Inés de la Cruz

STEPHANIE MERRIM

VANDERBILT UNIVERSITY PRESS

Nashville

99 00 01 02 03   5 4 3 2 1

This publication is made from paper that meets
the minimum requirements of ANSI/NISO Z39.48 (R 1997)
Permanence of Paper for Printed Library Materials ∞

Publication of this book was supported by generous grants from the
Program for Cultural Cooperation between Spain's Ministry of Culture
and Education and United States Universities, and from Brown University.

Library of Congress Cataloging-in-Publication Data

Merrim, Stephanie.
    Early modern women's writing and Sor Juana Inés de la Cruz /
Stephanie Merrim. – 1st ed.
    p. cm.
    Includes bibliographical references (p.) and index.

    ISBN 0-8265-1330-1 (alk. paper)
    ISBN 0-8265-1338-7 (pbk. : alk. paper)
    1. Juana Inés de la Cruz, Sister, 1651–1695–Knowledge–Women
authors. 2. Juana Inés de la Cruz, Sister, 1651–1695. Respuesta a
sor Filotea de la Cruz. 3. Women authors–History–17th century.
4. Women and literature. 5. Literature, Comparative. I. Title.
    PQ7296.J6 Z697 1999
    861–ddc21
                                    99-6029
                                    CIP

Manufactured in the United States of America

For Andrea Goff Merrim
In loving memory

Contents

Preface

When Sor Juana Inés de la Cruz surveyed the world of knowledge, she saw the interconnectedness of its many bodies. This book shares her vision and attempts to carry it into the field of early modern women's writing. To do so has entailed efforts to build bridges not only between Sor Juana's works and those of her sister writers of the early modern period but also between various special interest groups of the present. The book's introduction lays the groundwork for the first matter; here I want briefly to lay out some of the concerns that have pressed upon me in terms of the second.

My identity as a literary scholar can feel as dispersed as the pieces of Osiris's body that Isis, one of Sor Juana's most revered mythological figures, tried to assemble. As a Hispanist with comparatist leanings, I have been compelled by a desire to unite my field more fully with others. I repeat Isis's task: Hispanic literatures, as I discuss in the introduction, have too long been differed or differed themselves into a parochial insularity. More specifically, as a critic involved in women's issues, I have found it imperative to incorporate Hispanic women writers into the corpus of early modern women's literary and cultural history. As a Sor Juana scholar and as a teacher, I have committed myself to unpacking the intricacies of the Mexican writer's (and, of course, others') extraordinarily complex texts. As a critic writing in the theoretical ferment of recent years, I have found myself traversing not only several national literatures but also several of the theoretical languages or protocols that our climate affords us—and trading in an array of such languages according to the dictates of the texts.

Each component of my (happily) scattered identity and aims as a scholar may well speak to a different constituency. Though cognizant that I cannot fully satisfy often conflicting needs and interests, I have tried to keep each audience in mind. I have endeavored to provide the minimal necessary grounding for the Hispanist and for the non-Hispanist versed in any particular national literature to reach an understanding of each of the contexts that I treat. I would ask readers' indulgence with the introductory nature of some material presented and with the perhaps more than usual scrupulousness of certain arguments. Contending with Isis's task and serving Sor Juana's vision, I have striven to give this field- and bridge-building "City of Ladies" a solid granite-level foundation.

Writing with the conviction that in such a foundational enterprise the whole would speak more forcefully than its parts, and indeed, executing the book as an interconnected whole rather than as a series of autonomous essays, I have published only parts of chapter 1 (see n. 3 to chap. 1). The book has taken shape over the course of several years, basically reaching its final form at the end of 1996. During this period I have had the opportunity to lecture from it at Cambridge University, the Colegio de México, Emory University, the Graduate Center of the City College of New York, Harvard University, New York University, Princeton University, the University of Miami, the University of North Carolina at Chapel Hill, the University of Pennsylvania, Vanderbilt University, Wesleyan College, Wheaton College, Yale University, and at various conferences. Feedback from each occasion, and from colleagues and graduate students at Brown University, has greatly enriched my work.

I thank Brown University for the two sabbaticals that enabled me to complete substantial portions of the manuscript. Charles Backus and his staff at Vanderbilt University Press, particularly the editor, Bard Young, has brought the book to fruition with an enthusiasm and professionalism all too rare in the current publishing environment. Yet most of all I want to express my gratitude to the friends and colleague-friends who have sustained me during the tragic losses that have accompanied—and somehow moved—the writing of this book.

Providence, 1998

A Note on the Text: Given the comparative nature of the book and my desire that it serve various constituencies, I have presented all quotations in English, rendering only poetry and theater in both Spanish and a literal prose translation in English. For the reader's scholarly purposes, where possible and pertinent I have cited published translations and have provided page references for key texts to both the originals and the translations listed in my bibliography. *In all cases, the italicized page number refers to the English translation,* which in a few instances has been slightly modified to a more literal expression in accordance with the context of my argument. All cited translations of Sor Juana's "Respuesta," *Primero sueño,* and other poetry derive from Alan S. Trueblood's *A Sor Juana Anthology*. Original translations (i.e., where no italicized page number is given for a non-English text and/or where no translation is listed in the bibliography) in most cases owe to the good graces and skills of Frances M. López-Morillas, with my modifications. I warmly thank Frances M. López-Morillas for her efforts and the generosity that they represent.

Sor Juana Inés de la Cruz and Early Modern Women's Writing

I.

andando de texto en texto / buscando la conexión
[moving from text to text, seeking the connection]

–SOR JUANA INÉS DE LA CRUZ

One reason why I have given this book on baroque author Sor Juana Inés de la Cruz (1648–95) and other seventeenth-century women writers a title so puritanically stark, one that resists the metaphorical foreplay so common to titles, is that I suspect that the subject the title announces is provocative enough in its own right. It may provoke interest; it may even incite a not unreasonable skepticism. For on first imagining, the writings of a cloistered Catholic nun, living in colonial Mexico on the margins of the margins of almost anything embracing modernity, would appear to be an unlikely terrain for the enterprise my title announces.

Of course, Sor Juana Inés de la Cruz both bespoke, with a hyper- and self-consciousness, *and* transcended her milieu. From within the convent of San Jerónimo—whose walls were more permeable than one might assume—she corresponded widely, conversed with members of the court and her fellow intellectuals, and made contact, to a degree impossible to determine, with contemporary intellectual developments. Her knowledge of Latin gave her exceptional access to Western literature. She was extraordinarily well versed, vastly well read, in both religious and secular topics. She is considered to have amassed the largest private library in colonial Mexico; even in the small slice of it appearing in the portraits of the nun by Miguel Cabrera and Juan de Miranda, Sor Juana's collection was equipoised between science and literature, between theology, the church fathers, and the classics, between the ancients and the moderns. She wrote and published on secular themes as atypical for a nun as human love. Her remarkably extensive writings essayed and reenacted most of the (male) poetic, dramatic, theological, and even philosophical discourses of her times in the metropolis, making her works a compendium of baroque culture in its diversity and syncretism. Sor Juana's self-creation as

xi

a learned woman effectively toppled many of the walls in which she was materially enclosed and positioned her within the dynamic world of early modern European culture.

At the same time, her readings in tandem with her personal inclinations, genius, and circumstances attuned Sor Juana to the gender issues that had so greatly impacted her life, burdening it with struggles and ultimately with crises. Marginalized yet dangerously thrust into the public domain through her ever-growing fame, subordinated to church and gender hierarchies, Sor Juana developed an extraordinary radar capable of extrapolating—from the patriarchal and misogynist culture to which she was subject and in which she was an active writing subject—issues weighing on women inside and outside convent or Mexican walls, that is, certain central feminist and gender-related issues of the seventeenth-century Western world.

Yet there can be no doubt that Sor Juana's direct contact with contemporary women writers and women's writing was extremely limited; the walls remained standing. This "Tenth Muse" lived out the backhanded compliment of the denomination. Famed but painfully sui generis in her milieu, she had no female scholarly peers in Mexico, no imitators or successors in her religious order or among laywomen (Lavrin, 24). Utterly absent from Sor Juana's works are references to intellectual compatibility or collegiality with her religious sisters in the convent. Nor does it appear that Sor Juana's reading life was much richer in female companionship. Though the list of illustrious women in the nun's "Respuesta a Sor Filotea de la Cruz" [Reply to Sister Filotea de la Cruz] (1691) displays her cognizance of certain female forebears and of a few accomplished contemporary women (Christina of Sweden, the Portuguese Duchess of Aveyro, the Spanish Countess of Villaumbrosa), Sor Juana's writings as a body explicitly appeal to or echo—quite sparsely and quietly—only two women writers, both of them Spanish nuns: the Carmelite Saint Teresa of Avila (1515–82) and the Franciscan abbess, Sor María de Agreda (1602–65). I discuss at some length in chapter 4 Sor Juana's expedient conjunctions in the "Respuesta" with the voice of her famed foremother Saint Teresa; other critics have linked the two.[1] Sor María de Agreda, whose renowned mystical bilocations to New Mexico had attracted the attention of Philip IV and gained her a position as his spiritual and temporal advisor, gained Sor Juana's attention for her biography of the Virgin Mary, *La mística ciudad de Dios* [The Mystical City of God] (1670). Both the framework, of a mystical vision in which God shows Mary the mysteries of the universe over the course of nine days, and the feminist Mariolatry of the biography, its exaltation of the Virgin as equal to Christ and as a queen of wisdom, can be seen to bear on Sor Juana's "Ejercicios devotos para los nueve días antes de la purísima Encarnación del Hijo de Dios" [Devout exercises for the nine days preceding the Most Pure Incarnation of the Son of God] (4.406).[2] There, for example, in her sole reference to María de Agreda outside the "Respuesta," Sor Juana states, "The Venerable María de Jesús [de Agreda] tells of the ineffable favors that His Divine Majesty wrought for His specially chosen and most Christian Mother.

. . . Among them was showing her the whole creation of the Universe and causing all its creatures to proclaim her queen" (4.476).

The poetics of Sor Juana's connection in this and other of her works to María de Agreda, as well as their politics,[3] are a fascinating subject, one that certainly merits further study.[4] Nevertheless, and compelling as the matter may be, such is not the subject of this study. My subject here is more oblique, far more perverse, conceivably also more significant in a larger arena. Simply put, in the main I will be examining connections between the writings of Sor Juana and works not that she probably knew—but that in all reasonable probability she did not know—in order to map out certain signal features and concerns of early modern women's writing in Spanish, English, and French. My undertaking may strike the reader as suspiciously baroque in its propensity to the unusual or bizarre. Although I do perform some seemingly unlikely comparisons, my desire is not to startle but at once to tease out and to articulate commonalities between seventeenth-century women writers, and equally, to open a gateway to further comparative work: not only studies of Sor Juana in a wider framework but also the consideration of seventeenth-century women's issues that would do more justice to a Hispanic perspective.

The paucity of both types of outreachings, I believe, warrants consideration. Let me begin with my mother field. Hispanists, Sor Juana scholars, have naturally been daunted from comparative work by the formidable and respectable challenge of coming to knowledgeable terms with Sor Juana's work per se. Her oeuvre is not only vast (about nine hundred pages in an edition with no notes), but also generically varied, ideologically and philosophically complex, and remarkably difficult even on the entry levels of syntax and semantics. Scholarly work has only recently made inroads into encompassing Sor Juana's full corpus of works. Critics who have ventured into comparative work on Sor Juana and women's writing have generally attempted to establish connections with other Hispanic writers, in Spain or Spanish America. There they face another considerable challenge: a relative lack of subjects for comparison, especially in terms of women writing on secular subjects. Few Spanish and even fewer Latin American women writers published or gained renown at the time; the archaeological groundwork of exhuming forgotten voices is actively under way as I write. Even Octavio Paz's purportedly exhaustive, massive study (some 540 pages), *Sor Juana*, expansive and universalizing on so many other fronts, fails notably to add to our knowledge of her place in a colonial or wider female literary milieu.[5] The tendency to succumb to the Tenth Muse trap—that is, to view Sor Juana in isolation, as an isolated ex-centric phenomenon—persists.[6]

The last twenty years have witnessed an explosion of efforts to recoup the women's worlds of the early modern period on social, political, historical, and cultural grounds. I refer to such valuable contributions as *Beyond Their Sex: Learned Women of the European Past* (ed. Patricia H. Labalme), *The Creation of a Feminist Consciousness: From the Middle Ages to Eighteen-Seventy* (Gerda Lerner), *Female Scholars: A Tradition of Learned Women Before 1800* (ed. J. R.

Brink), *A History of Their Own: Women in Europe from Prehistory to the Present*, vol. 2 (Bonnie S. Anderson and Judith P. Zinsser), *A History of Women in the West: Renaissance and Enlightenment Paradoxes* (eds. Natalie Zemon Davis and Arlette Farge), *Renaissance Feminism* (Constance Jordan), *Women of the Renaissance* (Margaret L. King), *Women in the Middle Ages and the Renaissance: Literary and Historical Perspectives* (ed. Mary Beth Rose), and so on. All of these studies provide much-needed specific information and general paradigms on which to build. Yet even they, with their self-stated missions of inclusiveness, tend to focus on England, France, and Italy, or some combination thereof, often to the entire exclusion of Spain. Spanish (and, more so, Latin American) women generally appear, if at all, in an ancillary, token, or underinformed and undertheorized capacity. Where general historians of the early modern period or of the baroque as a (male) literary/artistic phenomenon would hardly neglect Spain, women's studies has not yet fully embraced the Hispanic context.[7] Do we ascribe this lack to default or to design? My previous paragraph could explain certain of the considerable barriers that would lead to default. With regard to design, one might speculate that the backwaters of the Counter-Reformation Hispanic worlds, so officially and militantly intransigent in the face of encroaching modernization, hardly afford a propitious territory for a feminist history of any heroic proportions. I hesitate to attribute any so skewed a design to the design of the above studies; suffice it to note the lesser prominence they accord the Hispanic worlds and to let readers draw their own conclusions.

In the introduction to my edited collection, *Feminist Perspectives on Sor Juana Inés de la Cruz* (1991), I wrote: "To my mind ... the most challenging act of revision facing us—practically a *terra incognita*—entails situating Sor Juana's work within the traditions of women's writing, both universal and within her own milieu" (25). The preceding discussion indicates that the situation upon which these lines reflect has not changed all that significantly in the intervening years (I write now in 1996). When I began to surmount my own provinciality as a Sor Juana scholar and to delve into the larger terrain in which I believe her works both warrant and merit positioning, I soon encountered a vast body of works establishing that Sor Juana's self-defense and defense of women's education, the "Respuesta," was neither sui generis nor did it emerge ex nihilo. Listened to carefully, Sor Juana herself articulates an awareness that she writes in a tradition of feminist debates: in her catalog of illustrious women mentioned above, Sor Juana employs the *brevitatis formula* and states that she will omit further names of women "to avoid relaying what others have said" (Trueblood *229*, 4.462; all translations of Sor Juana with a page citation, unless otherwise stated, derive from Trueblood). Sor Juana in all likelihood refers principally to Boccaccio's biographies of virtuous women in his *De Mulieribus Claris* (ca. 1380), yet her words need not limit us to pinpointing yet another of the nun's sources or to arguing for Sor Juana's direct knowledge of particular early modern feminist texts.[8] Rather, they may authorize us to re-place the "Respuesta" in the early modern feminist debates known as the *querelle des femmes* (which so often drew on Boccaccio). I will now proceed to do so, as a preliminary, concrete, and manifest indication of what can accrue from viewing Sor Juana without walls, that is, from situating her works within a larger context and from bodying forth the enhanced dialogue of commonalities that emerges from the interplay.[9]

The *querelle des femmes*, it is well known, formally began with Christine de Pizan's defense of women in her 1403–4 *Book of the City of Ladies* (which culled three-fourths of its examples of women from Boccaccio [Richards's introduction to Pizan, xxxvi]), sparked by Jean de Meun's misogynist attacks in his edition of the *Roman de la Rose*. Prior to Christine, no female had spoken out in the vernacular on issues pertaining to women (Richards, xxviii). Christine, revolutionary for her time, insisted that women be educated; she refocused the medieval debate on women onto the issue of misogyny itself and opened the debate to women themselves (Kelly, 15). The *Book of the City of Ladies* spawned feminist debates in several countries and languages that lasted well into the seventeenth century and that were conducted by women and men in genres as varied as histories, conduct books, pamphlets, letters, dialogues, romances, sermons, and treatises on government. The *querelle* as set by Christine de Pizan became the bedrock and staple of early modern feminist discourse on gender difference in Europe. Overly involved with moral issues to the neglect of social and legal concerns, often abstract, intellectual, and rhetorical—sometimes degenerating into mere exercises in logic—the entrenched lines of the *querelle* nevertheless helped build the foundations for a more activist feminism (Henderson and McManus, 31) and kept feminist issues alive over the course of three centuries.[10]

Subsequent chapters of the present study examine specific ideological and thematic concerns of the *querelle* as they pertain to Sor Juana and other of her female contemporaries. At this point I want to focus on the building blocks of the pro-female side of the debate, the most concrete links to the "Respuesta": its forms of argumentation. As did most of the ideological issues of the *querelle* remain constant (my chapter 5 brings out the most important evolutionary matters), so did its tactics. They have been grouped into three areas.[11] Be they male or female, participants in the *querelle* over the centuries argued, as I have already suggested, by example. Endowing historical, legendary, literary, mythical, and biblical women with an equal degree of reality, in their catalogs of illustrious females they cited exemplary women who belie and defy misogynist constructions of the female sex. Their select examples, as feminists were well aware, could not fully stanch the predominant tide against all women. Therefore, *querelle* debaters also turned to the powerful weapon of argument by authority, pitting the words of the patriarchs themselves against patriarchal misogyny. That is, employing proof texts to support their positions, they quoted a wide range of male writers considered authoritative—biblical, classical, or contemporary—who defended women. Though such authorities were not entirely lacking (Plato served them in good stead), pro-female writers hard-pressed by the weight of patriarchal tradition against their position often resorted to manipulation of that tradition, taking proof texts out of context and/or glossing them willfully to suit their purposes. Finally, the feminists argued by means of sheer reason. They constructed polemical texts that appealed to self-evident common sense, that displayed an admirable internal logic, and whose counterattacks deflected onto men precisely the same accusations that they had levied against women. When wielded by female authors, it is clear, all of the above techniques acquired a special pungency and implicit efficacy. For the impressive displays of erudition and logic that they manifest tacitly but patently deflated prevailing contentions that women were capable neither of learning nor of reason. Form merged with content and, moreover, propelled women into the audacious act, albeit at times under cover of male authorities, of challenging patriarchal authority and culture.[12]

Anyone familiar with Sor Juana's "Respuesta a Sor Filotea de la Cruz" will already have recognized in the foregoing description of general *querelle* techniques—which, I might note, was drawn from discussions of the controversy in England and France—the essential ploys it uses to defend women's learning. The same reader will also now begin to hear an uncanny doubling of voices in authors as far removed in space and milieu as the Mexican Sor Juana Inés de la Cruz and the French Marie de Gournay (1565–1645): a professional writer, a secular author, an uncompromisingly independent woman who led her own literary salon. In what Domna Stanton calls "a classic instance of the workings of the phallacious mentality" (1983, 11), Marie de Gournay's achievements have largely been linked with those of Montaigne, for he named her his "fille d'alliance" or adopted daughter, and she published eleven editions of his work. However, among other accomplishments, the magnificently learned yet self-taught Marie de Gournay was the first woman of her time to write on the French language, the author of one of the first *romans d'analyse* in France (*Le Proumenoir de Monsieur de Montaigne*, The Walking-Book of Monsieur de Montaigne [1594]), and most important for our present concerns, the first early modern female to publish separate feminist pamphlets in France: *Egalité des hommes et des femmes* [The Equality of Men and Women] (1622) and *Grief des dames* [The Ladies' Grievance] (1626). Both texts exhibit De Gournay's characteristic audacity and brio, for, unlike Sor Juana, she was unconstrained and unrestrained in asserting her radical opinions no matter what opprobrium they incited. Yet a reading of the first of her defenses of women, more impersonal and far-ranging in its arguments than the second, finds the outspoken, wickedly clever De Gournay structuring her argument along the same lines and using the same tactics as the restrained, equally clever (and at times wickedly so) Sor Juana. The parallels are at heart mechanical, and I mean them to be so; at the same time, they demonstrate how two learned, acutely intelligent women could and did similarly extrapolate from the set features of the *querelle*, to great polemical effect.[13] Neither author "swerves" from the *querelle*, which channeled and authorized her feminist voice. Rather, as if in chorus or in tandem, both maximize the potential of the debate in the same directions by bringing to bear on it their special energies and abilities.

Reason and erudition form the cornerstone of both authors' texts. In the spirit of the Christian doctrine of the baptismal equality of souls invoked more than once by Sor Juana in her poetry, De Gournay claims originality for her treatise by arguing reasonably not for the superiority of women but for the equality of the sexes ("I flee all extremes and am content to make women equal to men" [15]).[14] Sor Juana riddles her text, in both its autobiographical and its impersonal sections, with an erudition so dense as to make it almost inaccessible to the modern reader: with quotes in Latin, with citations, maxims, and proof texts from the classics and church fathers. De Gournay invokes in rapid succession a gamut of authorities ranging from Plato to Saint Jerome to Montaigne. Clearly, from their disadvantaged position as women, both argue primarily through authority. De Gournay articulates this very strategy ("I will not claim at this time that I can prove my point by arguments . . . only by referring to the authority of God himself and of the pillars of His Church and of the great men who served as guiding lights of the universe" [16]); Sor Juana consciously subscribes to it, among other ways by repeatedly and explicitly placing her most audacious arguments under the auspices of Dr. Juan Díaz de Arce, noted theologian and rector of the University of Mexico, and by revealing contradictions in Saint Paul (I will discuss the intricacies of her strategy in more detail shortly, and throughout the book). De Gournay goes so far as to transfigure that staple of the misogynists' arguments, Aristotle, into a defender of women (18); Sor Juana willfully transforms the arguments of another noted misogynist, Saint Jerome, by taking them out of context and manipulating them to support her contention that women should be educated. Nor does De Gournay fail to support women's education, proposing a radical view of women's unlimited abilities (that will be examined in chapter 5).

Radical as her views on education may be, both she and Sor Juana construct their most shockingly extreme and imaginative, yet most magisterially reasoned, key arguments around Christ himself. De Gournay queries: The sexes being equal, why was Christ not born a woman? She reasons the matter through on the basis of common sense: if Christ were a woman, he would not have been able to circulate so freely in society. In any case, Christ was born from the body of the most perfect of women (21). Further, she concludes with a flourish, there is no reason to assume that God is either masculine or feminine ("Beside, whoever is so stupid to imagine God to be either masculine or feminine openly shows that he is as bad a philosopher as a theologian" [21]). Sor Juana, for her part, devotes an extensive and astonishing section of the "Respuesta" to comparing herself, as a woman ostracized and martyred for her intelligence, with the suffering experienced by Christ due to his exceptionality (chapter 4 deals with this argument in more detail).

Neither Sor Juana nor Marie de Gournay, finally, could neglect argumentation through example, much as the latter says that she will ("I will not claim at this time that I can prove my point by means of . . . examples, since that is much too common" [*16*]), displaying, as does Sor Juana, the cognizance that she participates in a feminist tradition. Both authors, writing at the tail end of a centuries-long debate by example, utilize the *brevitatis formula* to render their lists of women self-consciously metonymical. Both "contemporize" their lists of women by mentioning women of recent times.

The question has been raised whether women's contributions to the *querelle des femmes* display traits different from men's. Henderson and McManus, for example, maintain that female debaters in England "infused the controversy with passion, conviction, and a new sense of purpose" (20). Certainly, both Sor Juana and De Gournay argue in deadly earnest, eschewing the tendency to jest and specious intellectual calisthenics found in certain male texts of the *querelle*. Further, both of De Gournay's defenses of women are infused with animus and crafted with what for the times would be labeled *virulence*. Even in *Egalité*, the more reticent of the two tracts, De Gournay shoots acerbic barbs at the other sex, asserting that men who denigrate women, and thus contravene all intelligent opinion of all times, must be idiots (*18*). And even Sor Juana, despite the very real risks involved in so doing, cannot resist hurling a few trenchant criticisms back at her accusers. De Gournay's tone is more inflamed, her attacks more frontal and frequent. Yet given Sor Juana's muffled and clearly stifled tendency toward sarcasm (as will be suggested further by her "Autodefensa espiritual," Spiritual Self-Defense) and the other striking similarities we have seen between the two learned women, one is left with the sense that the true voice of Sor Juana, if as unfettered as that of Marie de Gournay and were we to have heard it, might well sound even more remarkably like that of her French feminist counterpart.

When Marie de Gournay and Sor Juana undertake to frame effective defenses of women's rights to education, they cannot help engaging with patristic theology, and especially, as they both do, with Saint Paul, the voice most insistently cited throughout the Christian era in opposition to women's learning. Misogynist church tradition spurred the inception of the *querelle* and continued in the early modern period to present the most redoubtable obstacle to women's equal rights, shaping "ideas of gender of society in general" (Lerner, 24). The writings of Saint Paul served as the prime movers of Christian misogyny. In general, Saint Paul viewed women as responsible for the Fall, marriage as inferior to virginity, and the husband as the head of his wife much as Christ was the head of the church (Altman, 13). With regard to two of the central issues that so preoccupied the *querelle*, the subordinate place of women and women's learning, the most damning and oft-cited texts of Saint Paul were 1 Corinthians 14, especially verses 34–35 ("As in all the churches of the saints, the woman should keep silence in the churches. For they are not permitted to speak, but should be subordinate, as even the law says. If there is anything they desire to know, let them ask their husbands at home. For it is shameful for a woman to speak in church") and 1 Timothy 2:11–12 ("Let a woman learn in silence with all submissiveness. I permit no woman to teach or to have authority over men; she is to keep silent").[15]

"These biblical core texts," writes Gerda Lerner, "sat like huge boulders across the paths women had to travel in order to define themselves as equals to men. No wonder they engaged in theological reinterpretation before they could move on to other, more original and creative ideas" (138). Lerner also notes that women reinterpreting the Bible followed predictable patterns (159).

Biblical core texts, always looming in the way of feminists, created unlikely bedfellows. While Marie de Gournay, a secular writer, negates Saint Paul with two brief arguments,[16] both the religiously aligned Sor Juana, a Mexican Catholic, and Margaret Fell (1614–1702), a British Quaker activist, recognizing the centrality of Saint Paul's dicta regarding women to church and social policy, place the refutation of them at the very heart of their feminist apologetics. The scriptural hermeneutics of Margaret Fell's "Women's Speaking Justified by the Scriptures" (1667) and Sor Juana's "Respuesta" keep circling back compulsively to the epistles of Saint Paul, hammering away at them time and again from different angles in the tenacious effort to dissolve once and for all what Fell explicitly calls this major "stumbling block" (12).

The pronouncements of Saint Paul were a most critical stumbling block indeed to one of the central tenets of the Quaker movement, which, challenging the patriarchal relegation of women to the private sphere, maintained that they can speak in a public religious context. George Fox, the founder of the movement (and Fell's husband as of 1669), traveled widely to champion the establishment of women's meetings, entirely administered by women. Fell, one of the most remarkable women of the seventeenth century, defended pacifism as well as women's public speech through the meetings she held at Swarthmoor Hall and in her writings. Both Fox and Fell suffered imprisonment and penury for their beliefs. In 1656, George Fox published "The Woman Learning in Silence," in which he contended that "the spirit of Christ [may] speak in the female as well as in the male" (quoted by Latt in Fell, v). Though the title of his tract clearly alludes to Saint Paul, Fox builds his case from other scriptures; of the Pauline epistles he merely says, "[S]ome are hard to be understood" (Fell, vi). Margaret Fell took up the gauntlet of dealing directly with Saint Paul in her "Women's Speaking Justified," a text first published in 1666 and again, with two further discussions of the apostle's writings, in 1667.

Fell's treatise, a theological offshoot of the *querelle*, avails itself of the established techniques of the "woman question." Fell argues by example, limiting herself to biblical women who prophesied (like De Gournay and Sor Juana, Fell refers to the Sibyls) and to women favored by God and Christ. She also argues by reason: shrewdly pointing out, for example, that present-day ministers themselves use the words of Old and New Testament women in their sermons (14) or unabashedly labeling as heretics those who misinterpret Saint Paul (17). Fell's prime focus, however, is scriptural, and it is there that she performs her most brilliant maneuvers—among them, innovative uses of argument by authority. Structurally and scripturally, Fell subordinates Saint Paul (or as she would have it, the mistaken interpretations of his writings) to the higher authorities of God and Christ. While the very first paragraph of her text states that "the Apostles words" in Corinthians and Timothy have provided the fodder for "Objections" "against Women speaking in the Church" (3), she immediately segues to "how God himself hath manifested his Will and Mind concerning women, and unto women" (3). Here appear snippets of the wayward Genesis, and 1 and 2 Corinthians, pressed into service of the feminist cause.

After this, Fell begins in earnest her revisionist reading of the problematic Pauline texts. She contextualizes them in two extremely convincing ways. First, she reads the offending lines within the context of the whole chapter 14 of Corinthians where, she holds, Saint Paul exhorts "the *Corinthians* unto charity, and to desire Spiritual gifts, and not to speak in an unknown tongue" (8). Second, and significantly both for feminist hermeneutics and for our understanding of Corinthians in general,[17] she lays bare the specific historical context that his words address: faced with the general disorder and macaronic nature of the Corinthian congregation (with its share of "loose" women), when Saint Paul exhorts "women" to silence he in fact refers to *all* disruptive elements. In effect, women are but a metonymy for all persons "in confusion" (8). Fell then launches into an impressive anagogic reading of Saint Paul, maintaining (again in effect) that Saint Paul intends "women" not just metonymically but metaphorically. That is, "women" signify all those who "were under the Law"—those who had not yet received Christ. She later clarifies her allegorical argument, saying, "But *Jezebel*, and Tatlers, and the Whore that denies Revelation and Prophesie, are not permitted" (17). For De Gournay, Christ might have been born a woman; in Fell's metaphorical contestation to Saint Paul, "the Church of Christ is a woman, and those that speak against the womans speaking, speak against the Church of Christ" (5). If here Fell exercises her interpretive abilities on Saint Paul's mandates, throughout the essay she capitalizes on her knowledge of Scripture to allow Saint Paul to elucidate his own words, thus neutralizing their misogynist potency. Quoting a variety of Pauline texts, Fell brings to the fore the diverse attitudes toward women contained in the apostle's writings, a matter of great interest to present-day theologians.[18] In pointing out these inconsistencies Fell views them not as contradictions but as incontrovertible evidence that 1 Corinthians and 1 Timothy have been falsely interpreted as monolithic injunctions against women. For example, she questions, "for if he [Saint Paul] had stopt Womens praying or prophesying, why doth he say: *Every man praying or prophesying having his head covered, dishonoureth his head; but every Woman that prayeth or prophesieth with her head uncovered, dishonoureth her head?*" (9; italics in original).

Margaret Fell devotes her treatise, its addendum, and its postscript to the deconstruction of Saint Paul's seemingly unshakable dicta. Sor Juana directly and indirectly makes Saint Paul the magnetic axis of her entire *prueba* section, the section that adduces general proofs to support an argument. He even seeps into the more personal, emotive closing section, the *peroratio*.[19] The

broad patterns as well as the particular arguments of Sor Juana's destabilizing
reading of Saint Paul exactly parallel those of Fell (with the exception of the
allegorical angle). However, the Mexican nun's impeccable logic galvanizes
the elements I have just outlined vis-à-vis "Women's Speaking Justified" into a
strategy so imbricated and mercurial that only a line-by-line analysis could do
it justice. Out of consideration for my reader I will restrain myself, and just follow in their particularity and as representative of the whole the convolutions
of the early parts of her first assault on 1 Corinthians14.

As suggested in my preceding discussion of De Gournay's and Sor Juana's
arguments by authority, the "Respuesta" introduces Saint Paul through the
offices of Juan Díaz de Arce ("in virtue and cultivation a worthy professor of
Scripture" [*229*, 4.462]). Sor Juana has this authority raise the crucial question, as he does in his *Studioso Bibliorum*, of whether it is permissible for
women to study and to interpret the Bible. She then has Arce be the first to
present in the "Respuesta" Saint Paul's "Let women keep silence in the
churches: for it is not permitted them to speak," as an authoritative dictum
that the authoritative Arce himself counters in his work. He does so by calling upon other words by the apostle that contradict the foregoing: the passage addressed to Titus in which Saint Paul mentions the "aged women, in
like manner, in holy attire . . . teaching well" (*229*, 462; ellipses in original).[20]
From these words—suspiciously decontextualized—Arce concludes and
resolves, as Sor Juana recaps, "that to lecture publicly in the classroom and
to preach in the pulpit are not legitimate activities for women, but that studying, writing, and teaching privately are not only allowable but most edifying
and useful" (*229*, 462). Sor Juana now intervenes to reinforce Arce's party-
line Christian feminism with an equally inoffensive, yet clearly self-referential,
qualification of her own. Arce does not mean, she says, that all women
should study, etc., but only those "whom God has endowed with particular
virtue and discernment and who have become highly accomplished and erudite, and possess the talents and other qualities needed for such holy pursuits" (*229–30*, 462). Her mild statement, consistent with sixteenth-century
arguments linking education and virtue, at the same time serves as a jump-
ing-off point for more daring interpretive and rhetorical flights on the nun's
part. Sor Juana, like Fell, construes Saint Paul's reference to "women" as a
metonymy ("so the *taceant* applies not only to women but to everyone not
properly endowed" [*231*, 463]) and, interestingly, as a metonymy that
redounds sarcastically onto men: "So true is this that the interpretation of
Holy Scripture should be forbidden not only to women, considered so very
inept, but to men, who merely by virtue of being men consider themselves
sages, unless they are very learned and virtuous, with receptive and properly
trained minds" (*230*, 462). Taking her line of thought to its most extreme
consequences, Sor Juana attributes heresy itself to the contravention of the
doctrine she has just presented: "Failure to do so [to obey this doctrine], in
my view, has given rise precisely to all those sectarians and been the root

cause of all the heresies" (230, 462). Shortly after, in a higher register of invective, she proclaims: "Such the Divine Write became in the possession of wicked Pelagius, perverse Arius, wicked Luther, and the other heresiarchs" (230, 463). The Manichean, well-reasoned exegeses of both Sor Juana and Margaret Fell not only thoroughly invert Saint Paul's alleged misogynism, they also brand as heretical those who transgress the spirit of the apostle's words as the two feminists themselves have rescripted them!

Later portions of the *prueba* section of the "Respuesta" find Sor Juana cinching her inversion of Saint Paul's epistles: among several ways by using other writings by Saint Paul to contradict and undermine 1 Corinthians and 1 Timothy; by bending and conjugating his words with those of the other renowned misogynist, Saint Jerome, to translate them both into supporters of women's education ("Oh, how much harm would be avoided in our country if older women were as learned as Laeta and knew how to teach in the way Saint Paul and my Father Saint Jerome direct!" [232, 464]); by continuing to advocate a generalized understanding of his use of "women" ("women" refers not only to those who are incompetent to interpret Scripture but also to anyone who disturbs the silence in church [235, 467]). They also find Sor Juana explicating the historical context of Corinthians. Sor Juana's historical explanation differs from Fell's but displays an equal knowledge of the context. According to the Mexican author, Saint Paul's "Let women keep silence in the church" alludes to very particular circumstances. The women of the early church taught one another Christian doctrine in the temples, and the murmur of their voices disturbed the apostles who were preaching (233, 465–66). Sor Juana links one sententia of Saint Paul's to another, creating an explanatory system for "Let women keep silence in the church" by having the maxims illuminate each other: "And it is also written: *Audi, Israel, et tace* [Hear, Israel, and hold thy peace], words which address the whole conglomeration of men and women telling them all to maintain silence" (235, 467). This pair of Pauline texts well illustrates the significance of Sor Juana's historical contextualizations as described by Josefina Ludmer: "Here Juana teaches us a lesson in literary and ideological criticism. Dogmatic truths and hierarchical systems, she says, erase the traces of history in the text: from concrete and particular circumstances was derived an eternal and authoritarian dogma, a transcendental law regarding the difference of the sexes" (92).

That Ludmer's words are equally descriptive of Margaret Fell Fox's contribution to the *querelle* underscores the kinship between the two seventeenth-century women writers, lending further weight to the connections I have been drawing throughout the preceding pages. I believe that we can also draw several conclusions of defining import to the project at hand from the comparisons laid out to this point. As I suggested earlier and as can now be confirmed, the *querelle des femmes* constituted a pan-Western "language"— an ideological and discursive repertoire—for early modern debates of gender difference. Those familiar with the *querelle* (Margaret Fell probably among them) would inscribe their feminist polemics in its paradigms; those not necessarily familiar with the profeminist aspects of the *querelle* (Sor Juana—familiar with misogyny, with misogynist writings both secular and religious that fueled the *querelle*, and with the classics—probably among them) might just as readily coincide with them by dint of intuition, logic, rhetorical precepts, and a common cultural/ideological heritage. Due to Latin, the classics, and patristic texts, much of early modern culture transcended national boundaries. The last of the three elements I mention—patristic texts, with their never fully discharged legacy of misogyny—in particular both constantly spurred feminist debate and provided a pan-Christian imaginary with which each feminist would perforce engage. The years 1621, 1666, and 1691, as we have seen, witness feminists doing battle with the same Pauline stone wall or "stumbling block."[21] Feminism need not have been organized as such, as it is now, to evince either a feminist consciousness or a discursive commonality.

Indeed, if the texts I have analyzed are any indication, it is clear that the *querelle* and the pan-Christian imaginary gave rise to an unceasing, unwitting, almost inevitable, textual sorority between early modern feminists who were unaware of one another and who often worked in isolation. Isolation, one must note, was often their only means of negotiating a separate peace. Early modern women scholars, as Margaret L. King (1980) has established, tended to withdraw from life—from friendship, from cities, from public view—into self-styled prisons lined with books. Seventeenth-century French *précieuses* (female salon participants) may have exceptionally benefited from collective collaboration, but the solitude of, at best, book-lined cells was the fate of many early modern women writers. This puts a significant feminist contextual spin on Octavio Paz's interpretation of Sor Juana's solitude as characteristically Mexican and, in fact, renders her very isolation from her female contemporaries central and emblematic rather than ex-centric. The course of feminism was consigned by this isolation not just to an only de facto sorority but also, as Gerda Lerner so movingly tells us and as we can deduce even from the three texts we have shared, to Sisyphean repetition:

> Women were denied knowledge of their history, and thus each woman had to argue as though no woman before her had ever thought or written. Women had to use their energy to reinvent the wheel, over and over again, generation after generation. Men argued with the giants that preceded them; women argued against the oppressive weight of millennia of patriarchal thought. . . . Since they could not ground their argument in the work of women before them, thinking women of each generation had to waste their time, energy and talent on constructing their argument anew. Yet they never abandoned the effort. Generation after generation, in the face of recurrent discontinuities, women thought their way around and out from under patriarchal thought. (166)

II.

If you will walke without difference, you shall live without reverence: if you will conde[m]ne order, you must invite the shame of disorder.
—HAEC VIR, 1620

The *querelle des femmes* might have remained largely immutable over the course of the early modern period, but epochal earthquakes were taking place all around it, imbuing it with greater urgency and with the reactive virulence we have heard in the voices of De Gournay, Fell, and Sor Juana. To embrace the larger picture, which sets the stage for the following chapters, at this point I need to pan out almost immeasurably from concrete texts to the shaking contexts of the seventeenth century that bore as heavily on Sor Juana as they did on her European contemporaries. Neither here nor elsewhere do I mean to discount the specificity of each national context or to collapse the differences between them. Yet I believe that it is important to begin by delineating certain overarching patterns, deriving from negotiations between modernization and tradition, that obtained at least in England, France, and Spain: homelands of the women writers whose works the book examines and/or mother countries to the colonies from which they write. In what follows I will look (quite) synoptically at the fluctuating energies of modernization—at their circulation and containment—in these states, particularly as they pertain to women and to the concerns of the present study.

The conceptual tenets that resonate most emphatically throughout my book involve the semantic field around *tension*: paradox, ambiguity, contradiction, new economies, transvaluation, fissures, fractures, destabilization, and so on. Such terms speak equally to Sor Juana's baroque discourse and to the Januslike nature of the seventeenth century—for one scholar of the period, a series of "yoked incompatibilities" that reflect a world "disturbed to the point of schizophrenia" (Woodbridge, 325), for another, an "ambivalent phenomenon" with "one face peering perhaps at the sunset of feudalism, the other at the dawn of capitalism" (Beverley, 216). Michel Foucault characterizes the seventeenth century in more ethereal but still significant transitional terms, as a time of a shift between paradigms. (Although the Olympian abstractions of Foucault in *The Order of Things* stand at a considerable remove from social reality, not to mention women's social reality, he does raise issues that bear on these fields.) The theorist regards the seventeenth century before the onset of French classicism less as a fixed construction than as a time of unfixing, of unfastening and dissociation. For Foucault, the baroque does not constitute an episteme unto itself but instead, in a hypertrophy of what is often considered mannerism, largely entails the problematizing and dismantling of the Renaissance paradigm of similitude. Hence—and it is interesting that he takes Spain rather than France as his frame of reference—Foucault reads

Velázquez's paintings and *Don Quijote* as reifying the demise of the harmonious "prose of the world" based on an unbroken chain of similitudes and as typifying the new nonorder that dissociates signified from signifier, sign from referent. In the transitional times of the seventeenth century, similarity gives way to difference, and fixity to instability.

The profound upheavals taking place throughout Europe during the seventeenth century provide historical grounding and the necessary background for any theorizing of the era. It is practically incontrovertible that in political, religious, social, economic, and ideological terms, the seventeenth century was a time of disorder and change. "'Tis all in pieces, all coherence gone; / All just supply, and all Relation," wrote Donne (Rabb, 47). Financial recessions and poverty and plague, shifting demographics, inflation, a newly disempowered and impoverished nobility, among many factors, transformed its economic and social landscape. The revolutions of the Reformation and the Counter-Reformation continued to restructure the religious and political systems of Europe; the slow move toward the organization of the modern centralized state involved the breakup of empires and the configuration of national identities. Wars religious and secular, civil and international, consistently wracked Europe. Where the Reformation and Counter-Reformation had placed religious belief systems into question, the onset in certain countries of the scientific revolution during the latter half of the century subjected to systematic doubt all knowledge that had preceded it. In essence, and as been widely accepted by historians, these were *cultures of crises*, forged in the crucible of the larger battle between traditionalism and the questionable, problematic values of change and modernization. Antonio Maravall wrote of the seventeenth century in his *Culture of the Baroque*, "It was the spectacular and problematic breakdown of a society within which forces driving it to change struggle with other . . . forces whose object was preservation" (26).[22]

Several changes and upheavals of the seventeenth century conspired to shake women out of their traditionally prescribed places. As suggested earlier, the Quaker movement (as well as other radical Reformation sects) encouraged women to take on new, more public roles in the church. Increased urbanization in much of Europe and Mexico, bringing with it greater freedom and anonymity, began to redraw the lines of sex-specific behavior. Women in Spain chafed against their traditional near purdah confinement in the home to circulate around the cities in coaches, in disguise (as *tapadas*, veiled women), and to attend theatrical performances. Ludwig Pfandl, a twentieth-century author whose attitudes toward women will afford us dark comic relief more than once, inveighs against the new type of noble or bourgeois "worldly woman" who moved freely around Spanish cities of the Habsburgs, calling her the "corrosive product, the fruit of the dissoluteness of that period of decadence" (1929, 127). While Pfandl (without real substantiation) believes such women to be the real-life models for the stock figure in Spanish comedias of the woman who dressed as a man, women in early-seventeenth-century London are known to have worn men's clothing. There even exist reports of women attending church in male garb (Woodbridge, 142). Their behavior gave rise to the famous *Hic Mulier* pamphlet debate in 1620; its anonymous author attributes sexual inversion to city life. A woodcut on the title page of *Hic Mulier* shows one woman trying on a man's plumed hat with a diminutive man at her side, and another about to have her hair shorn. In the first paragraph of the text we read: "For since the days of Adam women were never so Masculine . . . Masculine in Number, from one to multitudes . . . Masculine in Mood, from bold speech to impudent action" (excerpted in Henderson and McManus, 265). Politically troubled times as well as urbanization undermined conventional gender roles. Especially in France, plebeian women took it upon themselves to guard the community's privileges not just by actively participating in riots but by actually inciting them (Gibson, 156; see also Davis, chap. 5). The English and French civil wars of the mid-seventeenth century, as does wartime generally, saw enhanced roles for women: the formidable French noblewomen known as the *frondeuses*, for example, played key parts in the Fronde (the Fronde, Joan De Jean asserts, "can be seen as a woman's war" [1991, 37]). Throughout Europe during the seventeenth century, the so-called manly woman and the cross-dressing woman also enter the literary arena, permeating it. Although given the insufficiency of information on women's conduct in the era, it is rather too deterministic to conclude, as does Woodbridge, that the frequency of assertive women in literature "is itself a testimony to the ubiquity of female aggression" (201), the fact that this phenomenon reached its apogee in the seventeenth century is certainly suggestive of real or widely spread *perceived* inversions of gender roles (a matter to which I return later on).[23]

Did women experience a Renaissance during the early modern period? The answer to this question remains vexed and equivocal in terms of the sixteenth century.[24] In terms of the seventeenth century, as I will proceed to argue (together with others) from perspectives that shuttle back and forth between the concrete and the symbolic, the answer must certainly be no. To begin with the first perspective, the economic developments with their attendant social changes that have led us to question the matter of a sixteenth-century Renaissance for women persisted and gained in the following century. The growth of capitalism over the course of the period tended to disenfranchise women from the labor force, to reduce women's roles, and further to polarize the sexes. Among the many manifestations of the new labor differential, one should cite the dwindling of female guilds and of women's participation in guilds, the appropriation by men of trades traditionally exercised by women, the exclusion of women from high-level productive work and their relegation to less skilled jobs, and the consequent decline of women's wages. The shift from a landed to a money economy literally devalued women's work, furnishing ever-stronger disincentives on economic and social grounds for women to work outside the home. Reformation Protestantism, fomenting the "formation of the preindustrial, patriarchal household as the basic social unit, as well as the economic unit of postfeudal society" (Kelly, 23), reinforced the transformation on ideological grounds.

With specific regard to the seventeenth century now, Evelyn Fox Keller has observed, "Alongside, and interlaced with, the economic, social, political and intellectual upheavals of this period, historians have recently begun to document a subtle but significant transformation in conceptions of and attitudes towards sexuality and gender roles" (47). A historian might well be inclined to impute such a transformation to the imperative to order generated by the reigning disorder. Absolute monarchies prevailed in seventeenth-century Spain and France; England strove over the course of the century to restore the order that had been gravely and consistently disrupted by conflicts between the concerns of the monarchy and those of Parliament. Referring to the cultures of crises across Europe, Theodore K. Rabb concludes that "throughout these metamorphoses the basic concern remained the same—in a world where everything had been thrown into doubt, where uncertainty and instability reigned, could one attain assurance, control, and a common acceptance of *some* structure . . . ?" (33). Further, and more to the point at hand, Maravall maintains that "baroque culture emerged as a complex of resources to overcome the forces of deviance or of opposition present in the society of the epoch" (125).

A feminist historian might well at this juncture make the following argument.[25] Cultures of crises devolve into crises of the patriarchy: as it strove to restore order, what Maravall denominates as pan-European baroque culture targeted women as symbolic of the general "forces of deviance" it needed to subdue.[26] Mary Elizabeth Perry, for one, in the introduction to her *Gender and Disorder in Early Modern Seville*, observes that

> symbolically, women performed roles of critical importance to a patriarchal order, signifying virtue and evil, providing a negative foil against which men could define themselves, and permitting a justification for male authority. On the basis of gender, "symbolic lines and boundaries" could be drawn, which anthropologist Mary Douglas has described as "a way of bringing order into experience." (5)

Natalie Zemon Davis, for another, states that "the female sex was thought the disorderly one par excellence in early modern Europe" (124), and then asks, "Can the unruly have been so much an issue when sovereignty was less at stake?" (150). Woman was identified with nature, and nature had changed sign in the seventeenth century from nurturing to disorderly (see Merchant, chap. 1). Woman's very physiology as then conceived—with its cold, wet humors that indicated a tricky, deceitful temperament, and its hysterical wandering womb—would render her disorderly (Davis, 124). Woman's conduct, when substantively transgressive or even when incurring minor infringements of established gender roles that provoked a disproportionate reaction, was perceived as the height of disorder.[27] It was construed to threaten the welfare of the ever more important state, one that increasingly utilized the relation of husband to wife as guiding metaphor for the relation of all subordinates to their superiors, including the sovereign (Davis, 127–28). We hear proof of Joan De Jean's important contention that "throughout France's so-called Great Century, it is clear that the principal architects of public policy promoted the belief that female rebellion posed a particular threat to the body politic" (1991, 17) in the following statements: "I cannot tolerate this liberty [of women] which can be pernicious to the whole species, prejudicial to the State, and fatal to the entire Universe," wrote Champelain in France (Albistur and Armogath, 143); Cardinal Richelieu coined the maxim in his *Testament politique* that "a Woman caused the world's fall; nothing is more capable of harming the State than this sex" (301). Further, the author of *Hic Mulier* excoriates the "monstrous" masculine woman, calling her "most pernicious to the Commonwealth, for she hath power by example to doe it a world of injury" (Woodbridge, 145).[28] Reactively, or probably more apt *proactively*, the theater of the times "insistently links female sexual excess with social disorder and disintegration" (Keller, 60), as have the foregoing paranoid pronouncements.

She who walks without difference, as the epigraph to this section—taken from the response to *Hic Mulier*—tells us, condemns order and invites disorder. The reinstituting of order, of the "Relation" that Donne found lacking, through the intransigent reinforcement of gender difference becomes a matter of great concern in the seventeenth century. As I will first examine, it entailed default on the modernizing sixteenth-century discursive position on women—and on the modernizing sixteenth-century episteme itself.

Humanist writers had broached women's issues as a consequence of their concern for the state. Attempting to bolster the secular social structure, they counteracted medieval exhortations to celibacy with defenses of marriage and of women, whom they attempted to reclaim from clerical misogyny. To vindicate women, they had to combat attitudes such as that of Saint John Chrysostom (whom Sor Juana, with yet another canny move, cites in her support): "What else is woman but a foe to friendship, an unescapable punishment, a necessary evil, a natural temptation, a desirable calamity, a domestic danger . . . ?" (Kors and Peters, 117). Though such attitudes would never disappear entirely, the humanists would rehabilitate women, reintegrating them into society. I take as an excellent example of their project the Spanish Fray Luis de León's *La perfecta casada* [The Perfect Wife] (1583), a work thoroughly invested in propagating the social and ideological norms of its time. Fray Luis outlines an ontological and pragmatic program to incorporate woman into the architecture of society and, by implication and design, into the Renaissance episteme of harmony, order, and similitude. Woman will cease to be the other, the disruptive element deleterious to society invoked by Saint John Chrysostom. She will instead become a crucial, if still subordinate, piece in the beautifully ordered, well-running machine of the Renaissance ("God wants no one in His house," says Fray Luis, "who does not perform the task He has set" [247]). To effect this transformation, Fray Luis delivers women into internal exile in the home, urges them to embody sweetness and gentleness there, allows for education to enhance their virtue, and charges them with the responsibility (no matter how harsh their husbands) of maintaining in the world of private life the tenets of an ideal public world. "Because it is a thing well known that, when a woman performs her office, her husband loves her, the family is in harmony [*concierto*], and the children learn virtue, and peace reigns, and material worth increases" (250). The *concierto* of which Fray Luis speaks resonates from regenerated woman to home to society in a symphony of seamless similitudes.

Now if at least on the programmatic level sixteenth-century humanism would extend to women its notions of inclusion and similitude,[29] the seventeenth century would resort to the principles of exclusion and difference. I take as a second emblematic example the fascinating situation surrounding the birth of modern science in England (a matter to which I return in chapter 5) examined by Evelyn Fox Keller in her *Reflections on Gender and Science*. Henry Oldenburg, secretary of the fledgling Royal Society of Science, stated its mission as that of raising a "Masculine Philosophy" (52). Joseph Glanville, one of the Society's chief propagandists, also resorted to gendered terms in delineating what the new "masculine" science opposed, that is: "the *Woman* in us who still prosecutes a deceit, like that begun in the *Garden*; and our *Understandings* are wedded to an *Eve*, as fatal as the *Mother* of our *miseries*." He concluded that truth has no chance when "the *Affections* wear the breeches and the *Female* rules" (53; italics in original). Glanville's resuscitation of medieval misogyny to launch the cause of the new science gives pause. It also supports on symbolic grounds Keller's claim, quoted above, that a renewed differential attitude toward gender had arisen in the seventeenth century. What is more, the trajectory leading up to the founding of the Royal Society traced by Keller discloses the symbolic and suggestive manner in which the new science renegotiated not the medieval but the Renaissance position on women. Appealing to the changing identification of nature with women mentioned above, Keller contrasts the sixteenth-century Paracelsians with seventeenth-century Francis Bacon. If the alchemists' root image of woman-as-nature, she writes, was "coition, the conjunction of mind and matter, the merging of male and female," that of Bacon placed emphasis "on constraint, on the disjunction between mind and nature, and ultimately on domination." Further, as "Bacon's metaphoric ideal was the virile superman, the alchemist's ideal was the hermaphrodite. Whereas Bacon sought domination, the alchemists asserted the necessity of allegorical, if not actual cooperation between male and female" (48). In sum, Keller's analysis of the new science gestures tantalizingly to an exclusivist construction of the masculine, the raising of a new masculine empire, and a relationship of domination rather than harmony between the sexes.

While Keller questions the existence of a direct relationship between the scientific issues under dispute and "the realpolitik of sexual domination" (53), evidence suggests the matter to be less problematic than she believes. For the seventeenth-century cultures of crises subjected women to ever-stricter controls. One might even maintain that women were targeted as symbolic of disorder and that they were also scapegoated in very tangible ways, as if control of the once-again disruptive element of women might restore a world turned upside down by change and turmoil. This argument gains in credibility when one considers the degree to which women, and particularly women's bodies, safeguard the essence of societal structures and order: lineage, inheritance, class, the family. As the agendas of the medieval misogynists and the humanists exemplify, and as is widely admitted, women and gender ideologies constitute a prime site for the state to enact its needs and desires. And if it were now desirable, to use the words of one seventeenth-century Spaniard, that the social orders "do not become changed, disturbed, mixed up or equivalent, but that each one preserves its place, order and harmony" (González de Cellorigo, quoted in Maravall, 132), then at the very least it can be said that an important step in achieving that world picture, which harks back nostalgically to the sixteenth century, was control of women.

Control assumed many forms. Under the guise of protection, laws clamped down on women's marital rights—to divorce, to remarriage, to their dowries. Natalie Zemon Davis stated, "Kings and political theorists saw increasing legal subjection of wives to husbands . . . as a guarantee of the obedience of both men and women to the slowly centralizing state" (128). Sumptuary laws regulated women's dress. Women's minds, and not just their bodies, came to the fore in the seventeenth century as a critical arena for subjugation: limiting access to education and severely delimiting the boundaries of that education, as my chapter 5 discusses at length, would rein in all aspects of women's lives. The church provided another, ever-present and potent, source of subject formation. Sermons, iconology, religious festivals, and so on kept their ideal and idealized women always in view. Subject formation itself, that is, vigorous didactic attempts to shape the subject (in this case, the female subject), infiltrated mass and high culture. Conduct books, *querelle* pamphlets, exemplary biographies, rolled off the presses. Broadsides, the theater, and literature alike satirized what they had catapulted into the stock types of the learned woman, the vain woman, the seductress, the shrew, the overbearing wife. Though Molière's satires of pedantic women may be the most famous, they are but one small piece of the avalanche of works produced in seventeenth-century England, France, and Spain against women climbing out of their prescribed places.

Mary Elizabeth Perry's superb *Gender and Disorder in Early Modern Seville* (1990) presents an inventory of the forms of control exercised by Counter-Reformation Spain on women as well as a paradigmatic case-in-point of reactions to disorder and the tides of change concerning the female sex. As Perry's book makes clear, chaos and bureaucracy converged in Seville. Port city for embarkation to the New World, first destination of the newly rich returning to the motherland, commercial center of the Spanish Habsburg Empire, and the fourth largest city in Europe, Seville epitomized the shakings of established order as they bore on Spain. When hordes of prostitutes plied their trade, when women whose spouses had left for the New World participated more actively in the life of the city, state and church began intensively to invoke gender prescriptions and to reinstate gender differentiation. Perry writes,

> Through the magnifying lens of early modern Seville, the order-restoring function of gender becomes especially visible. Secular and ecclesiastical officials increased their powers of social control in this city as they responded to religious schisms, developing capitalism, dramatic demographic changes, urbanization, the growth of a central state, and increasing imperial rivalries. (178)

Her book examines the concrete measures taken by civil and religious forces on several fronts. Perry brings into view that as men departed for the New World, leaving Seville largely "in the hands of women" (14), working women flourished. Gradually, however, women's work would be discredited, regulated, and displaced. In the face of changing women's roles, religious symbols emphasizing the weakness and passivity of women were called upon to fortify the traditional gender system. Those who broke sexual codes of conduct, the women who assumed leadership roles, such as the charismatic *beatas* (similar to the Beguines in other parts of Europe), suffered prosecution. More often, "transgressive" women of every sort suffered enclosure. The enclosure of women—be it in the legalized brothel, the convent, the disciplinary Magdalen houses (houses intended to reform prostitutes, a special creation of the times), or even the home, as several chapters of Perry's book demonstrate—served as the prime weapon of control. Perry concludes her study by observing that "the crisis of the patriarchy," to which such weapons correspond, "would be repeated in countless cities as they entered the modern period. Seville's response to this crisis *produced a pattern for gender and order that persisted in both Catholic and Protestant countries*" (179; italics mine).

As Perry's conclusion suggests, Counter-Reformation Spain affords what is perhaps just the most pronounced example of the conservative backlash against the progressive forces of modernization making its presence felt in other seventeenth-century European domains as well.[30] This recontainment of the energies of change manifested itself, among other ways, in a resurgence of traditional and medieval values. Maravall, who maintains that "only a conservative attitude was possible, one that would attempt to keep things in their order, reducing to whatever extent possible the crumbling of the prevailing system by the threat of time" (129), also contends that "the process of medievalizing restoration was not lacking anywhere or in any sphere of the collective life of western European peoples" (144). While one should certainly take his sweeping statement with a grain of salt,[31] the intensified preoccupation with "witches" throughout Europe and colonial America does signal a new medievalism cum new misogyny. In 1486 the medieval tract on witchcraft, *Malleus Maleficarum*, had identified witches with women's insatiable lust.

Almost three centuries later, the era that spawned the birth of modern science backslides into the same fearful identification of the woman with what Bakhtin calls the "grotesque body," the body symbolizing disorder that must constantly be surveilled, and renews its persecution of "witches" (see Stallybrass, 124–26).[32] Indeed, significantly enough, in the seventeenth century there was hardly any scientific revolution with regard to women's physiology. While the Copernican revolution reconfigured the universe, biology clung to the Aristotelian position that held women to be imperfect, passive, and hysterical from which medieval misogyny had drawn its principal sustenance.[33]

Seventeenth-century Western culture in general, state Katharina M. Wilson and Frank J. Warnke in the introduction to their pan-European anthology (*Women Writers of the Seventeenth Century*), "was not hospitable to the artistic and intellectual endeavors of women, its authoritarianism and increased centralization having tightened the grip of traditional conservative attitudes" (xvii). All told—given all the factors presented in the foregoing pages—one finds in seventeenth-century Spain, England, and France a widespread retrenchment vis-à-vis women and feminism.[34] We have gained some sense of the situation in Spain and will return to it in chapters 1 and 2. In England, the vicissitudes of the monarchy impacted forcefully on women's issues. With the accession of James I after the death of female ruler Elizabeth I in 1603, antifeminism broke out in earnest. The Stuarts aggressively promoted the image of the monarch as a father and husband of his country (Ferguson et al. 1986, xx), James I sought to rid his court of the women who had gained political power during Elizabeth's reign, and antifeminist satirists expressed themselves with vigor and vehemence. James I's actions and writings expose his discomfort with women's perceived ascendancy: his 1620 edict commanding the bishops of London "to inveigh vehemently and bitterly in theyre sermons, against the insolencies of our women" (quoted in Woodbridge, 142) prompted the *Hic Mulier/Haec Vir* controversies, as well as others. The events of the civil war and the interregnum, with their questionings of hierarchy and authority, produced a liberalizing effect on attitudes toward women's participation in public life (Latt in Fell, ix; also see Hilda Smith, chap. 1 et passim; Todd, chap. 1). However, the Restoration was soon to bring concerted efforts to restore order, to restore the traditional order. Keller notes that "after the Restoration, gender distinctions came to be drawn more sharply than ever before: male and female were separated by ascribed *nature* and function, with women reduced to new forms of dependency and the positions of men bolstered by new sources of authority" (62). In this connection, Laurie Finke states that the "monarchical political order that was restored after 1660 required, but was increasingly anxious about, patrilineage, an order specifically dependent on the control of female sexuality and on the naturalization of that control" (30). The conclusion of *Haec Vir*, in which man and woman promise to abandon their inverted sexual roles and to right society through adherence to the rules of difference, bespeaks the repatriation of gender difference that characterizes both the opening and the closing decades of seventeenth-century England.

Standing both apart from and at the heart of this drama, the Puritans merit special mention. Ben Barker-Benfield asserts that the male Puritan oligarchy eventually recoiled from the central Protestant doctrine that *all* humans should have a direct experience of the Spirit and thus be priests unto themselves. In Puritan New England, he claims, "the male need" gave "more definition to men and to God than the initial Protestant dynamic had allowed," and men found "an objective correlative for such definition in the sexual relationship" (66). The Puritan visible kingdom of God, founded as it was on what were considered divinely mandated principles of order, hierarchy, and subordination, necessarily reaffirmed and reinforced gender difference. According to Edmund S. Morgan in his now classic *The Puritan Family: Religion and Domestic Relations in Seventeenth-Century New England,* "the proper conduct of a wife was submission to her husband's instructions and commands. He was her superior, the head of the family, and she owed him an obedience founded on reverence. He stood before her in the place of God: he exercised the authority of God over her, and he furnished her with the fruits of the earth that God had provided" (Morgan, 45; see his chaps. 1 and 2 as well as Koehler, chaps. 1–3). Puritan New England, we see, defaulted on the progressive Protestant mission that carried important implications for women (and that was far better embodied by the Quakers) to instate a conservative utopia grounded in divinely sanctioned difference.

Ian Maclean entitles his path-breaking work on feminism in French literature from 1610 to 1652, *Woman Triumphant.* Since, as Maclean himself points out, he has not attempted to correlate literature with social reality (1), and his study leaves off precisely at the point at which Louis XIV's absolute monarchy began its ascendancy, the notion of "triumph" hardly encompasses either the chronological or the social sweep of the seventeenth century. Political and cultural developments in the first half of the century, such as the activities of the *frondeuses,* the reign of female regents that allowed women exceptional influence in political and cultural realms, and the salons led by the *précieuses,* certainly appear to warrant at least in some spheres the optimism announced by Maclean's title. Yet the consolidation of the absolute monarchy in France after midcentury brought with it a situation all too similar to what I have just described with regard to England.

Conceivably in reaction to the power exerted by the *frondeuses,*[35] certainly as a gesture toward reestablishing order through the reimposition of conventional social order, according to several studies the reign of Louis XIV clamped down on gender difference. Linda Timmermans has recently described the "ideological optic" of Louis XIV as "the will to social order, which implies the hierarchy of the sexes." She writes,

> The emancipation of women is an idea that grew ever-more frightening after the Fronde. . . . With the return to order and the

assumption of power of Louis XIV, a greater social conformism is restored which, in high society, entailed the insistence on the qualities and behavior specific to each sex and, in more traditionalist milieux, on the rigorous hierarchization of the functions (and knowledge) attributed to men and to women. (351–52)

Moreover, according to Albistur and Armogath, during the reign of Louis XIV, "ideology seemed to be arrested in the contemplation of the myth of the father, reproduced in every class and in every family" (134). The two critics christen this time the "great retrenchment" ("le grand renfermement") for women. In their words: "The reign of Louis XIV is extremely unfavorable to women. Like any authoritarian regime, it advocates 'a strong family in the image of a strong State.' In the political, religious, moral and social domains, one witnesses the triumph of concepts completely hostile to women." "This reaction of wrath," they go on to state, referring to royal legislation and unfavorable work conditions that created a negative environment for women, "often betrays anxiety on the part of those who feared being dispossessed of their authority and powers. The reign of Louis XIV is one of a great retrenchment towards women" (135). Similarly, Marjorie H. Ilsley calls attention to an important contradiction. On the one hand, women in seventeenth-century France "contributed increasingly to the development of the language and literature and to the refinement of manners" (215). On the other, "there remained a strange contrast between the role played by women in all these fields and the inferior position in which civil and religious law still held most of them" (215). Witchcraft panics in seventeenth-century France bolster claims of retrograde attitudes toward women (see Gibson, 133).

How, then, to explain the truly extraordinary cultural accomplishments of French women, such as the creation of the novel, during Louis XIV's repressive regime? Did they fall under official policy, thus extending to the second half of the century the triumphant position described by Maclean and rendering the monarchy's position equivocal? One approach would have it that in view of Louis XIV's desire that France represent the pinnacle of civilization, the refinement of culture advanced by the *précieuses* or subsequent learned females suited the purposes of the regime and warranted the integration of those often feminist women into the monarchist machine.[36] It was not necessarily their feminism but their contributions to culture that sanctioned the *précieuses*, allowing their writings to circulate and thus to be taken as representative of an official position. Moreover, Joan De Jean and Faith E. Beasley examine the contestatory role of such writing. Taking different examples, both of their books revolve around the belief that "seventeenth-century French women's writing offered the only articulate challenge to the Sun King's ever-more absolute rule" (De Jean 1991, 116). Beasley, for example, in *Revising Memory: Women's Fiction and Memoirs in Seventeenth-Century France*, submits that their privatizing and feminization of history through literature and memoirs represent women writers' concerted opposition to the official story, that

is, to the monopoly that the monarchist machine had begun to exercise on historiography.

⊰✠⊱

The *précieuses'* forays into history notwithstanding, much of our information
from the times regarding women's issues derives from male-authored or
mediated sources. To conclude my examination of seventeenth-century
retrenchments regarding women, therefore, I turn to the writings of two early
modern women, the French Marguerite de Navarre (1492–1549) and the
Spanish María de Zayas y Sotomayor (1590?–1661?), on the plight of women
in their respective centuries. Their texts have much to tell us about their times
and about each other, for María de Zayas (whose writings chapters 2 and 3
analyze extensively in seventeenth-century contexts) not only trenchantly
reads her own century's treatment of women, she also critically reads and
reinscribes Marguerite de Navarre's *Heptaméron*—and consequently, the sixteenth-century project for women and marriage.

Little besides her extremely popular novellas (the *Novelas amorosas*, 1637,
and the *Desengaños amorosos*, 1647 [translated into English as *The Enchantments of Love* and *The Disenchantments of Love*, respectively]) is known of
María de Zayas. In contrast, the life of Marguerite de Navarre, sister of
François I, has reached us in some detail. Renowned patroness of the arts and
of humanism, Marguerite wrote novellas, poetry, plays, and devotional literature. She espoused and sponsored the reformist tendencies of the Catholic
church: principally the need for monastic reform in clergy tainted by lasciviousness and corruption. The *Heptaméron*, a collection of sixty-seven stories
published posthumously in 1558,[37] makes it clear that Marguerite also
embraced the larger social reforms advocated by humanism in the apparent
belief that they would ameliorate the lives of women. Appealing to precisely
the same modernizing ethos found in Fray Luis de León, Marguerite advocates women's education and vindicates women from medieval misogyny
such as that expressed by her character Hircan: "I think you'll agree that ever
since Eve made Adam sin, women have taken it upon themselves to torture
men, kill them and damn them to Hell" (78). As the themes of each day of
storytelling reveal, Marguerite's moral tales showcase the virtue of women in
a corrective dialogue with clerical misogyny. The third day, for example,
treats "Of ladies who have goodness and purity in love and of the hypocrisy
and wickedness of the monks," while the fourth day contains tales
"Principally of the virtue and long-suffering of ladies in the winning over of
their husbands, and of the prudence of men with respect to their wives for the
preservation of the honour of their house and lineage." The focus of the
fourth day of tales exposes the very heart of Marguerite's text and of
Renaissance social reforms. For the overriding thrust of the book involves
deflecting love away from the vagaries of men's inevitable lust ("for our one
pride and joy, our one true delight, is to see you [women] caught, and to take

from you that which you prize more than life itself!" [208]) and toward long-lasting, stable, companionate marriage. Marguerite praises conjugal love through the group of storytellers' spiritual leader, Oisille, as "the finest and surest state in this world" (361). At the same time, the text does not fail to indicate an awareness of the political and social import of matrimony. The character Dagoucin voices his opinion that marriage should depend not on the promptings of the heart but on "the rank of families, the seniority of individuals and the provisions of the law," in order to "maintain peace in the state" and in order that "the monarchy should not be undermined" (374).

The moral love tales of María de Zayas—the most unabashed, militant Hispanic feminist of her age—twin and ultimately spin away from the *Heptaméron*. Zayas's direct borrowings from her female forebear's text on the thematic and formal levels leave no doubt as to their intertextual affiliation.[38] Several aspects of Marguerite's work lend themselves to Zayas's feminist and moralizing concerns. Most obviously, the defenses of women along *querelle* lines that Marguerite performs hold great attraction for Zayas, writing in the renewed misogynist climate of seventeenth-century Spain. Moreover, Marguerite exposes, albeit with a *Decameron*-like jocularity, the problematic nature of the relationship between the sexes: the fickle lust, false promises, adultery, and treachery that underwrite and undermine both courtly love and marriage. Her women fall victim to the violence of rape and incest. At the same time, as clever, virtuous, courageous, *active* subjects, they defend themselves and successfully wreak vengeance on their male aggressors.

Three-quarters of a century later María de Zayas looks up from the *Heptaméron* to read her world as she writes her socially aware novellas. She encounters, and registers in her works, a society in which the problematic relationship between the sexes has not only persisted but become dramatically—even irremediably—exacerbated. From Marguerite to Zayas, violence toward women escalates. Gone is the playful ribald eroticism of the *Heptaméron*'s seductions. In its place, Zayas's portrait of love (especially in the *Desengaños amorosos*) revolves around unmitigated, incessant strife and contains egregious abuse, scatalogical torture, and grotesque dismemberment, often rendered in naturalistic detail. Salacious friars assaulted women in the *Heptaméron*; here any and all men attack their female prey. Love, for the baroque Zayas, is war, women its undeserved victims. No matter what their virtue or cleverness, they cannot, and do not, in the *Desengaños amorosos* emerge victorious from the battles.

Implicitly but unmistakably, Zayas looks back at the world portrayed in the *Heptaméron* with a critical eye, seeing that its promise for women has not been fulfilled. Zayas's repeated, strident cries for women's education indicate that society has failed to realize that tenet of the Renaissance agenda. In fact, it has further chained women to the distaff, reinforcing their difference and "feminizing" them even more than nature intended (294 [Yllera ed.], *203*). Whereas women's education comprises the central plank in Zayas's feminist platform per se, subsequent developments in the harmonious marriage plot endorsed by Marguerite implicate every corner of the Spanish author's *Desengaños amorosos*. In the world of Zayas's second collection of tales, the marriage plot has clearly not been realized. Men have not ceased to pursue women only for pleasure, and marriage in the novellas is no solution—only the stage for further abuse. The sexes have not melded in companionate marriage but have become ineluctably polarized. Marguerite, as was to be expected in a Reformation climate that had taken a stand against monasticism, views the convent as secondary to marriage (for example, "no man will ever perfectly love God, unless he has perfectly loved some creature in this world" [228]); María de Zayas, as we will see in chapter 3, repeatedly has her characters withdraw to the convent as a refuge from marriage. Zayas's construction of the convent militantly changes the valence with which the patriarchy had endowed it: from the *man*dated space of enclosure, the convent becomes in Zayas's works the woman's chosen place of asylum from the noxious world of men, an idealized community of women. In sum, for Zayas the marriage project has failed, and the other benefits that were to have accrued from it have fallen away and been proven fraudulent. Marguerite de Navarre writes herself into the prevailing patriarchal ethos of the sixteenth century, supporting the interests of the state. The disillusioned María de Zayas of the seventeenth century feels compelled to defend women *against* the patriarchal ethos, as do more recent feminists, and to remove her sex from the injurious reaches of the state, turning to women's advantage the state's own imperious differentiating mechanisms.

⧯

III.

abiertas sendas al atrevimiento, / que una ya vez tri-
lladas, no hay castigo que intento baste a remover
segundo

[a pathway summoning the spirit to dare; once treading
this, no punishment can again deter it]
—SOR JUANA INÉS DE LA CRUZ
Primero sueño [First Dream]

The mere publication of María de Zayas's novellas, not to speak of their aggressive feminism and extraordinary popularity, insinuates that despite efforts to deter them seventeenth-century women were contributing notably and publicly to their cultures. Sixteenth-century educational reforms, combined with women's uncontainable urges to learn, had created "abiertas sendas al atrevimiento," that is, had set in motion forces of change that progressed inexorably. Educated women of the seventeenth century, while still subjected, would become increasingly active subjects and publish in ever-greater numbers. They would demand and achieve roles that far exceeded those that Fray Luis and other moralists had envisioned for them. This period, also transformative

and transitional for women in their own right, evinced changes that resonated from the previous century and would open doors to the subsequent more
enlightened one. During the seventeenth century per se, her-story would in
certain ways deviate more sharply than ever from his-tory, making the era
simultaneously a time of retrenchment and, at least in terms of women's contributions to culture, advances for the female sex. It is with good reason that
Natalie Zemon Davis and Arlette Farge chose *Renaissance and Enlightenment
Paradoxes* as the title of volume 3 of *A History of Women in the West.*

By far the most oft-noted transformation of the cultural scene accomplished by women is one that we have already seen in action with Marie de
Gournay, Margaret Fell, María de Zayas, and Sor Juana.[39] I refer to the fact
that for the first time in the seventeenth century significant numbers of
European women ventured into print to defend their own sex.[40] Heightened
misogyny spawned heightened feminist resistance: empowered by their learning, provoked by the tenacious subjugation of their sex at a time when so
many other enlightened changes had taken place in society, women took
advantage of the increased availability of print to enter into the *querelle* debate.
There, as can already be surmised, they executed defenses of the female sex
on collective rather than merely individual grounds, further signaling their
matrilineal awareness through their catalogs of illustrious women.
Interestingly enough, this phenomenon of women defending their own kind
in print arose for the first time in England, France, and Spain (to a lesser
degree) alike during the seventeenth century.

In more properly literary terms, compared to previous centuries, the seventeenth century also saw a considerable surge in women's writing and
publication.[41] Several general trends worthy of note emerged. Where sixteenth-century learned women tended to concentrate their scholarly efforts
on the reproduction of male learning through linguistic studies and translations, seventeenth-century women gained recognition as authors developing
their own ideas and publishing their own works (Hilda Smith, xii). Age-old
tradition had consecrated love poetry as the terrain for women's creative literary endeavors; seventeenth-century women made forays often fraught with
trepidation (as chapters 4 and 5 of my book detail) into many other fictional
and nonfictional genres. Similarly, women had traditionally exerted their writing energies on religious topics; the transvaluation of the early modern period, that is, the ever-increasing orientation of culture to secular issues, impelled
women into the arenas of nonreligious writing as well. There they placed their
mark on established genres (love poetry, the pastoral, and the novella provided particularly fertile territory) and contributed notably to the formation of literary phenomena such as the novel—especially in France, whose novel owes
its inception to women. Genres such as the novel and memoirs, with less
established rules and thus less burdened with male investment, particularly
attracted women writers of the seventeenth century. Female authors could
play an important part in mapping these forms. Given women's still generally limited sphere of experience, they gravitated toward various genres that

allowed for the inclusion of a personal element: including the novel and memoir, but also private history, letters, biographies, and autobiographies. Although many such texts remained personal and private and therefore desisted from infringing on male-dominated cultural capital, others blurred the lines between the public and the private. Hybrid works, such as Marie de Gournay's *Le Proumenoir de Monsieur de Montaigne*, welded the novel with the autobiography and essay. Biographies, such as the Duchess of Newcastle's of her husband, mixed the personal with political commentary. The *précieuses'* privatization of historiography through the historical novel collapsed the differences as well. Moreover, as was the case with Sor Juana's "Respuesta," forms developed for private exchanges were exploited in public exchanges (De Jean 1983, 6). All told, seventeenth-century women writers, like their present-day counterparts, performed a variety of generic formations and transformations.

One particular development involving women writers in the public sphere deserves special note: in the seventeenth century there arose the first small group of professional women writers. Christine de Pizan, the very first and unique for two centuries, had led the way. Seventeenth-century women like Marie de Gournay, Aphra Behn, Bathsua Makin, Mary Astell, and Ana Caro Mallén de Soto—generally incited by financial necessity, and sometimes by choice—earned their living by writing. Even Sor Juana wrote works (popular religious ceremonies to be performed in various cathedrals) on commission. Since it was writing for the court as well as the church that afforded Sor Juana the less tangible but still sustaining currency of continuing to pursue her chosen route as an intellectual, one could easily maintain that she, too, supported herself by writing. To live by the pen could be esthetically limiting *and* liberating. In the case of Aphra Behn, pandering to public tastes entailed writing bawdy works more risqué than those of any other known women writer of her times. In the case of Sor Juana, writing for mass consumption activated a carnivalesque popular voice (and voices: she includes speeches in Nahuatl) not found elsewhere in her works.

❧

The case of Sor Juana Inés de la Cruz—taking "case" now in a more legal sense—reveals that many of the significant accomplishments and tensions of the era with respect to women that I have discussed in the foregoing pages played themselves out in her life. In the context of the *Primero sueño* [First Dream], the epigraph to this section of my introduction relates to Phaeton and constitutes one of Sor Juana's poetic self-inscriptions; in a broader context, Sor Juana's life itself follows the lines of a seventeenth-century female Phaeton, evidencing his tragic daring and downfall. Sor Juana cultivated her mind. The court acquaintances she had cultivated guaranteed, for a time, her freedom to study and write. They published her complete works in Spain, including prose, poetry, and theater of a religious and secular nature. She gained public fame and, with it, mounting resentment on the part of the male clergy. When Sor Juana's writings infringed polemically and publicly on the masculinist domain of theology with the publication of her critique of Father Vieyra's sermon (her *Carta Atenagórica* [Letter Worthy of Athena]), she was censured. She defended herself and her sex in the "Respuesta." Soon after, she capitulated, apparently ending her life as a penitent and exemplary nun. Sor Juana, one might conclude, experienced the bounty of early modernity and the (unjust) deserts of its antifemale retrenchment.

Mindful of these microcosmic replays with their aftershocks in writing, the present book holds up the intricately wrought, erudite, encyclopedic, contestatory, gender-sensitive, and protofeminist works of Sor Juana as a potentially valuable lens through which to focus the literary production of her female contemporaries. I am interested in revealing here the aspects of seventeenth-century women's writing that can be seen through the lens of Sor Juana's oeuvre, and the dimensions of the works of Sor Juana's sister writers as well as of her own writing that become visible by virtue of this expanded optic. Indeed, the book is variously inflected, with certain chapters focusing primarily on comparisons of Sor Juana with another author and others invoking her work as an illustrative counterpoint to the main theme. Chapter 1, "From Anomaly to Icon: Border-Crossings, Catalina de Erauso, and Sor Juana Inés de la Cruz," examines the manner in which the cross-dressing Erauso, as did Sor Juana, exploited the dominant culture's own mechanisms and ideologies to legitimate her personal anomaly and to gain herself autonomy. Contradiction and category conflation serve as focal points both for the two women's advantageous fame and for the chapter's investigations. Chapter 2, "Women on Love, I: Love in a Choleric Time," continues to probe the Hispanic cultural climate vis-à-vis women by surveying the field of pro-female discourse in that terrain, paying special attention to its relationship with misogyny. Through an examination of the contestatory practices of Sor Juana's love poetry, María de Zayas's novellas, and Ana Caro's theater, the chapter brings to the fore the not inconsiderable resources that the Hispanic baroque afforded feminist discourse and literature. Chapter 3, "Women on Love, II: Sor Juana, María de Zayas, and Madame de Lafayette," comprises a sequel to chapter 2. By means of a reading of the framework story of Zayas's novellas and of Lafayette's *La Princesse de Clèves*, it demonstrates that the seventeenth century's disillusionment with love enabled women writers to forge a heroic and early modern form of the female bildungsroman. The problems of representation and narratability inherent in such an enterprise, for their part, ultimately illuminate the ending of Sor Juana's *Primero sueño*. Chapter 4, "Auto-Machia: The Self-Representations of Sor Juana and Anne Bradstreet," delves into the conflict-ridden inception of women's self-representation in the two continents of the New World, illustrating how both Tenth Muses contend with the oxymoronic situation of writing the self in contexts that militate for its erasure and destruction. The chapter treats, in the prose and poetry of the two authors, spiritual autobiography and redeemed subjectivity, humility topoi and anxiety of authorship, and instability in the representation of self and gender. Chapter 5, "The New Prometheus: Women's Education, Autodidacticism, and the Will to Signature," circles back to several of the epochal and generational matters I have expounded here in the introduction, bringing them to bear on issues of education, knowledge, and power. This culminating chapter of my study, which contains its general conclusions, contemplates the female Prometheus wresting knowledge from the patriarchal stronghold and explores the thematization and textualization of her drama in Sor Juana's *Primero sueño* and in various works of Margaret Lucas Cavendish.

Viewed separately, certain of the chapters tend to the capacious and exhaustive. They take on large and largely unexplored or underexplored topics and strive to confront the multiple issues that these topics bring into play. They often attempt to work through conundrums and oxymorons. Viewed collectively, the chapters flow into one another and assume a symphonic disposition. I return repeatedly to Sor Juana's inexhaustibly rich and paradigmatic "Respuesta" and *Primero sueño*. Matters treated in one chapter often reappear in others. Each different context discloses other implications, other wrinkles, or a new set of possibilities for core issues that I believe constitute a blueprint of significant factors in or preoccupations of seventeenth-century women's writing. These include (in random order) fame, the esthetic of the shocking and bizarre, women's education, melancholy, revisions of the consecrated theme of love, female homoeroticism, envisioning elsewheres, the *querelle des femmes* and misogyny, women and reason, philosophical and literary syncretism, multiple self-imaging, incursions into the public domain and into masculinist genres, unstable gender ideologies, and the phenomenon of the Tenth Muse. The last symphonic topic, the Tenth Muse phenomenon, brings several others into play and warrants a brief comment. The lens of Sor Juana focuses us on women writers, such as the Tenth Muses, of some renown—and quite tellingly so. Though not all the women writers I treat were denominated Tenth Muses, that is, exceptional female icons of their cultures, several of them were: Sor Juana, Anne Bradstreet, Ana Caro, Anna Maria van Schurman, and María de Zayas. They, as well as the blatantly nonconformist Catalina de Erauso and Margaret Lucas Cavendish, attracted considerable attention in their times. Each woman's spot in the public eye and domain raises in her writings, as we will see, a complex of concerns and consequences that places otherwise disparate figures on a continuum, creating—as does the *querelle des femmes*—the fascinating kinships specific to the seventeenth century that this book seeks to mine.[42]

Together with the topics that gain symphonic thickness over the course of the book, two larger questions have guided my inquiries. Both take their cue from a trenchant comment made by critic and novelist Sylvia Molloy in an interview with Magdalena García Pinto published in *Women Writers of Latin America: Intimate Histories* (1991). García Pinto raises the matter of continuity in women's writing over the centuries. Molloy responds in a cautionary vein, citing Sor Juana as a case-in-point:

> With Sor Juana, for example, people often give her work a kind of interpretation that makes it say more than she's saying, which happens when they take her out of context, and they impoverish her by doing that. That is, I can do a twentieth-century reading of Sor Juana and see certain elements, certain constants—like protest—that you see in contemporary women's literature, but I haven't nor should I forget that Sor Juana was writing in the seventeenth century, and that there is a series of literary conventions that inform her writing, just as there are literary conventions that inform my own. (143)

Bearing in mind Molloy's remarks on contextualization and anachronism, I have posed the following questions.

First, I have asked myself: What in the cultural repertoires of these seventeenth-century women writers' contexts provided the building blocks for early modern women's writing, particularly writing of a feminist cast? For every era in the Western world, including the apparently least propitious, has spawned some women writers and its own kind of feminism—conditioned by that era's ideologies, episteme, cultural and political climate, and so on. Constraints constrain but need not stifle and silence. They can stimulate and provoke, as Christine de Pizan's utopian feminist *Book of the City of Ladies*, springing from misogynist medieval polemics, demonstrates. Christine casts out from her context and shapes feminist debates to come. Yet even those who remain entirely within the dominant forms and norms of their context can open up a space for feminist writing. I refer the reader, for example, to the *Admiración Operum Dey* [Awe Before the Works of God] by the Spanish nun and Christine's contemporary, Teresa de Cartagena, the first Hispanic woman known to have defended in writing women's learning.[43] Such texts and considerations have prompted me to look in the following chapters at the resources that both the pancultural repertoire and individual cultures afforded the seventeenth-century woman writer. If in this introduction I have paid much attention to the ways in which patriarchal society thwarted women's advances, throughout the book and especially in its first three chapters I also endeavor to bring out aspects of the dominant cultures that in fact lent themselves to feminist appropriation, and the manners in which women writers instrumentalized them.

The second contextual aspect that interests me involves not only early modern feminist writing but also modern feminist critical practices—and the dynamics of the relationship between them.[44] Working in the early modern period leads one to interrogate and scruple what have come to be commonplace tenets of recent feminist criticism. That the bulk of them derive from our work on nineteenth- and twentieth-century women's writing gives rise to several weighty questions. Are these universals of women's writing, or historically conditioned and limited phenomena? To what degree are they applicable, without incurring in anachronism, to periods other than the liminal-modernist, modernist, or postmodern? Which of these paradigms (if any) hold in early modern women's writings, and how? How, in other words, does early modern women's writing rehearse and/or enact (if indeed it does) the attributes that would come to characterize its modern avatar? Although it lies outside the purview of my study to respond in any full way to the foregoing questions, I have had them much in mind. As the book unfolds, it should become clear that certain of our modern precepts—among them, anxiety of authorship, the angel/monster paradigm, gender-bending, generic hybridity, indeterminacy, category indistinction, questions of subjectivity—not only obtain without undue anachronism in the seventeenth century but also pertain with special relevance to that time.

The considerations just articulated, bearing on the connections between the early modern and the modern, lead me now to address one final question that implicates many of the matters raised in this introduction and treated in the book at large. Why, if I am primarily focusing on Sor Juana and other *seventeenth*-century women writers, do the title of the book and the title of the present introduction invoke the broader framework of the *early modern*?

For one thing, as the reader undoubtedly realizes, the designation *early modern* has been widely adopted to signal awareness of the expanded reaches of the period traditionally termed the *Renaissance*. Innovations of the Renaissance developed not in isolation but within a larger chronology now thought roughly to include the period between 1450 and 1700; the entire period, in which emerged "social structures previously unknown on the stage of world history" (Ferguson et al., xvii) and persisting to our day, introduces factors that render it *early* modern and that link it with the modern in fundamental ways. As Leah S. Marcus has written in *Redrawing the Boundaries: The Transformation of English and American Literary Studies*, "We are coming to view the period more in terms of elements repeated thereafter, those features of the age that appear to us precursors of our own twentieth century, the modern, the postmodern" (41). Therefore, to situate the seventeenth century in the compass of early modern is, as I have started to do in the foregoing pages, to view its distinctive traits as over/against the sixteenth century, its role as a pivotal time between the sixteenth (the earliest modern) and the eighteenth (the more properly modern) centuries, and to chart its connections with the modern per se.

Moreover, the term *early modern* gains particular relevance and urgency in the context of women's studies. *Renaissance* connotes a period of rebirth, of hope and shining optimism; traditional period definitions, we know, can take on quite a different look when viewed from the perspective of women. Although Jacob Burckhardt's classic study of the Renaissance maintains "that women stood on a footing of perfect equality with men" (395), we now recognize the naïveté and myopia of his claim. Catharine Stimpson has rightly noted: "'Early modern' is a far more sober, far less lyrical set of phonemes than 'Renaissance.' Despite this, the phrase points to an ambitious, energetic, fruitful effort to resee the Renaissance and to see it wholly" (foreword to Ferguson et al., vii). Revisiting the Renaissance and rechristening the period as early modern represent our ongoing efforts to restore to history and visibility phenomena that have been "ignored, marginalized, or distorted" (foreword to Ferguson et al., vii).

All of the above considerations underwrite my inscription of the book in the framework of the early modern. However, one further matter—pertaining specifically to seventeenth-century women's writing and illuminated by the optic of Sor Juana's work—drives my appeal to a wider perspective. Women might not have experienced the heart of the Renaissance, but they certainly registered the pulse of the contradictory early modern era, its dialectical beat. I allude particularly to the fact that much of seventeenth-century feminism and some of its women's writings were produced not only under siege but *dia-critically*. Several seventeenth-century women writers, for example, perceived or designed the sixteenth century as a women's Renaissance, however little truth that construction might have had in social reality;[45] they adopted conservative positions to further women's modernity. Female essayists of the time, more reformers than radicals, focus their sights on the relatively enlightened views of the sixteenth-century preceptists and lament their evanescence. María de Zayas reads Marguerite de Navarre with a critical eye. At the same time, she contrasts the "golden age" of Renaissance Spain under Queen Isabel with her present "age of iron" (*Desengaños*, 300–301, *209–11*) and states that although women are slandered in the present, they were more highly esteemed by men—and esteemed themselves more highly—in the past (*Desengaños*, 459, *357*). Mme de Lafayette situates *La Princesse de Clèves* in the sixteenth century, evoking its female-dominated court milieu and invoking Marguerite de Navarre (the novel begins in the year the *Heptaméron* was published). Mary Astell and Margaret Lucas Cavendish hark back to the convent, situating their female utopias in that now-banished realm. As the following pages will disclose in more detail, several female authors of the seventeenth century carried on a conservative romance with a recent yet idealized past, recuperating and mobilizing the recontained energies of the previous century to advance their own thinking or their own sex.[46]

Sor Juana, for her part, draws sustenance for women's education from Fray Luis and his fellow Spanish reformer, Juan Luis Vives, subscribing to their positions. She applies to her foremother, the great Saint Teresa—an activist writing nun of the sixteenth century. She summons up the stable, harmonious worldview of Renaissance Neoplatonism as one scenario of the Soul's quest for knowledge in the *Primero sueño*. Moreover, as the following pages will confirm, from within the confines of her "colonial echo chamber" (Harss, 17) Sor Juana begins to feel the heartbeat of the incipient Age of Reason. Critically and diacritically positioned between the old and the new, prescient of women's issues that obtain to this day, Sor Juana's work embodies and demands the wider economy bound up in the designation *early modern*. In chipping away at the walls in which scholarship has tended to enclose Sor Juana, we can make visible not only the walls but also the apertures, doors, and communicating vessels that describe the space occupied by the early modern woman writer.

Early Modern Women's Writing and Sor Juana Inés de la Cruz

CHAPTER ONE

From Anomaly to Icon:
Border-Crossings, Catalina de Erauso,
and Sor Juana Inés de la Cruz

Twenty years ago was born
a woman, a prodigy
at once honor and insult to her country
who amazes, affrights, and astonishes. . . .
–Carlos Coello, *LA MONJA ALFÉREZ (ZARZUELA,* operetta*)*

I am Eugenia! What gives you pause?
What astonishes you? What affrights you?
If not the contemplation of your blindness
when you see that, from a throne
that is both an altar and a judge's bench,
I can be both deity and delinquent?
–Pedro Calderón de la Barca, *EL JOSÉ DE LAS MUJERES*

The seventeenth century in Spain was a conflictive age[1] and an age of grave contradictions. Counter-Reformation Spain, with its absolute monarchy, endeavored to combat the modernizing thrust of the economic and social mobility, ideological aperture, growth of cities, and expansionism characteristic of the preceding century by reimposing the conservative values and hierarchical structures of the jeopardized feudal society. Especially in Catalina de Erauso's times, the besieged Spain of Philip IV (1621–65) and the Count-Duke Olivares subscribed to and propagated the belief that only a restoration of traditional values could achieve the revitalization of the country (Elliott 1989, 120). As George Mariscal demonstrates in his *Contradictory Subjects* (1991), there emerged from the intent to create a neo-knightly state in a modernizing world ideological clashes between dominant, emergent, and residual elements, clashes that gathered around issues such as bloodlines, virtue, wealth, family, and capitalism. According to Mariscal, "early modern social relations were the site of a pronounced struggle" (6) and early modern

Spanish writing "an intense competition between rival discourses and ideologies" (3) that framed what he terms "contradictory subjects." Overflowing the designs of subjection and figuring forth the dynamics of the era, in the baroque chiaroscuro of seventeenth-century Spain law and lawlessness, overweening morality and base licentiousness, the spirit and the flesh, the ideal and the real, the "deity" and the "delinquent," "honor" and "insult" all were celebrated in cultural products that oscillated madly between subject stabilization and destabilization. The paradox, antithesis, and incongruity that drove the rhetorical tropes of the times permeated both its larger discourse and its sociopolitical realities.

In testimony, first of all, to this dimension of baroque Spain, I unfold the following case study of the paradoxical Catalina de Erauso, the transvestite "Monja/Alférez" or Lieutenant/Nun who became a legend in her own time. I will examine from a largely cultural point of view the enigmas, tensions, and contradictions (baroque and otherwise) bound up in the astonishing phenomenon of Catalina de Erauso by exploring the reception accorded the Monja Alférez in the Hispanic baroque worlds as well as the displaying and disciplining of her story in an array of seventeenth-century texts: literary, legal, popular. As a case-in-point focusing the tensions of the Hispanic baroque age especially as they bore on literary discourse, publicity (with an emphasis on "public"), and gender, my discussion of Erauso takes on the disposition of an early modern wonder-cabinet. It will be a showcase for remarkable disjunctions of differing types and in essence for what, as we will see, the baroque deemed prodigies or "monsters."

Prodigies, of course, often accrue fame, a complex and multifaceted phenomenon. Leo Braudy, in his *The Frenzy of Renown: Fame and Its History* (1986), notes that fame "sits at the crossroads of the familiar and the unprecedented, where personal psychology, social context and historical tradition meet" (15). All of the broad issues that Braudy raises regarding fame will come into play here, and even into conflict, as I probe the following conundrum: that Catalina de Erauso's daring, participation in the male order, and exploits rendered her anomalous and indeed transgressive for her society. Though as a transgressor of, among several things, the foundational gender prescriptions of her society and thus as a potentially dangerous anomaly, she nonetheless achieved renown and official sanction. From an anomaly she became a cultural icon, as I have said, a legend in her own time. In other words, this chapter will investigate how, against apparent odds, Erauso catapulted–and, I should advance, catapulted *herself*–from anomaly to icon and thus achieved personal freedom in a restrictive context.

Erauso and her texts occupy a large portion of the chapter. However, the Lieutenant Nun's cross-dressing and the border-crossings,[2] that is, the breakdown of categories, that it entails will by the end of the chapter lead us into the negotiations of the actual nun, Sor Juana Inés de la Cruz, with fame, anomaly, iconicity, and the dominant cultural mechanisms. The conjunction of the two female phenomena blocks out issues concerning Sor Juana that subsequent parts of this book explore in greater depth. At the same time it consolidates the present chapter's formulation of certain contradictions *and* their implosion—such as the potency of baroque fame to construct from paradox a space beyond contradiction and prescription—that underwrote the seventeenth-century culture of both Hispanic worlds.[3]

❧❈❧

I.

For any society, and particularly for the regulated world of seventeenth-century Spain, even the bare bones of Catalina de Erauso's life story are wonderfully shocking. Born in San Sebastián, Vizcaya, toward the end of the sixteenth century, Erauso was raised from a young age in a Basque convent, from which she escaped at fifteen. She immediately cut her hair and fashioned her habit into male garb, vacating her identity as a female with the same alacrity and thoroughness as she shed her female dress. After moving around Spain under several assumed male names and serving a variety of masters, Erauso traveled to the New World, where she seems to have passed as a eunuch. The famed travel writer Pedro de la Valle described Erauso in 1626 as being "tall and strong of frame, rather masculine in appearance, she has no more breasts than a girl-child. She told me that she had used some remedy or other to cause them to disappear. . . . Her appearance is more that of a eunuch than a woman. She wears men's clothing in the Spanish style; she bears her sword with as much bravado as her life" (Ferrer, viii).

As de la Valle's reference to her bravado and sword suggest, Erauso became a fighter and a soldier. Feisty, contentious, and incorrigibly aggressive, she committed many crimes, often being saved from punishment by the political influence of her fellow Basques. She also acquitted herself bravely as a mercenary soldier in several battles of the Araucanian wars, serving unbeknownst to him under her own brother, and was awarded the minor title of *Alférez* or Second Lieutenant. Her sexual preference seems to have been for women; little wonder, then, that when under dire circumstances Erauso finally disclosed her biological sex to a bishop in Guamanga, Peru, she was found to be a virgin. Refusing to spend her life in the convent to which she was remanded, and having become a popular sensation, Erauso returned to Europe where, remarkably enough, she was granted dispensation from both the Spanish king, Philip IV, and Pope Urban VIII to spend her life dressed as a man, to be the Monja Alférez. The former soldier enjoyed her newfound celebrity for a while but soon returned to the New World. Launching the instrument of her gender change into the instrument of her livelihood, she spent the latter years of her life in Mexico as a merchant-muleteer who traded in clothing under the name of Antonio de Erauso. She died in 1650.

Many historical documents establish these facts. Indeed, a whole tangle of contemporaneous accounts that have come down to us both attested to and enhanced her considerable celebrity. Principal among these documents, which form the backbone of my study, figure Erauso's own petitions to the Crown requesting an annuity for her military services and compensation for a robbery to which she fell victim in France, a slew of eyewitnesses' *certificaciones* backing up Erauso's petitions, two *relaciones* or accounts of her exploits published in 1625 in Spain, and three published in Mexico. These broadsides sold to the public tell Erauso's life in installments. The first two Mexican *relaciones* duplicate those published in Spain, while the third, dating from 1653, follows Erauso's life up to her death. All three *relaciones* appear to issue from different (anonymous) authors. So famous had Erauso become that the *relaciones* do not even mention her name.[4]

None of these rich documents, however, is as tantalizing and controversial as Erauso's alleged autobiography, originally titled *Vida i sucesos de la Monja Alférez escrita por ella misma* [Life and Adventures of the Lieutenant Nun Written by Herself] and also published in modern editions as the *Historia de la Monja Alférez escrita por ella misma*. The principal question, still unresolved, that has arisen around this text is whether it was in fact and in toto written by Erauso. This is due first and foremost to the fact that we possess no autograph or original printed copies of the work, which was deposited for publication in the printing house of Bernardino de Guzmán in 1625. An alleged transcription of the original, with eighteenth-century calligraphy but seventeenth-century orthography and morpho-syntax (Vallbona 1981, 150) now housed in the Real Academia in Madrid, has served as the basis for the first modern (by Joaquín María de Ferrer in 1829) and, until recently, subsequent editions. In 1992, distinguished Costa Rican author and critic Rima de Vallbona published a superb critical edition of the *Vida* based on the manuscript in the Real Academia, redressing certain significant problems in the Ferrer version of the text (the original remains missing to this day). The weighty problems surrounding the *Vida* have with good reason rendered problematical and stymied literary analysis of the text in its own right.[5] Yet beyond these pressing textual issues, the very nature of the *Vida*, that is, its purposely shocking nature, inspires equal skepticism with respect to its authorship. For, as Rima de Vallbona has noted (1981, 236), it is difficult to understand how Erauso could have written such scandalous pages at the same time that she presented her case to the Crown for reward. Leaving aside for the moment the question of the text's authenticity, let us look at Erauso as she is represented in the *Vida*, as a Monja/Alférez–feminine/masculine–in a text that aggressively mines the shock potential, the difference, inherent in Erauso's public title and life.

A central passage from the *Vida* conveys the tone and stuff of the narrative. Here the character Erauso recounts how when finally disclosing her sex, she summarized to the bishop of Guamanga her life as a nun turned cross-dresser:

> Señor, all of this that I have told you . . . in truth, it is not so. The truth is this: that I am a woman, that I was born in such and such a place, the daughter of this man and this woman, that at a certain age I was placed in a certain convent with a certain aunt, that I

was raised there and took the veil and became a novice, and that when I was about to profess my final vows, I left the convent for such and such a reason, went to such and such a place, undressed myself and dressed myself up again, cut my hair, traveled here and there, embarked, disembarked, hustled, killed, maimed, wreaked havoc, and roamed about, until coming to a stop in this very instant, at the feet of Your Eminence. (*64*, 110)[6]

In colloquial language, with a matter-of-fact tone that but heightens the impact of her crimes, Erauso (for the sake of convenience in this discussion, I will say that Erauso wrote the text) unflinchingly parades her sins before the bishop *and* the reader. The staccato spate of harsh verbs at the end of the passage hammers them in, encapsulating the confession. Erauso's confession, however, hardly signals the beginning of her repentance and reform, for she remains unregenerate and true to herself to the end of the work. The text, in its themes and structure, is more of an exposé than a confession. The *Vida*'s largely formulaic chapters exhibit Erauso's transgressions with surprisingly little attention to her soldierly heroism (Vallbona 1981, 210–11, 294). Condensed, selective, highly emplotted with a compressed novelistic causality, the chapters focus with relentless singularity of purpose on the dire entanglements of a woman who has adopted male garb in order, as she says, to "travel and see a bit of the world" (*17*, 52).[7] Typically, they begin with brief background or filler material, then succinctly set forth whatever problematic situation the protagonist has brought upon herself, and end with Erauso escaping from the situation, unable or unwilling to resolve it. From chapter to chapter the protean Erauso rapidly changes roles, but not character: a thief, a war-mongering soldier, an inveterate gambler, a shameless murderer (with some fifteen homicides to her credit!), she persists, undeterred by many arrests, in "hustling, killing, maiming, wreaking havoc and roaming about."

Although action here predominates over psychology, a striking portrait of Erauso's iconoclastic and unabashedly "masculine" persona nonetheless emerges from the text. Most astounding for the times, the protagonist on several occasions displays her disrespect for religion: consistently and opportunistically claiming her right to asylum in a church to escape arrest or death ("Complete bedlam ensued. The [religious] brothers were scandalized and kept shouting, 'Heretic! Heretic!'" [*49*, 93]), mocking the priest about to hang her (*42*, 87), and resisting a life of enclosure in a convent ("I told the man that I had no order, and no religion" [*69*, 115]). Erauso, like Jesusa Palancares in Elena Poniatowska's *Hasta no verte Jesús mío* [Until I See You, My Jesus], styles herself as an incorrigible individualist who rejects conventional religion, and as a violent brawler and "macho" woman who scorns female behavior. Her textual persona corresponds precisely to the profile of the unadulterated (in humoral terms) male that her fellow Basque Juan Huarte de San Juan presents in his influential scientific treatise, *Examen de ingenios para las ciencias* [The Examination of Men's Wits for the Sciences] (1594): "The usual characteristics of men who are hot and dry in the third degree are courage, pride, liberality and insolence" (620). As a soldier, she also displays exemplary "male" valor, its being a natural outgrowth of her entrenched aggressiveness. Moreover, Erauso's assumed gender and role as a soldier configure the genre of autobiography—for the *Vida* displays not only the content but several of the traits of the soldier's autobiography outlined by Margarita Levisi in her *Autobiografías del siglo de oro* [Golden Age Autobiographies].[8] As in the autobiographies of Alonso Contreras and Ginés de Pasamonte that Levisi discusses, the almost complete lack of interiority and the absence of expressions of emotion or remorse substantially reduce the "I" in the *Vida* to the res gestae, a locus of external events. The author of the *Vida* abundantly documents such events with an attention to dates and names similar to that of soldiers' *relaciones de servicios y méritos* [accounts of services and merits]. Further, as we saw in the passage cited above, the language of the *Vida* assumes a quintessentially or conventionally masculine tone—laconic, understated, taut, and eminently "macho."

Erauso's rejection of the feminine and her iconoclastic "macho" voice come into play in the *Vida*'s provocative ending. Having become celebrated for her cross-dressing and military exploits, Erauso finds herself in Naples where two prostitutes taunt her, saying: "Señora Catalina, where are you going?" She replies: "Whore ladies, to give you both a hundred strokes to your necks and a hundred gashes with this blade to the fool who would defend your honor" (*80*, 124). Since the soldierly genres with which the *Vida* shares so many traits rarely indulge in symbolism, I am not sure how much one should read into this passage. Coming at the end of the text, however, it does take on the shape of an emblematic moment. Now fully invested as a male, Erauso takes umbrage at being addressed as "Señora." Using language far from ladylike, she inveighs against the prostitutes—her antithetical doubles, "public" women as transgressive as she but who, in a marginalized position and unlike Erauso herself, have subordinated themselves to male desire. "The hell with you," she says in essence to this kind of woman and perhaps to women in general. The prostitutes, reads the last line of the work, "fell dead silent, and then they hurried off" (*80*, 124). For once in the text others leave and Erauso stays, having displaced this type of female, negated the feminine in herself, and here claiming her own territory as a male.

In her actions and attitudes the character Erauso may reject the feminine, but the text by no means obliterates Erauso's dual nature as both masculine and feminine. Rather, it exploits her difference, titillating the reader with the character's sexual ambiguity. Erauso's effective disguise as a man fuels the drama of the text. As in a cloak-and-dagger play, Erauso's mother and father and even the brother at whose side she served for three years implausibly fail to recognize her. The text allows Erauso to maintain her disguise until her chosen moment of self-disclosure at the same time that it teases the reader: whenever she is injured and required to undress, priests presumably sworn to

secrecy cure her wounds. Even more inflammatory are the numerous eroti-
cally suspenseful episodes, so cleverly framed that they bear recounting. For
example, in chapter 3, reminiscent of *Lazarillo de Tormes*'s final adulterous triangle, her employer beseeches Erauso to marry his lover Beatriz, who at one
point locks Catalina in a room and vows, says Erauso, that "come hell or high
water I was going to sleep with her" (*13*, 47). In a cunningly double-edged section of chapter 7, Erauso states, first, that clergyman Antonio Zerbantes "took
a fancy to me, and gave me gifts and wined me and dined me at his house"
(egged on, we note, by the opportunistic Erauso) and then that he finally "told
me that he had a niece living with him who was just about my age . . . and
that he had a mind to see the two of us married" (*29*, 70). Erauso also makes
a thinly veiled reference to her lesbianism, complaining that a young woman
offered to her in marriage was "a girl as black and ugly as the devil himself,
quite the opposite of my taste, which has always run to pretty faces" (*28*, 70).
Although much emphasis is placed on Erauso's virginity when she discloses
her sex, the implication of homosexual attraction adds yet another layer of
ambiguous titillation to the text as it eroticizes the many, even apparently
innocent encounters with other females (one example among many: "I came
out of hiding, settled my affairs, and went quite often to visit my little nun and
her mother, and some of the other ladies there, all of whom were invariably
pleased by my company and made me many gifts" [*46*, 91]). The men in Erauso's text, Michele Stepto notes, "are never potential lovers. The women, by
contrast, almost always are" (xxxvii).

An extraordinary stylistic feature of the *Vida* also persistently assaults the
reader with Erauso's masculine/feminine difference. Constantly in view is the
fact that the "I" alternates between feminine and masculine adjectives in
describing herself. Rima de Vallbona, whose critical edition reinstates the
many feminine forms of the manuscript that Ferrer had suppressed,[9] discerns
a pattern of dramatic role-playing in the adjectives:

> It is worth pointing out how the narrator, perhaps unconsciously,
> adopts masculine or feminine forms according to circumstances,
> like a disguise that she uses to play a role at a given moment. In
> the passages dealing with courtship, coquetry, and love, she
> employs the masculine, just as she does in those referring to war
> and duels. However, when the register is neuter the narrator-pro-
> tagonist returns to the feminine form. (1992, 52)

However, at times the gendering of the adjectives in the *Vida* defies system-
atization, appearing unstable. It is highly conceivable that, due to the absence
of grammatical gender in her native Basque tongue of Euskera, Erauso paid
little attention to such matters.[10] Also conceivable in keeping with the rest of
the *Vida* is the possibility that its author contrived the adjectival instability for
its shock value, to position the text in the space of difference.

II.

As the foregoing discussion of the *Vida* has made clear, if Erauso's life was transgressive, her alleged text is even more so—even militantly so—on several fronts. Despite this, along with the dispensation from the pope and the Crown to spend her life in male garb, Philip IV awarded Erauso an allowance in perpetuity deriving from the rent on a land grant including Indian labor (an *encomienda de indios*) in Peru (Vallbona 1992, 148). Nor did the Inquisition ever trouble Erauso. Such facts, together with the *Vida* and Erauso's life, raise a burning question that runs in tandem with the enigma of the text's authorship: How could Erauso have lived as she did, made it known in a public way, and still have been officially sanctioned and rewarded? Although I cannot offer definitive answers to the question, I will engage in informed speculation revolving around the ways in which Erauso's life and texts spoke to various quarters of the official Spanish world and, ultimately, to its baroque esthetic.[11] Central to my ensuing argument is Erauso's own rough "Pedimento" [Petition] to the Crown seeking reward for her signal services, as conveyed through a scribe in 1625. The key portions of the Petition read as follows:

PETITION

Sir: the Lieutenant doña Catalina de Erauso, resident and native of the town of San Sebastián, in the province of Guipúzcoa, says that of the last nineteen years she has spent fifteen in the service of Your Majesty in the wars of the kingdom of Chile and the Indians of Peru, having traveled to those parts in men's garb owing to her particular inclination to take up arms in defense of the Catholic faith and in the service of Your Majesty, without being known in the aforesaid kingdom of Chile during the entire time she spent there as other than a man. Only some years later, in the lands of Peru, was it discovered under circumstances unfitting to mention here that she was a woman. And, being under the command in the kingdom of Chile of the Lieutenant Miguel de Erauso, her legitimate brother, she never revealed herself to him, though she knew that he was her brother; she denied their blood ties to avoid being recognized. In all the time that she served with him, as well as under the command of Field Marshal don Diego Bravo de Sarabia, she withstood the discomforts of military service like the strongest man, known only as such in every battle. Her deeds earned her the right to carry Your Majesty's flag, serving as she did as Lieutenant of the infantry company of Captain Gonzalo Rodríguez under the assumed name of Alonso Díaz de Guzmán. In that period she distinguished herself with great courage and valor, suffering wounds, particularly in the battle of Peru. The troops having been reorganized, she moved to the company of Captain Guillén de Casanova, governor of the fortress of Arauco, and was chosen as a valiant and fine soldier to go out and do battle with the enemy. . . .

She begs that Your Majesty be pleased to order that her services and long wanderings and valiant deeds be rewarded, thereby showing his greatness; rewarding her for the worthiness of her deeds and for the singularity and prodigiousness of her life/story [por la singularidad y prodigio que viene a tener su discurso], mindful that she is the daughter of noble and illustrious parents who are principal citizens in the town of San Sebastián; and for the rectitude and rare purity in which she has lived and lives, to which many have borne testimony; for which she would be honored to receive a yearly stipend of seventy pesos apportioned in twenty-two quilates per month in the city of Cartagena de las Indias, and funds to travel there, rewards that she hopes Your Majesty in his greatness will provide. (37; Vallbona 1992, 133)

In a blatantly self-serving act of self-fashioning or self-editing Erauso presents herself here as an exemplary military hero. She couches her petition in the conventional terms of a *relación de servicios y méritos*, playing up her service, her wounds, her valor, and her "manly" actions. She evokes the classical figure of the virago, of a woman who has dressed as a man to serve Crown and church. Four *certificaciones* from military superiors, who seem to be amazed but unperturbed by her true sex, support Erauso's claims.[12] The longest testimonial, by Field Marshal Juan Recio de León, swears to having seen her "respond with manly vigor to everything required of her in military life, living up to its demands, and that he knows her to have been virtuous and chaste . . . for all of which reasons she merits the favor of His Majesty" (Vallbona 1992, 146). The compelling defense of her military service mounted by Erauso in her well-orchestrated case apparently, or ostensibly, won her reward. A summary of Erauso's case, including the recommendations passed on to the king by the Council of the Indies, informs us that "having been received in the Council, it has seemed that, though dressing in men's clothing is prohibited, now that it has taken place and that she has served in this way for so many years, and so courageously in such persistent and constant war, and received wounds, it would be very fitting on Your Majesty's part to favor her, so that she can support herself and retire" (Vallbona 1992, 131).

We should note that Erauso's crimes, so prominently featured in the *Vida*, do not make their way into the Petition to mar its self-promotional contrivances. Omissions such as this prompt us, as perhaps did Erauso herself, to view the Petition as the "official" and the *Vida* as the unofficial versions of her story.[13] Yet, oddly enough, in the official story itself Erauso follows a dual line of argumentation that highlights her exemplarity *and* her anomaly. She focuses on her exemplary military service and at the same time, rather than suppressing it as she does her crimes, on her life as a woman who passed as a man. That Erauso had acted in the fabulous sphere of the New World, a frontier society for which norms of credibility as well as of behavior were suspended, might have rendered more plausible and indeed more acceptable her fabulous exploits as a cross-dressing *mujer varonil* or manly woman (a stock figure of golden age comedias) come to life.[14] Nevertheless, despite their favorable recommendation regarding her monetary reward, the matter of Erauso's cross-dressing gave serious pause to the Council of the Indies. Its members were undoubtedly aware that Deuteronomy 22:5 had stated that the "woman shall not wear that which pertaineth unto a man, neither shall a man put on a woman's garment: for all that do so are abomination unto the Lord thy God."[15] The document from the Council cited above, from March 7, 1626, and with seven signatures, immediately after granting Erauso the allowance states that the Council will leave it up to the *king* to decide the vexed issue of her refusal to change clothing ("and as for ordering her to wear women's dress, to leave it up to Your Majesty to command what would be most suitable, for she is not known to wish to change her present clothing, which is that of a man" [Vallbona 1992, 131]). Interestingly enough, another document from the Council on the same day, but with only one signature, remits the matter of the *allowance* to the king while contending that "as for changing her clothing, as it seems, it will be well for her to return to women's dress" (Vallbona 1992, 132). Therefore, an obvious question arises: Why did Erauso's second line of argumentation in the Petition, highlighting her cross-dressing, not utterly undermine her worthiness in the eyes of the officials?

Only by means of an excursus into the gender and sex ideologies of early modern Spain that bear implications for female to male cross-dressing–a fascinating mixture of rigid differentiation and fluid continuity–can I purport to respond to this deceptively simple question. I begin by registering Erauso's pointed insistence in the Petition that she had been known *only* as a man in the last fifteen years and had gone to great lengths to preserve the integrity of her male disguise, the emphasis in several *certificaciones* on her "manly" actions, the seeming calm with which her military superiors accepted her cross-dressing, and the significant convergence in Recio de León's testimony of two words, *varonil* [manly] and *virtud* [virtue]. Carrying the textual evidence into its social context, we can see that it responds to something much larger than Erauso's self-promotional campaign. It signals that on a level transcending that of the superficial disquiet occasioned by the transgression of her social role as a woman, Erauso's cross-dressing carries positive weight: according to the androcentric, patriarchal perspective of seventeenth-century males, she has transcended her lowly condition as a woman and acceded to the unequivocally superior realm of masculinity. Dekker and van de Pol have stated with reference to the generally favorable legal reception accorded to women warriors in the Netherlands that "[it] was judged that a woman who became a man strove to become something better, higher, than she had been, and that was considered an understandable and commendable effort in itself. If she was successful, one had to admire her" (74). The symbolic etymological connection between *vir*, man, and *virtue* had permeated the Western moral tradition, making the word *manly* a positive adjective that nullified gender descriptors.[16] Melveena McKendrick, noting that the use of the adjective *varonil* as a standard of excellence became widespread in the seventeenth century (53), submits that for the theater of the times "women who depart from the norm in an admirable, positive or at least forgivable way, are *varoniles*; those who do so in a totally reprehensible way are just wicked women" (62). *Jardín de las nobles doncellas* [Garden of Noble Maidens], a manual written for the education of Queen Isabel, accumulates examples of "manly women" from antiquity, even including "Amazons" (Bravo-Villasante, 102). Fray Luis de León insisted that the only way to be a good woman was to be a "manly" woman, which meant "virtue of spirit and strength of heart; industry and wealth and power and advantage, and finally, a perfect and complete being in those things to which this word is applied; and she who is a good woman treasures all this within herself" (256). In her *Camino de perfección* [Path of Perfection], Saint Teresa exhorted her nuns with words that speak directly to my point: "My daughters, I would not want you to be women in any way, nor to resemble them, but rather strong men, and if you fulfill your nature God will make you so manly that you will strike terror in men" (297).

It is clear that Erauso, by underscoring in the Petition her wholesale transfer into masculinity through transvestism, has written herself into the patriarchal gender ideology. The self-contradictory, border-crossing category of the "manly woman" provides a loophole in gender demarcations into which she easily writes herself as a cross-dresser, textually reinforcing prevailing norms rather than, as it would seem, placing them in crisis. Further, more than any virtuous *mujer varonil* whom Saint Teresa or Fray Luis would sponsor, the cross-dressing Erauso literalizes and viscerally embodies the manly woman. For according to Pedro de la Valle's account of the Monja Alférez cited earlier ("rather masculine in appearance, she has no more breasts than a girl-child. She told me that she had used some remedy or other to cause them to disappear"), she has mutilated and deformed her body into that of a man. Mary Elizabeth Perry insightfully concludes, "Catalina, in fact, refused feminization and embraced only masculine qualities. . . . Aware of the restrictions that gender imposed on her life, she did not try to change the inequity between the sexes. Instead, she chose to change herself, to deny her body, to repudiate the convent, habit, and submission expected of her as a woman, and construct for herself a male persona that would completely obliterate her as a woman" (134).[17]

The *gender* ideology of the "manly woman" literalized by Erauso finds its (equally constructed)[18] complement, and we perhaps an explanation of its self-contradictory, border-crossing nature as well as of the acceptance of Erauso's cross-dressing, in the *sexual* ideology of the times. That a woman can so readily achieve masculinity–be it quasi-metaphorically as a "manly woman" or quite literally through a change of appearance–synchronizes with the scientific model of the times, which places males and females on a single biological continuum rather than viewing them as incommensurable opposites. I refer to the so-called one-sex model that prevailed up to the eighteenth century and "where at least two genders correspond to but one sex, where the boundaries between male and female are of degree and not of kind," analyzed by Thomas Laqueur in his 1990 *Making Sex: Body and Gender from the Greeks to Freud* (25). Laqueur describes its fundamentals in the following way:

> For thousands of years it had been a commonplace that women had the same genitals as men except that, as Nemesius, bishop of Emesa in the fourth century put it: "theirs are inside the body and not outside of it." Galen, who in the second century A.D. developed the most powerful and resilient model of the structural, though not spatial, identity of the male and female reproductive organs, demonstrated at length that women were essentially men in whom a lack of vital heat—of perfection—had resulted in the retention, inside, of structures that in the male are visible without. (4)

In other words, as a doggerel verse cited by Laqueur spells out simply, "Though they of different sexes be, / Yet on the whole they are the same as we, / For those that have the strictest searchers been, / Find women are but men turned outside in" (4). The extraordinarily popular and influential (on seventeenth-century Spanish writers such as Cervantes and Lope de Vega) encyclopedic text of Juan Huarte de San Juan mentioned earlier, his *Examen de ingenios para las ciencias* (1594), recapitulates the one-sex model and establishes its currency in early modern Spain. Huarte writes: "And it is that man . . . does not differ from woman, as Galen says, other than in having the genital members outside the body. For if we examine the anatomy of a maiden, we find that she has two testicles within her, and two seminal ducts, and the uterus of the same construction as the virile member, lacking no feature" (608). Huarte proceeds to detail on a continuum ranging from the "pure" male to the "pure" female, with all the gradations in between, the manner in which within the one-sex model male shades into female (614–26); he also describes the facility with which one sex can theoretically convert into the other: "[I]f Nature had finished making a perfect man and wanted to change him into a woman, she would only have to place the instruments of generation within; and if, once made a woman, she wanted to turn her into a man again, she would need only to bring the uterus and testicles outside" (608).

As the statement by Huarte just quoted suggests, sexual dimorphism holds a host of implications for transvestism and thus for Erauso. Most significant, the sliding scale of the one-sex model, according to which the "body was far less fixed and far less constrained by categories of biological difference than it came to be after the eighteenth century" (Lacquer, 106), purportedly facilitated the easy slippage from one sex to the other—what Stephen Greenblatt calls the "myth of mobility" between sexes.[19] In the taxonomy of Huarte and other scientific writers, a male or a female could evince "male" and "female" characteristics being, respectively, effeminate or a virago when the characteristics of the other end of the continuum predominated. Men were understood to pass through a female stage in their youth before acceding to full masculinity (Greenblatt 1988, 78). In pre-eighteenth-century texts, bodies, such as those of lactating males or hermaphrodites, did "strange, remarkable, and to the modern readers impossible things" (Laqueur, 8). Consequently if, as Huarte's comment on convertibility began to imply, a transsexual transformation from female to male requires a simple flick of the switch by Nature and a little heat, then how would transvestism be viewed? In other words, if the body of a woman is a natural transvestite containing the male organs within, was not transvestism but a natural social extension of the "myth of mobility" intrinsic to the sliding scale?

Seen in the preceding light, transvestism takes its place among other ways in which I believe that the one-sex model was read back into or infiltrated gender constructions. The manly woman, I would argue, was one of them; the patristic notion that women will be resurrected more perfectly in heaven as men another; the fear that men witnessing transvestite female actors on a stage might backslide through propinquity and imitation into effeminacy yet another.[20] This anxiety around male to female gender instability in play-viewing gives one indication of how in the one-sex model, despite the superiority it accords the male (the scale, just as ideologically constructed as gender, is continuous but hierarchical, with the male considered superior), the fluidity of biological sex essentially opposes the rigidity and differentiating mechanisms of social gender. Laqueur states, "So-called biological sex does not provide a solid foundation for the cultural category of gender, but constantly threatens to subvert it" (124). Yet the examples of backreading I cited, transvestism among them, engage with the deep structure of biological sex not to the detriment of but to the benefit of gender difference, reinforcing it. In further support of my point let me note that in the comedia about Erauso (believed to date from 1626) by Spanish writer Juan Pérez de Montalbán, which I will discuss more fully later, one character asks Guzmán/Erauso why s/he has no facial hair. Guzmán replies, "Pues porque esté el valor más en su centro / Echo yo los bigotes hacia dentro" (Fitzmaurice-Kelly, 161) [So that valor be closer to the center, I grow my mustache inwards]. When we make the substitution of phallus for "bigotes" or mustache that the speech begs, we uncover the play's appeal to the one-sex model of women's internalized male sexual organs and its easy correlation of the one-sex model with transvestism and valor–alongside a subtle valorization ("So that valor be closer to the center") of the valiant manly woman.[21]

One final ramification of the one-sex model for transvestism and Erauso involves what Marjorie Garber calls the "transformative agency of clothing" (1993, 218); it ensues, somewhat differently from the above, from the opposition of the gender and sex models. Given that both sexes possess the same reproductive organs, albeit in different places, it follows from the one-sex model: first, that gender is, as Laqueur terms it, "theatricalized" (i.e., staged, constructed on top of a fluid continuum); and second, improbable as it sounds, that a penis would not absolutely qualify its bearer as a male. Laqueur notes that in the major Renaissance medical-jurisprudential text, Paolo Zacchia's *Questionum medico-legalium*, its author treats organs "as if they were contingent certificates of status" (140) because a penis was "a status symbol rather than a sign of some other deeply rooted ontological essence: *real* sex. It could be construed as a certificate of sorts, like the diploma of a doctor or lawyer today, which entitled the bearer to certain rights or privileges" (134–35). The phallus was thus, at least in theory, demoted to the status of one among many such certificates marking theatricalized gender and therefore could be conceived to occupy no more or less an important a place than other markers such as voice timbre, skin tone, temperament, beauty (see Huarte, 614–26)–or, might one add, clothing? Moreover, that gender was a theatricalized or staged construct conceivably fed, or was backread, into the theater itself. The conventions of seventeenth-century transvestite theater held that with the exchange of a few social markers a woman could convert her gender identity, arousing no suspicion. Whether it was the theater or theatricalized gender that conditioned the "transformative agency of clothing," the fact remains that the weight with which both paradigms invest external signs naturalizes a seemingly implausible dimension of Erauso's cross-dressing as presented in her texts: how it was that in fashioning her nun's habit into male garb she could henceforth be wholly accepted as a male.[22]

Had the situation been the other way around, had a man attempted to pass as a woman, his actions would undoubtedly have been construed quite differently. Sex and gender ideologies, the two of them constructed and clearly constructed from the same patriarchal fabric, both conspired to enshrine the male and thus to proscribe male to female crossings on either level. Despite or because of its potential for fluidity, the one-sex model interdicted male to female transsexuality (Huarte censoriously explains that males who in their mother's womb became women emerge as homosexuals with characteristics "indecent to the virile sex" [609]). In physiological terms, a woman might become a man by externalizing her internalized male organs through a burst of heat; Huarte's previous explanation of Nature's powers notwithstanding, logically the converse does not obtain. In more abstract terms, since as an author cited by William Harvey wrote, "nature always tends toward what is more perfect," "we therefore never find in any true story that any man ever became a woman" (Gaspar Bauhin, quoted by Laqueur, 127). We see that sexual dimorphism allows only for movement up, as it were, the Great Chain of Being.

The loaded, dichotomous attitude of the one-sex model toward biological transsexuality parallels that of gender politics regarding homosexuality. Here, following from the lines I have been drawing, it would not be the female but the male who is more severely judged for crossing "natural" bounds. Indeed, recent investigations have brought to light that a lesbian came under the scrutiny of the law only when she in effect threatened heterosexual marriage, either by being involved in sexual penetration (tribadism) or by entering into a marriage contract with another woman.[23] That is, only when she performed the male actions that held legal and the most profound social implications was a lesbian officially disciplined. Consistent and extraordinary opprobrium, on the other hand, was attached in Spain to male homosexuality. Ursula K. Heise, contrasting seventeenth-century England with Spain, maintains that Spain incurred "what is possibly the most violent history of persecution of [male] homosexuals in Europe." In 1497 the Catholic kings decreed punishment by burning for the so-called *pecado nefando* [abominable sin]; Philip II revalidated the decree in 1598. Burning, rather than hanging, was the punishment reserved for the most horrendous crimes (Heise, 362). Seventeenth-century annals, such as Barrionuevo's *Avisos* [Notices] (1654–58) in Spain and Robles's *Diario de sucesos notables* [Diary of Notable Events] (1665–1703) in Mexico, record many *autos de fe* of "sodomites." Most revealing for our purposes, however, is a case from 1530 noted by Rima de Vallbona of a male soldier who had fought bravely dressed as a woman in the conquest of Mexico; despite his admirable service to the Crown, he was condemned to death by burning (1992, 52). All of this further bolsters the conclusion that with regard to gender- or sex-crossings it was thought in the early modern period that the "man was demeaned, while the woman strove for something higher" (Dekker and van de Pol, 49).

❧❦❧

The higher thing that promoted Erauso's sanction may be something even higher, as it were, than masculinity. In the *Tercera relación* [Third Account] (1653) we find a rather confounding and presumably true anecdote describing Pope Urban VIII's reaction to Erauso.[24] Reportedly, after the pope had granted her permission to dress as a man, "a cardinal replied to His Holiness that he should consider carefully whether it was right to allow women who had been nuns to wear indecent clothing; to which His Holiness replied, 'Give me another Monja Alférez, and I will grant her the same privilege'" (Vallbona 1992, 171). That the pope himself, even in the face of opposition, should unwaveringly defend her intimates that the figure of Erauso held some religious value. We have seen Erauso assert in the Petition her desire to defend the Catholic faith. Further, in the portion I omitted from the Petition due to its length, Erauso portrays herself as being on a religious pilgrimage to Rome when she fell victim to a robbery (for which she also seeks compensation): "[I]n 1625 she tried to go to the Roman court to kiss His Holiness's feet, it being a holy year" (Vallbona 1992, 132). Despite the fact that none of the testimonials that accompanied this portion of the case describes her trip as religiously motivated, and despite the notable irreverence for religion encountered in the *Vida*, in the "official story" Erauso depicts herself as a pilgrim possessed of religious zeal.

Beyond overt professions of piety, the Petition, various of the *certificaciones*, and even the "unofficial story" (the *Vida*) also strike a chord of enormous religious resonance in emphasizing Erauso's virginity, the "rectitude and rare purity in which she has lived and lives" (Petition), and her cross-dressing.[25] Virginity, together with association of masculinity and virtue underlying Erauso's self-defense, forms the cornerstone of a Catholic tradition of transvestite female saints that dates from the fifth century. Although the Old Testament specifically forbids cross-dressing in either sex, the desire to imitate–the male–Christ and to maintain one's virginity and thus larger virtue are said to have incited a series of women to assume masculine dress in service, to use John Anson's phrase, of an ideal of androgynous perfection (5). Anson observes, supporting my earlier discussion of the connection between *vir* and *virtue*, that these women purified and elevated themselves by merging with the male, by becoming androgynous (9). Androgynous in the abstract, "manly women" in effect, they rallied to Saint Jerome's words (which perhaps reflect yet another backreading from the one-sex model) that a woman who "wishes to serve Christ more than the world . . . will cease to be a woman and will be called a man" (*Comm. in epist. ad Ephes.* 3.5). Following the pattern of Thecla rendered in the *Acts of Paul*, Saint Margaret of Antioch, Saint Theodora of Appollonia, Anastasia of Antioch, Hilaria, Theodora of Alexandria, Matruna of Perge, Eugenia of Alexandria (the Eugenia of my chapter's epigraph), and others, be they real or legendary, all followed the transvestite path to perfection.[26] Eugenia–who abandoned her pagan roots to become a Christian, dressed as a man, and eventually became provost of a monastery–justified her actions along lines uncannily evocative of Erauso's, saying, "Out of the faith I have in Christ, not wishing to be a woman but to preserve an immaculate virginity, I have steadfastly acted as a man" (Anson, 23).

Pedro Calderón de la Barca wrote a play based on the life of Eugenia that was published in 1660. Although Calderón casts Eugenia in the mold of a *mujer docta* or learned woman, his *El José de las mujeres* [The Joseph of Women] demonstrates that the tradition of female transvestite saints had not disappeared from view in seventeenth-century Spain. The most famous inheritor of the so-called "monachoparthenic" tradition of transvestite saints, Joan of Arc, also enjoyed a certain renascence in the seventeenth century.[27] During this period in France, according to Marina Warner, she came to represent not a heretic but the personification of virtue (see chap. 11). In Spain, Joan of Arc inspired Lope de Vega's play, *Pucella de Orleans* [Maid of Orleans] (now lost), later imitated by Antonio Zamora in his *Poncella de Orleans*. The legend of Joan of Arc conflates the woman warrior with the transvestite saint, with the latter dignifying the former. We hear reverberations of Joan of Arc's adamant and ultimately fatal refusal to abandon male dress in the statement regarding Erauso by the Council of Indies that "she is not known to wish to change her present clothing, which is that of a man" (Vallbona 1992, 131). The transvestite, the saint, and the virago, in sum, all join forces both in Joan of Arc and in Erauso to conjure the anomaly into a religious icon.

Echoes of the warrior-saint conjunction that underlies Erauso's Petition might elucidate but still cannot fully explain the incredible hagiographic version of Erauso's life by the Spanish Jesuit missionary Diego de Rosales (1601–77; the date of his text is unknown).[28] Rosales's text opens up the final matter I will consider in this section of the chapter: how in word and deed the anomaly was officially *staged* as an icon, rerouting but nevertheless feeding her fame. Rosales bases his version on the now, lamentably, lost chapter on Erauso by her and his contemporary, a certain Romay, "who wrote up this case" (Vallbona 1992, 181). The degree to which Rosales's account reproduces that of Romay can only be conjectured; some thing or things in the original must have provided Rosales with the fodder for his rendition. Whatever the content of the original, Rosales's document itself effects a religious rescripting of Erauso's persona of a most extreme and suggestive nature.[29]

Rosales's account builds features of warrior-saint legend into a more familiar story, of the prodigal son, of a "sinner saved" (Vallbona 1992, 183). In his version Catalina began as a fervent nun, but succumbing to the temptation to stray from the path of piety, she fled the convent and became a soldier. Characteristics familiar from the warrior-saint story surface in the depiction of this portion of Erauso's life, as soldiering provides the stage for purification and war a metaphor for spiritual struggle. Erauso's years as a soldier become a period of inner torment in that she resists the word of God, "fleeing from herself, for she could neither bear nor hold out against so harsh a battle, which was that of her thoughts" (180). She definitively assumes a male identity, using the name of Francisco de Noyola, "a name that she never changed" (180), and comports herself "with manly actions and a boldness so befitting a soldier that no one judged her to be a woman" (179)–both of which matters hark back to Erauso's Petition. Similarly, according to Rosales, Erauso "[a]lways preserved her virginity, with signal virtue" (180), being "always cloaked in the veil of virginal modesty" (181). And in a truly incredible addition to the Erauso story, Rosales states that she mortified her flesh when not engaged in military battle. Of Erauso's war wounds, Rosales writes: "It was her divine husband who was principally responsible for these wounds; like a lover, he wounded her in the breast to pierce her heart with the wound of the love she had so forgotten" (182). In the end this "strayed sheep," "wounded deer," and "weeping turtledove" (182) reportedly cedes to the divine Word and insists on professing as a nun.

A similarly pious construction of Erauso's life (minus the warrior-saint reverberations) is to be found at the end of the Mexican *Tercera relación* [Third Account] of 1653. After graphically recounting her transgressions, the final portion of the *relación* abruptly introduces a reformed Erauso who as a lay worshiper voluntarily adopted the religious regime of professed nuns. The *relación* has Erauso dying "an exemplary death . . . to the universal grief of all those in attendance" (Vallbona 1992, 174), in proof that God never abandons a sinner. The same urge found in Rosales and in the *Tercera relación*–the urge to normalize and naturalize a female figure celebrated for her anomaly–also manifests itself in the case of Sor Juana Inés de la Cruz. Sor Juana's *Fama y obras póstumas* [Fame and Posthumous Works] (1700), the very volume that as I discuss later eulogizes her prodigious idiosyncrasies, in a baroque counterpoint also includes Father Diego Calleja's conventionally hagiographic biography of the nun-writer. Calleja makes short shrift of Sor Juana's life as a writer to concentrate on the period after her supposed renunciation of humanistic pursuits and "conversion." The penitent Sor Juana of his biography so mortifies her flesh that she has to be restrained. As his famous line would have it, Sor Juana was not walking but flying to salvation.

In the case of both women and in all three texts we thus find an insistence on restoring, through textual means, the anomaly-turned-icon to a religious norm. Whether Sor Juana's penitential actions ever reached the extremes attributed to them by Calleja has prompted much heated speculation; that Erauso ever reached the heights of piety the texts ascribe to her inspires (at least in this reader) little more than incredulity. In any case, my point is not one woman's potential for piety versus the other's but that the radical rescriptings of Erauso–so dubious, so disjunctive with what we know of her–most tellingly lay bare the regulatory mechanisms of the Hispanic baroque church and state. Foucault, in *The History of Sexuality* (vol. 1, parts 1 and 2), asserts that in the seventeenth and eighteenth centuries the powers of the state begin to regulate the individual through discursive strategies rather than by means of physical force. Although, as the burning of "sodomites" makes all too patent, Counter-Reformation Spain hardly abjured physical punishment, it did make a concerted effort to extend its regulatory efforts to the sphere of discourse, creating a "guided culture" (*cultura dirigida*, cf. Maravall) devoted to the direction, subjection, and integration into the collectivity of the masses. J. H. Elliott writes that under Philip IV

> the government did not restrict itself to repressive measures. It also sought, where possible, to seize the offensive, mobilizing court preachers, playwrights, and artists on its behalf. There was no equivalent in Spain to the Gazette founded in France in 1631 by Théophrase Renaudot with Richelieu's blessing, but there was an unending stream of *avisos* and *relaciones* conveying officially inspired or authorized information. (1989, 183)

Public theater, reaching new heights during the golden age, was also pressed into the service of this regulatory enterprise. Theater, it is well known, provided a safe space where emergent elements such as the "manly woman" could cathartically play themselves out and be institutionalized and disciplined. The official scripting of the "manly woman," who was allowed a free sphere of action to fulfill her own and conceivably the public's rebellious fantasies only to be contained in marriage by the end of the comedia, at once dramatized the slipping out of their prescribed places of women–or by extension other elements–and emblematized the regulatory mechanisms of baroque guided culture.

As a "manly woman" who had materialized into real life, Catalina de Erauso, too, warranted official redirecting. We have seen that to a considerable degree Erauso had already regulated herself for official consumption in her Petition, a text shot through with culturally positive valences. Yet the popular appeal of the cross-dressing transgressive Basque woman, fanned by the sensationalizing *relaciones* and by word of mouth (and perhaps by the *Vida*, if it ever reached publication), overspilled that official document and might conceivably spin out of control. Whether, in accordance with Marjorie Garber's construction of the "transvestite effect," Erauso indexed a tangle of crises and thus incited to rebellion, I will not speculate; I am more interested here in the convolutions of the official staging of her fame.[30]

Rosales, for an at present undetermined audience and at an undetermined date, had pulled an exemplary and "readable" story of religious devotion out of a potentially contestatory and transgressive one. Equally regulatory and perhaps even more implausible–because it contradicted what was most likely taking place even as he wrote–is the play by Juan Pérez de Montalbán entitled *La Monja Alférez* that I briefly discussed earlier. Probably written while Erauso was in Rome, be it prescriptively or descriptively the play proclaims her rarity, her singularity: "Ser una muger soldado, / Y una monja alférez, es / El prodigio más estraño / Que en estos tiempos se ha visto" (Fitzmaurice-Kelly, 257) [To be a soldier-woman and a lieutenant-nun is the strangest prodigy that has been seen in these times]. Montalbán conventionally depicts Erauso as a "manly woman," that is, as a woman who has temporarily fled her socially determined role (and her sex) only to give in to both at the end. Although, unlike the conventional "manly woman," his Erauso would not marry at the end, Montalbán still manages to write a more socially acceptable chapter onto the life of the unregenerate Erauso. In a bizarre gestalt with the refusal to change her dress on which Erauso was insisting around the same time, the play culminates in Erauso's relinquishing her male identity, which action wins her high praise. The Viscount exclaims, "Nunca has mostrado el valor / Como ahora, de tu pecho" [Never have you shown your heart's valor as you do now], and Sebastián adds, "Más has ganado vencida / De ti misma, que venciendo / Ejércitos de enemigos" (Fitzmaurice-Kelly, 287) [You have achieved a greater victory in conquering yourself than in conquering armies of enemies]. Montalbán's simulacrum of the Monja Alférez as a former soldier now achieving the heights of "manly" valor by becoming a *woman* formed a smoke screen that perforce replaced the all too real and looming Erauso.

Despite all of this, I would assert that it was in the staging of Erauso's official reward rather than her literary staging, in praxis rather than in fiction, that Erauso was most stunningly recuperated as an exemplary figure. And here she herself, rather than any official figure, set the pace. I have just read the transparent maneuvers of Montalbán's play; let me now read the nuances of her reward.

If Montalbán and Rosales flagrantly rescript Erauso, her official reward reinflects her; while the first two authors write unreal chapters onto her story, the Crown and the pope simply reroute it in precisely the direction Erauso herself indicated. Erauso required subjection, and she had afforded them the means of achieving it. She had presented herself as a man. They would *make her a man*. Erauso's reward is multifaceted, and each piece of it signifies. The king, as stated earlier, granted her the rent on an *encomienda*. Moreover, according to Pedro de la Valle, the king granted her the title of *Alférez* (which she would henceforth ostentatiously use in official correspondence) and the right to *military* garb (Vallbona 1992, 127–28). All told, these are the signs of a man's reward, a hero's reward, specifically a conquistador's reward. The three aspects of Erauso's reward parlay an anomalous subject into a normative one, which (to a considerable degree) is exactly how Erauso had positioned herself. Further, as we also know, both the pope and the king allowed her to continue in male clothing. Since, as the Council of the Indies wrote, her cross-dressing had already taken place, it could not be changed. The past could not be changed, but it could be reinvented for the present and the future. Male garb, the external markers of masculinity, would replace the phallus—the only feature she lacked to make her a man—and, in a world conditioned by the one-sex model, serve not just to stage but functionally to regroup her as a male and into exemplarity. If a phallus was a contingent certificate of status, then it could be replaced by other status certificates that would overpower her problematic female identity. For Erauso, the myth of sexual mobility had effectively been translated into a means of upward mobility—one that provided her with the status she had requested and toward which she had angled the Petition and one that at the same time served the reformatory needs of the Crown vis-à-vis this socially anomalous figure.[31]

❧✧❧

III.

The life/story of Catalina de Erauso, we have seen at some length, unexpectedly embodied or could be construed to embody an array of culturally positive elements. Yet there is no denying that the Erauso of the three *relaciones*, of the *Vida*, and most likely of real life was unrepentantly transgressive. No matter how positively she was positioned or positioned herself, Erauso kept creating scandals, textual and real. The 1653 *relación* tells us that during her final years in Mexico, Erauso was asked to accompany a girl of marriageable age to the capital city. Unfortunately for Erauso, she fell in love with her charge, who was soon betrothed to a man. So taken was Erauso with the girl that she offered to pay her dowry as a nun and to enter the convent with her! The last document by Erauso herself that we possess, presented as authentic in the *relación*, is a letter James Fitzmaurice-Kelly describes as being "of incomparable arrogance" (xxiii) in which she challenges the girl's fiancé to a duel.

I believe, however, that here and elsewhere it was neither arrogance nor shortsightedness that led Erauso to commit the most audacious of her acts to writing and thus to jeopardize her prestige. A crucial justification for Erauso's risky textual strategy appears at the end of the Petition, where through the scribe she states: "She begs that Your Majesty be pleased to order that her services and long wanderings and valiant deeds be rewarded, thereby showing his greatness; rewarding her for the worthiness of her deeds and *for the singularity and prodigiousness of her life/story* [*por la singularidad y prodigio que viene a tener su discurso*]" (italics mine). I take this statement as the "smoking gun" of Erauso's writings. For even granting that in seventeenth-century Spanish *discurso* can mean either discourse or course (as in trajectory), here Erauso reveals a keen awareness of the worth of a singular and prodigious tale. In other words, her sensational and entertaining life/story, in equal measure with her service to the Crown, will merit her a reward. It is worth noting that Covarrubias's 1611 *Tesoro de la lengua castellana* [Treasury of the Castilian Tongue] presents the "singular" individual as a radically self-determining subject who disseminates novelty in public places (Mariscal, 91–92).[32]

What I call the smoking gun directs us to the moving force in Hispanic culture under Philip IV that countenances Erauso's *discurso*, and then back to the *Vida*. Things prodigious, striking, and bizarre, it is well known, held a magnified fascination for the Hispanic baroque worlds. Popular taste, sempiternally concerned with the scandalous and shocking, coalesced with the taste for extreme phenomena of the troubled times. Officialdom attempted to harness this current and to turn it to regulatory ends; awe is not a property of the state, but the state can manipulate and channel this fundamental emotion. As Maravall has outlined, from these designs there arose a seductive esthetic and politics of the amazing and peculiar: "Whatever is obscure and difficult, new and unknown, strange and extravagant, or exotic–all of this enters as an effective expedient [*resorte*] into the baroque code, whose purpose is to move the emotions, leaving them in suspense, astonishing them, exciting them with what they had never seen before" (*La cultura del barroco*, 467). To support his argument, Maravall cites López-Pinciano's contention that "the new thing delights, and the amazing more so, and the marvelous and wondrous even more" (1983, 215). In fact, Maravall argues that to mask the officially desired *lack* of change on more substantive fronts, baroque official culture displaced novelty into the less harmful arena of culture: "The irruption of outlandish elements in poetry, literature, and art compensated for the deprivation of novelty elsewhere" (138; also see chap. 9).

Particularly emblematic of this baroque tendency, and significant for the case of Erauso, is the matter of monsters. Octavio Paz aptly notes that the baroque intended to "astonish and amaze"; "hence it sought out and collected extreme phenomena, especially hybrids and monsters" (1976, 14).[33] What did the early modern Hispanic world understand as "monsters"? Naturally, the dwarfs and midgets so favored by the court and captured in Velázquez's paintings constituted monsters. Barrionuevo's *Avisos* and other documents of the times also present as monsters terrible curiosities such as the alleged individual with the feet of a goat and the face of a man (Barrionuevo, 73). Shockingly hybrid or contradictory phenomena, asserts Roberto González Echevarría, were considered monstrous and enjoyed extraordinary popularity. González Echevarría takes as an example of the hybrid monster Calderón's Segismundo, self-described in the play as "a composite of man and beast," which for the critic makes him "a double and contradictory entity in whom two natures coexist simultaneously" (34). Such monsters defy singular categorization; they incarnate incongruous conjunction, paradoxical encounter. In their residual implication as prodigies or omens sent by the Divinity with a message to be deciphered, they also signify undecidability. Further, according to González Echevarría and others (see Mullaney; Park and Daston), monsters in the seventeenth century were to be displayed–in the theater, in the wonder cabinet, in the public square, in paintings; recalling their etymological root in *monstrare* (to show), monsters purportedly incited not pity but the "curiosity and wonder of the spectator" (Reed, 176). And wonder itself, according to Descartes and Spinoza, precedes recognition of good and evil.[34] In practically all of the above terms, the phenomenon of Catalina de Erauso had something of the "monstrous" to it.

The baroque penchant for the bizarre also made its way into the nonfiction fields of popular journalism, such as annals and broadsides, and historiography. "In this monarchy prodigious things have happened," writes Almansa; "Miracles and rare prodigies have recently been seen," recounts Pellicer; "One sees portents and what are almost miracles," declares Barrionuevo–all journalists of the mid-seventeenth century (Maravall, 229). The *Anales de Madrid* [Annals of Madrid] of León Pinelo abound in tales of miracles, absurd cases, and prodigious phenomena. Similarly, New World historiographical texts of the period display a baroque sense of the marvelous quite unlike that of the sixteenth century. In the period of the early encounters and conquest the "otherly" flora, fauna, and customs of the indigenous peoples inspired high wonder. In seventeenth-century chronicles such as Juan Rodríguez Freyle's *El Carnero* (1638) the improbable and scandalous lives of the colonists were the currency on which writers traded to capture the public's interest, bringing the marvel to the micro-level of the quotidian where it intersected with the real.

The *relaciones* or broadsides that take Erauso as their subject exemplify the baroque esthetic I have been discussing. In these texts directed to the masses the timeless popular taste for scandal–Erauso would probably be portrayed in similar terms today by tabloids such as the *National Enquirer*–links up with the baroque esthetic of the bizarre and its regulatory aims. Together they further sensationalize Erauso's already sensational story by working all the extreme angles of her life at once. Rima de Vallbona states that the first two broadsides, written at the same time that the Monja Alférez was presenting her case to the Crown, aimed to support Erauso's petition (1981, 81–82, 143). Thus each of them attempts to redirect Erauso's story in what we by now recognize as predictable directions: by presenting her as either patriotically valiant (first and second *relaciones*) or pious (third *relación*). The first and third *relaciones* hold particular interest for the contradictions they accommodate. The *Primera relación* melodramatically recounts how Erauso overcame her weak nature and cowardly soul as a woman to perform the brave deeds of a man in service of her honor and that of her country. Directly derived, as its title (in Toribio Medina) tells us, from the scandalously provocative *Vida*, the broadside also abundantly regales the reader with pungent details of her gambling, crimes, and imprisonment, reproducing the tone, material, and even actual phrases of the *Vida*. For its part, the *Tercera relación* extensively titillates the reader with Erauso's lesbian passion for her young charge. The final paragraphs of the 1653 *relación*, as I suggested earlier, abruptly and incongruously splice in references to Erauso's piety and exemplary death. What emerges from this surprise ending, and indeed from both *relaciones* in their entirety, is an implausible, disjunctive concoction of subject formation and deformation. In this unregenerated textual embodiment of the contradictory subject, the two Erausos, the scandalous and the exemplary, the social anomaly and the social icon, share equal textual space and time.[35]

My larger point is the following: in these texts on the "monstrous" Erauso the regulatory functions of the esthetic of the bizarre short-circuit and in so doing destabilize categorization. For as they pander to the bizarre (to sell copies as well as to lend support to Erauso), the broadsides unabashedly burn the candle at both ends. They celebrate the Monja Alférez as both saint and sinner, law-abiding and lawless—according to my epigraph, as "honor" and "insult" to "her country." Popular taste for scandal, never fully harnessed, overflows regulation: the malformed subject naturally and "monstrously" coexists with the re-formed subject, disclosing the manner in which the exploitation of public taste can implode or boomerang. When the esthetic of the bizarre, predicated on extremes, connects with the textualization of a "monster"—that composite of contraries in whom opposites naturally coexist—contradictions remain standing, and stand out. Binary categorization is fractured, and a category-conflating textual space is produced. From the esthetic of the bizarre there thus emerges a space of exceptionality that both allows contradictions to stand and, significantly, subsumes them under its aegis. The very architecture of the *Primera relación* speaks to the border-crossings immanent in this volatile esthetic. The title and first lines of the work place it under the rubric of the extraordinary and monstrous; the first paragraph then inscribes Erauso in the exemplary; the rest of the work oscillates between showcasing her crimes and her heroism. The text may ostensibly purport to re-form Erauso into an exemplary male soldier, but its *dispositio*, a reification of the category-blurring potential of the bizarre, effectively does otherwise. In the undecidable realm of the monstrous and in these texts that follow lines introduced by Erauso's own Petition, contradiction becomes *paradox*: "a statement that may seem contradictory, unbelievable, or absurd, but that may actually be true in fact" (*Webster's New Universal Unabridged Dictionary*, 2d ed.).

In view of the untamable nature of the popular taste for the prodigious and bizarre, that Erauso was allowed to continue dressing as a man takes on one last implication. Seeing that the popularity of Catalina de Erauso, fomented by the broadsides, threatened to career out of control, the king pacified the public by devising what can easily be understood as a solution that fit the crime, a "monstrous" solution. The ultimate regulatory gesture led Erauso in a different direction from that undertaken by Montalbán. Erauso would not be reformed into a conventional woman; her cross-dressing, a major source of the Lieutenant-Nun's popular appeal, would be accommodated. She *would* be remade and re-marked, as I have already observed, into a man, but she would also remain a cross-dresser—an oddity, a monster, a prodigy. This double-pronged solution that kept her double edge alive, a fabulous finessing of regulation, reengages with the esthetic of the bizarre and creatively exploits border-crossing to the gain of all involved.

As the reader may already have deduced, in spotlighting rather than stifling certain transgressive aspects of her life in the Petition, Erauso also capitalizes on the esthetic of the bizarre to her own gain. The scandalous *Vida* utilizes and hyperbolizes the same strategy as the Petition in that its author omits any exemplary or extraneous material to focus almost exclusively on events that will shock and titillate the reader. Analogously, the *Vida* branches out from the esthetic of the bizarre to embrace other aspects of the prevailing baroque literary esthetic, galvanizing their melodramatic charge. The vicissitudes of Erauso's roguish life story as presented in the *Vida* exemplify the turbulence, mutability, and dynamism so characteristic of baroque literature in general. Erauso's life also warrants, and the text houses in its understated and underwritten way, gestures toward several specific literary modalities of the times.[36] Almost needless to repeat, the entire premise of the book dovetails with the popular dramatic theme of the woman disguised as a man: as Lope de Vega declared in his *Arte nuevo de hacer comedias* [New Art of Playwriting], women dressing as men "tend to please the audience greatly" (17). The erotic titillation of the would-be or might-be lesbian love scenes in the *Vida* has its match in the "equivocal episodes" not uncommon to cross-dressing theater in which a woman falls in love with another woman, one of the two taking the other for a man (Ashcom, 56). In passing from master to master, in evincing a completely malleable identity changes in which are self-consciously marked by changes in clothes, Erauso also figures in the *Vida* as a *pícaro* [picaresque hero] come to life. Or better, as a *pícara* [picaresque heroine], for her insouciant attitude recalls the female picaresque novels such as *La Pícara Justina* (1605) in vogue at the times. If the *Vida* displays the outer structure of the picaresque, the inner configuration of each chapter uncannily resembles a cloak-and-dagger play. Each chapter, I suggested earlier in discussing the *Vida*, frames a neat dramatic imbroglio. Despite the token descriptions of different Latin American cities that head several chapters, this is not the New World but a two-dimensional theatrical world in which characters such as "The New Cid," "Antonio Zerbantes" [Cervantes], and "Antonio Calderón" make their appearance. Chapter 13 of the *Vida*, in which Erauso rescues the adulterous wife of Antonio Calderón from his murderous rage after discovering her *in flagrante delicto* with a lover, could easily have been taken from the plays of the character's namesake. Erauso's life unwittingly imitated art, and the *Vida* exploits the points of confluence.

Did, then, the none too ingenuous Erauso write this text, so attuned to baroque culture and to the "smoking gun" and other aspects of her own calculated Petition? Beyond its transgressive nature and the question of the manuscript, the *Vida*'s tight emplotment and literary echoes cast doubt on Erauso's authorship, for it is unlikely that she possessed such authorial skills. Sporadic factual errors and anachronisms (including an incorrect birth date and misidentification of her brother's title)[37] also argue against Erauso's having written the text. On the other hand, the overriding historical veracity of the work and its author's intimate familiarity with circumstantial minutiae, along with the points of connection with her known writings that I have analyzed, support Erauso's participation in the genesis of the work. Scholars, in the main, have proposed three quite plausible theories in answer to the question of authorship.[38] First, Erauso herself wrote the work, which is entirely her own. Second, Erauso told her story to a more cultivated author, who then wrote it down, giving it form and perhaps texture. In other words, Erauso might have commissioned or authorized a ghostwriter to immortalize her story. I myself am inclined to accept this alternative, especially in view of the many mentions in the *Vida* of Catalina telling her tale. It is interesting to note that if indeed the second alternative is the case, we can consider the *Vida* an early form of testimonial literature, as was the *Infortunios de Alonso Ramírez* [Misfortunes of Alonso Ramírez] (1690) of Mexican baroque author Carlos de Sigüenza y Góngora with which it shares several features.[39] A third possibility would have it that a later author elaborated on Erauso's original, interpolating episodes. This would explain the literary resonances as well as what I call the "copycat" chapters, that is, the several schematic chapters (11–16) relating Erauso's exploits after she leaves military service and before her confession to the bishop, each of which finds her being blamed for crimes she did not commit.

All of this leads us to conclude that even if the *Vida* is not entirely of Erauso's making, she did have a direct hand in it. Moreover, and to my mind of equal importance, the text reflects–*be it metonymically or metaphorically*–Erauso's larger strategy vis-à-vis her own anomaly. And that strategy entailed her actively seeking to convert anomaly into notoriety, notoriety into gainful celebrity. The Petition flaunts her anomaly, the *Vida* even more so. Erauso is always pushing the envelope. These textual strategies find their complement in her extratextual actions. The Erauso we have seen is a woman eminently capable of mounting an effective self-defense and of what Leo Braudy calls "self-naming," that is, of greasing the wheels of her own renown. Litigious and astute in legal matters, on several occasions she mounted an elaborate machine of self-promotion comprised of numerous testimonials and *certificaciones*. A theatrical woman with a flair for the dramatic, Erauso openly courted notoriety: she sat for at least two portraits with famous artists, wrote several official appeals to the Crown without trepidation, never ceased her increasingly public transgressions, and told the story of her life hither and yon. The *Vida* alone has her telling her tale on at least four separate occasions. Royal historian Gil González Dávila describes a visit that Erauso paid him (Vallbona 1992, 157–58) and Pedro de la Valle recalls that Erauso "spoke to me of diverse affairs and incidents from her life, all very strange; I have recounted only the most remarkable and trustworthy ones here, as [the testimony] of a bizarre person of our times" (Vallbona 1992, 128), confirming her predilection for sensational self-disclosure.

From notoriety Erauso reaped the considerable fruits of fame. In this regard, the *Vida* provides both an emphatic testimony to her celebrity and, de facto, a prescriptive blueprint for the continued good treatment she hopes to receive. The *Vida* narrates in pathos-eliciting detail how the bishop of Guamanga responded to Erauso's confession: "My tale lasted until one in the morning, and all the while that saintly gentleman sat there motionless, without speaking or even batting an eyelid, listening to my story, and when I had finished he didn't say a word but remained there motionless, his face bright with tears" (*64–65*, 111). After receiving proof of Erauso's virginity, he pledges his respect–"I esteem you as one of the more remarkable people in this world" (*66*, 112)–and promises his support. Her story quickly becomes public: "News of this event spread *throughout the Indies*, and it was a source of amazement to the people who had known me before, and to those who had only heard of my exploits in the Indies, and to those who were hearing of them now for the first time" (*67*, 113; italics mine). The last chapters of the *Vida* show Erauso basking in her sudden fame and preferential treatment, both of which have extended from the New World to the Old. Having secured her dispensation from the pope, Erauso writes that in Rome: "My fame had spread abroad, and it was remarkable to see the throng that followed me about–famous people, princes, bishops, cardinals. Indeed, wherever I went, people's doors were open, and in the six weeks I spent in Rome, scarcely a day went by when I did not dine with princes" (*79*, 123).

High society has opened its doors to her. Erauso has become a cultural icon to the powerful and the norm-brokers as well as to the masses. In trading on her anomaly, which as I have endeavored to show found improbable favor with the state and the church, Erauso has discovered an escape valve from the rigidity of a regulated society. Unwittingly walking and perhaps quite wittingly writing herself into spaces that exploit and implode the contradictions of the baroque world, she has attained both social and gender mobility. Her official story and her unofficial story, official regulation, and publicity have together theatrically "produced" this phenomenon. Moreover, the sensational corpus of Erauso's life and works, so consistent with the sensationalizing esthetic of the body politic, has unlocked that zone of permissiveness and flexibility reserved for the prodigious and unusual. That is to say, in writing herself as a man and in mining her masculine/feminine difference, Erauso has achieved what in the baroque, thanks to its penchant for the bizarre, (and perhaps even now) is the ultimate category beyond categories and beyond the pale of normative social codes: fame.

✦

IV.

The familiar and the unprecedented, personal psychology, social context, and historical tradition, all join forces in distinctively baroque ways to enable Erauso's fame and autonomy. To further illustrate the contradictions and category-conflating dynamics of the Hispanic baroque that facilitated the transformation of a seventeenth-century anomaly into an icon, I conclude this chapter with a discussion of Sor Juana Inés de la Cruz's celebrity, surprisingly similar to Erauso's—as was Sor Juana's agency in producing it. I will argue that what Catalina de Erauso accomplished in the milieu of the Spanish world in part by tapping the resources of baroque mass culture, Sor Juana negotiated, using similar means and successfully for a time, in the sphere of Mexican baroque court culture. Given the extraordinary complexity of Sor Juana's mind and the absolute centrality of fame to Sor Juana's life and works, her tactics will at once be more elaborate, more transparent, more self-conscious, and more anguished than Erauso's. Given, too, the discrepant responses the issue of her fame generated in the nun's writings, I will not attempt to encompass it in a single discussion. Chapter 4, on Sor Juana's humbled self-representations, seizes the (perhaps ultimately unseizable) issue of fame from another angle, looking at what amounts quite precisely to the other side of the coin.

Sor Juana's acute self-awareness shines through from beneath the baroque acrobatics of her works. Poems such as "Let us pretend, sad Thought, that I am happy" (Romance #2), with its searing analysis of her own intelligence, show us a woman painfully in touch with her problematic place in the world. Sor Juana did not fail to recognize the incongruity of her position as a woman, a nun, an intellectual, and a writer. More than merely recognizing her anomaly, Sor Juana drew attention to it. In a variety of genres, and in registers ranging from the light to the mortally serious, many of Sor Juana's works openly address the incongruities of her position. For example, her first comedia, *Los empeños de una casa* [The Trials of a Household] (1683), has the character Leonor declaim Sor Juana's life story—a story of intellectual prodigiousness, beauty, and whirlwind celebrity. As I have argued elsewhere, Sor Juana encodes her dilemma as a daring creative woman into all of her major theatrical works, and not just into *Los empeños de una casa*.[40] Treating a serious theme in a jocular tone, Sor Juana's Romance #48 ("Replying to a gentleman from Peru who had sent her some small clay vessels, telling her she should become a man" [27]) flirts with the ideal of androgynous perfection. She glosses the notion that "si es que soy mujer / ninguno lo verifique" [that if I am a woman, let no one find it out] with the provocative declaration: "y sólo sé que mi cuerpo, / sin que a uno u otro se incline, / es neutro, o abstracto, cuanto / sólo el Alma deposite" [and I only know that my body, without inclining to one sex or another, is neuter or abstract, serving only to house the Soul]. Passing from body to mind, the *Primero sueño* inserts Sor Juana's "I" into a magnificently erudite portrait of the soul's daring nocturnal quest for knowledge. Finally, in her fraternal-twin autobiographical documents, the so-called "Autodefensa espiritual" [Spiritual Self-Defense] (1681–82?) and the "Respuesta a Sor Filotea de la Cruz" (1691)–the first in a tone of high invective and suggestively, the second with subdued militance yet extensively–the embattled Sor Juana magnifies her life story into an object lesson, to argue for all women's right to knowledge.

The anomaly that Sor Juana so openly acknowledged, rather than blocking her public renown, in characteristic baroque fashion fed into it. The weighty scaffolding of panegyrics that framed her works celebrated Sor Juana's prodigious singularity. Among the 105 (!) pages of laudatory poems in the nun's *Fama y obras póstumas* (1700), we find the following titles: "Pondering the erudition of Mother Juana Inés, from such an early age"; "For having acquired such wide knowledge without the aid of teachers"; and "To the incomprehensible elevation of the miraculous intelligence of the Singular Muse, Sor Juana Inés de la Cruz." Epithets such as the "Tenth Muse," "Phoenix of Mexico," and the overblown epigraph by Carlos de Sigüenza y Góngora to Sor Juana's Silva #215, "Mother Juana Inés, professed nun in the convent of San Jerónimo of Mexico: Phoenix of erudition in all bodies of knowledge: Rival of the most refined minds: Immortal glory of New Spain," further confirm Sor Juana's status as an anomaly cum cultural icon. Even today one is astonished at the extraordinary prominence and recognition bestowed upon the transgressive nun in her own times.

Georgina Sabat-Rivers insightfully remarks, "We may wonder whether the glory accorded to this woman in her own day . . . was due to her genius itself or to those Baroque ideas of being unusual, extraordinary, and amazing in a topsy-turvy world" (1992, 144). Both factors that Sabat-Rivers mentions authorize Sor Juana's baroque fame and the early modern model for learned women it reflects. In the early modern period learned women increasingly made their way into the public sphere. Nuns or otherwise, they continued (as subsequent chapters of my study detail) to incite far more anxiety and disapproval than admiration. However, a means was carved out of the antifeminist climate to accommodate the learned woman when, for example, her achievements–as did Sor Juana's–could serve as a monument to Culture.[41] No new paradigm, embracing the learned woman without qualification, yet emerged; instead the seventeenth century drew on the classical construct of the Tenth Muse (first applied to Sappho) to frame a space of exceptionality for learned women. Should it be so desired, the learned woman would be celebrated as an *exception* to her sex, as prodigious, as a rara avis, as a freak. This early modern paradigm allowed for an uneasy acceptance of the woman into the public sphere as well as for her containment, in a circumscribed and exclusive third space. The affinity between the gender-numbing category of the Tenth Muse and the baroque esthetic of the bizarre deployed in the case of Erauso also to the default of categorization hardly needs to be underscored. In any case, we can plainly hear the conjunction of the anxious Tenth Muse paradigm and its baroque orchestration in the overblown praises of Sor Juana's singular and prodigious achievements: hyperbolic comments in keeping with a baroque sensibility that still perhaps protest too much.

Keenly attuned to the baroque mechanisms that had produced her fame, Sor Juana played into them and played with them.[42] Engaging with her iconic status as a rara avis, Sor Juana not only drew attention to her incongruity but in her poetic self-representations also developed something of an iconography of anomaly. Romance #48, we have seen, humorously reconstructs her body into a logic-confounding sex beyond sex (I will return shortly to this loaded characterization). The self-invective of Sor Juana's last poem (Romance #51), from her most embattled days, vilifies her body as monstrous: "un casi rústico aborto / de unos estériles campos, / que el nacer en ellos yo, / los hace más angostados" [an almost rustic abortion miscarried by barren fields, themselves made all the more fallow by giving birth to me, *105*]. Sor Juana subjects her body, together with her anomalous position as "Phoenix of Mexico," to parodic treatment in the epistolary Romance #49. Here the nun answers a poem (included in vol. 1 of Sor Juana's works as Romance #48bis) sent to her by a gentleman recently come to New Spain in which he compares the Mexican writer, for her everlasting fame, to the phoenix, with its everlasting life. The gentleman also compares Sor Juana's fame with that of the Monja Alférez. Erauso unequivocally promoted her fame as a "monster"; in this magnificent burlesque of the baroque esthetic of the bizarre and of her role as a prodigious Phoenix of Mexico within it, even as she writes herself as a literal monster Sor Juana proves herself eminently aware of the contradictory, "monstrous" implications of being considered one. She is not unmindful of the benefits that accrue from her position as a rara avis, which makes her sui generis ("tengo solamente yo / de ser de todo mi linaje," I have only I as my whole lineage [ll. 31–32]), autonomous ("¿Hay cosa como saber / que ya dependo de nadie . . . ?" Is there anything like knowing that I now depend on no one? [ll. 133–34]), and safeguards her from others ("ni me ha de moler a mí / quien viniere a visitarme," nor need I be annoyed by those who come to see me [ll. 163–63]). "I did not think of such a thing," writes Sor Juana, "mas si él gusta gradüarme / de Fénix, ¿he de echar yo / aqueste honor en la calle?" (ll. 109–12) [but if he wishes to raise me to a Phoenix, must I toss this honor into the street?]. Nevertheless, Sor Juana does not fail to register that the phoenix who thus finds herself exempt from categories and regulation is *also* a monster and a freak. In an abrupt turnabout, the poetic speaker takes grave exception to the manner in which circus people have turned the phoenix into a sideshow freak (a "Monster" or, fittingly enough for a learned woman considered to possess a hypertrophied intelligence, a "Cabeza del Gigante," or Giant's Head) whom they parade from town to town, charging those who love novelty ("amigas de novedades" [l. 182]) an admission fee to see her. "No, not that!" the poem exclaims. No one will see this Phoenix, who to avoid display has shut herself away under lock and key (in the convent?). As befits the equivocal expedience of being a phoenix, the poem ends on an ambiguous note. The diction of the last stanza leaves it unclear whether Sor Juana grants only her addressee the right to compare her to the phoenix or to anything else, or whether—in full awareness that the advantages of baroque fame outweigh its disadvantages—the poet desires that she be compared *only* to the phoenix and to nothing else.[43]

Sor Juana derives a considerable portion of her Romance #49 from a poem by a male baroque writer: from Francisco de Quevedo's "La fénix" [The phoenix] (vol. 2, 245–46). Quevedo's third-person portrait of the phoenix depicts an isolated, melancholy creature (an "eternal hermaphrodite," another manifestation of the hybrid monster of the baroque) to whom praise is a burden. Sor Juana's first-person portrait of herself as a phoenix clearly resonates, directly and indirectly, with Quevedo's poem, but adds an extremely telling coda to it. Nothing in Quevedo's poem would suggest the ending of Sor Juana's *romance*, which constitutes her most penetrating comment in the poem on the downside of being a celebrated woman writer and on the baroque sensibility so fond of novelty ("amigas de novedades") that sponsored her as such. Indeed, further confirming her heightened awareness of the problematic dynamics of her fame as the Phoenix of Mexico, Sor Juana's coda on the phoenix as a sideshow freak whom the public must pay admission to view swerves away from Quevedo's poem and into a rather unsavory implication of early modern women in the public sphere. *"Quien ver el Fénix / quisiere, dos cuartos pague"* (ll. 185–86; italics in original) [*Whoever wants to see the Phoenix, let him pay two coins*]: Sor Juana here comes very close to equating her fame with prostitution, publicity with the "public" woman. "Whore's the like reproachful name, as poetess—the luckless twins of shame," wrote Robert Gould in his *Satirical Epistle to the Female Author of a Poem* (London, 1691; Gallagher, 69). Misogynist seventeenth-century males would have it that the publication of a woman's work automatically implied a public woman or prostitute (Gallagher, 69); the literarily and personally hypersensitive Sor Juana recognizes that her fame as a phoenix brings her freedom but is a tacit sellout to the popular taste for novelty. Quevedo's phoenix shrank from a burdensome fame; Sor Juana as Phoenix of Mexico must nevertheless embrace it.

Though its dates are uncertain, by the time that Sor Juana wrote Romance #49 on her monstrous fame, she certainly knew whereof she wrote. In *Los empeños de una casa* (1683), through her alter ego Leonor, the nun describes her mushrooming fame: "Era de mi patria toda / el objeto venerado / . . . / llegó la superstición popular a empeño tanto, / que ya adoraban deidad / el ídolo que formaron" (4.37–38) [I was the venerated object of my entire country; popular superstition reached such a pitch that they adored as a deity the idol that they made]. No mere self-promotional campaign, Leonor's speech corresponds to the fact that in the 1680s Sor Juana found herself in an exceptional position of fame and privilege. In Mexico and in Spain she was the famed mix of a nun-poet, an icon of New World culture. Published in Spain, her *Inundación castálida* [The Overflowing of the Castalian Spring] had obtained the remarkable success that had it reprinted nine times. Beyond her prodigious talent, what during most of this period bolstered and guaranteed her privileged position was the support of the viceroy, the Marquis de la Laguna, and vicereine, the Marquise de la Laguna and Countess de Paredes in her own right, who reigned from 1680 to 1688. They had taken her up, they visited her frequently, and the Marquise de la Laguna had her works published. In the *Advertencia* [Foreword] to what is now Romance #16, Sor Juana expresses her love and "gratitude from one favored and celebrated" to her dear friend, the vicereine. In sum, Sor Juana had free access to the power center of colonial Mexico. She thus enjoyed conditional immunity from reprobation or regulation, even though as we will see here and more extensively in chapter 4, disapproval of her activities circulated continuously. Enjoying conditional immunity, Sor Juana wrote with notable impunity. Her lighthearted comedias, her love poetry, that is, the majority of her secular works, date from this period. In the early 1680s, Sor Juana also dismissed her confessor Antonio Núñez de Miranda with a letter so vehemently defiant as to be unique in her repertoire. "Sin temor en los concursos / defendía mi recato / *con peligros del peligro* / y con el daño del daño" (4.38; italics mine) [In poetry contests I fearlessly defended my modesty, *from dangers with danger*, from injuries with injury]. These were her glory days, and personally and literarily Sor Juana availed herself of the freedom they afforded her.

During this period in which she largely found herself beyond categories and regulation, Sor Juana literarily cross-dresses. Breaking literary rules, she free-falls between male and female personae; playfully making herself "diversa de mí misma" (Romance #51) [different from myself], she evinces boundless sexual permutability in a literary space that, very much in the terms of José Donoso's novel, constitutes a *lugar sin límites* or limitless place.[44] Sor Juana effectively reenacts the potency of fame and favor to defy limits with her literary cross-dressing, coextensive and coterminous with her glory days. In this figuration of freedom, a host of poems finds Sor Juana freely crossing boundaries by speaking as a female lover *or* as a male lover. The blazing gap or *écart* between Sor Juana's known status as a nun and her assumed poetic roles as male and as lover invites the reader to imagine Sor Juana freely reimagining and positioning herself. Just the opposite of a fully embodied poetic presence that presumes a relationship of identity between poet and poetic speaker, these poems are the space of free-flowing reembodiment. Moreover, in a couple of poems, Sor Juana reimages herself into a third sex outside sex–that is, into (not just boundary but) border-crossing incarnate. In Romance #19, as chapter 2 of my study will elaborate, she draws on the Neoplatonic solution that souls have no gender to write love poems to another woman ("Ser mujer, ni estar ausente, / no es de amarte impedimento: / pues sabes tú que las almas /

distancia ignoran y sexo," Being a woman or far away is no hindrance to my love: for the soul, as you well know, distance and sex do not count [ll. 109–12]). In Romance #48, referred to earlier, Sor Juana tells the gentleman from Peru who told her to be a man that she is not even a woman. If, as Saint Thomas maintained and as Sor Juana appears to follow,[45] woman was created solely to fulfill a reproductive function, then "a mí no es bien mirado / que como a mujer me miren, / pues no soy mujer que a alguno / de mujer pueda servirle" (ll. 101–4) [it is not right to look on me as a woman, since I am not a woman who can act as one]. Her condition as a virgin, as was the case with the transvestite nuns, constitutes androgyny ("es común de dos lo Virgen," a virgin has no sex at all [l. 100]). Hence, as the nun goes on to state, her body is neutral, abstract, only a repository for the soul. Here Sor Juana verbally fashions herself into a third sex and tacitly refashions her neutralizing nun's habit into a kind of "monstrous" cross-dressing. As are her poems, it is a site of privileged border-crossing, of transformative potency, of gender undecidability.

Sor Juana writes in Romance #48 that her body "inclines" to neither the male nor the female sex (l. 106). Whether or not her statement appeals to the one-sex model, it is clear that the boundary- and border-crossings of the poems just discussed replicate its sliding scale.[46] In effect or in fact they pit this construction of "sex" against gender, that is, the essentially fluid against the (socially, punitively) differentiated. Erauso's life may well have played into the myth of sexual mobility as it bore on transvestism; very differently but still partaking of a fluid field, the poems of Sor Juana's glory days invoke and correlate to mobility per se through the device of sexual permutability. In this way, too, beyond what we have already seen, the Mexican nun writes herself as a phoenix: "yo soy la Fénix / que, burlando las edades, / ya se vive, ya se muere, / ya se entierra, ya se nace" (ll. 53–56) [I am the Phoenix who, outwitting the ages, now lives, now dies, now is buried, now is born]. Similar to the phoenix, in both literature and in life she has crossed imposing boundaries. Moreover, like the phoenix with its self-regenerative powers, Sor Juana may by means of her poems be actively *birthing herself* into invincibility. As did Erauso's, Sor Juana's writings can function preemptively to make her invincible by broadcasting and thus solidifying her fame. For all told, in calling such constant attention to her freedom, her iconicity, and her anomaly, Sor Juana's writings function prescriptively as well as descriptively. Like Erauso, she engages in self-naming to ensure and insure her fame, her mobility.

The humor and wit of such poems as her phoenix-fable, along with the other baroque literary mechanisms I have discussed, comprise potent weapons in Sor Juana's arsenal of fame-maintaining instruments. In the witty Romances #48 and #49, Sor Juana capitalizes on what Bakhtin calls "the permanent corrective of laughter" (55) to turn inflammatory issues into a non-threatening comedics of gender. Humor generates border-crossings, producing a mental reaction that subverts the "lofty direct word" (Bakhtin, 55) and the physical reaction of laughter that can neutralize anger. Far more significantly, the wit (*ingenio*) so highly prized by the baroque served as an important calling card for Sor Juana into the court and into fame. She traded on it constantly, producing reams of witty, ephemeral, occasional poetry. This poetry, practically devoid of literary merit, was rich with cultural capital. Light and frothy, it is also a weighty indication of the expert manipulation of cultural structures that so marked Sor Juana's life and works.

For, as I have already intimated, even as she reveled in and literarily reenacted the freedom of her glory days, Sor Juana was also taking steps to preserve it. Fully cognizant of the precariousness of her anomalous situation, as one can conclude from the nun's dismissal of her confessor (she accuses him of "fiscalizando mis acciones con tan agria ponderación como llegarlas a *escándalo público*," denouncing my actions with such bitter exaggeration as to create a *public scandal* [Tapia Méndez, 15; Paz, *495*; italics in original]), Sor Juana literally wrote herself into the esthetic and structures of the ruling order. We have seen in considerable detail how, like Erauso, she played to the baroque cult of the bizarre. Erauso may or may not have been attuned to baroque literature per se; the eminently well-read Sor Juana systematically essayed, with constant displays of wit, all of the major poetic and dramatic genres in vogue during the baroque period: sonnets, *silvas*, *ovillejos*, *endechas*, *romances*, *villancicos*, *ensaladas*, comedias, eucharistic plays, and so on. From within the walls of her convent, Sor Juana insistently positioned herself as the star of an imaginary literary academy.[47] Yet the astonishing compendiumlike nature of her works, I submit, is no mere display of baroque virtuosity. By undertaking all the genres of the ruling discourse, Sor Juana legitimated herself beyond all question as a writer and effectually rendered herself the quintessence of the baroque. Further, in so doing, she rendered herself indispensable to the court, to the ruling class. More than two-thirds of her work is occasional or commissioned. The *Neptuno Alegórico* [Allegorical Neptune], written to welcome the new viceroy, the scores of *villancicos* and religious ceremonies performed throughout Mexico, the comedias and eucharistic dramas, as well as her reams of encomiastic poetry, all fulfilled crucial societal functions while serving her personal needs. Through them, from her marginalized position Sor Juana became a pillar of Mexican court society, its unofficial official poet.

It is clear that, like Catalina de Erauso, Sor Juana needed fame to maintain her autonomy—in her case the freedom to pursue a life of the mind despite her gender and her status as a nun. Fame was Sor Juana's bulwark. She had to cultivate and promote it. Hence, she incurred outright contradiction to self-serving purpose with her multiple self-fashionings. Chapter 4 of the present study demonstrates how Sor Juana, who as we have seen here underscored her anomaly and fame, also labored consistently to undo them—among several ways, by writing herself out of anomaly and into the conventional script for women of her society. The two transgressive women, Sor Juana and Erauso, verbally regulated themselves in accordance with the gender ideologies of their times: the former by writing herself as a "woman," the latter by writing herself as a "man." And as did Erauso, Sor Juana not only actively produced her fame but also managed it with the skill of an expert impresario. She encouraged patrons to publish her works and participated in their publication. She maintained an extensive correspondence with other savants, entertained important guests, and, as María Luisa Bemberg's film on the nun ("Yo, la peor de todas," I, the worst of all) dramatizes, created a salonlike atmosphere in the convent's locutory.

When for reasons completely beyond her control the protective structures that Sor Juana had so zealously cultivated collapsed, her fame and anomaly finally worked against her. Briefly summarizing a very complex situation, I will say that after the departure of the Marquis and Marquise de la Laguna in 1688, the *mala fama* or notoriety–deriving from baroque misogyny, from social and religious interdictions of writing females and nuns, from jealousy of court figures and prelates–that had always accompanied Sor Juana's fame definitively prevailed over the *buena fama* or positive renown–eventuating from the baroque sensibility, from her own exceptional talent, and from her alliances with the power center–that had in the previous decade safeguarded her.[48] The loss of her viceregal protectors, the unauthorized publication of her *Carta Atenagórica* [Letter Worthy of Athena], the reprimand of Sor Juana by Bishop Fernández de Santa Cruz, a climate of political and economic tension in Mexico City, among several other issues, all conspired to give advantage in the 1690s to those who would diminish her. Sor Juana then found categories and limits reimposed, her *lugar sin límites* razed. As Verónica Grossi states:

> Sor Juana's literary project was initially supported by the court hierarchy because it was looked upon as an exceptional endeavor, the prestige and extraordinary quality of which would reinforce the values and aspirations of the aristocratic community. That very project was later restricted, rejected, and censured by the political and religious hierarchy (including the Bishop of Puebla, Manuel Fernández de Santa Cruz). The officials came to view her literary activity as threatening and autonomous, as "different" (and, moreover, as flaunting its strangeness, its otherness, its marginal nature), as impossible to integrate into the socio-literary structures of the hegemony and as unfitting to the symbolic values of the reigning political order. (38)

From a cultural icon the nun saw herself plummeting to a pariah. Even the publication in Spain in 1692, sponsored by the Countess de Paredes, of the second volume of her works–with an engraving of *Fame* on its cover–could not sufficiently affect her fortunes in Mexico.[49] Before renouncing humanistic pursuits, Sor Juana would write her eucharistic plays, the "Respuesta a Sor Filotea de la Cruz," the *Primero sueño*, her series of feminist *villancicos* to Saint Catherine of Alexandria. Figuring herself implicitly or explicitly in each of them, the besieged Sor Juana at this point abandons literary cross-dressing to assume the exclusive literary identity of a female and, in the latter three efforts, to defend the rights of women in general. The almost desexed/almost inaudibly gendered body and almost invisible "I" of the poetic speaker in Sor Juana's extraordinarily cautious summa, the *Sueño*, present a pained counterpoint to and echo of the free crossings of her earlier period. Shortly after writing these works, to forestall her total undoing, Sor Juana surrendered her difference to become a model or conventional nun. She recalled her confessor, renewed her vows, subscribed to abject penitential documents, and assumed at least something of the self-mortifying stance that Calleja exalted in his hagiographic biography of the nun.

Unsuccessful as Sor Juana's ability to manage her own anomaly proved to be in absolute terms, the tragic ending to her story does not nullify or even diminish her achievements. Nor should it mitigate the argument I have set out in this final section of my chapter regarding the manner in which two women of the baroque age manipulated the dominant culture's very mechanisms to consolidate their autonomy. By exploiting rather than effacing their own male/female difference and trespasses to enhance their fame, both Catalina de Erauso and Sor Juana Inés de la Cruz advantageously availed themselves of a counterhegemonic space latent in the dominant culture itself.

The full measure of Erauso's sentience regarding her public position and writings, I must admit, still remains somewhat elusive to me, open to speculation. Sor Juana's trenchant awareness both of her self and of her circumstances, on the other hand, provides us with an apt statement of what I believe to have been the border-crossing pragmatics of baroque fame that favored both women. In her last poem (Romance #51), later entitled "In recognition of the matchless pens of Europe, whose praises enhanced her works. Lines found unfinished," Sor Juana observes that in the eyes of those who would praise her, the *extraordinary and bizarre have replaced the perfect*: "Si no es que el sexo," she states with uncanny insight, "ha podido / o ha querido hacer, por raro, / que el lugar de lo perfecto / obtenga lo extraordinario" [Might it be the surprise of my sex that explains why you are willing to allow an unusual case to pass itself off as perfection? *109*]. This is the only justification for her fame that Sor Juana allows herself (because, as she says, it obliquely redeems her sex), and the last full portion of her last poem. Following it, the poet opens a new movement with a suggestive reference to the leveling power of (baroque) tastes–"Quien en mi alabanza viere / ocupar juicios tan altos, / ¿qué dirá sino que el gusto tiene en el ingenio mando?" [One who found such lofty wits praising me could only say that their tastes had overruled their minds, *109*]–and then the tantalizingly incomplete Romance #51 evanesces. Sor Juana's statements dovetail with my chapter's two epigraphs, which read in the light of the preceding pages suggest that for the contradictory age of the baroque, phenomena such as prodigious women who amaze, astonish, affright, perturb, and strike mute could occasion a blindness–and a fame–that undercut antitheses such as the deity and the delinquent, honor and insult.

CHAPTER TWO

Women on Love, Part I: Love in a Choleric Time

To lead an autonomous life and to relate her life story in official or extra-official contexts, Catalina de Erauso essentially rendered herself a man. We have seen that to finesse her sanction and renown, she represented herself as a man and appealed to the patriarchal ideology as well as to its esthetic. Despite the similarities in the two women's manipulation of dominant cultural structures, then, Erauso's gender stratagems contrast rather than interface with those of Sor Juana, who wrote qua woman and in defense of her sex. To underscore this contrast is to open up a large, significant, and imbricated issue, all too literally a Pandora's box: *How could, and did, pro-female literature of women writers exist in the resistant climate of seventeenth-century Hispanic cultures?* The burdens against it would lead us to expect the outcome for feminist discourse that María de Zayas pessimistically predicts in her *Desengaños amorosos*: "Well, if those of us [women] who are appointed today to disenchant are to tell the truth and if we wish to teach them [men] a lesson, what can we expect except hatred and rancor?" (*204*, 294). That, as the case of the best-selling yet militantly feminist Zayas itself testifies, the opposite could obtain, prompts the investigations of the present chapter.

This chapter offers a selective overview of the field or what might be called the ontology of the pro-female discourse, especially by women writers, of the Hispanic baroque: the climate surrounding feminist discourse, the sites in which that discourse was produced, the strategies to which it took recourse, what enabled and authorized and naturalized it, the dynamics of its reception. My agenda within this overview will establish, among other things, that it is a field laden with conscious or de facto negotiations with tradition and with ironic returns of conventions.

In laying out the topography of the field of feminist discourse, the present chapter pivots, hingelike, between those that precede and follow it. As did chapter 1, chapter 2 rallies around improbable situations, around the conundrums of "how they got away with it"; I also examine and historicize more fully here the counterindicative, misogynist dynamics of the Hispanic context. At the same time, chapter 2 raises issues of love and disillusionment that provide the scaffolding for its sequel, chapter 3. In essence, where chapter 1 looked at the aporias in baroque articulations of gender that facilitated Erauso's and Sor Juana's successes, here I broaden out to the matrices of baroque discourse that facilitated the voicing of feminist positions; similarly, where chapter 3 will look at the poetics of a feminist space (the convent), this chapter will look at the "spaces," in elite and popular literature, that baroque culture afforded a feminist poetics or discourse as well as how they were instrumentalized by women writers, notably by Sor Juana, María de Zayas y Sotomayor, and Ana Caro Mallén de Soto.

Before proceeding, three quick clarifications are in order. First, by "feminist discourse" specifically in the seventeenth-century context, I mean texts that articulate a defense of women and women's rights such as the right to education, often along lines advanced by the *querelle des femmes*. In keeping with one central argument of the chapter, I include in my purview anything that purposefully on the face of it *or* merely on the face of it, *or* deeper within its machinery and machinations, fits this criterion. The overall designs of text and context will be taken into account, but matters such as satirical or regulatory intent will not exclude these works from consideration (or, I will argue, agency) in the field under survey. Therefore, in the first section of the chapter I will be surveying the discursive sites in which pro-female articulations either manifested themselves or masqueraded as such. Second, I will not be examining religious discourse, which has received more attention than secular writings.[1] Third, because to my knowledge the question of feminist discourse in the secular literature of the seventeenth-century Hispanic worlds has not yet been broached or treated in precisely these (abstract and admittedly ambitious) terms, I can only purport here to lay out some broad, seminal lines of an issue with vast dimensions and ramifications that merit further fleshing out, I hope, by many other scholars.

Hence, while I settled on straightforward titles for the book itself and its introduction, I have purposely overloaded the title of this chapter with familiar literary allusions in order to suggest the multiplicity of issues that its subject will call into play. "Women on Love" not only invokes the central site of seventeenth-century gender discourse, love, but also ironically evokes that "counter-revolutionary sexual politician" (Millet, 233), D. H. Lawrence. Lawrence's misogyny, inveighing against the feminine as the lower half of being and the masculine as the higher, perpetuates the terms of the antifemale side of the *querelle des femmes*—so pervasive in the seventeenth century and that women perforce combat—and signals the unchanging persistence of *querelle* constructions from the fifteenth to the seventeenth to the twentieth century. His particular argument that involvement with women seriously hinders the male project—"It is not woman who claims the highest in man. It is a man's own religious soul that drives him on beyond woman, to his supreme activity. . . . He may not pause to remember that he has a life to lose, or a wife and children to leave" (*Fantasia of the Unconscious*, 138)—replays, with remarkably little difference, the aims of the Spanish state that as I will argue together with Ruth El Saffar drove its official barring of the feminine. "Love in a Choleric Time," for its part, summons up Gabriel García Márquez's *El amor en los tiempos del cólera* (1985). This neobaroque novel's esthetic of excess and extremes and its equation of love with illness refigure the choleric, disturbed world of the baroque per se and its prevailing picture of the dementia of love, so suggestive for male and female writers alike. Both García Márquez and Lawrence, of course, wrote best-sellers–as did, curiously enough, certain Hispanic women writers of the seventeenth century. Finally, the allusiveness of my title in its own right signals the modus vivendi and modus operandi of baroque discourse, an architectonics crucial to any discussion of seventeenth-century writing and particularly crucial for women's writing. All of these issues, in ways I have already begun to suggest, will exert pressure on the focused examination of feminist discourse in the Hispanic baroque that follows.

❧

I.

THE RETURN OF THE REPRESSED

What exerted the most determining pressure on feminist discourse in the Hispanic worlds was, of course, their especially virulent misogyny. An exceptionally enlightened seventeenth-century Spaniard, Martín González de Cellorigo, lamented that Spanish women had been reduced to "a worse condition, in every respect, than in other countries" (Maravall, *Picaresca*, 663–64); Maravall states that "the seventeenth century was probably one of the worst in terms of men tightening their pressure on women" (Maravall, *Picaresca*, 654). Misogyny, as the case of Lawrence and countless others like him throughout the ages illustrates, remains a transhistorical phenomenon attributable to a variety of power-mongering motivations. Yet it takes on special import and contours in certain historical contexts. That a neomedieval misogyny should reassert itself in seventeenth-century Spain with such particular force has traditionally been ascribed to the demands of the Counter-Reformation and to the unyielding Catholicism of a country that, in the eyes of some, for this reason did not absorb the full impact of Renaissance humanism. Fray Luis de León's *La perfecta casada*, written in the sixteenth century and still fettering females to religious norms while tepidly favoring their education, supports the latter contention in terms of women. The Counter-Reformation, bent on conserving Spain as a bastion of pure Catholicism and on conserving the status quo, strove to squelch what advances had derived from humanist efforts and also, as I discussed in the introduction, targeted the control of women as a means of managing crisis. Rather than repeating the lines already established, yet still keeping them present, let me now bring forth Ruth El Saffar's recent and deeper probings into Spanish misogyny for what they tell us about it on both the local and the transhistorical levels: the extreme misogyny of seventeenth-century Spain, especially as construed by El Saffar, proves to be, if not an exemplary, an extremely telling phenomenon–one that redounds into Latin America as well as into both anti- and pro-female discourse.

In the last book that El Saffar wrote before her untimely death, *Rapture Encaged: The Suppression of the Feminine in Western Culture* (1994), and in a series of previous articles on similar themes, the critic offers a fascinating reading of the Spanish Empire on historical and psychoanalytic grounds addressing how it was that there and then the "balance of masculine and feminine energies that was the dream of so many Renaissance thinkers . . . gave way in the period we have come to call the Baroque to visions instead of separation, suppression and dominance" (1988, 7). Demonstrating that a broad range of factors–"the drive for religious and political unity, the insistence on an unbending Catholic orthodoxy, the shift in population distribution away from the country and into the cities, the establishment of the military, the growth of the colonies, the development of male schooling, the sharp separation of gender roles, the practice of wet-nursing"–bolstered a "separative consciousness oriented toward dominance and progress" (1994, 78), El Saffar maintains that the demands of empire (and especially a crumbling empire) warranted a male atmosphere that precluded and rendered deleterious maternal female influence. Called into service in the cities, the court, the military, and the New World, men and boys were forced to abandon their connection with the land, the family, the mother, and were plunged into an exclusively masculine world based on values of dominance, discipline, independence, loyalty, emotional repression. To respond to this Oedipal situation, to this "call of the father" (1994, 66), to this "male genesis" (1988, 9) compelled and promoted by the needs of the state, entailed in males "a suppression of feeling and rejection of all taint of feminine nature and maternal influence" (1988, 9), influence that had become the embodiment of what men feared and despised in themselves (1994, 62). "The integral self, the autonomous subject that became the accomplishment and hallmark of masculine identity, was purchased at the price of connection to the mother" (1990, 4).[2] Thus was produced, by the state and in the individual, a barring of the feminine (I might add: the replacement of one partial object, the mother, with another, gold), like that which Hélène Cixous's poetic lines neatly encapsulate: "and dream of masculine / filiation, dream of God, the father / emerging from himself / in his son,–and / no mother then" (Keller, 43).

The barring of the feminine surfaced explicitly in official texts and contexts. As the Spanish Empire declined, *effeminacy* became a scare word invoked to explain its demise. Male writers repeatedly denounced the self-emasculation of their fellow countrymen, their vacating of male values, their abdication of the warring spirit in favor of frivolous pastimes. In 1621, for example, Fray Juan de Santa María quotes Sallust to the effect that "when a kingdom reaches such a point of moral corruption that men dress like women, . . . that the most exquisite delicacies are imported for its tables, and men go to sleep before they are tired, . . . then it can be regarded as lost and its empire at an end" (Elliott, 251). Unlike England, where similar anxieties about male effeminacy in an urban society can be heard (as in *Hic Mulier*),[3] in Spain women were not directly accused, at least in these treatises, of assuming masculine roles. They were, nevertheless, not just rhetorically but ideologically implicated as the symbolic scapegoat for Spain's failures. For a man to be "effeminate" was not simply for him to adopt "feminine" ways but to betray the aims of State.

The year 1639, which saw the events coming to a head that would definitively mark the dissolution of the Spanish Empire, also witnessed the production of a play by Pedro Calderón de la Barca, *El mayor encanto amor* [Love, the Greatest Enchantment].[4] If Calderón's play reifies the impending crisis and its alleged causes in thinly veiled terms, it dramatizes the barring, indeed the demonizing, of the feminine in unmistakable terms. *El mayor encanto amor*, performed in the palace gardens at the request of the Count-Duke Olivares's wife, remythologizes in tacit service of the Spanish state Ulysses's struggles with the enchantress and temptress Circe. In it, Circe exercises her magical powers on the quintessential warrior, attempting to retain him for herself and for love, and away from war. A *mujer esquiva* (in the context of golden age theater, a woman who resists marriage) who despite herself falls in love, Circe also incarnates the *mujer varonil*–one who, interestingly, employs her "manly" powers in the efforts to divest Ulysses of his "manliness," to render him effeminate. Against a backdrop of music pleading "Love, love" and cries sounding the notes of "War, war" (406), Circe tries to drown out the latter: "¡Calla, calla, no prosigas, / Ni lleguen ecos marciales / A los oídos de Ulíses! / Aquí tengo que dejarle / Sepultado en blando sueño, / Porque el belicoso alarde / No pueda de mi amor nunca / Dividirle ni olvidarle" (407) [Quiet, quiet, don't continue. Don't let the echoes of war reach Ulysses's ears. I must leave him here sunk in soft slumber so that the bellicose display can never divide him from my love or make him forget it]. His men, as well as Ulíses himself, recognize the love-induced effeminacy to which he has fallen prey: "No soy sin duda el que fuí, / pues à delicias süaves / Entregado, ¡ay de mí! estoy, / y tras los ecos no voy" (405) [Doubtless I am not who I was, for alas! I have succumbed to soft delights and do not follow echoes]. Yet this is no mere "manly woman" play; rather, it is *The Empire Strikes Back.* The spirit of Achilles, calling Ulíses an "effeminate Greek" (409), comes forth to rouse the hero from his stupor and quickly effects the male protagonist's anagnorisis and return to his warrior ways. Says Ulíses: "Reason freed me from love, the greatest enchantment" (409). Clearly, that "love is the greatest enchantment" is precisely the axiom whose pernicious effects the comedia seeks didactically to play out and forcefully to defuse. Love is the greatest enchantment and thus the most threatening to the state. The calls of the battle horn and the sword, the call of the Father, must prevail over the degraded yearnings of the (emasculated) phallus.

Calderón stages this battle as an encounter not only between war and love but also between two mythical, archetypal, archipotent forces: Ulysses the invincible warrior and the previously unvanquished Circe, empress of all she surveys. Circe–who possesses the magical capacity to turn men into *animals* and to leave them "without free will" (394), who is depicted as fearsome, arrogant, vindictive, all-knowing, and as ruler of nature, the heavens, and men–

figures something more than love. She embodies the barred feminine, here vilified and radically demonized into the all-powerful woman and, equally radically, depotentiated and eradicated. The end of the play finds the former *mujer esquiva*, having surrendered to love for a man who repudiates her, now humbled, pleading for his affections, destroying her own kingdom, and as a spectacular volcano issuing flames appears (a spectacular symbol of the womb, the *vagina dentada*, as well as of vanquishing male potency), announcing her impending suicide! Circe, who early on in the play figuratively shakes up the waters of gender relations by proclaiming that women can surpass men in arms and letters (394), is replaced in the final scene with the counterfemale figure of Galatea riding in a "triumphal chariot." Galatea proclaims her debt to Ulysses and literally calms the waters to pave the way for his victorious journey. The threatening Circe, in other words, not only suffers total defeat but is also replaced by a regenerated construction of the feminine, ally and symbol of the demands of empire.

Love, woman, power, and empire are all thus at stake in the temptress Circe. Though the conjunction is potent and important, I now want to pull one thread out of Calderón's construction of Circe that, like Ariadne's, will lead us through the labyrinth of misogynist discourse and ultimately into its opposite. That strand involves the all-powerful mother–the fear and force of whom Circe so clearly manifests–and together with the all-powerful mother, the return of the repressed. Sigmund Freud, Karen Horney, and Nancy Chodorow, among others, have provided us with vivid pictures, traces of which strongly imprint El Saffar's project, of the power that a mother wields for her son. As she who initially has complete control of his needs and socialization, who is his "first love, first witness, and first boss" (Chodorow, 81), the mother remains in the boy's psychic life as an omnipotent figure. When the boy heeds to a masculine identity, he attempts to repress his attachment to the mother, devaluing the feminine. Chodorow's summary of the attainment of masculine gender identity succinctly articulates this process:

> First, masculinity becomes and remains a problematic issue for a boy. Second, it involves denial of attachment or relationship, particularly of what the boy takes to be dependence or need for another, and differentiation of himself from another. Third, it involves the repression and devaluation of femininity on both psychological and cultural levels. (51–52)

In these words we hear El Saffar's reading of the collective Spanish psyche and its Oedipal crisis; from them we also begin to form an understanding, on psychological grounds, of the maternal subtext informing Spain's virulent misogynist discourse.

For it can be argued that in the psychic economy of an individual or a collectivity, nothing is lost, but rather displaced and transformed; the repressed returns. It stands to reason, then, that the more repressed, the more violent the return: in morbid anxiety, or with respect to the cases to which we turn, in a morbidly anxious misogynist discourse bent on demonizing and depotentiating the all-powerful mother.[5] When the barred and devalued feminine returns in misogynist discourse, then, it carries the same vengeful power that we saw in the representation of Circe and that Cixous describes in "The Laugh of the Medusa" with regard to women's writing: "When the 'repressed' of their culture and their society returns, it's an explosive UTTERLY destructive, staggering return with a force never yet unleashed and equal to the most forbidding of suppressions" (886). And even when, as it undeniably does in the hegemonic, disillusioned Hispanic worlds of the seventeenth century, misogynist discourse on women and love serves as an available platform for social critique, it will nevertheless manifest itself extremely, often as a phobic critique of the all-powerful mother. Gender issues, as I suggested in the introduction and as is commonly the case in literature throughout the ages, constitute a symptomatic and overdetermined space in which the manifold represseds of society assert themselves.

The proliferation of misogynist literature in seventeenth-century Spain takes its cue from a variety of tensions, among them the fact that what is socially peripheral frequently becomes symbolically central to the imaginary of the dominant culture.[6] During this period, then, "when moralist and creative literature became so often indistinguishable, poets and other writers surpassed churchmen in pouring upon women a stream of invective never before equalled, even by the misogynists of the feminist debate" (McKendrick, 11). In an array of venues and registers, from popular to elite and from comical to austere, Spanish writers opened the floodgates of woman-hating in literature that proved to be as lucrative as it was purportedly edifying. The major literary figures of the golden age turned their hands and passions to the tarnishing of women. Clergyman Baltasar Gracián, for one, fashioned the "Falsirena" or False Siren ("our wicked inclinations, the depraved propensity for evil" [23]) of *El Criticón* [The Critic], who, like Circe, entraps men into lust. Gracián's "Falsirena" signals the centrality of negative constructions of the female in Spanish literature as well as the particular contours those constructions assumed: the entrenched paradigms of patristic misogyny and of the antifemale factions of the *querelle des femmes* persisted and were reinvigorated in the Counter-Reformation Hispanic context. Much as baroque misogyny responded to the political and social circumstances of the times, and much as writers took advantage of the prevailing taste for *conceptismo* [verbal conceits] to sharpen their satires of women, seventeenth-century attacks on the female sex continued to derive their arguments from the frozen lines of the *querelle* established centuries earlier. The terms and cited authorities of the *querelle* debate both for and against women had remained remarkably stable over the centuries, with the antifemale ranks harking to Aristotelian and biblical imperatives in viewing women as devoid of reason and as the embodiment of passion. From medieval to seventeenth-century Spain, from Spain to the colonial Hispanic worlds, we find women being vilified as inconstant creatures of passion. As Gracián wrote of the female sex in *El Político*: "In this sex the passions reign to such a degree that they leave no room for counsel, for respite, for prudence, which are the essential elements of government, and with power their tyranny increases" (60).

Gracián's references to "power" and "tyranny," appended to words resonant with medieval and Aristotelian sentiments, betray the imprint of the all-powerful mother and thus align the didactic churchman with the scatological satirist Francisco de Quevedo. The poems of Quevedo, the most copious and acute Spanish literary misogynist of the century, encapsulate the energies of misogyny I have been discussing, bringing them to bear with particular weight on the female body. Quevedo's satirical poetry displays a repulsion for the biological functions of the female as well as for women's cosmetic artifice and, importantly, for their entrapping sexuality. His work abounds not with mothers per se, but with patent mother-substitutes (the female go-between, the aunt, the mother-in-law), characteristically portrayed as devouring, loquacious, and powerful. Open, sewerlike, toothless (depotentiated), voracious, demanding mouths, repugnant orifices such as vaginas artificially restored to virginity, together with fleshy breasts and protruding bellies or emaciation all write Quevedo's fetishization of female corporeality into the carnivalesque grotesque body. That body is open, disproportionate, overflowing, unfinished, becoming; the bodies of Quevedo's parodic females are porous and transformable, often depicted at the limen of metamorphosis (from ugly to beautiful through artifice, from life to death, from promiscuity to virginity). If, according to Bakhtin, the closed classical body represents the state with all that it holds on high and the grotesque body its low comic inversion, the release of the taboo, in Quevedo we can easily read the emphatic return of the socially repressed in a violent grotesque mode that endows the barred feminine with extraordinary potency even as it strives to debunk it.

In the burgeoning societies of the New World, misogyny had yet another mission: to contain, by controlling the sexuality of European-born men, the miscegenation that threatened the hierarchical divisions of Creole social order. "Misogyny," writes Kathleen Ross, "thus served a social purpose beyond religious piety and the ultra-orthodoxy of Counter-Reformation Spain" (11). Social satire conducted by marginalized individuals also gained new magnitude as Latin American writers sought through pointed critique to combat the pervasive colonialist ideology that promoted the New World as the realization of utopian projects.[7] "Women are often singled out as symbols of both physical and moral decay in satiric works, and their denigration provides the most common theme in colonial Spanish American satire," states Julie Greer Johnson (1993, 29). The imperatives of social critique together with urbanization and rampant prostitution, the need to indoctrinate the native populations, and the increased leisure of upper-class Creole women afforded new impetus and literary types to misogynist literature. Yet the Spanish mentality and prototypes held their ground and were enjoined in the battles. We therefore find in the New World not only renewed propagation of the patristic misogyny that the clergy, with their stranglehold on the colonies, so staunchly defended, but also a proliferation of misogynist discourse proportionate to that of Spain–notably in writers such as Juan Rodríguez Freyle, Mateo Rosas de Oquendo, and Juan del Valle y Caviedes (all of whose works circulated extensively in manuscript). Moreover, we find Latin American writers imitating and retrofitting Spanish misogynist discourse to New World circumstances. Rodríguez Freyle, denouncing in *El Carnero* the Spanish women of Nueva Granada (Colombia) for the chaos their adultery has wrought, hinges his view of the female sex on Sempronio's lines in Fernando de Rojas's *La Celestina*: "Women are called limbs of Satan, the fountainhead of sin, and the destroyers of paradise" (Johnson 1983, 92). Rosas de Oquendo translates Quevedo's greedy, deceitful women onto the streets of Lima as does, in terms so scathing and obscene that only recent years have seen the publication of his complete works, that "Quevedo of the New World" Juan del Valle y Caviedes. The social ills that these writers satirize by means of the (M)Otherly woman may have emerged in the colonies, but the paradigms from which they draw imaginative sustenance hark back to the metropolis.

While the history of misogynist discourse in the Hispanic worlds follows an unbroken course, of strong influences and a strong male lineage, that of pro-female articulations emerges as broken and riddled with contradictions. No male equivalent of the French essayist François Poullain de la Barre, an uncompromising defender of women (to be discussed in chapter 5), seems to have appeared on or at least strongly impacted the Hispanic scene; certainly, the pro-female side of the *querelle* did not find its home in the essay.[8] Instead, its main arena shifted to the Spanish theater,[9] a vibrant space that, in Michael D. McGaha's words, "accurately reflects the teeming diversity, intellectual ferment, and social tensions of the milieu that gave it birth" (Casa and McGaha, 11). There the exacerbated misogyny of the times spawned its counterface or counterpart (as we will see, its equally hegemonic counterpart) in the persons of strong female protagonists. As is well known, though the mother herself rarely appears on the Spanish stage, the *mujer varonil* in her multiple manifestations of the *mujer esquiva*, female bandit, learned woman, warrior woman, huntress, the woman disguised as a man, and so on, populates and dominates the Spanish comedia following the vogue initiated by Lope de Vega. Whatever form she assumed, the "manly woman" of the comedia generally took into her own hands the defense of her love-besmirched honor and the pursuit of a spouse. Dramatists foraged far afield for female models, drawing their "manly woman" from the pantheon of admirable women available from history, mythology, and literature (McKendrick, 276). These women, and especially the learned woman, both incarnated and often amply voiced the feminist side of the *querelle* with defenses of women's education, power, and right to choose her own spouse. The misogynist edge of the *querelle*, for its part, was often relegated to the mouths of the *gracioso* or buffoon, where it received comic, parodic treatment.

If the repressed feminine and the pro-female debates of the *querelle* returned with constancy and vigor on the eminently public Spanish stage, their return hardly constituted a satisfactory revenge on misogyny. Theater was literally the prime stage on which the "guided culture" of the hegemony responded to pressures and negotiated with them, reaffirming itself. Spanish dramatists produced women for the state and thus, as I stated in the previous chapter, officially scripted the "manly woman" who reified both sexes' rebellious impulses only to squelch and efface them by the end of the play, reconciling her (and presumably them) to social structures. Even recent feminist readings of the comedia, as in the 1991 collection edited by Anita K. Stoll and Dawn L. Smith, *The Perception of Women in Spanish Theater of the Golden Age*, focus ineluctably on the plays' rebellion-quashing conclusions.[10] The question, however, remains, and remains hotly debated, as to the mendacity of what precedes the ending. In other words, to what degree are the feminist exertions of the plays a sham (and a con)? Lope, for example, persistently maintained in his plays and in *La Dorotea* that women's inferior intellectual acuity owes to their inferior education rather than to an intrinsic lack of abilities. Daniel Heiple argues in the above-cited collection that Lope specifically refuted the pseudoscientific misogyny of Huarte de San Juan's *Examen de los ingenios* in his play, *La prueba de los ingenios* [The Proof of Wits]; in the same collection, Michael D. McGaha imputes the pseudofeminism of one of Lope's ostensibly most pro-female comedias, *Las mujeres sin hombres* [Women Without Men], to his desire to court the favor of his lover, Marta de Nevares. I suspect that the debate on the sham or real properties of the comedia's feminist positions, revolving around elusive issues of intentionality, lends itself not to resolution but only to definition. For example: "The complexity of the problem is exemplified by the fact that for every critic who assures us that Tirso was a feminist, another can be found who supports the opposite view" (Stoll and Smith, 22).[11]

Around 1647 María de Zayas wrote in her *Desengaños amorosos*: "Without a single exception, there is no play staged or any book printed that is not a total offense against women" (*42*, 124). Neither to support her position nor to resolve the debate just broached but to place in view the important dynamics of what is clearly in this case—as it is in so many others—a regulatory sham feminist discourse, we will briefly turn our attention to another ostensibly ardent feminist play by Lope de Vega, *La vengadora de las mujeres* [Woman Avenger of Women] (published in 1621). The play immediately sets up its female protagonist, Laura, as a hyperbolic *mujer esquiva*: one who refuses to marry and, what is more, styles herself as a militant man-hater and as the avenger of her sex. She is also a learned woman who prefers the cultivation of her intellect over marriage and something of a *mujer varonil*, an "Amazon" who issues a battle cry for women's rights.

The multiple conventional prototypes that Lope builds into his exaggeratedly feminist Laura signal the satirical function of her character and bode nothing if not her defeat. And indeed Laura's extreme feminist positions are at each juncture undercut by males and females alike, leaving no doubt about where the play stands on them. The more Laura's feminism is touted, the harder it falls. By the conclusion of the play her positions have been systematically discredited, she has succumbed to suitor Carlos, and she ends up giving lessons to other women on how to love rather than to hate men. What began as a diatribe against men ends as a paean to them (and even against women's inconstancy in act 3, scene 7), capped off by a *gracioso* who under the sway of a spell proclaims his love for another of his own sex. Yet along the way the extremely transparent and extreme contrivances of the comedia have allowed free rein for the most inflamed feminist discourse. A lengthy speech by Laura in act 1, scene 2, as one example among many, replays in crystalline form the traditional *querelle* complaints of men against women and counters them with bold accusations: "Desde el principio del mundo / se han hecho tiranos grandes / de nuestro honor y albedrío, / quitándonos las ciudades, / la plata, el oro, el dinero, / el gobierno, sin que baste / razón, justicia ni ley / propuesta de nuestra parte; / ellos estudian y tienen / en las Universidades / lauros y grados; en fin / estudian todas las artes" (p. 1572) [From the beginning of the world men have been great tyrants of our honor and our will, depriving us of cities, silver, gold, government; and neither reason, justice, nor law proposed by us has sufficed. They study, and in the University gain honors and degrees; indeed, they study all the arts]. What we can take away from Laura's speech, and from my admittedly predictable analysis of the all too obviously sham feminist discourse of the play, is at least the following: that in theater the hegemony produced and managed its own counterhegemonic discourse and that pro-female discourse had thus found a rather troubled and equivocal home in the theater–but one that nevertheless insistently kept in the public eye a repertoire of strong "liberated" women and kept alive the pro-female side of the *querelle*. If I began the discussion of *La vengadora de las mujeres* by invoking the words of María de Zayas, it was in part to suggest the special currency that this sham feminist discourse, as we shall see, garners for her works and those of other women writers.

While Spanish theater almost invariably debunked the manly woman and mocked the learned woman, the Neoplatonic courtly love poetry that persisted into the seventeenth century set woman on high, providing an important forum for the positive imaging of the feminine. Though the degree to which the poetry that originally arose in fourteenth-century Provence corresponded to actual love practices remains a disputed issue,[12] it is clear that by design or in effect courtly love's construction of women countered that of medieval misogyny. In acknowledging the superiority of the female beloved (the high-ranking feudal lady) over the supplicant male lover who pays constant verbal tribute to her, in endowing her with absolute power over him, courtly poetry from its inception elevated and ennobled women. The Neoplatonism that beginning with Petrarch and Dante supplemented the courtly tradition spiritualized it and further exalted women and love. Neoplatonism catapulted both into philosophical categories, stepping-stones to the ideal forms of Beauty and Knowledge, and from there, to the Divinity. By the seventeenth century, courtly love poetry had also established a highly codified repertoire for the representation of the ideal courtly woman's physical attributes and emotional attitudes. This repertoire passed unmodified and deracinated into the Hispanic context, some pieces of it (such as light eyes and hair) standing out incongruously there and other pieces (such as the *belle dame sans merci*) interacting synergetically with the new milieu.

The *belle dame sans merci* in particular, and the sonnet mistress in general, "is as potent a symbol of feminine dominance and power as the Renaissance ever provided" (Woodbridge, 189). Accordingly, it can easily be argued that the vengeful Laura and the demonized Circe are but one face of the all-powerful mother and of the return of the repressed. Ruth El Saffar refers to the occluded mother as the "figure the seventeenth-century imagination loved to dehumanize on the side of the angelic or the demonic" (1988, 12); Nancy Chodorow sees men attempting to deal with the powerful mother by naming and externalizing her, either in dread images or in glorification of her (in other words, as the script Chodorow mimes runs, "There is no need for me to dread a being so wonderful, so beautiful, nay, so saintly" [35]). Their formulations offer an expanded explanation for the classic virgin-or-whore dichotomy and a frame in which to set the exaltation of women by courtly love poetry. Misogynist satire and courtly exaltation take their place within that framework as two faces of the same coin, as twin essentializations of the feminine into the dark underworld images of the Evil Mother or the frozen idealizations of the Good Mother. Both female figures are powerful lovers. Both are unrealizable loves: the Evil Mother (seductive but) undesirable, the Good Mother unavailable.

R. Howard Bloch demonstrates the complicity and deep structural identity between the French discourse of asceticism and that of courtly love on both historical and literary grounds in his *Medieval Misogyny and the Invention of Western Romantic Love*.[13] That negative and positive fetishizations of women conspire and intertwine in the poetry under study here can be demonstrated, first, in the cross- or undercurrents of misogyny that make their presence strongly felt in the disenchanted love poetry of the Hispanic baroque. Though it is a truism, I must call to mind the fact that the choleric conflictive times produced a literature infused with *desengaño* [disillusionment or disenchantment]. *Desengaño* did not fail to permeate love literature as well, reducing amorous relationships to a tragic battleground rife with conflict, hatred, betrayal, lasciviousness, and cruelty. The disillusioned field provided fertile grounds not only for heightened enactments of the courtly *belle dame sans merci* in all her potent cruelty and rejection, but also for the amorous complaint that again activated *querelle* invective against women's inconstancy and duplicity *and* for ascetic palinodes rejecting women and love. That misogynist invective and courtly idealization of the woman form two Januslike heads of a single body can, second, be deduced from another current prevalent in the baroque: the same male poet would write works in both registers. This *odio et amo* syndrome obtained in medieval poetry and in Capellanus's *The Art of Courtly Love*, but as María del Pilar Oñate and other critics note,[14] it asserts itself particularly in baroque literature: "A systematic accounting would find a large number of poets who simultaneously praise and insult women. The matter is not new, but it is more pronounced than in other periods" (123). To wit, Quevedo in Spain and Valle y Caviedes in Latin America incurred the supreme paradox of satirizing women in one work and celebrating them, with full-fledged courtly vigor, in another. While the phenomenon lends itself to a gamut of explanations (the following of tradition; extreme times fostering a literature that falls into extremes; the divorce of a decentered literature from truth claims; poets writing in multiple modes, each of which had its own generic and formal dictates; and so on), it indisputably situates love and hate, the Good Mother and the Evil Mother, on a continuum.

From the foregoing survey of male discourse on the opposite sex, of its crosscurrents and equivocations, we can extract at least one firm conclusion: the theme of love constitutes the prime site for the imaging of women and of gender relations. Whatever its intentions, in order to create a rich dramatic or poetic situation a love plot must enfranchise women into powerful and generally active subjects. Moreover, as the locus of intensely patriarchal formulations, love entails a theme ripe for the appropriation and instrumentalization of women writers. Love poetry was the venue of obligation and opportunity for the preponderance of seventeenth-century women writers. Since literary gender decorum had traditionally closed off to women the public genres of the epic, tragedy, and political and philosophical theory, "love lyric," Ann Rosalind Jones notes, "as an ostensibly private discourse, an art of the in-house miniature, could conceivably be allowed them" (1990, 7). While confining on social and intellectual levels, the fabulous capaciousness of the theme of love still permitted the venting of an almost unlimited spectrum of emotional states and of a plethora of ideological issues, along with the erecting of widely ranging scenarios. Like the "cowboy-and-Indian" Western for males, love poetry for women is a foundational, malleable ur-genre, one that has accommodated the shifting desires and pressing concerns of seventeenth-century women and of women throughout the ages. The sedimented features of courtly love poetry I outlined earlier held special access for feminist responses. Courtly love poetry, though long dissociated from its original feudal context, would endure and be reideologized in later eras precisely because it remained an important problem-solving model for both men and women.[15]

The 1993 anthology *Tras el espejo la musa escribe: Lírica femenina de los Siglos de Oro* [The Muse Writes Behind the Mirror: Feminine Lyric in the Golden Age], edited by Julián Olivares and Elizabeth S. Boyce, has made a singular contribution to our understanding of the women poets of the golden age and their handling of the theme of love.[16] Olivares and Boyce have published, often for the first time ever, generous selections of the poetry of ten secular and religious Spanish women writers of the sixteenth and seventeenth centuries. Their anthology also includes a lengthy introduction that, also in several ways for the first time (as I am both pleased and sorry to say), effectively uses a range of recent feminist critical tools to elucidate the subversive and contestatory practices of these early modern Spanish women poets. All of the poets Olivares and Boyce examine, though exercising varying degrees of resistance to contemporary representations of women, remain within what Jean

Franco calls the "language games" (25) of the times and make them speak to women's concerns; the women poets' works, taken together, demonstrate the panoply of feminist possibilities that this panoply of lyric modes enables. The following summary of the pertinent points of the anthology's hundred-page introduction thus briefly aims to suggest, opening up areas on which the rest of my chapter expands, not only *how* women writers in general maneuvered within the given field but also *why* they found the male-dictated language games (including those we have been viewing up to now) apposite to the expression of their gender-specific concerns.

Golden age love poetry encompasses a vast repertoire of canonical registers, genres, and techniques. Building on Ann Rosalind Jones's notion of "negotiation" from her excellent *The Currency of Eros: Women's Lyric in Europe 1540–1620* (which, however, does not include Spain), Olivares and Boyce examine the manners in which women poets reinflected that ample repertoire. From mythology, as chapter 5 of my study will detail vis-à-vis Sor Juana, women writers extrapolated a legion of female figures, heroic and tragic. Tortured Philomela, as Cheryl Walker's *The Nightingale's Burden* shows with regard to North American women's poetry from colonial times to the present, and Echo, who also appears in Sor Juana's sacramental play *El Divino Narciso*, pointedly encoded the encaged voices of women in patriarchal society. The pastoral mode furnished a highly exploitable scenario for women's agency. Its freedom from social constraints, utopian equality of men and women, vernacular speech, stock figures of the shepherdess reluctant to embrace love and the beautiful huntress, all lent themselves to women's appropriation.[7] Courtly love poetry proper, for its part, allowed negotiated and overtly subversive effects. Women writers such as Leonor de la Cueva y Silva ventriloquized through the male courtly lover's hyperbolic praise of the beloved, using his conventional encomiastic speeches to extol her virtue and beauty. Although this technique kept woman in her traditional objectified place while still serving as a defense of the woman poet's sex, other female poets' desublimation of amorous discourse affronted courtly love's objectification of their sex. From the poems satirically disarticulating the topoi of Petrarchan portraiture of women by Catalina Ramírez de Guzmán to outright burlesque of courtly love matching Quevedo's but now from the other side (by Leonor de la Cueva y Silva, Catalina Clara de Guzmán, and Marcia Belisarda), courtly love poetry suffered parodic reversals at the hands of women. At the outer limits of the feminist reappropriation of courtly love poetry we find Sor Violante del Cielo's published poems that literally regender the love triangle, making all three actors women. Well within the bounds of courtly love poetry, baroque disillusionment, the *querelle des femmes*, and the popular *cantigas de amigo* [female love lyrics], on the other hand, we find poems of amorous complaint authored by women and with female speaking subjects. Though Octavio Paz myopically (if with a certain national pride) claimed Sor Juana's "Hombres necios" [Foolish men] (Romance #92) to be unique for its time, several early modern Hispanic women writers wrote—and even published, as did María de

Zayas—poems of amorous complaint in which they aimed their harsh sights at men in general and at men's criticisms of women.[18] The terrain of amorous complaint sanctioned and reinvigorated by the baroque, in fact, would be the launching pad for women's literary activism in the theater and the novella as well as in poetry.

The findings of Olivares and Boyce establish that rather than accepting the barring of their subjectivity, early modern women poets could be mobile within the systems of male discourse and begin to suggest what it was in those systems that licensed their mobility.[19] If these women writers worked within the language games of the times, it was in no small measure because they *could*, that is, because aspects of that apparently counterindicative force field created diverse spaces and apertures to be mined. I in no way mean to discount the formidable personal and social obstacles to women's writing and publishing: chapters 4 and 5 treat them in great detail. Yet I do wish to suggest and to bear out in what follows herein that to the degree that, as Elizabeth Ordóñez points out, the Spanish women's texts she analyzes were imagining a new female economy (6), the baroque afforded them considerable resources with which to do so and the means to get away with it. The foregoing words, however, open up another side of the question. Many of the writers studied by Olivares and Boyce were never published, though some of their works, as did those of so many golden age poets, circulated in manuscript. Conceivably, they could write whatever they wished—which, incidentally, makes their adherence to established discourses all the more significant. To our knowledge none of the works of those who published, furthermore, gained high recognition. As fully as possible to problematize and to disclose the drama of baroque pro-female discourse, I now turn to three women writers whose literary efforts did: Sor Juana, María de Zayas, and Ana Caro. Sor Juana and María de Zayas will work out their feminist polemics in the two traditions, the two sides of the all-powerful mother, to which I have already devoted considerable attention: courtly love and satire. Moreover, the test cases of the public writings of these three women—places where the problematics of women's participation were the sharpest[20]—allow us further to probe the resources that the baroque, despite its flagrant and pervasive misogyny, allotted the woman writer in the three genres of poetry, novella, and theater; to formulate two larger strategies or protocols inherent in the baroque literary environment; and to examine how the three women managed and marketed their feminism for public consumption in elite and popular milieux.

II.

ENDGAMES: SOR JUANA INÉS DE LA CRUZ

To scrutinize the love poetry of Sor Juana is, I believe, almost ineluctably to call into play the lines of the feminist criticism largely performed during the

1980s, that is, to focus on "contestatory responses to signifying practices" (Jones 1990, 2). Our earlier feminist critical practices bear a strong situational resemblance to the practices of early modern women's poetry itself. Both are operating within an orbit still essentially dominated by the masculine (masculine theory and/or masculine literature) and are attempting to articulate spaces of feminine/feminist resistance. To *voler* or steal paternal discourse, to explode it, describes both the basically thematic and formalistic thrust of 1980s feminist criticism and the erudite, intertextual baroque culture in which writers such as Sor Juana moved. Sor Juana in particular could say with Jorge Luis Borges that she had experienced relatively little but read a great many books. I also take recourse to a 1980s mode of criticism in reading Sor Juana's love poetry to compensate for a critical, in both senses of the word, lack. Although the Olivares and Boyce anthology does much to bring the feminist criticism of golden age poetry up to speed and although many feminist critics have effectively applied themselves to the works of Sor Juana, crucial areas of her contestatory designs still remain to be recuperated. I maintain that the feminist implications of her copious and dense love poetry are one of them, and will now proceed to disclose them following a protracted, somewhat sinuous course that befits the dimensionality of Sor Juana's own designs, protocols, and literary culture.[21]

Why did Sor Juana write so much love poetry? Not only was it untoward for a nun, but love is a topic and emotion that seems to inspire true repugnance in Sor Juana. Consider the titles of the following poems, that revile love: "Which describes the catastrophe of the joys and desires of lovers" (Glosa #140), "Which resolves the question of which is more troublesome in conflicting emotions [*encontradas correspondencias*]: to love or to hate" (Sonnet #166), "On a reasonable reflection which allays the pain of a passion" (Sonnet #172), "Which offers a means to love without much grief " (Sonnet #176). Sor Juana, as the titles suggest, is hardly a woman happy with love, an entranced woman in love. Happy or not, the sheer abundance of Sor Juana's love poetry—nearly fifty poems, about one-fifth of her poetry—has provoked scores of commentators to speculate about her motivation in writing it. Did Sor Juana write her amatory poetry in wake of a lost love? Conversely, was it a mere exercise, yet another of her experiments with a literary tradition, of her literary academy–inspired attempts to try her hand at them all? For to be a lyric poet was to be a love poet; love was poetry and poetry love (Luciani, 183). Or, as Irving Leonard's influential interpretation would have it, did Sor Juana cipher into some of the love poetry an allegorical meaning, using the conventionalized forms of love poetry covertly to express the struggle between her love for church and for knowledge? Or was Sor Juana burdened less with abstract than with emotional struggles, with a melancholy for which the consecrated and depersonalized topics of courtly love provided an acceptable outlet?[22]

Sor Juana's love poetry can, I believe, display genuine emotion. It can also sound like a mere exercise in courtly love and degenerate into a showcase for

Scholastic argumentation or *conceptista* wordplay. Such antitheses in the unstable and ample universe of Sor Juana's poetry need not be explained away. Still, I would like to propose yet another approach to the issue of why she wrote so much love poetry, one that will eventually incorporate both poles. And that is the following: I consider Sor Juana's love poetry, taken as a corpus, to entail her exploration of the counter-realm to the *Primero sueño*, to be the counterpart and conceivably the prelude to that work, her masterwork. While in the *Sueño* Sor Juana exhaustively investigates the pure world of reason and knowledge, in her love poetry she extensively interrogates the passionate world of *un*reason and *not*-knowing. The universe of knowledge and reason clearly enthralls Sor Juana; the universe of love, construed as its counterface, would exercise an equal fascination for the poet as well as provide opportunities for a wide variety of poetic effects and registers. Hence, among other reasons, the sheer bulk of her love poetry.

These are unusual claims. Let me briefly expand on them by setting out the opposing terrain over and against which Sor Juana's underworld of love stands. In the *Sueño* we witness the Soul/Intellect separating from the body, and thus from the world and its strife, to ascend in its nocturnal flight to the overworld of pure thought. "[Y] juzgándose casi dividida / de aquella que impedida / siempre la tiene, corporal cadena, / que grosera embaraza y torpe impide / el vuelo intelectual" (1. ll. 297–301) [Almost loosed from that bodily chain that always blocks her path, obstructing crudely and grossly interfering with the flight of the intellect, *177–78*], the Soul contemplates the spark of divinity contained in herself (ll. 293–96, *178*), and then begins her journey through the "mental orilla" (1. 566) [vast sea of knowing, *185*]. Questing for knowledge, the Intellect tests out the two major ways of knowing the world, ways that represent metonymies of *all* of reason's (versus faith's) means of knowing the world. In Sor Juana's male-female love poetry, on the other hand, the soul remains united to the body, attached to the lower appetitive faculty of the will that in Scholastic terms opposes free will (Luciani, 97). The intellect remains mired in an emotional underworld in which, as I will detail, *reason and knowledge lose their sway*. I would assert that the love poetry probes the realm of passion that one must leave behind to move unencumbered into the world of ideas, into the world that the Soul "mounted so high above herself" considered to be "a new region" (*182*, ll. 433–34). That is, we can view Sor Juana's love poetry as part of an incremental philosophical inquiry, as the necessary first step toward the *Sueño* in both chronological and conceptual terms. My contention assumes greater credibility when we take into account the fact that the *Sueño* was one of Sor Juana's last humanistic works and her self-stated most personal poem, summa and capstone of her efforts.

Viewed as a corpus, Sor Juana's love poetry frames an underworld, with its own distinctively dark nature and governing principles, that rivals the overviewing overworld of the *Sueño*. At the core of this underworld lies the tragic baroque conception of male-female love that Sor Juana defines in the opening stanzas of her Sonnet #184, "Which consoles a jealous lover, with an epilogue to his series of loves":

Amor empieza por desasosiego,
solicitud, ardores y desvelos;
crece con riesgos, lances y recelos,
susténtase de llantos y de ruego.

Doctrínanle tibiezas y despego,
conserva el sér entre engañosos velos,
hasta que con agravios o con celos
apaga con sus lágrimas su fuego.

[Love begins with unease, supplications, ardor, and insomnia; it
increases with risks, quarrels, and rejections; it feeds on tears and
pleas. Indifference and coolness instruct it; love remains itself amid
cloudy veils, until, with insults or with jealousy, it quenches its
own fire with its own tears.]

Sonnet #184, it is clear, details the miseries attendant upon each phase of the
love process.[23] The poem instantiates in programmatic form Sor Juana's slant
on love–her slanted picture of it–as well as what comprise the obsessive topics upon which she expounds in her love poems. Repetitively, systematically,
and exhaustively, Sor Juana will probe every corner of the dark side of love as
she erects the abhorrent underworld of passion into a universe unto itself.

Sor Juana's boundless ingenuity extracts from the kernel theme of the suffering of love and from the matrix of courtly love an enormous range of situations, attitudes, poetic personae, lyrical stances and registers, and effects
them in a sweep of metrical forms. Her thoroughgoing investigation of love
appropriates the poetic resources of each metrical form to its own purposes,
with the result that each form treats the subject in a discernibly different way.
The almost narrative quality of the *romances* allows Sor Juana to treat at length
such broad philosophical questions as the fundamental role of jealousy in love,
or that of fated inclination versus true sentiment. The *endechas*, which traditionally involve laments or complaints, on the other hand, lack a philosophical dimension. Instead, as in the famous poem #78 ("She expresses the pain a
loving wife suffers upon her husband's death" [75]), which some consider to
be Sor Juana's most genuinely emotional love poem, they serve as the vehicle
or channel for intensely felt and candidly expressed emotions.[24] The neat
rhyme and compact stanzas of the *redondillas* lend themselves to light battles
of opposing terms. Here, with the contentious attitude typified in her
Redondilla #92 ("Hombres necios"), Sor Juana treats the minor disputes, mis-
understandings, and complaints of love. The *décimas* combine features of the
redondillas and the *romances*. They escalate the small battles of the former into
full-scale wars against love, with an allegorical/philosophical thrust that harks
back to the latter. Contentiousness often swells into ripe invective. Sor Juana
utilizes the *glosas* to translate courtly love and traditional popular themes into
the idiom of the baroque. Finally, in her heterogeneous sonnets Sor Juana follows the dictates of the form to contract large philosophically or emotionally
charged situations into small packages. Among the sonnets we thus find the
"encontradas correspondencias" or ironic symmetries series (poems #166 to

#171), with their dispassionate ratiocinations on amorous questions,[25] and the exquisite vignettes of her most renowned love poems: Sonnet #164, "In which she allays misgivings with the rhetoric of tears" (*81*) and Sonnet #165 ("Which contains a fantasy satisfied with a decent love"), better known as "Deténte, sombra de mi bien esquivo" [Semblance of my elusive love, hold still, *81*].

Sor Juana compounds both the monotony and the diversity of her amorous universe by systematically exploiting the scenarios furnished by courtly tradition. Her love poetry, the dates and order of which we have not been able to determine,[26] forms a de facto *canzoniere* (Luciani, 30), in the sense of a dictionary of the phases and postures of courtly love. Frederick Luciani observes, "Practically the entire gamut of courtly love situations and sentiments can be found somewhere in Sor Juana's lyric" (28). Though a woman writer usually speaking as a female poetic voice be it to a male or female addressee, Sor Juana exercises all of the traditional roles of the courtly lover. She devises the recently enamoured *fenhedor* who suffers in silence: "que te asisto y no me sientes, / que te sirvo y no me miras" (Romance #42) [I attend you and you do not hear me, I serve you and you do not look at me]. Wounded by the poisoned darts of love, her *fenhedor* experiences the physical symptoms of *hereos* or lovesickness–"strangled cries," a "troubled expression," "stifled breath" (Endecha #75). In expressing his (or in this case, her) love to the beloved, the courtly lover passes from *fenhedor* to *precador*. Many and diverse are Sor Juana's poems of the *precador* stage, directly addressing the lover in amorous entreaty or complaint. Courtly love eventually enlists the lover into the feudal service of the beloved. As the *servidor* or servant devoted to the needs of the beloved and the higher good of love, the courteous lover manifests a certain serenity (Luciani, 82). We encounter a calmness of this sort in poems to Lysi, Countess de Paredes and vicereine of New Spain– for example, Sonnet #179, "Which explains love's most sublime quality."[27] At the end of love's long trajectory, the courtly lover often throws off its madness, expressing the rejection of love in palinodes, songs of retraction. Given her focus on love's miseries in action, Sor Juana wrote only a few palinodes (Endecha #79, Romance #99, Sonnet #171), but they are remarkable for their originality. In Sonnet #171, for example, the poetic speaker ends up reviling her unworthy lover and despising herself for having loved him.[28]

As the preceding discussion suggests, despite its encyclopedic sweep of the domain of courtly love, Sor Juana's love poetry displays a predilection for certain phases in the courtly process. It favors not the initial and hopeful stages of enamorment, but the later phases of the *precador* and *servidor*. That is to say, of those who have known love in all its force and verbalize their complaints and laments, often directly to the beloved. Sor Juana derives from these traditional courtly postures the anything but conventional (for courtly poetry) cast of female poetic personae who most frequently appear in her love poetry. Consistent with her passion for self-imaging, Sor Juana's poetic "I" assumes the guise of the widow, the jealous lover, the lover separated from her beloved, the *belle dame sans merci*, the spurned lover, the supplicant *servidor*. Her female subjects, even the *belles dames sans merci*, inevitably find themselves on the losing end of love. Neither devouring nor all-powerful, they demythify the potent mother and, in a variety of scenarios and emotional shadings, expose the subjectivity of the female side of the courtly equation. The poet may bracket off a particular field of courtly love, but her chosen theme of amorous complaint knows no bounds.

Extraordinarily multifaceted, Sor Juana's underworld of love can appear bewilderingly amorphous. Arthur Terry, one of the most astute exegetes of Sor Juana's love poetry, analyzes certain contradictions in her philosophy of love (299–302); Frederick Luciani with his customary eloquence describes the body of poems as "a kind of brilliant mosaic in which disparate, sometimes contradictory ideas are juxtaposed" (28).[29] While agreeing that it admits a range of at times discrepant attitudes and scenarios (and while taking certain of them as the frame for my next chapter), I would still argue that Sor Juana's love poetry displays a notable consistency in its diversity. What emerges from an examination of the corpus of poems is an overriding picture of male-female love as a battleground that produces suffering; in other words, love as strife, discord, and disillusionment. For Sor Juana, love's constitutive principles include jealousy ("Son crédito y prueba suya; / pues sólo pueden dar ellos / auténticos testimonios / de que es amor verdadero," They are both credit and proof; for only they can offer authentic testimony that love is true [Romance #3]) and (according to Sonnet #174) a mutability tantamount to that of fickle Fortune. Jealousy and mutability, among other things, generate what Alan S. Trueblood nicely terms the "thematic nexus of separation-distance-absence" (13), that is, Sor Juana's many poems of solitude accentuating the breakdown of affective ties. The nun-poet, Trueblood further notes (12), often dwells on obstacles to the fulfillment of love, to the achievement of an *amor correspondido* or requited love. In all of the love poems I find only one strong tribute to mutual love between a man and a woman, and it is literally a postmortem conceived in the beloved's absence: the poetic narrator of Lira #213, "Which expresses feelingly the pain a loving wife suffers at her husband's death," acknowledges that "Ni Fabio fué grosero, / ni ingrato, ni traidor; / antes, amante / con pecho verdadero, / nadie fué más leal ni más constante" [Fabio was not coarse, nor an ingrate nor a traitor; rather, a lover with a true heart; no one was more loyal or more constant].

Even the love of God—and even when requited—results in suffering. Sor Juana's three personal religious compositions (versus those written for religious ceremonies), Romances #56, #57, and #58, provide a window onto the travails of spiritual life as their speaker struggles with divine love. Romance #56 tells us that unlike the always chafing planes of human love, "de contrarios compuestos" [built on warring tensions, *87*], the very different "amor que se tiene en Dios, / es calidad sin opuestos" [love placed in God is a quality without inconsistencies]. Infused with Pythagorean harmony, God's own love is sublimely Neoplatonic because spiritual, rational, and noncorporeal. Sor

Juana's poetic characters, however, to their dismay prove incapable of transcending their conception of human love fully to partake of divine love's bounty.[30] In Romance #58, the poetic speaker has achieved a rare "amorous union" with the Divinity (the fleeting and unusual nature of the event marked by an insistent chorus of "today's") who has entered her heart "in person." Uplifted by her arguably mystical experience of the divine presence, the poetic speaker still cannot help asking a very human question: Is it love or jealousy that has motivated the Divinity's "careful scrutiny" of her person? Thus, while the love of God in and of itself must be the height of good, the poetic "I" remains rooted in the intermediate zone, of pain. As Sor Juana states in Romance #56, "que siendo el término el Bien, / todo el dolor es el medio" [since its terminus is the Good, it is in between that suffering lies, 87]. This intensely personal zone, which the poet delivers with a naked candor that surpasses customary protestations of unworthiness found in religious love poetry, is fraught with self-imposed conflicts and contradictions. Romance #57 depicts the speaker's struggle between her virtue, excited by Grace to ascend to the celestial sphere, and her custom, the "peso de mis miserias" [the weight of my miseries] that succeeds in impeding the woman's flight. Thus encumbered by her own nature or will (voluntad) and sabotaging herself, the narrator recognizes that "[d]e mí mesma soy verdugo / y soy cárcel de mí mesma" [I am my own executioner and my own prison]. Similarly, and even more explicitly, the speaker in Romance #56 laments her inability to love God in any other than a human way. She has endeavored to renounce human love, a "bastard love," for a sublime love, "tan en su natural centro" [so fully in its natural center] and fueled by virtue and reason. Incapable of doing so, she laments "our human weakness," "adonde el más puro afecto / aun no sabe desnudarse / del natural sentimiento" [where the purest affection cannot divest itself of merely natural feeling]. Darkly evoking Saint Teresa's enraptured professions of mystical love, her "I die because I do not die," the speaker states: "Muero, ¿quién lo creerá?, a manos / de la cosa que más quiero, / y el motivo de matarme / es el amor que le tengo" [I die, who would believe it? at the hands of what I love best, and what puts me to death is the very love I profess, 89].[31]

Romance #56 ends with Sor Juana's characteristic determination to keep on trying: "Pero valor, corazón: / porque en tan dulce tormento, en medio de cualquier suerte / no dejar de amar protesto" [Still, take courage, heart: when torture becomes so sweet, whatever may be my lot, from love I'll not retreat, 89]. The last stanza of the poem presents two issues worthy of comment. First, the attempt to attain divine love, a superior love in itself but still the source of so much suffering, can be even more anguishing than the efforts of secular love. Secular love can be renounced, but divine love must be pursued incessantly (the title of Romance #56 reads: "In which she expresses the effects of Divine Love and proposes to die loving, despite the risk" [89]). And second, Sor Juana portrays the pain of divine love as a "dulce tormento," a sweet torture. In contrast, Sor Juana's male-female love poetry fails to glorify love's suffering.[32] This returns us for a moment to the wellspring of courtly tradition. The notion of love as suffering is alien to neither religious nor secular love poetry ("Happy love," Denis de Rougement famously remarks, "has no history" [15]). It is well known that *the* theme of courtly poetry was a lover's laments in the face of an unrealizable adulterous love. The very unnrealizability of their passion together with the ennobling qualities of Neoplatonic love I mentioned in the first section of the chapter, however, caused courtly lovers to rejoice in their suffering as an end unto itself: "To love love more than the object of love, to love passion for its own sake, has been to love to suffer and to court suffering all the way from Augustine's *amaban amare* down to modern romanticism" (Rougement, 50). Petrarch wrote, for example,

> At times, however, this ill invades me with an obstinacy that grips and torments me for days and nights on end. The ordeal affords me no ray of light nor tremor of life; it is an infernal night and a cruel death. And yet–here is what may well be called the height of woe!–I feed on these particular pains and sufferings with a kind of delight so poignant that if I am snatched away from them it is against my will. (Rougement, 183)

And the seventeenth century still registers, as one example among many, Pedro Espinoso's claim that "the true lover lives when he dies" (1605; Green 1963, 171). In failing to share its passion for suffering for suffering's sake, Sor Juana notably parts ways with the courtly tradition. To her way of thinking, there is nothing redeeming in the suffering a woman experiences in loving a man.

What renders heterosexual love so unredeemable, so despicable? What is the Prime Mover of the underworld, and what are its ways? Sor Juana does not, as one might expect from a nun, condemn the pleasures of the flesh. Rather, she repeatedly excoriates the *sin razón* or Unreason of love, which in robbing them of their intelligence can (as a follower of Saint Thomas would naturally see it) reduce humans to beasts: "¡Oh discurso irracional! / ¡Que quepa en pechos humanos / lo que al examen de un bruto / sale siempre condenado!" (Romance #7) [Oh irrational discourse! That human hearts can contain what is always condemned in brutes!]. Simply put, love for Sor Juana is mad love, and in Redondilla #84, "In which she describes rationally the irrational effects of love" (79), she denounces the "loving torment," "grave agony," "blind madness," "fierce pain," and the loss of free will that Unreason creates. Declaring in the same poem that she understands not the logic of irrational love, the speaker perhaps unwittingly gives us a clue to its peculiar ways: "No sé en qué lógica cabe / el que tal cuestión se pruebe: / que por él lo grave es leve, / y con él lo leve es grave" [I know not in what logic this lies, when it is tested: for in it the heavy is light and through it the light is heavy]. Unreason, the stanza implies, has its own contrary logic, one that twists causal propositions into paradoxical syllogisms. Romance #6 supplies an even more explicit statement of the same phenomenon: "Mira que es contradicción / que no cabe en un sujeto, / tanta muerte en una vida, / tanto dolor en un muerto"

[This is a contradiction that a single subject cannot contain, so much death in a life, so much pain in a death]. Here, in philosophical terms, lie the despised offense of Unreason and, in literary terms, its attraction–which links the two poles of emotion and poetic exercise mentioned earlier. For, in Sor Juana's formulation, the perverse modus operandi of Unreason both engenders and lends itself to the punning cherished by baroque poetic discourse, that is, the *conceptismo* that seems to flow so naturally from Sor Juana's pen (another reason, undoubtedly, why she wrote so much love poetry).

Sor Juana further expounds on the hated logic, and the truth, of illogic in Romance #4. Stanza 4 of the poem yields the key formulation that, in the world of love's Unreason–versus that of the "razón de estado" or customary logic–actions produce inappropriate and opposite reactions: "Ved que es querer que, las causas / con efectos desconformes, / nieves el fuego congele, / que la nieve llamas brote" [See how love causes contradictory effects, how fire freezes snow, how snow bursts into flames]. Later on in the poem, she terms the discordant effects of Unreason "encontradas golpes," ironic blows. Clearly, and importantly, the ironic blows of love's Unreason beget the thorny sentimental problems on which the poet meditates in this and in the sonnets of "encontradas correspondencias" or ironic symmetries mentioned above. They generally revolve around the question of "whom should I love: he who loves me or he whom I love?" The poet rails against so intolerable a situation and its cause, saying: "¡Oh vil arte, cuyas reglas / tanto a la razón se oponen[!]" (Romance #4) [Oh vile art, whose rules are so opposed to reason!]. Nevertheless, in Romances #3 and #4 she grants love's Unreason some small measure of truth. Romance #3 acknowledges with regard to lovers mad with jealousy that "[c]omo de razón carecen, / carecen del instrumento de fingir, / que aquesto sólo / es en lo irracional bueno" [since they lack reason, they lack the faculty of dissembling; in that sense alone is the irrational good]. The speaker of Romance #4 shows us Unreason's truth in action, declaring herself incapable of dissembling her love for Fabio, much as "customary logic" would dictate otherwise. Already compromised by love and removed from reason, her "noble heart" maintains a minimal dignity.

The truth of Unreason hardly compensates for its ravages. Irrational love condemns the female poetic narrator to a nightmarish upside-down world of perverse contradictions and emotions that she can neither understand nor at times control. It is the Hades of the *no saber*, of not-knowing. Romance #4 concludes that we can never know love, only its effects. Redondilla #84's opening stanzas directly oppose feeling to knowing. The former cancels out the latter and, as stated earlier, deprives the poem's speaker of the ability to extricate herself from the situation. Divine love, desired and not attained, can have similar effects on knowing: "Tan precisa es la apetencia / que a ser amados tenemos, / que, aun sabiendo que no sirve, / nunca dejarla sabemos" (Romance #56) [To see our love returned is so strong a craving, that even knowing it to be useless, we never know how to renounce it]. Even though Sor Juana considers divine love to be a superior Neoplatonic love, in Romance

#56 and the poems on not-knowing and Unreason with a secular focus she allies with the tradition of mad love to contravene the important aspect of Neoplatonism that views love as a route to ultimate knowledge.

These and yet another important devastation wrought by Unreason on reason figure prominently in Romance #6, "In which, with deep feeling, she foresees the pain of separation" (*69*). Its deictics ambiguous, the poem begins as a self-conscious epistolary poem of farewell to the beloved, commenting on its own creation; later, somewhat confusedly, it implies his direct presence. Whatever the actual scenario, it is clear that, deeply and lovingly in love, the poetic speaker has given herself up to the despair of her lover's absence even before it takes place. Love has undone her completely, transmuting her heart and soul into the basic elements of water and wind (stanza 11). Furthermore, at three separate points in the poem she states that love has reduced her to pure sentiment; for instance: "Ya no me sirve de vida / esta vida que poseo, / sino de condición sola / necesaria al sentimiento" [This life that I have is of no use to me as life, but only as a requisite for sentiment]. In so doing, love also sabotages the writer's tool, words: "Y aun ésta [my pen] te hablará torpe / con las lágrimas que vierto / porque va borrando el agua / lo que va dictando el fuego" [Even my pen's speech is blurred by the tears I shed, for they keep washing away what passion's fire dictates]. Words, natural language, are replaced with the language of *hereos*, of the emotions, conventionally depicted.[33] However eloquent this mute language may be–"Oye la elocuencia muda / que hay en mi dolor, sirviendo / los suspiros, de palabras, / las lágrimas de conceptos" [Heed the eloquent silence of sorrow's speech and catch words that breathe through sighs, conceits that shine through tears, *69*]–I do not believe that the poet-speaker (or the poet herself) regards it as entirely advantageous. Rather, I would maintain that especially in such a self-conscious poem the loss of language along with the other torments described in the *romance* cumulatively build into the complaint that augurs the poem's change of tone from loving to almost adversarial. The narrator asks, "¿Por qué me llevas el alma, / dejándome el sentimiento?" [Why do you take my soul, leaving me the pain?] (we recall that Sor Juana generally equates the soul with the mind). Impotence and incomprehension eventually overwhelm the speaker, and the poem concludes: "Y a Dios; que, con el ahogo / que me embarga los alientos, / ni sé ya lo que te digo / ni lo que te escribo leo" [Farewell; with the anguish that chokes my breath, I no longer know what I am saying to you, nor can I read what I write]. I have argued elsewhere that mad love galvanizes the female protagonists of Sor Juana's plays into creative activity (1991); here it would appear to shut down their creative efforts.

The female voice of Romance #6, I suggested above, does not simply resign herself to being love's victim. By the final movement of the poem, before succumbing to emotion, she has attempted to exercise some control over the situation. Using an ever sharper language for which she eventually apologizes (proving the poet to be eminently aware of it), and issuing a series of commands, the poetic subject enjoins her lover not to forget either her love for him or his own noble promises to her, his honor. This woman's act of resistance against love pales on several fronts in comparison with those of the poems I will now consider. In them, from the forbidding (for a nun) mode of courtly love will slowly emerge the even more forbidding image (for the patriarchy) of woman as the defender and locus of reason. Courtly love, amorous complaint, will thus provide the matrix for Sor Juana's often subtle contestations to misogynists' claims of the woman's irrationality and inconstancy, that is, as the springboard for a particular kind of "wild zone" within the underworld of love. Ironically but tellingly, it is a wild zone that in transgressing two taboos is perforce subdued and, in responding to the invective of the times, is adversarial to claims of women's wildness.

Sor Juana's polemical mind gravitates toward traditional dualisms such as body versus soul, reason versus passion (Terry, 302). Several love poems or poems on love take the latter opposition as their explicit theme. Décima #104 assumes a philosophical stance to contrast elective or rational love (which I discuss below) with the "affective" sensual love imposed on the lover by "imperious influence." It makes a strong case for love born of reason, the more noble of the two. Sonnet #174 ("Although in vain, she wishes to reduce the pain of a jealous lover to a rational method"), Redondilla #84 ("In which she describes rationally the irrational effects of love," analyzed above), and Décima #100 ("Soul which at last succumbs to a love it has resisted, allegorized through the fall of Troy"), all in the first person, self-statedly pit love against reason, albeit to reason's defeat. Military imagery functions to ingenious effect in the allegorical battle of the last poem mentioned, Décima #100. In violent battle, love lays siege to the female poetic "I," who successively figures herself both as the male Priam–"Intelligence" and "King of Powers"–and as the female Cassandra–"Reason" and Princess of the Soul. Military allegory with its attendant imagery also pervades the poem that precedes and dramatically counters Décima #100, reversing reason's defeat. Décima #99, "Which shows reason's decorous resistance to the vile tyranny of a violent love," contains Sor Juana's most forthright and impassioned treatment of the love versus reason battle. The battle motif gives rise to open invective as the poem launches its verbal and thematic attack on Love, a tyrant and "Rapacious conqueror," and his ways. Love's vile weapons have ignited in the female speaker a flaming "civil war" between passion and reason. The famous lines read: "En dos partes dividida / tengo el alma en confusión: / una, esclava a la pasión, / y otra, a la razón medida" [My soul is in confusion divided into two parts, one a slave to passion and the other to cool reason]. Love, the "conquered conqueror," may have vanquished the castle, but it will not take its chatelaine. Valiantly and triumphantly she resists, with the result that "podré decir, al verme / expirar sin entregarme, / que conseguiste matarme / mas no pudiste vencerme" [I will be able to say, when I die without surrendering, that you succeeded in killing me but could not defeat me].

That the verb *poder* [to be able] is in the future tense indicates a negotiation between two strands of courtly tradition. Above I listed Décima #99 as a palinode, a retreat from mad love. This it undoubtedly is. Yet Sor Juana does not allow her speaker the less problematic route of the repentant lover who speaks in retrospect of a love that has proven impossible. Rather, to heighten both the battle and its victory, the poet conflates the repentant lover with the *belle dame sans merci*. In Sor Juana's construction, the *belle dame sans merci* becomes a warrior, something of an Amazon. And Sor Juana presents her character, unlike the traditional palinode narrator, still in the throes of amorous struggle, waging successful war against a very present enemy ("y hoy, que estás dentro del alma, / es resistir valentía," and today, when you are within my soul, it takes courage to resist) and foreseeing her eventual victory. No other poem so specifically proclaims the triumph of reason over passion, but we do come upon analogous victories. After deliberating on the love triangles in which she finds herself enmeshed in Romance #4 and Sonnet #168, the poetic speaker reaffirms her free will to choose whom she desires to love, instead of contenting herself with he who loves her.

Victorious or not, rather than entrapping men into lust female characters do battle against love's offenses. The "I" of Lira #212, though reclaiming rather than refuting love, defends herself against the unjust accusations of her jealous lover. Similarly, the poetic voice of Romance #7 contrives an ingenious strategy to make of herself the "victor" and not the "vanquished" of the amorous fray. In the hopes of unthawing her icy lover, she decides to use love's Unreason, its "irrational discourse" and "warring affections," to her own benefit. Because "tal vez en el mundo / hay caprichos tan extraños, / que conceden al desprecio / lo que al amor le negaron" [perhaps in this world there are whims so strange that they grant to scorn what they denied to love], in order to return her lover to his courtly path she styles herself as a glacial Diana and, to capitalize on the power of that figure, as more conventional *belle dame sans merci* than that of Décima #100. Sor Juana herself, or at least her poetic self, attempts in her revisionary sonnet to Portia (#156) to rescue a woman who was decimated by love. The nun craftily uses all three sonnets to classical female personages who committed suicide (poems #154 to #156) both to celebrate the women's virtue and to denigrate the actions for which they have become famous. (Sor Juana appears not merely to be spouting Catholic dogma against suicide but to be lamenting the loss of such outstanding women.) The poetic narrator expresses her quarrel with Portia, who died a gruesome death by her own hand after learning of her husband's demise, in the strongest terms of all three sonnets. "¿Qué pasión," she asks Portia, "¿qué dolor tan ciego / te obliga a ser de ti fiera homicida?" [What passion, what blind grief, forces you to be your own ferocious assassin?]. As if she could change history, the narrator places herself at the scene of Portia's suicide and admonishes her not to use the burning coals, their fires being unworthy of the fire of her love. Portia, blinded by love and unable to see its grandeur, or her own, may not have been able to defend herself; Sor Juana assumes her defense, ordering Portia to resist love's passion.

The paradigm for Sor Juana's most personal defense against love can be found in Sonnet #165, "Which contains a fantasy satisfied with a decent love" (*23*). In this magisterial composition the poetic "I" subjugates her evanescent lover by taking him prisoner in her mind. Addressing the beloved as a shadow, an image, an illusion, and a fiction, the opening quatrain would appear to reference the transformation announced in the title. However, as we deduce from the second quatrain, the chain of synonyms equally (or actually) refers to the fugitive beloved's characteristic male offenses of having seduced and abandoned the speaker; in deceiving and eluding her, he has become phantasmagorical. As the tercets progress, implied defeat cedes to its opposite. In a triumph of mind over matter, and of the female lover over her male beloved, the speaker wrests power from him: "poco importa burlar brazos y pecho / si te labra prisión mi fantasía" [it matters not to evade my arms and breast, since my fantasy holds you captive in its grasp, *81*].[34] "Fantasía" is and has the last word in the sonnet's amorous battle. Carlos Blanco Aguinaga's analysis of the sonnet suggests that this mental act distinguishes Sor Juana's sonnet from one of Quevedo on a quite similar theme, "A fugitivas sombras doy abrazos" [I offer to embrace fugitive shadows]. The lovers in both poems pursue their shadowy and elusive beloveds, but using different weapons: "Where in Quevedo all is force, a physicality which breaks things into 'pieces' and seeks 'revenge,' Sor Juana strikes us as interiorized, quite calm. . . . In contrast to the violence of masculine expression, a subtle yet paradoxically obstinate affirmation of the spirit" (159).

Sor Juana also reaffirms the powers not so much, as Blanco Aguinaga would have it, of her spirit as of her mind in Glosa #142, addressed to Lysi ("Because she holds her in her thoughts, she scorns the sight of her eyes as useless"). The poem plays on the Neoplatonic notion that love enters through the eyes, dazzling and thus blinding the lover. Although the narrator has lost her physical sight, she has been granted in its stead a superior interior vision that internalizes the beloved in her soul or "pensamiento" (thought; Sor Juana uses the two terms interchangeably). Appropriated, transmogrified, the image of Lysi affords the poetic speaker a bittersweet ecstasy shot through with a now pleasurable suffering–not the "torments of the body" but the "pleasures of the soul." "Así tendré, en el violento / rigor de no verte aquí, / *por alivio del tormento*, / siempre el pensamiento en ti, / siempre a ti en el pensamiento" (italics mine) [So, in the violent pain of not seeing you here, *to allay my torment*, I shall have my thought always in you, you in my thought]. The exercise of mental powers permits the female speakers of both poems just analyzed efficaciously to neutralize or transform the beloved's capacity to inflict pain. It turns dialogue, an adversarial "I" versus "you," into a kind of monologue where the powers of the mind have made the "you" a function of the "I."

Octavio Paz has written, "Absence is the territory where desire and imagination display their creations" (284). Certainly, the absence of the beloved obliges the lover to re-create him or her in her mind. The poetic speaker of Redondilla #91 has been all too successful in this regard. So thoroughly has she internalized her beloved Lysi ("y dentro de mí tenía / todo el bien que deseaba," enjoying within myself all the joy I desired) that she has foregone her presence. Lysi presumably has complained; Sor Juana replies, justifying

the overly long absence. Other substitutes, such as the portraits that Sor Juana's female characters address in a host of poems, can also compensate for the
beloved's absence. All of the above poems, together with all of the poems
lamenting separation from the beloved, undoubtedly reflect the absences and
solitude that Sor Juana must have felt so keenly in the enclosed world of the
convent. But a biographical explanation hardly suffices.[35] For, if as Paz's statement suggested, solitude can stimulate the mind, the themes of solitude or
absence can provide the poet a forum in which to make a case for the powers of the mind. In other words, much as the love poetry may attest to Sor
Juana's solitude certain poems also attest to her belief in the powers of the
mind, and in the foregoing examples, the mind of the *female* lover. Indeed, this
representation of the female speakers as minds rather than bodies does more
than transcend the nun's personal circumstances or exchange the violent
physical weapons of Quevedo's "A fugitivas sombras doy abrazos" for "fantasía." In importing the realm of the idea to the feminine, it exchanges the
grotesque female body of misogynist satires such as Quevedo's for its opposite, the classical closed body. Sor Juana shifts women's being from the flesh-
dominated body to the head, seat of reason and core of the classical body, and
from the open mutability of the grotesque body to the stable, hermetically
sealed world of Platonic ideas. Her female poetic speakers feel and emote, but
they resolve their emotionality into the realm of the idea. In the forum of the
"high" genre of courtly love poetry, therefore, Sor Juana recuperates the low
grotesque body of the "low" genre of satire, at the same time pitting the Neoplatonic edges of courtly love poetry against its own misogynist undercurrents.

Arthur Terry observes that absence is the only state in which the imagination can exercise its powers to the full (308–9) and incisively comments that
imagination affords Sor Juana "a possible means of dominating the experiences which she presents" (308). A possible means and a very particular one:
in bringing the beloved into her mental sphere the female speaker overcomes
the not-knowing of Love and subjugates it to her own knowing. The desire to
exercise some control or power over the love situation also receives expression in a series of verbal techniques, stock devices that appear in poem after
poem. They are all highly conventional, part of the repertoire of baroque
poetry. However, through insistent repetition Sor Juana makes them characteristically her own, functional pieces of her poetic system. I have already
alluded to most of these devices; let me recap them here. The first is the use
of command forms, which Gary J. Brown has identified as the most popular
nonrhetorical technique of baroque sonnets (29). Many of Sor Juana's love
poems directly address the beloved, employing a variety of phatic devices to
establish contact. These include the use of the addressee's name or other
forms of direct address, and questions and exclamations. Contact with the
addressee often ends in command forms that order, exhort, implore, and so
on, the receiver to heed the speaker's words or will and redress their wrongs
to her. The extremely frequent use of command forms in such a manner cap-

italizes on the structures of courtly love poetry that allow the woman to instruct her lover and endow Sor Juana's poetry with a lively performative dimension. The second is the logical syllogistic development of the poems that, as I stated earlier, often play out binary oppositions and can take on the air of exercises in legalistic or Scholastic argumentation. Exercises or not, they are virtuoso performances, displays of the poet's logical capabilities in face of *querelle* arguments to the contrary as brilliant as the polemicizing of the "Respuesta a Sor Filotea de la Cruz" discussed in the introduction. The verbal conceits that inform and structure every corner of Sor Juana's love poetry serve the same function as they at once bespeak the poet's ingenious logic and the perverse illogic of love. By means of both devices, as the title of Redondilla #84 has articulated, Sor Juana manages to describe in rational terms the irrational effects of love. She tames its unreason into a geometry of the emotions. Finally, one should not fail to mention the efficacy of invective and biting humor in attacking love. Sor Juana brings the two to bear on men most strikingly in the famous Redondilla #92, best known as "Hombres necios . . ." [Foolish men]. A comically acerbic verbal war, with its skein of conceits, "Hombres necios" showcases Sor Juana's impeccable reason at the same time that it exposes the absurdity and lack of reason entailed in men's treatment of women.

"Hombres necios," availing itself of the prevalent satiric mode as did other female-authored works, establishes the only outspoken link between Sor Juana's love poetry and the outspoken feminism of her autobiographical documents and the *villancicos* to Saint Catherine of Alexandria. Bénassy-Berling neatly describes the feminist message of the *redondilla*'s ending in saying: "Discreetly but firmly, the nun performs a small Copernican revolution in the last line as she assigns men . . . the role of object, object of desire, object of scandal" (277). In a direct counteroffensive to *querelle* misogyny, "Hombres necios" turns the table on men and their "sin razón" or lack of reason by attributing to them the negative qualities that misogyny imputes to women: men are, she concludes, "carne, diablo y mundo" [the flesh, the devil and the world]. No other love poem or poem on love of Sor Juana's so explicitly defends women per se against men's constructions of them: in accordance not only with social but also, as we will see shortly, with literary etiquette, Sor Juana's contestatory responses prefer a more subtle protocol.

As audacious in ways as "Hombres necios" yet at the same time a more comfortable fit with her muted, layered protocol are the poems in which Sor Juana expands on the image of women as rational beings to celebrate the rational love of one woman for another. I refer, of course, to Sor Juana's many love poems to her protectoress, the Countess de Paredes, which comprise a full 15 percent of her personal lyric (Scott 1993, 159). The nun inscribes her affection for the vicereine (whom she poetically calls Fílis or Lysi, the latter name not improbably an echo of the female interlocutor of Plato's treatise on friendship [Scott 1993, 161]) in a kind of secular scripture, one that follows the same paradigm as the divine love, with its attendant human emotions, discussed above in terms of Romance #56. Several critics (see, for example, chap. 15 of Paz's book, "Religious Fires") have aptly described the love that Sor Juana's poems profess for women as being essentially Neoplatonic—a pure love, of the soul and mind and not of the body—that is, the rational or elective love described in Décima #104. Terry, in particular, has discerned in the nun a "tendency to think in terms of a spiritual love which does not appear to lead to the love of God. This love is an 'amor del entendimiento' [cerebral love] which resides in the soul and which scorns the senses" (305). Sor Juana, drawing on Christian tradition to support her Neoplatonism, sees gender as presenting no impediment to the love between souls: "Ser mujer, ni estar ausente, / no es de amarte impedimento; / pues sabes tú, que las almas / distancia ignoran y sexo" (Romance #19) [Being a woman or far away is no hindrance to my love: for the soul, as you well know, distance and sex don't count].[36] The title of the same poem, however, reminds us that sublime as it may be, Neoplatonic love can generate very human feelings: "Puro amor, que ausente y sin deseo de indecencias, *puede sentir lo que el más profano*" (italics mine) [A pure love, however distant, eschewing all unseemliness, *may feel whatever the most profane must feel, 37*]. In her poems to the female beloved, as we saw in Glosa #142 to Lysi, although the poetic character suffers love's intense effects, she no longer feels their sting. This very human and characteristically Sor Juanian dimension anchors the poems to Lysi and Filis in courtly tradition. Neoplatonic in their conception, they are courtly in their enactment.

Indeed, in the poems celebrating the superior rational love of one woman for another and its conceivably more real affective ties for Sor Juana (I think of Paz's statement that one "can see Sor Juana's women; her men are 'ghostly shadows'" [226]), the courtly model that exalts the beloved asserts itself in full force. It is no longer problematized or viewed as problematic. Sor Juana consistently invokes the courtly framework of love as a religion in her poems to Lysi and Filis, be they the love poems or the occasional poetry or the poems of praise. She deifies the vicereine and depicts herself as the goddess's willing slave.[37] Brought to bear on many contexts, these courtly topics lend themselves, for example, to an ingenious tactic in Décima #125, a petition to the Countess de Paredes to free a captured Englishman. Sor Juana prostrates herself before the deity—"como a Deidad os adoro / y como a Deidad os ruego" [as a Deity I adore you and as a Deity I implore you]—to beg the Countess to grant the poet her servitude of love and the Englishman his freedom. Poems #19, #90, and #179, all to women, return the courtly topics to their natural context of love poetry. There they proliferate and stand in contrast to or even directly reverse the stances of the male-female love poetry. Romance #19 houses the full stock of courtly attitudes. Filis is the sun goddess to whom the poet pays homage and feudal tribute, using the archetypal lexicon of courtly love: sacrifice, service, idolatry, hyperbolic praise, and so on. "Contraverting" the natural "order," as well as that of Sor Juana's heterosexual love poems, the miracles of love here have been able to "hacer el dolor amable / y hacer glorioso el tormento" [make pain delightful and torment glorious]. They render erstwhile conflicts unconflictive: "Yo, pues, mi adorada Filis, / que tu desdén idolatro / y que tu rigor venero" [I, my adored Phyllis, who worship your disdain and venerate your rigor]. The poet revels in her captivity: invoking Saint Teresa's lines once again but now quite joyfully, the poem concludes, "que vivo asegura, sólo en fe de que por ti muero" [I only live to prove that I die for you]. In poems #90 and #179 we find further revision of male-female stances on love, and continued reversion to the courtly model. Both are *servidor* poems in which, contentedly and calmly dedicating themselves to the service of the female beloved, the narrators of the two poems emphasize that their actions are based on knowing. For example, the speaker of Sonnet #179 states, "No emprender, solamente, es lo que emprendo: / pues sé que a merecer tanta grandeza / ningún mérito basta, y es simpleza / obrar contra lo mismo que yo entiendo" [Simply not to try is what I try to do, for I know that no merit suffices to merit so great a thing and it is foolish to act against what I know is true]. What is more, such pleasure does the narrator of Redondilla #90 derive from unrequited service that she begs her mistress not to grant her favors, "pues me quitáis con la dicha / el mérito de la pena" [for with this joy you deprive me of the merit of suffering]. The courtly positions embraced in all of the poems just discussed, interestingly enough, contrast strikingly not only with those of the male-female poems in a woman's voice that I have examined, but also with those of the poems in which Sor Juana assumes a male voice to address the female beloved (most notably, poems #77, #141, #177, #178, #183). The male voice of these poems confronts his *belle dame sans merci* and (in all but poem #141) protests, sometimes vehemently, the service she requests of him or the power she exercises over him.[38] Sor Juana's male-to-female love poems reactivate, and her woman-to-woman love poems erase, the traces of the Evil Mother in courtly lyric.

One naturally wonders what at heart motivated Sor Juana to write such impassioned (and conventional) courtly love poems to a woman. I broach the subject with neither prurience nor militancy, but to round out our sense of Sor Juana's celebration of women in the love poetry. Octavio Paz acknowledges that the nun's love poems to women are more heartfelt and less disembodied than her poems to men and raises the possibility of a homoerotic attraction between Sor Juana and the Countess de Paredes (e.g., 217). In chapter 14 of his book, however, Paz directs our attention not to Sor Juana's homoeroticism but to her self-*interests* as he asserts that Sor Juana's poems of loving friendship express her affection more for the body politic than for the "body" of the vicereine. Paz writes, "In Sor Juana's poems to the Countess de Paredes we find all the motifs of traditional amatory poetry [i.e., courtly poetry] transformed into metaphors of the relationship of gratitude and dependence that united the nun with her Vicereine" (202). Sor Juana's love poems to women would thus be poems of vassalage raised to an amatory power. To support his contention, Paz traces the seamless, constant exchange between erotic language and the language of vassalage in courtly poetry, which C. S. Lewis calls the "feudalisation of love" (2). Arguing along the same lines as would Paz later, Luciani maintains that "those who read Sor Juana's love lyric written to members of her own sex as a confessional outpouring of emotion would do well to remember the degree to which love was official discourse, institutionalized parlance, and the prime vehicle of social mobility" (188).

No doubt the unswerving—in both the literal and the Bloomian senses—adherence to the courtly model, found more in the love poetry to women than elsewhere in Sor Juana's lyric, supports Luciani's point and favors a political explanation of the poems. Yet given the fact that Sor Juana had at her disposal, and indeed, extensively utilized vehicles other than outright and fervent love poems to express her ties to the body politic (i.e., praise poems and occasional poetry), I believe that a balanced view is called for, one that does not discount any of the factors in this unresolvable conundrum. Alan S. Trueblood, among others, provides such a view.[39] Trueblood describes Sor Juana's love poems to women as containing "a mixture of love and friendship in which affection, devotion, gratitude, respect and a Neoplatonically accented idealization all have a part. There is more than a touch of flattery at times and, most all perhaps, a need for closeness to another person" (13). The explanatory note or *advertencia* to Sor Juana's *Inundación castálida* (Madrid, 1689), conceivably by Sor Juana herself, also posits this tangle of factors:

> Either her appreciation for being favored and celebrated, or her acquaintance with the illustrious gifts bestowed by Heaven on the Lady Vicereine, or that secret influence (which until today no one has been able to verify) of the humors or the stars, known as sympathy, *or all of these together*, generated in the poet a love utterly pure and ardent for her Excellence, as the reader will see in the whole of this book. (Romance #16, quoted in Paz, 199; italics mine)

Not only self-interest and gratitude, but also intimate acquaintance with and love for the Countess de Paredes, and an appreciation of woman-to-woman rational love all arguably feed the secret sympathies that motivated Sor Juana's love poems to women.

The love poems to women more clearly signal to us not why but *how* Sor Juana wrote her pro-women love poetry in general—that is, by means of the "endgames" whose protective maneuvers I will now proceed to describe, pulling together various pieces of my previous discussion. We have seen that at precisely the point in which Sor Juana's love poetry becomes highly audacious, it also reverts most undisjunctively to the courtly mode. I might say of Sor Juana in this regard what Mary Gaylord Randel has said of Lope de Vega, that "the most intensely confessional verses tend also to be the most profoundly imitative" (224). Sor Juana writes at the end of an era whose poetic culture was, among other things, profoundly imitative. As Thomas M. Greene's now classic *The Light in Troy: Imitation and Discovery in Renaissance Poetry* amply details, the calculated dissolution of literary voice in the face of tradition that was *imitatio* ruled both sixteenth- and seventeenth-century poetic operations. Yet in her Ovillejo #214 Sor Juana explodes literary clichés and expounds on the burden of literary tradition:[40] in the Gongoresque climate of Hispanic baroque poetry and in the Creole climate of the Hispanic baroque New World poetic practices had surpassed the citational mode of the Renaissance to move into far more elaborate reworkings of the inherited texts.[41] Moreover, as suggested by chapter 1's discussion of Mariscal's *Contradictory Subjects* and by my earlier discussion in this chapter of the extensive repertoire of golden age poetry, the modernizing climate of the seventeenth century manifested itself in a plurality of discourses. As society, despite hegemonic rule, became more differentiated, so did art and philosophy. The discursively polyglot or heteroglossic disposition of societies in transition provided a rich playing field for writers of the time.

At the end of the era of empire, in slow and surreptitious transition to the Enlightenment, the baroque culture of crisis nevertheless remained more conservative than forward looking. The ecological economy of the baroque in literature, ideology, and philosophy strove to conserve rather than to discard tradition. Anachronism was anathema; syncretism countermanded and undermined it. In the spirit and with the aims of patristic Scholasticism, baroque neo-Scholasticism and Jesuit syncretism (to which chap. 5 returns) melded and harmonized the most diverse and even opposing currents. As a consequence of all these epochal endgames, in the words of Severo Sarduy, the synchronic diversity of baroque styles reflected a notable diachrony: "The European Baroque and early Latin American Baroque present the image of an unstable and decentered, *but still harmonious* universe; they are constructed as bearers of a certain consonance" (102; italics mine).

Sor Juana's own endgames in her love poetry draw sustenance from and sustain this special fin de siècle perspective. As court games for an elite public, they traffic in the imitative erudition so prized by what Angel Rama calls the *ciudad letrada* or educated community and allude to Plato, Saint Thomas, Quevedo, the centuries-long traditions of courtly love poetry, and so on. In an article on the nun's love poetry, Georgina Sabat-Rivers writes, "Sor Juana, in the history of Hispanic poetry, was clearly the last grand poet in the tradition that had begun in Spanish with Boscán and Garcilaso and that came to an end with her death" and "in her literary world she was the poet who commanded the widest range of previous poetry. She was of course conversant with the Renaissance practice of *imitatio*, which in her case was never servile" (1995, 104). As court games for an elite public that contest the misogynist representation of women, Sor Juana's love poems operate under the triple veil of a nun writing in a courtly mode and redeploying Scholastic debates on reason versus passion. Otis Green, in *Spain and the Western Tradition: The Castilian Mind in Literature from* El Cid *to Calderón*, recaps those debates. The words that Green quotes from Fray Luis de Granada, for example, clearly echo Sor Juana's argumentation:

> If all the dignity of man qua man consists in two things, which are reason and free will, what is more inimical to the one faculty and

to the other than passion, which blinds reason and drags will in its
train? Wherefore you will see how injurious and harmful is any
unduly violent passion; since it thus throws man down from the
seat of his dignity, obscuring his reason and perverting his free
will, without which two things man is not man, but a beast. (1964,
170–71)

To regender the debate and to contest the negative contentions of the *querelle
des femmes* while remaining, as I have already suggested, within both social and
literary etiquettes, Sor Juana acts as a *bricoleuse*. That is, to be "simply" oppositional on feminist grounds, she performs the complicated operations of
deterritorializing and refunctioning the polyglot "languages" of her times. *This
is the essence of her endgames*. A *bricoleuse* juggling shards of male tradition and
making them function transitively, Sor Juana does not in her love poetry
instrumentalize existing aporias in patriachal constructions of gender but de
facto produces them.

As a further example of this deterritorializing or *contaminatio*, where different currents jostle each other in a purposeful and "eclectic mingling of heterogeneous allusions" (Greene, 39),[42] and of Sor Juana's fin de siècle
conservative and critical endgames, let us look at her stance on reason. The
question of whether or to what degree Sor Juana's works reflect an influx of
Enlightenment ideas has been debated extensively. In chapter 5 I take up the
issue on a larger scale; here I will comment schematically on one corner of it,
that is, on how Sor Juana's love poetry positions itself vis-à-vis the Neoplatonic and Thomistic currents that so molded seventeenth-century Hispanic
thought as well as the nun's own. I have already discussed the importance of
Neoplatonism to Sor Juana's love poetry. We have seen that even in her Neoplatonic poems on divine love Sor Juana eschews the ultimate tenet of Neoplatonism that posits love as a route to knowledge. Instead of being a
Neoplatonic stepping-stone to knowledge, male-female love for Sor Juana is a
low force that has to be vanquished by reason. Yet in contravening the Neoplatonism that informs her poetry to so significant a degree, Sor Juana is not
necessarily signaling her adherence to Enlightenment thinking. Rather, it is
more likely that she is locating herself squarely within the bounds of neo-
Thomism. Saint Thomas, it is well known, valued the intellect over the other
faculties of the mind and above all else–as the spark of the Divine in
humankind, as what distinguishes humans from beasts.[43] I quote Bénassy-
Berling's conclusion that "if there is rationalism [in Sor Juana], it is perhaps
much closer to the rationalism of St. Thomas" than to that of the Enlightenment (194).

Descartes's radical rationalism subjected the past and all thinking to categorical skepticism, attempting to wipe the slate clean. The orthodox rationalism *and* the contestatory feminism (particularly as manifested in her
woman-to-woman texts) of Sor Juana's love poetry craft the elements
bequeathed to her at the end of an era by tradition into a jigsaw puzzle of
interlocking pieces. As we have seen at many junctures in the readings of the

poems, each piece in its turn is called upon to authorize or facilitate the poet's own assertions. The ideological or philosophical ungrammaticalities that Sor Juana commits on one level are resolved by resorting to other discourses: one strand can take over where the other falls short. In the capacious fin de siècle repertoire of Neoplatonism, Scholasticism, courtly love, baroque thematics, debates on love versus reason, poetic satire, and in their internecine contradictions, there can generally be found a piece, a tradition, to legitimate what the poet wants to say. It is this special *ars combinatoire* inherent in baroque imbrications and actualized by Sor Juana's wide-ranging and erudite endgames that, to use Arthur Terry's words, accounts for the contrast between "the almost line-by-line derivativeness of many of her poems and the extraordinary freshness of the whole" (303) and that, despite the conservative nature of her ratiocinations, sets her on a continuum with the most Enlightened women thinkers of her day.[44]

A weaving and harmonizing apposite both to the stratagems of much early modern women's writing and to baroque syncretism thus characterize Sor Juana's endgames.[45] Hence (rather than invoking the quintessential icons of women's writing, the distaff and the needle), Sor Juana often meditates on musical harmony and invests it with extraordinary significance: "For Sor Juana the function of music does not depend on its sonorous properties as much as on its metaphysical properties. Hence this discipline can act as a *speculum* of the universe" (Lavista, 201). The reference to music as a simulacrum of the universe, recalling Sarduy's depiction of the decentered yet still harmonious baroque worldview, alludes to Sor Juana's Pythagorism. A handful of recent studies have explored the nun's conservative romance with that world picture, tracing her notions of music to Neoplatonic sources.[46] Moreover, in several religious compositions Sor Juana associates the Virgin Mary, as mediator between the divine and human realms, and Christ himself (in *El Divino Narciso*) with harmony. Music is Beauty of a divine or worldly nature and Beauty itself is relationship: "Así, la Beldad no está sólo en que las partes sean / excesivamente hermosas, sino en que unas a otras tengan / relativa proporción. / Luego nada representa a la Belleza mejor / que la Música" (vol. 3, Loa #384) [Thus Beauty is not only surpassing loveliness in each single part but also proportion kept by each to every other. Hence nothing represents Beauty half so well as Music, *85*]. If this role of music well depicts the harmonizing dialogical tendencies of Sor Juana's own endgames, another well depicts the discordant, subversive notes her love poetry secretly sounds. In the same *Loa*, the effects of music are said to occasion both disquiet and peace: "proporcionando a sus modos / ya el alterar sus quietudes, / ya el quietar sus alborotos" [with a distribution that at times disturbs the quiet of the emotions, at times quiets their turbulence]. Sor Juana, as her overdetermination of harmony indicates, may partake of the syncretic *concierto barroco* of her era, but she maneuvers decorously within this end zone to produce a feminist discourse that can disturb its concerted complacency.

III.

EXTREME GAMES: MARÍA DE ZAYAS, ANA CARO

Such decorum is a rare commodity in the novellas of María de Zayas, whose textualized voice, Lisis, proclaims: "And I caution you that I write without fear" (*The Disenchantments of Love, 369*; *Desengaños amorosos*, 471; henceforth I abbreviate her *Disenchantments* as D., *The Enchantments of Love* as E., and Amezúa's prologue to the *Novelas amorosas* as N.).[47] I focus now on Zayas in order to examine what the extraordinary differences between her writings on love and those of Sor Juana have to tell us about baroque feminist discourse in the Hispanic context. Although both authors' published works circulated widely, if in her love poetry Sor Juana played discreet and recondite endgames for an erudite, elite public, in her novellas on love María de Zayas played extreme games for a mass audience with popular tastes. The extreme games of Zayas's novellas—and of Ana Caro's comedias—engage in an extreme feminism, in extreme violence, and with the extremes of contemporary discourse. Like our present-day "Extreme Games," they are outrageous, codified but not canonized, on the cutting edge and the limits of the acceptable. The very acceptance and success of Zayas's extreme games fascinate me: chapter 3 will analyze the novellas in some depth, but here I want to interact with their surfaces (and in so doing, inevitably, to reenact some critical commonplaces) precisely because it strikes me as significant that their feminism was so readily apparent, so "out there" yet so heartily consumed. The success of Zayas's extreme games, as we will ultimately see, does in part derive from patriarchal discourse and from the imitative patterns intrinsic to Sor Juana's endgames. Yet first it is essential to form an idea of the most overtly outrageous aspects of her works.

María de Zayas immediately begins her *Novelas amorosas* (1637) on the defensive and the offensive. The first lines of the prologue, more a brash assault than a *captatio benevolentiae*, read: "Oh my reader, no doubt it will amaze you that a woman has the nerve, not only to write a book but actually to publish it" (*1*, 21). The prologue and later moments of the text go on systematically to parade the techniques (especially lists of learned women from the past and present) and topoi of the pro-female lines of the *querelle des femmes*: that women's souls and minds are the same as men's, that women's humoral constitution in fact sharpens their intelligence, and that men in their "cruelty and tyranny" (*1*, 22) deny women an education.[48] The frequency and vehemence of her diatribes only increase in the even more embittered *Desengaños amorosos* (1647), where they infiltrate the framework story and the frame stories alike. There we find such impassioned accusations as the following:

Men have always been the authors of deception, scriptures and history tell us that. Although I could cite some examples, I won't because I wish to earn the title of disenchantress, not scholar. Men have usurped this latter title from us by feminizing us more than nature did. While nature gave us tender hearts and little strength, at least she infused in us a soul every bit as capable as a man's soul. Because this is true, let men enjoy their dominance even if it is despotically acquired. (D., *203–4*, 294)

"What is new," writes H. Patsy Boyer, "is that Zayas wedded the philosophical arguments in defense of women with exemplary fiction" (E., intro., xxiii). Those philosophical arguments also feed the thematic axis of both her collections, the fundamental and exemplary thrust of which is to expose the inconstancy of *men* in love in contrast with *women's* constancy and thus to oppugn men's slander of women's evil libidinous nature ("The burden of all blame falls upon the feminine sex as if men's fault were not greater, insofar as they pretend to be nature's perfection" [D., *114*, 200]). Zayas deconstructs the courtly love practices of men, exposing their injurious intents and effects on innocent women. Disarming with hundreds of pages the attacks of misogynists such as Quevedo on women's fidelity, and matching his arguments and tone point by point, Zayas restages the pro-female side of the *querelle* not only in the novella but also in the exacerbated, disillusioned register of the baroque.

Female subjectivity, repressed or misrepresented in male discourse, and female anger, socially silenced, return with violent, extreme force in Zayas's works. Only women, the "disenchantresses," tell tales in the *Desengaños*. The women whose stories the tales tell, as has often been observed, are active, desiring subjects. While generally virtuous, Zayas's strong women can play out a misogynist's worst nightmares. Actively vindictive, they exercise their powers (especially intellectual powers) to defeat and humiliate men. They go to extraordinary lengths to pursue their love and to defend their honor: dressing as men, performing heroic deeds in the male arenas of the battlefield and the court, refusing marriage. The extraordinary and the shocking in fact form the cornerstones of Zayas's thematics and esthetic. In the introduction to the *Novelas amorosas* we are told that the characters will recount not novellas but *maravillas* or marvels, a term that implies wonder and amazement; the *Desengaños* praise novelty ("people love to try new things [*novedades*] whether they're savory or not" [*167*, 257]). Marcia Welles says of this new slant on the novella that "the change in the designation of her stories from 'novelas' to 'maravillas' shows that the cultivation of the surprise and wonder of the audience was of primary concern to María de Zayas" (303). Zayas courts and astonishes her public in a manner reminiscent of the broadsides on Catalina de Erauso, with their tabloid esthetic. Zayas's tales include cases of witchcraft, prophetic dreams, miracles, supernatural apparitions, miscegenation, and homosexuality. The most extreme violence enters her text under the aegis of inspiring *admiratio* and cementing the texts' didactic message. Baroque love, as it was with Sor Juana, is again war: "Love represents a battlefield and a combat zone where, with fire and sword, it struggles to vanquish honor, guardian of the soul's fortress" (E., *38*, 71). Men abuse, rape, torture, dismember, and murder innocent women. "Innocence Punished" (the fifth "Desengaño") finds Inés living in a cell for six years surrounded by her own excrement; "Triumph Over Persecution" (the ninth) finds Beatriz blinded and locked in a cage. Male violence against women escalates in the *Desengaños*, but in the *Novelas* women extract their own bloody revenge. Storyteller Matilda notes of women that "we should be learning how to avenge ourselves, since honor stained can be cleansed only with the blood of the offender" (*45–46*, 81). Her tale has Aminta plunging a dagger into Jacinto's heart, a scenario evocative of Calderón's wife-murder plays. Zayas's female protagonists, her shocking esthetic, the violence her texts and their heroines perform on men, together with her outspoken feminism all conspire to confirm "the UTTER-LY destructive, staggering" return of the repressed in the woman writer's novellas.

Poised as they were to shock and affront, Zayas's "maravillas" in the *Novelas* did not alienate their seventeenth-century readership. Rather, they attained instant best-seller status, quickly went into many editions, and were circulated in England and France. Exceeded only by Mateo Alemán's picaresque *Guzmán de Alfarache* and Cervantes's *Novelas ejemplares* [Exemplary Novellas], they became, together with the *Desengaños*, the most read works of entertainment in seventeenth-century Spain (Amezúa, N., xxxi; Yllera, 64). Moreover, to our knowledge, neither of her two collections met with any objections from the Inquisition or its censors (Amezúa, N., xxxii). Zayas herself comments on the success of her *Novelas* in the *Desengaños*: "What a challenge for the mind, and the person who understands it is will appreciate it while the one who doesn't is excused by his ignorance. This is what happened with the first part of our soiree. If a few people criticized it, a hundred applauded it. Everyone rushed out to buy it and they're still buying it. It's already been through three printings, two legitimate and one pirated" (*168*, 258). Her remarks inject a negative note into the overwhelmingly positive scenario of the works' reception that gives us pause: Had she been attacked for her feminist positions? In both of her books, as do other women writers of her time, Zayas displays considerable anxiety about their reception. She often attempts to channel that reception, among several ways by a special pleading that her works receive the courteous response due to the efforts of a woman and (like Erauso) by depicting in the framework story of the text the favorable reaction of the public within the work to the tales they have heard. However, the comment in the *Desengaños* quoted above would appear to respond to actual criticisms levied against the *Novelas*. Those criticisms, indeed any criticism, have not come down to us. Based on texual evidence from the *Desengaños*, however, Susana Paun de García offers the interesting possibility that Zayas was criticized by members of her own literary group for her lack of literary skill or originality. The storytellers' repeated defense of their lack of art (that may derive from men depriving women of an education), simple style (essential to reach a large public and thus to spread the lesson of the work), and the novellas' originality (they "have not simply been taken from any old source as some invidious critics stated about the first part of our entertaining soirees" [D., *113*, 199]) bolster Paun de García's contentions. Textual evidence would not, on the other hand, suggest that Zayas had been criticized for her intemperate feminism. Given her obvious concern with the success of her works, had such been the case why would she neither address nor redress rather than, as she does, redouble her feminism in the *Desengaños*?

All of the above most exquisitely begs the question that I posed earlier: How did she get away with it? That Zayas's works attained such popularity is not terribly problematic; it may be attributed to popular taste. Their sensational esthetic appeals to popular taste; the public in general may have welcomed Zayas's radicalism as an expression of the rebellious impulses of a restive population; popular taste may stand in advance of or supersede official norms. Yet the lack of official resistance to her works or of published negative responses to them in the patriarchal climate of the baroque still perplexes. To probe this perplexity, let me examine the aspects of Zayas's texts that despite their radical nature naturalized them, making them not only readable but acceptable and even laudable.

The single most readable feature of Zayas's novellas must undoubtedly be their moralistic, didactic cast. Zayas herself insistently and consistently positioned both collections of novellas as exemplary and moral. The full title of her first work reads *Novelas amorosas y ejemplares* [Amorous and Examplary Novellas]; the second she entitled *not Desengaños amorosos* (a title that Amezúa imposed and that has been retained in recent editions) but *Parte segunda del Sarao y entretenimiento honesto* [Second Part of the Soiree and Honest Entertainment]; until 1736, her combined works were issued under the title of *Primera y segunda parte de las novelas amorosas y exemplares* [First and Second Parts of the Amorous and Exemplary Novellas] (Kaminsky, 377). The anonymous "Prologue by an Objective Reader" to the *Novelas* (as in the case of Sor Juana's explanatory note, conceivably by Zayas herself) hastens to mention the moral the works contain and, sounding the sine qua non of didactic literature, states: "This book is not only good for the reform of customs, it's a tasty dish in and of itself" (E., *4*, 27). Thus, if the self-statedly exemplary and far more moderate *Novelas* had established Zayas as a moral writer, the original title of the more problematic *Desengaños* would solidify the association with the earlier work and its intentions. Moreover, Lisis's demand in both volumes that her storytellers relate only true cases, little as the stories actually correspond to her dictum, clearly fulfills the didactic function of exemplum (Welles, 302).

These superficial inscriptions of the novellas into the genre of moralistic literature were no mere gestures; the texts' self-stated purpose of defending women and calling women to defend their own honor and reputation against male offenses reinforces rather than belies them. The unjustified offenses against women so intensely presented provoke the readers' sympathies for the powerless female victims ("for not their beauty, their virtue, their intelligence, their royal blood, not even their innocence, could keep them from becoming victims, sacrificed on the altar of misfortune" [D., *222*, 338]), sympathies that might conceivably be extended to the victims' "manly" actions in seeking justice. On the face of it and in almost all of her stories, Zayas is merely reissuing the theme of honor, allegedly with the purpose of mending men's ways: if the "disenchantresses" "had declared war upon men," it was "not because they hate men but to try to correct them" (D., *167*, 258). The male characters obligingly concede their faults (as don Juan, of all people, says, "we admit our defeat and confess that there are men who through their deception and cruelty, stand condemned, thus vindicating women" [D., *270*, 366]). In direct contradiction of what is really going on in the feminist diatribes, they also realize "that the ladies were blaming them only for the vice of deceiving women and then speaking ill of them" (D., *305*, 403). At heart equally ironic, the female characters' retreat to what my next chapter will establish as the subversive feminist space of the convent to become exemplary nuns allows Zayas to play the religious card that consolidates the affiliation of her novellas with upstanding moralistic literature.

Zayas need not necessarily have gone to such lengths. In a Spain so profoundly concerned with subject formation, the demand that literature possess an instructive dimension had become so obligatory that, paradoxically enough, even summary, spurious compliance with the dictates of utilitarianism was acceptable. As the various misprisions of problematic works that Maxime Chevalier details in *Lectura y lectores en la España del siglo XVI y XVII* [Reading and Readers in the Spain of the Sixteenth and Seventeenth Centuries] demonstrate, moral discourse was a most flexible and accommodating umbrella. Almost anything could be written and legitimated under its aegis. The author(s) of the bawdy *La Celestina* presented the work as a "breviary of practical morality" (Chevalier, 154), and its readers tended to accept it as such.[49] Best-selling literature of the seventeenth century of negligible or equivocal moral value proclaimed its exemplarity: we can think of picaresque novels and of Cervantes's *Novelas ejemplares*. So-called courtly novels (the *novela cortesana*), like those of Alonso de Castillo Solórzano, imposed perfunctory morals on their works to placate the censors. "[Courtly novels] present immoral examples only to state later, with false horror, that they must not be imitated" (Val, xlvii). That the censors should have accepted the novellas of María de Zayas, with their more organic moralism, exactly as she had positioned them therefore hardly surprises. The censors' attention was captured not by the innovative feminist message but by the more familiar exemplarity of the novellas. Following the traditional formula, the two censors of the 1637 edition of the *Novelas amorosas* state that the work contains nothing that goes against the faith or "decent customs" of society; Josef de Valdivielso echoes Zayas's own appellation to call the *Novelas* an "honest and entertaining soiree" (N., 4–5). A comment by Fray Pío Vives in the "Approbation" of the *Desengaños* goes even farther. After stating, "I find nothing in it that is contrary to our Holy Faith and decent customs," he

adds, "rather, I see in it a refuge where feminine weakness, assailed by flatter-
ing importunities, can take shelter, and a mirror of what man most needs in
order to direct his actions properly; and so, I consider it very useful and worthy of being communicated to the world through publication" (N., xxxiii).

"An odd recommendation indeed," exclaims Amezúa, "turning the novellas of doña María into nothing short of a moral and devout work!" (N., xxxiii). Quite odd, but hardly unmotivated, is the fact that the violent return of the
repressed unleashed by Zayas's novellas should have been naturalized into
exemplary tales and rendered almost invisible. In official readings her feminist
discourse takes its place as a subgenre of didactic literature; moralistic literature subsumes and obviates the category of feminist discourse. A similar phenomenon occurs with Sor Juana's *Inundación castálida*, a work that contains
the conceivably jarring woman-to-woman love poetry analyzed above. Once
again sounding the sine qua non of didactic literature, the frontispiece of the
volume proclaims it to be: "For instruction, recreation, and wonder" (87). That
neither the works of Zayas nor those of Sor Juana were explicitly concretized
as feminist also suggests the possibility of an official rerouting or reading strategy. Especially in the case of the popular and would-be populist Zayas, it is
conceivable that the censors' readings aimed to channel the readings of the
public itself, creating an optic that privileged the culturally salutary features of
the texts. I cannot help noting that Amezúa's readings of Zayas in his important prologues to the first full twentieth-century editions of her works respond
to and reflect a similar temptation. Attempting to justify Zayas's popularity in
her times and thus to redeem both the tastes of the golden age and Zayas herself (from prudish nineteenth-century criticisms of her prurience), Amezúa
recasts Zayas as pure, moral, romantic, realistic, and "feminine." When, as
heard above, he exclaims at Pío Vives's radical rerouting of Zayas's extreme
texts, we realize that Amezúa himself has performed a similar, and similarly
motivated, misprision!

Amezúa's claim that Zayas had been an excellent housewife (*Desengaños*,
xiv) may have been misguided, but his claims regarding the peculiar morality
of her times bear consideration. In pondering why Zayas's violent, sensationalizing, lurid texts escaped from the Inquisition unscathed, Amezúa suggests
that "clerics or friars, censors of our recreational reading, were at that time
more tolerant and liberal than they are today on these matters of chastity and
lechery, and were more open-minded than we" (N., xxxiii). H. Patsy Boyer's
words bolster Amezúa's hypothesis:

> Following upon the Council of Trent and the Catholic Counter-
> Reformation, Spanish Catholicism permitted moral freedoms
> unthinkable to the Victorians at the same time that there was dog-
> matic control and harsh repression of heresy under the Inquisition.
> Zayas's novellas are in no way unorthodox and were lauded as
> exemplary by the censors, yet they treat moral issues and present
> material (e.g., rape, battering, murder) with a frankness that seems
> shocking to us. (E., xxv)

Religious rather than social heresies, obscene language more than sensuality, most exercised the Inquisition. The officially sponsored baroque esthetic of the bizarre and shocking that promoted Erauso and promoted Zayas's ability to tell shocking feminist tales demonstrates the permissiveness for transgression–a kind of vacation from morality–endemic in Counter-Reformation Spain. Where Erauso reinforced the male ideal, Zayas attacked it: here then is concrete proof that, even in a most egregious case, the Inquisition could extend its license for licentiousness to feminist discourse.

The licentiousness and novelty that Zayas's works so clearly embraced were also endemic in the *novela cortesana*. Zayas wrote in a genre, and Zayas and Ana Caro belong to a literary group, that strove to extract new and sensational aspects from the novella tradition (another corroboration of the contention that Zayas's literary peers criticized her lack of originality) in order to cater to the tastes of a growing mass public of readers. The literary group, whose trademark was extremism, included Alonso de Castillo Solórzano and Juan Pérez de Montalbán (the author, as the reader will recall, of *La monja alférez*). Both writers wrote prefatory poems praising the *Novelas amorosas*; to the two authors has been attributed the so-called decline of the Spanish novel.[50] By this is meant its alleged decline from Cervantes's *Novelas ejemplares* into a commercial form that bears the earmarks of mass production from readymade parts, that cultivated action and sensation at all costs, that traded in the most extreme immorality, and that–as Lope de Vega had also claimed he did–sacrificed "art" for popularity. Even more so than Lope, they wrote vulgarly for the *vulgo* or populace, a public in which women figured prominently. Accordingly, several features of María de Zayas's extreme novellas that might strike us as uniquely attuned to her feminist program had already been essayed by the male members of her extremist literary coterie. In Castillo Solórzano's courtly novels, for example, can be found a female framework story with all-women storytellers, insistence that he writes in a simple style, the retreat to the convent, strong pursuing female characters, and far less than admirable male protagonists. Moreover, the masculinist, prudish criticism of Zayas's novels by Ticknor and Pfandl as filthy and obscene (see Boyer, E., xii) would more appropriately have been directed at those of Pérez de Montalbán ("It can be stated without hesitation," writes Joaquín del Val, "that they are the most obscene novels of their time" [lvi]). Yet the Inquisition did not disturb his, Castillo Solórzano's, or María de Zayas's novels.

The courtly novels of Castillo Solórzano and María de Zayas, as is characteristic of the early modern novel in general, housed the whole span of contemporary discourse. Recapitulatory, and self-consciously so, they drew on the resources of the chivalric, Byzantine, Italianate, exemplary, Moorish, and picaresque novels, on motifs popularized by comedias and tragedies, and in their interpolated poetry, on a range of lyrical modes as well. The heteroglossia of the times and the dialogical nature of the seventeenth-century novel equate Zayas's extreme games with Sor Juana's endgames. Both authors extensively avail themselves of the expanding circle of discourses of the times, each of which discourses authorizes and renders readable their works. Sor Juana may lament in her Ovillejo #214 the burdens of a century "en que todo lo hallamos servido" [in which we find that everything has been used up], but in fact she and Zayas expediently utilize the established economy. Zayas's almost kitsch novellas not only deploy this vast repertoire in ways too numerous to recount here, but in their perspectivism also *emblematize* the heteroglossia of the baroque discursive landscape. Much critical attention has been paid to the manner in which Zayas, distancing herself from her texts, builds "male" and "female" perspectives and tales into them.[51] Marina S. Brownlee, for one, contends that Zayas "is committed to exploring perspectivisim in all its complexity . . . with a degree of intensity that is hard to equal" (119) and that in so doing the novelist dramatizes "totalizing discourses–feminist, masculinist, canonical, and uncanonical–all vying for power" (125) in paradigmatically baroque fashion. That Zayas includes masculinist tales by male storytellers about women who cruelly deceive men can conceivably, and probably correctly, be seen as concessions to patriarchal attitudes, concessions that create tensions and inconsistencies in her otherwise feminist project.[52] If they vitiate her feminist designs, such apparent inconsistencies nevertheless expose the polymorphousness of the baroque discursive field in general and of Zayas's omnivorous novellas in particular–a matter that she uses to purposeful effect. For in exhaustively dramatizing the panorama of baroque masculine discourse and literary conventions, including misogyny, she can also significantly recontextualize them, appropriating them to her own playing field and aims.

Zayas culls the strands of her extreme discourse from an end zone already burdened with its own tensions. "[E]very day, as surely the world draws to its end, things go from bad to worse," state the *Desengaños* (*402*, 507). The choleric, disillusioned tenor of baroque literature, as I have already suggested on several fronts, dovetailed with Zayas's own. Symbiotically interrelated, one fed off, fomented and, obviously, legitimated the other. As was the case with Sor Juana's love poetry, the disillusioned baroque construction of love as a space of strife and discord proved for Zayas to be a potent tool, one that could desublimatize romantic love and counter stereotypical visions of women in love. Similarly, social critique was rampant in the times, and Zayas joined forces with it in her *Desengaños*. The lengthy final diatribe of the text rehearses the scare topic of the effeminacy and cowardice of the men of the times, attributing to it not only the decline of Spain but also Zayas's signature theme, their deplorable treatment of women: "Respect and honor women and you will see how your lost valor returns" (D., *401*, 506). While *arbitristas* (authors of projects) submitted to the Crown or published their recommendations for the amelioration of Spain's deplorable situation, picaresque novels took up the exposé of social conditions on the literary front. Picaresque social satires, such as Quevedo's *El Buscón* [The Swindler] (1626) with its male protagonist, or the male-authored female picaresque (e.g., Francisco López de Ubeda's *La pícara Justina*, 1605; Alonso Jerónimo de Salas Barbadillo's *La hija de la Celesti-*

na [The Daughter of Celestina], 1614; Castillo Solórzano's *La Garduña de Sevilla y anzuelo de las bolsas* [The Weasel of Seville and the Hook for Purses], 1642) proliferated in the seventeenth century, criticizing even more acerbically than their sixteenth-century predecessors the degraded society from which they originated.

Zayas's *courtly* novellas improbably but transparently partake of the resources of the *picaresque* novel, particularly of the female picaresque. Her aristocratic heroines avail themselves of the tricks of a *pícara* and share her aggressiveness and mobility (see Amezúa, N., xxix; Pérez-Erdelyi). Indeed, the male-authored female picaresque, with its celebration of its heroine's freedom, would appear to be the ideal springboard and authorizing model for Zayas's feminist discourse. *La pícara Justina*, for example, delivers "feminist" pronouncements such as the following that coincide practically verbatim with those of Zayas: "[I]t is as natural as it is necessary for man to be the natural master of his wife; but that a man should entirely subjugate his wife, even against her will, is not natural but rather against human nature, for it is captivity, sorrow, a curse, and a punishment" (Maravall, *Picaresca,* 651), or "we women, since we were made from the bone of a man's rib, have the privilege of receiving and even demanding, to the point of stripping a man's bones for justice's sake" (*Picaresca,* 691). These are bold statements from male authors—too bold, I am afraid, to be taken at face value. Recent readings of the female picaresque, in fact, expose the foregoing as but another instance of the regulatory or sham feminist discourse I discussed earlier in the context of golden age theater. Anne J. Cruz argues that the male-authored *pícara,* who inevitably is a prostitute, both sexually and textually comes under the male control only to be censored and disempowered. The male-authored female picaresque acts in collusion with rather than in subversion of male structures of power;[53] female characters, once again, "act out" male fears and prejudices.

Cruz's points are extremely well taken, but my point veers off in another direction. I want to argue that—as the almost verbatim reproduction by Zayas of the "feminist" pronouncements of López de Ubeda's Justina suggests—established satirical and/or sham feminist discourse can be mobilized for authentic feminist purposes. The more extremist the male satires of "liberated" or cultured women, the more they lend themselves to appropriation by feminist discourse; on the other hand, the more strident and shrill the feminist discourse, the more it fuses with the misogynist satire that endows it with cultural authority. When patriarchal discourse is willfully read or dissociated from its context, the two adversarial discourses can become virtually indistinguishable, rendering misogynist discourse both self-contradictory and highly serviceable to feminist ends. Laura's incendiary feminist diatribes in *La vengadora de las mujeres* and the *pícara* Justina's biting accusations, together with the legions of other avatars of the all-powerful mother that misogynist discourse with its unchecked return of the repressed had placed in circulation, can circle back and come back to haunt—not as the *unheimlich* but as their own opposite. Let one last example suffice to consolidate my point. That most inflamed misogynist Quevedo wrote in 1635 (Zayas's *Novelas*, we remember, date from 1637) a cutting political satire entitled *La fortuna con seso y la hora de todos* [Luck with Shrewdness and Everyone's Hour]. In it, all the oppressed and/or marginalized elements of the Spanish Empire are given one hour, "everyone's hour," to voice their complaints. When women take the platform, they vehemently lambaste men for encarcerating both their bodies and their minds. In Quevedo's *La fortuna con seso* we read,

> Tyrants, why (when women are one part of the two that make up the human race, forming half of it) have you alone made laws against them without their consent, exactly as you please? You prevent us from studying out of envy that we will surpass you; from arms for fear that those of you will be vanquished who are vanquished by our laughter. (273)

In Zayas's *Novelas* we read,

> Why, vain legislators of the world, do you tie our hands so that we cannot take vengeance. Because of your mistaken ideas about us, you render us powerless and deny us access to pen and sword. Isn't our soul the same as a man's soul? . . . For a sword you give us the distaff, instead of books, a sewing cushion. (E., *175*, 241)

In Quevedo, again, we read, "Among us women adultery is a sin punishable by death, and among you men merely one of the amusements of life. You want us to be good so that you can be bad, chaste so that you can corrupt us for yourselves" (273). In Sor Juana's uniquely extreme Redondilla #92 we read, "Hombres necios que acusáis / a la mujer sin razón, / sin ver que sois la ocasión de lo mismo que culpáis: [new stanza] si con ansia sin igual / solicitáis su desdén, / ¿por qué queréis que obren bien / si las incitáis al mal?" [Foolish men, who unjustly accuse women, without realizing that you are to blame for the very things of which you accuse us; and if you assiduously seek her scorn, why do you expect a woman to behave well when you do your best to make her sin?], and in Zayas's *Desengaños*: "You make women bad, indeed you expose yourselves to a thousand dangers to make them bad, and then you go about telling everyone that women are bad. You never consider the fact that if you're the ones who keep them from being good, how, then, can you expect them to be good?" (*238*, 332).

Such then is revenge on the repressed and on the oppressor of Zayas's extremely efficacious, omnivorously incorporative extreme games. If, as we see in chapter 3, Zayas could write such a "perfect" feminist bildungsroman, it was, interestingly enough, because patriarchal discourse had given her the building blocks and the textual authority to do so. Zayas may have been almost unique in her milieu, and radical, but she was not a radical innovator. She need not, as the ultimate irony of Quevedo's *La fortuna con seso* most pungently discloses, have transgressed the language games of her times. She only needed to know how to exploit them and how to assume literary agency within their pluralistic and inflamed baroque bounds. While her work, so intertwined with a skein of sanctioned norms, could be muffled and subsumed in them, it was not stifled or even significantly constrained by them. The following words of Raymond Williams well capture the complicated mechanisms that come to bear on the emergent feminist discourse of Zayas's extreme games: "It would be wrong to overlook the importance of works and ideas which, while clearly affected by hegemonic limits and pressures, are at least in part significant breaks beyond them, which may again in part be neutralized, reduced, or incorporated, but which in their most active elements nevertheless come through as independent and original" (114).

Margarita Nelken's *Las escritoras españolas* [Spanish Women Writers] (1930) offers the unique and uniquely tantalizing comment that María de Zayas's popularity gave rise to a literary school of writers who followed her lead (153–54). Without elaborating fully on her claim, Nelken offers only the questionable example of the discreet Mariana de Carvajal as a disciple of Zayas. A far more likely candidate for membership in this possible "school" was Ana Caro Mallén de Soto (1600?–1650?). Much has been written on Zayas but little is known of her life; relatively little has been written on Caro and equally little is known of her life.[54] What we do know is as tantalizing as Nelken's comment. Ana Caro moved and wrote almost exclusively in the effervescent ambit of Seville, an important cultural center. There she garnered considerable renown, being lauded as Tenth Muse (Serrano y Sanz, 179) and described, by Rodrigo Caro, as a "distinguished poet" who has written much poetry, comedias produced in Seville, Madrid, and elsewhere, and who has participated in many literary competitions, usually winning first prize (Luna's introduction to *Conde*, 2–3). As far as we know, Caro wrote poetry about events in Seville, two short theatrical works, three sacramental plays that have been lost, and the two love comedias I will study here: *Valor, agravio y mujer* [Courage, Outrage and Woman] (date unknown; first published in the twentieth century by Manuel Serrano y Sanz) and *El Conde Partinuplés* [Count Partinuplés] (first published in 1653 in *Laurel de comedias. Quarta parte de diferentes authores* [Garland of Comedias. Fourth Part, By Various Authors] but likely to have been written decades earlier), both probably performed in Seville and Madrid (Luna, 10–11).[55]

Two more pieces of Caro's sketchy extant biography particularly arouse our interest. First, she was a professional writer. Documents in Seville register that she received monetary recompense for her sacramental plays from the "Commission for the Festivals of Corpus Christi." Lola Luna, the foremost expert on the author, also believes that Caro was paid for her comedias and notes, "In that time of crisis, a woman of letters succeeded in turning her writing into legal tender by obtaining 300 reales per play from the best public source of money, the municipal council and ecclesiastical chapters. The same

authorities who criticized women as a factor in social decay and tried to regulate their behavior paradoxically accept her authorship" (6–7). Zayas's works
attained best-seller status; Caro, unlikely to have achieved best-seller status,
achieved the equally unlikely position of well-paid author. Second, Caro and
Zayas formed a fast friendship. Caro resided briefly in Madrid in 1637, it is
believed in Zayas's own home (Castillo Solórzano, 95; Serrano y Sanz, 179).
Zayas and Caro both praise each other in print: Zayas in the *Desengaños* (230)
and Caro in a prefatory poem to the *Novelas* (10–11). The imprint of that
friendship runs deep in Caro's works. Castillo Solórzano's description in *La
Garduña de Sevilla* of Caro, whom he met in 1637, *only* as a poet suggests that
she had not yet written plays by the time she spent in Madrid (96): I would
suggest that Caro wrote her plays not necessarily in Madrid but still under
Zayas's influence, that she carried Zayas's project into that genre and to
Seville.[56] Questions of direct influence aside, for our purposes Caro's plays–
displaying features akin to Zayas's novellas but with their own unique stamp–
bring into clearer relief the extremist pro-female agendas both authors share,
the *querelle* paradigms that Caro shares with Zayas and with Sor Juana, and
finally, the baroque "marketing strategy" of the two women authors.

When I first read Caro's plays, I was immediately struck and surprised by
how remarkably easy they are to analyze in feminist terms, be they ours or
those of the seventeenth century. Refining my reactions, I realized that taken
together her two comedias present a veritable thesaurus of the golden age
theatrical conventions that lent themselves either to contestatory inversion or
to feminist exploitation–and that she performs both. By *contestatory inversion*,
I refer to the manner in which Caro upends conventions and constructs, of
the theater or of the *querelle*, denigratory to women. Like Sor Juana and Zayas,
Caro directly assails misogyny, imputing to men precisely the vices that they
attribute to women. *Feminist exploitation* refers to the manner in which Caro
instrumentalizes theatrical conventions regarding women and suggests the
specific profile of Caro's extreme games, which depend on an exaggeration
that verges on parody. Palinodes not to love but to theatrical tradition, Caro's
extreme plays "push Baroque theatrical devices to the limits of parody and
shape them according to [her] will" (Ordóñez, 12). The literarily self-conscious
comments sprinkled throughout her works as well as the patent intertextuality on which I comment in what follows all betray Caro's hyperawareness of
the conventions in which she writes. Caro's plays are not "about" intertextuality or parody but to a considerable degree about the representation of
women in her chosen models: in rebutting offensive lines, in exploiting to the
extremes of parody and to the maximum the "feminist" discourse of the theater, she tacitly reveals its fraudulence and unmasks the protective moves of
the countercultural discourse produced by the hegemony itself. Like María de
Zayas, Caro in essence responds to the assertion that no printed work has
faithfully represented women. What is remarkable and extremist is that she
does so in the arena of theater, that repository of official values and most public forum.[57]

Caro scans contemporary theater with a radar for gender issues so acute and marked as almost to be uncanny. From its very title and first scene, *Valor, agravio y mujer* takes us into a space where women are exorbitantly empowered, men mocked and reformed, and myths of the masculine debunked. The play opens with Estela and Lisarda, dressed as huntresses and carrying javelins, caught in a fearsome storm. That storm quickly comes to symbolize the magnitude of don Juan's offenses against the female protagonist Leonor: following shortly thereupon don Juan boasts to don Fernando that he had seduced Leonor, giving her his word in marriage, and then abandoned her. With this speech he establishes himself as an unregenerate fickle male, the typical Don Juan (the principal and fickle male figure of the framework of both of Zayas's collections also bears the name don Juan). Over the course of the play male and female characters alike voice their disapproval of don Juan's actions, thoroughly discrediting him. Caro's reimagining of Tirso de Molina's *El burlador de Sevilla* [The Seducer of Seville] (1624?, 1630) purports not only to mock the mocker but also to reform him, and by extension, the male audience of the plays.[58] Leonor, disguised as the male Leonardo, achieves this goal by providing men with a new script for their amorous endeavors. An incensed Leonor/Leonardo accuses don Juan of inconstancy: ". . . porque sois / Aleve, ingrato, mudable, / Injusto, engañador, falso, / Perjuro, bárbaro, fácil, / Sin Dios, sin fe, sin palabra" (196) [because you are perfidious, thankless, fickle, unjust, a deceiver, false, a perjurer, savage, wanton, with no God, no faith, no honor]. S/he exposes the perfidy of his obsession with female beauty (199) and the bankruptcy of his amorous discourse. Pretending to court Estela, Leonor/Leonardo reinvents a lover's discourse as modest and divested of Petrarchan embroideries ("No hay en mí satisfacción / De que me puedas amar / Si mis partes considero," If I think of my qualities, I have no hope that you may love me [204]) and reinvents the image of the male lover itself, promising to avenge and love his/her beloved (Leonor herself!) as that lady deserves: "Mas yo, *amante verdadero*, / La prometí de vengar / Su agravio, y dando al silencio / Con la muerte de don Juan / La ley forzosa del duelo, / Ser su esposo; y lo he de ser" (210; italics mine) [But I, *as a true lover*, promised to right her wrong and upon the death of don Juan, silenced by the inexorable law of the duel, to be her husband; and so I will be]. To state the obvious, Leonor as the male Leonardo, and in her own pursuit of don Juan, embodies the constancy and loyalty of the female lover in direct contradiction both of the Don Juan figure and of men's portrayals of women.

Leonor/Leonardo–the ideal "male" lover–is at the same time a most inflamed "manly woman," a real Fury. Quasi-literalizing the convention of the woman who dresses as a man to avenge her honor, Leonor states that she has not merely disguised herself as a man but become one ("Mi agravio mudó mi ser," The outrage against me changed my whole being [185]). In what can be construed as a parody (and a criticism) of bloody male honor plays, Caro has her female protagonist swear violent revenge on don Juan. When cautioned to temper her bloodthirsty rage, Leonor/Leonardo responds with the familiar *querelle* list of women warriors celebrated for their ferocity. Like Zayas's Aminta, Leonor has become a man's worst nightmare, proof that hell hath no fury like that of a woman scorned: "que tanto puede en un pecho / Valor, agravio y mujer" (211) [all this can be accomplished by valor, outrage and a woman]. Leonor/Leonardo will not, in the end, carry out her violent threats. Rather, by exercising her intellectual powers to ignite don Juan's jealousy, she manages to reignite his love for her and to achieve his anagnorisis. The play does end conventionally, with Leonardo reassuming her identity as Leonor and as don Juan's now acknowledged wife, but she, as deus ex machina of the drama, has pursued on her own and won her lover, conceivably reforming him in the bargain.

If *Valor, agravio y mujer,* with its none too subtle rejoinders to antifemale *querelle* accusations and its exaggerations of theatrical prototypes, is incredibly easy to unpack in feminist terms, Caro's later play, *El Conde Partinuplés,* is if anything even easier–and, for this reader, an even more interesting performance of them. *Valor* inserts a virago into the territory of the male myth of Don Juan, and there her presence unthrones it and exalts her; *Partinuplés* transports the spectator into an emphatically matriarchal realm, refashioned from male discourse, to witness a rich display of gender-bendings. *Partinuplés* stages the myth of Cupid and Psyche within the intertextual scaffolding of Calderón de la Barca's then recent (1635) *La vida es sueño* [Life Is a Dream]. In Caro's play, Empress of Constantinople Rosaura lives under the prophecy that she and her country will be dishonored at the hands of her suitor. Her ministers force her to submit to marriage and to choose a suitor. Willfully, she selects the only candidate who has already been promised in marriage: the heir to the French throne, Count Partinuplés, engaged to his cousin Lisbella. Exercising magical powers, her cousin Aldora introduces Rosaura to the images of her possible suitors, introduces Partinuplés to Rosaura through a portrait, and transports Rosaura to an island. There, under cover of darkness and invisibility, she proceeds to enamor the count with mysterious maneuvers reminiscent of Ana in Calderón's *La dama duende* [The Phantom Lady] (1629). The Count, against his word, succumbs to curiosity about his lover's identity and shines a light on her. Discovering his treachery, Rosaura (unlike Calderón's Circe) demands that the Count go off to war to defend his besieged country. The war gives rise to a confrontation in which the two female leaders eventually face off peacefully, to Rosaura's victory on the front of love.

As even my brief summary suggests, Caro has once again set up a scenario thick with feminist implications and refigurations. This matriarchal world features the *esquiva* Rosaura who, with "proud courage" (89) and declaring herself an Amazon (82), protests having to submit herself to the yoke of marriage. Where Calderón's Rosaura largely remains a shifter and a blank in his play, Caro's Rosaura–her mind, will, "manliness," and subjectivity–dominates the *comedia* (Ordóñez, 10–11). Male characters here take a backstage to female, and the female characters present exemplary traits in a feminist vein: they are no more beautiful than intelligent ("if of equal perfections" between physical charms and brains "is beauty comprised / she is the most discreet and beautiful" [141]) and heroic and strong. In the female-dominated love triangle, the two "manly" female leaders emerge as equal and worthy adversaries (Lisbella describes herself as "una mujer sola que / viene de razón armada," a lone woman who comes armed with reason [168]). Indeed, the play contains neither conventionally submissive women nor subservient ones. Rosaura's cousin Aldora stands in for the usual role of female maid or *graciosa*, and her stereotypically "feminine" magical abilities, identified with Circe's (112), provide the motor of the play. Favorably presented, they redeem Circe from conventional associations with evil magic such as those we saw played out so fearfully in *El mayor encanto amor*.

If Aldora redeems Circe and Caro's Rosaura reinfranchises Calderón's, echoes of Psyche unmake Partinuplés. To him is imputed the blind mad love that Sor Juana so excoriated; it is he who is guilty of the damning "female" curiosity that Psyche represents in androcentric myths. Partinuplés, exhorted by Rosaura to show his bravery, thus exhibits "feminine" characteristics and Rosaura "male." However, the play calls into question exactly where Rosaura can be situated in the categories into which women have been locked. What is the Phantom Lady, wonders don Manuel of Calderón's *La dama duende*, "Angel, demonio o mujer" (261) [Angel, demon or woman]? Similarly, the Count in Caro's play repeatedly displays his inability to locate Rosaura in any single or set category, for example: "Cuando *fiera* te seguí / *monstruo, mujer* o *deidad*" (105; italics mine) [when as if chasing a *beast* I followed you, *monster, woman* or *deity*]. Demon woman or deity? Rosaura, feminist character of a female author, is neither and both. In precisely the terms discussed in my previous chapter, she *is* a "monster" who defeats and fractures categorization.

The destabilizing, gender-bending tactics of the text find ultimate expression in its ending. There the unrepentant male *gracioso* (there is a *male* if not a female comic figure) Gaulín, who has galled us throughout the play with his patently risible misogynist comments, ends up without a partner; he says: "Bueno, todos y todas se casan, / solo a Gaulín, santos cielos, / le ha faltado una mujer / o una sierpe, que es lo mesmo" (172–73) [Well, all the he's and she's are marrying, and only Gaulín, by heaven, has no wife–or serpent, which is the same thing]. The Count, on the other hand, actually cedes his kingdom to Lisbella so that he may marry Rosaura: "que sin Rosaura no quiero bien ninguno" (172) [besides Rosaura, nothing else matters].

This fairy-tale feminist ending and the other feminist features of both plays should by now have provided ample evidence of Ana Caro's extraordinary, even implausible, gender radar. I should note that I have not exaggerated but if anything understated the case, for the sake of brevity. Indeed, no exaggeration whatsoever is necessary for–as I will now argue in conclusion to this section–I have every reason to believe that I have done no more than bring to the surface the plot that Caro and Zayas themselves very purposefully devised for their own gain as well as their audiences' edification. Elizabeth J. Ordóñez states: "If we perceive difference in these works by women, we still cannot assume that Zayas or Caro, or any woman writer for that matter, necessarily made the conscious choice to create alternative texts" (13). I have profited in many ways from Ordóñez's important article,[59] yet I must take issue with this one statement and assert my strong suspicion that the extreme, extremely feminist games of both Zayas and Caro reflect a conscious, shared program of writing differently, that is, a concerted quest on the part of the two women to create alternative texts. I believe that in the climate of the Hispanic baroque where novelty held such extraordinary cachet, Zayas and Caro seized upon the notion of "writing as woman" as a trademark, a signature, a marketable commodity. Zayas, from the very first lines of the *Novelas amorosas*, pugnaciously places in view her status as a woman writer; Caro includes in *Valor, agravio y mujer* what sounds very much like an advertisement for women dramatists and poets, past and present (193).[60] Their self-advertisement joins forces with the mutual advertisement of Caro and Zayas discussed earlier. Since they were that oddity, a woman writer, they would capitalize on their difference: not simply by advertising themselves as women writers but also by exploiting their generic difference to write stridently feminist works as a means of enhancing rather than detracting from the market value of their production. Zayas, as we have heard, cultivated her popularity; Caro would be paid for hers. If Zayas was criticized for her lack of originality, she, and Ana Caro, would be original with a vengeance: Zayas heightening rather than diminishing her feminism in the *Desengaños*, Caro deepening hers in *Partinumplés*. Their main moral point, that someone had to defend women against men's misrepresentations, would also be their main selling point and women would be a significant part of their target audience. Both the novella, as we have seen, and golden age theater, as is well known (Lope stated that he wrote for "the populace and women" [12]), counted on a female audience. Zayas in particular appears to gear her works to a female public. Her novellas contain declarations of the simplicity of her style ("I've not sought rhetorical or cultivated style . . . because I would like everybody, both ordinary and cultured, to understand me" [D., *367*, 469–70]),[61] the female cast of storytellers, an emphasis on the "feminine" details of clothing uninteresting or even incomprehensible to male readers (see Kaminsky), appeals directly to women (to which I return shortly), and so on. In courting the renown that might accrue from writing on women's issues qua woman and in part for women, Caro and Zayas courted the border-crossing pragmatics of fame that favored Erauso and Sor Juana; though distinct in significant ways from the nun's feminist discourse, the two Spanish women writers' extreme games reproduce the tactics of Sor Juana's wonder-producing, self-advertising iconography of anomaly.

One final caveat before moving to general conclusions: the conceivable market value of Zayas's and Caro's conceivable program to write "differently" raises the question of opportunism and places the authenticity of their bla-

tantly feminist discourse in question. Zayas's heteroglossia and Caro's intertextuality and parody, as we have seen, draw from established discourses and
capitalize on the currency of sham feminist discourse. Susan C. Griswold
writes, "Precisely because Zayas's works make use of themes which are part of
a recognized and vital literary tradition, one must regard 'herófeminism as a
topos and be very wary about believing that feminism to be a sincere expression of her personal beliefs on the subject" (100). As I hope my discussion of
the oppositional efficacy of Zayas's and Caro's discourse-devouring extreme
games has established, Griswold's argument can easily be reversed–but still it
raises qualms. Not having access to the writers' intentions, I cannot definitively put these qualms to rest. The depth and complexity of Zayas's feminism, which chapter 3 will expose, perhaps allay them. For the purposes of
this chapter's investigations, however, I will rest with the conclusion that the
success of Zayas's and Caro's works proves that a woman writer's overt and
hard-hitting feminist discourse could and did successfully exist in the misogynist climate of the Hispanic baroque, and with the suggestion that women
writers themselves perceived the circulation of such discourse as an oppor-
tune rather than a disadvantageous means of placing themselves in commercial circulation.

⸎

IV.

CONCLUSIONS: THE CURRENCY OF FEMINIST DISCOURSE

Toward the end of his *Woman Triumphant: Feminism in French Literature
1610–1652*, Ian Maclean elucidates the affinity between baroque topoi–such as
metamorphosis, mutability, fusion, the upside-down world, *admiratio*, war–and
seventeenth-century French feminist discourse. He concludes his discussion
with the provocative words: "All of this leads to the question of whether feminism has closer links with the baroque than anti-feminism" (264). On the disembodied level of literary topics, Sor Juana's and Zayas's works have
indisputably attested both to the rightness of Maclean's assertion and to its
applicability to the Hispanic literature of *desengaño*. What my chapter has
sought to establish, however, is that such an assertion holds even in the seemingly unpropitious literary *and* larger cultural context of the Counter-Reformation Hispanic worlds. I must once again disavow any desire to glorify or
idealize the Hispanic baroque vis-à-vis women's issues or writing: what I have
endeavored to emphasize are its malleable spaces, tacit fissures, and ironic
returns. Exploring them, we have seen that the extreme misogyny of the times
gave heightened currency to gender issues: the more the feminine was barred
and repressed, the more virulently and predominantly would it reassert itself,
infiltrating a panoply of genres and assuming a wide variety of phobic forms.
The barring of the feminine in actuality endowed gender discourse with extraordinary cultural capital, as manifested in the thick "mother lode" of courtly
love poetry, extreme misogynist satire, and sham feminist discourse. These

patriarchal discourses legitimated and made readable feminist discourse. The Hispanic culture of crisis also spawned a syncretism and heteroglossia that lent themselves to feminist discursive mobility. All told it can be said that, in paradoxical contradistinction to the more enlightened official cultural politics of France, the more conservative, more misogynist, more extreme, more quintessentially baroque Hispanic worlds actually provided a highly fertile climate for discourse with feminist features and immanence.

Indeed, far from there having been an absence of feminist discourse, there was an overabundance of it. Be it due to the return of the repressed, to the availability of gender issues as a platform for social critique, to their marketability, or to all these factors combined, the Hispanic cultural scene was in fact *saturated* with quasi-feminist discourse. Piling irony on irony, I would assert that so saturated was the market with quasi-feminist discourse and so thoroughly had the discussion of gender issues been transferred into popular and comic genres that gender discourse had dissolved into white noise. In other words, by virtue of its saturation of the market and its popular cast, feminist discourse was de-ideologized and neutralized, made numb and numbing; what could have been "noise" (entropy, disruption, disorder) became an impotent white noise. The sensationalizing aspects of the baroque that canceled out moral issues could also cancel out ideological ones. Like the specious intellectual calisthenics of certain male renderings of the *querelle* I referred to in the introduction, feminist discourse was both readable and almost invisible. In sum, as the "Approbations" to Zayas's work well attest, much in the baroque worked for the telling of feminist tales, but much worked against their being recognized as such or acted upon.

I make the above assertions based not only on the degeneration of the pro-female *querelle* into high-visibility popular forms and satire but also on the fact that we have basically no knowledge of activity on the part of the state to improve women's lot *or* of substantive female rebellion in the seventeenth century (besides the works of Zayas!). Sumptuary laws and laws regulating the conduct of such women as the *tapadas* or veiled women may indicate an increase in female licentiousness, but only with regard to the extremes of aristocratic women or prostitutes. Mariló Vigil's disappointing *La vida de las mujeres en los siglos XVI y XVII* [Women's Lives in the Sixteenth and Seventeenth Centuries] declares but fails to document the rebellious activity of seventeenth-century Spanish women.[62] We know of a female reading public, but not of collective female action. The Hispanic seventeenth century has, then, bequeathed to us a considerable amount of feminist discourse but negligible evidence of its praxis. That disjunction between discourse and praxis, for its part, not only corroborates my contention regarding the excessive and ultimately counterproductive currency of feminist discourse but also speaks to the crises of the times. Gender discourse, for or against women, served as a site of symbolic struggle symptomatic of tensions rather than directly catalytic of action. In terms of women's issues per se, only in the next century—when, I must note, María de Zayas's popularity if anything *increased*[63]—would the disjunction be resolved, as the state acted upon this discursive legacy, in part its own, and legislated conditions more favorable to women. Sor Juana, working at the end of an era and the forefront of another, had seized on precisely the strand, reason, that would turn around the situation for women.

In light of the scenario I have just outlined, María de Zayas's extreme games take on two final shadings. The first is ironic and poignant: if indeed inflamed "feminist" discourse was little more than white noise, then the outspoken feminism of Zayas's extreme games may have been no more audible than Sor Juana's more muted endgames. The second depends on the first and seeks to combat it: in writing as woman for women and in as shrill a voice as possible, Zayas was attempting to de-automatize sham feminist discourse, to make it more than white noise. The features of her texts that invoke a female public, as described earlier, find their most explicit articulation in exhortations that call a female public to action—"Come, let's give up our finery, our curls, and our flowers; let's defend ourselves, some with wit, others with weapons! That would be the best kind of disenchantment for women living today and for all days to come" (D., *141*, 231). The stridency of her voice would perhaps rise above the fray of sham feminist discourse, her calls to action would hope to convert discourse into praxis, thereby overturning the dynamics of a feminist discourse that in the seventeenth-century Hispanic baroque world led an all too plethoric life.

CHAPTER THREE

Women on Love, Part II:
Sor Juana, María de Zayas,
and
Madame de Lafayette

(for FWG, in memoriam)

But I began to think there can never come much happiness to me from loving; I have always had so much pain mingled with it. I wish I could make myself a world outside it, as men do.
—George Eliot, THE MILL ON THE FLOSS

I.

INTRODUCTION(S)

This chapter focuses on endings that contravene the characteristic comedia script conclusion: on three seventeenth-century women writers who attempt through the endings of their texts to envision for their female characters, and to narrate, a life outside the conventional love and marriage plot—a life elsewhere portrayed otherwise.[1]

The complexity of the endings of their texts spills over into my task of beginning a discussion of them; I will begin twice. Starting simply, I repeat that this chapter comprises a sequel to the previous one. In chapter 2 we gained a sense of Sor Juana's philosophical stance on love, her rejection of love and passion in favor of reason. We examined certain resources that the pessimistic baroque vision of love afforded three feminist writers of the seventeenth century as well as their "thefts" of established discourses. The bulk of the present chapter will extend these issues deeper into the novellas of María de Zayas and carry them into various fictions by Mme de Lafayette (1634–92, almost Sor Juana's exact contemporary). Unpacking my themes in the context of the two women's works as well as that of other poems of Sor Juana, I will show how they all conspire to produce a significant development in women's writing–an incipient yet "heroic" form of the female bil-dungsroman. The bildungsroman, for its part, derives sustenance from yet another facet of baroque literary conventions and social reality, the retreat to the convent.

I begin again. This time, in keeping with the *esprit géometrique* of the texts and their times, I will start to flesh out the central tenets and themes of the chapter through a reading of Sor Juana's geometry of metaphysics.[2] The open-ing stanza of the *Primero sueño*, with its stunning landscape of a triangle and a circle, establishes the basic opposition of her geometrics: pyramidal, the shad-ow born of earth pushes heavenward toward the orb of goddess Diana. Circles, such as Diana's orb, repeatedly come to the fore when Sor Juana broaches divine themes. In the introduction to the *Neptuno alegórico* [Allegorical Neptune] Sor Juana notes that "[i]t was a custom of antiquity, and quite particularly of the Egyptians, to worship their deities in various hiero-glyphs and in different forms: hence they used to represent God with a circle" (4.355). In the *Sueño* we find the "First Cause" or Divinity being described as the ". . . circunferencia / que contiene, infinita, toda esencia" (ll. 410–11) [the circumference containing every essence ad infinitum, *181*]. Moreover, Sor Juana represents harmony, identified with the Divinity, as a spiral (Romance #21); as we saw in the last chapter, divine love "es calidad sin opuestos" [is a quality without inconsistencies] from which emanate Pythagorean harmony, Neoplatonic reason, correspondence. If in Sor Juana's geometrics *circles* repre-sent the perfect realms of Divinity and heaven, in the *Sueño* and elsewhere *tri-angles* come to signify what is earthbound and problematic.[3] "[S]iendo el término el Bien, todo el dolor es el medio" (Romance #56) [since its terminus is the Good, it is in between that suffering lies]: where circles entail divine har-mony, perfection, and correspondence, triangles are the shape in Sor Juana's poems for all too human dramas embodying paradox, unhappiness, and the jagged planes of the perverse illogic of love.

I have especially in mind Sor Juana's love triangle poems, the poems of "encontradas correspondencias" or ironic symmetries discussed in the previ-ous chapter. Her love triangle poems play out weighty issues within the deceptively light format of "cuestiones de amor o de discreción" [questions of love or discretion], a genre dating from classical times and enjoying particular currency in seventeenth-century court settings.[4] The "cuestiones de amor" of the seventeenth century debate piquant issues of courtly or court love. Sor Juana's own "cuestiones de amor" always revolve around a woman's choice between two men, one whom she loves but who does not love her, and one whom she does not love but who loves her. In Romance #4, which contains Sor Juana's major pronouncements on the nature of ironic symmetries (for example, "¿. . . cómo la razón puede / forjarse de sinrazones?" [how can rea-son be forged from unreason?]), the poetic subject must choose between her beloved Fabio and the loving Silvio. Going against both "obligation" and pub-lic opinion, she reaffirms her free will by choosing Fabio. In Sonnets #166 and #167 the poetic speaker puzzles through the same issues, arriving only at the realization that one suffers either way, in loving or in being loved. On the other hand, pondering the choice between two unnamed males in Sonnet #168, the "I" comes to a conclusion apparently opposing that of Romance #4. To safeguard her "honor," she says, "escojo / de quien no quiero, ser violento empleo, / que, de quien no me quiere, vil despojo" [I choose to be violently employed by one whom I do not love rather than to be the vile spoils of one who does not love me]–that is, she chooses the Silvio figure of Romance #4. Sonnets #171 and #172, though not properly triangle poems of ironic symmetries, disclose the aftermath of that choice. Palinode poems, they express in no uncertain terms her hatred for Silvio.[5]

Placed in the context of María de Zayas's and Mme de Lafayette's texts, with their far thicker love triangles, these seemingly flighty and slight poems of Sor Juana's acquire wonderful resonance and an emblematic value. On the most immediate level, they present precisely the same triangle and "cuestión de amor" encountered in the other two authors' works of fiction. Fueled by mad love's perverse logic that (as Sonnets #166, #167, and #170 demonstrate) can breed only unhappiness, the triangular situations of Sor Juana's poems bespeak, as ever, the pessimistic vision of love that effectively informs the works of all three authors. The poetic "I" attempts to achieve some respite from the clutches of illogical love by working her way through the triangles of passion. In so doing, she tries out different, even contradictory, positions. She works the problem through in characteristically baroque fashion–producing ambiguity, restless shifting, and dynamic instability. Similarly shifting and unstable grounds underlie the works of Zayas and Lafayette and, as we will see, give special poignance to the woman's drama.

For this is a woman's drama, one that in its own unprepossessing way opens up the issue of the refusal of love in the name of reason and self-determination that will prove to be as central to Zayas and Lafayette as it is to Sor Juana. The apparent contradictions between the resolutions of Sor Juana's Romance #4 and Sonnet #168 harbor a subtle commonality. In Romance #4, the poetic speaker extricates herself from Unreason's cruel ironies and declines requited love ("No es amor correspondencia," Love need not be requited to be love) to assert her freedom: "Él es libre para amarme, / aunque a otra su amor provoque; / ¿y no tendré yo la misma libertad en mis acciones?" [He is free to love me, though his love distresses another woman; shall I not have the same freedom in my actions?]. Similarly, the poetic speaker of Sonnet #168 endeavors to salvage some small shred of self-dignity from the impossible situation that the poet has been at pains to detail in the two preceding sonnets by avoiding at least her own passion.[6] The sustaining of self-will and dignity, it is clear, underwrites both poems. And like the Duc de Nemours–Ne-amours, the negation of love–whom the Princesse de Clèves will ultimately reject in the novel that bears her name, the schematic male figures of Sor Juana's triangle poems in the final analysis serve as shifters in the game or "question" of love, springboards upon which the female speaker erects her self-determination.

II.

PASSION VERSUS REASON
IN MARÍA DE ZAYAS AND MME DE LAFAYETTE

Literary criticism to my knowledge has yet to equate Sor Juana, Zayas, and Lafayette. Indeed, the three authors—writing in three different genres from different countries and cultural contexts—may well appear to be rather unlikely partners. To inaugurate the dialogue, I will establish some primary affinities between them by extending to Zayas and Lafayette the discussion of love versus reason carried out in the last chapter in terms of Sor Juana.

As the reader will recall, the previous chapter has already examined in some detail Zayas's stance on love and its integral relationship with Sor Juana's as well as with the baroque worldview of their sister societies. Zayas is not as specifically concerned with the issue of reason versus passion as Sor Juana, yet it does undergird her position and contribute to the rejection of love she advocates. Nor is Zayas's treatment of the matter as philosophically informed as that of Sor Juana (or of Lafayette). However, what Zayas's works lack in depth or precision they make up for in vehemence and in sheer persistence as they prosecute their case against love.

To literary and didactic effect, Zayas places her emphasis on passion and its madness rather than on reason. She formulates, and her novellas illustrate, a love that functions on a principle similar to Sor Juana's "ironic symmetries," both for ideological reasons and for its efficacy in generating literary plots: "It appears that Love isn't doing his duty if he doesn't create impossible situations" (E., *277*, 377). Most often in Zayas's works, as might be expected, men are the agents of love's madness and are described as mad or as having lost their reason. Men's brand of love exemplifies a dark variant of the Tristan phenomenon outlined by Denis de Rougement as a central feature of courtly love: love can remain strong only as long as obstacles remain in its way. In Zayas, the Tristan phenomenon shades into yet another manifestation of love's illogic, men's own mutability: "This is what often happens when love rules: men promise things they later deny when their desire has been satisfied and their passion waned" (E., *197*, 270). Such is the ruling message of Zayas's *Novelas amorosas*–that women should not be deceived by men's unreliable professions of love. In the *Desengaños amorosos* everything, as we continually see, grows more dire. Men's actions reach a frenzy of cruelty as they become ever more crazed and even less capable of upholding their reason: (one example among many) "No matter how he tried, don Juan was in such a state that he could no longer restrain the runaway horse of his passion through the use of reason" (D., *117*, 203). In a rare moment of psychological penetration, through interior monologue Zayas shows us the male protagonist of the penultimate "Desengaño" thinking through his mad love and trying to choose between his "burning desire" and his "reason" (*313*, 412–13). The former wins out.

Mad love's agents in Zayas's text are mostly men, its victims women. But women, too, can fall prey to mad love, for a young woman whose "beauty, vanity, and folly are governed by the will . . . tends not to heed reason or judgment, and, instead, lets herself be carried away by lascivious desires" (E., *183*, 253). Nevertheless, Zayas's beleaguered female characters, generally more virtuous and principled than the males, tend to heed reason and to resist the importunities of mad love–if not to the end, at least for an admirably long period of time. When women do fall victim to love, it is usually as a manifestation and result of their fidelity to unworthy lovers. The female characters evoke, and one of them directly invokes, Ariadne, whose lover repaid her "constancy with disloyalty and deception," making her "suffer such great torment" (see E., *168–71*, 233–36). Yet because the women's basically laudable constancy often abrogates their reason to lead them down the path of mad love, the lesson offered by the very first tale of the *Novelas amorosas* and tacitly echoed throughout both volumes holds equally true for women and for men: that a person should not trust "in the frail bark of his weakness" or throw "himself into the ocean of unrestrained appetites lest he drown in it" (E., *12*, 37). Lisis, protagonist of Zayas's framework story in both volumes, takes this advice quite literally: at the end of the *Desengaños*–and this shall be the subject of much of my later discussion–she rejects love altogether and retreats to a convent.

The above advice from the *Enchantments* could easily be mistaken for that of Mme de Lafayette (or Sor Juana). "But wait," as Shreve says to Quentin in *Absalom, Absalom!* whenever Quentin's narrative makes an unexplained leap. How can a hallmark of French classicism such as Lafayette concur in tone and substance with Zayas or Sor Juana, exemplars of the Spanish baroque? The question bears addressing.[7]

Contemporary interest in the baroque as a pan-European phenomenon and as a reaction to the Renaissance optimism and its neoclassicism has inspired scholars to reevaluate the rubrics traditionally utilized to classify French seventeenth-century literature. What was previously seen as an essential, and heuristically or even nationalistically convenient, opposition between classicism (order, measure, reason, law) and the baroque (disorder, excess, fantasy, freedom) has subsequently been modified into a more dialectical relationship. Critics now allow that topics, themes, and techniques of the baroque infiltrated French seventeenth-century literature, especially that of the first two-thirds of the century. Metamorphosis, mobility, life's ephemerality, disguise, plays within plays, mirror reflections, perspectivism, elemental images, the love of decoration, nonlinear language and, most important, the theme of *paraître* versus *être* [appearances versus reality] comprise the central elements of the baroque that would meet with both acquiescence and resistance from French writers before Racine. On the level of doctrine, French classicism would define itself over/against the baroque; in practice, writers were reluctant to abandon these literarily attractive baroque elements.[8] Jean Rousset concludes, "Baroque work, classical work: two poles of attraction rather than two strict and symmetrically opposed patterns; there can be contamination, vacillation, or alternation within the compass of the period in a single artist's works" (249).

One need not by any means have a direct knowledge of critical debates to discern the baroque resources, so familiar from Spanish golden age literature, upon which *La Princesse de Clèves* (published anonymously in 1678; to be abbreviated as *LPDC*) draws from its language on up.[9] Lafayette's lapidary prose relies heavily on key words repeated time and again in different contexts. While her language is classical in its minimalism, among the key words we find several characteristically baroque locutions of surprise and amazement: *surprise, épouvant, s'étonner, éclat* or *éclater, s'admirer,* and so on. For example, when M. de Clèves first meets his future wife:

> Il fut tellement *surprise* da sa beauté qu'il ne peut cacher sa *surprise*; et Mlle de Chartres ne peut s'empêcher de rouger en voyant *l'étonnement* qu'elle lui avait donné. . . . M. de Clèves la regardait avec *admiration*, et il ne pouvait comprendre qui était cette belle person qu'il ne connaissait point. (138; italics mine)

> He was so *surprised* by her beauty that he was unable to hide his *surprise*, and Mlle de Chartres could not help blushing when she saw the *astonishment* she had caused. . . . M. de Clèves gazed at her in *amazement*, wondering who this beautiful young girl could be whom he had never seen before. (*10–11*)

Both the novel's style and its sequencing of events often turn on such reactions and (as I will discuss in detail in section V here) on their analogues: chiaroscuro contrasts or about-faces of extreme and antithetical emotions. Moreover, as Leo Spitzer might put it, the locutions of surprise function as "spiritual etymons" or indices of the deeper baroque structure of the text and of its court milieu. Mme de Chartres, mother of the Princesse de Clèves, articulates that framework in warning her daughter about the world of the court and its love affairs: "If you judge by appearances in this place . . . you will frequently be deceived: what you see is almost never the truth" (*26,* 157). The Princesse and the reader, as they delve deeper into the court milieu represented in the text, come to a greater awareness of the veracity of Mme de Chartres's advice, that is, the fact that both court and text revolve around appearances versus reality, deceptions versus disillusionments. Or, in Spanish, the quintessentially baroque themes and structuring principles of *engaño* versus *desengaño*, orchestrated in *LPDC* with conventional devices of masked balls, secret chambers, and clandestine meetings.

The court atmosphere rife with intrigue and profoundly enmeshed in issues of love depicted in *LPDC* also reflects (though transposing it safely to the reign of Henri IV) the position of the French nobility during the reign of Louis XIV, which was not dissimilar to that of its Spanish counterparts. The increasing impoverishment of the French aristocracy to which the Fronde or civil wars of 1648–53 gave violent expression and the establishment of an absolute monarchy resulted in the dependency of the nobles on the monarch for much-needed funds and favors. Their fortunes in decline, the French nobility converged upon the court, which became a center, among other things, of power-mongering.[10] Reduced to so limited a sphere of action, the aristocracy availed itself of all of its resources, including love, as bartering chips in the ploys for power. As Lafayette wrote in *LPDC*: "Ambition and love affairs were the life-blood of the court, absorbing the attention of men and women alike. There were countless interests at stake, countless different factions, and women played such a central part in them that love was always entangled with politics and politics with love" (*14*, 142).[11] Hence, if not experiencing quite the same conflictive times as in Spain, the French aristocracy was certainly subject to pressing conflicts; love became party to them. And as the wars of state were increasingly fought on the battlegrounds of love with women as principal actors, women writers stepped in to chronicle them. In writing memoirs and novels such as *LPDC*, they wed History with private history and merged the two meanings of *histoire* (history and story).[12]

Mme de Lafayette's great theme of love—so akin to Zayas's—takes shape against this backdrop propitious to women's writing, unpropitious to genuine affection, and as we have seen, evocative of the Spanish baroque on more than one level. Like Zayas, Mme de Lafayette would not only write exclusively about love but would also appear heartily to despise that emotion. At the age of nineteen, Lafayette penned to her friend Ménage the famous lines, "I am so convinced that love is an uncomfortable thing, that I am delighted that my friends and I are free of it"; at twenty-nine, in a letter to Huet, she mentions having written an "argument [*raisonnement*] against love" (*Correspondance de Mme de Lafayette*, 1:34, 193).[13] Not surprisingly, then, the works of Lafayette present no model for happy love. Married love fails to be mutual love; love outside marriage may be reciprocated, but proves catastrophic, even fatal. There *are* model and worthy figures—the Princesse's husband, M. de Clèves, or the would-be lover of the Princesse de Montpensier, the Comte de Chabanes—but they end up as the most tragic figures, martyrs of doomed love (which is perhaps why Lafayette thought to entitle her novel *Le Prince de Clèves*). In the battleground that is, yet again, love, man tries to conquer, woman to resist. Man may succeed, but happiness will not result for either partner.

The intensity of the strife that produces the debasement of these two worthy figures suggests the violent exacerbation of the trials of courtly love that informs Lafayette's conception. Rather than ennobling, love debilitates its subjects: "We are very weak when we are in love" (*La Princesse de Montpensier*, *179*, 64). And love weakens its victims due to its indomitable destructive forces that wreak jealousy, madness, and disorder. Lafayette, Camus has stated, attributes even greater powers to love than the Romantics do, powers of "dementia and confusion" (Laugaa, 254). The dementia of jealousy invariably accompanies love, and love engenders jealousy because of its fundamentally inconstant nature. Even more explicitly than in Zayas's novellas is the Tristan principle operative in Lafayette. Love, with its ever-perverse logic, redoubles in the face of rejection: only when he realizes that his wife loves the Prince de Navarre does the Comte de Tende fall in love with her (*La Comtesse de Tende*, *199*, 328). The Princesse de Clèves, for her part, definitively rejects Nemours out of fear that once the obstacles so essential to the persistence of (courtly) love have been removed, his love will prove inconstant and wane, destroying her in the process:

> But how long does men's passion last when the bond is eternal? Can I expect a miracle in my favour? If not, can I resign myself to the prospect that a passion on which my happiness depended must infallibly come to an end? M. de Clèves was perhaps the only man in the world capable of remaining in love with the woman he had married . . . perhaps, too, his passion only endured because he found no answering passion in me. But I should not be able to keep yours alive in this way: it seems to me, indeed, that *your constancy has been sustained by the obstacles it has encountered.* (148–49, 306; italics mine)

Courtly love in its pure form induces a benevolent and bittersweet pain, always redolent of love. In the near invective of the Princesse's *refus* or refusal of love, shading into the stridency of Zayas's diatribes against men's mutability, we hear a love tinged with its opposite, hatred. As Lafayette's companion, La Rochefoucauld, wrote: "If one judges love by most of its effects, it resembles hatred more than friendship" (Maxim 72, p. 52).

To say the very least, María de Zayas's culture provided little ideological (if much unexpected discursive) support for an outspoken feminism such as hers that declaimed against men and amorous entanglements and culminated in the rejection of marriage at the end of the *Desengaños*. Mme de Lafayette, on the other hand, wrote in a palpably more advantageous context. She could, as the following synoptic discussions of issues familiar to early modern French scholars suggest, draw on the ideas of the *précieuses* and Jansenists for her tragic vision of love and for her protagonist's lucid *refus*–that is, for the three interlocking pieces of the drama of love as she so often depicted it: the *refusal* of love in the name of *reason* and *repose* (*repos*: peace, tranquillity).

The very title of *précieuse* or "precious woman," applied to the women who led and participated in salons, announces the currency with which elite French culture endowed those who warranted the sobriquet. Female-dominated salon culture, which reached its apogee after the Fronde in the 1650s, spearheaded what has been called the feminization of French culture (Treasure, 479). By this is meant the refinement of the manners, tastes, and language of those who frequented them. Flying in the face of the fear of "effeminacy" that so perturbed their contemporaries in other European countries, and in the face of traditional *querelle* debates, defenders of the *précieuses* argued for the civilizing role of women. It is to women, wrote Nicolas Pradon, that men owe "wit, refinement, / Good taste, a gallant manner, and delicacy. / In contact with beauty the crudest spirit / In order to please, is quickly smoothed and polished" (Lougee, 39). As arbiters of culture, the *précieuses* themselves accentuated their own refinement and leading edge by espousing a rarefied style (*preciosité*) akin to that of the Spanish baroque. Like Caro, Zayas, and Sor Juana, but in a communal and collaborative setting probably unique to seventeenth-century Europe, the *précieuses* embraced and promoted novelty as an important selling point of their matriarchal empire.

If the *précieuse*, as Michel de Pure tells us in his 1656 *La Précieuse ou le Mystère des ruelles* [The *Précieuse* or the Mystery of the Receiving Room], was she who placed singular value on what she said and deemed worthy (Bray, 137), even higher was the value that she attached to her own sex and self. The so-called feminization of seventeenth-century French culture gave rise to the extremist feminism that the *précieuses* advocated in their discussions, correspondence, and literary works. Marriage was an issue of pressing concern, constantly problematized and reformulated. In general, the *précieuses* viewed the institution with tremendous disfavor, considering it a form of slavery for innocent female victims. The *précieuses* tended to value their own sisterhood over motherhood or conjugal ties.[14] In their bold pronouncements they envisioned marriages based on convenience and interest, experimental marriages, short-term marriages that could end with the birth of the first child and spare women the dangers of excessive childbirth, marriages that would allow women to exercise the privilege allotted to aristocratic males of taking lovers, marriages where male and female partners would operate as equals.[15] Marriage was to be separated from love, but passion of any sort was regarded as perilous to the self and thus to be avoided. The preeminent *précieuse* and friend of Mme de Lafayette, Mlle de Scudéry (who herself, like other *précieuses*, did not marry) propounded in her novel *Le Grand Cyrus* [The Great Cyrus] a love disengaged from sensuality. Following the lead of Honoré d'Urfé's pastoral novel *L'Astrée* [Astrea], she and other *précieuses* favored a platonic love or friendship that would not trouble the soul. Cotin wrote: "In so sweet a relationship, there is no conflict between reason and sense, between passion and duty; all is great calm and profound peace" (Bray, 153). Letters exchanged between Mlle de Montpensier and Mme de Motteville in the 1660s find the two *précieuses* proposing a renunciation of the world of the court and a rejection of marriage in order to create a corner of the world in which women are "their own mistresses" (De Jean 1984, 899). A jealous regard for self-possession, viewed by the *précieuses* as the sovereign good (Vigée, 731), and for the *repos* that ensues from such an attitude, best obtained by rejecting love and marriage, motivates their—and as we will see, the Princesse de Clève's—positions on love.

Mme de Lafayette not only figured as "one of the *précieuses* of highest rank and farthest flight" (*Correspondance*, 1:131), but also frequented the hôtel de Nevers, a gathering place of the Jansenists, read Pascal with pleasure, and collaborated extensively with Jansenist La Rochefoucauld. Moreover, for their ascetic attitudes, the *précieuses* were termed by a contemporary "the Jansenists of love" (Bray, 161). To approach the weighty subject of Jansenist philosophy in seventeenth-century France, it is appropriate to turn to Paul Bénichou's influential *Morales du grand siècle*. Bénichou maintains that all moral literature of the French seventeenth century addresses the problem of the grandeur or baseness of humanity. If Corneillian idealism, deriving from Descartes, exalts the heroism of the individual and human spirit, the Jansenists embrace a wholly pessimistic theory of humankind. In the Jansenist view we are all sinners after the Fall and cannot save ourselves, no matter what our actions or merit; only God can save us, and the Divinity does so not necessarily according to our merit. Jansenist theory thus crushes all idealism to deny human virtue or greatness or values. With this, it damns human nature, the self, as fundamentally and utterly weak—as a tempestuous conglomerie of passions. Pascal wrote of the inconstancy and the *bizarrerie* of humankind (Bénichou, 158), awash in a perpetual flux of passions that leaves no room for free will or reason. For Bénichou, the Jansenist view culminates in the dissolution of self:

> Pascal . . . , having disarticulated the individual into variable qualities, separated from the individual's will and judgment, asks pathetically, "Then where is the 'I'?" By reducing man to a blind and dependent sensibility, absolutely irreconcilable with our notions of freedom and reason, by wholly returning him to brute nature . . . the Jansenists or their sympathizers ended up actually dissolving that "I" on which they purported to base everything. (160–61)

The preceding quotation also gives us a sense of where the Jansenists, and by extension Lafayette, stand on the issues of passion versus reason under study here. Camus, in a single crystalline phrase describing her "very special notion of love," sums up what I believe happens when Lafayette imports into her fiction Jansenist, and *précieuse*, notions of love: "Her singular premise is that this passion places one's very being in peril" (Laugaa, 253–54). To illustrate in Lafayette not only the accuracy of Camus's observation but many of the issues discussed thus far surrounding love and reason, I offer a reading of her earliest short novel: the clear-cut morality play of *La Princesse de Montpensier*.

All of the novels attributed to Lafayette, it has often been noted, treat a single dilemma or "question of love": an unhappily married and virtuous young woman falls in love with a man other than her husband. Will she be able to defend her virtue? What will be the consequences of her actions? *Montpensier* dramatizes in no uncertain terms the grievous consequences of a weak self ceding to fatal passion, to the detriment of her reason and *repos* and to the ruin of all concerned. It also discloses the consequences of the lack of a principle that plays so crucial a role in *LPDC*, the need for self-vigilance or mistrust of the self ("défiance de soi-même").

In this oppressively single-minded tale of inevitable downfall we witness the surrender of the Princesse de Montpensier to adulterous love for her former suitor, the Duc de Guise. What appears on the surface to be a simple morality tale is, however, a platform for Lafayette's intense exploration of the issue of unchecked loss: loss of reason, loss of self, loss of self-control (which would explain why one of the key words of the text is *ôter*, to remove). Upon reencountering her former suitor and realizing that her passion has been rekindled, the Princesse confesses it to her confidant and would-be lover the Comte de Chabanes, resolving to resist: "[N]othing was capable of shaking the resolution she had made never to become entangled" (*169*, 51). Yet her resolve quickly dissipates as her passion grows, and "despite all the lovely resolutions she had made" (*170*, 54), she moves from prudence to *hardiesse* or imprudent daring in ceding to what the text often calls a "violent love." Since "we are very weak when we are in love" (*179*, 64), once the all too feeble scaffolding of self-restraint and virtue has been dismantled, the Princesse emerges as a dehumanized sadistic monster. Possessed by passion, she is scheming and manipulative; cruelly insisting that he serve as her go-between, the Princesse "torments" Chabanes and makes him swallow long draughts of the barely metaphorical "poison" (64) of hearing her love for another. Much as Chabanes hopes that "the Princesse de Montpensier would recover her passion and resolve not to see the Duc de Guise" (*182*, 68), the text builds to its inexorable conclusion: the Prince de Montpensier's discovery of a secret tryst between the lovers, the death of Chabanes, and ultimately that of the Princesse herself.

As the dénouement suggests, love undoes not only the Princesse, but also all those who surround her. The acid of their fatal attraction to the Princesse or hers to them corrodes the male characters' weak façades of self-control and reason as well. Her husband explodes with jealousy. Another of her failed suitors, the Duc d'Anjou, takes out his rage on the more successful Guise ("Jealousy, vexation, and rage, mingling with the hatred he already felt for the Duc de Guise, produced the most violent effect imaginable in his soul" [*173*, 57]). Chabanes—"hard pressed by his own feelings, whose violence sometimes deprived him of all consciousness" (*180*, 66)—suffers the debasement I have described.[16] The case of the Duc de Guise, however, introduces a different tragic twist. Whereas the Princesse, consumed by shame and love for him, soon dies, he soon transfers his affections to the Marquise de Noirmoutier, "who gave him more to hope for than the princess" (*187*, 73), and lives out his life with her. As she does with Nemours in *LPDC*, Lafayette builds on the connotations of the names of historical personages, rendering the names and figures allegorical. Here Guise—fancy, whim—tropes yet another of love's perils, its caprice and inconstancy.

Stirling Haig calls *Montpensier* "a kind of program note" for *LPDC* (73); I acknowledge the unmistakable resemblance between the two texts, but prefer to understand *Montpensier* as a counter-fable to *LPDC* for the following reasons. The last lines of the earlier work read: "She died within a few days, in the flower of her youth: she was one of the most beautiful princesses in the world, and would doubtless have been the happiest, if virtue and prudence had guided all her actions" (*188*, 74). Both the Princesse de Clèves (and her analogue, Belasire in *Zaïde*) and the Princesse de Montpensier (and *her* analogue, the Comtesse de Tende) are shown to die at the end of their stories, but for different reasons and in the service of different moral points. The Princesse de Montpensier's death speaks compellingly and tellingly to the unmitigated *absence* of reason, *refus*, and *repos* in the desolate landscape of her text. The retreat to the convent and eventual death of the Princesse de Clèves, on the other hand, ensue from the overweening *presence* of reason, *refus*, and *repos* in her personal universe. So, too, given the continuity between their constructs of love, does Lisis's retreat to the convent at the end of Zayas's *Desengaños amorosos* imply her attainment of repose. "Fortunate many times over are the women who remain free of such terrible entanglements, who live their lives quietly without having to please a tyrant," writes Zayas in her text (*97*, 183). I turn now to an examination of the good fortune that the convent embodies in the seventeenth century on several levels.

III.

THE CONVENT SCRIPT

The patriarchal arbiters of the early modern Christian worlds provided a place on the margins of society for women who in a multitude of ways fell between the cracks of the social structure. That space was the convent. Needless to say, women over the ages would retreat to the convent to pursue a spiritual vocation. But, as is well known, convents in the seventeenth century accommodated more than one type of woman. Wayward, dishonored, or otherwise displaced women could be remanded to a convent or *recogimiento* [shelter] when no other place could be found for them: we recall Erauso, sent to a convent after her disclosure to the bishop of Guamanga. As the alleged Erauso of the *Vida* openly stated in her text, she had no religious vocation whatsoever. Nor necessarily did the great numbers of women who *chose* to withdraw from society and to live in the convent.[17] The example of Sor Juana, of course, comes immediately to mind. Sor Juana makes it clear in the "Respuesta" that given her "total disinclination to marriage" and dedication to knowledge, she would have preferred to "live alone" and to have had no "fixed occupation which might curtail my freedom to study" (*212*, 446). The convent came as close to that life as contemporary social structures allowed, and it was common practice in Spain, France, and the New World for women lacking spiritual fervor but seeking an alternative to society to choose enclosure in the convent over enclosure in the "world." The enclosure to which the patriarchy consigned them, be it in the secular or religious worlds, could be used to advantage by women who elected conventual life. There, in comparison with their secular sisters, in order to perform their religious duties they would at least learn to read and at best be empowered to exercise their talents in a wide range of occupations from which they were restricted in secular life. For in the convent women could teach, prophesy, write, correspond with eminent personages, carry on business transactions with the outside world (nuns were often allowed to hold their own property), perform administrative tasks, and even rule.

Perhaps for these reasons premodern convents became veritable Cities of Women. Women of every age would retire to them, often with their children and relatives in tow. The devout nun, the divorcée, the street woman, the criminal, and the young girl could all converge in these multiplex communities. By the mid-seventeenth century there were nearly three thousand nuns in Venice, some 3 percent of the whole population (King 1991, 83); even more astonishing, by the end of the seventeenth century Lima's *grandes conventos* housed more than ten thousand cloistered women, that is, more than a fifth of the female population (Martín, 179, 172). Convent culture offered a wide variety of lifestyles and regimes. This single space could combine the functions of hotel, primary school, shelter, and religious center. In France, as does the Princesse de Clèves, aristocratic women could retreat to "des maisons de [houses of] repos" where they could live as laywomen, without taking religious vows. In Spain, too, women could lead a relatively secular life, surrounded in the sheltered confines of the convent by the comforts that their wealth afforded them. In the New World, Lima's *grandes conventos* were notorious for their lavish entertainments. Mexico was home to conventual worlds of the most dramatically different natures. For example, nuns in the Convent of Santa Mónica in Puebla, an order of Augustine Recollects founded by Bishop Fernández de Santa Cruz and home to the writing nun María de San José, slept on narrow slabs of rough wood and practiced mortification of the flesh at least three times a day. Sor Juana, who had rejected the ascetic climate of a convent of Discalced Carmelites, eventually found her place in the far more lax environment of the Convent of San Jerónimo where she inhabited a comfortable apartment that she herself owned, was afforded the benefits of servants and slaves, and was subject to relatively little communal life.

Outside the "Respuesta" and her final penitential testimonies, Sor Juana has remarkably little to say in her writings about conventual life itself or about her retreat to the convent in lieu of marriage. Other female religious, of course, depict conventual life in as many ways as there were individuals writing, figuring the convent as heavenly or hellish, as sublime or mundane, according to their personal experiences. At a greater remove from conventual life, and thus with greater license for refiguration, lie the secular writers who are the subject of the present chapter. They, too, avail themselves of the retreat to the convent, making of it a literary device or topic as multivalent as the convent itself was in social reality. In other words, retreat to the convent comes to comprise a significant option in reality and, particularly as a textual ending, for the literary imagination. Though I do not claim to be familiar with all of the texts that utilize this device, my readings indicate that retreat to the convent in a withdrawal from society as a theme and as a textual closure—what I see as the convent script in its most fully realized form—is likely to assume different shadings when wielded by (secular) male as versus female writers.[18] When taken up, reembroidered, by women writers, it assumes a far more dimensional and utopian cast. I will support my assertions by surveying representative or significant texts from each camp, beginning with works by male writers.

The convent script comes to secular literature with its own baggage from religious practice and literature. Christian hagiography contains numerous examples of male saints who renounced the world, its riches and women, in favor of an ascetic life. Similarly, as Sandra Foa discusses in "María de Zayas: Visión conflictiva y renuncia del mundo" [María de Zayas: Conflictive Vision and Renunciation of the World], male writers of the Spanish golden age utilized the topic of the renunciation of the world to cap off ascetic treatises warning against the dangers of lascivious love and sensual appetite (133–35). The first variant of the convent script (more properly a monastery script, but operating according to the same principles) I examine, Jerónimo de Contreras's *Selva de aventuras* [Jungle or Miscellanea of Adventures], incorporates both dimensions. Written at some point between 1569 and 1615,[19] *Selva de aventuras* is a barely secularized and conventionally novelized version of a saint's life. By this I mean that it combines the conventions of hagiography with those of the novel of chivalry to tell the story of its protagonist Luzmán's [*luz*: light] spiritual voyage away from love for a woman to love of God, inner knowledge, and retreat. After being rejected by his childhood sweetheart Arbolea, Luzmán begins his wanderings. At each step of the journey he meets up with individuals from whose stories he gleans the moral lessons that guide him toward transcendence of the world. At first Luzmán hears the laments of lovers, which begin to turn him away from earthly love. Later he encounters a series of figures who have foregone both love and material wealth to renounce the world. Gradually, then, Luzmán becomes ensconced in a textual landscape of figures who incarnate the neo-Stoical philosophy that the novel at heart propounds. Upon returning home after many travails, Luzmán visits Arbolea in her convent and proposes to place the love he still holds for her "somewhere else" (505); that is, he renounces the world to build the monastery in which he lives out the rest of his life in saintly purity.

Contreras's displaced hagiography, of more interest as an example of a male-authored convent ending than as a text in its own right, advocates a rather predictable ascetic misogamy. In *Selva de aventuras* and Gonzalo de Céspedes y Meneses's *El español Gerardo, y el desengaño del amor lascivo* [The Spaniard Gerardo, and the Disillusionment of Lascivious Love] (1615) we find the female characters being similarly employed as the ultimate choice in and emblem of renouncing the world. Other male-authored texts of seventeenth-century Spain, such as Castillo Solórzano's, intermittently use retreat to the convent as a merely textual as well as a hagiographic device.[20] The convent can serve the textual function of providing a way station or parking place of last resort in which characters are temporarily stowed until they can resume their lives in the plot. Given Miguel de Cervantes's idiosyncratic genius and his magnificent theme of freedom for men *and* women, one would expect no such unidimensional conventionality from him. Indeed, his exemplary novel "El celoso extremeño" [The Jealous Extremaduran] (1613) constitutes one of the most multilayered, suggestive manifestations of the convent topos and probably provided the model for Zayas's "El prevenido engañado" [Forewarned But Not Forearmed].[21]

On one level, Cervantes's slippery moral tale subverts the honor plays of the times by sidestepping the tragic dénouement that affronts to honor conventionally entail. Child-bride Leonora marries the jealous Carrizales, who goes to extreme lengths to keep her out of other men's way, imprisoning her in a fortresslike house. His efforts, as one might imagine, come to naught, for the golden-tongued Loaysa sweet talks (and sings) his way into the house and into Leonora's arms. Carrizales discovers them in what he believes to be an amorous coupling; although in reality Leonora has resisted Loaysa's advances, she is unable to convince Carrizales of her innocence. Carrizales's blindness to the truth, however, opens the door to a more important insight. Rather than impelling him to greater fury, the breach of his honor prompts the jealous husband to realize the error of his ways, and he grants Leonora her freedom to marry Loaysa after he dies.

"El celoso extremeño" ends with Leonora, having refused Carrizales's offer as proof of her virtue, entering "one of the most enclosed convents of the city" (*180*, 135) and with the narrator posing a question that goes unanswered: Why was Leonora, who fell mute as she tried to protest her innocence, so incapable of defending herself? Certainly, as I argued above, her impotence promoted Carrizales's realization, his "growing up." Beyond that, I read Leonora's muteness and her withdrawal to an austere convent as indices of the other story that Cervantes's tale purports to tell in an ironic mode. And that is the story of Leonora's lamentable "growing down," a story in which her *refus* and retreat signify the rejection of freedom. Carrizales has managed to liberate himself from the bonds of jealousy. But the seemingly virtuous and exemplary Leonora, whom the text often mocks as "simple-minded" and "ignorant," has condemned herself forever to the prison that her husband had foisted upon her. "Madre, la mi madre, / guardas me ponéis, / que si yo no me guardo, / no me guardaréis" (125) [Oh Mother, my mother, don't guard me so close. I'll guard my own honour in the way I shall choose, *170*], sings Leonora's duenna: her young and impressionable charge, who still plays with dolls, has assimilated the husband's rules of conduct and placed shackles on her own freedom.[22]

(Pre)figurations of the convent to which Leonora eventually retires provide the telltale signs of the second plot. Here, as distinct from the displaced hagiographies I just discussed but equally conventionally, the convent presents a negative valence—of enclosure, of all that opposes freedom. On numerous occasions the house in which Leonora has been imprisoned, and in which reside only virgins and eunuchs, is explicitly equated with a convent; for example: "Never was monastery more enclosed, nor nuns more withdrawn, nor golden apples more strictly guarded" (*153*, 106). Leonora's life is compared to that of a nun: "In this way they spent their novice year, and went on to make their profession in that way of life, resolving to continue in it to the end of their days"(*153*, 106). At the same time, Cervantes portrays Leonora's existence as a death-in-life, for her parents surrender their daughter to Carrizales's custody as if they were taking her to the grave (104). If, then, the house is a grave and a metaphorical convent (and not the Bachelardian "female space," as Harry Seiber would have it [*Novelas ejemplares*, 18]), in retiring to the real convent Leonora is but duplicating the life she left behind.[23]

The mythic overlay on "El celoso extremeño" adds the final ironic note to Leonora's story. Through the character of Loaysa, Cervantes introduces the story of Orpheus and Eurydice.[24] Loaysa's Orphic song wins him entry into the impregnable house (the black servant "welcomed his teacher inside like Orpheus himself" [*158–59*, 112]) and almost succeeds in charming Leonora as well. As Orpheus, Loaysa would undertake to rescue his Eurydice from the Hades in which she is held prisoner. Here he fails—due not primarily to his own flaws but to those of the simpleton, Leonora, who refuses the opportunity to ascend from Hades, to grow upward or up into freedom.[25]

I have analyzed Cervantes's exemplary novel in some detail not only because I want to do some small justice to the text, but also because "El celoso extremeño" introduces several issues of import to my consideration of the convent script as deployed by women authors. In its negative rehearsal of what would later crystallize into the female bildungsroman, "El celoso extremeño" gestures toward that genre and toward a more positive dénouement; if only in an ironic mode, it gives equal weight to woman's freedom, shading into the position of the female-authored convent script. At the same time, on its literal level Cervantes's exemplary tale both conventionally represents the convent as a space of austere enclosure and dramatizes an extreme case of exactly what women must flee in order to achieve freedom. And that is patriarchal marriage with its literary correlate, the marriage plot.

To lay out the implications of the marriage plot from the viewpoint of women's writing, let us revisit for a moment another by now familiar exemplary tale or parable, that of Penelope as construed by Carolyn Heilbrun in her essay "What Was Penelope Unweaving?" (1990). For Heilbrun, in weaving her web Penelope is writing her own story, the as-yet-unwritten story of a woman who charts her own course. Why does Penelope lack a plot? Heilbrun responds:

> Because all women, having been restricted to only one plot, are without a story. In literature and out, through all recorded history, women have lived by a script they did not write. Their destiny was to be married, circulated; to be given by one man, the father, to another, the husband; to become the mothers of men. Theirs has been the marriage plot, the erotic plot, the courtship plot, but never, as for men, the quest plot. Women have been tempted into

romantic thralldom, and then married, like the heroines of our great novels of the eighteenth and nineteenth centuries, or like the heroines of Harlequin romances. Their story was over. (126)

Heilbrun goes on to make the following pronouncement: "The question women must all ask is how to be freed from the marriage plot and initiated into the quest plot" (126). Although I am not so sure that "all" women "must" ask the question, this is exactly the issue that I will address on literary grounds in the remainder of the chapter. For I aim to demonstrate how, unlike eighteenth- and nineteenth-century male and female writers, at least some early modern women writers of the seventeenth century were able to transpose a social reality—the convent—into a literary script that allowed freedom from the marriage plot, and the freedom intrinsic to the quest plot. In its literary refiguration, the convent and convent ending afforded seventeenth-century women writers a means of writing beyond the ending of the marriage script, an option that rendered the female heroic script narratable in what was in most cases a still intensely patriarchal world.

In literary convention, as in life, the most acceptable alternative to marriage for the seventeenth-century woman lay in the convent. Women writers effectively took possession of that alternative and utilized it as an umbrella that embraced and figured other "heroic" options: early feminists, according to Constance Jordan, almost invariably praised women who sequester themselves from the world in institutional or private settings (57).[26] As women authors reinscribe the convent, we witness a broadening of its image in secular as well as utopian directions. This could be seen, to a degree, in Sor Juana's "Respuesta"; *La Princesse de Clèves*, with its convent ending, is so notably devoid of a religious dimension that Auguste Comte included the work in his *Bibliothèque Positiviste* [Library of Positivism]![27] Religion and a triumphant feminism can just as easily coexist, as they do in the texts of María de Zayas (though the heroines of both Lafayette's and Zayas's texts fail to take religious vows). To demonstrate how the convent lent itself to the envisioning of "heroic" and utopian female communities, I will examine the writings of two seventeenth-century British women writers who reinscribe the topic of the convent, one with a religious redefinition, the other with an irreligious one.[28] I should note that because the Protestant Reformation had taken a stand against monastic life, the convent—while still a living part of the cultural imaginary—was for both of these Anglican women already on the brink of becoming a nostalgic abstraction that they labored to revive.

Mary Astell (1661–1731), who has been called "the first systematic feminist in England" (52), published in 1694 a widely circulated essay entitled "A Serious Proposal to the Ladies for the Advancement of Their True and Greatest Interest." Addressing, on the one hand, the growing numbers of unmarried women in England (she herself had chosen to remain unmarried) and, on the other, a society that viewed semi-enclosed spinsterhood as the only respectable route for unmarried women (Hill in Astell, 14), Astell proposes in her treatise a new direction. She seeks financial support for a "Religious Retirement" with "a double aspect, being not only a Retreat from the World for those who desire that advantage, but likewise, an Institution and previous discipline, to fit us to do the greatest good in it" (150). The double aspect of the convent to which Astell refers is actually triple. First, the institution shall devote itself to the "service of GOD," creating a true community of women with "but one Body" (157). Second, since Astell ardently championed education for women, it will provide its residents with a broadly based humanistic education, including a knowledge of French philosophy and *lettres* such as those of *précieuse* Mlle de Scudéry. Finally, this "Monastery," which will require "no Vows or irrevocable Obligations" (158), will train its unorthodox postulants as teachers so that, if they wish, they can go back out into the world and educate young women. The walls of this woman activist's design for the enclosure of her sex, we see, are utterly porous and yielding.[29] Other temporal advantages accrue from Astell's proposal, for the Religious Retirement will provide a refuge for heiresses from "the rude attempts of designing Men" (165), and the revenues from the teachers' work will allow them to educate the "Daughters of Gentlemen who are fallen into decay" (166). In its ever-widening wave of benefits, Astell's brilliantly conceived convent furnishes unmarried women with knowledge and with a respectable profession at the same time that it makes provision for the betterment of the lot of women in general.

The necessity pinpointed by Astell of saving the wealthy heiress from the designs of greedy men literally occupies center stage in *The Convent of Pleasure*, one of many plays by the prolific Margaret Lucas Cavendish, first Duchess of Newcastle (1623–73).[30] Cavendish's play contains several remarkable feminist features, from a sympathetic portrait of lesbian attraction to a play within a play on the miseries of marriage. Most remarkable of all for our purposes is the elaborate refiguration of the convent that we find therein. Heiress Lady Happy, besieged by suitors in pursuit of her fortune, prefers to flee the "folly, vanity and falsehood in Men" (act 1, scene 2) by fleeing marriage and to employ her wealth in outfitting a truly idyllic convent. Religion plays no role whatsoever in Lady Happy's brave new world. Here the convent changes sign entirely to become a sybaritic realm of the senses: "My Cloister shall not be a Cloister of restraint, but a place for freedom, not to vex the senses but to please them" (act 1, scene 2). Over the course of three scenes Lady Happy outlines with relish her plans for the convent of pleasure. A particularly wonderful disquisition in act 2, scene 2, previews in extravagant detail the sumptuous furnishings of the women's chambers, different for each season, the delicacies they will consume, and the magnificent garments they will wear ("of the newest fashion for every Season, and rich Trimming"). Replete with pleasing "feminine" detail that captivates a female audience, the play transfigures the convent into a veritable utopia for women and a world without men.

The female audience of *The Convent of Pleasure* may well have experienced a rather unpleasurable jolt when this whole magnificent construct vanishes into thin air at the end of the play. Not known as such to the audience, a man disguised as a woman who dresses as a man (!) has entered the convent. He and Lady Happy fall in love, giving rise to what for several scenes is present-ed as an overtly lesbian relationship. Then, in the three brief scenes of act 5, the Prince discloses his real identity and marries Lady Happy. No further mention is made of the Convent of Pleasure—which at least is not explicitly canceled out but just ignored—and the play abruptly and rather awkwardly reverts to the comedia formula that dictates an ending in marriage and rec-onciliation with society. We saw in the last chapter how seventeenth-century comedias, with their "Taming of the Shrew" agenda, erase and efface the woman's flight of self-determination; in the terms of the present chapter I would say that the erotic and quest plots are intertwined in the body of the play but not integrated in the ending, where the quest is suspended. With Cavendish's comedia the artificiality and pathos of that formula are both most keenly felt *and* laid bare by the rhythm of the play. For the hastily patched-on marriage ending (perhaps patched on by Cavendish's husband),[31] the wealth of attention devoted to Lady Happy's convent plan and *esquivez* or reluctance to marry, and even the very title of the play tell us that the real effective and affective heart of the work lies in its feminist center rather than in its more socially sanctioned ending.

Would a life elsewhere be depicted otherwise in the seventeenth century? The case of María de Zayas's novellas and Mme de Lafayette's *La Princesse de Clèves* establish that it would. In their works the two elements of female rein-scriptions of the convent that I have discussed up to now—female protagonists, feminist authors—join forces with the third component, the convent *ending*, and actualize the potential of the topic in the following ways. First, in shifting the protagonist's refusal of marriage and withdrawal to the space of the con-vent from the middle to the ending, the texts eschew reconciliation with soci-ety and enable their heroines to continue to pursue their personal goals at a remove from the forces that might constrain them. In breaking with the sacro-sanct comedia ending, our authors employ what I call the "convent script" proper in such a manner that it provides a platform for the heroic female nar-rative that Heilbrun envisions, a narrative of self-realization outside society and outside the marriage plot. If in literary texts women are heroes when questing and heroines when they concede to the social script, here the female protag-onists move from heroines to heroes.[32] Second, in walking away from the con-ventionalized story of their lives, the protagonists walk into another space and another plot that bring not only self-actualization but also the boon of the heroic quest: transcendence of their personal situation, a wider perspective, a critique of society. Third and perhaps most important, as it traces the woman's progress toward that more lofty position, the female convent script feeds into an early form of one type of bildungsroman, the sentimental education (*édu-cation sentimentale*).[33] These sentimental educations follow their protagonists' development from marriageable age to the rejection of marriage. They chart, as does the prototypical bildungsroman, the character's passage from igno-rance and innocence to wisdom and maturity together with the conflicts she suffers between self and society. As a bildungsroman that ends in withdrawal from society, the female convent script hooks up with the displaced hagiographies discussed earlier. But as now should be quite clear, it both builds on and deviates from the male model: figuring the woman's rebellion within a conventional plot and space while straining toward another economy.

⌘

IV.

THE CONVENT SCRIPT/BILDUNGSROMAN IN THE NOVELLAS OF MARÍA DE ZAYAS

Taken as a unit, María de Zayas's two volumes of short novels comprise a perfect, and perfectly "heroic," prototype for the female bildungsroman. I make this statement and generic transposition (from novella collection to bildungsroman) based on the framework story that weaves the two volumes into a single continuous fabric, and on the story it tells—the story of the development of Lisis.[34] Over the course of the two volumes Lisis grows and changes in unpredictable ways, culminating in her anagnorisis, self-determination, and retreat to a refigured convent. Her round character and characterization stand out against the backdrop of Zayas's other characters. For faithful to the conventions of romance representation, Zayas generally reduces her characters to mere plot functions, loci of action or ideological vehicles schematically characterized by only a couple of traits. In her characterization of Lisis, Zayas does not go so far as to represent her protagonist's interiority per se, but she does offer an aperture into that inner world through the rich interaction between the framework story and the tales themselves. Lisis grows and changes by virtue, first, of her own direct experience of love's afflictions as described in the framework story and, second, due to her exposure to others' even more dire experiences through the tales to which she listens over the course of the many nights of storytelling.[35] The tales overflow into the framework story as Lisis articulates her reactions to them. This dynamic interplay between framework story and frame tales, quite different from the oblique relationship between the two in Boccaccio's *Decameron*, constitutes one of Zayas's most notable contributions to the genre. It also gives rise to the multilayered sentimental education whose unfolding I will detail first in the *Novelas amorosas* and then in the *Desengaños amorosos*.

The mercurial developments of the framework story in the *Novelas* issue from the same triangular situation found in Sor Juana's ironic symmetries poems and display similar contradictions. At first, Lisis is in love with don Juan, who has transferred his affections to her cousin, Lisarda. Humiliated and jealous, Lisis gradually shifts her favors to don Diego, who loves her but for whom she appears to bear an only spurious attachment. The framework story, bracketing the beginning and end of each storyteller's tale, advances incrementally and circuitously. Each step that Lisis takes toward don Diego

is undercut by the displays of jealousy that they arouse in don Juan, indications of his residual passion for her. Further, in the fifth and final night of the
framework soiree, by which time Lisis has formally accepted don Diego's suit,
don Juan tells the story of a man falsely accused of inconstancy ("The Magic
Garden"), as if to persuade Lisis to reconsider her perhaps still mutable position. Lisis, in turn, responds by manifesting her jealousy for Lisarda, proof
that she still harbors strong feelings for the man who has scorned her. We see
that not only don Juan but also Lisis is playing two games at once: playing up
to the man who loves her but whom she does not love, and to the man who
does not necessarily love her but whom she loves.

My intention here, however, is not merely to point out the similarities
between Sor Juana's poems and Zayas's novellas but to suggest the implications
for the sentimental education of this game of emotional musical chairs. Viewed
from the perspective of a bildungsroman, it becomes clear that Lisis, while listening to the tales, is also living out her own story–and a packed story it is. In
the accelerated time and compacted space of the framework story, Lisis has
experienced the pivotal emotions of love (rejection, humiliation, jealousy,
desire), its unstable course, and the affections of two suitors, who themselves
represent two principal variants in the drama of courtly love (the unloving
beloved, the unloved lover). In other words, in this dance of shifting grounds,
Lisis has arguably undergone quite a substantial sentimental education.

While Lisis inches forward toward her engagement to don Diego and
loops back toward her love for don Juan, yet another movement is surreptitiously taking place: the first stirrings of what we could call Lisis's feminist
radicalization. The tales of love that Lisis hears and that supplement her sentimental education impel the character's radicalization. A couple of common
threads, as my previous chapter suggested, run through the tales of the
Novelas amorosas. Women are betrayed by inconstant men; emboldened by
their disillusionment, the women take action to avenge themselves, in general successfully. Like the fragments of Osiris's body distributed by Isis (in the
myth so dear to Sor Juana and perhaps even to Zayas), bits and pieces of
Lisis's own situation with don Juan reassemble in the tales. Ruth El Saffar
notes the *mise-en-abîme* quality of the frame tales, their "ever-receding replica-
tion of the theme of failed love" (1995, 203). With so many love triangles in
the tales, so many fickle men, and so much jealousy, Lisis in effect sees her
own quandary and future being paraded before her. The lesson of the tales,
one might surmise, motivates her decision to be "violently employed" by the
more promising don Diego rather than being the "vile spoils" of the fickle don
Juan (the words, of course, belong to Sor Juana). However, Lisis is also on her
way to learning a larger principle about men that transcends her particular circumstances. The protagonists of the first tale of the third night, "The Power
of Love," are, I believe purposefully, named Diego and Laura–Laura being the
name of Lisis's mother. This Diego proves himself "mutable like all men" (*166,
230*) in a story that builds to the following moral: (says the storyteller, Nise)
"Seeing so many painful examples of the way men behave, what woman can

be so foolish as to want to get married? And the very woman who thinks she's most likely to find happiness will be the one to fail most dismally" (*175*, 241). It takes but a small leap of the imagination to see Nise's message as implicating *Lisis's* don Diego and as eradicating her hopes for happiness with him or, by extension, with any other man. Lisis would appear to have performed that very leap, for at the beginning of the subsequent and penultimate night she sings the song that gives voice to what she has learned from the frame tales about men's intrinsic unreliability. "When you hear a man tell / a woman she is fickle," sings Lisis, "when he is like a weathervane, / can you fail to laugh? / They pretend loyalty / without seeing that they'll lose; / one should look carefully / when he pretends to be loyal, / that would be like a magic spell / that promises what it cannot give" (*214*, 292). Here, for the first time, Lisis takes a stand against men in general.

The *Novelas amorosas* leave Lisis at a delicate point in her development, fraught with unresolved tensions. Lisis's final actions belie the words we have just heard her speak. She has learned a lesson from the tales about the ways of men, but it results only in a tepid action still directed toward marriage. Unlike several of the heroines of the "Enchantments," Lisis will neither defend herself boldly nor retire to the convent forsaking men entirely. Instead, her resolve to marry don Diego by all indications remains strong, and the ending of the *Novelas* announces that in the second part we will see Lisis's wedding. But beyond the asymmetry of the tales' impact on the framework story heroine, the text has given other mixed and deconstructive signals regarding Lisis's development. During the first night of storytelling, Lisis sits on a green couch ("the green symbolizing a hope she did not really feel" [*9*, 32]) and wears a dress of blue, the color of jealousy. By the third night she has arrayed herself in black and diamonds, black representing uncertain fortune (cf. E., *245*, 333) and white purity and *chastity* (cf. D., *239*, 334). When the final night finds Lisis dressed in gold, symbolizing firmness (cf. D., *239*, 334), the reader is left wondering exactly what that means. Even more pungent is the fact that Lisis's wedding has been scheduled for the Day of Circumcision, a powerful suggestion of castration. The *Novelas amorosas*, we see, retain Lisis within the marriage plot but waffle in their—and her—position. For, to paraphrase Ruth El Saffar, the *Novelas* cry out for a resolution that the text does not provide.[36]

Where the reconciliatory *Novelas* take place at Christmas time, "a happy time perfect for the celebration of parties, games, and friendly joking" (*7*, 29), the *Desengaños* take place during Carnival time (*Carnestolendas*). Fittingly, the *Desengaños* do their part to turn the world upside down as they drop any pretense of reconciliation to assail marriage (and the marriage plot) and men. Women preside over this subversive world: according to the rules set by Lisis for the new game, only women, the "disenchantresses," can tell stories. Their stories, too, have changed sign from the *Novelas*, becoming violent tragedies. Six of the ten protagonists die at the end of their respective stories. The other four, dishonored, take refuge in a convent. While women in the *Novelas* undertook heroic revenges and met with success, the *Desengaños* present an almost unrelieved landscape of female characters victimized by marriage and utterly incapable, no matter what their actions or virtue, of saving themselves. When women do take action, it often backfires, leaving them worse off than before. By declaring an open "war on men" (*167*, 258), the female agents of disenchantment fight back with another weapon, their tales. What is more, an unidentified "I" (to whom we will return in a crucial moment) surfaces subtly and intermittently over the course of the framework story of the *Desengaños*,[37] setting up a correlation between the narrator and author and implying the author's heightened investment in the militant matriarchal world of her second collection of novellas.

In the charged context just described, the framework story that follows Lisis's evolution resumes and changes course. The introduction to the *Desengaños* returns to the tensions latent in the ending of the *Novelas*, now even more exacerbated and explicit. Lisis has been on the brink of death for a year, not from quatrain fever as in the first text but from her "sorrow at seeing herself in the power of a new and different master" (that is, an "undesired master" [*35*, 115]) and due to her still strong feelings for don Juan, "since it was the chilling of his affection for her that had caused the lady's burning fever" (*36*, 116). Though don Diego has renewed his suit and Lisis has once again set her wedding date, Zayas has injected a new element into the scenario, one that will eventually break the no-exit situation of the love triangles: female companionship, in the form of the slave Zelima who has roused Lisis from her illness. Now a recovered Lisis, dressed in black and gold (i.e., uncertain fortune), takes her place as the president of the second entertainments and sets their female-dominated itinerary.

After this introduction, significantly enough, the framework story as we have come to know it virtually disappears from the *Desengaños*. There will be no new developments in Lisis's erotic plot, which is basically abandoned during the nights of storytelling. Instead, diatribes against men, soliloquies previewing the morals of the tales to be told, and the reactions of the audience to the tales they have heard inhabit the space allotted to the framework story in the *Desengaños*. The framework story thus shifts from providing a counterpoint to the tales to being a function of them and their aggressive feminism, and from recounting one woman's story to focusing on the plight of all women. Lisis herself, however, does not cease to develop. Rather, throughout this long period of gestation during which we hear her process the object lessons of the tales, Lisis develops not in terms of the love plot but in terms of the quest plot. She moves from a socially conditioned to a socially subversive plot of self-actualization. The rhythm of Lisis's evolution in the framework story, formerly so action packed, changes to one of meditation and reaction. And the submerged framework story as we knew it, with its erotic plot, will resurface only in the last night of the entertainment, its triangles exploded by the changes that Lisis has undergone in the interim.

Lisis's development in the *Desengaños* along the lines of the heroic plot, her now unmitigated radicalization, owes its existence almost exclusively to the tales she hears. Once again aspects of Lisis's situation are woven into the tales to connect her to them. For all of the tales deal with marriage rather than courtship (the theme of the *Novelas*). The stakes have grown higher for Lisis as the date of her marriage rapidly approaches; so too, as I stated above, have the tales escalated, growing more didactic, violent, and tragic. Lisis can escape the tragic fates of the female protagonists only by listening well and learning from the tales. In this, she may take her example from another signal listener, don Martín of the fourth tale, "Too Late Undeceived." The only character in the tales whose role is essentially that of listening,[38] don Martín is exposed to the ghastly story of don Jaime, who has turned his once beloved Elena into a slave and her lying maid into his beloved due to Elena's alleged betrayal of him. By the time that don Jaime learns of Elena's innocence, she is already dying. Having heard the story of don Jaime's misjudgment and been witness to its consequences, don Martín (in one of the few happy endings to a tale) rushes off to marry his fiancée: "He returned to Toledo and married his darling cousin and there they live happily to this day. He learned a harsh lesson from the events he himself had seen with his own eyes: not to be deceived by the plotting of disloyal servants" (*163*, 254). The basic function of this tale, I conclude in view of its moral, can only be to demonstrate the importance of learning from listening.

That Lisis has followed the lead of her textual mirror, don Martín, to become an active and reactive or proactive listener is amply evidenced by her readings of the tales as presented in the framework story. Moreover, the role that Lisis plays vis-à-vis the many other readers posited by the text serves as a crucial barometer of her development. As part of her didactic strategy, Zayas sets up a dialogical scenario for the framework story of the *Desengaños* in which members of the audience express their diverse opinions of each successive tale. They "read," and often misread, the tales. It is generally Lisis who then provides the corrective and clearly correct readings of the tales, articulating their morals and redressing (particularly the male) misinterpretations. At the end of the second *desengaño*, for example, Lisis counters the interpretations offered by don Juan and doña Isabel of "The Most Infamous Revenge" in a passage too long to quote, and concludes, "The best thing [*fineza*] about love is the sense of mutual trust and confidence, although some ignoramuses say jealousy is. I believe they're wrong" (*110*, 196). Here not only do we hear Lisis offering the definitive reading of the text, we also hear her embracing friendship as the essence of love. Even more significant, in commenting on the sixth *desengaño* ("Love for the Sake of Conquest"), Lisis pronounces her first substantive disquisition in the *Desengaños* against men in general. She takes as her theme the topic central to Sor Juana's "Foolish Men," men's double standards: men corrupting women and then accusing them of being evil (*238–41*, 331–35). The narrator, with one of her rare statements in the first person, commends the positive reception of Lisis's position (*240*, 335). Lisis has emerged as the ideal reader of the tales—and, by extension, as an embodiment of the ideal reader of *this* text. Her "consciousness," so to speak, has also evolved to the point where, to the approval of the narrator, she has made her debut as the spokeswoman for the text's ideology.

Lisis's radicalization, motivated by the tales she has heard, builds to its unmistakably "heroic" climax as the text draws to a close. Lisis introduces the last tale by proposing the outcome of her own life story as the final *desengaño* and as an example for all women: "I myself shall put to the test the greatest disenchantment"; "I am fighting for all of us [women]" (*368*, 470). The lengthy tirades against men that she offers at the beginning and end of the final tale confirm that Lisis has definitively assumed the role of the spokeswoman for all women and against men. Clearly, Lisis has achieved a larger perspective, the boon of the quest. She has managed to do so, as the character explicitly states, by virtue of the vicarious *desengaños* she has experienced in listening to the tales: the frame heroine now turning hero justifies her long-awaited refusal to marry Diego by summarizing in detail what she has learned, not through personal "experience" but from "knowledge" gleaned from each of the tales (*403*, 508). Lisis, who had previously leaned toward the same choice as the poetic speaker of Sor Juana's triangular Sonnet #168, decides to opt out of the patriarchal love system entirely. Accompanied by her companion Isabel (the true name of the slave Zelima), and later by their respective mothers, Lisis withdraws to the convent where she will remain as a lay nun ("seglar" [510]). The final synoptic paragraphs of the *Desengaños* register the dissolution of the love triangle. They describe the tragic ends of the male figures—don Diego dies in the war and Lisarda rejects the unworthy don Juan—which stand in a marked contrast with Lisis's happiness and triumphant heroism:

> [T]he beautiful Lisis lives in the cloister. . . . This end is not tragic but rather the happiest one you can imagine for, although court-ed and desired by many, she did not subject herself to anyone. If you still wish to see her, seek her with chaste intent and you will find her at your service, with a firm and honorable will as she has promised. As always, your humble servant as befits your merits, and even in acknowledging that, no woman excels her. (*405*, 511–12)

In rejecting the marriage plot ("she did not subject herself to anyone"), Lisis has risen to exemplarity ("no woman excels her") and achieved self-determination ("with a firm and honorable will"). The tension of the triangles finally broken by Lisis's refusal of don Diego, she has attained repose.

The *Desengaños* have followed Lisis from the brink of physical death to a spiritual resurrection in the convent. There, surrounded by her female companions and remaining a lay nun, she will re-create the ideal matriarchal world previously incarnated in the scenario of the framework story, a salon not dissimilar to those of the *précieuses*. Lisis's parlor, the setting of the soiree of the *Novelas*, boasted "heavy Flemish tapestries whose woods, groves, and flowers depicted exotic landscapes like Arcadia" (E., *9*, 31); the scene of the framework story of the *Desengaños* is described as an "abbreviated version of heaven," occupied by "hierarchies of angels," "the Divine Lisis," and men "feeling quite unhappy" (*39*, 120). The Divine Lisis and her mother, Laura, reign supreme over their Arcadia, imposing the rules discussed above that allow women to prevail. But as emblematized by the fact that the telling of the stories takes place only at night, theirs is a temporary Arcadia—a liminal space, a limbo. Their "abbreviated" City of Women, like Scheherazade's stay from execution, will endure only as long as the stories are still being told. Yet here, as distinct from Cavendish's play, the female utopia will not be erased at the end. Rather, it is displaced to and given permanent form in the convent. For in the convent Lisis will achieve female community. According to Ruth El Saffar, she effects a version of the recovery of Persephone by Demeter so celebrated by women writers (1990, 6–7).[39] In a conceivable counterecho of the myth of Orpheus and Eurydice, the Demeter of the myth descends to the underworld to rescue her daughter Persephone, who has been kidnapped by Hades. Here Lisis's move to enter a convent and to withdraw from the "unremitting hell" of the world of men (El Saffar 1990, 6) inspires her mother to do the same. The daughter rescues the mother: their female bond will be upheld and the community of women preserved in the confines of the secularized convent presented at the very end of the *Desengaños*.

The striking dénouement of the *Desengaños* that I have just explicated prompts me to make a couple of remarks about the dynamics of the endings of the two convent scripts under study. It almost goes without saying that literary texts generally build toward an ending. More interesting is the way that endings overdetermine texts, allowing the reader to discern what has been called the "retrospective patterning" or telos of the narrative (see Miller 1980, xi; Torgovnick, 5, Herrnstein Smith, 10–14). Endings, it is well known, are also ideologically charged spaces, important sites of cultural encoding. Rachel Blau DuPlessis states that "one of the great moments of ideological negotiation in any work occurs in the choice of a resolution for the various services it provides. Narrative outcome is one place where transindividual assumptions and values are most clearly visible and where the word 'convention' is found resonating between its literary and social meanings" (3). In the case of Zayas and Lafayette, the endings of their texts at once flout the fundamental social code of marriage, reinscribe the cultural code of the convent, and privilege the feminine. Subversive and in that sense culturally underencoded, two dimensions of the endings—the convent and female-to-female relationships—reverberate all the more emphatically into the body of the texts for reinforcement .

The oppositional ending of Zayas's *Desengaños* quite literally and forcefully overdetermines the text, which places the convent before us in almost every novella. The convent appears in a variety of guises. From the point of view of the male characters (similar to the textual function it assumes in male-authored texts), the convent often represents a space of refuge from the law or a place in which to leave unwanted or dishonored women. One male character, Enrique of the eighth *desengaño*, goes so far as to malign the eternal captivity of religion (*277*, 373) a convent entails, thus articulating the position latent in Cervantes's novella.[40] Zayas's overriding position vis-à-vis the convent as showcased in the attitudes of the female characters, however, contradicts that of Cervantes and Enrique. The majority of female protagonists of female-narrated tales end up in a convent, where they find happiness and freedom rather than austerity, for example: "Today Jacinta lives in a convent, so happy that she thinks she never desired to live any other way or could ask for any greater pleasure" (E., *44*, 74). The female characters also extol the religious merits of convent life. Similar to many real female religious in their own writings, the fictional characters laud Christ as a husband far superior to the mortal men they have left behind. Each of these tales praising the convent and describing the aftermath of encloisterment prefigures and bolsters, in both structural and ideological terms, Lisis's final decision to withdraw from the world. Where Cervantes equates marriage with convent life, Zayas diametrically opposes the two.

Not only Lisis but Jacinta of the first "Enchantment," Gracia of the fourth "Enchantment," and Beatriz of the last "Disenchantment" enter the convent with either their mothers or other female companions. This fact signals the unmistakably compensatory and contestatory valorization of female-to-female relationships found in Zayas: we recall, once again, her statement that "[w]ithout a single exception, there is no play staged or any book printed that is not a total offense against women." Male authors of the Spanish golden age extensively imagined and propagated their notions of what an unchained woman might want or how she might act through the "manly woman," the bandit, the *esquiva*, the castrating feminist, and so on. We should remember that these were *male* fantasies and ask ourselves what the fantasies of seventeenth-century women in their own right might look like. I would suggest that they might well incline not necessarily to rebellion against men but to the female bonding and loving female relationships so extensively depicted in the works of María de Zayas (and Mme de Lafayette).

For where golden age dramas expunge the maternal presence, Zayas's novellas accentuate it.[41] Her characters *do* have mothers; the mothers act in concert with the fathers; the mother-daughter bond prevails over the father-daughter relationship. Zayas fills gaps in the literary representation of mothers by presenting several instances of mother-love, of empowered active mothers, of mothers protecting daughters from the abuses of fathers, and of a mother's psychology. Zayas extends her recovery of the feminine for literature to other female-female relationships as well. We see a caring relationship between sisters (E., *304–5*, 412–13), and nonhierarchical friendships between mistress and slave or maid. The sixth *desengaño* ("Love for the Sake of Conquest") sympathetically broaches the theme of lesbian relationships under the same protective coloring to which Cavendish took recourse: the seemingly homoerotic passion of a character disguised as the opposite sex. When the male Esteban disguised as Estefanía falls in love with Laurela, s/he audaciously states that "the power of love can also include a woman's love for another woman just as it does a suitor's love for his lady" (*214*, 306). Later s/he justifies homoerotic love in precisely the same Platonic terms found in Sor Juana's poetry: "[W]ith regard to love, since the soul is the same in male and female, it matters not whether I'm a man or a woman. Souls aren't male or female and true love dwells in the soul, not in the body" (*224*, 317). Indeed, Esteban proves to be a far more worthy lover as Estefanía than as a man. In what is perhaps the most brutal reversal of all the *Desengaños*, Esteban abruptly abandons Laurela once he has conquered her, and returns to his wife.

Zayas's representation of women, I should note, is not always so favorable nor is it one-sided. A host of false female friends, and evil aunts, mothers-in-law, and stepmothers also populate the stories, fueling their plots. The tale that Lisis herself tells at the end of the *Desengaños* focuses on a wicked woman possessed by mad love. But the author makes even this apparent inconsistency with her pro-female stance redress the literary balance in women's favor: Zayas repeatedly implies or declares that for a *woman* to be bad is the worst of all evils, and that the existence of some bad women does not justify men slandering all womankind.[42]

The female bonds cemented at the end of the *Desengaños* form the final link of yet another thematic chain: the irremediable polarization of the sexes. The baroque breakdown of love that I discussed in the last chapter results in a world where women ally with women, and men with men to the detriment of women. Two details betoken the magnetic repulsion between the sexes. First, the incongruous piece of information about the entertainment's guests unobtrusively dropped into the introduction of the *Novelas*: "[F]or it just so happened that none of the ladies had a father and none of the gentlemen had a mother" (E., *9*, 31). And second, the fact that Tantalus is the mythical personage most mentioned in the poetry of the *Desengaños*. As the text's tutelary god, Tantalus denotes the insatiable desire of one sex for the other and the equally impossible chance for its fulfillment that the tales so clearly illustrate.[43] To wit: increasingly toward the end of the *Desengaños* a new type of triangle comes to the fore.[44] As in Borges's "La intrusa" [The Intruder] and to similar effect, it is a triangle of two men bonding against a woman. Fathers turn sons against their respective wives in the seventh and eighth tales. That the son in the seventh tale turns out to be homosexual, and that Zayas should risk depicting a taboo subject, intimates the weight she attaches to the theme of male bonding. Treacherous Federico of the ninth tale, on the other hand, creates a schism between his *brother* Ladislao and Ladislao's wife that can be summarized using Borges's words from the conclusion of "La intrusa": "Cain was rearing his head, but the Nilson brothers' affection for each other was considerable . . . and they preferred to discharge their tensions on a third party" (1970, 20–21). Moreover, the narrator's comments on the wife's situation in Zayas's ninth *desengaño* gives voice to the plight of all the women faced with male triangles: "But in this case the accuser was his own brother and the accused his wife. When the traitor is a man and the betrayed a woman, no matter how innocent she may be, no one will believe in her innocence, least of all her husband. In this kind of situation, *he is her arch-enemy*" (*327*, 428; italics mine). In my view, these male triangles have no small impact on Lisis. Despite the victories of the "disenchantresses" reflected in don Juan's acknowledgments of men's errors on more than one occasion, and despite the subsequent agreement of *all* the men present that they have wronged women, Lisis chooses the company of women. In opting for the convent and out of Tantalus's dilemma, it would appear that Lisis not only rejects men but also confirms the impossibility of reconciling the polarized sexes.

With all of its pieces now in view, it is clear that the convent script as activated by the passionate María de Zayas makes for a heroic feminist bildungsroman. In exploiting the potential of (yet another) extant literary option and of a contemporary social alternative, Zayas's convent script opens up a space beyond the purview even of most nineteenth-century renditions of the bildungsroman. Their female protagonists, as has often been remarked, generally become heroines and marry. If they choose to remain heroes, they go mad or die. And they die, for one reason, "because a female hero has no alternative community where the stain of energy will go unnoticed or even be welcomed" (DuPlessis, 16). Here, in contrast, female community is reified in the convent, Lisis "did not subject herself to anyone," and the male rather than female protagonists are dealt tragic ends. Yet triumphant as Lisis's destiny may appear to be, it too contains a certain tragic dimension. Nancy K. Miller has written, "In so much women's fiction a world outside love proves to be out of the world altogether" (1988, 45). I will explore this issue further in discussing *LPDC*. For now let me merely say that wittingly or not, the narrator's appraisal of Lisis's fate—"This end is not tragic but rather the *happiest one you can imagine*" (italics mine)—constitutes an apt and balanced judgment on the situation of the female hero of the seventeenth-century bildungsroman.

⌘

V.

THE CONVENT SCRIPT/BILDUNGSROMAN
IN La Princesse de Clèves

A few critics have noticed the tantalizing similarities between the convent endings of Zayas's *Desengaños* and Lafayette's *LPDC* and have cautiously suggested that Lafayette had read Zayas.[45] The relationship they suggest is not all that implausible given the vogue of Spanish literature in France at the time, as reflected in the Spanish setting of Lafayette's own *Zaïde*. Other of the idiosyncratic features of Lafayette's novel—the famous *aveu* or avowal by the Princesse to her husband that she is struggling with an adulterous passion, and the anomalous intervention of an unidentified "I" in the narrator's voice (*LPDC*, *1*, 131)—appear in Zayas's *Desengaños*.[46] If the feminist aspects of

Zayas's *Desengaños* also exercised an influence on *LPDC*, that interaction between the two authors could place an interesting slant on the subject to which I devote considerable attention in the following pages, the novel's indeterminate ending. Whether or not there was direct contact between Zayas's novellas and Lafayette's novel, both texts undoubtedly present the same profile of a sentimental education that culminates in the protagonist's *refus* and withdrawal to the convent. Therefore, reading *La Princesse de Clèves* through the lens of the convent script (and María de Zayas), I will proceed to treat the text as a heroic female bildungsroman, a story of self-affirmation. Although to my knowledge no one has discussed the bildungsroman dimension of Zayas's novellas, here I am hardly in uncharted territory. So my reading will draw selectively—and in the end, metacritically—on the many fine existing analyses of *LPDC* as a sentimental education.

As is the case in Zayas's bildungsroman, and as may well be the case in any example of that genre, the protagonist of *LPDC* gleans knowledge of the world through both indirect and direct experience. The Princesse de Clèves finds herself in something of an academy of life replete with would-be mentors, each of whom furnishes another building block for her apprenticeship to the court, lessons that she, like Lisis, will carry into her own action. Raising her daughter sequestered from the court and men, her widowed mother, Mme de Chartres, has laid the cornerstones of the Princesse's moral "education" (137, *9*). She has spoken to her of love, of men's infidelity, of the need to avoid extramarital entanglements at all costs. She has outlined a model existence for her daughter, the life of the "honnête femme":[47] grounded in virtue, marital harmony, and most important of all, the exercise of extreme mistrust of oneself ("extrême défiance de soi-même" [137, *10*]) in order to preserve her virtue in the face of the temptations that meet a woman at every turn. The mother's advice, a still point in the Princesse's churning world, will impact all of her subsequent actions. Distinct from the *précieuses* but akin to Zayas, Lafayette emphasizes rather than excises maternal ties.

Mme de Chartres and others also supply object lessons, parables encoded with multiple messages for the Princesse to decipher. These object lessons, the seemingly digressive anecdotes recounted by several characters to fill in the gaps of the Princesse's knowledge of the court, at times so dominate the text as to convert the narrative of the Princesse's own bildung into something of a framework story. The Reine-Dauphine and Mme de Chartres inaugurate the series. After the latter's death, the Prince de Clèves takes over the mother's role in his wife's moral education and tells the tale of the Comte de Sancerre's relationship with the duplicitous Mme de Tournon. The Prince's polyvalent tale is cautionary on several levels: it details the corrosive effects of passion, features a woman who has betrayed her own resolve to avoid love, and warns against the wildfire spread of gossip in the court milieu. The Prince also interjects in the tale his own appreciation of complete sincerity in matters of the heart, which provokes the Princesse's later avowal to him of her passion for another, the *aveu* that proves to be M. de Clève's undoing. Laden as his and the other anecdotes may be with divergent messages, a common thread runs through them all and reaffirms the mother's lesson. And that is the dangers of adulterous love, the moral ruination and unhappiness it invariably brings. The Princesse sees that the most powerful women in Europe–Diane de Poitiers, Anne Boleyn, the queen of France herself–are at the same time the most unhappy. Hence, like Lisis, the Princesse embarks on her own amorous adventures amply provisioned with examples of women whose experience previews that of the young woman herself, didactically playing out its tragic results even before Mme de Clèves has lived them.

All of these academic lessons are simultaneously being subjected to the crucible of direct experience. The world of the court and her illicit passion for Nemours hurl the reluctant Princesse from innocence into an abhorred duplicity, from harmony to discord between her inner and outer selves, and as a consequence, from confiding in her mother to dissembling from her. To do justice to the Princesse's movements in the moral testing ground of the court, let me begin by elaborating on Jules Brody's indispensable treatment of the subject in "*La Princesse de Clèves* and the Myth of Courtly Love" (the references in parentheses indicate Brody's contributions). Viewing *LPDC* as a novel of apprenticeship, Brody details the steps in the young heroine's sentimental education without which "her *éducation morale* would have remained no more than academic" (116). Mme de Clèves has already learned the moral side of love from her mother; she has everything to learn, says Brody, about the "nature of passion itself" (117). The Princesse's relationship with Nemours thrusts her into the maelstrom of that epistemological dilemma. Not only does it set off the ruptures I framed above, but particularly after her mother's death, it forces the Princesse to forge her conscience on her own terms. One of the first milestones in these developments is the night of unmitigated, if chaste, pleasure that the Princesse shares with Nemours (the only such unmixed pleasure she will experience with him) as they collaborate on a letter that exculpates Nemours from a presumed affair with another woman (119–20). Reflecting sadly on that night, the Princesse realizes that the whole situation had aroused in her the intolerable new emotion of jealousy that has led to the loss of her tranquillity or repose: "Although the suspicions the letter had given her had been set at rest, they none the less opened her eyes to the risk of being deceived and gave her intimations of distrust and jealousy that she had never known before" (*LPDC, 91,* 236). Worse yet is the suggestion implanted by jealousy in her mind that Nemours may not indeed be capable of a sincere and lasting attachment. Brody summarizes the implications of the letter-writing incident, saying, "Whereas prior to this incident Mme de Clèves had founded her avoidance of Nemours on abstract moral principles and authoritative advice, at this point she stands beyond her mother's strictures; she has begun to suspect the real nature of the passion and of the man that had but recently exposed her to the complementary extremities of happiness and misery" (119).

The lessons of the letter radiate into the second milestone event in the Princesse's sentimental education, the *aveu*. In mustering the courage necessary for the avowal to her husband of her adulterous attraction, the Princesse displays the hard-won fruits of her own inner struggles in wake of the void left by her mother's death. She actualizes her mother's guidance, combining it with her own most distinctive trait, sincerity ("Mme de Chartres marvelled at her daughter's great frankness, and with good reason, for it was unmatched" [*LPDC*, *21*, 150]). The courageous *aveu* reaps at least two tragic but instructive consequences. First, in contributing to the death of M. de Clèves, it teaches the Princesse that the jealousy that had wrought such havoc on her own repose can kill (Brody, 121). Second, when the Princesse learns that Nemours had broadcast the *aveu* to which unbeknownst to her he was party, she attains direct proof of her mother's assertions about men's unworthiness and indiscretion. Previously, she had known in principle *why* she should resist Nemours; now she knows exactly *what* she is resisting (Brody, 120). In sum, through these two incidents Mme de Clèves learns "for herself, at first hand, that her mother's descriptions of the ways of love were neither one-sided, nor arbitrary, nor abstractly moralistic" (Brody, 116).

It is not without arduous effort, as I have said, that the Princesse gains the moral high grounds of the *aveu*. Nor, I add now, are those grounds in any way stable or definitive, for love both forms and deforms the Princesse. Throughout the text, we witness the Princesse's inconclusive attempts to preserve her self when confronted with precisely the destructive effects of love (which "places one's very being in peril") described in section II above. Yet unlike the basically unchecked and inexorable descent of the Princesse de Montpensier into passion, up to the end of the novel the Princesse de Clèves will constantly shuttle back and forth between self-control or containment, and explosion or "decontainment," all the while straining to assert lucidity and self-vigilance. This struggle within the Princesse is, of course, the very core of the novel, and in its depiction lie the origins of the work's fame as a watershed in the development of the novel, which with Lafayette is emerging from flatter romance forms.

Hence, the first part of *LPDC* pans from the larger circumstances of the court and its personages into an ever tighter close-up onto the Princesse. As the Princesse acquires emotional depth through the vicissitudes of her personal situation, the narration moves from the outer world into her inner recesses, and we are given increasing access to the character's anguished interiority. Thus we are directly privy to the efforts at self-control galvanized by the Princesse's attraction to Nemours, for the "attraction she felt for M. de Nemours threw her feelings into such a turmoil that she was no longer mistress of her emotions" (*56*, 193). As she battles to remain mistress of her self, the Princesse becomes a paradox incarnate in whom contradictory states of love and shame, containment and decontainment, alternate in rapid succession. Jean-Baptiste Trousser de Valincour, the first seventeenth-century critic of

LPDC, calls her "the most flirtatious prude and the most prudish flirt ever seen" (Laugaa, 99); Kaps sees her as a baroque "oxymoron," "the embodiment of fatal passion and rational lucidity" (69). The constant flux of the Princesse's emotions, her chiaroscuro consciousness, can be most strikingly illustrated by the letter-writing incident discussed above. Here, as the Princesse experiences the untroubled pleasure of Nemours's company, the decontainment that she usually confines to her inner musings spills over into her external actions: "She felt only the pleasure of seeing M. de Nemours, a pure, unmixed delight [une joie pure et sans mélange] that was new to her, and from this delight came a mood of gaiety and freedom which M. de Nemours had never before seen in her" (*89,* 234). Immediately after Nemours leaves, sublime pleasure cedes to its opposite. The Princesse's decontainment, be it in public or private, is often described by the text as a dream state; indeed, only then does her libido prevail. Now, passing directly from the realm of libido to that of superego with no intermediate ground, "she awoke as from a dream" (*90,* 235) and bitterly recriminates herself for the night's actions. Guilt over the implications of her behavior, memories of the jealousy she had suffered, and suspicions of Nemours crowd her mind; "she could no longer recognize herself" (*91,* 235–36). The third-person narration, as it often does in recounting moments of profound internal agitation, plunges into interior monologue, and the Princesse concludes: "I am conquered and overcome by an inclination that carries me with it in spite of myself. All my resolutions are of no avail" (*92,* 237).

The preceding vignette exemplifies the young woman's dilemma of decontainment, a dilemma further encapsulated in one of the most oft-repeated phrases of the text: "elle ne put s'empêcher de . . ." [she could not help but . . .]. Yet not all is weakness, for the Princesse goes to great lengths to repossess her self. The salutary decontainment through honesty manifested in the *aveu* to M. de Clèves (and later, as we will see, in her *refus* of Nemours) is one of them. Mme de Clèves takes the unheard-of step of confessing her passion to M. de Clèves in order to enlist his help. He must assist his wife in achieving the self-control she so ardently desires but is unable to effect on her own: "Be my guide" (*95,* 241), "dispose of my conduct" (*100,* 247), she pleads. Despite her supplicant tone, as the Princesse herself states, the *aveu* issues not from weakness but from strength: "It was not weakness that made me confess: it needs more courage to admit such a truth than to seek to hide it" (*96,* 242). From her strength to tell the truth will result the aid that will produce renewed self-mastery and virtue. But how is her husband to help her? He must permit her to withdraw from court life into the tranquillity of the countryside. Not only here but at many other points in the text the Princesse takes recourse to the formula for achieving victory over passion prescribed by her mother—retreat from the offending temptation. On her deathbed, Mme de Chartres exhorted her daughter: "Have strength and courage, my child, withdraw from the court, persuade your husband to take you away" (*40,* 172). Accordingly, at each dangerous juncture, when she is most cognizant of the threats to her virtue, the Princesse withdraws from the court or attempts to do so. One such moment, paradigmatic of the rest and embodying all the elements of the drama, takes place after the Princesse has allowed Nemours to steal her portrait:

> [S]he gave thought to the *violence of the passion that was irresistibly drawing her towards M. de Nemours*; she discovered that she was *no longer mistress of her words or her expression*; she reflected on the fact that, since Lignerolles had returned, she need have no more fears about the English affair [Nemours's marriage to the queen of England], and that her suspicions with regard to Mme la Dauphine had been set at rest; she saw, in short, that there was nothing that could protect her now: *she would only be safe if she went away*. (65, 204; italics mine)

Each retreat from the court, each exertion of "extreme mistrust of self," accomplishes its purpose, but only temporarily: the Princesse recovers her repose and believes she has effaced her passion for Nemours until she sees him again and the cycle begins anew.

The ending of the novel takes on relief and heroic stature against the backdrop of the Princesse's instability, reminiscent of Sor Juana's mutually contradictory triangle poems, that I have just detailed. Harriet Allentuch notes the innovative congruence between the body and ending of the text, saying: "The *Princesse de Clèves* is the first of French novels to move relentlessly towards its conclusion" (185). Allentuch refers specifically to the contrast between Lafayette's novel and earlier romances, but her words also point to the extraordinary symmetries of this most geometrical and overdetermined of texts. Like a hall of mirrors, each piece of the text at once echoes into another and contains its own reflection. The magnificently limited lexicon of the text, the key words and phrases that provide a map of the novel's affective terrain, enhances and reifies its repetitions. "To repeat and to know how to repeat," in Camus's words (Kaps, 3), comprises the essence of Lafayette's novelistic art and, I add, contributes to the intense retrospective patterning of the novel. Hence, the Princesse's final *refus* of Nemours and retreat to the convent may unsettle her suitor and destabilize the marriage plot, but her actions need not surprise the vigilant reader. The ending has been richly prefigured by the "precise play of foreshadowings, echoes and affinities" (Borges 1947, "El arte narrativo y la magia," Narrative Art and Magic [90]) of this most modern early modern text. In what we have already seen, one *aveu* of the Princesse's sentiments (to her husband) previews and leads to another (to Nemours); numerous retreats from the court in search of repose auger the final withdrawal to the convent; inconclusive efforts at self-control culminate in definitive resolve. Taking into account this retrospective sense of an ending and refracting the novel's ending into the various aspects that exhibit its heroic dimensions, I will now analyze the bildungsroman conclusion of *LPDC*.

The very topography of the novel reflects and interprets its convent ending. The circumscribed topography of *LPDC* contains two basic spaces with their own connotations—the court and the noncourt. In the problematic space of the court both inner and outer turmoil reign supreme for the Princesse. In the noncourt spaces (the country home at Coulommiers and its pavilion, and ultimately the convent), the Princesse regains her composure. We recall that the Princesse was raised outside the court, which fact has led some critics to identify the noncourt spaces with the realm of the female. The space of the convent certainly bears out this identification (see Hirsch, 76; Kamuf, 91) as does the historical genealogy of Coulommiers: a seventeenth- (rather than, as would befit the novel's historical setting, sixteenth-) century residence filled with busts of illustrious women, one of whose inhabitants founded at least two convents and another of whom was a former *frondeuse*.[48] It is in the pavilion at Coulommiers that the first *aveu*, a product of the Princesse's strength, takes place. Her second retreat to Coulommiers produces an even more dramatic act. Alone in the pavilion (or so she thinks, for once again Nemours lurks in the background), the Princesse performs a private ritual of love. In a scene charged with eroticism, she lies on a couch to contemplate a portrait of Nemours and, transported to a dream state, strings ribbons around his cane. Flushed from the sultry night breezes, her head and breast covered only by her hair (*128*, 281), "grace" and "sweetness" are written on the Princesse's face as she abandons herself to the second moment of idyllic decontainment in the text. Yet as distinct from the first moment (the letter-writing episode), here the Princesse safely rehearses her love in solitude and takes enraptured possession of her beloved through an act of symbolic displacement.

The private drama of the pavilion at Coulommiers holds particular import for our understanding of the Princesse's final retreat to the convent as its homologue (cf. Miller 1988, 37) and on its own terms. The Princesse's refusal of Nemours's suit after the death of her husband—an act on which, as we will see, so many critics place a negative interpretation—is hardly the absolute disavowal of love it might appear to be. Rather, as Faith Beasley has written, "Mme de Clèves does not reject her passion, as Valincour and many modern critics argue, but channels it into a mode of action where it can be perpetuated instead of destroyed" (242).[49] Incapable of obliterating completely her love for Nemours but refusing entirely to see him, she performs a delicate negotiation with passion parallel to her actions in Coulommiers. She internalizes her love and relegates it to the hermetically sealed confines not of the pavilion but of her self ("do not doubt that my feelings for you will exist eternally and unchangeably whatever I do" [*151*, 309]). The *précieuses*, intent on self-preservation, often took recourse in their literary works to similar acts of internalized appropriation. According to Claude Vigée: "Often, among the *précieuses*, memories and mental images advantageously replaced the real person of the lover" (743). The operative word here is *advantageously*. For in an action and a scenario wonderfully evocative of Sor Juana's sonnet, "Semblance of my elusive love, hold still," the Princesse consigns her rebellious passion and lover to the space of self where, as Sor Juana puts it, she need no longer fear their "tyranny": "poco importa burlar brazos y pecho / si te labra prisión mi fantasía" [it matters not to evade my arms and breast, since my fantasy holds you captive in its grasp].

The preservation and definition of that self occupy the forefront of the scene with Nemours in which the female bildungsroman culminates. In a sentimental romance, free of their previous encumbrances the two lovers would triumphantly come together and marry, ennobled by the trials they had endured (Pingaud, 101). Instead, in this psychologically acute bildungsroman the Princesse decides in the name of reason, virtue, obligation ("devoir"), and repose to save herself above all else by rejecting marriage to the man she loves. Claiming, as I already stated in section II that his possible unfaithfulness would destroy her were she to cede to his suit, the Princesse rejects Nemours, "more from self-love than from love for you" (303) and "in the interest of my repose" (308). The Princesse's stunning disavowal of passion–"I confess . . . that my passions may govern me, but they cannot blind me" (*149*, 306)– impels her definitive resolve to follow the "austere principles" that obligation dictates (*146*, 303).[50] Her resolve is all the more heroic because the Princesse succeeds in maintaining it even though her inner struggles will not cease with the *refus*: "Little as I trust myself [quoique je me défie de moi-même], however, I believe that I shall never be able to vanquish my scruples, nor can I hope to overcome my attraction to you. It will make me unhappy, and I intend to remove myself from your sight, however violent the pain it will cost me" (*150*, 308). Indeed, they so continue to torment her as to weaken the Princesse's health, setting her on the course to an early death. Yet after her illness, at long last, "she overcame the remains of a passion already weakened by the sentiments her illness had inspired" (*154*, 313). Her *refus* may not bring unmitigated happiness, but it does entail anagnorisis and the *repos* that, in broad strokes, seventeenth-century French culture understood as "withdrawal from the movement and activities of the world to a retreat where man, relieved of disquieting passions and desire, could be spiritually reborn and enjoy uninterruptedly a stable, independent and virtuous life" (Stanton 1975, 102). And that, given the dark picture of love and human nature that informs the novel, is perhaps the most one can hope for. As Pascal wrote: "One must know oneself: even when that does not suffice to find the truth, at least it suffices to regulate one's life, and there is nothing more just" (Allentuch, 196). Particularly when viewed in its own ideological context, the *refus* emerges not as a defeat but as a victory over the forces that undermine lucid self-knowledge. The Princesse's passionate being is not *her* being but its undoing; mistrust of the self, tautologically enough, *is* her being, the being she has now managed to preserve at great cost.

The strength of the Princesse stands in marked contrast to the male characters of *LPDC*. In the matriarchal world of the court of Henri IV represented in *LPDC*, women reign supreme and men are weak: Diane de Poitiers, mistress of the king (a man whom the narrator portrays as not possessing "all the great qualities" [7, 134]), has obtained so complete a dominion over him "that one may say she was mistress both of his person and of the State" (*6*, 133). Power factions form around female personages of the court (cf. *14*, 142). The novel ends at the point at which Cathérine de Médici, the first of a series of female regents, takes power. What can be said of the court also holds true for courtly love, in both senses of the phrase. Madame de Tournon, for example, emerges triumphant from her amorous machinations, but the Comte de Sancerres is undone by them. All of these unequal alliances set the stage for the central misalliance of the text, the union of the Prince and Princesse de Clèves. Given his defining characteristic of prudence and his desire for mutual love in marriage, M. de Clèves appears to be the strongest, most admirable figure in the text. Claudine Herrmann has even suggested that he represents Lafayette's ideal "feminized" man (38).[51] Yet when his virtues are put to the test, M. de Clèves crumbles. And he crumbles to illustrative effect, for Lafayette contrives his trials in such a fashion that they echo those of his wife. Hence, the knowledge that his wife has been tempted by another man shakes the very foundations of his being, his reason, and repose ("There is, in short, no last shred of tranquillity or reason in me" [*124*, 277]), and as does she on so many occasions, he loses mastery over himself ("I have fallen prey to violent, shifting emotions which I cannot master" [*124*, 276]). Upon realizing that someone has divulged his wife's *aveu*, the Prince finds himself encompassed by "precipices and chasms on every side" (*112*, 261). Now, on her deathbed Mme de Chartres had warned her daughter against an affair with Nemours, saying, "you are on the edge of a precipice" (*39–40*, 172). Both the Princesse and her husband, we see, find themselves on the edge of a precipice, but here the resemblances end. For, unlike the Princesse, M. de Clèves cannot find the strength in himself to surmount the chaos of decontainment, the shaking of what have proven to be his spurious reason and repose. Where the Princesse retreats from society rather than betray her self, or the female hero of the nineteenth-century bildungsroman dies rather than succumb to the inauthenticity of the social script, M. de Clèves's own weakness sends him to his death.

I will conclude my examination of the ending of *LPDC* by taking a close look at the implications in terms of the female bildungsroman of a couple of crucial phrases from the final pages. Working backward, I begin with the last two words of the text. They read: "et sa vie, qui fut assez courte, laissa des exemples de *vertu inimitables*" (315; italics mine) [Her life, which was quite short, left *inimitable examples of virtue*, *156*]. The word *virtue* harks back to the mother's moral code and marks the return of the Princesse, not unlike that of Lisis, to the maternal realm. Early on, the novel tells us that Mme de Chartres dreamed of making her daughter "love virtue and be virtuous" (*9*, 137); again on her deathbed the mother counsels her daughter to hold paramount her self, her virtue, and her duty (*40*, 172). The Princesse thus retreats to the female space of the convent if not literally, at least figuratively, accompanied by her mother. The daughter reinserts herself in the mother's discourse; Demeter has rescued Persephone from the Hades of passion. Yet as we can now see fully, the daughter has not circled back but spiraled toward the maternal terrain. She has carried Mme de Chartres's teachings to greater heights than ever envisioned or even desired by her mother. Mme de Chartres inculcated her daughter with virtue in order to fit her for a husband and the court. The mother's ambition and pride (she is described as "exceptionally proud" [*10*, 137]) led her to sanction the loveless marriage for the Princesse that set all of the novel's tensions in motion. The daughter, for her part, has transcended the hubris of social ambition to realize her mother's dictates in their most pure and absolute form—and outside society, outside marriage, outside the marriage plot designed for her.

But why is the daughter's resulting virtue termed *inimitable*? Does the narrator, with a stroke of irony perhaps similar to Cervantes's descriptions of the virtuous Leonora, mean to insinuate that no one else would be so foolish or extreme as to follow the same austere path away from marriage as the Princesse? One explanation of this puzzling word (whose negative implications, I will soon argue, cannot be entirely discounted) lies in yet another of the Princesse's heroic transmutations of her mother's advice. At the end of the deathbed scene the mother leaves her daughter with the following thought: "I would say that, were anything capable of troubling the happiness I hope for in leaving this world, it would be to see you fall *like other women*" (*40*, 172; italics mine). Henceforth the Princesse does assume the quest of preserving her perhaps inimitable difference from other women as prescribed by her mother, but she carries it out through extremely unorthodox and "different" measures. The word *inimitable* so emphatically positioned at the end of the novel, I would argue, recapitulates not only the actions undertaken by the Princesse to preserve her difference but also the assertion of her uniqueness bound up in those actions. The Princesse's *aveu* to her husband, of course, is the first such effort. There, as we have seen, the Princesse draws on her signal quality of sincerity. What is more, she performs an action that is repeatedly described as singular: "I will make you a confession which no woman has ever made to her husband" (*95*, 240); "[t]he singular nature of such a confession, for which she could find no parallel, brought home to her all the risks it entailed" (*98*, 244). Subsequently, the Princesse decides to reject Nemours precisely because his commonness has jeopardized her difference: "And yet it is for this man, whom I believed so different from other men, that I have become like other women, I who resembled them so little" (*113*, 262). Nemours himself articulates the singularity inherent in the second of the Princesse's extraordinary actions, the *refus*: "It is harder than you think, Madame, to resist someone who both attracts you and who loves you. You have succeeded so far, thanks to a virtue so austere that it is almost without parallel" (*150*, 307–8). Although the Princesse, as Nemours's statement indicates to the reader, may not have evolved outside the *moral* parameters projected by her mother, she has—as the plays of similarities and differences in the novel's symmetrical construction conspire to show—personalized that terrain with her unique imprimatur.

The second phrase is equally significant but requires less comment. I have said that after her illness, the Princesse banishes the last vestiges of passion from her inner world. Sensing the approach of death, she retires to the convent, possessed of a new and larger perspective: "*The passions and attachments of the world now appeared to her as they do to those whose vision is more elevated and more detached*" (*155*, 313–14; italics mine). The Princesse, as this phrase tells us, has done more than exempt herself from love itself–she has exempted herself from the marriage plot and acceded to a heroic state. She has attained the boon of the quest, a perspective on the world of passion and appearances here extolled as a godlike tragic wisdom. And now as the Princesse lives half the year in the convent and half the year in austere retreat within her home, subjecting herself to no man, leading a saintly life, and leaving an example of great virtue, her persona and story merge almost indistinguishably with those of Zayas's heroic Lisis.

Having sounded this rather apocalyptic note, I must step back from my reading of the text's conclusion through the lens of the female bildungsroman as heroic to problematize it, opening up an issue that has significant bearing on the convent script as developed by Mme de Lafayette. I refer to the enigmatic indeterminacy of the ending, and take as a point of entry into the issue the fact that many critics have quite convincingly–even for this reader–construed the very same final pages in ways utterly different from mine, and hence also from the critics on whose arguments mine has built.

Over the course of *LPDC*'s critical reception the text's ending has proved to be a lightning rod for readings of the most opposing sorts. Since the critical parameters of the seventeenth century reflected the emerging shift from romance to novel and largely centered on issues of verisimilitude, Valincour found many of the Princesse's actions–the *aveu* even more than the *refus*–implausible and extraordinary.[52] His take on the *refus* in *Lettres à Madame la Marquise xxx sur le sujet de* La Princesse de Clèves [Letters to Madame the Marquise xxx on the subject of the *Princesse de Clèves*] (1678), reminiscent of concretizations of Zayas's work and perhaps indicating equal success on Lafayette's part in diluting the novel's incendiary potential, highlights the Princesse's "courage" and "virtue" in sacrificing Nemours for the sake of her *husband's* memory (Laugaa, 99). In contrast, the more wide-ranging twentieth-century critical reception of the text finds conflicting interpretations clustered insistently around the novel's ending, which has raised the following questions: Is the *refus* to the benefit of the Princesse's self or to its detriment? Does it comprise a growing up or a growing down? Is *LPDC* a novel of growth toward authenticity or one of inauthenticity and atrophy? The nature and vocabulary of these questions suggest the identity of the two most directly opposing camps: feminist versus existentialist critics. I will briefly summarize their respective approaches.

Most feminist critics tend to view the ending of *LPDC* as heroic; their readings have informed mine. For example, Harriet Ray Allentuch makes a strong case for "The Will to Refuse in the *Princesse de Clèves*," arguing that the protagonist attains maturity and freedom at the end of her sentimental education. Allentuch notes that although the Princesse dies prematurely, "she fails to die of emotional paralysis. On the contrary, in the scene in which she confronts Nemours for the last time she is self-possessed, active, more in control of her situation than at any other time in the novel" (195). Nancy K. Miller (1988), Joan De Jean (1984), and Faith Beasley all consider the *refus* to be a specifically female victory, not only over the self but also over the bounds of narratability of the times—an "inimitable" deconditioning of literary scripts, an early appropriation of narrative by a woman writer, the expression of Lafayette's desire that her heroine retain control over her own plot. Yet the feminist camp is far from uniform. Marianne Hirsch diverges from Allentuch (and from the position I have presented) in her excellent "A Mother's Discourse: Incorporation and Repetition in *La Princesse de Clèves*," to argue compellingly for the stifling effects of Mme de Chartres on her daughter: "It is my contention that the mother's lesson is at the center of a nexus of scenes that reflect and echo one another, trapping the heroine in a structure of repetitions which ultimately preclude development and progression" (73). In an article written concurrently with Hirsch's piece, Peggy Kamuf arrives at similar conclusions by filtering the text through the Girardian triangle of desire: the mother is the model and object, the Prince de Clèves the mediator, and the Princesse the subject striving to reproduce the model.

The readings of the *refus* as heroic to which I have referred (and my own) function on their own terms and in effect restore the balance skewed against the female protagonist by critics along existentialist lines. One can all too easily imagine how Nemours's characterization of Mme de Clèves's *refus*—"you alone have made for yourself a law that virtue and reason could never impose" (*151*, 309)—could incense those who valorize the existential constructs of freedom, authenticity, and commitment. Helen Kaps summarizes the prefeminist critical history of the *refus*, noting that whereas in previous centuries the heroine's final renunciation had most often been considered "a moral victory, a triumph of duty over passion somewhat in the manner of Corneille," prefeminist contemporary readers are "more inclined to see the renunciation as a defeat— a failure to meet the challenge of life, a selfish withdrawal from the risks of self-giving, a semineurotic flight from reality" (x). Indeed, Camus, Sergei Doubrovsky, Bernard Pingaud, Georges Poulet, and Stirling Haig, for example, all devaluate the *refus* along one or another of these lines. Haig assumes a particularly vehement stance, describing the *refus* as life-denying, as "retrenchment, a truncation and semi-suicidal mutilation of the self that results in that traumatism that goes by the name of *repos*" (133).[53] Claude Vigée, author of one of the most respected and worthy articles on *LPDC*, at times incurs in equally incensed vituperations against the Princesse's actions. Nuancing in important ways the earlier understanding of the novel as a Corneillian moral victory, Vigée portrays *LPDC* as a meeting place between two irreconcilable currents, the Jansenists' pessimism and Corneille's idealism. The two converge without melding, which results in a half-triumph of love (the Princesse's internalization of her passion, as discussed above) and in a half-triumph of the self. For Vigée, the Princesse's ego is only half-triumphant because her rejection of love in favor of self–"more from self-love than from love for you"–constitutes an act of incomparable egotism. Revealing a bias similar to that of the existentialists and certainly anathema to a feminist (or *précieuse*), Vigée writes, "There isn't a page in which a matchless egotism does not burst forth from beneath the outer trappings of modesty and dignity" (74). Vigée's article, we can plainly see, both presents an implicit challenge to and unwittingly lays the groundwork for a feminist approach.

As all of the above readings suggest, the very theme of the novel's ending–the rejection of love and society, particularly by a woman–is a provocation to a variety of sensibilities. Inserted in the context of their own times, the two refusals that inhere in the ending of *LPDC* may have been either socially or literarily shocking, or morally justifiable; inserted in the postromantic context of our times, they may be laudable (to a feminist) or damnable (to an existentialist). It all depends on what moral shading one places on abnegation. Nevertheless, and significantly, I note with Allentuch (186), the fact remains that critics of the most opposing camps find ample corroboration of their views *in the text itself.* This fact leads the reader who has carefully worked his or her way through the novel and its formidable critical scaffolding to conclude that the malleability of the ending does not owe its existence merely to the willfulness of critics who would use it as a stomping ground for their respective agendas, but derives from the equivocal nature of the text itself. In other words, it is not a critical but a textual phenomenon.

In textual terms, then, what renders the ending so malleable, so indeterminate? For one thing, the final episodes of the *refus* and the retreat operate on a principle of nonexclusivity–as Nancy Miller sees it, of both/and rather than either/or.[54] Critics have readily noted that the inimitable *refus* and retreat *themselves* contain both negative dimensions (the Princesse refuses a love she could freely accept, consigns herself to an austere life, dies an early death, and so on) and positive ones (the many heroic aspects involving self-preservation discussed at length above). This fact, inherent in the multiple valences of the convent in reality and as a literary topic, transcends whatever personal interpretation one places on abnegation. Less noted are the other oxymorons present in the final episodes: the Princesse decontains herself to Nemours to ensure her definitive containment; she renounces Nemours *and* retains him in her inner recesses; she displays egotism, saving herself, *and* denies it, rejecting the man she loves; she remains faithful to the memory of her husband *and* to Nemours; she lives in society *and* outside it, and so on. In sum, if the Princesse's only moment of true happiness with Nemours, the letter-writing incident, was described as "pure et sans mélange" (234) [pure and unmixed, *89*], here she finds herself in a space where contradictions coexist and coalesce, a space of *mélange* and *sans mélange*. We the readers find ourselves in a similar space, one that in accommodating opposing elements also accommodates opposing lines of interpretation.

Second, there is the extraordinarily important matter of the abrupt shift in narrative perspective of the text's last two pages. Suddenly–as the narration switches into an external, synoptic, third-person mode–we are deprived of the protagonist's interiority, which has been the focus and stuff of the whole narrative. We are shifted back from novel into romance representation. The epilogue, which telescopes years of the Princesse's life into the last three sentences, gives no indication whatsoever of the Princesse's perspective on the events. Helen Kaps characterizes the whole circular narrative movement of the text, stating, "The reader has moved from a position of a superior [i.e., external] understanding at the start of the novel, to a direct . . . view of the heroine's consciousness, to the completely 'outside' view of the final pages." This "allows for a measure of uncertainty, a measure of speculation, within the framework of a closed circle" (64). The Princesse has remained faithful to her quest, but the narrator has abandoned its transcription.

Yet this is not the first time, even within the most intensely focalized sections, that the narrator has abdicated at a crucial moment. Almost routinely when the Princesse or other characters have reached a state of extreme (and extremely interesting to the reader) agitation, the narrator withdraws, using phrases such as, "it is easy to imagine," "one cannot represent," "one can only imagine" what a certain character was feeling at the time. The absence of moral judgments and the ambiguous elliptical language of the text, which Joan De Jean has termed a "poetics of lack" or suppression and which frustrated the readers of its own era,[55] are all signs of what could be called a *renunciation of representation*. The renunciation of representation, for its part, is I believe but one sign of a still larger phenomenon: the whole text intermittently gives mixed signals that implicate our interpretation of the ending. *La Princesse de Clèves* tells an exemplary, even allegorical tale, with hagiographic echoes and a transparent symbolism (such as the eroticism of the pavilion scene). But at the same time, as one of the first modern novels and distinct from Lafayette's novellas, it undercuts its own and its protagonist's exemplarity. Mme de Lafayette praised the novel (which, I repeat, was published anonymously), stressing its complexity: "I find it most agreeable, well written without being overly polished, full of wonderfully fine things that even merit a second reading" (*viii; Correspondance*, 2:63). Following her advice, let us briefly reread the Princesse's *refus* through the figure of Nemours.

The protean, shadowy, unresolvably ambiguous figure of Nemours comprises the second–if not absent, certainly unseizable–center of this arguably baroque text. Lafayette has rewritten the historical personage of Nemours into an insoluble (in both senses of the word) mixture of *honnêteté* or virtuous respectability, and *hardiesse*, impetuous daring. Basically, she has taken the *hardiesse* and aggressive sensuality of the historical figure and combined them with the positive features of a courtly lover,[56] which produces a character in whose speech the Princesse discerns "a note of chivalry and respect," but which she also finds "a shade too bold [*hardi*] and explicit" (56, 193). As readers we gain a larger view of Nemours than the Princesse, but in a sense to lesser avail. Simply put, it is absolutely impossible to determine on the basis of the information with which the reader is provided whether Nemours has been so transformed by his passion for Mme de Clèves as to have abandoned his Don Juan-like *hardiesse* for the *honnêteté* that she can love and respect. Is he worthy of her love and unworthy of the *refus?* Nemours's actions reveal him to be rash, imprudent, weak, egotistical, and dishonest, *and* remorseful, faithful, controlled, self-sacrificing, and honest (see Brody, 112). While we remain bemused, the Princesse remains firm in her willful reading of Nemours as *hardi*, something of a self-fulfilling prophecy. As Stirling Haig puts it, "she prepares a conclusion of past and future in order to crush the present" (130).[57] Thus from the vantage point of the reader, the fact that the Princesse has based her decision on such slippery and inconclusive evidence almost makes a mockery of her virtue and virtuous resolve.

La Princesse de Clèves, we see, is a self-problematizing artifact. The ending speaks in more than one tongue; it is indeterminate, a point of pertinence (Todorov, 26), what Roman Ingarden has called "opalescent" (144). It is possible, as Bernard Pingaud would have it, that any exemplary text betrays its own exemplarity: "Perhaps any great work is necessarily equivocal, in that whatever efforts it makes to be exemplary also bear witness to the futility of exemplariness" (106). Of course, we can never know exactly why Lafayette undermined the Princesse's exemplarity even as she enacted it, but I would argue that the framework of the convent script I have been developing in this chapter, and the context in which Lafayette wrote, open up a different generic and a more genderic (gender-specific) perspective on the ending's ambiguity than what Pingaud offers. The convent ending of this text shakes the social foundations of patriarchy and its construction of the female subject. It also pushes the bounds of narratability—but only so far. For Lafayette's representation of a woman in the heroic act of rejecting society and love, as we have seen, proves to be vacillating, unstable, not fully realized. As such, it lays bare the conflictive dynamics of the representation of female "heroism" in the seventeenth century. And here it is pertinent to bring in a conceivably antibaroque pronouncement by Valincour regarding verisimilitude: "Novelists are not permitted to abuse [poetic license] by creating monsters and utopian dreams, nor to invent things that shock the mind of everyone who reads them" (Beasley, 243). Writing a new kind of fiction that discloses the previously untold depths of a woman's interiority, Lafayette publishes her text anonymously and signals her heroine's "inimitability," thus signaling awareness of her own temerity. The novelistically rendered story of the Princesse de Clèves, despite its grounding in Jansenist and *précieuse* ideas, is still inimitable, partially unnarratable.

Even the passionately feminist María de Zayas, writing in a baroque climate so disposed to "things that shock the mind of everyone who reads them," hesitates in the *Novelas amorosas* to remove Lisis from the marriage plot. Perhaps in her first collection Zayas still held out some hope for the redemption of marriage (El Saffar 1995, 211); or perhaps, bowing to convention and as another manifestation of her syncretism, she only made a show of doing so, all the while developing a submerged plot subversive of marriage. The far less equivocal *Desengaños* can also display a certain coy shiftiness, with some of the female *desengañadoras* declaring a conciliatory attitude toward men that their inflammatory stories overtly negate. Lafayette affords us a far richer insight into her heroine's development than Zayas, but with that step forward–perhaps inevitably–come greater ambiguity and retrenchment. Her convent retains more conventional associations than those of her sister writers. Her convent ending falters. Nonetheless, in the larger scheme of things, Lafayette's text *is* a large step forward, into the heroic plot and register of present-day women's writing. Even its retrenchment is exemplary and illustrative, of the dynamics of an early modern female bildungsroman–still inchoate, not fully in another economy.

VI.

SOR JUANA REDUX: CONCLUSIONS

Mme de Lafayette's love triangle undeniably stands at a far remove from Sor Juana's schematic poems of ironic symmetries. In the early pages of the chapter I noted that the authors under study here may well appear to be unlikely partners; I hope to have dispelled that doubt with respect to the relationship between Zayas and Lafayette. At this final juncture, then, let me return to Sor Juana to suggest that the convent script, particularly as developed in Lafayette's novel, creates a context that allows us better to understand certain aspects not of Sor Juana's love triangle poems but of her *Primero sueño*.

This assertion ceases to sound so improbable as soon as we recognize that the *Sueño* operates outside the erotic plot, and entirely within the quest plot. The female "I" of the *Sueño* frees herself from all external ties to undertake the most heroic and pure of quests, the quest for true knowledge. Where the female protagonists of the convent script venture outside the marriage plot into the otherly female space of the convent, the protagonist of the *Sueño* realizes her quest within the equally otherly space of the night–obverse of the day and effacement of the diurnal world with all of its attending constraints. She leaves behind the conflict-ridden triangular world to aspire to the circular orb, an orb, I note, that is first identified not with the male godhead but with the adamantly female moon goddess Diana: "que su atezado ceño / al superior convexo aun no llegaba / del orbe de la Diosa / que tres veces hermosa / con tres hermosos rostros ser ostenta" (1.ll. 11–15) [that even its frowning gloom stopped short before it reached the convex side of that fair goddess's orb–she who shows herself in threefold beauty, the beauty of her three faces, *171*]. In her three incarnations Diana rules the underworld, the earth, and the heavens. It is within Diana's realm, something of a utopian space, that the unencumbered female soul can pursue her quest. Interestingly enough, the *Sueño* will draw on the erotic imagery of mystical poetry in detailing its protagonist's heroic quest, not so much for loving union with God or any male figure as with wisdom; the erotic, for once, becomes a function of the heroic.

What remains of the daring quest at the end of the *Sueño*? An enigma, at best: "quedando a luz más cierta / el Mundo iluminado, y yo despierta" (ll. 974–75) [leaving the world illuminated by a more certain light, and I awake]. The ending destabilizes the poem on more than one count. It discloses the previously veiled identity of the poem's "I," and it appears to ascribe some kind of revelation to that "I." But what is the nature of that revelation, the boon of the quest? The final lines shimmer with opalescence. Sor Juana shuts us out of her protagonist's inner world in the ending of the poem in precisely the same abrupt manner as does Lafayette at the very end of her novel: both works retreat from representation at the crucial climactic moment. We are left, in the *Sueño*, with the protagonist's eminently suggestive but ultimately undefined awakening, an awakening that accommodates the most opposing interpretations. Has she awakened to a conventionally baroque *desengaño*, to an acceptance of the failure of her quest? Or like the night, "segunda vez rebelde" (l. 965) [rebelling once again, *195*], has she determined to pursue her quest in the next night or in another sphere? Has she awakened to faith as the path to true knowledge? Has she gleaned, with the coming of day, some unstated illumination? The possibilities are legion, and I will not pretend to exhaust or to explicate them here. My intention is not to resolve the enigma of the poem's conclusion but to highlight its similarity to the indeterminate ending of *La Princesse de Clèves*. Like Phaeton, one of the Mexican writer's most oft-invoked characters, Sor Juana has performed an act of great daring in the *Sueño*. But like Mme de Lafayette, Sor Juana will only go out so far–then she shuts down and walks safely away, leaving the revelation shrouded in mystery. Certainly (as we saw in the *Vida i sucesos de la Monja Alférez*), the literary taste for things left unfinished, for open endings that surprise and titillate, forms part of the baroque esthetic.[58] I believe, however, that the enigmatic ending of the *Sueño* also reflects, in yet another context and comprising yet another manifestation of Sor Juana's circumspection, the perils of unleashing an "other" script, of writing otherwise.

Sor Juana's earthly triangles and utopian circles, straining to meet, have one last thing to tell us about the convent script that I have laid out in this chapter. Not only the poetic speaker of the *Sueño*, but also Lisis and the Princesse de Clèves must all avail themselves of an "elsewhere" as the scenario for self-realization. The poetic subject of the *Sueño* can take unfettered flight only in a nocturnal space, the space where Zayas's storytellers perform their "Enchantments." Lisis and the Princesse de Clèves (and Sor Juana herself) must retreat to the convent. Theirs is a remarkably heroic but still dysphoric plot, of exclusion and alienation rather than social integration.[59] The Princesse herself, in the *aveu* to M. de Clèves, had made a notable attempt to reform marriage, to ground it in sincerity, honesty, and genuine communication– which is perhaps why the *aveu* provoked so much discussion in its times. We

have seen the abysmal results of her efforts. The Princesse and her female contemporaries in literature could only hope for self-realization and self-determination in a space beyond the reaches of patriarchy, not mutual understanding
or happiness in marriage. I return to Nancy K. Miller's observation that "in so
much women's fiction, a world outside love proves to be out of the world
altogether." Though the convent script, in the ways that I have detailed, can
afford its protagonists a more positive scenario and dénouement than the
nineteenth-century female bildungsroman, only the twentieth century would
allow female characters and women themselves (in general, not just a select
few) to achieve some measure of self-realization within marriage or society.
Heroic yet dysphoric, the literary efforts of these three early modern women
writers figure their female protagonists' self-realization and determination into
possible spaces, the only spaces where the triangle can approach the circle. To
paraphrase María de Zayas, theirs are not tragic endings but the happiest then
conceivable, and narratable; like Sor Juana's masterpiece, they are *first* dreams.

CHAPTER FOUR

Auto-Machia:
The Self-Representations of
Sor Juana and Anne Bradstreet

I sing my SELF; my Civil Wars within;
The Victories I Howrely lose and win;
The dayly Duel, the continuall Strife,
The Warr that ends not, till I end my life.
–George Goodwin, "AUTO-MACHIA" (1607)

I.

A Good poet, must know things Divine, things Natural,
things Moral, things Historical, and things Artificial.
–BATHSUA MAKIN (1673)

*L*a Princesse de Clèves has, as we can tell, with good reason been vaunted as the first modern psychological novel in Western literature. With an unprecedented richness of texture and nuance, it transcends the two-dimensionality of romance representation to unfurl before the reader the complex interiority of its complex female protagonist. We see a character whose struggle with herself enunciates, problematizes, and defies conventional categorizations of woman as either virgin or whore, angel or monster. We see an interiority in process: we witness the battles of the Princesse's self-civil war or *auto-machia* between virtue and vice and passion and reason unfolding in their full contradictory ambivalence. The novel's surprisingly modern narrative mode, indirect free style, delves so deeply into her consciousness that it eventually all but crosses the line into interior monologue.

The contrast between the thick interiority of the Princesse de Clèves and that of the "I" at the end of Sor Juana's *Primero sueño* could therefore hardly be more stunning. We have followed in the *Sueño* the flight of a depersonalized soul to the point where it or she begins to assume a personal identity (as

138

an "I," as a female, perhaps as Sor Juana herself) and to connect with a more concrete reality. At this very point, as discussed in the previous chapter, the poem shuts down and shuts us out. Where the poem's third-person "Soul" unabashedly detailed its audacious quest for knowledge, its first-person "I" denies us precisely the details that *La Princesse de Clèves* so amply affords. Although in the seventeenth century lyric poetry would seem to be the most appropriate and conventional space for the examination of the self, Sor Juana places closure just where we could expect disclosure. One might surmise, then, that not only the "writing otherwise," but also the terrain of first-person self-representation held certain interdictions for the nun.

This chapter takes up where the *Sueño* leaves off. Incited by the disjunction just described to probe more deeply into the realm of autobiographical writings, I will examine in detail not the origins of the novel's depiction of a woman's inner self but its correlate, the inauguration of women's literary self-representation in the two continents of the New World. The nature of early modern writing, I note, warrants a certain latitude in my definition of self-representation. I will take as works of self-representation first-person writings that address their authors' personal circumstances—be it as individuals or as writers—and that either directly bespeak their interiority or present an image of themselves that has entailed self-scrutiny and self-judgment. I will be analyzing works of self-representation, in prose and in poetry, by Sor Juana and by her sister Tenth Muse in the New World, Anne Bradstreet.[1] Near contemporaries, Sor Juana and Anne Bradstreet were the first two published female poets in the New World.

A necessary aside before continuing to lay out the parameters of the chapter: Anne Bradstreet and Sor Juana are the most likely and unlikely of the pairings in this book, which thus far has dealt in rather unlikely matches. Beneath their contemporaneity and shared title of Tenth Muse, which certainly invite comparison, lie seemingly unbridgeable gaps. Let me draw some pictures: Anne Bradstreet moving with her large family from frontier town to frontier town, always in the avant-garde of the Puritan errand into the wilderness / Sor Juana enclosed in the relative comfort, luxury, and solitude of her convent cell; Anne Bradstreet, the fiercely devoted wife and mother / Sor Juana, with her self-stated aversion to marriage; Anne Bradstreet as daughter and wife of major public figures in the Puritan movement and herself a devout exponent of their common beliefs / Sor Juana, a nun, writing in the milieu of the Catholics whom Bradstreet once excoriated as "bloudy, Popish, hellish miscreants" ("Four Ages," 62); Anne Bradstreet, exemplar of the homely, transparent "plain style" of the Puritans / Sor Juana, expert technician of the baroque *conceptismo* and elaborate metaphors that also characterized the British metaphysical style so abhorred by the Puritans.

Despite all of this, the work of the two authors presents the many compelling similarities that a handful of critics has not failed to notice and even to dramatize, as does Electa Arenal in "This life within me won't keep still." Arenal's moving and beautifully choreographed play sets Anne Bradstreet and

Sor Juana side by side, speaking words from their own works. At various moments in the play, and especially in the final act devoted to the themes of "Fame/Woman/Lineage and Tradition," the two poets utter sentiments, images, and ideas so alike as to be practically of one voice. Arenal's play dramatizes as well the challenge of juxtaposing the two poets. Wonderfully suggestive, the dramatic piece essentially relegates to the audience the task of establishing the connections between Anne Bradstreet and Sor Juana and the reasons behind the connections. In undertaking this comparison I have been provoked by works such as "This life within me won't keep still" to seek the significant core of commonality that might explain the uncanny similarities that their works present despite the extraordinary differences in the two writers' contexts, personal predilections, and literary styles.[2]

For example, wending back to our subject now, among the affinities that have been noted between Anne Bradstreet and Sor Juana is one that strikes me as quite significant for the seventeenth-century woman writer and that bears implications for her self-representations. I refer to the fact that both Anne Bradstreet and Sor Juana qualify as what British writer Bathsua Makin (epigraph above) terms a "Good" or what I would call a "Complete Poet" in that both write about matters divine, moral, natural, historical, as well as personal or sentimental. Sor Juana, of course, came late to her "completeness." Her work built to the *Sueño*, her summa, that almost encyclopedic compendium of scientific and philosophical knowledge, storehouse of myth and esoterica. On the way to the *Sueño*, however, Sor Juana had dealt with topics private and public (such as the *Neptuno alegórico*), of a secular and sacred nature. Indeed, in a little discussed *silva* that I will analyze here, her "Epicinio Gratulatorio al Conde de Galve por la victoria de la Armada de Barlovento sobre los Franceses" (Silva #215) [Ode Lauding the Count of Galve for the Victory of the Windward Fleet Over the French], she even endeavored to address a theme of historical import. Anne Bradstreet, on the other hand, inaugurated her poetic career with the extraordinarily ambitious series of poems designated as the "Quaternions" because each lengthy work encompasses four global themes: "The Four Elements," "Of the Four Humours," "Of the Four Ages" (of man), "The Four Seasons," "The Four Monarchies." After a turning point that most recent critics attribute to the death of her father and poetic mentor in 1653,[3] Bradstreet's poetry moved increasingly away from such large public themes and toward the more personal and religious subjects as well as idiom that comprise her later and arguably her best poetry. So "complete" a poet was Bradstreet that–be it with a significant pun or from a genuine confusion–in praising her, Makin says, "How excellent a poet Mrs. *Broad*street is (now in America) her works do testify" (White, 284; italics mine).

Bradstreet's biographer, Elizabeth Wade White, states that no British woman had previously dealt with "such hitherto entirely masculine topics as history, war, politics, and the 'natural philosophy' or science" (256). The same could in all likelihood be said of Sor Juana vis-à-vis Hispanic poetry. Such published women's poetry as there was up to the seventeenth century mostly dealt with love, as does so much of Sor Juana's poetic production. Yet here we have two women poets who also established themselves in the then distinctly unfeminine, as it were, arena of more external topics. This is no longer a case of a woman "writing otherwise" but one of a woman invading the Other's poetic space. Anne Bradstreet acutely observes in the Apology at the end of her historical survey "The Four Monarchies," "This task befits not women like to men" (172); she glosses the comment on a more personal level in the "Prologue" to *The Tenth Muse*, saying: "To sing of wars, of captains, and of kings, / Of cities founded, commonwealths begun, / For my mean pen are too superior things" (15). Truly, then, the "completeness" of the two poets is a fraught similarity, paradoxically both an incursion into a menacing domain and an important reason for their having been celebrated as prodigious and elevated to the status of Tenth Muse. Personally, I also find it a fraught issue with regard to self-representation, for it raises the following questions in my mind: How does the Complete (early modern woman) Poet, mistress of the external, write her self? With equal temerity? With equal depth and breadth, with an equally encyclopedic scope? And if not, within what parameters and according to what norms?

As the present chapter responds to the preceding questions we will find ourselves, perhaps not unexpectedly in view of Bradstreet's "Prologue" and what we already know of Sor Juana, dealing with some of the darkest aspects of the self and of self-representation: with confessions of sins and flaws, with melancholy, and particularly with a broad range of acts of self-abnegation. In sum, with the signs, or more appropriate to the context, the stigmata, of violently waged *auto-machias* or self–civil wars. Disheartening as it may be to delve into this, the Complete Poet's heart of darkness, we will find it a fertile territory, one that despite its almost uniformly negative cast proves to be far from unidimensional. Hence, rather than discounting it or explaining it away (for example, by teasing out subtexts of self-affirmation, layers of irony), I will mine this terrain largely on its own terms with the aim of unlocking its dimensionality. For, as the ensuing pages will strive to demonstrate, the *under*mining and undoing of the self that results from a searing auto-machia can be seen to constitute an *over*determined site. Its supremely contradictory bounds contain both the intricate dynamics of the "languages" that seventeenth-century—particularly religious—culture afforded writers engaged in self-representation and the double bind in which Bradstreet and Sor Juana found themselves as early modern women writers. As Cheryl Walker has stated with reference to early North American women poets: "One need not believe that these poems reflect in uncomplicated ways the 'true' feelings of their authors to assert that their existence helps us imagine more fully the nature and dimensions of women's experience in American culture" (xii).

Mindful of another of Walker's keen statements, her suggestion that scholars form a picture of women's self-representation and "the laws governing its intelligibility" (xii), I shall proceed to examine in Sor Juana and Anne Bradstreet three large areas: issues of selfhood versus self-erasing subjectivity as emerging from spiritual autobiography; humility topics as expressions of anxiety of authorship; and instability in the representation of self and gender. Throughout, as stated above, I will be attempting to elucidate the inception of women's self-representation in the two continents of the New World.

◦◦✥◦◦

II.

. . . not to set forth myself, but the glory of God.
–ANNE BRADSTREET
"To My Dear Children"

As literate and invested members of the Catholic and Puritan worlds, Sor Juana and Anne Bradstreet availed themselves of their communities' paradigm for self-examination, the spiritual autobiography. Their options for self-representation were more limited than one might expect. Although it is a commonplace that secular autobiography began to emerge in the Renaissance, humanist autobiography prevailed neither in their predominantly religious worlds nor in their respective countries. Broadly speaking, secular autobiography had not yet evolved in England or in Spain beyond the objective external model of the res gestae, chroniclelike representations of the self limited to the events that configured it and embodied in political, military, and travel memoirs. Spiritual autobiography remained the major forum for introspection in both cultures. Paul Delany writes with regard to England that "it was in religious rather than secular autobiography . . . that the greater progress away from the objectivity of the res gestae took place" (172), and Margarita Levisi says of Spain that "except in the case of religious reflection, to speak of one's own inner world would have been considered almost lewd, and certainly impertinent" (1988, 114). Particularly for women writers, and for women writers in religiously oriented communities, spiritual autobiography entailed the only culturally viable form of self-representation in prose (see Myers, 468; Weber, 20). Hence Sor Juana wrote the "Respuesta a Sor Filotea de la Cruz" (1691), appropriating to her pressing purposes the structure and topoi of the nun's *Vida* or Life. Of Bradstreet we possess not only the diary entries in prose and poetry that comprise the preliminaries to a Puritan spiritual autobiography, but more significant, "To My Dear Children" (ca. 1656, cf. Stanford 1974, 126), a missive to her progeny whose few pages contain most of the essential elements of that genre in a more fully realized form.

These two documents, the spiritual autobiographies of poets, are essential to our investigations here on various levels. Obviously they reveal, within the constraints of the conventions I will be describing, the struggles and vicissitudes of their authors' lives and thus provide windows onto their personal worlds. Of equal importance, I will argue that they contain the keys to the writers' self-representations *in general* as patterns deriving from the spiritual autobiography reverberate between their prose and their poetry. In view of the limited lexicon for self-description at their disposal such errancy was to a degree inevitable. Therefore, certain codified aspects of the spiritual autobiography—formulaic epithets, religious terminology, structural patterns—can easily be identified in the poems of self-scrutiny. Yet at the core of the genres of spiritual autobiography in which Bradstreet and Sor Juana inscribe their prose and poetry lies another less readily apparent auto-machia as essential to their autobiographical texts as the struggles with sin that the authors purport to describe in their confessional documents. And that is the battle of representation between self-assertion and self-erasure intrinsic to both Puritan and Catholic spiritual autobiography, the matter of constructing a subject position from the very building blocks that deny such a thing. Sor Juana—baroque, literarily self-conscious, ingenious, beleaguered—imitates, manipulates, and plays with this conundrum to great effect and gain. The Puritans, and the Puritan Anne Bradstreet, characteristically utilize it in great earnest. I begin, therefore, with them and with her as the most direct means of introducing the dynamics of spiritual autobiography at large.

However lacking Puritan writing may be in imaginative qualities, it can and often has been credited with launching the intensely individualistic and introspective cast of New England or North American writing. The Puritan poetics of self-exploration derives (as does the Catholic version) from the ur-text of Saint Augustine's *Confessions* but heightens the stakes of self-revelation immeasurably. Perry Miller eloquently summarizes the Augustinian strain of Puritan piety, remarking that "the same subjective insight, the same turning of consciousness back upon itself, the same obsession with individuality . . . these qualities which appear in Augustine almost for the first time in Western thought and give him his amazing 'modernity,' reappear in force among the early Puritans. Like his, their meditations are intensely introspective" (22). Saint Augustine was the quintessential quester, for knowledge of an abstract and of a personal nature. No mere technician of grace but magnificently human, Saint Augustine recounts his struggles toward conversion and his quest to purge himself of carnal longings in a manner that the twentieth century could well describe as "authentically" introspective. Indeed, it would not be inappropriately anachronistic to bring the existential notion of authenticity to bear on Puritan self-scrutiny. Whereas Saint Augustine writes from the relatively confident stance of one who has already received divine illumination, their Calvinism consigned the Puritans to what Perry Miller has called "the wheel of doubt" (53). Not knowing whether they had been "elected" (predetermined) for salvation, the Puritans searched their souls for some assurance of grace. Having received what they believed was the call, the Puritans felt that even the state of "regeneration" could be ephemeral or perhaps counterfeit. This fact impelled the Puritans to further self-doubt, moral accountings, and self-scrutiny as they strove to forestall any possible deception. In such an intensified climate of soul-searching the slackening of self-vigilance could mean the loss of salvation. The introspection that began in Saint

Augustine as a personal and moral imperative, for the Puritans became imperative to their immortality.[4]

The Puritans performed their scrupulous self-analyses in the diaries and autobiographies devoted not primarily to the events of their lives or res gestae, but to the minute and exhaustive tracing of their spiritual quests. As is proper to confessional writing and appropriate to the search for salvation, their personal texts essentially limited the representation of the self to the most punishing aspects of interiority, that is, to emotional duress and the recounting of sins and shortcomings. Although largely one-sided, these parameters nevertheless allowed for an unusual amplitude of self-expression. Religious confession in general, it almost goes without saying, knows few bounds and little decorum (if much ritual). Anything can and must be confessed since God knows all. Indeed, for confession to be effective, the individual must strive to display a knowledge of self approximating that possessed by God, whom Saint Augustine called the "physician of my most intimate self" (180).

Puritan autobiography in particular prescribed a most extraordinary latitude in the discourse of confession. One of the most notable and oft-noted aspects of Puritan personal writings is the allowance it made for the venting of doubts, not only of one's worthiness but also—in acts of seeming dissidence—of religion itself as it affected the individual.[5] Daniel Shea observes in his *Spiritual Autobiography in Early America* that "God's mercy to sinners, and the ultimate wisdom of Providence, would never be subject to persistent doubt; but whether these were truths for other men or for oneself might be an open question" (249). Shea's subdued statement masks the often anguished expression of doubt and questionings of God's mercy and righteousness found in Puritan writings. The Puritans wrote in heartfelt terms of their souls-in-the-making; as Shea also notes, they were pilgrims and seekers within their own narratives (249). Moreover, the Puritans were in effect obliged to remain strapped to their "wheel of doubt" and to record its effects in their writings. As I stated above, a categorical posture of doubt combated the ephemerality and deceptiveness of regeneration. "The faithfull," wrote Arthur Hildersam in 1629, "have not this assurance so perfect, but they are oft troubled with doubts and fears. . . . But they that have this false assurance are most confident and never have any doubts"; Ezekiel Culverwell proclaimed "an unfeigned griefe for the want of faith" to be a sign of faith (Morgan 1963, 70). The Puritan belief system and its accompanying discourse, we see, exercised an intricately contrived hegemony. Omnivorous, the system sanctioned, absorbed, and even prescribed its antithesis, with the result that its discourse accommodated its own counterdiscourse and thus allowed for the assertion of a questing and iconoclastic self.

We arrive now at an issue of signal importance to both Puritan and Catholic spiritual autobiography: the other auto-machia, what I will call the process of selfhood nihilating into subjectivity.[6] Stephen Greenblatt lays out the general terrain in which this process is located: "It has been traditional, since Jacob Burckhardt, to trace the origins of autonomous individuality to the

Renaissance, but the material under consideration here [transvestism in seventeenth-century British theater] suggests that individual identity in the early modern period served less as a final goal than as a way station on the road to a *firm and decisive identification with normative structures*" (75–76; italics mine)– that is, to *subjectivity*. More specifically for our concerns, Sacvan Bercovitch in his *Puritan Origins of the American Self* (1975) and Ivy Schweitzer in her *Work of Self-Representation: Lyric Poetry in Colonial New England* (1991) have mapped the dynamics of selfhood nihilating into subjectivity with regard to the Puritans (I will discuss the specifically Catholic aspects later), beginning with its fundamental contradiction. Schweitzer writes that the "whole process of Puritan conversion affirmed the existence of a new kind of interiority, of a private, unique, inner space . . . only to demand its sacrifice, renunciation, and occupation by Another" (22). And Bercovitch, discussing spiritual autobiography and other personal writings, astutely notes that we "have been told that the Puritans' personal literature is a major 'manifestation of a growing self-consciousness,' that every one of them 'had to speak honestly of his own experience.'" Yet "their writings yield a different conclusion: there, self-examination serves not to liberate but to constrict; selfhood appears as a state to be overcome, obliterated; and identity is asserted through an act of submission to a transcendent absolute" (13, quoting Owen C. Watkins, *The Puritan Experience: Studies in Spiritual Autobiography* [New York: n.p., 1972], 40, 164).

Bercovitch and Schweitzer's theses cap an argument that, again, resonates from Saint Augustine to the Puritans. Saint Augustine repeated several times in the *Confessions* that all virtues issue from God, all evil from the individual. For example, addressing God, he wrote, "My good points are instilled by you and are your gifts. My bad points are my faults and your judgments on them" (181). The Calvinist conception of the inherent depravity of humankind after the Fall exacerbated such beliefs and rendered the self a site to be cleansed so that it might be entirely inhabited by God. Simply put, the self must be purged of self. As Richard Baxter wrote in a treatise called *The Benefits of Self-Acquaintance*, "Self-denial and the love of God are all [one]. . . . The very names of Self and Own, should sound in the watchful Christian's ears as very terrible, wakening words, that are next to the name of sin and satan" (Bercovitch, 17). The Puritans engaged in "powerful counter-subjectivist moves" (Bercovitch quoted in Schweitzer, 6) to incite a loathing of the self that would compel self-effacement, that is, the delivery of the self unto God. They railed against the self–"the great snare," "the false Christ," the "figure or type of Hell"–and demanded that the Puritans seek their identity in God. "Not what the Selfe will, but what the Lord will," urged Puritan Thomas Hooker (Bercovitch, 18). Their goal was to replace the "old man in Adam" with the "new man in Christ" and thus to move from a fallen to a *redeemed subjectivity*" (Schweitzer 7; italics mine). Having annihilated their selfhood into a redeemed subjectivity, when Puritans looked in the mirror or mirrored themselves in a text they should see, not (as did the humanists) the self, but the Christic image (cf. Bercovitch, 14).[7]

The Puritans codified the battle between selfhood and subjectivity through the construct of "humiliation." The fourth step of the morphology of conversion, humiliation comprised the final phase available to all rather than only to the elect. As such it had a broad appeal and played an important part in the Puritan splinter movement termed Preparationism. Preparationism, for its part, maintained that by preparing the heart through introspection, the individual could work in covenant with God to merit salvation (see Pettit, especially chap. 1). Running counter to Reformed theology's denial of the individual's ability to affect his or her fate, Preparationism brings humiliation in line with the more mainstream Christian notion of humility so crucial to Catholic spiritual autobiographies and to Sor Juana's "Respuesta." Like humility, Puritan humiliation entails the individual submitting entirely to God, divorcing himself or herself from vanity and pride (Pettit, 18). William Perkins, outlining in Cambridge the ten steps of the Puritan morphology of conversion, defined humiliation more particularly as the phase in which "the individual perceived his helpless and hopeless condition and despaired of salvation" (Morgan 1963, 68). And leading American Preparationist Thomas Hooker further characterized humiliation as a loosening of the man from himself that made him see "an utter insufficiency in what he hath or doth" and an "emptying" of the soul from "whatsoever it hath that makes it swell" (Pettit, 96–97). Puritan countersubjectivism thus articulated its principal goal in humiliation as, broken, submissive, and perhaps despairing, the individual will succumbs to God.

The convolutions of Puritan spiritual autobiography that we have followed in the preceding discussion–its introspective nature, its circumspection of the self, its amplitude within those circumscribed parameters, its countersubjectivism–all find their definition in two brief phrases by George Goodwin, author of "Auto-Machia": "I cannot live, with nor without my Selfe," "Unto myself my Selfe my Selfe betray" (Bercovitch, 19). Goodwin's lines convey as well precisely the dynamic that imbues Anne Bradstreet's conventionally "humble" letter to her children with special textual interest. As it sets forth the self "for the glory of God," Bradstreet's letter "To My Dear Children" registers the acts and effects of humiliation on her person; at the same time it dramatizes the consequences for textual representation of the self nihilating into subjectivity.

Saint Augustine and Saint Teresa of Avila alike comb their early years for sins, foregrounding their own wickedness by magnifying peccadilloes such as Saint Augustine's theft of the pears into signs of the autobiographers' innate evil. In the properly autobiographical section of her letter (up to "Many times hath Satan troubled me," 243), on the other hand, Bradstreet makes surprisingly little reference to her wickedness and sins. Of sin in her early years, she says, "I avoided it" (240). Instead, she foregrounds God's attempts to break her self–to deliver her "I" unto humiliation–and the emotions they provoked.[8] Her autobiography of the undoing of the self chronicles the unrelenting afflictions that God has visited upon her: smallpox, the trials of arriving in a New World (captured in her famous line, "I found a new world and new manners, at which my heart rose," 241), lameness, barrenness followed by the "great pains" of giving birth to eight children, their illnesses, and the family's "losses in estate." She interprets the afflictions as corrections and as acts of humiliation: "After some time I fell into a lingering sickness like a consumption together with a lameness, which *correction* I saw the Lord sent to *humble* and try me and do me good, and it was not altogether ineffectual" (241; italics mine). Effectual or ineffectual as the corrections might have been, they occasioned the considerable anguish of an auto-machia that Bradstreet does not fail to voice in her text. The emotional spectrum of the early pages of the text includes pains, weaknesses, cares, fears, doubts, and afflictions, punctuated only intermittently by moments of thankfulness for prayers answered and moments of "refreshment after affliction" that but led to "more circumspection" (242). In the final portion of the autobiographical section devoted to her "humiliation" by God, Bradstreet admits, "yet have I many times sinkings and droopings" (243). The conventionalized Puritan language she employs here prompts us to ponder the manner in which seventeenth-century religion subsumed and its religious vocabulary encoded the true workings of psychology—a subject shunned by the Puritans (cf. Miller, chap. 10, "The Nature of Man"). One can only guess at the depths of the psychological and emotional struggles wrought by "humiliation" that Bradstreet compacts into her formulaic expressions.

Truly and literally has Bradstreet been at pains in her life to transform affliction into what she calls "the times of my greatest getting and advantage" (242). As the pilgrim-writer strives to effect a parallel alchemy in the letter, we will see, her writing displays a notable slippage. The first three pages of the letter treat aspects of humiliation imposed on her by God through affliction. Then Bradstreet turns inward to focus on herself and her meditations in pages marked by locutions of introspection (make conscience, understanding, communed, thought, troubled, argued with myself, and so on). The word *perplexed* (243) signals the transition into this more personal vein. Bradstreet begins with the perplexities that have induced the personal despair that is part and parcel of humiliation. In the most moving section of the letter, she confesses that "I have not found that constant joy in my pilgrimage and refreshing which I suppose most of the servants of God have" (243). Though she has "sometimes tasted of that hidden manna that the world knows not," she has also experienced the many "sinkings and droopings" to which I referred above as well as a dearth of "felicity" (243). Bradstreet recounts how she has beseeched God to "lift the light of His countenance" upon her at those dire moments when she found herself "in darkness" and saw "no light" (243). Having opened the floodgates to her perplexities on an emotional level, Bradstreet's narrative spins off into an account of her grave theological misgivings. I say "spins off" because, as we will note more fully in her poem to Sir Philip Sidney, Bradstreet's pen can in effect escape her control when she has a deeply personal story to tell. Here the wrenching story is that of her doubts whether God exists, whether such a God as exists is the God she and hers worship or the God worshiped by the Catholics, and finally, whether there is faith on earth. She expresses her concerns through a spiraling series of questions in which each "trouble" or "block," after reaching a certain resolution, generates another. For example: "When I have got over this block, then have I another put in my way, that admit this be the true God whom we worship and that be his word, yet why may not the Popish religion be the right?" (244). The exposition of her doubts occupies a disproportionate amount of space in the letter, more than a third of it.

Critics have characterized Bradstreet's agitated spiritual autobiography as more "drooping" than those of her male contemporaries. Wendy Martin asserts that the "diaries of her male counterparts reveal a certainty of God's love that Bradstreet did not experience" (54; see also Shea, 116–18). It is not only the substantial space devoted to her doubts and pained cast of the letter that warrant such a conclusion, but also the near absence in Bradstreet's text of the driving force of spiritual autobiography: a description of regeneration, of the receiving of grace.[9] Most Puritan autobiographies follow their author's progress from illumination to repentance and then to conversion (see Edkins, 42–43). While admittedly a cross between a letter and a spiritual autobiography, Bradstreet's narrative displays no such trajectory. Moreover, when she does address her elect status, Bradstreet does so with enigmatic reticence. It is, significantly enough, in the context of her passage on humiliation's despair discussed above that the author cautiously alludes to her regeneration, in a language burdened with qualifications and equivocations: "I have often been perplexed that I have not found that constant joy in my pilgrimage and refreshing which I supposed most of the servants of God have, although He hath not left me altogether without the witness of His holy spirit, who hath often given me His word and set to His seal that it shall be well with me" (243). She goes on to confirm that she has "sometimes tasted of that hidden manna that the world knows not" (243) but then fails to elaborate on exactly what that taste entailed, relating instead her times of darkness. Is this a "feminine" reticence such as Bradstreet is wont to exhibit? A reluctance to assert what others would proclaim? The copious expressions of personal doubt that directly succeed it, the imbalance between what is left almost unsaid and what is said abundantly, suggest not. In the case of Bradstreet's letter, they effectively displace the core of spiritual autobiography onto the questioning space of a woman who "never saw any miracles" (243).

I am reminded here for more than one reason of Jorge Luis Borges's marvelous lines at the end of his essay, "A New Refutation of Time." "*And yet, and yet,*" he says in the coda to a long refutation of time, space, and individual selfhood, "[t]he world, unfortunately, is real; I, unfortunately, am Borges" (64; italics in original). Anne Bradstreet, being who *she* was and writing in her world, necessarily returns from her questionings to the reality of the doctrine she perforce knew was true. Thus, after the series of transitional but not inconsequential resolutions of her doubts that serve as the shifters in her theological argument,[10] Bradstreet veers definitively at the end of the letter from the misgivings of faith to its reaffirmation, from doubts to certainties: "I *know* all the Powers of Hell shall never prevail against it [faith]. I *know* whom I have trusted, and whom I have believed" (245; italics mine). In a predictable about-face, her personal voice cedes to the doctrinaire praise of God (and to an injunction to herself to praise him?) with which she ends the letter: "Now to the King, immortal, eternal and invisible, the only wise God, *be honour*, and glory for ever and ever, Amen" (245; italics mine). Where Borges in his essay moves from the negation to the grudging affirmation of selfhood, here Bradstreet and her text take the necessary steps to move from selfhood into subjectivity—that is, to use Borges's words, to move into (her form of) "the nothingness of personality."[11] With regard to textual representation, she abdicates her richly voiced subject position on the levels of both language and substance. In so doing, Bradstreet in effect joins forces with God to "correct" herself, to purge herself of selfhood.

And yet, and yet, I must say again, together with the numerous critics who have commented on the shifting subject positions of the letter, Bradstreet's voice and self have hardly been subsumed in the archetype.[12] The letter has succeeded in conveying with dimensionality both the fallings of her soul and the risings of her heart; as the pilgrim progresses in her writings toward subjection, the conventions of Puritan spiritual autobiography have enabled a thickness of self-representation that far transcends formulaic mea culpas. Though the debate—of such interest to certain feminist critics—will undoubtedly continue, in light of the Puritan poetics of spiritual autobiography the question of whether Bradstreet should be considered dogmatist or rebel can, I believe, best be understood inclusively rather than exclusively. Ann Stanford concludes, "Rebellion and a struggle for or against conviction form a pattern which runs through her [Anne Bradstreet's] writing. It is the statement of dogma and the concurrent feeling of resistance to dogma that give much of the writing the vitality we are still conscious of today" (1983, 77).

As Stanford aptly notes, the counterpoint of dogma and resistance constitutes a strain, in both senses of the word, present in much of Bradstreet's work after the first edition of *The Tenth Muse*. From the poet's renowned "Contemplations," a symphonic orchestration of the temptations of the worldly versus the otherworldly, to her personal notebooks and occasional poetry, with their exhortations to God and alternating expressions of despair and gratitude, this pattern can be seen as a matrix of Bradstreet's later work.[13] Since Stanford has amply treated the theme in her book *Anne Bradstreet: The Worldly Puritan* (1974), and since, in any case, it is far too vast a subject for me to treat in depth, I have narrowed my arena for analysis of her verse in the terms of this section to a set of three deeply personal poems that I consider to exemplify the manner in which Bradstreet translates the Puritan poetics of spiritual autobiography into actual poetry: the elegies to her grandchildren, Elizabeth, Anne, and Simon.

The early deaths of her grandchildren, none of whom lived to see their second year, incite in the poet a tremendous anguish that, in the poems,

shapes itself into an anguished self–civil war between emotion and belief, outrage and resignation. The battle, not unexpectedly, evolves into one of selfhood versus subjectivity as Bradstreet unleashes her personal affect only to
negate and dissolve it into the impersonal statements of doctrine that provide
closure, if not for her emotions, at least to each of the three poems. Dating
from August 1665 (Elizabeth), June 1669 (Anne), and November 1669
(Simon), the elegies form a series of interlocking poems that itself evinces a
progression from the assertion to the effacement of self. Where the first elegy
exposes the imperfectly resolved doubts of the "I" as to the rightness of the
child's death, and the second inward musings of a self-accusatory nature, the
third elegy–which was Bradstreet's penultimate poem–shades into a resigned
and impersonal voice. Their conclusions may be foregone and doctrinaire, but
the elegies are absorbing as poems of process in which we witness the self
deploying several strategies in order to cajole itself into subjectivity.

The title of a poem by Emily Dickinson, "After great pain, a formal feeling
comes," captures the drift of Bradstreet's elegy sequence.[14] If the last poem of
the series embodies the formal feeling, the first labors to stanch great pain.
Her elegy to Elizabeth Bradstreet (Hensley ed., 235) commences with the
apostrophe and farewell and apotheosis in which the third elegy ends ("Go
pretty babe, go rest with sisters twain; / Among the blest in endless joys
remain" [237]). Yet in the elegy to Elizabeth the first two farewells are immediately brought into a personal zone: "Farewell dear babe, my heart's too
much content, / Farewell sweet babe, the pleasure of mine eye." A third more
moralistic farewell follows, noting that the child had merely been lent to the
world by an unspecified force that Bradstreet does *not*, maybe significantly,
explicitly identify with God at this point ("Farewell fair flower that for a space
was lent, / Then ta'en away unto eternity"). The weight of emotion returns
the poetic speaker to her "I" in the tercet that concludes the first stanza, and
it prompts her to reach out to doctrine for comfort: "Blest babe, why should
I once bewail thy fate, / Or sigh thy day so soon were terminate, / Sith thou
art settled in an everlasting state." Why indeed? The statement can be construed as a question, and as a question expressing doubts that go unanswered.

For the poem essentially begins again in the second stanza (demarcated,
unusually, with a "2"). The "I" and its markers (my, mine) disappear as the poet
weaves an extended comparison between nature and God. Bradstreet's imag-
istic repertoire tends to the earthy and sensual. Here, in what one can hardly
help interpreting as an invidious comparison, she contrasts the just cycle of
nature and time that allows its produce to ripen to maturity before dying with
the metaphorical "plants new" and "buds new blown" unnaturally eradicated
by God's hand. Be it through the emotional catharsis the comparison brings
or be it–conversely–due to the distancing from the "I" and her personal emotions it effects, the recourse to metaphor leads the speaker immediately to end
her poem with an acknowledgment if not a celebration of God's power: "His
hand alone that guides nature and fate." The final tercets of the poem that convey this statement, together with the rhyme scheme in-*ate* that they share

with those of the first stanza, link the two halves of the disjunctive poem and structurally equate their respective invocations of doctrine. Yet the two invocations would not appear to entail a question and its subsequent answer or resolution. Rather, they parallel each other; they are both the inchoate gestures toward doctrine of an insufficiently humbled subject. As Randall Mawer comments in his article on the first elegy, the poem's "deepest theme is the speaker's failure to achieve the religious resignation she purports to describe" (211).[15]

The second elegy is the most inward-looking poem of the series and one of the most exclusively and explicitly introspective of all of Bradstreet's poems. The auto-machia it contains responds again to Bradstreet's bereavement but also (at least in effect) to the first elegy to such a degree that the second elegy appears to have ensued as much from the first as from the death of another grandchild. Structurally, the elegy to Anne follows the same pattern as the first elegy and the letter–the familiar pattern of emotions and doubts and ceding to reason and ultimately to the mouthing of doctrine. Thematically, it enters into an integral dialogue with the posture of the speaker that underlies the first poem. She is a speaker, Mawer speculates, who may be disenchanted with God for having "eradicated" her grandchild or with herself for having failed entirely to relinquish her "heart's too much content" (Mawer, 211) and who now, I add, strives to check the spleen vented in the first poem. Indeed, what I have just presented as a dialogue with the elegy to Elizabeth gives rise to soliloquy in the elegy to Anne, a poem that is *not* about the child but emphatically about the poetic speaker. The personal focus of the poem is immediately evident in the "I's," "my's," and "me" that (rather than apostrophe) dominate the opening five lines. Bradstreet devotes the first movement of the poem to the "sorrows," "disappointments," and "hopes" of the poetic subject. Instead of God's guiding hand, as at the end of the first elegy, her own "troubled heart and trembling hand" as she writes occupy center stage here and throughout this self-scrutinizing poem that details the process of resolution to which we now turn.

Looking backward and inward, the poetic subject attempts to accomplish *for* herself the humiliation *of* herself that, it would seem, her afflictions have not. Audibly reviewing the past, she works her way through the lessons that previous experience should have taught her about the value of worldly ties and chastises herself for not having become more "wise." Her lines put us in mind of another *prise de conscience*, the point in Bradstreet's "Upon the Burning of Our House" when, after lamenting the loss of her home and all her worldly goods including her writings, the speaker says, "Then straight I 'gin my heart to chide" (293). The chidings take an interesting twist in the second elegy. Reproving herself for what she knew from reason but could not assimilate into feeling, the speaker launches into a sequence of similes, the only images in the poem: she "knew" that the child was but a "withering flower," "a bubble," "brittle glass," "a shadow." Similar to the first elegy and for reasons equally impossible to pinpoint, recourse to poetic imagery provides the buffer or distancing in the poem that permits a change in subject position. Feeling finally allies with reason as the speaker mockingly calls herself a "fool" and, after this last self-accusation, bids farewell to the child with a "cheered" if still "throbbing" heart.

Kenneth R. Ball demonstrates that the third elegy, "On My Dear Grandchild Simon Bradstreet, Who Died on 16 November, 1669, Being But a Month, and One Day Old" (237), is inscribed in the patterns of the morphology of conversion, with humiliation standing at its center. The poem begins with a description of the infant's death (once again compared to that of a flower), then addresses the indisputability of God's will and need for humility, and ends, as I have said, with images of anticipated paradise (Ball, 29–30). Though the direct invocation of humility comes in the seventh of the brief poem's twelve lines–"With humble hearts and mouths put in the dust"–the entire poem can be said to have been written from a humbled stance. The "I" of the poetic speaker, which figured prominently in the first two elegies, has indeed rendered itself unto the dust and practically withdrawn, wrapping itself into the first-person plural (e.g., "caused us weep," "our losses," "let's say"). Bracketed between two doctrinaire statements that unequivocally affirm resignation to God's will ("the last i' th' bud, / Cropt by th' Almighty's hand; yet He is good"; "He will return and make up all our losses"), the speaker inserts a spate of exhortations to an unspecified addressee that simultaneously articulate and squelch any remaining doubts. Bradstreet writes, "With dreadful awe before Him let's be *mute*, / Such was His will, but why, let's not dispute, / with humble hearts and mouths put in the dust, / Let's *say* He's merciful as well as just" (italics mine). These exhortations, I maintain, also articulate the terminus of the process we have witnessed in the other two poems. Almost metapoetically her exhortations contain the essence of what the self must do, and has done, over the course of the elegies in order to attain the hard-won posture of subjectivity into which the "I" has finally erased itself here. Only by a "muting" and an injunctive "saying" can the subject attain the humbled position well expressed in the first lines of the poem that chronologically precedes the elegy to Simon in Bradstreet's production: "As weary pilgrim, now at rest."

By means of the processes of self-scrutiny and saying, the speaker has transformed a "troubled" into a "cheered" heart and undone herself "for the glory of God" (Elegy to Anne). Indeed, as I have suggested, something would seem to inhere in the resources of lyric itself–the metaphors and similes, commonplace as they may be, which Bradstreet employs–that facilitates the conversion. The literary skill that Bradstreet denies herself in the prose letter ("I have not studied in this you read to show my skill, but to declare the truth" [240]), but allows herself in the elegies, is an important enabling aspect that poetry adds to Bradstreet's Puritan poetics of self-exploration, with which it shares so many other features. All told, I believe that the three elegies in their sequential unfolding and each unto itself illustrate with enhanced poignance one of the lines that introduced our discussion of Bradstreet's personal writings: "I cannot live, with nor without my Selfe."

With a *conceptismo* akin to Sor Juana's own, Goodwin's other line captures the very heart of the nun's auto-machia: "Unto myself my Selfe my Selfe betray." It feeds into a phrase that Sor Juana repeats in several contexts—"de mí misma soy verdugo" [I am my own executioner]—a phrase that encapsulates both her embattled interiority per se and the evolving strategies of her self-representations. To do justice to the extraordinary complexity of the issue, I will examine several of Sor Juana's purportedly autobiographical works, at times in considerable detail. I begin with the conjunctions and disjunctions between the so-called "Autodefensa espiritual" and Leonor/Sor Juana's auto-biographical speech in *Los empeños de una casa* that provide the framework for her self-fashioning, proceed to her introspective poems of a secular and religious nature, and end my examination with a related set of conjunctions and disjunctions in the "Respuesta a Sor Filotea de la Cruz." We will see throughout that the errant topics and tactics of the *Vida* provide the glue that binds together Sor Juana's varying self-representations.

Most scholars have accepted as authentic the recently uncovered letter that has been titled the "Autodefensa espiritual" or Spiritual Self-Defense (for reasons that will become clear, I prefer simply to call it her "Autodefensa" or Self-Defense) from Sor Juana to her then confessor, Antonio Núñez de Miranda.[16] Yet even if the work were an elaborate hoax, it would be something of a necessary fiction—necessary as a scholium for the self-assertions and self-negations of Sor Juana's "Respuesta" to which I turn later, necessary in a broader sense to help us understand the problematic situation of women and of the woman writer in the patriarchal context of the early modern Western world. The letter is the only piece of Sor Juana's personal correspondence that we possess, and in it, as I mentioned in chapter 1, Sor Juana responds to Núñez's slander of her person. His attacks, for their part, seem to have been ignited to a considerable degree by the nun's fame (see Scott 1988, 431). Why, beyond the expectable issues of jealousy, was her fame such an inflammatory issue? Renaissance iconography represents fame as a woman. Nevertheless fame, as Ann Rosalind Jones explains and as my chapter 1 suggested, was generally *not* for women in the Renaissance. The word *fame* in English comes from the Greek root *phanei*: "to speak and to be spoken about." Both, Jones argues, were proscribed for early modern women in the Western world. Virtual blanks, women were to remain silent, enclosed in the home, not attracting public attention (see Jones 1986, 74, 93 et passim). In the synchronic system of battling energies circulating in the early modern Hispanic worlds, the expedient Tenth Muse model made limited provision for exceptional women's fame. However, it coexisted in tension and disalignment with traditional patriarchal constructions such as those articulated by Jones, constructions that, in the misogynist climate of the times, maintained their stranglehold on women.

A text by a Spaniard who lived in Spain and England provides ample proof of Jones's assertions. Humanist Juan Luis Vives, in his extremely influential *Instrucción de la mujer cristiana* [Instruction of the Christian Woman], makes it painfully clear that women should keep silent: "I praise silence as most useful to the chaste life [of the maiden], and especially in cases where it is not particularly necessary to speak." The maiden should speak only "when keeping silent does damage to her virtue or speaking assists it" (24). Women may be learned, but they cannot display their knowledge: "And I want her to learn for learning's sake, not to show others what she knows, for it is good for her to keep silent, since then her virtue will speak for her" (28). Vives reiterates the dicta of Saint Paul that "women should keep silence in church, for they are not permitted to speak," and that "if there is anything they desire to know, let them ask their husbands at home" (27). Moreover, Vives's text establishes with regard to women the almost inescapable connection between *fama* and *mala fama*, good and ill repute. In the Spanish word for fame one is never far from the other, but given, as Vives interestingly concedes, that "our [men's] judgment is naturally perverse, and more inclined to believe evil than good" (63–64), any public actions of women are bound to attract negative comment and to jeopardize their honor.

I consider the above evidence crucial to Sor Juana's letter and to her situation at large because it signals the incendiary potential of the crisis that the nun was experiencing at the hands of her confessor and others who would malign her fame, a crisis (I will soon argue) accompanied by a crisis in her self-representation. In the "Autodefensa" we see Sor Juana having reached that dreaded juncture in which *fama*, dangerous enough in itself for a woman, has with Núñez's slander become outright *mala fama*. Deeply aware of the double valence of a woman's fame, Sor Juana asks Núñez why he had to discredit her "publicly before everyone" (Paz, *501*; Tapia Méndez, 23) rather than restricting his reprimands to their proper private sphere ("in secret as mandated by fatherly discretion," *501*, 21).[17] The Sor Juana who, as we saw in chapter 1, literarily and personally capitalized on her fame, appears also to have understood all too well that received notions such as those of Vives can transform any public attention whatsoever, be it slander or praise, into a "martyrdom" (*497*, 17); she is eminently conscious of the fact that for a woman in her context "applause" is converted into "stinging thorns of persecution" (*498*, 17). Such painful persecution, she tells us at length, has infiltrated her life and circumscribed her actions,

> for as all know the facility I have [of writing poetry], if to that were joined the motive of vanity (perhaps it is a motive of mortification), what greater punishment would Y. R. wish for me than that resulting from the very applause that confers such pain? Of what envy am I not the target? Of what malice am I not the object? What actions do I take without fear? What word do I speak without misgiving? (*497*, 17)

As the timbre of the above statement makes clear, together with its reference to her well-known facility for writing verses, Sor Juana may be suffering, but she is far from chastened. In fact, the "Autodefensa," a private document, flaunts that rarest of all emotions in early modern women's writing, *anger*. Anger permeates the letter for, as Sor Juana herself puts it, she has reached the boiling point: "But to Y. R. I cannot fail to say that by now my breast is over-flowing with the complaints that over the course of the years I could have spoken, and that as I take up my pen to state them, responding to one I venerate so highly, it is because I can stand no more" (*501*, 23). Attacking Núñez before she dismisses him as her confessor, Sor Juana here assumes an offensive subject position that is almost unique in her writings. She marshals an arsenal of verbal devices that include sarcasm, irony, caustic accusation through rhetorical questions, and the vocabulary of invective ("vituperation," "hatred," "repugnance," "horror," and so on). Outrage links up with the impeccable logic Sor Juana never abandons to produce such superb frontal attacks as the following:

> Because if in gainsaying an opinion I were to speak passionately against Y. R. as Y. R. speaks against me, innumerable times your words have been exceedingly repugnant to me . . . ; I do not for that reason, however, condemn them but, rather, I venerate them for being yours and defend them as my own; and even turn them against myself, calling them kind devotion, extreme affection, and other titles that my love and reverence know how to invent when I speak with others. (*501*, 23)

Eroded by sarcasm, the language of loving fealty to her confessor here and elsewhere in the letter reveals itself as mere rhetoric, a ballast against his hatred.

In the even more ironic "Respuesta" Sor Juana refers more than once to her candor (e.g., "the truth and clarity natural and habitual with me" [*208*, 4.443]). In the nakedly emotional context of the "Autodefensa" we are more inclined to accept her statement at face value when she refers to the "simplicity of heart that does not allow me to say things except as I feel them" (*502*, 25). One is similarly inclined to believe two of the most modern-sounding of all of Sor Juana's self-descriptive statements: "nor do I have so servile a nature that I do under threat what reason does not persuade me" (*501*, 21) and "I am not as humbled as other daughters in whom your doctrine was better employed" (*501*, 23). Writing *to* a man (as distinct from the Sor Filotea of the "Respuesta," a man masquerading as a woman), for once Sor Juana writes with anger *like* what the seventeenth century would call a "man" and represents herself almost *as* a "man." This is no servile woman or nun; this is the opposite of humility, be it religious or secular. Though the letter has been taken as a blueprint of the "Respuesta" that draws its model from the spiritual autobiography, we can see that it was not entirely appropriate for its discoverer, Aureliano Tapia Méndez, to have entitled the text a "Spiritual Self-Defense."

Tapia Méndez and Paz, I repeat, have situated the writing of the "Autodefensa" around 1681–82; Sor Juana's comedia, *Los empeños de una casa*

[The Trials of a Household], was first performed in October of 1683, and written at an earlier date that has not been ascertained. Though no one to my knowledge has yet made the connection, I believe that the "Autodefensa" and *Los empeños de una casa* should be placed together, for thematic as well as chronological reasons. They address the same situation in different arenas and as self-representations ultimately explain each other. Where the "Autodefensa" shows us Sor Juana's crisis of fame and her private response geared to a single individual, the speech saturated with details from her own life that Sor Juana places in the mouth of her protagonist Leonor dramatizes and performs the crisis of fame in a public forum. *Los empeños de una casa* was first performed at a reception in honor of the Marquis and Marquise de la Laguna that coincided with the arrival of the new archbishop, Francisco Aguiar y Seijas, to Mexico City. The speech of the idealized heroine Leonor can thus be seen as a personal statement by Sor Juana in a political context, one that counters public slander with a public self-defense. In it Sor Juana not only replays her crisis, but also recasts her story and, conceivably in response to the crisis, refashions her own image.[18]

As mentioned in chapter 1, Sor Juana avails herself of Leonor's speech to *melo*dramatize her own story. She creates a "readable" version of her life fit for mass consumption. To the facts that we know derive from her life–she was beautiful, intelligent, prodigious, the object of fame–Sor Juana adds a fictionalized noble birth and the love affair with a "perfect" man that has prompted much speculation on the part of her biographers. Yet at the same time and in practically the same breath as she constructs her legend for the public, she deconstructs it. Sor Juana undermines her established public image by showing through Leonor the deleterious effects that natural gifts and fame have produced. What might strike an audience familiar with Sor Juana's reputation as her good fortune or *dicha*, she systematically reveals to have been misfortunes or "desdichas" (4. 36). To wit: the good fortune of Leonor's noble birth has been tempered by an innate sadness, her celebrated beauty by an inability to love, her prodigiousness by the "burning sleeplessness" and "anxious concerns" the acquisition of knowledge has cost her. The "fama parlera" [garrulous fame] to which Leonor devotes several stanzas has only distorted the reality of her person ("La pasión se puso anteojos / de tan engañosos grados, / que a mis moderadas prendas / agrandaban los tamaños," Passion put on such distorting spectacles that they exaggerated the size of my mediocre gifts [38]) and parlayed her into a false "idol" (38). Falling prey to Leonor's public image, her own parents relaxed their vigilance and allowed her to fall in love with Carlos–a love that, in typically Sor Juanian terms, has only occasioned "unease and concern," "tragedies," and "injuries" (41). In sum, nobility, beauty, intelligence, and fame have landed Leonor in the sorry position she describes with unbridled pathos at the end of her speech as "sin crédito, sin honor, / sin consuelo, sin descanso, / sin aliento, sin alivio" (43) [without credit, without honor, without consolation, without respite, without breath, without relief].

Sor Juana has pressed the resources of drama into the service of autobiography and self-defense in order to inspire the audience's sympathy and to mitigate her potentially inflammatory public image. She furthers this *captatio benevolentiae* by having Leonor speak like a "woman." Befitting the angel heroine Leonor incarnates, she now regrets her transgressions and invites her audience in the play to share her woes (36). As do the real women of accomplishment whose autobiographies Patricia Meyer Spacks describes in "Selves in Hiding," Leonor exposes the dark personal underside of an outwardly successful life. In so doing, the angel figure underscores the painful emotional consequences of the "martyrdom" deriving from fame to which Sor Juana alludes in the "Autodefensa." The resemblance between the two works and their female subjects, however, ends there. In what effectively constitutes a striking abjuration of the nonservile persona of the "Autodefensa," Leonor refers to her "reserve" and to the "modesty" with which she defended herself against fame's praises (39). The angry persona of the "Autodefensa" gives way to a female character who is so conventionally modest that she recoils from discussing the reasons for her fame and who, in an insightful pronouncement, perfectly articulates the double bind of humility: "si digo que fui / celebrada por milagro de discreción, me desmiente / la necedad del contarlo; / y si lo callo, no informo de mí" (37) [if I say that I was praised as a miracle of discretion, the foolishness of saying so disproves my words; and if I remain silent, I tell you nothing about myself].

If, as its autobiographical details prompt, we view Leonor's speech as an act of self-representation by Sor Juana, then the gap between it and the "Autodefensa" involves more than mere autobiographical indirection warranted by adherence to comedia conventions. Clearly, the crisis of fame and slander (which, we know, neither originated nor ceased with Núñez's comments) has entailed for the nun-writer what can be understood as a crisis in self-fashioning. On the largest scale, the crisis devolves into the competing literary self-images that span her works. Caught in a maelstrom of emerging and residual elements, Sor Juana writes herself into the two readable (albeit contradictory) scripts of humble woman and flaming Tenth Muse. She slides from one fiction of self-representation to another, bridging the stories that patriarchal culture has written for women (see Sidonie Smith, chap. 3). While she fragments herself for sale in the public marketplace (recalling the Phoenix), in her brief moments of self-assertive "unreadability" she fractures prevailing paradigms. As it is with other early modern women writers equally compelled to hyper-self-awareness and self-defense by their anomalous positions, this is clinical narcissism but of a most social and literary sort: a casting about for identity, a restless shifting between prescribed and proscribed selves. Chapter 1 of my study foregrounded Sor Juana's iconography of anomaly from her glory days, which pandered to the baroque esthetic of the bizarre; chapter 5 will demonstrate how the nun thickly ciphers her self–perhaps her deepest self–into a variety of mythological figures in the *Primero sueño*. Between the two lie the preponderance of Sor Juana's self-representations. In them, as the figuration of

Leonor has begun to suggest, Sor Juana's crisis assumes its most palpable and even poignant form as the nun projects herself as a modest "woman" and as a chastened and conflicted subject.[19]

Sonnet #150, "She shows distress at being abused for the applause her talent brings" (97), takes us deeper into the interiority of this persona as it struggles with fame and into its writer's characteristically melancholic world. The poem contains a series of dissolving oppositions that build to the same improbable equation driving Leonor's speech: that the "dones" or gifts of seeming good fortune are in fact "males" or misfortunes that call for sympathy. Addressing Fate familiarly with the *tú* form, the poetic subject presents herself in the opening lines as the object of its "torments" and "punishments," merited by her unspecified "crime." In grammatical terms, all of the poem's verbs but two insistently present the speaker as a direct object who has been acted upon, first by fate and then by the onlookers who "viéndome rica de tus dones" [seeing me rich in your gifts] would fail to have "lástima a mis males" [pity on my misfortunes]. The speaker's passivity, her victimization, acquires special significance when linked with the fame referred to in the poem's title (a title, of course, not necessarily of Sor Juana's making) and discussed above with regard to the "Autodefensa." Yet even more significant in this poem is the speaker's admission that fate's or fame's punishments have only extended into the public sphere the torments that the subject has privately effected *on herself*: "no basta el que adelante el pensamiento, / sino el que le previenes al oído" [beyond that torture which the mind foresees, you whisper you have yet more in store, 97]. Like Leonor, she is innately "sad." When juxtaposed with the mention in lines 11–12 of fate's "afflictions" and her own "misfortunes," it becomes even more obvious that the speaker's misery anteceded that inflicted by fate and that the "I" and the "you" are engaged in complementary, not opposing, wars to destroy her person. The poem's only two verbs in the first person, "me persuado" [I persuade myself] (rather than the "you persuade me" one might expect, given that she is addressing Fate) and "pienso" [I think], voice the interiorized civil war that collapses the seeming oppositions between subject and object, public and private, "I" and "you," destruction and self-destruction.

The oppositions may be dismantled, but their consequences do not disappear. The poem still presents the interaction between external and internal forces that results in a pained melancholic speaker who "thinks" and "persuades herself"—the paradigmatic features of the majority of Sor Juana's self-representations. Whether melancholy constitutes part of a mask designed to produce the sympathy that Sonnet #150 requests and Leonor inspires, whether for Sor Juana it was a seventeenth-century malady and topic (a subject to which I will return more than once), whether it was a central element of the nun's personality, or whether it was a product of circumstances such as those that the "Autodefensa" and the "Respuesta" detail, is impossible to determine absolutely. That is to say, as I intimated in the discussion of Sor Juana's woman-to-woman love poetry in chapter 2, we have to allow for an indeterminable mix of authenticity and convention, of experiential *bios* and constructed *autos*, in the self-representational works of any writer and can hope only to elucidate both the personal circumstances and the topics that bear on the mix. Whatever the case–and it is certainly not a simple one–as we saw in the love poetry and see again in her more patent self-representations, the expression of brooding and sadness, of trials and tribulations, is a constitutive feature of Sor Juana's lyric voice and lyrical persona. The poet's impassioned "Afuera, afuera, ansias mías" [Out, out, my worries] (Romance #9) both declares the function of that lyric voice–"Salga el dolor a las voces" [Let pain cry out], "salgan signos a la boca / de lo que el corazón arde" [let signs issue from my mouth of what is burning in my heart]–and enunciates the melancholy of her signature poetic subject: "Mayor es, que yo, mi pena; y esto supuesto, más fácil / será, que ella a mí me venza, / que no que yo en ella mande" [My grief is greater than I; and once I realize this, it will be easier for it to conquer me than I it].

The reader may well have recognized by now another "signature" evident in all of Sor Juana's divergent self-representations discussed above: the inscription of hagiography. The trials and tribulations the texts are at pains to showcase together with their references to persecution and martyrdom ineluctably evoke Catholic hagiography and, in Sor Juana's context, a hagiographic autobiography such as Saint Teresa's *Vida* [Life]. Given Sor Juana's relatively infrequent mentions of Teresa, Bénassy-Berling has questioned the Mexican nun's familiarity and sympathy with her precursor.[20] I do not purport to argue that Teresa's *Vida* provided the direct intertext for all of Sor Juana's hagiographic self-representations. I do, however, maintain that it can be considered, if not an intertext, an "archetext" for Sor Juana.[21] Teresa's *Vida*, as Electa Arenal and Stacey Schlau have established in their *Untold Sisters*, was the most representative and influential such work for sixteenth- and seventeenth-century writing nuns, one that united texts as disparate as Sor Juana's erudite "Respuesta" and the spiritual autobiography of the uneducated Mexican nun, María de San José. The elements of spiritual autobiography elaborated earlier in addition to those I will discuss now reach important expression in Teresa's self-hagiographic *Vida*, where they are rewritten in a "feminine" mode that, as do other Teresian features, feeds significantly into Sor Juana's self-representations.

Saint Augustine's *Confessions* provide the principal model for both Puritan and Saint Teresa's spiritual autobiographies.[22] Certain of the essential elements I analyzed with regard to the Puritan writings therefore reappear in Teresa's *Vida*. Once again, the individual attributes her evil qualities to self and her positive qualities to God ("Eventually I found that He, on His side, had done all the good things, and I had done all the bad things" [*382*]). Teresa defines the still central notion of humility in terms parallel to the Puritans and to Augustine: as purging the wicked self of its imperfections. In obliging individuals to reflect "on our lowliness and our ingratitude to God, on the great things that He has done for us" (*120*), humility also affords the *Vida* its modus operandi. The goal of humility as before is a subjectivity that involves self-erasure and filling oneself with God. Teresa appeals to this notion in her own defense and in defense of her form of prayer, saying: "From this point onward, I am speaking of another and a new book–I mean, of another and a new life. Until now the life I was describing was my own; but the life I have been living since I began to expound these matters concerning prayer is the life which God has been living in me. . . . Praised be the Lord, Who has delivered me from myself!" (*219–20*). Subjectivity, of course, finds its ultimate embodiment in the mystical trances and visions that Teresa narrates elsewhere.

Saint Teresa efficaciously makes her case by framing her life as a martyrdom in a *Vida* that has been called a "hagiography written by herself" (Sabat-Rivers 1992, 421). The formulae of hagiography to a degree supplant the more individualistic texture of Saint Augustine's *Confessions* as Teresa presents her life as one of unremitting tribulations and trials. Tribulations: from the confessors who have not served her well, who force her to write and dictate the course of her writings, from the many individuals who have opposed her form of prayer and founding of convents. Trials: the constant illness and other afflictions that she, like Bradstreet and Sor Juana, says she has endured and that, as does Bradstreet, Teresa portrays as hidden favors from God (e.g., "At this time, though I was not careless about my own improvement, the Lord became more desirous of preparing me for the state of life which was best for me. He sent me a serious illness" [*74*]). What the *Vida* may be lacking in individualistic self-analysis it makes up for in the force of its writer's sentiments; the hyperbolic emotionality of the *Vida* overcomes the formulaic nature of the sentiments expressed.[23] For example, in but two pages of chapter 35 concerning her reactions to her possible election as Mother Superior, Teresa details her "torment," "martyrdom for God's sake," her "gladness," her "worries," her "weeping," her "inward restlessness," and her "fears" (*334–35*). The first lines of Sor Juana's Romance #9 cited above, "Afuera, afuera, ansias mías," well describe the cathartic function of both her and Teresa's texts. Given this, even writing becomes a form of martyrdom for Teresa: "I began to think over my general confession and to write down all my good and bad points and prepare the clearest account of my life that I possibly could, leaving nothing unsaid. I remember that, after writing it, I found so many bad points and so little that was good that it caused me the greatest distress and affliction" (*227*).

The preceding statement illustrates, as well, Teresa's penchant for Manichean self-abasement. Throughout the text she insistently vilifies herself in absolute terms, proclaiming her wickedness and sinfulness and denying herself any worth, virtue, or inherent ability. Employing the conventionalized humility topics that will occupy much of my later discussion, Teresa assumes a stance akin to Aristotle's self-effacing *eiron* who disavows all laudable qualities (Weber, 87). Among the qualities she categorically denies is, significantly, knowledge. Teresa echoes the church's prescription of *santa ignorancia* or "Holy Ignorance," the notion that the faithful should know only what they need to know and not what they do not, in disclaimers such as: "Do not suppose that learning and knowledge have anything to do with this, for I am wholly destitute of both" (*281*; on Teresa and Holy Ignorance also see Egido 1983, 592). Most often, however, Teresa will deprecate herself in conjunction with hyperbolic praise of another, be that God or a powerful, virtuous individual. In one famous example she writes, "For my Lord well knows that I have no other desire than this, that He may be praised and magnified a little when it is seen that on so foul and malodorous a dunghill [herself!] He has planted a garden of sweet flowers" (*124*). Saint Augustine and other men of the church performed similar acts of self-deprecation in conjunction with another and in isolation, but much less systematically (and with a less purple rhetoric). Alison Weber confirms that

> there are few humility topics in Saint Augustine's *Confessions.* They are surprisingly rare in the devotional writers preferred by Teresa—Luis de Granada and Francisco de Osuna, for example. When the topics do appear, they are found only in the prologue—that part of the text, which, after all, is devoted to the purpose of *captatio benevolentiae.* In contrast to the one or two humility topics found per prologue, Teresa's text offers two or three topics per page. (50)

I can envision at least three reasons for this disturbing contrast. First, Teresa, like Sor Juana after her, is a woman engaged in a public self-defense to which the emphatic denial of any personal merit could only prove beneficial.[24] Teresa, as we heard in chapter 1, also demeaned her own sex along patriarchal lines. Second, the matter lying at the heart of Weber's book, *Teresa of Avila and the Rhetoric of Femininity*: Saint Teresa has rewritten Saint Augustine into a language appropriate to a woman writer and accessible to a female public. Weber states:

> As I read more and understood more clearly the conditions under which Teresa wrote, I was convinced that Teresa's self-deprecation was rhetorical but that it had a very non-traditional function. It seemed possible that Teresa's "rhetoric for women" was a "rhetoric of femininity," that is, a strategy which exploited certain stereotypes about women's character and language. Rather than "writing like a woman," perhaps Teresa wrote as she believed women were *perceived* to speak. (11)

Whether self-consciously or not, Teresa has deployed a language that resolves the woman's double bind of speaking in a context that proscribes public speech, perhaps the only self-referential language available to women that was acceptable to the patriarchy. In so doing and conceivably for these reasons, Teresa has also effectively determined the language of writing nuns to come. The *eiron*, Weber notes, denies positive qualities "to avoid parade" (15). A third explanation for Teresa's self-deprecation returns us to the familiar terrain of religious rhetoric.[25] Electa Arenal observes that whereas the Puritans (and, I add, Saint Augustine) "were to get to heaven on a road paved with circumspection," the Catholics "were to do so on roads of penitence" (1986, 159).

Penitence involves confession, confession self-accusation, and self-accusation the beginnings of humility. If humility entails the emptying of the self to clear the space for God's presence, then its markers are formulaic self-denigration, the verbal steps toward subjectivity.

The wordplay of Saint Teresa's poetry, among other aspects, makes its way into Sor Juana's Romance #56 ("Así alimentando, triste, / la vida con el veneno, / la misma muerte que vivo, / es la vida con que muero," Thus, with deadly poison I keep my life alive; the very death I live is the life of which I die [*89*]), one of the three personal religious poems I analyzed in my second chapter to elucidate Sor Juana's conflictive sense of divine love. It is instructive to return to two of them now (Romance #56, "In which she expresses the effects of Divine Love and proposes to die loving, despite the risk," and Romance #57, "*Romance* on the same subject") and to examine the twin compositions within the framework of our present discussion. In this light they reemerge as poems of self-scrutiny and as illustrations in an explicitly religious context of a theologically based auto-machia with Teresian echoes on which Sor Juana places her own stamp.

In commenting on the two poems I am prompted to remark again, as I did in the second chapter, on the extremely limited and repetitive nature of Sor Juana's poetic economy—perhaps inevitable in such a prolific writer. It contains points and contradictory counterpoints, but also statements and ever-deepening restatements. Romances #56 and #57, for example, delve further into the same internal conflicts expressed by the poetic speaker of Sonnet #150. Their tormented poetic speaker, risking the possibility that broadcasting her "penas" [afflictions] will turn them into "culpas" [faults] (#57), like Teresa gives rein to her tribulations and at the same time gives the reader a thicker understanding of the self-victimization to which Sonnet #150 refers more cryptically.

In Romances #56 and #57, the reader may recall, the poetic subject bemoans her inability to accept God's love. "Gracia" [Grace] (#57), the "finezas" [demonstrations of love], and "cariños" [affections] of God (#56) lie within reach, inciting her to ascend to the divine sphere, but she cannot accept the summons. She scrutinizes her self with eyes not blinded by love (#56) and recognizes the self-punishing nature of the dilemma: that she is too encumbered by a misery-ridden self to achieve the abdication of agency ("y hace mi voluntad mesma / de lo que es alivio, cruz," and my own will makes a cross from what is actually relief [#57]) necessary to attain what Méndez Plancarte recognizes is an Augustinian state of conversion (1.453). Simply put, she cannot disabuse herself of self. Poem #57 insinuates that the speaker's suffering may be trials sent by God ("Padezca, pues Dios lo manda," Suffer, for God wills it). However, the thrust of the two poems diverges from Teresa's orthodox view of divinely mandated afflictions to situate the drama squarely within the realm of the problematic self: "Bien ha visto, quien penetra / lo interior de mis secretos, / que yo misma estoy formando los dolores que padezco" (#56) [The one who has power to probe the secrets of my breast, has seen that I am the cause of my suffering and distress, *89*]; "Mientras la Gracia me excita / por elevarme a la Esfera, / más me abate a lo profundo / el peso de mis miserias" (#57) [While Grace inspires me to rise into the heavens, the weight of my miseries plunges me into the depths]. "The weight of my miseries" hooks up with the brooding self we heard question the gift of a brief union with God in Romance #58 ("¿Es amor o celos / tan cuidadoso escrutinio?"; Is so careful a scrutiny love or jealousy?). That brooding self now turns on itself. In full recognition and articulation of her auto-machia, the poetic speaker vilifies herself in both poems for being her own executioner. "De mí mesma," she says in Romance #57, "soy verdugo / y soy cárcel de mí mesma" [I am my own executioner and my own prison]. Unpacking this play of conceits, we see that the self has presented the speaker with a double obstacle to happiness. Sad and brooding, it has been the agent of her execution; incapable of disabusing herself of that self, she remains locked in its prison cell and cut off from Grace.

We turn now to the last and, I believe, the most important poem of self-representation to be examined in the present section: Sor Juana's Romance #2 (which begins, "Finjamos que soy feliz, triste Pensamiento," Let us pretend, sad Thought, that I am happy). It was, I admit, the richly self-revelatory nature of "Finjamos" that provided another significant impetus for this chapter. In my early readings the poem struck me as unique in Sor Juana's repertoire, and as the uniquely nuanced self-revelation of an intellectual woman's inner turmoil. Now I see Romance #2 as responding at least in part to the external situation of fame and censure and, paradoxically, as laboring to expose the depths of an at least in part strategically constructed persona. Moreover, I find that when examined closely—which, as far as I know, no one has truly done—the dense and challenging poem yields up theological dimensions that display an unmistakable kinship with the two religious poems just discussed, dimensions that inscribe the secular poem of self-revelation in a theologically conditioned context of self-negation. That "Finjamos" appeared in Sor Juana's first collection of poems and the sacred *romances* I have just discussed in her third makes the matter all the more interesting, for here we find an inversion of the golden age's customary process of rewriting secular poems *a lo divino*, that is, in a religious mode. Working backward, as it were, Sor Juana crafts her self-representation from a host of theological elements that would later find expression in their more proper context.

In Romance #2 the poetic speaker personifies the force within herself that in the other poems we have examined has brought her such misery. She identifies it with the mind and names it variously "Pensamiento" [Thought] and "Entendimiento" [Intellect]. She attempts to isolate it, to dialogue with it, and to control its relationship to her. The poem thus begins with the speaker entreating Thought for once to use its powers of imagination to her benefit: "Finjamos que soy feliz, / triste Pensamiento, un rato; / quizá podréis persuadirme, / aunque yo sé lo contrario" [Let us pretend for a little while, sad Thought, that I am happy; perhaps you can convince me, though I know it is not so]. She pits her *saber*, her self-knowledge, against its powers of illusion and asks Thought to be her ally in the enterprise of reversing, if only temporarily, her mournful state. Why is the speaker so unhappy? The answer comes in the third stanza and in stanzas 13–17. Surprisingly or not for an intellectual woman, it is because none other than her presumed ally, sad Thought, has been her enemy, one that she now seeks to control. "Sírvame el entendimiento alguna vez de descanso" [let my intellect serve, for once, as a source of relief], she beseeches of Thought in the third stanza. Sor Juana's *romances* attain their (often inordinate) length by accumulating parallel stanzas. Here stanzas 13–17 all basically repeat the same accusation against Thought. Of the many possible positions it could assume, Thought has unfailingly taken an adversarial one, controlling her and doing her damage: "Si es mío mi entendimiento / ¿por qué siempre he de encontrarlo / tan torpe para el alivio, / tan agudo para el daño?" [If my intellect is mine alone, why must I always find it so inept at relieving me, so keen at harming me?]. This is the determining factor in the speaker's self–civil war and, from a different perspective, a defining feature of Sor Juana's self-representations. For along with the poetic speaker, we as readers have been asking of Sor Juana–and I attempting to answer–the loaded question posed in stanza 14: "¿O por qué, contra vos mismo, / severamente inhumano, / entre lo amargo y lo dulce, / queréis elegir lo amargo?" [Oh why, against your very self, so sharply inhuman, must you always select the bitter when choosing between the bitter and the sweet?].

Despite the overtly personal nature of the *romance*, Octavio Paz classifies it as a moral poem of the type so in vogue in the seventeenth century (298). I do grant that, not unlike Lope de Vega's famous moral poem "A mis soledades voy, / de mis soledades vengo" [To my solitudes I go, from my solitudes I come], Romance #2 uses the personal as a platform for musings on larger issues (perhaps even to deflect attention from the self).[26] Yet as distinct from Lope's interestingly fragmented and disjointed poem, Sor Juana's first-person passages and philosophical meditations feed into and bolster each other in a seamless fabric. The first such disquisition (stanzas 4–12), an essentially phenomenological argument relativizing truth into perspectivism, builds to the accusations levied against Thought for having adopted to the speaker's detriment a consistently negative perspective. The second, in two parts, occupies the majority of the poem and treats the conventional theme announced by its inflated title: "Acusa la hidropesía de mucha ciencia, que teme inútil aun para saber y nociba para vivir" (well translated by Trueblood as "She condemns the bloatedness of much learning, which she considers useless even as knowledge and harmful for living" [*91*]). Much of the latter part of what has by then become a full-blown diatribe against Thought, we should note, attacks the unrestrained free play of *ingenio* or wit more than *ciencia* per se.

The first part (stanzas 18–21), however, holds more interest for our purposes. In it, proving learning to be "useless even as knowledge," Sor Juana makes a case for ignorance in terms clearly evocative of Holy Ignorance. The argument, like most of the poem, is not easy to follow. In stanza 18, Sor Juana returns to the relativist position taken earlier: "que el saber consiste sólo / en elegir lo más sano" [that knowing simply consists in choosing the healthiest path]. It soon becomes clear that the healthiest path for knowledge does not entail, as earlier, choosing "the sweet" over "the bitter," but choosing a wise ignorance. Stanzas 19 and 20 associate knowledge with brooding on disasters to come, which turns into a self-fulfilling prophecy. Given the pernicious effects of knowledge, stanza 21 exclaims: "¡Qué feliz es la ignorancia / del que, indoctamente sabio, halla de lo que padece, en lo que ignora, sagrado!" [How happy is the ignorance of he who, unlettered but wise, finds sanctuary from suffering in what he does not know!]. Happiness enters the poem for the first time. With a gesture to orthodoxy the speaker identifies ignorance as a happy wisdom and implies the sacred nature of such wisdom. I say implies because the hyperbaton of the stanza maneuvers the word *sagrado* into accepting a double meaning: as sanctuary, according to the expression "acogerse a sagrado" (i.e., the phrase as translated above) and, in the conventional association elicited by the contraposition with *ignorancia*, as sacred ("en lo que ignora, sagrado"). The subtle maneuver sets up what in the context of Sor Juana's works can be seen as an uneasy alliance. Sor Juana had spoken forcefully and explicitly in the "Autodefensa" *against* Holy Ignorance: "Y. R. wishes that I be coerced into salvation while ignorant, but, beloved Father, may I not be saved if I am learned? . . . Why for one's salvation must one follow the path of ignorance if it is repugnant to one's nature" (*499–500*, 21). Her defense of Holy Ignorance in Romance #2 is therefore all the more telling–telling of a nun famed for her learning who now disavows it.[27]

The fact that the Romance #2 links a learning "useless even as knowledge and harmful for living" with a sad speaker ruled by an imperious *Entendimiento* or Intellect connects "Finjamos" to the complex of religious and secular issues bound up in golden age Spain's construction of humoral melancholy. Saint Teresa denounces humoral melancholy in chapter 7 of her *Libro de las fundaciones* [Book of the Foundations] as the step before and toward madness, as caused by the devil, and as an illness obscuring reason to which women are particularly prone. Already dire, earlier notions of melancholy such as Teresa's acquire the added dimensions of an epistemological peril in the Counter-Reformation world of the Hispanic seventeenth century. Teresa Scott Soufas's path-breaking study, *Melancholy and the Secular Mind in Spanish Golden Age Literature* (1990), demonstrates that in seventeenth-century Spain melancholy becomes the literary site in which intellectuals play out the battle between conservative ideas of a more medieval, God-centered universe and a new epistemological order that values the autonomous secular mind (ix). Seventeenth-century Spanish intellectuals, she says, view humoral melancholy as the double-edged "condition of body and mind that intensifies the tendencies for isolation, self-conscious contemplation, and a hyperactive mind–considered historically, and depicted literarily, either as an attribute of brilliance or as a dangerous and marginalized aberrant pathology" (2). Hence, the "superiority and distemper known as melancholy" provided the perfect medium for those who "in the face of a growing body of opinion that affirms the superiority of the autonomously functioning mind, endeavor to reaffirm the traditionally appropriate application of human thought in a God-centered universe" (xiii). "In few instances," Soufas states in a chapter on her paradigmatic melancholic, Don Quijote, "does the melancholy figure receive unequivocally positive treatment by Siglo de Oro authors" (4).

Don Quijote may, in Soufas's interpretation, epitomize the melancholic figure, but her argument certainly sheds light on the melancholic speaker of Sor Juana's poems. Where Don Quijote, in his brilliance and madness, embodies the whole dialectic of values or "transvaluation" of the times, we can see that Sor Juana's poetic persona embodies the conservative position in a pained alliance with traditional values. Through acts of self-conscious contemplation, her poetic speaker depicts the workings of a hyperactive mind. She censures them as dangerous to herself and advocates in a secular context an orthodox ignorance. Soufas's portrayal of melancholy so fits Sor Juana's as to suggest the nun's awareness that melancholy constituted not only a perennial *topic* but a perilous phenomenon as well (the dangers of secular thought being an issue that occupies center stage in the "Respuesta"), which matters should no doubt give pause to those, like Ludwig Pfandl, who are all too eager to psychoanalyze Sor Juana herself on the basis of this poem.[28]

The melancholy, moralistic considerations, and auto-machia of Romance #2 all culminate in its final self-sacrificing stanza: "Aprendamos a ignorar, / Pensamiento, pues hallamos / que cuanto añado al discurso, / tanto le usurpo a los años" [Thought, let's learn to not know, since we find that whatever I add to my discourse I take away from my years]. Two aspects of the last stanza in particular demand our attention: its unequivocal summons to ignorance, and its equivocal tangle of verb forms. The first, while a shocking pronouncement from the author of the *Sueño*, ensues naturally from the gist of the poem in general and from its previous movement (stanzas 30–32) in particular. There the discussion of the dangers of Thought escalates into a full-scale attack, with biblical echoes, on *Ingenio* or Wit. Unleashing a flurry of invective, the speaker characterizes Wit as a vassal who rebels against his Master, and as a "duro afán pesado" [hard and heavy urge] imposed on humankind by God as a trial. In this biblical environment the antepenultimate and penultimate stanzas of the poem return to the theme of ignorance, again identifying it with happiness and calling for a "seminary" where one could learn to not know. Now *desengañada*, the speaker would appear to have recognized that a happiness less illusory and more enduring than that which she requests of Thought at the outset (Let us *pretend for a little while*, sad Thought, that I am happy [italics mine]) can accrue from ignorance. Somewhere, invisibly, in the course of her diatribe she has decided not to ask that Thought exercise its powers on her behalf but to cancel it out entirely! Even more mystifying is the possible identification of the speaker herself with Thought, which acquires a certain urgency in view of its obliteration. From the very first stanza the poem has been none too clear whether Thought *is* the Self or the governing *part* of the Self (i.e., Let *us* suppose that *I* am happy if *you* can persuade *me*). The final stanza only adds to the confusion and to the interest of the poem's conclusion. The first-person plural "hallamos" [we find], not a command form now, further bolsters an identification between the "I" and Thought by suggesting that the two "sad" entities have been thinking together throughout the well-thought-out poem. If such is the case, the attempt to purge herself of Thought in the aims of achieving a sacred ignorance no longer tainted with melancholy would logically imply a purging of *self* as well.

I have devoted a good deal of space to Romance #2 not only because the difficult poem has received insufficient critical attention but also and primarily due to its importance for Sor Juana's self-representations. Capping off the series of melancholic self-scrutinizing texts we have been examining, "Finjamos" adds to them one final piece that together with the others will form the key weapons of Sor Juana's self-defense in the "Respuesta a Sor Filotea de la Cruz." That piece, fascinatingly transposed in the "Respuesta," is the poem's theme of knowledge and its depiction as a devastating force within the self, a force if not entirely alien to the speaker's "I," then certainly alien to her will. When we bring this and the other pieces to bear on the "Respuesta," we will begin to understand Sor Juana's self-representations not only as a limited economy of statements and deepening restatements but as an *ars combinatoria* in which elements that have become "topics" in the nun's self-representations are combined and restyled according to the pragmatic context. Put more simply, we will see that in the "Respuesta" (in all likelihood written after the poems) Sor Juana refashions the established elements of her self-fashioning to suit her self-defense. Moreover, when we view the "Respuesta" within the series of her self-representations, it emerges that the two inimical elements or modes previously separate in her works now coincide in a single site. The self-assertion of the "Autodefensa" and the multifaceted self-negations of the other poems implausibly coexist in the "Respuesta," in effect constituting a *civil war of self-representations.*[29]

To perform the tactics just outlined, Sor Juana once again avails herself of the Teresian discourse that we have been following and that, for its efficacy in throwing into relief Sor Juana's civil war of self-representations, will frame my discussion of the "Respuesta." In the "Respuesta" Teresa's "language" takes on both its richest and a parodic significance as Sor Juana re-places the Teresian topics from her own poems into their proper context of a spiritual autobiography and reinscribes them with notably self-serving swerves from their precursor.[30]

Kathleen A. Myers has opened up the subject of the relationship between the "Respuesta" and the *Vida* in general. In her important "Sor Juana's *Respuesta*: Rewriting the *Vitae*" (1990), Myers discusses how Sor Juana utilizes the consecrated topics of the spiritual autobiography such as the "story of my life," writing as an act of obedience, *vos me coegistis, imitatio Christi*, and Holy Ignorance. Certain of these topics will prove central to my discussion, but I prefer to begin with an aspect of Sor Juana's *vitae* that has an unmistakably Teresian and humble ring: how she contrives to write like a self-effacing "woman."

Both the "Respuesta" and the "Autodefensa" allow me to assert with reasonable confidence that Sor Juana *contrives* to write like a meek woman. Seething with irony, at the end of the "Respuesta" Sor Juana lays bare the disguise of her male/female interlocutor in begging him/her to forgive the "homespun familiarity" of her style and stating that she has not dared "to exceed the limits of your style nor to infringe the margins of your modesty" (*243*, 475). The presumed style of Sor Filotea adopted by Sor Juana, as the reference to "homespun familiarity" would signal, is none other than that of Saint Teresa–whom, in fact, "Sor Filotea" in his/her reprimand had urged Sor Juana to take as a model.[31] Though far more erudite than homespun, like Teresa and for similarly self-defensive reasons Sor Juana does incur in formulaic acts of self-vilification at various moments of her Reply. Such self-vilification figures prominently in the poems on writing to be considered shortly and is illustrated by the following phrases from the "Respuesta": "Am I, perchance, anything but a poor nun, the least of all the world's creatures, and the most unworthy of engaging your attention?" (*206*, 441), and "I readily confess that I am base and vile" (*239*, 470).[32] Elsewhere she asserts her humility (*asserts* being the appropriate word, however contradictory) by denouncing her intellectual abilities, personal qualities, writings, and even her condition as a woman. As did Teresa, Sor Juana presents writing as an act of obedience and an excruciating martyrdom: "And in truth I have never written except when pressured and forced to and then not only without enjoyment but with actual repugnance" (*209*, 444). The two positive qualities Sor Juana strategically allows herself–a penchant for the truth and a sweet, affable nature–she attributes to God. Sor Juana, despite the fact that she had so often proclaimed the rational nature of women, also gestures in the *exordio* or salutation of the text to Teresa's emotionality. She alludes to Teresa's emotive, digressive style in asking forgiveness for "the digression wrung from me by the force of truth" (*207*, 441). She associates emotionality with genuine modesty and with truth: "It is no affectation of modesty on my part, Madam, but the simple truth of my entire soul, to say that when the letter that you chose to call Athenagoric came into my hands, I burst into tears of embarrassment, something I do not very easily do" (*206*, 441).

The personal and literary self-consciousness implicit in Sor Juana's reference to the rhetorical topic of "affected modesty" in combination with the irony of her comments on Sor Filotea's "style," the theatricality of her confessions of unworthiness, and the hyperbolic renunciation of her vocation as a writer, compel us to consider the possibility that Sor Juana is not just imitating Teresa's "feminine" language but parodying or mimicking it. The successes and the writings of Sor Juana's activist foremother render Teresa's *Vida* a sixteenth-century feminine "classic" for the seventeenth-century Mexican nun. Conversely, Sor Filotea's injunction to Sor Juana that she follow the lead of

Saint Teresa authorizes and appropriates the *Vida* for patriarchal discourse and thus renders it a site ripe for mimicry, in which one assumes the subaltern role deliberately, even subversively.[33] On its own, or compared to the unabashedly angry style of the "Autodefensa," the Teresian language of the "Respuesta" reveals itself as "affected."

With predictable humility and self-accusation, Teresa invokes the imitation of Christ's martyrdom or *imitatio Christi* in remarking: "At such times I turn straight to the life of Christ and to the lives of the saints and realize that I am travelling in the opposite direction from that which they took, for they experienced nothing but contempt and insults" (*Life, 293*). Sor Juana will eventually take the topic to places unthinkable for Teresa. As she did in Leonor's speech, in narrating her life story in the "Respuesta" Sor Juana frames it as martyrdom akin to that of Christ and the saints. She has martyred herself for the sake of knowledge (by cutting her hair, denying herself pleasures) and, more gravely, has been subjected to "contempt and insults" by those who would forbid her to study. The passage that introduces the latter theme replays the false legend whose underside of suffering both the "Respuesta" and Leonor's speech are anxious to expose: "Who could fail to believe, in view of such widespread plaudits, that I have sailed with a following wind on a glassy sea to the encomiums of general acclaim?" (*218*, 452). Sor Juana packs the passage on her pursuit of knowledge with the vocabulary of martyrdom appropriate to a model nun following the *camino de perfección* or path of perfection: arduous difficulties, persecutions of a noxious and painful nature, mortification, torment, a reference to martyrdom itself. Significantly, strategically, and transparently, before detailing the specifics of her martyrdom at the hands of her religious community, Sor Juana refers even more explicitly to the *imitatio Christi* topic and inserts a lengthy digression into her text on the pain and ostracism suffered by Christ for his superiority (*219–24*, 453–57). The textual proximity to Sor Juana's own story alone would be sufficient to conjure up the association between the two. Yet at the end of the section the author actually *invites* comparison between herself and Christ, writing herself into the topic. In a brilliant conjunction of Teresian rhetoric of self-deprecation and a self-assertion that Teresa could only consider blasphemous, Sor Juana concludes her discussion of Christ's wisdom in the following way:

> There was not a single alien soldier who did not give him trouble nor any maidservant who did not bother him. I confess that I am far removed from wisdom's confines and that I have wished to pursue it, though *a longe*. But the sole result has been to draw me closer to the flames of persecution, the crucible of torture, and this has even gone so far as a formal request that study be forbidden me. (*224*, 457–58)

Not even the Teresian locutions of this passage can mitigate its presumptuousness; the arrogant iconoclastic swerve that Sor Juana here places on the *imitatio Christi* contradicts her more humble texts of martyrly affliction and exceeds even the contra-*diction* of the rhetoric of humility found in the "Autodefensa."

The "Respuesta" rises from a humbly defensive to a noticeably un-Teresian offensive position even more akin to that of the "Autodefensa" at least twice. The first involves the important theme of ignorance or Holy Ignorance, and knowledge. Sor Juana tells us in the "Respuesta" that she had been reproved for a learning that contravened Holy Ignorance: "*This study is incompatible with the blessed ignorance to which you are bound. You will lose your way, at such heights your head will be turned by your very perspicacity and sharpness of mind.* What have I not gone through to hold out against this?" (*218*, 452; italics in original). In the self-defensive "Respuesta," the author remaps the fields of ignorance and knowledge. When recounting her intellectual travails, Sor Juana had reiterated the contention found in the "Autodefensa" that God is knowledge and that all knowledge issues from God, associating it with the Great Chain of Being linking secular and theological wisdom ("All things proceed from God, who is at once the center and the circumference from which all existing lines proceed and at which all end up" [*216*, 450]). She had characterized her ignorance as an inability to pull all the pieces together, to make the holy connections (*215*, 449). Having laid this groundwork, Sor Juana comes back to the theme of ignorance and knowledge in the *prueba*, the section that adduces general proofs to support an argument. She provides a *catalogue raisonée* of learned women in support of her right to knowledge and then focuses her sights and formidable polemical abilities on the issue of *men* and knowledge. Here in a biting offensive attack, she depicts ignorance not as the holy tabula rasa seen in "Finjamos" but, when placed in the wrong hands and minds, as a travesty of knowledge. Knowledge, she says, can be "the best sustenance and the very life of the soul" (*231*, 463). Yet many men, "who merely by virtue of being men consider themselves sages," "study in order to become ignorant" (*230*, 462). Knowledge only perfects the stupidity of these "arrogant, restless and overbearing" (*230*, 462) individuals. In essence, then, Sor Juana redefines ignorance as being fit only for arrogant males: "Of these the Holy Spirit says: *In malevolam animam no introibit sapientia* [For wisdom will not enter into a malicious soul]. Learning does more harm to such than remaining ignorant would" (*230*, 463).

The end of the *prueba* finds Sor Juana returning one last time to her personal circumstances and arguing them through with an airtight logic and with the very same self-assertive voice of the "Autodefensa" (which lends further credence to the document's authenticity). Far here from humility, Teresian or otherwise, she asks, "Is not my mind, such as it is, as free as his [of Father Vieira, whose opinions she countered in the *Carta Atenagórica*], considering their common origin?" (*237*, 468). She contends, "I was free to dissent from Vieira" (*237*, 469). The voice we are hearing connects the "Respuesta" to the "Autodefensa," and the circumstances under which it writes do so even more. Sor Juana, with characteristic literary self-consciousness, goes on to justify her "slip of the pen" into a harsher register as deriving from the fact that her words responded to the remarks of one of her *slanderers* ("in talking of my detractors, I recalled the points made against me by one who has just appeared, and without realizing it my pen slipped into attempting to answer him in particular" [*237*, 469]).

It is, however, humility and even a "redeemed subjectivity" that form the crux of the self-representation and self-defense of the "Respuesta's" most personal pages. By resorting to a construction of redeemed subjectivity grounded in Catholicism, Sor Juana at once explains, tempers, and belies her daring assertive voice; finessing an expedient "border-crossing," she effectively resolves the civil war of self-representations. In the properly autobiographical section or *narratio*, which Sor Juana significantly terms "the narration of my inclination" (*210*, 445), the nun repeatedly and humbly disclaims responsibility for her gifts and proclivity for learning.[34] Drawing on the topic of "Vos me coegistis," she attributes them instead to a God-instilled inclination over which she has no control:

> From my first glimmers of reason, my inclination to letters was of
> such power and vehemence, that neither reprimands of others–and
> I have received many–nor my own considerations–and there have
> been not a few of these–have succeeded in making me abandon
> this natural impulse which God has implanted in me. (*210*, 444)

If in "Finjamos," Thought was the wicked part of selfhood that had to be purged in order for the speaker to attain the subjectivity of a sacred ignorance, here Thought is her God-given core and sacred in itself. It is still, nevertheless, an alien force. The "I" has been filled up with and completely (reminiscent of Teresa's mysticism) *possessed* by a divinely infused tendency to which her selfhood has finally and fully succumbed. Obeying God's will, however, has allowed her no peace. Yet again Sor Juana recasts the seeming gifts or *dones* as *males* or misfortunes and associates them with melancholy: "I brought my greatest enemy, given me by Heaven whether as a boon or a punishment I cannot decide" (*212*, 447). She terms her thirst for knowledge "mi locura" [my madness] and presents it as a God-sent trial of humiliation that has caused her only pain: "This type of observation would occur to me about everything and still does, without my having any say in the matter; indeed, it continually irritates me because it tires my mind" (*225*, 458–59). Though God-given, interestingly enough its effects have been as diabolical as those of the melancholy Teresa condemns; Sor Juana laments that "even my sleep was not free from this constant activity of my brain. In fact, it seems to go on during sleep with all the more freedom and lack of restraint" (*226*, 460).

All told, this argument speaks to the orthodox heart of the *imitatio Christi* and comprises a remarkable self-defense. It singles out Sor Juana as chosen by God and thus divests her of agency, selfhood, or responsibility for her actions. It renders those who would thwart her sinners for their opposition to God's will. And as the concluding lines of the *narratio* indicate, it *exculpates her from any perceived arrogance or sins*:

> Even if these studies were to be viewed, my Lady, as to one's cred-
> it (as I see they are indeed celebrated in men), none would be due
> me, since I pursue them involuntarily. If they are seen as repre-
> hensible, for the same reason I do not think I should be blamed.
> Still, though, I am so unsure of myself, that neither in this nor in
> anything do I trust my own judgment. (*226*, 460)

Sor Juana here lays claim to a humbled and "redeemed" subjectivity worthy
of Teresa and–despite the differences in voice, argumentation, and context–fit
for Anne Bradstreet as well. By abdicating a subject position, by nihilating her
self into subjectivity, Sor Juana paradoxically *assumes* a subject position that
allows her openly and boldly to discuss the most intimate, cherished aspects
of her life as a learned woman.[35]

III.

*What strange madness: to take more pains to destroy one's
own reputation than one might have taken to gain it!*
–SOR JUANA, "Respuesta a Sor Filotea de la Cruz"

In her Romance #8 (one of three "Texts for singing") Sor Juana cat-
achrestically refigures the mythological Narcissus as feminine, as a female
Orpheus and Cupid, and as a homicidal Siren. Sor Juana's play, *El Divino
Narciso* [The Divine Narcissus], revamps (the male) Narcissus into a Christ
who banishes the (female) Devil-Eco, restores harmony to the world, and kills
himself in the effort. The Orphic song of the female "Narcisa" in Romance #8,
while capable of paralyzing the movement of the stars and bringing a harmony that eradicates "discord," reduces its male targets to the female Eco's imitative babbling. Like Cupid's arrows, it wounds them; as the song of the
"Sirena," it can ultimately kill them. It may kill *them*, but the implication contained in Narcisa's name, if left unstated in the poem, is that the song also kills
her, the poet-singer.

Though a love poem of sorts, Romance #8 is uncannily emblematic of the
anxiety of authorship of the seventeenth-century woman poet whose harmonious song threatens and imperils her male cohorts. It is also eminently suggestive of the manner in which the female poet's "narcissistic" representations
of herself as a writer will decimate their subject. They will do so through
protestations of personal unworthiness or humility and, more specifically, by
employing humility topics. The introductory poem of Anne Bradstreet's *The
Tenth Muse* (1650), entitled "To Her Most Honoured Father, Thomas Dudley
Esq. These Humbly Presented," for example, is a veritable thesaurus of such
topics. She exalts the poetic skill of her father (whose poetry, as far as we
know, was never published!) and decries her own "lowly pen" and "humble
hand," lacking in "strength" or "skill."[36] She subordinates herself to another

male precursor, the leading French Calvinist poet Du Bartas whose poems provided the model for aspects of Bradstreet's Quaternions, saying, "I honour him, but dare not wear his wealth." All too similarly, in her Romance #45, "She excuses, modestly, the composing and sending of verses," Sor Juana spends several stanzas praising her male patron (either the Marquis de la Laguna or the Count de Galve) with rather fulsome hyperbole. She then proceeds to excuse her "rustic talent" and her "daring" in placing before him the scribblings that she deems mere inconsequential products of "wasted moments." Cringing with humility, both Sor Juana and Anne Bradstreet present themselves as overreachers. Sor Juana refers to her "daring" (inevitably associated in the nun's oeuvre with Icarus and Phaeton). Anne Bradstreet contrasts her verse to her father's, saying, "To climb their climes, I have nor strength nor skill. To mount so high requires an eagle's quill; Yet view thereof did cause my thoughts to soar" (another evocation of Icarus). Overreachers, they appeal to humility—a word that originally meant lowness in the concrete and spatial sense (Curtius, 408).

Writing, fame, and entering the public domain induce a posture of shame in the woman writer. Although it is by now a (well-founded) commonplace in feminist criticism that many women writers internalize the patriarchy's derogatory views of the opposite sex and, suffering from an anxiety of authorship, externalize them in their writings, the point bears repeating here. Where most such commentary has been directed to nineteenth-century women writers, we should be aware that the same phenomenon was operative even—or particularly—in the earlier modern writings of seventeenth-century women authors. Cheryl Walker, for one, raises our awareness of the matter. In examining the works of pre-nineteenth-century women poets, she was struck by "the way so-called 'internal' and 'external' become confused as women's conceptions of themselves are mediated through patriarchal language" and by "the effectiveness of these [patriarchal] imperatives, the regularity with which one can find their imprints on generations of writers' works" (1982, xi). Explicitly, in the above poems, and implicitly elsewhere, both Bradstreet and Sor Juana write for a patriarchal audience. They write over/against the shadow story of male expectations for women and to a considerable degree write themselves into the scripts for women that their societies sanction. In their writings they take up self-abnegating subject positions for which conventionalized humility topics provide an apt channel and outlet. Once again, but now in a wholly secular context, self-erasure and humility will be the keynote of the women's self-representations.

Humility topics, as I mentioned with regard to Saint Teresa, resolve the woman's double bind of how to speak in a context that *man*dates silence and furnish the woman writer with a socially sanctioned self-referential language. Seventeenth-century women writers, closer than those of subsequent centuries to classical rhetorical conventions and generally speaking in an even more antagonistic climate than they, would find these tactics particularly accessible and appropriate. Ernst Curtius has apprised modern readers of the multiple provenance and wide range of the topics. Deriving from classical judicial oratory, they later merged with courtly and devotional formulae (which, of course, underscores the connection with spiritual autobiography). They served the function of *captatio benevolentiae* and over the course of their development came to encompass excuses for the author's feebleness, inadequate preparation or talent, rude speech, and personal unworthiness of a variety of sorts as well as the formulae of "affected modesty" and "writing by obligation" (see Curtius, 83–85, 407–13). Diverse in provenance and form, humility topics also arguably fulfill a variety of needs for the writer. Psychologically, they supply a conventionalized vehicle for emotions or interiority and can act as enabling disclaimers; rhetorically, they capture the reader's sympathy and ally the writer with tradition. Yet as is the case with any formulaic discourse, they are inevitably more translucent than transparent. They can be read (among several ways) as mere gestures to tradition, as ironic, or as genuine. Each and every one of the above forms and functions obtains for the woman writer—and yet another one. For all the reasons just listed, humility topics also afford women writers a prefabricated mold in which to encode their conceivable anxiety of authorship. Multiple in form and function, unseizable in intent and meaning, they are apt vehicles for the vexed situation of the woman writer.

Not unexpectedly, then, the erudite Sor Juana appeals to humility topics with great frequency, explicitly applying them to her position as a woman writer. In the "Dedication" of her *Neptuno alegórico* (1680), Sor Juana refers specifically to Cicero's humility topic of *mediocritas* and, warding off anticipated criticism, explains why she rather than a man is writing a public text to celebrate the arrival of the Marquis de la Laguna to New Spain: perhaps those who requested it of her deemed "the unlettered softness of a woman more apt than the eloquence of so very many learned pens" (4.358). For a woman writer in Sor Juana's circumstances, as suggested earlier, praise can be as dangerous as criticism. Therefore, in the "Prologue" to the first edition of her works (1690; Romance #1), Sor Juana undertakes the task announced by the epigraph to this section of my chapter. Deflecting attention from the poems to her negative opinion of them and to her implied humility, the very first stanza states her thesis: her poems "sólo tienen de buenos / conocer yo que son malos" [the only good thing about them is that I know they are bad]. As she does so often in her sonnets, here Sor Juana constructs her interlocutors as adversaries and seeks to control them. She invites their criticism ("Dí cuanto quisieres de ellos, / que, cuando más inhumano / me los mordieres, entonces me quedas más obligado," Say whatever you like of them, for the more inhumanly you attack them, the more you are in my debt) and grants her readers freedom only to censure her verses. This perverse, and perversely effective, form of *captatio benevolentia* draws on several humility topics (writer by obedience, the author as the reader's servant, inadequacy of style) and culminates in a capsule autobiography of its author. Endeavoring to capture the reader's sympathy by openly refusing to request it, the speaker says that she will not excuse the defects of her poems as deriving from her own poor health (another topic), lack of time for writing, or the constant obligations of her "status" as a nun. To do so would be to suggest that the poetry could have been otherwise.

The autobiographical vignette caps off Sor Juana's concerted effort in the "Prólogo" to disabuse herself and her writings of any credit–an effort, I note, unmatched in the prologues of her male contemporaries. No male author of any of the prologues Alberto Porqueras Mayo includes in his extensive collection of mannerist and baroque prologues (Sor Juana's being the lone female voice in the anthology) presents his work as totally lacking in redeeming features. Only Cervantes, in the prologue to the first part of *Don Quijote* from which Sor Juana may be taking her cue, vilifies his work in similar if more jocular terms.[37] For the most part, however, male writers attack their readers and defend their works against anticipated criticism. They use the prologue as a kind of advertisement intended more to capture sales than sympathy. Though clearly economics as well as gender determine the tenor of a prologue, in the prologue to his *Viaje entretenido* [Amusing Voyage] (1603) Agustín de Rojas takes a position diametrically opposed to Sor Juana's: insulting his readers, taking issue with their criticism, denying that his work has no positive qualities, and in an undoing of conventional topics, disclaiming his own humility (in Porqueras Mayo, 93–99).

For Sor Juana, the precarious situation of writing so copiously and of depending on the court's protection to continue to do so would seem to have generated a need for a similarly copious unwriting of the self–and particularly of the "self-as-author." In addition to the poems already discussed, several epistolary *romances* addressed to well-placed figures (Romances #21, #37, #38, #43, #45, #49, #50, #51) find her commenting on her inabilities as a writer, either in response to praise and/or in the attempt to praise the eminent addressee of the poem. While several of these poems hold interest on other fronts or as comic virtuoso performances, as self-inscriptions they rather monotonously strike the same chords of humility noted up to now. As ritualized as the court environment of which they form a part, the epistolary *romances* lack the texture and intricacy of Sor Juana's other self-representations; they are too conventionalized to tell us very much.

Sor Juana's little-analyzed (if much-mentioned) last *romance*, however, literally and figuratively speaks volumes. Octavio Paz maintains that she composed the poem on receipt of the second volume of her works at the end of 1692 or the beginning of 1693, that is, after the "Respuesta" and immediately preceding her alleged conversion. The title of the unfinished poem, "In recognition of the matchless pens of Europe, whose praises only enhanced her works. Lines found unfinished" (Romance #51, *103*), would thus refer to the twelve poets and seven theologians who praised her in the second volume (Paz, 302–3; unfortunately, Paz has little more to say on the poem in and of itself). Sor Juana's friends in Spain, as we saw in chapter 1, may have published the volume to salvage her, but the rescue mission could easily backfire by merely enhancing the Tenth Muse's ever more dangerous celebrity.

Whatever the circumstances, in the poem Sor Juana makes a desperate final effort to combat praise and fame. In a proliferation of stanzas all addressing the same theme, throughout the poem she questions and discredits the false public image that has grown up around her. Sor Juana pungently articulates her point in the famous lines of the fourth and fifth stanzas: "No soy yo la que pensáis . . . y diversa de mí misma / entre vuestras plumas ando, / no como soy, sino como / quisisteis imaginarlo" [I am not who you think I am; and different from myself I am borne among your pens' plumes not as I am but as you insist on imagining]. The context and the heightened rhetoric of the Europeans' praise occasion the most inflamed of Sor Juana's self-vilifications. She combats the falsely exalted image with a hyperbolically abject one, reviling herself as an "ignorante mujer, / cuyo estudio no ha pasado de ratos" [ignorant woman, who has studied only in snatches], as a "casi rústico aborto" [almost rustic abortion] whose literary sterility only enhanced the infertility of her native lands, and her poetry as "scribblings" and "humble strokes." Together with a full array of humility topics, the saving self-knowledge of "Finjamos" (Let us pretend for a little while, sad Thought, that I am happy, though I *know* it is not so) makes another appearance here: farther would she have fallen than Phaeton or Narcissus "a no tener en mí misma / remedio tan a la mano, como conocerme" [had I not within me the remedy so close at hand, of knowing myself].

Why was the poem found unfinished? The reasons are completely beyond our knowledge, yet the nature of the poem itself prompts me to think that it was not finished because it *could not* be finished, because its theme was neverending. Markedly different from Sor Juana's other *romances*, however prolix, this one is not only long and accumulative but shapeless. All of Sor Juana's poems, even her most Gongoresque, display a logical development and progression. Here, however, she keeps circling back to the same central and obsessive theme of "I am not who you think I am" in different contexts. She redevelops it time and again much in the same way as she treats Saint Paul's stumbling block that women should be silent in church, but now with virtually identical arguments. Neither she nor her writings are what have been made of them by the words of others, and Sor Juana is using the writing of this poem in the impossible effort to undo them all. I am reminded of her Sonnet #145, which begins, "Este que ves, engaño colorido" [These lying pigments that you see]. There the poet aims to destroy yet another object that purports to be her mirror image, a portrait. Through logic and mounting invective, in and by means of the poem, she decimates the portrait into "cadaver," "dust," "shadow," and "nothing." Sor Juana's last poem and so many others seek to destroy not only the object but the subject herself. Yet in Romance #51, however forceful or extensive the arguments she marshals to give the lie to praise, however strong the invective she exercises on herself and her writings, they would not appear to be sufficient or sufficiently copious for the beleaguered poet to reduce either the words—be they her own or others'– or the self to the necessary "nothing."

Three of Anne Bradstreet's most cited lines read: "I am obnoxious to each carping tongue / Who says my hand a needle better fits, / A poet's pen all scorn I should thus wrong, for such despite [contempt] they cast on female wits" ("Prologue," 15). Much as this sounds like a protofeminist statement, I must make it clear that in seventeenth-century English *obnoxious* appears primarily to have meant "exposed to (actual or possible) harm, subject to injury or evil." The lines, Patricia Caldwell explains, in all likelihood signify "I am vulnerable to criticism" and not, as the present meaning of *obnoxious* would indicate, "I am repellent to my critics" (7). That the publication of Bradstreet's poetry, as did that of Sor Juana's, would set carping tongues wagging is hardly surprising in the Puritan setting. An intransigently hierarchical world with a ruling oligarchy that was all male, a society that civilly disenfranchised women and disallowed their public testimony (hence the domestic nature of Bradstreet's letter), that did not permit women to attend university, that scapegoated rebellious women like Anne Hutchinson, and that placed extraordinary emphasis on marriage, could be no more expected than Sor Juana's to countenance either a woman's public speech or her public devotion to intellectual pursuits.[38] Though Bradstreet had (unusually) been raised in an intellectual environment, recorded comments of carping tongues show the culture actively militating against learned and publishing women. Thomas Parker, upon learning that his sister's writings had emerged in print, composed a public letter in which he said, "Your printing of a Book beyond the custom of your sex, doth rankly smell" (Walker, 5). John Winthrop, governor of the Massachusetts Bay Colony of which Thomas Dudley was second governor, in a journal entry from 1645 criticized Anne Hopkins, "who was fallen into a sad infirmity, the loss of her understanding and reason, which had been growing upon her divers years, by occasion of giving herself wholly to reading and writing, and had written many books." He speculated that had she "attended to household affairs, and such things as belong to women, and not gone out of her way and calling to meddle in such things as are proper for men, whose minds are stronger &c. she had kept her wits, and might have improved them usefully and honourably in the place God had sent her" (Stanford 1974, 64). Winthrop's categorical denunciation of learned women far exceeds the reprimand "Sor Filotea" attached to Sor Juana's *Carta Atenagórica*; Ann Stanford suggests that the criticism to which Bradstreet refers in her "Prologue" may have issued from Winthrop himself (1974, 64).

Male anxiety regarding female authorship permeates the extensive–like that of Sor Juana's *Fama y obras póstumas*, unusually extensive–prefatory material to Bradstreet's *The Tenth Muse* (Schweitzer 1991, 147). Gender issues dominate the introductory texts as their male authors tackle the uncomfortable task of justifying the excellence of a woman's verse and the temerity of placing a woman's writings in the public domain. Their task is made easier by the matter that John Woodbridge, Bradstreet's brother-in-law, hastens to disclose in the "Epistle to the Reader" placed at the head of the collection: he has published the volume without the poet's knowledge or consent and therefore "presumed to bring to public view what she resolved should (in such a manner) never see the sun" (3). As the preceding comment illustrates, Woodbridge's "Epistle" domesticates Bradstreet, taming her image and showing that she has not stepped out of her place as the "angel" in the house (Schweitzer 1991, 147). Woodbridge confronts the assumed "unbelief" that will make the reader "question whether it [poetry] be a woman's work, and ask, is it possible?" by portraying Bradstreet and her volume in the following manner:

> It is the work of a woman, honoured, and esteemed where she lives, for her gracious demeanour, her eminent parts, her pious conversation, her courteous disposition, her exact diligence in her place, and discrete managing of her family occasions, and more than so, these poems are the fruit but of some few hours, curtailed from her sleep and other refreshments. (3)[39]

Modesty is thus attributed to Anne, the audacity of publishing her work to him.

Each of the succeeding authors of prefatory material negotiates a different path through the thorny issue of gender, some by demeaning the female sex but praising the author, others by condescendingly and humorously conceding her incursion into the superior male domain ("Mankind take up some blushes on the score; / Monopolize perfection no more; / In your own arts, confess yourselves outdone"; by a friend who signs himself B. W., 7). Close family friend Nathaniel Ward and an unidentified author presumed to be the Boston anagrammatizer John Wilson (Schweitzer, 147) compare Bradstreet's work to that of her model, Du Bartas. In cunning and telling sleights of hand, they solve the problem of "which best, the woman or the man" (4) by pronouncing Bradstreet "epicene" (9): Ward calls her "a right Du Bartas girl" (4); Wilson verbally transmutes her into a man with an epigram that begins, "Anna Bradestreate Dear neat An Bartas" (9).

Why, given the oppositional climate and the palpable anxiety that the volume produced even in relatives and close friends, would Bradstreet's family undertake to publish her verse? Speaking broadly, I return to the Tenth Muse model outlined in chapter 1: it is conceivable in the cases of both Bradstreet and Sor Juana that the two continents of the New World needed a poet to stake their claim to the (old) world of culture.[40] So "complete" a poet as Sor Juana and especially Bradstreet in this volume (mostly given over to the masculinist Quaternions) prove themselves to be, could add the luster of civilization to the two errands into the wilderness. The only problem, as it were, was the gender of the poet. Speaking more narrowly and with specific reference to Bradstreet, I draw on Ivy Schweitzer's convincing answer to the question. As she maintains, Puritan New England had been grappling with a host of rebellious women, such as the antinomian Anne Hutchinson and her followers. Anne Bradstreet's birth family itself had been dishonored by the conduct of their allegedly rebellious daughter, Sarah Keayne. Keayne was excommunicated, divorced, and disinherited for publicly preaching in London. Just at the time Keayne returned home from England, Woodbridge left for London with Bradstreet's manuscript (1991, 150–53). The Puritans and the Dudleys had had their "monster" women; they now needed an "angel" to place in a public position. Anne Bradstreet, Schweitzer argues, fit the bill. Possessing the "feminine" virtues touted by Woodbridge in his "Epistle," her writing was "eminently acceptable" as well, "being a rather modest imitation of men's speech" (152).

It is therefore instructive to observe in the "Prologue" to *The Tenth Muse* (originally the prologue to the masculinist Quaternions) not only Bradstreet's self-styled "angelic" qualities but the degree to which the question of imitating men's speech and other issues regarding men pervade the poem, activating the speaker's anxiety and humility. The categorical denial of her abilities contained in the first four stanzas begins with the lines quoted at the outset of this chapter: in an echo of Virgil's *Aeneid*, Bradstreet declares the singing of wars, captains, kings, and cities too superior for her "mean pen" (15). Her childishly "wond'ring eyes" and "envious heart" nevertheless respond to "Great Bartas's sugared lines" and inspire her to write. When in addition Bradstreet states, "A Bartas can do what a Bartas will / But simple I according to my skill," we recognize in her words the humility formula familiar from religious writings of self-deprecation through hyperbolic contrast with another. Both here and in the poem to her father discussed above, Bradstreet so lionizes the male personages who have catalyzed her writing as to figure them as displaced deities—deities with whom she longs to unite but cannot. (As Bradstreet matured as a poet and wrote properly religious works, however, the humility topics employed to protest her inadequacy as a writer shade off into the protestations of humility as God's unworthy subject from which they appear here to spring—that is, into a re-placement of God as the father.)[41] Bradstreet's literary models are all and always male, never female. Thus, passing from Du Bartas to the orator Demosthenes, the poet-speaker compares herself to him in equally unfavorable terms. She then focuses her sights on the larger matter of women versus men. Wittily, this "right Du Bartas girl" refers to the no-exit situation of a woman poet such as she. The carping tongues, Bradstreet writes, cast such "despite on female wits" that "If what I do prove well, it won't advance, / They'll say it's stolen, or else was by chance" (16). Her ironic expression of umbrage, however, quickly cedes to a conciliatory posture in which the speaker allows that "men have precedency and still excel," and that "Men can do best, and women know it well. / Preeminence in all and each is yours; yet grant some small acknowledgement of ours" (16). Changing addressees at the end of the poem from men in general to male poets in particular ("And oh ye high flown quills that soar the skies"), the poet asks only that they concede her a thyme or parsley wreath, allowing her a small space so that her "mean and unrefined ore" can "make their glist'ring gold but more to shine" (17).[42] Though not all acts of self-representation, these comments on the woman poet's plight bear weight for Bradstreet's self-fashionings. They give us a fleeting glimpse of the inner conflicts that she resolves into the voice of the patriarchy (not a redeemed subjectivity, but a subjectivity nonetheless) and, in confirming that she positions herself vis-à-vis men throughout the poem, impute Bradstreet's humble voice as a young poet not only to her fledgling literary status but also to her gender awareness.

Each time that Bradstreet takes up the pen in *The Tenth Muse* to render homage to a male figure, it wanders–back to its author. Bradstreet, like Sor Juana, returns compulsively to her self-as-author and her unworthiness in the early poems of the collection. As Ann Stanford notes in terms of the North American poet, "Over and over again she was to take a current genre, emphasizing certain of its customary elements, and turn it into a personal form in which she as the poet often plays a central role" with the result that "her 'expression of inadequacy' becomes a theme uniting the poems, revealing to the reader the poet's own motives and aspirations" (1974, 15). The author tries to sing the praises of her male precursors, but I believe that she defaults to the story she needs to tell, one akin to the unwitting "other story" contained in the narrative an analysand recounts to a psychoanalyst–that of her anxiety of authorship.

Bradstreet's elegy to the knight-poet Sir Philip Sidney at once enacts and articulates the process of telling the "other story." Written in 1638 and her very second poem, the unwieldy and overburdened elegy underwent the most severe emendation of all the poems included in the second edition of Bradstreet's verse. Bradstreet excised a full sixty-one lines from it in what was to a significant degree an effort to downplay herself and to reroute the poem back to its intended subject of Sidney (White, 37). The self-representational lines, both those omitted and those remaining, involve her unworthiness to praise Sidney. Two renowned male poets, Du Bartas and his British translator Sylvester, had already done so. Who, then, was she to attempt such a feat? Finding herself in a "labyrinth" of doubt about how to speak of Sidney, having "too late" become aware of her presumptuousness, Bradstreet's first-person speaker launches into a comparison of herself with the daring of Phaeton and his unruly chariot. In this substantial passage excised from the second version, Bradstreet's poetic speaker compares her pen running "head-long" with Phaeton's "hasty hand" and ungovernable chariot (Piercy ed., 194). Such literarily self-conscious words mirror what I construe as the ungovernable psychology of the young author. While aiming to make her way through a labyrinth whose center is Sidney, despite herself she keeps losing sight of the prescribed course and twisting back to her own anxious person. "Endless turns," "the way I find out not," "doubt," "ambitious," "error," "presume," "faltering lines," "ill-guided," "proudly foolish," "terror struck," "too weighty charge": in and out of context the language of the whole section (194–95) tells the story and the "other story."

Bradstreet must certainly have succeeded in deflecting criticism for her daring and in garnering her readers' sympathy with the pathos of her self-figurations in the elegies to Du Bartas and Sidney and in the "Prologue." They could scarcely be more abject or a more transparent reflection of patriarchal imperatives.[43] In each of the three poems Bradstreet adds to her first-person protestations of humility a different portrait of her Muse, who represents the authorial part of her self. The speaker in the early elegy to Du Bartas (1641) declares herself dazzled, ravished, and muted by the splendor of the French poet's verse. She compares her Muse to a little boy who admires the glitter of a fair and attempts futilely to convey his impressions to his mother. The terms in which the speaker describes the boy fit Aristotle's category of the "natural slave," an insidiously enduring notion that equates children, women, and barbarians as all needing (the civilized) man's rule. Analogous to the natural slave, Bradstreet's child-Muse is inferior (to Du Bartas), dependent (on the mother to whom he turns for comfort), bereft of "understanding" and reason (he "speaks no word of sense"), and passive (thwarted by his inability to speak, he "[s]its down in silence"). The superior civilized male naturally dominates the natural slave. Similarly, Bradstreet's Muse and the speaker's "weak-brained" "I" are overwhelmed by the accomplished Du Bartas whose praises they vainly seek to sing. Childish too, and an antithesis of the classical figure, is the "foolish, broken, blemished Muse" of the "Prologue." Like a "schoolboy," she lacks rhetoric; the now female Muse lacks beauty and harmony as well. In an image painfully suggestive of the instrumentalization of women by patriarchal society, Bradstreet refers to her Muse's "broken strings." The instrument in question, Caldwell notes (7), may have been a virginal!

Bradstreet's innately imperfect Muse ("nature made it so irreparable," 15), the figure of lack, faces the classical Muses in the elegy to Sidney only to have her pen—a metaphorical penis?—taken away. The female Muses of this poem (and of the "Prologue," stanza 2) have allied themselves with males and against their own sex. When the poetic speaker and her doubting Muse apply to the nine Muses for aid, they discover that the Muses "had no will / To give to their detractor any quill; / With high disdain, they said they gave no more, / Since Sidney had exhausted all their store" (191). The first version now interpolates: "That this contempt it did the more perplex, / In being done by one of their own sex" (Piercy ed., 195). The "injured" Muses confiscate the speaker's "scribbling pen" and drive her "from Parnassus in a rage." Finally, Errata throws her the pen with which the speaker concludes the poem. The message of this anxiety-ridden poem is all but self-evident. In praising Sidney, Bradstreet's female speaker has attempted to storm the male domain of Parnassus.[44] A transgression of such magnitude ires even her own sex, who divest her of authorship because she is a woman. The male-aligned Muses brand her as an errata and, for "blemishing" their fame (Piercy ed., 195), exile her and her blemished Muse from heaven. The two remain disinherited, orphaned, and alone of all their sex.[45]

❧

We now move into a series of striking coincidences between the works of Bradstreet and Sor Juana, coincidences generated at least in part by the humble postures their cultures oblige them to assume. The first concerns the lamentably similar relationship of the Tenth Muses to the nine consecrated

Muses. Where the Muses in Bradstreet's elegy to Sidney, as we have just seen, grudgingly grant her the pen of Errata, those of Sor Juana's Romance #50 deign to throw her the leftovers from male poets. Sor Juana writes her epistolary poem in reply to the laudatory verses (1, #49 bis) that the Count de la Granja had directed to her. With characteristic baroque excess and hyperbole he described her poetry as having robbed the Muses of their function and as surpassing the works of a host of male poets (Virgil, Góngora, Quevedo, Ovid, Camões, and so on). With equal hyperbole and great comic prowess Sor Juana offers the Count in return the story of how she came to her poetic inspiration. The first-person speaker tells us that she began, "por modo de vicio" (155) [out of bad habit], by poking around in the vessels containing water from the Castalian fount of poetic inspiration. After finding some dust in them that allowed her to start writing, she consulted the nine Muses. Seeing her "tan hambrienta de ejercicios, / tan sedienta de conceptos / y tan desnuda de estilos" (156) [so hungry for something to do, so thirsty for conceits, and so lacking in styles], the Muses took pity on her and jokingly threw her the crumbs of inspiration that remained from the classical male poets. From whence it follows, writes Sor Juana, that she cannot be a "worthy object" of the Count's praise. "Y no es humildad" (157) [And it's not a question of humility]—or so she says.

Together with humility formulae, Sor Juana and Bradstreet avail themselves of yet another classical topic to manifest their unease with authorship: the book as child. In representing themselves as writers and in their writings, both either employ the topic directly or allude to it by linking procreation with literary creation. Though it might seem quite natural for a woman writer to take recourse to the topic, our authors make it perform two very similar unnatural acts. The first manifests itself in Bradstreet's elegy to Du Bartas and Sor Juana's Silva #215, the second in the same *silva* and Bradstreet's "The Author to Her Book."

The first two poems mentioned expose the ravages of being a "Complete Poet," that is, of incursions into "male" literary territory. Both Bradstreet's elegy to her precursor Du Bartas, a male, and Sor Juana's *silva* celebrating the victory at Barlovento (poem #215), a masculinist historical/epic theme, find the authors responding to their overwhelming subjects with female corporeal imagery. The male subjects of the poems, as we will see, implicate and even denaturalize the female body or its progeny. Bradstreet's poem effects a fairly straightforward, yet still disturbing, reversal as the poetic speaker surrenders her role as fertile female to the poetically fecund Du Bartas. His is the "pregnant brain" filled with the "vast comprehension" (194) that makes him intellectual master of the universe. If master, why not mistress too? Indeed, he is the natural force that causes "flowers and fruits soon to abound" (192). She, on the other hand, is "barren," and if by chance the female speaker should produce any fruits or flowers, she will yield them unto him in homage. Bradstreet's depiction in this poem of her Muse as a little *boy* now becomes more significant, for we see that in face of the all-consuming Du Bartas she has defeminized her speaker on two counts: making her both barren and a diminutive male.

Sor Juana 's *silva* headed a volume of poetry published in 1691 to celebrate the victory over the French of the armada of Barlovento (the Windward Islands fleet) led by the Count de Galve. Hers was the only female voice in the collection. As far as we know, neither before nor after did the poet again treat such a theme. The poem is her only *silva* besides the *Sueño* and boasts the same dense, convoluted language as that poem–and a similarly elided "I." All of the preceding factors have a bearing on the singular structure and nature of the poem. Of the poem's 138 lines Sor Juana devotes only 26 to narrating the events of the victory per se. The rest of the poem concerns itself with the impossibility of doing justice to its lofty subject: the Count and his victory. The "I" appears only indirectly but in a strategic enough position to make it patent that the travails pertain to the speaker: "No cabal relación, indicio breve / sí, de tus glorias, Silva [the third last name of the Count] esclarecido, / será el débil sonido / *de rauca voz*" (ll. 1–4; italics mine) [Not a detailed description, but a brief indication of your glories, famous Silva, will be provided by the feeble sound of an *already hoarse voice*].

The impossible theme and the impossibility of writing catapult the speaker into the corporeal. We recall that the *Sueño* presents the body as inimical to the mind: only sleep allows the mind unfettered flight and the need for food curtails its flight. Silva #215, for its part, employs corporeal imagery to excoriate as monstrous the speaker's imperfect thought and writing. In a flood of maternity imagery, the speaker reviles her writings as malformed aborted concepts, shapeless embryos rather than mature offspring, imperfect progeny, an aborted son–and compares herself to a cloud pregnant with rain. It is important to note that neither here nor elsewhere does Sor Juana's poetry display any conventional maternal longings. She refigures even the archetypal mother, the Virgin Mary, into mother of the Word (see the *Ejercicios de la Encarnación*, vol. 4; my chapter 5 discusses the role of maternal imagery as a function of the *Sueño*'s quest for knowledge). In Sor Juana's personal idiom, maternity is at heart a giving birth to learning and writing. I can therefore accept neither Alfonso Méndez Plancarte's parochial and summary dismissal of the maternity imagery of the poem as "high-flown poetic Latinisms" (573) nor Ludwig Pfandl's prurient contention that the poem represents Sor Juana's "stifled cry for a child" (138).

In fact, what Pfandl sees as a cry for a child, I see as the expression of a rape. Classical notions of procreation derived from Aristotle and persisting to the end of the seventeenth century considered the female womb to be inactive, to provide merely the inert material activated by the male's vitalizing sperm. Similarly, and again echoing Aristotle (for whom "conception is the male having an idea in the female body" [Laqueur, 35]), the only redeeming features the speaker allows her monstrous progeny derive from the "divino ardimiento" [divine burning] that the Count "engendró en mi entendimiento" [engendered in my mind]. The engendering takes on far more violent sexual connotations in the poem's third stanza. There, as I have said, the speaker compares herself to a cloud pregnant with rain–a cloud, moreover, forced into giving birth by the tyrannical and disharmonious thunder ("que al cielo descompone la armonía," which disturbs the heaven's harmony) that *rips* it ("rasga") and aborts the child ("el hijo aborta, luminoso," luminous, aborts the child). A pregnant image indeed! The fourth stanza compounds the eroticism by showing the virginal oracle of Delfos, impregnated by Apollo with ideas ("preñada de conceptos divinos," pregnant with divine concepts), in a quasi-orgasmic frenzy ("encendida, / inflamada la mente," on fire, the mind inflamed) that reduces her to babbling. The two subsequent stanzas directly link the extended metaphorical comparisons to the speaker's struggles with her theme. Once again, as in the "Respuesta" (conceivably written in the same month), Sor Juana has called on imagery of possession to exculpate herself; yet now, in the face of an impossible theme of a distinctly "unfeminine" nature, possession shades into a sexual violation that produces unnatural offspring.

The metaphor of the book as child, Curtius tells us, derives from Plato's *Symposium*. There Diotima remarks that instead of actual children, poets would rather produce the books that bring them everlasting fame. Traditionally, then, the brainchild that ensures his immortality has been lauded and loved by the male writer (see Curtius, 132–34). Such is hardly the case of Sor Juana's misshapen "abortions" or of the "ill-formed offspring of my feeble brain" to whom Bradstreet addresses her poem entitled "The Author to Her Book." In fact, as it did in Sor Juana's *silva*, the denaturalizing of maternity will form the axis of Bradstreet's poem and self-representation. Bradstreet composed the piece for the second edition of her collection, published (unlike the first) with her knowledge. She clearly had the first edition in mind. The prefatory material of the first edition, with its obsessive focus on gender issues, had brought home to Bradstreet (as if it were necessary) the problematic nature of her work. This introductory poem, "The Author to Her Book," takes advantage of the second edition to reassert her humility and to domesticate and naturalize her writing into a child. In availing herself of the book as child metaphor, Bradstreet would also appear to be responding to the prefatory poem ("To My Dear Sister, The Author of These Poems") that drew on the topic to justify the publication of the book or "infant": "I know your modest mind, / How you will blush, complain, 'tis too unkind: / To force a woman's birth, provoke her pain, / Expose her labours to the world's disdain" (6). Woodbridge presents the publication of his sister-in-law's work as a violation of a woman's "labours," and Bradstreet responds in kind, lamenting the manner in which her ill-prepared offspring was snatched prematurely from her side "by friends, less wise than true," and "exposed to public view."

The book may be a child, but there the correspondence between creation and procreation ends. Ironically enough, to situate herself in the topic and at the same time to preserve her modesty, Bradstreet must do violence to both child and mother. If in her elegy to Du Bartas he was pregnant and she barren, now she is a mother, but the mother of a monster: "ill-formed," a "rambling brat," "unfit for light," of "irksome visage," full of "blemishes" and "defects" (like Bradstreet's Muse), crippled. Well worth pondering is the connection between her book as monstrous child and the putative monstrous births of rebel Anne Hutchinson—reportedly thirty misshapen creatures!—and of her follower Mary Dyer as punitively described by Puritan Governor Winthrop:

> God himselfe was pleased to step in with his casting voice, and bring in his owne vote and suffrage from heaven, by testifying his displeasure against their opinions and practices, as clearly as if he had pointed with his finger, in causing the two fomenting women in the time of the height of the Opinions to produce out of their wombs, *as before they had out of their braines*, such monstrous births as no Chronicle (I thinke) hardly ever recorded the like. (Barker-Benfield, 82; italics mine)

Bradstreet may have produced just one rambling creature, but its existence sufficed for the poet to contravene her self-identified maternal instincts. Unlike Sor Juana, Bradstreet had raised eight children to maturity in the wilderness, had addressed her spiritual autobiography to them, and had written a most loving poem about them: "I had eight birds hatched in one nest, / Four cocks there were, and hens the rest. / I nursed them up with pain and care, / Nor cost, nor labour did I spare" ("In Reference to Her Children," 232). In "The Author to Her Book," however, while admitting that "being mine own at length affection would / Thy blemishes amend, if so I could," Bradstreet's speaker considers her literary child a "brat" of "irksome visage" and tries ineffectually to correct his flaws. Expanding on Spenser's metaphor and lines from *The Shepheardes Calendar* ("But if that any aske thy name, / Say thou wert base begot with blame" [Stanford 1974, 73]), she ends up sending him out of the door with the injunction that he declare his mother poor and his birth illegitimate: "If for thy father asked, say thou hadst none; / And for thy mother, she alas is poor, / Which caused her thus to send thee out of door." Illegitimacy was hardly a matter to be taken lightly in the Puritan setting, but then again neither were a woman's verses—which no pater or patriarchy was overly disposed to sanction.

Both Bradstreet and Sor Juana, we have seen, were keenly aware of this fact, and each in her own way skewed the book as child metaphor into yet another humility topic. Women using the book as child metaphor, Susan Stanford Friedman writes, tend to defy the division between creation and procreation, reconstituting "woman's fragmented self into a (pro)creative whole uniting word and flesh, body and mind" (75). Mindful of the transgressive nature of their enterprises and the criticism it could elicit, on the other hand, Bradstreet and Sor Juana invoke a possible (pro)creative whole only to dismantle it. By means of the familiar topic they summon a natural association between motherhood and authorship that might neutralize their trespasses and then for the same reason proceed to set up a de facto disjunction between the two by reviling their unnatural literary offspring. Indicative of the punishing and self-punishing situation of women writers in the public domain of the early modern Western world, for both authors creation ultimately becomes a travesty of procreation, and authorship of motherhood.

IV.

*Here, there her restless thoughts do ever fly, / Constant
in nothing but inconstancy.*
    –ANNE BRADSTREET, "The Four Humours"

Yo sé que es frágil / la naturaleza, / y que su constancia / sola, es no tenerla.

*[Well I know how frail Nature's nature must be since she
is constant only in inconstancy.]*
    –SOR JUANA, Endecha #70

The poems analyzed up to now have afforded ample and rather discouraging evidence of Bradstreet's and Sor Juana's complicity in their self-representations with patriarchal norms regarding women and women writers. Other, contradictory, aspects of their poetry, however, allow me to end the chapter on a somewhat more heartening note. I will therefore conclude by examining very briefly one last coincidence between the two writers: the shared fissures in their positions regarding women, the contradictory instability of their writings on this subject and on the subject herself qua woman. That Bradstreet and Sor Juana at times defend their own sex and even themselves as writers places into question if not their humbleness–which I concede may be genuine–then certainly the complicity with patriarchal attitudes involving women that they have displayed elsewhere. It provides the telltale signs of a halfhearted internalization of and adherence to imposed norms common to other women writers as well (Walker observes that "such vacillation is the one fundamentally pervasive feature of American women's poetry up to 1945" [9]).[46] The deconstruction of their unfavorable view of women insinuates that yet another auto-machia, one implied by the imagery of violation and in the unnatural rending of creation from procreation just discussed, underwrites the poems on authorship: that of a woman betraying herself and her sex.

Where chapter 2 of this book, together with the "Respuesta," the *villancicos* to Santa Catarina, and numerous other texts leave little doubt (if doubt there was) as to Sor Juana's defense of women in the abstract and in general, the present chapter has shown her speaking in what is unmistakably another voice about the self as woman. However, we have seen that Sor Juana constructs competing versions of her self in the "Respuesta" and throughout her oeuvre, and a militant version of the self in the "Autodefensa." Not an angry but a rather self-congratulatory "I" also makes its appearance in two of the nun's most famous sonnets, #146 (which begins, "En perseguirme, Mundo, ¿qué interesas?"; World, in hounding me, what do you gain? [*95*]) and #152 ("Verde embeleso de la vida humana," Green allurement of our human life [*101*]). Both credo poems favor knowledge over the transitoriness of material things. Both emphatically foreground their speaker's "I" as a paragon of the philosophical virtues the poems advocate: a baroque neo-Stoicism in Sonnet #146, *desengaño* in Sonnet #152. Inserted in the tissue of baroque commonplaces that constitute the poems and perhaps form a smoke screen for the speaker's self-defense, the "I" almost dissolves into impersonality. Nevertheless, autobiographical references to persecution (by a "World" that in the context of the poem could craftily refer to the worldly world or to a hostile public), and to learning and reason, inevitably would foment an identification in the reader's mind between two "I's" and their author. Not fully dispelled and hardly unassuming, the "I" of both sonnets promotes herself and contradicts the posture of her other self-representational poems.

Scholars have pinched and probed and pored over Bradstreet's self-depictions, hoping to eke out some protofeminist posture that would mitigate their apparent humility. One can quibble about the meaning of "I am obnoxious to each carping tongue," but for the most part I am afraid that we will have to let Bradstreet's words stand at face value and accept the posture she proffers. It takes a "practiced, interested, and modern eye," notes Schweitzer (1991, 167), to read Bradstreet's feminist leanings. That interested eye finds the going easier in the poet's less personal works. As the following lines that describe the Quaternions in the poem to her father suggest, the argument can be made (and has been; see Watts) that Bradstreet favored a more "female" relational unity over the "masculine" aggressiveness she descries in her father's poetic figures: "Yours did contest for wealth, for arts, for age, / My first do show their good, and then their rage, . . . And yet in equal tempers, how they 'gree / How divers natures make one unity" (14).[47] The real smoking gun, however, Bradstreet's only forthright statement in favor of women, is her poem "In Honour of That High and Mighty Princess Queen Elizabeth of Happy Memory" (1643).

That Queen Elizabeth had restored Protestantism and created an atmosphere of relative religious tolerance established her as a fit subject for praise from a Puritan pen. Yet Bradstreet does not limit herself to exalting those halcyon days of Elizabeth's England. She also utilizes her subject as a model and a platform for a vindication of the female sex, on which the poet herself had cast aspersions: "She [Elizabeth] hath wiped off th' aspersion of her sex, / That women wisdom lack to play the rex" (196). In the poem to Queen Elizabeth, Bradstreet allows herself to envision a different script for a woman, radically unlike her own and that of her mother, who died in 1643. Whereas in the same year that she wrote the poem to Elizabeth the poet elegized her mother as a "worthy matron of unspotted life, / a loving mother and obedi-ent wife" ("An Epitaph on My Dear and Ever-Honoured Mother Mrs. Dorothy Dudley," 204), she depicts the monarch as a manly woman. Elizabeth acts in the public sphere ("The world's the theatre where she did act," 195); a "virago," and an "Amazon," "[f]rom all the kings on earth she won the prize" (196–97). Elizabeth may be a manly woman, but she is also heiress to a proud female lineage. The queen ranks with Minerva and Pallas Athena for her learning and wisdom. Even more interesting, Bradstreet gives over many lines of her poem to a list of illustrious women rulers from antiq-uity analogous to Sor Juana's catalog of learned women in the "Respuesta." Elizabeth, surpassing them all and creating what Bradstreet depicts as a veri-table utopia ("Was ever people better ruled than hers? / Was ever land more happy freed from stirs?" [196]), carries the proud female tradition from antiq-uity to the present. And to the future: ending the poem in an apotheosis that portends the Puritan millennium, Bradstreet predicts the rebirth of the "Phoenix" Queen–a Second Coming of Elizabeth Regina that will restore not only "happy England" but a gynocracy in which men's "slander" of women will once again be treason (198).[48] Bradstreet's backward glance to a strong female forebear of the sixteenth century, far less conflicted than Sor Juana's, epitomizes the conservative romance of a seventeenth-century woman writer with an idealized recent past that may serve as a model for the future.

The early portions of the poem to Elizabeth seem to augur a renascence of another kind, of Bradstreet's self-imaging. In a faintly positive statement, the speaker asserts her belief that Elizabeth *will* accept her praise, however rough. Unlike Sidney's Muses who betrayed their own sex, Elizabeth will not snatch her pen away. That the subject's is a "loyal brain" suffices for Elizabeth, whose "clemency" allowed her to esteem the acclamations of rich and poor (195). Moreover, the accomplishments of Elizabeth leave *male* poets equally rapt and inadequate to "compact" the monarch's works and wars. The political combines with the poetic to render the speaker a worthy subject of Elizabeth and to grant the poetic voice a tenuous authority as a writer. In a later passage of the poem, nevertheless, the speaker retrogresses. Whoever would do jus-tice to the perfections of Elizabeth, the speaker tells us, must "dip his pen in th' Heleconian well," which contains the origins of a poet's creative impulses. "Which I," the speaker adds in a return to Bradstreet's familiar humility, "may not, my pride doth but aspire / to read what others write and so admire" (197). Yet immediately afterward, in a dramatic about-face that leaves the reader reeling and asking precisely the same question, the speaker queries, "Now say, have women worth? or have they none? / Or had they some, but with our Queen is gone?" (197–98). The poetic voice then proceeds to attack men head-on, indignantly responding to the "despite they cast on female wits" ("Prologue," 16): "Nay masculines, you have thus taxed us long, / but she, though dead, will vindicate our wrong. / Let such as say our sex is void of rea-son, / Know 'tis a slander now but once was treason" (198).

This cameo moment perfectly encapsulates the instability of Bradstreet's position on her sex as well as that of her sister writer Sor Juana. Bradstreet's speaker demeans herself in the first person as writer and defends her sex in the third. What Bradstreet enacts in the span of a single stanza, Sor Juana apportions, for example, between the autobiographical *narratio* and the erudite *prueba* of her "Respuesta." The disjunction between their first- and third-person representations of women and its implicit auto-machia suggests that Bradstreet and Sor Juana prefer to sacrifice or scapegoat the self in order to keep on writing. A posture of self-abnegation serves as an enabling disclaimer that allows the two early modern women poets to write, to infringe on the domain of masculinist themes and the male domain of the public sphere, and to keep on writing not always otherwise but always in spite of.

The preceding conclusion invites us to revisit the interdiction of the "I" encountered in the *Primero sueño*–that curiously incomplete complete poem, replete with un-"feminine" themes, split between the third and first person. It leads us to consider why Sor Juana relegates the "I" to the margins (and to margins suggestive of failure) in what is arguably her most personal, most intimate, most autobiographical poem. No doubt she wishes to universalize the search for knowledge, eschewing associations with a particular individual. The foregoing chapter, however, argues that this is not the only reason for the elided and peripheral "I" of the *Sueño*. As our expedition into the self-representations of the New World's first published female poets has endeavored to establish, in the cases of both Bradstreet and Sor Juana the "I" remains a battleground or, as I stated at the outset of the chapter, an overdetermined site in which the manifold tensions bound up in the milieux of the early modern writing women oppressively and perhaps even ineluctably impose themselves. These literally civil wars redound into self–civil wars from which the "I" cannot emerge intact, victorious, or unequivocally defiant, for both the "languages"–religious and otherwise–at their disposal and the strictures of the societies in which Bradstreet and Sor Juana wrote induce the two women writers to assert their selves in self-nihilating contexts. The origins of women's self-representation in the New World, in poetry and spiritual autobiography alike, it follows, lie in self-erasure and self-abnegation.

How can the self be written in a context that militates for its erasure and destruction? As we have discovered, the nihilating of self need not entail an entirely impoverished self-representation or the utter forgoing of a distinctive subject position: the less agreeable sides of life, as the hundreds of pages of Robert Burton's 1621 *Anatomy of Melancholy* well attest, have a considerable life and scope of their own; the road toward verbal compliance with subjectivity allows Bradstreet brief pungent flashes of individualism; Sor Juana's characteristic posture of melancholic self-reviling makes for nuanced inquiries into the various dimensions of her life as a celebrity, a thinker, and a nun–all seen through a glass darkly rather than heroically. The mechanisms of spiritual autobiography allow interiority and selfhood to be expressed on the way to subjectivity, and indeed, the two Complete Poets go to great lengths and depths in exposing their own incompleteness or inadequacy. Nevertheless, the bulk of their self-representational works supports the conclusion that both Sor Juana and Anne Bradstreet would appear to consider the patently autobiographical "I" far too dangerous an arena for the rehearsing of radical and dearly held positions such as the *Sueño*'s association of the female self with the indomitable ("segunda vez rebelde," rebelling once again) quest for knowledge. This kind of writing otherwise, we conclude, was best enacted elsewhere.

CHAPTER FIVE

The New Prometheus:
Women's Education, Autodidacticism,
and the Will to Signature

sirtes tocando / de imposibles
[brushing the shoals of impossible things]
—PRIMERO SUEÑO (LL. 828–29)

Ireturn to the wellspring of my inquiries, the *Primero sueño* or "First Dream." Now it is the overture and not the ending of the liquid poem that affords us an aperture into this chapter and its investigations of the relationship between early modern women and knowledge. For it is in the overture (vol. 1, ll. 1–64; Trueblood, *171–73*), in a penitential register harking back to the spiritual autobiography,[1] that Sor Juana tropes a gripping portrait of the New Prometheus and her labors–that is, of the female Prometheus wresting knowledge no longer from the gods but from the patriarchal stronghold.

Walking into the poem's overture, let me say that for reasons that will become increasingly clear over the course of the present chapter, I visualize the *Primero sueño* (henceforth to be abbreviated as *PS*) both as a river and as a richly figured, variously woven tapestry that depicts multiple scenes. As a tapestry, its patterning alternates between the reembroidering of set pieces or topics and the crafting of what I call matrix moments: densely wrought sections, thick with symbolic implications, that in spiraling *ritornellas* repeatedly cipher the larger message of the poem. The overture is one such matrix moment. Consonant with the feminine connotations of the word *matrix*, it unfurls a series of female characters each of whom is cast from the same mold or paradigm–of daring transgression–and each of whom at the same time adds the nuances of her own particularity to the paradigm. The pyramidal shadow, undoubtedly the poem's most resonant and emblematic symbol, is the first to make her appearance. External manifestation of the soul aspiring to the First Cause (cf. ll. 400–408, *181*), Neoplatonic archetype of spiritual wisdom and of the soul's rise to enlightenment, embodiment of human vanity challenging the Divinity (Harss, 74), the pyramid initiates the Soul's daring

search: "escalar pretendiendo las Estrellas" (l. 4) [Bent on scaling stars, *171*].
Beset by ill omens, this lugubrious "punta altiva" (l. 3) or towering tip immediately sees herself mocked by the heavens in the form of the stars and granted access only to the border of Diana's realm, the lowest of the celestial
spheres.

The cosmic aspirations of the Shadow quickly take on more specific
dimensions as that border region is constituted as her "imperio" or empire (l.
20) and populated by the nightbirds who at once define the quest, delimit it
as feminine,[2] and mark it as transgressive. Untying the knotted mythological
allusions of the next two stanzas, we find in them the stories of Nyctimene
and of the Minyades, all female figures who committed transgressions against
the patriarchal order related to knowledge, all of whom were dealt fearsome
punishments for their sins. Sor Juana builds the disgrace of Pandora and Eve's
original sin into her construction of the "shamed" Nyctimene as the very figure of a *female* Prometheus. This maid of Lesbos committed incest with
her father and was turned into an owl who, in Ovid's words from the
Metamorphoses,[3] "flies from sight of men and from light of day" (book 2, 74) in
shame. The owl, for its part, was considered an unholy creature that desecrated church altars by drinking the oils of the candles and thus extinguishing
the sacred flames (Harss, 79). Stalking the holy temple for a place that will let
her in ("que capaz a su intento le abren brecha" [l. 31]), as did the Shadow,
Nyctimene attempts to enter the sacred realm. The Shadow assaulted the
whole heavens; the chastened Nyctimene, like the "Sor Juana" of Romance
#50 who scavenged around the leftover vessels of the Castalian fount of poetic creation, consigns herself to the nooks and crannies of the temple. Sor Juana
avails herself of the traditional identification of the owl as the bird of Minerva
in order to cement the association between Nyctimene and stolen knowledge.
"Sacrilegious," Nyctimene extinguishes or, significantly, *defiles* ("infama" [l.
34]) the sacred olive oil of Minerva.

That Minerva's sacred oil was squeezed from the presses by dint of arduous labor (ll. 37–38) betokens Sor Juana's portrait of hard-gained knowledge
in the "Respuesta" and leads into her treatment of the Minyades in the *PS*.
The three daughters of Minyas ("a la deidad de Baco inobedientes" [l. 41])
refused to participate in the orgiastic cult of Bacchus, god of wine and fertility. Eschewing the festivals of the male god, eschewing bacchanalia, they
remained at home hard at their labors and firm in their worship of the female
goddess Minerva. In Ovid we read: "While others run away from household
duties / To waste their time with dubious priests and prayers, / We choose to
give our faith to chaste Minerva, / A better goddess than the god they know"
(book 4, 112). The labors of the Minyades entailed the quintessentially "feminine" occupation of weaving, accompanied by the quintessentially transgressive activity of female authorship, in the form of storytelling ("historias
contando diferentes" [l. 42]). Over the course of several pages in Ovid's poem
(book 4, 112–22) we see and hear the Minyades telling their stories, which
are–in a *mise en abîme* effect likely to have appealed to the ever literarily self-

conscious Sor Juana–stories of the metamorphoses to which the Minyades themselves would fall victim. In fact, given Sor Juana's self-conscious tendency to portray her authorship as transgressive and her penchant for creating in the *PS* what Harss terms "floating self-images" (80 et passim), it may not be misguided to interpret her first and rare use of a first-person verb in the description of the Minyades's daring ("digo," I mean–the rhetorical *figura correctionis* [l. 47]) as an inscription of herself into their portrait. However we interpret it, the "digo" introduces Sor Juana's grotesque description of the Minyades's punishment for their scorn of the male god and defiant insistence on their own goddess and storytelling: their metamorphosis into bats with featherless wings, into a fearsome parody of Sor Juana's much-invoked Icarus.

Ascalaphus joins the bat-women in the final emblematic image of the overture, the nightchorus. The first active male figure to appear in the *PS*, he nevertheless plays an eminently "female" role in this drama of transgressive knowledge. As gardener of Hades, Ascalaphus informed Pluto that Persephone had eaten some pomegranate seeds, thereby condemning her to the underworld for half the year (Harss, 80). With a sprinkling of river water he was turned into a screech owl in punishment of his betrayal of Persephone. The punishment fits the crime as well as the feminist context of the *PS*. For having betrayed a woman, and moreover, for incarnating the proclivity to gossip seen by misogynists as stereotypically feminine,[4] Ascalaphus becomes the caricatured metonymy of womankind. Ascalaphus's ill-conceived use of knowledge, his function as the double of sacrilegious fellow owl Nyctimene, and the association of the screech owl ("supersticioso indicio al agorero," the diviner's superstitious omen [l. 55]), with evil genius (Harss, 80), all ally him with the Promethean implications of the overture. They also call to mind the Devil/Eco of Sor Juana's *El Divino Narciso*–in the play's rendition of the myth, a woman punished for telling tales out of school.[5] Echoes of the metamorphosed and muted Eco seep into the final image of the *Sueño*'s overture as Ascalaphus joins his crippled ruin of a voice to those of the Minyades. Together they form the screechy, halting, terrifying lament of the nightchorus: "la no canora / componían capilla pavorosa, / máximas, negras, longas entonando, / y pausas más que voces" (ll. 56–59) [the fearsome jangling choir, droning long and longer lengthened notes, and pausing more than singing, *173*]. In *El Divino Narciso*, Christ/Narciso signifies and embodies harmony and sacred similitude; the Devil/Eco entails their opposite.[6] Here the nightchorus, inversion of an angelic choir and antagonistic counterpoint to the Pythagorean harmony of the spheres (cf. Harss, 82), introduces a fearful dissonance that comprises a fitting theme song for the foregoing tableaux of the shamed yet defiant learned ladies of the night.

Learned ladies, the early modern Prometheus–their voicing of the seventeenth-century crisis in women's education, their arrogating of knowledge to themselves, their defiance and circumvention of patriarchal structures–are the subject of this final and in many ways capstone chapter of my study. Here, among other things, I will attempt more fully to engage with the texture and totality of the *Primero sueño* than I have in previous chapters. The reader may ask: Why do I return so consistently to the *Primero sueño*? Yes, it is Sor Juana's masterpiece, the sum and summa of her works. Of equal importance, in the course of my investigations on seventeenth-century Western women writers I have also found the inexhaustibly rich *PS* to entail a magnificent (if unwitting) scholium for many of their common concerns and for many of the issues of representation that their texts raise. The foregoing chapters have in important ways borne out my contention. In terms of the present chapter, we have already begun to glimpse how the *PS* speaks to the desire of certain seventeenth-century learned women to storm the world of knowledge, part of what I will be calling the *will to signature*. By *will to signature* I mean the woman's desire to dominate (especially in the Spanish sense of the word *dominar*: control, master, stand out), to make her mark, to stake out her place, in the City of Knowledge—that is, in the seductive, institutionalized, male-controlled, and almost exclusively male world of learning. Since in the seventeenth century the City of Knowledge was anything but a City of Ladies, the will to signature entailed self-authorizing through autodidacticism, an education outside institutionalized structures and strictures. The actual signature of her works, as we have seen at various junctures, presented no small problems for the seventeenth-century female author;[7] the will to signature, I believe, imposes itself in default or defiance of that problematic self-broadcasting. The *PS*, I will argue, not only articulates the will to signature, but also literally em-bodies it. Therefore, in the first part of the chapter, continuing the line of inquiry begun in my own overture, I will examine the relationship of the early modern woman to knowledge and its fablelike *thematization* in the *PS*. In the second part, through an excursus into the works of Sor Juana's near-contemporary, Margaret Lucas Cavendish (1623–73), we will come to see how the *PS* in fact *textualizes* the same issues, issues that constitute the overriding concerns of seventeenth-century female feminists and form the crux of their generational impulse.

I.

It is commonly understood that knowledge and power go hand in hand. Knowledge is power in and of itself; knowledge can and should function as the cornerstone of social power. Simple logic then leads to the conclusion that to withhold knowledge is to limit power, to disenfranchise those from whom it is withheld. This truth being self-evident, as did the gods of classical mythology keep fire from humankind, so has the patriarchal state consistently barred women from access to knowledge and thus to power by controlling their educational opportunities. Gerda Lerner categorically states in *The Creation of a Feminist Consciousness* that the "disadvantaging of women in gaining access to education and in participating in educational establishments has been a consistent feature of patriarchal power in every state for over two thousand years"

(18). Seventeenth-century feminists across Europe, addressing what they perceived to be the *crisis in women's education*, were no less cognizant of the intimate connection between education and power, and the monopolization of both by men. Marie de Gournay wrote in her "Grief des Dames" [The Ladies' Grievance] (1626): "Happy are you, reader, if you do not belong to this sex to whom all good things are forbidden, since to us freedom is forbidden; and whom they [men] prevent from acquiring almost all virtues by keeping us away from power, in the moderation of which most virtues are formed, to leave us as our only form of happiness and as our only sovereign virtues: ignorance, foolishness, and subservience" (*23*). François Poullain de La Barre (1647–1723), whom Simone de Beauvoir has called the "leading feminist of the age" in France (121), notes in his 1673 *De l'égalité des deux sexes* [The Equality of Both Sexes] that, "according to the manner of dealing familiar to all *Men*, it is only by force and Empire that they have reserved for themselves these Extrinsical Advantages [of education and action in the public sphere]; from which, the Female Sex is debarred" (74; I quote from the 1677 English translation of his work). British educator and learned woman Bathsua Makin (1612?–74?) pinpoints in 1673 the crux of the prevailing situation: "Let Women be Fools, and then you may easily make them Slaves" (34). And the Spanish María de Zayas, even more cynically, conjectures in the *Desengaños amorosos* that men have excluded women from arms and letters, limiting them to domestic labors, due to fear: "It would be a good thing for women to use swords, then they would never suffer affront from any man. It would be even better for women to profess in letters, for then they would cost men fewer doubts and more jobs. Because of men's fears, women are put down and obliged to do only household tasks" (*140*, 228–29).

The preceding statements speak to the fact that over the course of its history the patriarchy has utilized knowledge as a prime mechanism of social and political control as well as to the fact that it has fashioned the world of learning into what I call the City of Knowledge, a male-controlled domain from which women are excluded or to which their access is severely limited. The specific roots of the patriarchal City of Knowledge, Poullain recognized, lay in the formation of universities: "[S]everal *Men* had received some tincture of this new Learning, they began to assemble themselves in certain Places, to discourse thereof more at leisure; where every one speaking his Thoughts, Knowledge ripened, and Colledges and Accademies were appointed, where the *Women* were not admitted; but in the same manner were excluded from Learning, as they had been from all the rest" (72). Recent women's historians have substantiated Poullain's assertion by tracing the dramatic changes in the relationship between women and knowledge from the twelfth to the thirteenth century.[8] The twelfth century had provided a favorable climate for women's learning in monastic settings: double monasteries run by female abbesses, convent schools teaching the trivium and running scriptoria where women copied manuscripts, male teachers with female disciples, and what appears to have been a general appreciation for the learned lady. The thirteenth century witnessed the institutionalization of knowledge through the birth of universities, which effectively functioned as corporations licensing teaching and the professions of law, medicine, and theology. Since women could neither attend universities nor exercise the professions for which they prepared their students, a much larger gender gap in education than had previously existed resulted from the institutionalization of learning. Education in convents deteriorated. Early Christian misogyny, the vilification of woman as Eve in order to promote the chastity of male monks (as well as the subjugation of females), increasingly and vehemently reinforced the exclusion of women from the City of Knowledge.

"An Essay to Revive the antient Education Of Gentlewomen" (1673), by Bathsua Makin, aptly identifies a second dramatic development in the City of Knowledge, one that pressed even more directly than the medieval constitution of universities on the seventeenth-century crisis in women's education. In the essay's preface, Makin contrasts the present with the past: "I verily think, Women were formerly Educated in the knowledge of Arts and Tongues, and by their Education, many did rise to a great height in Learning. Were Women thus Educated now I am confident the advantage would be very great: The Women would have Honour and Pleasure, their Relations Profit, and the whole Nation Advantage" (3–4). Makin's argument in itself as well as the examples she later provides of sixteenth-century learned women from England and Italy make it clear that the "antient Education Of Gentlewomen" to which she refers was that practiced by Renaissance humanists. William Wotten, in his 1694 *Reflections upon Ancient and Modern Learning*, echoes Makin's perceptions of the decline in women's education from the previous century (with a statement that Mary Astell in turn cites in her "Proposal" [153]). During the sixteenth century, Wotten says, to educate women "was so very modish that the fair Sex seem'd to believe that Greek and Latin added to their Charms; and Plato and Aristotle untranslated were frequent Ornaments of their Closets. One wou'd think by the effects that it was a proper way of Educating them, since there are no accounts in History of so many great Women in any one Age, as are to be found between the years 15 and 1600" (Brink, 86). Speaking from a distance–albeit a relatively small one–and suiting their polemical purposes, all three essayists extol the sixteenth century's attitude toward women's learning. As did María de Zayas regarding the treatment of women, they invoke a supposed golden age of the past as a viable model for a present reality that has degenerated from it. Though idealized, their visions of the past contain certain indisputable truths. To understand the full weight of the crisis of women's education in the early modern period as it had emerged historically and as it was perceived by early modern feminists, let us review in more concrete terms the shifts in positions and realities from the sixteenth to the seventeenth century.

The Renaissance rehabilitation of women to serve the interests of church and state, as is widely known, entailed a new educational project–beginning with Leonardo Bruni's *De Studiis et Litteris* (1423–26). In the sixteenth century, the interconnected and highly influential circle of Desiderius Erasmus, Sir Thomas More, and Juan Luis Vives opposed the entrenched medieval belief that learning detracts from a woman's virtue.[9] If anything, they argued, education could improve a woman's nature (which, especially for Vives, remained base) and at the same time enhance her allotted role in society, rendering her a more fit companion for her husband and a more skillful mother and household manager. While emphatically restricting to the private realm of the household her sphere of action, the space in which her education would take place, and the demonstration of her knowledge, they advocated a high level of literacy for the upper-class woman. Within these parameters and still with an eye to her virtue, Erasmus and More allotted the female sex a broadly based humanist education (Vives, on the other hand, would limit her readings to Christian doctrine). The humanists' proposals, though clearly far from a full vindication of women or an acknowledgment of the equality of the sexes, did carve out a space within patriarchal discourse and society for the private cultivation of women's minds.

"The Abbot and the Learned Lady," Erasmus's famous colloquy between a foolish clergyman and the erudite Magdalia (modeled on Sir Thomas More's daughter, Margaret Roper) to the former's detriment, was published in 1524. By that time, as Magdalia observes, there already existed a fair number of humanistically educated women in Europe. Deriving from the normative discourse of the humanists or from the importance that humanist culture itself attached to learning, secular education for women expanded during the Renaissance, and several learned women even rose to prominence beyond the domestic sphere.[10] In the rich humanist culture of Italy, for example, women such as Laura Cereta, Cassandra Fedele, Isotta Nogarola, and Olimpia Morata followed the finest quattrocento curriculum, mastered the classics, and composed in several of the usual genres of the times (see King, 1991, chap. 3). In Spain there existed under Catholic Queen Isabel a fairly liberal atmosphere for women. Queen Isabel ensured her daughters' education; the literacy of upper-class women grew; a few women classicists such as Francisca de Nebrija and Beatriz Galindo emerged (see Bomli, chap. 4; McKendrick, introduction; Navarro, introduction). We should, of course, be at pains not to exaggerate the breadth of this phenomenon in Spain or elsewhere. For one thing, Renaissance learned women were generally of the nobility, educated at home (educational institutions per se for women had not yet evolved beyond the convent), often from families that exceptionally favored education. And as Margaret King (1980) has detailed with regard to Italian women humanists, even in that propitious humanist climate they rarely fulfilled their early promise. With no professional outlet for their learning, they generally capitulated to marriage, retreated from secular to sacred studies, and/or as I mentioned in the introduction, withdrew like pariahs from society into the "book-lined cells" that symbolize their still anomalous social position. For another, Renaissance learned women were in fact proportionately few in number. Erasmus's Magdalia mentions only a handful. King has found about thirty-five such women in Renaissance Italy: a dozen who could be easily named, perhaps three who had gained renown (1980, 67). Although I would imagine that the statistics are still in flux, Lerner states that historians have identified just three hundred learned women for the entire Christian era in Europe up to 1700 (29).

The Protestant Reformation appeared to augur a more appreciable renaissance in women's education.[11] Basing his religious doctrine on the authority of Scripture, Luther believed that men and women alike should have access to the source and therefore advocated universal instruction in reading. The Reformation thus fostered literacy and resulted in expanded elementary education for girls, especially in the German territories where school attendance was made mandatory for both sexes (Lerner, 32). Further, as the case of Margaret Fell Fox demonstrates, the radical sects not only supported women's education but made inroads into the prohibition against women's speech by allowing them to preach. Early modern advances for women, however, inevitably involved retreats and serious qualifications. Conceivably in reaction to the intellectual emancipation of women, Reformation theology aggrandized the role of the patriarch as ruler of the home and of its subservient females. While the Reformation promoted universal literacy, in revolting against Catholicism it also disbanded the convents and convent schools that historically had been the most significant venue for women's education and a refuge for educated women. Astell's revisionary convent and Cavendish's Convent of Pleasure reflect a mourning professed by many for this valuable institution.[12]

By the seventeenth century, discrepancies in women's education had naturally evolved between Protestant and Catholic countries (where, for one thing, convents still existed but continued to wed women's education to religious indoctrination); variations had long existed between individual European countries. Nevertheless, certain common denominators of the seventeenth century cross national lines.[13] First, theory inevitably lagged behind practice in instituting women's elementary education (Sonnet, 103). Second, as discussed in the introduction, especially Spain and England and their colonies experienced a misogynist backlash against whatever enlightened attitudes toward women had arisen from humanist, Erasmian, or Reformation ideologies. Third, and perhaps most prominent in the minds of the learned ladies writing during the seventeenth century, is the situation regarding upper-class women that Phyllis Stock describes:

> While primary education was having its first effects on the lower classes in the early modern period, the *formal education of upper class women was deteriorating from its Renaissance level.* In Protestant areas the noble or wealthy bourgeois woman was viewed as ideally a homemaker and mother, for whom an elementary education, with emphasis on religion and housewifery, was sufficient. In Catholic countries, such as Spain and Italy, noble women were almost totally confined to the home; the learning provided them

> during the Renaissance, in the wake of the Catholic Reformation, viewed as pagan and dangerous. (81; italics mine)

Almost universally in the seventeenth-century Christian world, the education of upper-class women (be it in convent schools, boarding schools, or the home through private tutors) was directed toward preparing them to be an attractive commodity on the marriage market. Given women's disenfranchisement from commercial activity, that was basically the marketplace remaining to them. Hence, women's training centered on the "feminine" accomplishments of domestic skills, dancing, drawing, needlework, and perhaps some French or Italian. The scores of women humanists with a broader training of earlier years had shrunk in the seventeenth century to the exceptional Tenth Muses—sometimes to one icon, if any, per country.[14] Incited by the sorry state of affairs, which she clearly understood as a crisis in women's education, British educator Hannah Wooley remarked in 1675, "The Right Education of the Female Sex, as it is in a manner every where neglected, so it ought to be generally lamented. Most in this depraved later Age think a woman learned and wise enough if she can distinguish her Husband's bed from another's" (Stock, 98).[15]

Extremely significant developments in feminist activism ensued from this resealing of the City of Knowledge; I believe that it would not be unwarranted to view the seventeenth-century crisis in women's education as a watershed in feminism, be it early modern feminism or feminism in general. Privately or self-taught women took action. New Prometheuses, they sought to bring knowledge to their sex. In England, Mary Ward, Bathsua Makin, Hannah Wooley, and Mary Astell labored to found schools for girls. In and beyond England, others—to whom I next turn—ventured into print to argue for women's education. Their efforts effected a breakthrough in the discourse on knowledge. Breaking the silence, breaking the prohibitions on women's public speech, for the first time a group of women publicly took their place among those who would dictate the terms of women's access to knowledge, tacitly claiming the word from the male preceptists who had monopolized it. No longer would men only wield the keys to the City of Knowledge, particularly on the level of doctrine. Though seventeenth-century feminists have been faulted for focusing their sights almost exclusively on education,[16] as Lerner maintains, "discussion of this subject became the main instrument for the development of feminist ideas" (210).

The incipient feminist consciousness, the breaking of the silence, the rallying cry of education—all entailed a limited yet important rupture in the traditional isolation of women thinkers. It created one of the first (if not the first) public cross-cultural cross-fertilization of ideas among learned women.[17] The Dutch Tenth Muse, famed Oriental linguist Anna Maria van Schurman (1607–78), corresponded with many learned men and women of Europe—among them, Marie de Gournay. Schurman read De Gournay's *L'Egalité des hommes et des femmes* and commented on it in her own work; De Gournay read Schurman's *Dissertatio logica de ingenii muliebris ad doctrinam et meliores litteras aptitudine* (1638), and critiqued it in her correspondence with the author. Supporter of women's education Clement Barksdale in 1659 translated Schurman's treatise into English under the title of *The Learned Maid: or Whether a Maid may be a Scholar? A Logick Exercise. The Learned Maid* exercised a determining influence on Bathsua Makin's "Essay" discussed earlier (which also contains the praise of Anne Bradstreet cited in chapter 4, as well as favorable reference to Margaret Lucas Cavendish as a self-taught scholar). Makin corresponded with Schurman, mentioned the Dutch scholar in laudatory terms at various points in her piece, and utilized in it Schurman's polemical tactic of confronting an "Objector." Finally, Mary Astell's "A Serious Proposal to the Ladies" subscribes to several positions put forth by Makin and (although Astell does not cite her outright) even uses her words.[18] From here the chain would extend into the future as the writings of Astell, bearing the marks of her predecessors, resonated into the eighteenth century.[19]

As a group and individually, the essays just named reflect the transitional, transformative dynamic of the early/modern period. Commensurate to the shifting, disjunctive grounds of the times, the essays fall into two groups that follow two different lines of argumentation. I view the first line of argumentation as more *early* modern or traditional and call it "accommodationist." I view the second line of argumentation as more properly modern, and call it "radical." The majority of the essays—those by Schurman, Makin, and Astell—fall into the first category. These religiously aligned authors were at pains to establish, in effect, that a female Prometheus need *not* be a Pandora or Eve, that is, a threat to the patriarchy. They framed their arguments for women's education in such a fashion that they either avoided a direct challenge to traditional gender definitions or reinforced them. They acknowledged, if not women's inferiority, then their continued subservience to men. Since traditionalism and feminism were anything but inimical in the seventeenth century, by design or reinvention the "accommodationists" follow in the footsteps of the Renaissance humanists. Therefore, each of the three women in question voices the following positions, most of which can be found in Schurman's treatise: the domestic sphere remains the woman's place; learning should be for private ends and to the benefit of domestic order, marriage, and motherhood; education enhances virtue; secular knowledge is intimately allied with religion—supplementing, reinforcing, and heightening the understanding of theology, pinnacle of knowledge; education best befits upper-class women who have leisure time to fill, to keep them from frivolity and vice. Carrying the precepts of the humanists into a more modern age, they recuperate and expand on the most enlightened corner of Erasmus's and More's program, that which prescribes a broad education for girls in secular subjects. Even Schurman, the most conservative of the three, contravenes the limited "feminine" curriculum of the times, stating: "I clearly affirm all honest Discipline or the whole . . . Circle and Crown of liberal Arts and Sciences (as the proper and universal Good and Ornament of Mankind) to be convenient for the *Head* of our *Christian Maid*" (4). She goes on to list the broad range of subjects in which a girl should be instructed, a list that includes rhetoric, the language of the public sphere specifically outlawed for women by Bruni and Vives.[20]

Similarly, I should note that in their writings neither Schurman, Makin, nor Astell conforms to the mold of the unassertive dulcet female promoted by Vives or by Fray Luis de León. Perhaps taking their cue from the outspoken Magdalia (whom Makin herself discusses on p. 23), these female essayists as well as their more radical counterparts can be not only sharp-witted in their logic but also sharp-tongued in their criticisms of the opposite sex. They underscore, responding to the *querelle des femmes* that they have much in mind, the faulty reasoning of men who limit the opportunities of women and then criticize them for their inferior accomplishments and brute nature. Projecting out from another line of the *querelle*, Makin sarcastically observes that men injure women exceedingly "to account them gidy-headed Gossips, fit only to discourse of their Hens, Ducks, and Geese, and not by any means to be suffered to meddle with Arts and Tongues, lest by intollerable pride they should run mad" (16). None of the female essayists fails to observe the irony that men have not universally profited from their superior education. Mary Astell, for instance, says that quite the opposite is often the case: "If any object against a Learned Education, that it will make Women vain and assuming, and instead of correcting encrease their Pride: I grant that a smattering in Learning may, for it has this effect on Men, none so Dogmatical and so forward to shew their Parts as your little *Pretender* to Science" (167). Thus, much as the accommodationists generally uphold the patriarchal ideology, their logic and invective betray a not inconsiderable outrage with the order of things.

Nevertheless, a significant gap remains between the accommodationists and the essayists whom I deem more radical, that is, Marie de Gournay–and, outside the cross-fertilizing circle, María de Zayas and Poullain de La Barre. As I see it, the crucial dividing line between the two groups lies in their definition of an educated woman's proper sphere of action. These three more radical writers not only deplore the inferior education of women and desist from yoking education to religion, but also reject the premise that an educated woman should limit the exercising of her knowledge to the domestic realm. The boldest Prometheuses yet, they break the foundational law of the patriarchy that consigns women to the home. De Gournay, the oldest member of the interrelated group (perhaps still partaking of Renaissance optimism), takes a stance in *L'Egalité* from which the younger members would undoubtedly recoil in horror. An uncompromising and unqualified egalitarian, she contends that women and men being equal, women should perform the same public functions as men. De Gournay rails against the Salic law that bars women from holding the French crown. Even more daringly for her times (and even ours), she suggests that females serve as priests. Since women have been granted the right to administer the sacrament of baptism, De Gournay shrewdly asks: "[W]hich faculty necessary to administer the others do we justly lack?" (*20*). María de Zayas, with a keen satirical wit that matches De Gournay's, goes so far as to assert not just the equality but the potential superiority of women, were they not educationally disadvantaged by men. According to Zayas, if women were trained in arms and letters, they could rival and perhaps outdo men. Poullain de la Barre, for his part, outdoes both the female and the male[21] authors of the seventeenth century by bringing a Cartesian posture of categorical doubt to bear on the received arguments that have been adduced to prove the inequality of women. Among the many astonishingly modern-sounding defenses of women by Poullain, we find extensive discussions of how women, once educated, could and might admirably discharge the then male offices of king, church pastor, medical doctor, lawyer, statesman, businessman, politician, and so on (see especially the Second Part of his essay). Though clearly prompted to his systematic militancy regarding women by his philosophical methodology, though already in 1673 representating views more characteristic of the Enlightenment, the influential Poullain nevertheless recapitulates in a higher gear the views of his radical female forebear, De Gournay.[22]

What place does Sor Juana occupy in this panorama? The impersonal *prueba* section of the "Respuesta" contains her most explicit and conventional contribution to the debate on women's education. Though Sor Juana had no knowledge of her sister writers' efforts, her polemic corresponds almost exactly to the accommodationist stance of the other religiously aligned female writers. Pilar Gonzalbo Aizpuro observes in her study of Mexican education during the colonial period, "Nothing revolutionary can be found in these statements, which speak of indoctrinating rather than instructing" (332). Isolated from other feminists and their arguments, Sor Juana gears her hardly revolutionary views on education to the patriarchy and more specifically to the relatively–very relatively–enlightened position assumed by Sor Filotea in her introduction to the *Carta Atenagórica*, which states: "I do not subscribe to the commonplace view of those who condemn the practice of letters in women, since so many have applied themselves to literary study, not failing to win praise from Saint Jerome" (*200*, 4.695).[23] Sor Filotea goes on to say: "Letters that breed arrogance God does not want in women. But the Apostle does not reject them so long as they do not remove women from a position of obedience. No one could say that study and learning have caused you to exceed your subordinate status" (*200*, 695). Accordingly, when discussing education in her Reply, Sor Juana takes care to underscore not so much the right of women to an education but, as did others following sixteenth-century lines, the connections between religion and learning as well as the subordinate status of women's study. She posits the Bible as a kind of encyclopedia, as "the book which takes in all books, the knowledge which embraces all types of knowledge, to the understanding of which they all contribute" (*214*, 4.449), and gives copious examples of the interlinkages between logic, rhetoric, physics, mathematics, history, music, etc., and theology. With characteristic willful ingenuity, Sor Juana bends the letter of Saint Jerome to Laeta and other sources into stating that females be taught the Scriptures by older educated women (see Scott 1985, 516–17).[24] She appeals to and espouses the view put forth by yet another male authority, Juan Díaz de Arce, that (as I quoted in the introduction) "to lecture publicly in the classroom and to preach in the pulpit are not legitimate activities for women, but that studying, writing, and teaching privately are not only allowable but most edifying and useful" (*229*, 462). Here, and in discussing her own scholarly activities, Sor Juana upholds the crucial patriarchal dividing line between private and public, studying and publishing, demarcating the first term of each pair as the woman's preserve. For example: "My purpose in studying is not to write, much less to teach (this would be overbearing pride in my case), but simply to see whether studying makes me less ignorant" (*210*, 444).

Trenchant barbs of irony reminiscent of those of other accommodationists punctuate Sor Juana's would-be patriarchal position on education in the "Respuesta." Arguing that only women of aptitude be granted an education, she suddenly turns the tables on men to suggest that the same holds true for them. Saint Paul's dictum of quiet (*taceant*) in the church, she contends, "applies not only to women but to everyone not properly endowed" (*231*, 463). The hyperbolic protestations of personal unworthiness of learning that I discussed in the previous chapter also render Sor Juana's statements suspect. Yet it is the fulsome little scene she paints of a virginal maid and her threatening male tutor that goes far in convincing us of the demagoguery bound up in Sor Juana's accommodationist position. When discussing the benefits of female teachers, Sor Juana employs her dramatic skills to depict the "impropriety of having a strange man sit beside a bashful woman (who blushes even when her father looks directly at her) and treat her with offhand familiarity and with the informality of the classroom" (*233*, 464). She plays to the conceivable prurience and concern for honor of her male readers by suggesting that "from the ease of contact and the close company kept over a period of time, there easily comes about something not thought possible" (*232*, 465). This grandstanding, with its feel of a *costumbrista* vignette, smacks of both pathos and parody.

Even to achieve the modest goals for women's education set forth in the "Respuesta" would have been a notable improvement over the rudimentary "Amiga" schools and most private education of girls in colonial Mexico, limited almost entirely to the essentials of literacy, the catechism, and domestic accomplishments.[25] I do not mean to underrate Sor Juana's project. Nevertheless, that her most deeply held aspirations for women and herself vis-à-vis knowledge exceed the narrow bounds laid out in the "Respuesta," as well presumably as the capabilities of that genteel female tutor teaching the basics of Scripture, is readily apparent from the contrast between the impersonal and the more properly autobiographical sections of the text. Sor Juana, as Gonzalbo Aizpuro observed, may have advocated an education for women in general directed toward the inculcation of Christian doctrine, but in the *narratio* of the "Respuesta" we see her own omnivorous mind ranging feverishly over all knowledge, sacred and secular and empirical. Sor Juana appeals to the interconnectedness of all things, to one another and ultimately to God through the Great Chain of Being, in order to justify her voracious study of secular works. With this, the "Respuesta" hooks up with the aspirations to total knowledge of the *Primero sueño*. And the *PS*, as I will now consider in some detail, for its part adumbrates the early/modern tensions inherent not only in Sor Juana's stated positions on knowledge but also in the struggles of the seventeenth-century female Prometheuses in general, as they engage with patriarchal imperatives.

My reading depends on the divisions, symmetries, and metamorphoses built into the very fabric of the *PS*. Although commentators have waged small wars over the internal divisions of the poem,[26] here we need consider only its broadest and most evident structuring units: the distinction between inside/outside the nightworld. That is, the distribution of the poem into the three large blocks of (1) the coming of sleep and night, (2) the nightworld itself with its "intellectual voyage" (l. 301), and (3) the arrival of day and the poetic speaker's awakening. Symmetries and repetitions linking these three units abound. Jean Franco (32) has aptly likened the *PS* to the symmetrical mirrored house, rife with reflections, of Triste-le-Roy in Jorge Luis Borges's story, "La muerte y la brújula" [Death and the Compass]. I would state in more concrete terms that elements and images pass from one part of the poem thus divided to another, and–this is crucial–undergo metamorphoses or transformations as they proceed. Returning to my initial metaphor of the *PS* as a tapestry, I suggest that we view the poem as a tightly interwoven triptych in which the same threads pass from one segment to another, changing color and configuration as Sor Juana skillfully and purposefully spins them out. The central portion of the poem, the nightworld, becomes the space of privileged transformations, of transmographies with special import for a feminist reading. For example, the pyramids that symbolize the Soul, cloaked in shadow in the first part but incongruously bathed in light in the nightworld of the second part, most apparently call our attention to the poem's internal transformations. I will return to the metamorphosis of the pyramids; for now, in reading the *PS* as Sor Juana's fable of the woman's struggle for knowledge, I would like to follow the redemptive transformations embodied in several of the poem's mythological figures, especially in the seemingly secondary figures of Arethusa and Aurora.

Phaethon, the final metaphorical mask the poetic speaker assumes in the nightworld before heading toward day, has generally been construed as the poem's central mythological presence and as the most definitive representation of the questing Soul. And with good reason: image of tragically heroic daring despite all odds or risks, of unfettered ambition, of freedom, and of transgression, Phaethon well encapsulates the multiple aspects and moods of seekers of knowledge such as the *Sueño*'s Soul or, by extension, the early modern woman. Over the course of the poem, Sor Juana develops a complex and idiosyncratic genealogy for Phaethon. Conflating him, as is her wont, with fellow daring aerial artist, Icarus, Sor Juana maneuvers the Phaethon of the nightworld into recapitulating the transgressive winged nightbirds of the over-ture as well as the eagle, Jupiter's bird and symbol of the flights of the soul. As distinct from her construction of Icarus, however, Sor Juana endows Phaethon with the properties of the phoenix and of renewed flight ("que alas engendra a repetido vuelo," causing wings to sprout for further flight [l. 805, *191*]) that prefigure the cyclical efforts of the Dark Empress of night ("segunda vez rebelde," rebelling once again [l. 965, *195*]) to renew her quest at the end of the third segment of the poem.[27] Inside the nightworld, Phaethon partially redeems both the Dark Empress and the Promethean nightbirds. I say par-tially because, working the opposing poles of the baroque topic of Phaethon as emblem both of hubris or ambition and of immortal glory (Sabat-Rivers 1976, 86), Sor Juana figures Phaethon as unresolvably ambiguous: "Tipo es, antes, modelo: / ejemplar pernicioso" (ll. 803–4) [Rather, that youth is the model: a most pernicious example]. Traditional symbol of poetic daring, he constitutes a superb reification of baroque contradictions and of the poet's auto-machia. Conceivably salving her inner battle and clearly salvaging her transgressive female personages, Sor Juana asserts that Phaeton ultimately merits exceptional mercy. Where, outside the *Sueño*'s nightworld, the crimes of the daring birdwomen met with punishment, inside its sacrosant space those of their new avatar, Phaethon, should be punished secretly or not at all (ll. 816–26, *191*).

Compared to the undeniably central character of Phaethon, convergence of so many of the *Primero sueño*'s lines and one of Sor Juana's most favored mythological references, the spring Arethusa would appear to cut a rather small figure. Relegated to a corner of the poem (ll. 712–29, *189*), tucked into the diegesis as a tiny example of the world's confounding complexity, Arethusa occupies a marginal position in the *PS*. However, one cannot dis-count Sor Juana's propensity to make large statements in small margins. Therefore, building on recent discussions of Arethusa by Franco and Sabat-Rivers (1991), I would like to focus here on her redemptive potentiality vis-à-vis women and knowledge, and later on her heuristic value for the textuality of the *PS*–and thus to recuperate Arethusa as a significant tutelary goddess of the poem.

The *PS* disarmingly embeds its fleeting emblem of a woman who acquires knowledge and uses it to positive ends in an epistemological excursus intend-ed to illustrate all that the Soul does *not* know. In the immediate context Arethusa represents the stream, object of the Soul's questioning wonderment. Yet meandering like the very stream it describes, the poem takes a detour to flesh out Arethusa and thus to remove her from the status of a simple mytho-logical allusion. From the biography of this nymph of Diana whom the god-dess mercifully transformed into a stream so that Arethusa could escape the pursuing river god Alpheus, Sor Juana excerpts an episode germane to the poem's concerns. She portrays the crystalline course of the stream Arethusa traversing the overworld and the horrific underworld, catching a glimpse of Persephone, and informing Ceres of her daughter's whereabouts:

> *clara pesquidora* registrando
> (*útil curiosidad*, aunque prolija,
> que de su no cobrada bella hija
> *noticia cierta* dio a la rubia Diosa. . . .)
> (ll. 722–25; italics mine)

[*bright searcher*, showing *useful*, though prolix, *curiosity*, brought to the fair-haired goddess *true word* of her beautiful missing daughter . . .] (trans. López-Morillas; the episode can be found in Trueblood, *189*)

As the italics added to the lines just quoted signal, Sor Juana's depiction of Arethusa's heroic relationship to knowledge contains a rich network of luminous echoes and redemptive reversals. Protected (rather than mocked, as in the opening) by the moon goddess Diana, Arethusa evinces a daring worthy of Phaethon, a daring unadulterated by ambiguity. Even more than Phaethon, then, within the unexpectedly en-lightened confines of the nightworld, Arethusa reclaims the overture's nightbirds of knowledge. Their torpid darkness becomes light and lucidity. Nyctimene's defiling of the lamp of knowledge changes valence to become "useful curiosity." The Minyades's worship of the female goddess finds its reward in Diana's protection of Arethusa. Ascalaphus's infamous betrayal of knowledge and of Persephone directly reverses itself in Arethusa's "true word" that relieves the distraught Ceres. The dissonant nightchorus reverts to harmony in Arethusa, proprietress of pastoral poetry (Bell, 61). Each and all of the transgressive nightbirds, in sum, meet their redemptive counterpart in Arethusa, whose "useful curiosity" erases the taints of Eve/Pandora in the female Prometheus—leaving her shining, sanctioned, and validated.[28]

The reader may have noticed that to establish the contrast between the contradictory Phaethon and the unambiguously positive Arethusa, I have reversed the chronology of the poem. In actual fact, Arethusa precedes and shades into Phaethon who, as I have stated, is the last mask the Soul assumes before proceeding into the diurnal segment of the poem. According to Paz, the Soul recognizes it/herself in Phaethon and then withdraws (380). Much as Arethusa entails the highly desirable yet brief apotheosis of the female quester for knowledge, the chiaroscuro contradictions of Phaethon bespeak Sor Juana's more pragmatic or full-bodied understanding of the the the woman's plight. I maintain that within the *PS*, but in the no longer dream space of its final diurnal portion, Aurora personifies that pragmatic position. Given the invariable carryovers from one section of the poem to another, the bi-polar Phaethon directly preceding Aurora augurs and predicts her. Consequently, as distinct from Paz, I will argue that not Phaethon but Aurora can be seen as the Soul's final mask, and that this mask, in turn, ultimately gives us a clue to the nature of the veiled final "I" of the poem.

The well-hidden road toward Aurora begins long before the appearance of Phaethon. It begins at the very outset of the poem where we find a subtle

reconstruction of the universe and a definition of the quest in terms of opposing female personages, light and dark heroines. The audacious Shadow wages
her "war" (l. 7, *171*) on the heavens as metonymized in the orb of Diana, the
moon. From the first, then, a dark transgressive presence pits itself against a
celestial source of light. The unmistakable religious connotations of Sor
Juana's Diana further magnify and exalt the goddess. Critics have recently noted the surprising paucity in the *Sueño*'s nightworld of Christian iconology, and
especially of explicit references to the Christian God as male, to Christ, to the
conventional Trinity.[29] At the outset of the poem, in accordance with Sor
Juana's tendency in the poem to refigure the Divinity in feminine terms, the
first heavenly figure to be mentioned is the Moon, a defiant antimale goddess
positioned as a godhead: "del orbe de la Diosa / que tres veces hermosa / con
tres hermosos rostros ser ostenta" (ll. 13–15) [of that fair goddess' orb–she
who shows herself in threefold beauty, the beauty of her three faces, *171*]. The
emphatic references to "three's"–also the perfect number of Pythagorean harmony (Harss, 77)–invoke a new Trinity, an alternative female Trinity, an
empowering of the feminine. Sor Juana's characterization has the thrice-beau-
tiful Moon Goddess, in her three incarnations as Persephone, Diana, and
Selena, ruling the underworld, the earth, and the heavens. The also empowered Shadow, armed with her "punta altiva" or towering tip (perhaps a symbol of re-placed phallic potency, a reversal of the rape scene in Sor Juana's
other major *silva*, poem #215), hurls herself at the female godhead.

When we combine this initial tableau with what we have already seen of
the subsequent unfolding of the poem's overture, a wonderfully suggestive
scenario emerges. In a baroque chiaroscuro the shining triple Moon Goddess
encounters her dark adversarial counterparts, and the Shadow her profile, in
the set of *three* mythological figures presented (Nyctimene, the [3] Minyades,
Ascalaphus). The dissonance of their nightchorus contrasts with the implicit
Pythagorean harmony of the three-faced Moon Goddess. Their search for
knowledge elevates the Shadow's assault on the Moon Divinity into what
could easily be construed as a quest for mystical union with Her. We are thus
left at the end of the overture with a picture of two contrasting sets of female
characters: the empowered, shining, harmonious Moon Goddess versus the
punished, dark, dissonant women of the nightshadow, who are attempting to
scale the heights. This, for its part, insinuates that another allegorical layer
beyond that of the search for knowledge is woven into the poem: the drama
of the transgressive dark heroine, proponent of knowledge and literary creation, seeking union with the divine light heroine (Diana); that is, seeking
redemption for her knowledge-related sins. Sor Juana dramatically contrasts
yet implicitly allies her dark and light heroines. Twins in their daring and defiance, they represent two different inflections of a single shared impulse or
body.

The above battle is played out inside the nightworld through the figures
of Arethusa (fleeting redemption of the Shadow) and Phaethon (reincarnation
of the duality). It reaches its dénouement in the outside margin of the poem

with the enigmatic Aurora. Aurora warrants our close attention because she is the last female mythological icon to be introduced before the final "I" comes forth. She also provokes our confusion because we are hard-pressed to understand what she represents, where her allegiance lies, and where she stands with regard to the other characters of the poem. Does Aurora negate the other female characters, and particularly the Shadow, punishing them for their quest? For, on the one hand, the poem and mythology clearly ally her with the Sun. As his standardbearer ("signífera del Sol" [l. 918]), Aurora leads the Sun's battle to rout the chastened, shamed Nightshadow. And the Sun, potent patriarchal presence alien to the feminine cast of the nightworld (a matter on which I will elaborate further in the third part of the chapter), clearly stands in for the traditional Christian God. Etching ("pautando" [l. 944]) the sky with the lines of golden light that "salían / de su circunferencia luminosa" (ll. 947–48) [sprang from his luminous circumference, *194*], "The Father of Light" (l. 887) patently harks back to earlier brief allusions to the Christian Godhead (as "Eterno Autor," Eternal Author [l. 674, *188*]; in Nicholas de Cusa's famous metaphor, as center of all lines and as boundless circumference [ll. 408–11, *181*]). Herself "de mil luces vestida" [arrayed in countless lights] and "contra la noche armada" [armed against the night] (ll. 899–900, *193*), the dayworld's Aurora has joined forces with the masculine powers, with the male Christian God, enemy of the questing Shadow.

On the other hand, when we view Aurora as part of the whole fabric of the text rather than in isolation, she changes sign completely. Though the nightworld has technically come to an end and we seem to have moved out of something resembling Plato's cave into the light, the poem remains a continuous skein, and elements do not cease to carry over from one section to the next. For instance, "aurora" (if not "Aurora") had earlier made a small appearance as part of the coloration of the rose in the stanza following Arethusa's story (ll. 745–46, *190*) and thus as part of the poem's epistemological questionings. Harss interprets this mention as a suggestion of morning slowly filtering into the dream (124). I would call attention to the fact that here, as in the final segment, A/aurora is linked to Venus: first, in Venus's flower, the rose (ll. 741–42, *190*) and, ultimately, as the companion of Venus the morning star (ll. 895 ff., *193*). As revealed in the *Neptuno Alegórico*'s equation of Venus with Isis, goddess of wisdom, Sor Juana takes the former goddess to represent not only female beauty but also intelligence.[30] Ovid casts Aurora as the quintessence of femininity ("all my talents are of feminine gifts" [208]). Sor Juana simultaneously grants her feminine beauty ("la bella esposa," the fair wife [l. 898, *193*]) and presents her as an "Amazon" (l. 899, *193*), who thus recalls the Diana and the bold Shadow of the opening.

As do her boldness and intelligence, the multiple connections between Aurora and Phaethon make her complicity with Father Sun all the more puzzling: in trying to take his place, tradition has it, Phaethon revolted against his father the Sun. Semantic and graphic effects conspire in the *PS* to draw a firm connnection between Aurora and Phaethon. In the *PS*, Sor Juana makes notable if select use of alliteration, only in A's and E's. At different moments in the poem an alliteration of A's signifies ascencional daring, with positive connotations (e.g., "del empeño más arduo, altivo aspira, / los altos escalones ascendiendo" [ll. 607–8]).[31] Such A-words cluster ostentatiously around Phaethon: "auriga altivo del ardiente carro," "alto impulso," "donde el ánimo halla," "abiertas sendas al atrevimiento," "ánimo ambicioso," etc. (see the section on Phaethon: ll. 781–810). The A-words, some of them the same, reappear around Aurora: "apacible lucero," "rompió el albor primero," "amazona," "contra la noche armada," "hermosa si *atrevida*" [daring], "valiente aunque llorosa," "*animosa*" [courageous] (see ll. 895–905; italics mine). In addition, the dew, here conventionally represented as the Dawn's tears ("valiente aunque llorosa," valiant though tearful [l. 902, *193*]), together with the very valor to which that line refers and her phoenixlike nature (her cyclicality, shown in contrast to the ineluctable aging of her husband, Tithonus), all situate Aurora in the lineage of Phaethon.[32]

By now it should be clear that the dauntless Aurora constitutes a rather unlikely and even an unseemly companion for Father Sun. But this, I believe, is precisely Sor Juana's larger point and the resolution of the battle begun in the poem's first lines. Sor Juana gathers the daring, transgressive female (and male) characters of the poem into Aurora. She bathes Aurora in light and unites her with the Father—as "Eternal Author" representative of knowledge, as "luminous circumference" representative of the Christian Divinity—who by all indications bestows upon her in the diurnal world that redemption or sanction prefigured in the overture. He thus resolves the auto-machia of the light and dark heroines and writes an appropriate ending onto the *PS* as a spiritual autobiography. The poem has literally and symbolically come full *circle*. The Nightself, with whom we can now see Aurora also shares certain traits, has been banished to another sphere. In her place arrives Aurora: a diurnal, consecrated, more tame reiteration of the shining Moon Goddess ("the beautiful goddess" becomes "the lovely wife") who has not relinquished her central qualities or aspirations. Perhaps, just perhaps, in view of the poem's constant metamorphoses and "floating self images," Aurora affords the model and mask for the "I" who awakens in the poem's last two lines to a more certain light. If so, that "I" should certainly not be read as thoroughly *desengañada* or defeated, but as one who has negotiated her own separate peace with the powers that be.

I cannot help noting that this redemptive resolution of the woman's drama of knowledge, though itself calm, and as reconciliatory as any words an accommodationist might have written, is not devoid of jarring implications; its apotheosis contains apostasy. By the end of the poem, the Father of Light has replaced the female Moon Goddess as a possible source of redemption. Light inevitably summons up conventional associations with revelation, spiritual illumination, anagnorisis. Yet when we look back over the whole poem, we discover a destabilizing of the connotations of light and dark that bears intensely negative, even heretical, implications for the Sun God. "Neither light nor dark," Franco has noted, "have a stable, Manichean set of connotations" (33). Franco refers particularly to the fact that within the nightworld light can signify either illumination or confusion and bedazzlement; I take her comment as an illustration of the fact that, within that same disordering semantic field, the symbolic grounds of dark and light are constantly shifting. Elements such as the pyramids change valence in the nightworld, passing from dark to light. At the same time, dark assumes the positive connotations of freedom and free will, while light can reverse itself into an antagonistic force, an ever-present omen of all that will eventually undo the Shadow's flight. In the lengthy passage after the Soul's attempt at intuitive understanding of the world fails, for example, blinding light (ll. 501–2) becomes the deadly poison (l. 521) for which the Soul's own powers of darkness serve as antidote (ll. 495–539, *184*). Moreover, any of the several evocations of Icarus or Phaethon carries with it the recollection that it was the Sun who caused each one's death. The description of Phaethon refers to "el vengativo rayo fulminante" (l. 798) [the vengeful lightning bolt, *191*]; that of Icarus contains the powerful lines:

> –contra el sol, digo, cuerpo luminoso,
> cuyos rayos castigo son fogoso,
> que fuerzas desiguales
> despreciando, castigan rayo a rayo
> el confiado, antes atrevido
> y ya llorado ensayo (ll. 460–65)

[against the sun, I mean, the shining body whose rays impose a punishment of fire which, scorning unmatched forces, chastises beam by beam the self-assured, originally bold, now lachrymose attempt] (*182–83*)

How, then, are we to read the Father Sun of the poem's last segment? Conventionally, as the benign, merciful Christian God, the diurnal segment's wholesale metamorphosis/reversal of the punishing vengeful Sun of the nightworld? Or–and the implications are truly fearsome–as the vengeful Sun's new avatar? For obvious reasons, and in keeping with the ambiguity of the poem's ending, the question must remain open. However, that the Sun is shown cruelly attacking, even raping, the Shadow lends weight to the second alternative. In a striking inversion of the opening's metaphorical suggestion of female potency (the phallic "punta altiva," towering tip), here the Shadow shrivels into her "funesta capa," "de los tajos claros heridas recibiendo" (ll. 929–30) [funereal cape, that took short wounds from the stabbing brightness, *194*]. As Night sounds what Trueblood translates as her "raucous horn" ("ronca tocó bocina" [l. 936]), the Sun "assaults" her with a "burst of bouncing light" (*194*) that bathes in radiance the highest tip (again, "punta" [l. 941]) of the world's loftiest or most erect ("erguidos" [l. 943]) towers. Sor Juana's description of the phallic force assailing the Shadow and energizing the world with its masculine potency leaves little to the imagination. It also leaves the female Prometheus violated and disenfranchised (if only temporarily) by an unsavory force identified not only with the Christian Divinity but also quite emphatically with the masculine—the patriarchy? And finally, it closes the poem with Sor Juana's distinctly dissentient innuendo worthy of her more radical counterparts that redemption (or accommodation), if such has occurred, has been gained by dint of what now takes on the outlines of a Faustian pact.

II.

But I fear my ambition inclines to vain-glory, for I am very ambitious; yet 'tis neither for beauty, wit, titles, wealth, or power, but as they are steps to raise me to fame's tower, which is to live by remembrance on after-ages.
    –MARGARET LUCAS CAVENDISH, Memoirs of the Duchess

If you will but direct me, said the Duchess [the character, "Margaret, Duchess of Newcastle"] to the spirits, which world is easiest to be conquered, her Majesty will assist me with means, and I will trust to fate and fortune; for I had rather die in the adventure of noble achievements than live in obscure and sluggish security; since by the one, I may live in a glorious fame, and by the other I am buried in oblivion.
    –MARGARET LUCAS CAVENDISH
The Description of a New World Called the Blazing World

The first Duchess of Newcastle, Margaret Lucas Cavendish (whom we met briefly in chap. 3), was clearly no Sor Juana. Sor Juana concealed her innermost "I" in dark and light masks; Cavendish flaunted her "I" in the first secular autobiography written by a woman to promote her own fame (Todd, 43, 57) and turns her fictional masks into ostentatious renditions of her "I." Sor Juana retained her lucidity under even the most difficult circumstances; Cavendish, as one can already sense, could be rather batty. Sor Juana denounced what fame had accrued to her; Cavendish, in what can be seen as one of the most overriding concerns of her life, touted her fame however she could.[33] Nor was the Duchess of Newcastle any respectable sort of Tenth Muse. She disdained the conformity that certain male-designated Tenth Muses of the seventeenth century (we think of Bradstreet, Sor Juana, van Schurman) each in her own way espoused, to aspire to utter singularity in all aspects of her life: "For I always took delight in a singularity, even in accoutrements of habits, but whatsoever I was addicted to, either in fashion of cloths, contemplation of thoughts, actions of life" (*Memoirs*, 209). We will find no "redeemed subjectivity" here! Avid for fame, she fashioned her own fantastical clothing and performed outlandish self-fashionings in her many fictional and nonfictional works. Such tendencies prompted the famous comment by Pepys that the "whole story of this Lady is a romance, and all that she doth is romantic" (quoted by Lilley in *Blazing World*, to be abbreviated to *BW*, xii). Pepys's characterization of Cavendish is an unusually generous one. For unlike the Tenth Muses chosen as icons of their cultures, this self-designated star occasioned the mockery and revilement of her contemporaries on both personal and intellectual grounds. She was then and, thanks to Virginia Woolf's treatment of her in *A Room of One's Own*, continues to be known as "Mad Madge." Even in the present climate of feminist revisionism, where Cavendish has aroused a certain amount of attention for her pioneering efforts on several fronts, most critics can muster only a qualified enthusiasm for her writings and thinking in their own right.

What Cavendish *was*, was an extreme overreacher, the personification of Phaethon in all his brave hubris. Value judgments aside, I hold that her restless, omnivorous, overreaching mind and the many fruits it yielded also make her a noteworthy example both of the early modern female Prometheus and of many of the trends that this book has discussed. For in the seclusion of her country estate of Welbeck after the English civil war—well back from the fray, well ensconced in her own endeavors—Cavendish managed to "act out" (in the psychological as well as the theatrical sense) with a notable impunity the drama of the learned woman's early modernity. Her life and works display the self-styled freakishness and shameless self-naming, the desire to create new matriarchal worlds, the melancholy, the anxiety of authorship, the incursion into "masculinist" themes and into the male domain of publishing, the unstable positions on her own gender coexisting with an overt feminism along the lines of the *querelle des femmes*, and finally, the calls for improved women's education that I have observed in other women writers of the times. Recapitulating various strands of the book, in the course of my analysis of Cavendish I will examine these important issues. At the same time, I intend in this section to build toward another goal. I aim to demonstrate how, by virtue of her autodidacticism and overweening will to signature, the contours and dynamics of Cavendish's works illuminate the *textualization* (the textual em-bodiment) of the seventeenth-century woman's search for knowledge in general and that of Sor Juana in particular. As we will see, one of the places where Cavendish and Sor Juana most diverge—the issue of fame—is precisely what sets the Duchess on a parallel course with the Mexican Tenth Muse.[34]

Ironically enough, it is Virginia Woolf's mixed portrait of Cavendish rather than Cavendish's self-aggrandizing writings that has most widely perpetuated the Duchess's fame in modern times. Woolf vividly calls attention to Cavendish's autodidacticism:

What could bind, tame or civilise for human use that wild, generous, untutored intelligence? It poured itself out, higgledy-piggledy,
in torrents of rhyme and prose, poetry and philosophy which
stands congealed in quartos and folios that nobody ever reads. She
should have had a microscope put in her hand. She should have
been taught to look at the stars and reason scientifically. Her wits
were turned with solitude and freedom. No one checked her. No
one taught her. The professors fawned on her. At Court they
jeered at her. (64–65)

Although inaccurate in certain details (she did use a microscope; professors
hardly fawned on her), which demonstrates the relative oblivion into which
Cavendish had indeed fallen by the 1920s, Woolf's comments accurately
depict the shortcomings of Cavendish's intellectual formation in all their
pathos. Like many aristocratic women of the seventeenth century, Cavendish
received an education geared to the "womanly" arts. "As for my breeding,"
wrote Cavendish in her *Memoirs*, "it was according to my birth and the nature
of my sex" (188). She goes on in the *Memoirs* to discuss the tutors she had "for
all sorts of vertues, as singing, dancing, playing on musick, reading, writing,
working, and the like," noting that "they were rather for formality then benefit" for "we were not kept strictly thereto" (190). Like almost all aristocratic
women of her times desiring a broader education, Cavendish would create it
for herself outside institutional structures. At the age of twenty-two Margaret
Lucas married the amateur intellectual, playwright, and poetaster, William
Cavendish—a monarchist forced into exile for twelve years by the civil wars.
During their exile, he and his brother Sir Charles, a professional mathemati-
cian, introduced the Duchess to the world of the intellect. Pierre Gassendi,
Descartes, and Hobbes, among others, dined with them in Paris. Their conversations and the sympathetic tuition she received from her husband and
brother-in-law galvanized the Duchess's intellectual curiosity. Snippet by snippet she gained familiarity with and interpolated herself into the current universe of knowledge. Cavendish punningly wrote, "[T]ruly I have gathered
more by piece-meals than from a full relation, or a methodical education for
knowledge; but my fancy will build thereupon and make discourse therefrom,
and so of everything they discourse (I say they, that is my husband and brothers)" (*Philosophical and Physical Opinions*, 1655 [quoted in Grant, 94]).

Whereas Cavendish's love of knowledge and wealth of fancy or imagination would spur her on for the rest of her life, her egregiously informal education would never cease to hinder and vex her. Because she had not studied
Greek, Latin, or French, her familiarity with the foundations of knowledge
remained spotty: "But my Ignorance of the Mother Tongues makes me ignorant of the Opinions, and Discourses in former times; wherefore I may be
absurd, and erre grossely. I cannot say I have not heard of Atomes, and
Figures, and Motion, and Matter; but not throughly reason'ed on" (*Poems and
Fancies*, to be abbreviated to *P&F*, prefaces, n.p.). Cavendish's ignorance even

of her Mother Tongue ("for there are many words, I know not what they sig-
nifie" [*P&F*, prefaces, n.p.]) manifested itself most blatantly in the idiosyncrasies of her spelling, which far outstripped the usual vagaries of
seventeenth-century English (Hilda Smith, 93).

Such sorely felt inadequacies combined with her dauntless yearning for
fame to make Cavendish hypersensitive to criticism. Of her *Poems and Fancies*
she wrote, "If it be prais'd, it fixes them; but if I am condemn'd, I shall be
Annihilated to nothing: but my Ambition is such, as I would either be a
World, or nothing" (*P&F*, prefaces, n.p.). None of her works contains fewer
than five prefaces, prefaces in which she strove to defend herself and her writings against the criticism she awaited with bated breath. Painfully aware of her
lack of credentials for the City of Knowledge, she was always excruciatingly
and excessively on the defensive. Hence, unlike Sor Juana and Bradstreet,
Cavendish does not limit herself to employing humility topics in the prefaces.
She draws on an arsenal of often incompatible weapons to defend herself:
sometimes denigrating (as the above comments exemplify), sometimes exalting, and sometimes (as I will substantiate in discussing her theories) elabo-
rately justifying her relationship to knowledge.[35] However, there is one topic
familiar to us from the last chapter that Cavendish finds particularly useful in
her prefaces. To cajole her critical reader into a benevolent stance, she resorts
to the "book as child" topic and equates literary creation with procreation:
"True, it may taxe my Indiscretion, being so fond of my Book, as to make as
if it were my Child, and striving to shew her [!] to the World, in hope Some
may like her" (*P&F*, prefaces, n.p.). Though clearly manipulative, her conventional use of the topic also possessed more than its usual measure of truth.
Cavendish was unable to bear children, and thus it fell to the writings that her
prefaces so zealously defended to ensure her immortality.

Of equal importance, Cavendish utilized her prefaces and writings as platforms from which to lament the imperfect state of women's education.
Cavendish's unstable, contradictory views on women's education do not fall
squarely into either the accommodationist or the radical camp. In one of her
major statements on the subject, the Preface to the Reader from *The World's
Olio* (1665, reprinted in Goulianos), while waffling infuriatingly on the subject
of women's intrinsic merits, she tends to depict women as inferior to men but
still worthy of a better education—even if it only involves reading in her clos-
et (59). In another, "To the Two Most Famous Universities of England"
(*Philosophical and Physical Opinions*, 1655; reprinted in Ferguson, 85), she rues
that women have been barred by men from an education and thus have been
"Shut out of all Power and Authority" and "never Imployed in Civil or Martial
Affairs," implying that women might aspire to anything. For the most part,
Cavendish appears to view women as well endowed with understanding by
nature yet denied opportunities to develop their potential by male-dominat-
ed culture and the entrenched male institutions that regulate knowledge. She
repeats the position familiar from the *querelle des femmes* that women have
"Rational Souls as well as Men" (Ferguson, 85) and asserts, "Whereas in nature

we have as clear an understanding as men, if we were bred in schools to mature our brains and to mature our understandings, . . . we might bring forth the fruits of knowledge" (Goulianos, 56).

The fact that Cavendish, in the hope that they would include her books in their libraries, did not shrink from paying obsequious tribute to the very male institutions of Oxbridge that had excluded her sex (see Ferguson, 85) exemplifies the matter to which I will now devote considerable attention: her aggressive efforts literally and figuratively to storm the male City of Knowledge. Consumed by the desire to learn as are most true autodidacts, self-motivated, driven by ambition ("The Duchess answered, that neither she herself, nor no creature in the world was able to know wither the height, depth or breadth of her ambition" [*BW*, 183]), back in England Cavendish comported herself as a scholar and surrendered herself to the acquisition and deployment of knowledge. With her husband's moral, intellectual and, not insignificant, financial support, she published some fourteen works in fifteen years. Hilda Smith states that the "production of five scientific treatises, five collections of poetry and works of fantasy, two groups of essays and letters, and two volumes of plays was a feat unequalled, in scope at least, by any other seventeenth-century woman and rarely matched by later English women" (76). Smith is clearly unfamiliar with Sor Juana, but her point and the shared hyperproductivity of the two female writers are telling.

Moreover, in certain of the "competing self-representations" (Sidonie Smith, 89) so characteristic of the Duchess's unstable production, Cavendish contrives to represent herself not as a scholar *manquée* but as a born intellectual. In the unusually penetrating self-portrait at the end of her *Memoirs*, Cavendish refers to the restless activity of her mind in terms equivalent to Sor Juana's "Respuesta" and illustrative of the autodidact in general: "[Y]et I must say this in behalf of my thoughts, that I never found them idle; for if the senses bring no work in, they will work of themselves, like silk-wormes that spinns out of their own bowels," and "I would walk two or three hours, and never rest, in a musing, considering, contemplating manner, reasoning with my self of everything my sense did present" (*Memoirs*, 208). As did Sor Juana, here (and in the frontispiece that adorns various of her books; see James Fitzmaurice) Cavendish presents herself as musing and melancholy: "[A]s for my disposition, it is more inclining to be melancholy than merry, but no crabbed or peevish melancholy, but soft, melting, solitary and contemplating melancholy" (*Memoirs*, 209). When, in yet another description, she associates her melancholy with both authorship and solitude, we begin to associate it with the *topic* of melancholy discussed in the previous chapter and are struck by the pertinence and usefulness of that topic for the learned lady of the seventeenth century. A faithful depiction of the isolated, troubled circumstances in which the learned lady worked, the topic also allows her literally to inscribe herself into the profile of the male intellectual. The regendering of the historically male construct of melancholy effected by Cavendish and Sor Juana endows their isolation and alleged temperaments with cultural prestige.[36]

In terms of Margaret Lucas Cavendish's efforts to lay claim to the male spheres of knowledge, the foregoing is only one small piece of the picture. Like Bradstreet and Sor Juana and other British women in the second half of the seventeenth century, Cavendish was moving into areas outside the patriarchally designated "feminine" subject of love. She did occasionally write romances, but for the record she scorned the conventional genres of women's writing of her time: "[M]ost commonly when any of our sex doth write they write some Devotion, or Romances, or Receipts of Medicine, for Cookery or Confecioners, or Complemental Letters, or a copy or two of Verses" (quoted in Jones, 83). Bradstreet made forays into history; Cavendish staked out her territory in the masculinist world of science. It can hardly be lacking in significance that Cavendish, the ambitious autodidact, was the first British woman to publish works on what we now understand as science (Meyer, vii; Todd, 24) and Sor Juana, a woman, the author of the only major scientific poem of her century in the Spanish language (Rivers, 262; Bellini, 84). Therefore, I would like to ponder for a moment some implications of science for the seventeenth-century learned woman such as Cavendish, as she inched away from love and toward modernity.

Up until the eighteenth century, *scientia* meant all learning; in the seventeenth century, at the dawn of the scientific revolution, *scientia* was evolving into science (Harari in Serres, xii). Science, or what was then generally called natural philosophy, stood at the forefront of *scientia*. It thrust *scientia* toward modernity, gradually disengaging it from the theology that for so long had controlled the world pictures of Christian civilization. To practice science was to reappropriate the world, to form part of the prestigious avant-garde of knowledge, and to wield the summa and marker of *scientia* (as signaled by the ingenuous exclamation from Fontenelle's treatise for women on science: "I have the whole system of the universe in my head! I'm a scholar!" [73]). The cachet of science dovetailed with its exclusivist gender mission, as described in my introduction. If women were encroaching on the City of Knowledge through their literary endeavors, science would be masculine in its construction and practice; if women were climbing out of their prescribed places, a new space excluding them would be erected. Science would reinforce gender ideologies as well as rescue men from the anxieties of "effeminacy" as they discharged their intellectual, rather than soldierly, tasks. The masculine force of arms would be imported into letters.

For these and other reasons too numerous to mention here, from its early modern inception up to now the practice of science has continued to be a preserve dominated by men. In the case of seventeenth-century Great Britain, women were barred from the Royal Society of Science (chartered in 1662). Gerald Meyer writes in *The Scientific Lady in England 1650–1760* that before Cavendish, "Englishwomen were permitted by their male custodians to seek intellectual refreshment from the study of languages, art, poetry, and music. The sciences remained the wares of Oxford and Cambridge—wares well beyond the reach of undisciplined feminine intellects" (2). Needless to say, feminine intellects remained undisciplined due to male institutions such as the Royal Society and Oxbridge, which excluded them and which, as they had with so many fields of knowledge, claimed science for its confines. Since advances in science required specialized tools and a highly specialized education, the avant-garde of science was ripe for institutional appropriation (cf. Hilda Smith, 63).

Certain instruments, notably the microscope and telescope, and a certain presentation of science nevertheless made their way into the hands of women. I draw my examples here from Great Britain and France, but also have in mind Sor Juana's fascination with the science of optics (a matter I will discuss later). Meyer notes that some of the novelties revealed by the telescope and microscope did not contravene but bolstered the Christian world picture: "The two-way extension of the Book of Nature into the incredibly great and small seemed to give a new and greater dimension to the all-powerful, all-wise God who had written it" (1). Therefore, even though women were kept out of the forefront of science, in the minds of the male arbiters of culture some of its advances could profitably be shared with the opposite sex. The telescope and microscope drew women into the conjectural and speculative aspects of science. In contrast with the more professionalized experimental science, this was a pursuit appropriate for amateurs (Todd, 24). Moreover, as did the world of science for so many seventeenth-century writers, its unbounded possibilities sparked women's imaginations. The burgeoning "science" of the seventeenth century, not yet limited by sharp disciplinary boundaries and glimmering with the potential of other worlds and worlds inside worlds suggested by the microscope and telescope, easily comingled with fantasy. Especially for the less tutored minds of early modern women, it might be said that the less one is wedded, by default or design, to the factuality of science, the more science can serve the imagination.

Bernard le Bovier de Fontenelle's superb *Entretiens sur la Pluralité des Mondes* [Conversations on the Plurality of Worlds] (1686; an instant best-seller quickly translated into English in 1688 by none other than Aphra Behn) fomented and propagated the imaginative possibilities of science specifically for women. Though it appeared shortly after Cavendish's time, Fontenelle's work gives us insight into the appeal that recent discoveries held for her and others. Indeed, one could scarcely hope for a more apt or appealing purveyor of science to women than Fontenelle (1657–1757). He was a serious intellectual whom the Academie Française received in 1691 and who played an important early role in the Académie des Sciences; he was also a friend to the *précieuses* and a frequent participant in their salons.[37]

In order, as the sympathetic Fontenelle says, to "encourage women through the example of a woman who, having nothing of an extraordinary character, without ever exceeding the limitations of a person who has no knowledge of science, never fails to understand what's said to her, and arranges in her mind, without confusion, vortices, and worlds" (4), he arranges his text as an attractive intellectual dialogue cum flirtation between the

Marquise of G. and her male scientist friend. The mention of "vortices, and worlds" in the preceding quote brings out the two principal aspects of physics that his book renders palatable to women by packaging them as a "spectacle for the imagination which please it as much as if they had been made expressly for that purpose" (5). Meyer nicely describes Fontenelle as deftly portraying on his "space-canvas" "the themes of infinite space, countless worlds, eons of geologic time, and the attendant conjecture of life on other planets" (21). Fontenelle's *Entretiens*, its author tells us, uses "verifiable physical tenets" (5). However, he says, "the true and the false are mixed here," which matter "is the single most important point of the work" (5). The main character spins out the imaginative possibilities of hidden worlds to the Marquise's growing enthrallment. She says: "Finish driving me to madness–I can't control myself any more; I no longer know how to hold out against philosophy" (53). The work concludes by shading off from science into speculation and by handing over the reins of those speculations to the Marquise: "You've arrived at the last vault of the heavens, and to tell you if there are more stars beyond that, one would have to be more able than I am. You may put more systems there or not, it's up to you. . . . I'm satisfied to have taken your mind as far as your eyes can see" (73).

Margaret Lucas Cavendish succumbed as fully as the Marquise of G. to the pleasures of science with its promise of many new worlds. She rhapsodizes about science in her *Philosophical and Physical Opinions* (1655), construing the discipline itself as a New World for the activities of the mind: "[I]t is a great delight, and pleases the curiosity of men's minds; it carries their thoughts above vulgar and common objects; it elevates their spirits to an aspiring pitch; it gives room for the untired appetites of men to walk or run in, for so spacious it is, that it is beyond the compass of time" (quoted in Grant, 22). Given Cavendish's native "fancy," her unusual exposure to the new science, and her lack of training in older forms of knowledge (we recall her statement that she lacks an education in the classics but has some familiarity with "Atomes," etc.), it was almost predictable that she be attracted to science. The privileged position of science in her culture also exercised considerable influence on her agenda. Critics have attributed Cavendish's enthusiasm for science at least in part to a motivation even more personal than its suitability to her circumstances.[38] They agree that due to the cachet, prohibitive aspect for women, and topicality of science, Cavendish viewed it as a golden opportunity to obtain the fame she required. Jones states that Cavendish was drawn to natural philosophy "by her own natural curiosity, and then driven on by the knowledge that she was the only woman working in an exclusively masculine field. Here was the chance to achieve the fame she so ardently desired" (118). All that I have read of Cavendish's work leads me to agree with Jones's statement and, indeed, to take it a step farther. I believe that to satisfy both her yearning for knowledge and the height-depth-breadth of her ambition, Cavendish was hell-bent on arrogating to herself–and by a self-interested extension, to her sex–the full male-dominated world of knowledge. Although

Cavendish would not touch theology ("For God, and his Heavenly Mansions, are to be admired, wondred, and astonished at, and not disputed on" [*P&F*, prefaces, n.p.]), she would exercise her inflamed will to signature on the summa of man-made *scientia*, science.

With her usual defensive candor, Cavendish confesses in the prefaces to *P&F* that she wrote science in verse because poetry left her less vulnerable to criticism. The mediocre scientific verse of the first part of her first book certainly warrants this justification. Its main claim to poetry, at least to my mind, lies in the ingenious and willful license that it takes with science. Cavendish expounds an all-encompassing theory of atoms arising from her musings on the microscope that she summarizes with the following words:

> Thus the *Fancy* of my Atomes is, that the foure Principall Figures as Sharpe, Long, Round, Square, make the foure Elements; not that they are of several matters, but are all of one matter, onely their several Figures do give them several Proprieties; so likewise do the mixt Figures give them mixt Proprieties, & their several composures do give them other Proprieties, according to their Formes they put themselves into, by their several Motions. (31; italics mine)

Lisa Sarasohn has stated that Cavendish's theories did bear some relation to others of the times and were not all that more fanciful than they. She also admits that Cavendish's atomistic cosmology "was indeed very extreme and reflects her rejection of all kinds of intellectual authority" (291). Sarasohn goes on to remark that what in particular distinguishes the Duchess's system from the corpuscular philosophies of Descartes, Hobbes, and Gassendi is the "disregard of the Divinity" (291). For Cavendish's atoms, among other things, act out of their own volition and with a fine disregard for Divine Providence (291). Cavendish exploits the atoms as a means of placing her signature on a gamut of issues as weighty as Divine Providence and as flighty as earrings. That "All things are govern'd by Atomes" (*P&F*, 16) enables Cavendish to theorize about all matters scientific. The most ponderous questions of physics, astrology, meteorology, and so on fall prey to her theorizing, not infrequently to bizarre effect. For example, in "The Attraction of the Earth," Cavendish deals with its magnetic properties. Why is the earth magnetic like the sun? Because little atoms arise from the earth like bees, "[a]nd as they wander, meet with duller Formes, / Wherein they sticke their point, then backe returnes" (21). The zeal with which Cavendish encroaches on science, evinced from the prefaces on into her elaborate theories of all the world's phenomena, makes it difficult to ascribe such outlandish explanations solely to poetic fancy.[39]

In May of 1667 the Duchess of Newcastle obtained an invitation to its quarters from the Royal Society of Science. Her visit, in a dress with a train held by six attendants, prompted Pepys to remark: "I do not like her at all, nor do I hear her say any thing that was worth hearing, but that she was full of admiration, all admiration" (Meyer, 10). Nor was Cavendish, despite her alleged protestations of admiration, reportedly all that pleased with what she saw. The technical complexities of experimental science, of the telescope and microscope in their full scientific context, detracted from the imaginative possibilities that had so compelled her previous scientific reasonings. They also shook Cavendish's already shaky confidence in her earlier theories. In fact, Cavendish's disappointing visit to the Royal Society only consolidated the sui generis position regarding experimental science she had earlier begun to adopt after reading in 1665 Robert Hooke's *Micrographia*, with its jarringly graphic pictures of microscopic investigations (Grant, 204–5). In her *Observations on Experimental Philosophy* (1666), she had already rejected the microscope in favor of the naked eye (or "I") and had set to evolving a more "natural" natural philosophy that validated herself and her sex. Sarasohn sums up the situation:

> The only option left to the duchess, since she could not be admitted into the male preserves of learning, was to develop her own speculative philosophy, rejecting not only the teachings of the ancients, but the system of the moderns as well, at least in theory. If the Scientific Revolution can be considered an attack on the authority of Aristotle, the medieval world-view of Margaret Cavendish was a further attack on the authority of a male-dominated science, and, by implication, an attack on all male authoritarianism. In adopting the role of the female scientist, Cavendish implicitly turned the world upside down. (294)

Cavendish put forth her new theory of nature and motion most vividly in *Description of a New World Called the Blazing World*, a utopian science fiction novel that she appended to *Observations Upon Experimental Philosophy*. Her new cosmogony further magnified the deification of an emphatically female Nature already inaugurated in *Poems and Fancies*. Sarasohn rightly noted the almost complete dethroning of the Christian Divinity in *P&F*. However, Cavendish endows atoms with some of the Divinity's properties and Nature, even more explicitly, with others. The first poem of *P&F*, for example, is no less than an alternative creation myth, a rewriting of Genesis. It begins with the lines: "When Nature first this World did create / She cal'd a Cousell how the same might make" (1). In both *P&F* and *BW*, Cavendish tacitly transforms Nature, Scholasticism's Second Cause, into the First. The central statement of her theory in *BW* makes clear the importance Cavendish attaches to Nature:

> [B]oth by my own contemplation, and the observations which I have made by my rational and sensitive perception upon nature, and her works, I find, that nature is but one infinite self-moving body, which by the virtue of its self-motion, is divided into infinite parts, which parts being restless, undergo perpetual changes and transmutation by their infinite compositions and divisions. Now, if this be so, as surely, according to regular sense and reason, it

appears no otherwise; it is in vain to look for primary ingredients, or constitutive principles of natural bodies, since there is no more but one universal principle of nature, to wit, self-moving matter, which is the only cause of natural effects. (*BW*, 154)

Sarasohn characterizes Cavendish's system as manifesting "a full-scale skepticism" (292) and as favoring over the mechanistic theories currently in vogue an "organic materialism" that harks back to Renaissance theories of natural magic (295, 297). I note with interest that to place her own stamp on male modernity and at the same time to appropriate that modernity for the feminine, Cavendish (like other early modern women we have seen) resorts to a conservative position.

I also note with interest a significant corollary to her scientific position on Nature. In many of her writings, Cavendish's valorization of Nature serves to justify her not only as a scientist but also as a scholar/writer. Much as Cavendish stands on the brink of the Enlightenment and appeals frequently to reason (as in the above statement of the observations made by her "rational and sensitive perception upon nature"), she more often appeals to a self-styled and self-serving *avant la lettre* Romantic position that disparages formal rhetoric, writing, or learning. Of the many examples to this effect in her works, I will reproduce only a couple of particularly resonant ones.[40] First, a brief poem from *P&F* that bears a striking resemblance to Romanticism's unbound Prometheuses:

> Give Mee the Free, and Noble Stile,
> Which seems uncur'b, though it be wild:
> Though it runs wild about, it cares not where;
> It shewes more Courage, then it doth of Fear.
> Give me a Stile that Nature frames, not Art
> For Art doth seem to take the Pedants part.
> And that seemes Noble, which is Easie, Free,
> Not to be bound with ore-nice Pedantry. (110)

Second, a couple of remarks demonstrating that Cavendish considered herself to be the ideal exponent of a natural style: "[F]or I must tell my readers, that Nature, which is the best and curiosest worker, hath paved my brain smoother than custome hath oiled my tongue, or variety hath polished my senses, or art hath beaten the paper wheron I write; for my phancy is quicker than the pen with which I write" (*Memoirs*, 185), and "though I am but poetess, yet I am but a poetastress, or a petty poetess; but howsoever, I am a legitimate poetical child of nature" (*Sociable Letters* [in Grant, 128]).[41] By exalting natural philosophy, natural poetry, and natural style, and in creating herself as their proprietress, Cavendish cannily turns to good use the pernicious equation between woman and nature, and man and culture. Her philosophy seizes science away from (male-dominated) culture and makes it a function of a female-dominated Nature. The association between nature and fancy also bolsters the claim on poetry of women in general ("Besides, Poetry, which is built upon Fancy, Women may claime, as a worke belonging more properly to themselves" [*P&F*, prefaces, A3]). Perhaps most important, in all its facets Cavendish's philosophy of Nature sanctions her own self-generated, undisciplined knowledge. "A true poet," she wrote, coining a rather grotesque natural metaphor, "is like a Spider that spins all out of her own bowels," and who draws upon "observation, and experience, got by time and company" (*World's Olio* quoted in McGuire, 202]). With this, autodidacticism becomes not an obstacle but Cavendish's license to the City of Knowledge.

Theorizing and writing about science, we see, fulfilled important needs for Cavendish. Science provided a means for her to take on the quintessence of the world of knowledge and the world itself in its minute and broad dimensions. Yet science was not world enough. Cavendish's mind wandered voraciously and randomly over all creation. "A Dialogue Between Melancholy and Mirth" (*P&F*, 76), a poem by the Duchess curiously similar to Bradstreet's "Contemplations," purports to let us into its author's mind:

> As I sate Musing, by my self alone,
> My Thoughts on several things did work upon.
> Some did large Houses build, and Stately Towers,
> Making Orchards, Gardens, and fine Bowers:
> And some in Arts, and Sciences delight,
> Some wars in Contradiction, Reasons fight [and so on].

Cavendish would appear to have dignified whatever thoughts crossed her mind, on whatever subject, by writing them down and then publishing them. The very titles of her works betray their diverse, miscellaneous disposition: *Divers Orations, Philosophical and Physical Opinions, Nature's Pictures, The World's Olio*. One might aptly term all of Cavendish's works "olios," a highly spiced hodgepodge of things (Grant, 140).

Lilley asserts that "Cavendish's response to the narrow territory with which women were supposed to concern themselves was a desire for encyclopedic coverage" (*BW*, xvi). Be it a response to the limitations placed on her sex or to the indomitable freeplay of her mind—or, as I see it, a reflection of her will to signature—Cavendish's works often manifest both a miscellaneous and a totalizing encyclopedic tendency. Her *Blazing World* provides a stunning illustration of Cavendish's tendency to put her hand to *all* bodies of knowledge, as well as of other tendencies I have noted in the British writer. Compared to *The Convent of Pleasure*, *BW* is not merely a matriarchal space of self-governance and self-possession, a world almost without men, but also one where women—its author, its female characters (one of whom, as seen in an opening extract of this section, is "The Duchess of Newcastle")—can wield all the interdicted male discourses of knowledge. Cavendish *erects* a new City of Knowledge in *BW*: a domain in which she can expound her theories on almost everything, where she can exhibit her knowledge with no constraints.

The world's olio becomes a world unto itself, a monument of its author's knowledge; what blazes here is Cavendish's all-consuming unfettered mind.

The Blazing World, as the preceding comments suggest, is basically a geographic structuring device for a spectacle of knowledge. The text quickly makes this clear. It begins as the improbable story of a young Lady's abduction, shipwreck, arrival at Paradise, and coronation as its Empress. This seeming romance adventure immediately reveals itself to be only a framework story, a pretext. The frame tale of sorts that occupies the rest of the text revolves around the efforts of the new Empress to inform herself about her new kingdom and thus to assert herself as its ruler. Our blazing Empress creates herself as leader of both church and state and as a patronness of the arts and of learning ("she erected schools, and founded several societies" [134]). She summons priests and statesmen to give her accounts of the empire. In the lengthy dialogue that ensues, the informants inform and the Empress comments on every aspect of their world: political theory, religion, science and mathematics, rhetoric, gender roles, architecture, logic, metaphysics, and so on. The real adventures of the Blazing World are those of the mind. Although the final section of the text briefly returns to the romance mode (allowing the Empress and the "Duchess of Newcastle" successfully to defend the empire against enemy forces), for the most part it remains an encyclopedia of the Blazing World, purposefully titled *The* Description *of a New World Called the Blazing World* (italics mine).

All of the major characters in Cavendish's encyclopedic work are engaged in a display of (her own) knowledge, and the author uses their dialogue to advantage. By this I mean that in a game of shifting positions, sometimes the informants act as vehicles for Cavendish's particular notions of things and sometimes as their foils. Given that the Blazing World is at once Cavendish's own utopian textual space and her projection of a utopian world, her own cherished theories—for example, of a harmonious uniform, monarchy with but one religion and no dissension (135)—find their home in it. The Blazing World's venerable intellectuals voice Cavendish's personal theories and others of which she approves, legitimizing them. Yet Cavendish must also establish the superiority of the female Empress, which in the context of the novel involves establishing her as the most shining mind in the Blazing World. She does so by having the Empress on occasion sharply assert her own opinions over those of the intellectuals of her realm. The Empress expounds Cavendish's "natural philosophy" in the central passage (154) cited earlier. Analogously, the Empress mocks experimental science and commands the "Bear-men" to break their telescopes: "[N]ature has made your sense and reason more regular than art has your glasses, for they are mere deluders, and will never lead you to the knowledge of truth; wherefore I command you again to break them; for you may observe the progressive motions of celestial bodies with your natural eyes better than through artificial glasses" (141–42). The reply of the "Bear-men" to the Empress's command contains Cavendish's parody of institutional academics: "[the 'Bear-men' say that were they to break their telescopes] we shall want employments for our senses, and subjects for arguments; for were there nothing but truth, and no falsehood, there would be no occasion for dispute, and by this means we should want the aim and pleasure of our endeavours in confuting and contradicting each other" (142). The Empress/Cavendish reserves her greatest spleen for the final movement of the interview with her native informants, a colloquy on yet another set of subjects traditionally reserved for men. In a conversation with the Blazing World's mathematicians, geometricians, orators, and logicians, the Empress acerbically mocks their artifice-ridden disciplines as inimical to nature and banishes at least one of them from her realm. This final touch makes it all too clear that Cavendish has manipulated the dialogical play of voices in *BW* to serve her own monological impulses.

As if it were not enough to have discussed all things worldly in the Blazing World, the Empress now extends her ever more dizzy sights to the "spirit" world and to the Earth. Having had her way with the native informants, the Empress calls in the spirits. She exploits their presence to discourse on a grab-bag of subjects, that is, on whatever shards of ideas Cavendish had not managed to include earlier—from the Bible to theories of constant motion to the corporality of ghosts (e.g., "Then she asked them, whether spirits could be naked? and whether they were of a dark, or a light colour?" [175]). With this, the somewhat orderly inquiries into the Blazing World descend into a real "olio" that verges on utter randomness. The native informants then suggest that the Empress summon the spirit of the Duchess of Newcastle, to aid her in writing a "caball."[42] The disembodied soul of the Duchess eventually takes the disembodied soul of the Empress on a tour of Earth, which allows both of them to comment on its flaws in comparison with the utopian Blazing World. The tour ends at Welbeck, where the soul of the Empress becomes enamored of and enters the soul of the Duke of Newcastle: "which the Duchess's soul perceiving, grew jealous at first, but then considering that no adultery could be committed amongst Platonic lovers, and that Platonism was divine, as being derived from divine Plato, cast forth of her mind that Idea of jealousy" (194–95).

By now the reader must be asking: Can Cavendish possibly be serious? Is *Blazing World* philosophy? Is it comedy? Is it autobiography? Is it satire or caricature? Is it science? Is it fiction? Having asked myself the same questions, I would have to answer all of them affirmatively. Lilley considers Cavendish to be a student of genre, fascinated with impure and unexpected hybrids, and "engaged by that which troubles or resists categorization" (*BW*, xi). I suspect that Lilley's characterization of Cavendish accurately captures the hybrid nature of her works but magnifies the author's prescience beyond its rightful limits. For what we have seen of Cavendish suggests that the author's most earnest will to signature can cause her displays of erudition to spin out of control—blurring generic boundaries, infusing knowledge with an overdose of fancy that can result in an unwitting caricature of erudition, incongruously conflating registers, and weaving diverse islands of knowledge into a single encyclopedic body. *BW* rather disingenuously introduces its "Duchess of Newcastle" by saying, "[A]lthough she is not one of the most learned, eloquent, witty and ingenious, yet she is a *plain and rational* writer, for the principle of her writings is *sense and reason*" (181; italics mine). I believe it is not unfair to state that Cavendish's aspirations to learnedness and ingenuity often lead her to stray from sense and reason and to transform her purportedly plain and rational writings into original hybrid concoctions.

Cavendish's insistently original *Blazing World* places her stamp on the world of knowledge and on seventeenth-century utopian fiction. From her very first work and extending to her novellas, plays, and novel, Cavendish displays what can only be taken as an obsession with creating new worlds, ideal or not.[43] In addition to the *Convent of Pleasure*, we find in *P&F* an alternative Genesis, the modeling of a utopian island that rectifies England's woes ("Of an Island" [116]), and a sequence of microscope-inspired poems, each of which explores a different world within this one (e.g., "A World in an Eare-Ring," "Several Worlds in Several Circles" [45–46]). Cavendish's play *Bell in Campo* draws up the constitution for a more perfect world (see Tomlinson, 149). Her novella "Assaulted and Pursued Chastity" contains a quasi-anthropological portrait of a new world that bears notable traces of sixteenth-century representations of *the* New World.[44] Each of these worlds, nevertheless, is pronouncedly Cavendish's own creation. Particularly in her most fully elaborated world, the Blazing one, Cavendish sets her idiosyncratic imagination to all we survey—from the theories of natural philosophy to the jewel-encrusted architecture to the brightly colored skins of its inhabitants and their costumes. With the "feminine" sense of sensual detail mentioned in terms of *The Convent of Pleasure* and a striking visual imagination, Cavendish showily reimagines the world piece by piece and marks it as her own.

Fontenelle's *Entretiens* had inspired hundreds of utopian novels and imaginary voyages (Fontenelle, xxv). Moreover, other women of the times had tried their hands at utopian fiction (see Lilley's article). Cavendish's utopian text distinguishes itself from others for its absolutely hyper-self-consciousness. The Duke of Newcastle introduces his wife's work by praising her accomplishment in making a "World of Nothing, but pure wit" (121); *BW* not only purports to have created a world ex nihilo, as do some utopian fictions, but also loudly thematizes the matter. In the *mise-en-abîme* of created worlds in this text, Cavendish as author first fabricates the Blazing World and then glosses her own enterprise. She writes herself into the text as the "Duchess of Newcastle" who, with the aid of the spirits, engages the Empress in the explicit activity of creating worlds. "What, said the Empress, can any mortal be a creator? Yes, answered the spirits; for every human creature can create an immaterial world fully inhabited by immaterial creatures, and populous of immaterial subjects, such as we, and all this within the compass of the head or scull. . . ," etc. (the spirits then elaborate profusely on the subject; 185–86). The Empress finds it practically impossible to imagine a world superior to her–read Cavendish's–own Blazing World, "by reason it was so well ordered that it could not be mended" (189). The "Duchess of Newcastle," on the other hand, at first finds herself at a loss as to how to proceed. She rummages through the utopian models proposed by a variety of philosophers such as Pythagoras, Plato, Epicurus, Aristotle, and Descartes. She then rejects these male models in favor of her own invention: "At last, when the Duchess saw that no patterns would do her any good in the framing of her world; she resolved to make a world of her own invention, and this world was composed of sensitive and rational self-moving matter" (188). Like an Escher engraving, the "Duchess of Newcastle's" created world replicates the Duchess of Newcastle's Blazing World, which recasts the actual world.

In yet another vertiginous proliferation of reflections, both Duchesses, the author and the character, make it abundantly clear why they so strive to create worlds. After the "Duchess of Newcastle" has informed the Empress of her boundless ambitions, the text tells us outright that she "was most earnest and industrious to make her world, *because she had none at present*" (186–87; italics mine). Remarkably enough, the "Duchess's" confession is but a pale echo of those of the "real" Duchess[45] at the beginning and again at the end of *BW*. I will quote only the first, and most famous, such statement. In her Preface to the Reader, Cavendish writes,

> . . . for I am not covetous, but as ambitious as ever any of my sex was, is, or can be; which makes that though I cannot be *Henry* the Fifth, or *Charles* the Second, yet I endeavour to be *Margaret* the *First*; and although I have neither power, time nor occasion to conquer the world as *Alexander* and *Caesar* did; yet rather than not to be mistress of one, since Fortune and the Fates would give me none, I have made a world of my own. (124; italics in original)

This statement has great impact and several implications. First of all, it bolsters the picture of Cavendish as overweeningly ambitious that I have been drawing throughout my discussion. Second, it links the 'Duchess' (author of the preface) with the "Duchess" and with the Empress specifically in terms of *power*. The two fictional Duchesses are now Empresses. They have achieved dominion over their worlds through their intellectual capabilities, the original Empress over hers through her mind and her appointed position (appointed by the text!). Power and knowledge go hand in hand, in the Blazing World and the real one. *BW* gives its female characters full scope to exercise both of these male-dominated and male-proscribed activities in its utopian space. It is not by chance that the single most striking image of the text is that of the blazing apotheosized Empress, whose shining jewels illuminate her face:

> which added such a lustre and glory to it, that it caused a great admiration in all that were present, who believed her to be some celestial creature, or rather an uncreated goddess, and they all had a desire to worship her; for surely, said they, no mortal creature

can have such splendid and transcendent beauty, nor can any have so great a power as she has, to walk upon the waters, and to destroy whatever she pleases, not only whole nations, but a whole world. (215)

BW, as do most of Cavendish's fictional works, empowers and deifies its female characters.[46]

Finally, the pronouncement of Empress "Margaret the First" in her preface clearly cements the equation of the 'Duchess' or Cavendish herself with the Empress, an equation already built into the Empress's theories of natural science. It reveals both principal characters of *BW* to be the fictional masks of the 'Duchess' or of the author. This, for its part, undermines Cavendish's apparent redemption of her sex in general by rendering her feminism distinctly *unipersonal*. Such a position is perfectly consistent with Cavendish's inconsistent gender ideologies. Almost all of her commentators have been taken aback by the British author's alternating denunciations and defenses of her sex.[47] *BW* does not fail to evidence Cavendish's characteristically split attitude. On the negative end, the utopian Blazing World leaves much to be desired as a woman's utopia. In her discussion with the priests, for example, the Empress learns (and does not take issue with) the fact that in her empire "women and children have no employment in church and state" and that "although they are not admitted to public employments . . . they are so prevalent with their husbands and parents, that many times by their importunate persuasions, they cause as much, nay, more mischief secretly, than if they had the management of public affairs" (135). This is pure Pauline misogyny! The text has little else to say about women (except that their quick wits fit them to be nuns, [162]) of a praising or a denigratory nature. Far more positively, the Blazing World is a paradise for the Empress and the "Duchess." The autobiographical details that Cavendish builds into both characters, as well as the other identifications I have noted, sign them as glorified self-portraits.[48] They confirm her never interdicted, ever-proliferating "I" as the nerve center of the Blazing World and her self-centered desire to make a world for that "I" as a driving force of the text. Paradoxically, in our modern climate this is one of Cavendish's greatest claims to fame. As Janet Todd writes of seventeenth-century female writers, Cavendish "was certainly not the first woman to publish fictional material and she was certainly not the first to publish. But she *was* the first to use published fiction to create a fantastic, wish-fulfilling, compensatory world" (68).[49]

III.

Perhaps a significant figure in her own "write," certainly a significant phenomenon in the panorama of seventeenth-century women writers, Margaret Lucas Cavendish is still no Sor Juana—a world-class writer. However, the cartoonish outlines of Cavendish's work, when projected onto the *Primero sueño*, expand the map of our readings of that epistemological text. Up to now, what comparative studies there are of the *PS* tend to concentrate on its links to male-authored texts (of Cicero, Fray Luis de León, Trillo y Figueroa, Kircher, and so on). Much can be gained from comparison of the *PS* to the texts of a female author, even a less distinguished one, who labored under conditions similar to Sor Juana's. The dialogue between the two authors' works will show us, among other things, how the textuality of the *PS* relates to Sor Juana's situation as an autodidact trying to storm the City of Knowledge: what Cavendish audibly states, Sor Juana visibly and unmistakably enacts in her texts. Cavendish and Sor Juana took different public positions with regard to fame, but both manifested an ambition to besiege the bastions of knowledge. Sor Juana's not inconsiderable will to signature would compensate for the effacement of her "I" and produce a text that bears meaningful resemblances to Cavendish's *Blazing World*.

To better understand the placement of Sor Juana's text vis-à-vis that of Cavendish and of Sor Juana herself vis-à-vis the world of knowledge, it will be valuable to consider the broader implications of a couple of tendencies observed in the British author. First of all, we have noted at length Cavendish's encyclopedic urges. Bradstreet, too, in her compendiumlike Quaternions, evidences a thirst to write the whole world.[50] In effect what we are seeing here is a pre-Enlightenment encyclopedism, an encyclopedism in the age of the baroque or the metaphysicals. While the seventeenth-century spirit of abundance and excess, together with its love of erudition and spectacle, no doubt promotes the totalizing display of knowledge, the woman's will to signature also plays a significant role. I maintain that Cavendish's work represents not only an *avant la lettre* but a *gendered* encyclopedism, driven by the exclusion of women from the world of knowledge.

Second, in recuperating the encyclopedia for learned women, Cavendish replicates the epistemological properties with which the work of philosopher Michel Serres has endowed it. In his conception, the encyclopedia represents a totalizing way of knowing the world, one achieved by the free circulation among disciplines and bodies of knowledge. Josué Harari says that for Serres, "to know is to navigate between local fragments of space, to reject techniques of classification and separation in order to look for units of circulation along and among displacements. To know is to adopt the comparative and pluralistic epistemology of the journey, to implement a philosophy of transport over one of fixity," and "what counts in this [encyclopedic] space constituted of fragmented local spaces is less the circumscription of a region than the circulation along and among paths" (Serres, xxii–xxiii). I grant that *BW*'s crazy hybrid mixing of science with fiction, of philosophical fact with philosophical fancy, stands at a far remove from Serres's epistemological justifications, but I believe that Cavendish's text speaks to his notion of the encyclopedia–albeit for rather different reasons. For Cavendish the autodidact, working outside

disciplinary formations, fact becomes more tractable and disciplinary boundaries more fluid. Moreover, *her* version of an encyclopedic urge impels
Cavendish to weave all matter of knowledge together into a single sui generis creation. If Serres's chosen emblem is Hermes, transgressor of boundaries,
Cavendish's is more of a spider-woman ("that spins all out of her own bowels") and, by extension, Penelope the transgressive weaver. All told, Serres's
poetics of the encyclopedia becomes in Cavendish what I call the "poetics of
the autodidact."

Autodidacticism (together, as we will see later, with its attendant poetics)
plays a crucial role in the works of Sor Juana. In essence, we can read the *PS*
as an autodidact's dream or nightmare: a solitary confrontation of the
Intellect, lost in space, with the cosmos's floating bodies of knowledge. Also
lost in space is *Theo*didactus, protagonist of Athanasius Kircher's *Iter
Exstaticum Coeleste*, an epistemological dream poem considered by Paz and
others to be a central source for the *PS*. Yet he, Theodidactus (transparent
mask of Kircher himself [Paz, 363]), receives a divine revelation from God's
messenger. Cosmiel, "minister of the God of Heaven and earth," rescues
Theodidactus, saying, "Arise; do not fear, Theodidactus; your desires were
heard and I have been sent to show you, insofar as may be permitted to mortal eye, the supreme majesty of the God Optimus Maximus, who shines in
spendor in all his works" (Paz, 363–64). Paz makes much of the lack of a
divine guide or divine revelation in the *PS*, seeing their absence as the poem's
prefiguration of modernity. Yet neither Paz nor anyone else to my knowledge
has drawn one self-evident conclusion: the *PS* has a female voyager (a transparent mask of Sor Juana), and that female voyager fails to receive enlightenment.[51] The female *auto-didactus* has been denied the privileges and the
ecstasy of a male *Theo-didactus* taught by God.

Sor Juana's discussion in the "Respuesta" of her quest for knowledge
makes this poignantly clear. Her formal education at the "Amiga" school
taught her reading but ended in what would now be primary school years.
Like other women of her times, Sor Juana found herself barred from a university education and turned to private study in a home library. Unlike certain
aristocratic women, she had no tutor to guide her study. Sor Juana gives us a
very real sense of what it meant to learn under these conditions:

> What I might point out in self-justification is how severe a hard-
> ship it is to work not only without a teacher but also without fel-
> low students with whom to compare notes and try out what has
> been studied. Instead I have had nothing but a mute book as
> teacher, an unfeeling inkwell as fellow student, and, in place of
> explanation and exercises, many hindrances . . . (*216–17*, 4.450–51)

Sor Juana also gives us a remarkably precise portrait well worth reproducing
in full of the diversified, eclectic, autodidact's education that resulted from
these conditions:

Thus, for the acquisition of certain fundamentals, I would constantly study divers things, without inclining in particular to any
given one, inclined rather *to all generally*. So it happened that my
having concentrated on some more than others was *not a matter of
choice* but came about through the *chance* of having found books
dealing with the former subjects closer to hand, which gave them
preference without any decision of mine. As I had *no material goal
in mind*, nor any limitation of time constraining me to the study of
any one thing to meet *degree requirements*, almost at once I was
studying different things or dropping some to take up others,
although this was not wholly unsystematic since some I called
study and others diversion. The latter brought me relaxation from
the former. It follows from this that *I have studied many things*, yet
know nothing because each one always interfered with some
other. (*215*, 449–50; italics mine)

Sor Juana's description brings out, once again, her extraordinary thirst for total
knowledge. Though obviously an attempt to justify her study of unorthodox
subjects, it also brings out the possible pitfalls of an education outside an institutional framework and contravening disciplinary bounds. However, the
author hastens to state that the ostensibly haphazard education has worked
to her benefit by revealing to her the interconnectedness of all phenomena: "I
should like to convince everyone by my own experience not only that different subjects do not interfere with one another, but that they actually support
one another, since certain ones shed light on others, opening a way into them
by means of variations and occult connections" (*215–16*, 450). Sor Juana may
not have attained Theodidactus's cosmic illumination, or even—as she states
in the "Respuesta"—have dared to touch theology, but by virtue of her all-
encompassing autodidacticism she has achieved the enviable overview of a
comparatist.

Students of Sor Juana will recall that Karl Vossler and Ludwig Pfandl
have exploited the above descriptions of her education to demean the nun's
scholarly qualifications (despite the fact that she passed an examination
administered by the luminaries of her time).[52] Vossler, for example, says,
"Unsystematically, indefatigable and an audodidact, one might even say an
insatiable filibuster, she violently persists in seeking knowledge," and "she
loved all the branches of knowledge in a fresh feminine way, as one loves
delights and adventures" (Bénassy-Berling, 94). If he were referring to
Cavendish, I might be inclined to see more truth in Vossler's remarks. But the
rigor of Sor Juana's mind, her seriousness of purpose, and the depth of her
intellectual curiosity place the Mexican writer in a different league. In my
view, Alan S. Trueblood assesses Sor Juana's autodidacticism far more appropriately: "The lack of a formal education, though deplored by Sor Juana, had
the compensatory effect, in throwing her on her own resources, of fostering
both vast intellectual ambition and the self-reliance needed to pursue it; both
might have been inhibited by a more systematic and supervised training" (21).

The final portion of Trueblood's statement raises an important point, one particularly pertinent to Sor Juana's context. "¡Oh siglo desdichado y desvalido / en que todo lo hallamos ya servido" (Ovillejo #214) [Oh unhappy and impoverished century, in which we find that everything has been used up]: in writing these lines Sor Juana could easily have had in mind the stagnation of institutional learning in seventeenth-century Mexico. With Mexican universities given over as they were to the monolithic propagation of a rigid neo-Scholasticism tied to Christian orthodoxy, Sor Juana may well have profited from being excluded from them.[53] In what constitutes an effective reply to Vossler, Tonia León sums up the advantages that Sor Juana most likely gleaned from being self-taught:

> While Sor Juana may not have fulfilled her fantasy of attending the University, she did successfully escape its restrictive intellectual atmosphere committed to Scholastic philosophy. An autodidact, she was not only able to master the orthodox philosophy of her time and adroitly employ its methods and logic in both her poetry and prose, but also become familiar with the unorthodox thought of the seventeenth century. (76)

Moreover, like Cavendish, Sor Juana made good use of available resources. Direct observation, a prolific correspondence, conversations, experimentation with different technical instruments, and an array of secondhand sources all supplemented her education, giving it a broad base.

Over the course of her life Sor Juana pieced together her own world of knowledge. She would display it throughout her works and especially in the *Neptuno alegórico* and the *Primero sueño*.[54] Paz, in words lamentably similar to Vossler's, refers to the "charming pedantry" (1951, 37) of the *PS*. While pedantry was certainly rife among the bureaucrats of what Angel Rama calls the *ciudad letrada* or educated community of seventeenth-century Mexico, Sor Juana's displays of erudition also lend themselves to a gendered explanation. Harss notes the "*criollo*'s obsessive display of bookish learning that showed his mastery of cosmopolitan skills," and goes on to comment: "An even stronger obsession in a woman who had to keep proving herself in her own eyes as well as those of a skeptical world" (21). As a literate individual and sometimes accountant and archivist of the convent, Sor Juana belonged tangentially to the *ciudad letrada*. However, the "Respuesta" made it painfully clear that as a nun and a woman, Sor Juana did *not* belong to the City of Knowledge. In other words, when we take gender (and, in other cases, race) into consideration, the *ciudad letrada* and the City of Knowledge split into two very distinct entities. For genuine intellectual and for personal reasons, Sor Juana sought a place in the City of Knowledge, which had excluded her. Totalizing encyclopedic spectacles of knowledge would serve as her passport and modus operandi—the telltale signs of her will to signature. María de Zayas forsook erudition, which had only brought her criticism that she lacked originality, to flaunt her feminism ("I wish to earn the title of disenchantress, not scholar"

[D., *203*, 294]) as a trademark or signature; the opposite would hold true for Sor Juana, who flaunted her will to signature.

A verbal spectacle based on a visual one, the *Neptuno alegórico* (1680) illustrates one of the paths taken by Sor Juana to stake out a place in the City of Knowledge. In her ecphrastic explanations of the arches painted to welcome the new viceroy and his wife, Sor Juana demonstrates an exhaustive command of sources pertaining to the mythological figure of Neptune. The excessive *Neptuno alegórico* contains two twin texts, one in verse (read on the occasion) and another in prose (later published). The prose explanation in particular bears all the earmarks of a baroque scholarly text: an abundance of quotes in Latin, theoretical pronouncements, a dense Gongoresque language, citations from an apparent wealth of sources biblical and classical.[55] In both texts of the *Neptuno*, Sor Juana ingeniously manipulates her sources to create an image of Neptune that profiles the ideal leader she hopes the new viceroy will be and to exalt learned women through the figure of Isis, goddess of wisdom. These manipulations reflect Sor Juana's intellectual and personal agendas. For with the *Neptuno* Sor Juana indelibly establishes herself as an intellectual with an extraordinary depth of knowledge on a specific subject. Propelled by the personal and political motivations discussed at the end of my first chapter, she also establishes her value as an icon of Culture to be supported by the Marquis de la Laguna. Isis becomes her mask and the *Neptuno* another act of self-fashioning in a public context as Sor Juana almost imperceptibly writes herself into the text: "Este, Señor, triunfal arco, / que artificioso compuso más el estudio de amor / que no *el amor del estudio*" (403; italics mine) [This triumphal arch, Señor, built skillfully by the study of love, rather than by the *love of study*]. Georgina Sabat-Rivers observes that through the *Neptuno* Sor Juana intended to "be recognized by the Viceroy as an erudite woman, and to earn his respect" (1983, 69). In the *Neptuno* as well as in the *PS*, Sor Juana subdues her "I" but blazons her will to signature.

Where in the *Neptuno* Sor Juana scripts her will to signature for a public and political venue, in the *PS* (according to Sor Juana the only work she wrote for her own pleasure) she enunciates her most intimate yearnings for knowledge. If the *Neptuno* establishes the depth of Sor Juana's knowledge, the *PS* also establishes its encyclopedic breadth. Her *silva* harks back to the origins of the metrical form as a miscellanea—a *selva* of random material, an olio, what Serres calls a *randonée* or expedition filled with random discoveries (xxxvi). Along these same lines, we can view the *PS* as a curio cabinet stocked with wonders: the Egyptian pyramids, the lighthouse of Alexandria (one of the seven wonders of the ancient world), the magic lantern. Cavendish's olios certainly had something of the curio cabinet to them as well. The British author fancied the ultramodern; hers was a wonder cabinet. Sor Juana embraces ancient and modern knowledge; her work is something of a museum. In fact, like a museum, the *PS* aspires to be not a miscellanea but a repository of all human knowledge. As Diego Calleja's summary of the poem in the *Fama y obras póstumas* would have it: "I dreamed that I wanted to understand totally and instantly all things of which the universe is composed" (Paz, 359). The *PS* encompasses an amazingly encyclopedic range of subjects, ancient and modern: astronomy, astrology, poetics, history, politics, law, physiology, philosophy, optics, mythology, experimental science, mechanism, and metaphysics (see Gaos, 60–61). Of great importance, as I stated earlier, Sor Juana makes her mark both on the world of knowledge and on literary history by including science in her repertoire. Neither her stated model, Góngora's *Soledad primera* [First solitude], nor what Sabat-Rivers (1976; part 1, chap. 3) has shown to be her partial working model, Francisco de Trillo y Figueroa's *Pintura de la noche desde un crepúsculo a otro* [Portrait of the night from dusk to dawn], evinces the scientific leanings of the *PS*.

Sor Juana's masterpiece often articulates its own totalizing bent. The section of the *PS* that depicts the coming of sleep reads like a reverse Genesis, an uncreating of the entire Earth. The synecdoches of this and succeeding sections emphatically speak for the whole cosmos. For example: "El sueño *todo*, en fin, lo poseía; / *todo*, en fin, el silencio ocupaba" (ll. 147–48; italics mine) [*All* was now bound in sleep, *all* by silence occupied, *175*]. Similarly, Fantasy ("fantasía") reproduces the entire world for the mind to see: "así ella, sosegada, iba copiando / las imágenes de *todas* las cosas" (ll. 280–81; italics mine) [so the fantasy was calmly copying the images of *everything*, *178*]. Metaphors of the poem's compendiumlike nature proliferate in the section on intuitive knowledge. In lines 280–91, Fantasy becomes an artist capable of painting, in potential colors, not only "*all* created things" in the "sublunary world" (*178*, ll. 285–86; italics mine) but also all invisible, immaterial ideas. The mirrored lighthouse of Alexandria that reflected all movement on the seas, for its part, functions as a metaphor of Fantasy's all-encompassing representational activities. Interestingly, even and much as the poem becomes the global body of nature and culture, all of the Soul's wanderings take place *inside* herself. She, like the poem's author, contemplates the enormous world compacted into her mind.

From the "Aleph" inside the mind of the *PS*'s dreaming Soul emerges a vision of the interconnectedness of all phenomena and all bodies of knowledge. We recall from the previous chapter Sor Juana's depiction in the "Respuesta" of her mind's associative dream-work:

> [E]ven my sleep was not free from this constant activity of my brain. In fact, it seems to go on during sleep with all the more freedom and lack of constraint, putting together the separate images it has carried over from waking hours with greater clarity and tranquility . . . including certain thoughts and subtleties I have arrived at more easily while asleep than while awake. (*226*, 460)

In the context of our present discussion this statement speaks to the *Sueño*'s poetic and philosophical sense of similitude: its linking of one thing with another, of the microcosm with the macrocosm. The hierarchical animal kingdom, with its king and queen, reproduces the human world. The human body reproduces the machinery of the world. Human beings contain a spark of the Divinity and comprise a mysterious "compendio que absoluto, / parece al Angel, a la planta, al bruto" (ll. 692–93) [complete compendium resembling angel, plant, and beast alike, *188*]. All phenomena are interrelated through the Aristotelian categories.

Sor Juana's sense of similitude asserts itself even more notably in the poem's "encyclopedic" (in Serres's usage) textuality, its all-melding syncretism.[56] The *PS* syncretically harmonizes the diverse languages and bodies of knowledge. It creates channels of communication between myth, science, philosophy, history, and so on. For one thing, the body of the text moves seamlessly between mythology and science (for example, from the overture's mythological panorama to the physiology of the sleeping person). More significant, discrete sections of the poem weave together seemingly incompatible modes of knowledge. The elaborate "intermezzo" on the pyramids (ll. 340–424, *180–82*), for instance, draws on esoteric philosophy (the pyramids as external manifestations of the soul according to hermetic Egyptology), history (of Memphis, of Alexandria), religion (the Tower of Babel), science (optics), mythology (the giants who attacked Olympus, Icarus), and poetry (Homer). To introduce the neo-Aristotelian method (ll. 617–703, *187–88*) Sor Juana avails herself of mythology (Thetis), Scholasticism (man as linked to the Divinity and to all things), religion (book of Revelation), and mechanism. Truly does the *PS* chart a fine course between local fragments of space, rejecting classification and finding units of circulation.

Sor Juana's dreamy vision of a universe of harmonious similitudes is far from sui generis. It clearly derives sustenance from the Renaissance episteme as well as from the enduring world picture of the Great Chain of Being (with Neoplatonic and Aristotelian roots; see Paz, 375–76) that she invokes in the "Respuesta":

> It was to form this universal chain that the wisdom of their Author so put them in place that they appeared correlated and bound together with marvelous concert and bonding. This is the chain that the ancients pretended emerged from Jupiter's mouth, on which all things were strung and linked together. So much is demonstrated by the Reverend Father Athanasius Kircher in his curious book *De Magnete* [On the Magnet]. (*216*, 450)

Nor, as the quote makes clear, is her syncretism unique. A host of recent studies have demonstrated that Sor Juana's most erudite work, largely inspired by Kircher, situates itself in the syncretic traditions of the Jesuits and of Florentine Neoplatonism, Hermeticism, and neo-Scholasticism.[57] "The key factor" in all of these syncretic paradigms, summarizes Harss, "was the humanist sense of an expanding world that required a new unifying scheme capable of accounting for cultural diversity" (15). Following on the discussion of Sor Juana's endgames in chapter 2, we can see that the notion of an overarching heuristic model that harmonized diverse currents certainly suited Sor

Juana's way of thinking; in view of recent studies, we can accept as a given that she partook of some or all of these syncretic models.

I would introduce one more element into the already thick mix. The fact that Sor Juana appeals to the Great Chain of Being in an attempt to legitimize her own eclectic pattern of study tells us something crucial. It suggests a relationship between her autodidacticism and her philosophical disposition in the *PS* to similitudes and syncretism. Sor Juana divulges in the "Respuesta" that she journeys somewhat haphazardly from text to text; unconstrained by either institutional or disciplinary boundaries and seeking total knowledge, she makes what connnections she can. As was the case with Cavendish, under these circumstances the already fluid disciplinary boundaries of seventeenth-century *scientia* grow more fluid, the passage between them more open. The poet, like Arethusa, travels easily between different worlds, joining them. I do not in any way mean to displace or discount the importance of existing heuristic models for Sor Juana. I do wish to suggest that the conditions under which she labored lent themselves to syncretisms and similitudes, and that the "encyclopedic" nature of the *PS* (together with its totalizing inclinations) reflects what I have called the *poetics of the autodidact*. If necessity is the mother of invention, then I would say that had such models not existed, Sor Juana might well have invented them.

Sor Juana's Jesuit-trained fellow intellectual, Carlos de Sigüenza y Góngora, also performed some astonishing syncretic gymnastics in his historical works.[58] However, be it due to his academic interests or to his more easily established place in the City of Knowledge, as far as we know from his extant works Sigüenza never undertook to write the whole world in one tome. While he could be extraordinarily pedantic and polemical, his works lack the vigorous will to remake the entire world of knowledge found in Sor Juana. Sigüenza openly polemicizes, as in his famous manifesto arguing for the comet as a scientific rather than a religious phenomenon. Sor Juana eschews overt polemic (we recall the unfortunate results of her one attempt at it, the *Carta Atenagórica*) and exerts her will to signature by tacitly refiguring, subverting, and re-creating the world of knowledge and the world itself.

To begin to substantiate my assertion, let us consider the manner in which Sor Juana reembroiders literary set pieces in the *PS*: as Harss states, the poem is "made up of several more or less set pieces woven of traditional themes" (22). Of course, the seventeenth and preceding centuries held a notion of authorship that sanctioned rather than discouraged literary borrowings. Even so, not only Sor Juana's literary borrowings (which I have elsewhere called the signs of "textual friendships" [1991, 22]) but her reembroiderings strike me as exorbitant, almost compulsive. Méndez Plancarte has devoted endless pages to documenting Sor Juana's sources; Sabat-Rivers has devoted an entire book to the literary traditions refigured in the *PS* alone; Paz gives lengthy account of the relationship between the *PS* and other dream poems. Rather than reiterate their findings, I will bring forward a couple of others as examples of the poet's desire to place her signature on literary tradition. First, building on the equation between sleep and death, Sor Juana shapes her portrayal of the coming of sleep into a medieval Dance of Death (ll. 174–91, *175–76*). An armed Morpheus urges all the earth's creatures, from the peasant to the pope, into slumber. The second example returns to the baroque motif of strife. In lines 243–51 [*177*], Sor Juana reworks a set topic, the digestion of food, into a mock epic battle between the head and the stomach (Harss, 91). A parody of the epic, the battle also plays on the fascination that food held for baroque poetry by showing us the precise aftermath of the many "Baroque banquets" so vividly noted by José Lezama Lima in *La expresión americana*. Sor Juana's ingenuity, the baroque worldview, and physiology all join forces in this virtuoso performance.

A couple of lines from the *Neptuno alegórico* bring Cavendish to mind and well describe the yearning for a new world that Sor Juana satisfies in the *PS* by actually creating one. Addressing the viceroy, Sor Juana writes: "El mundo solo no encierra / vuestra gloria singular, / pues fue a dominar el mar / por no caber en la tierra" (4.397) [In itself the world cannot hold your singular glory, which went on to rule the sea since land could not contain it]. In the *Neptuno*, Sor Juana utilizes the otherly realm of the sea as the site for her display of erudition. In the *PS*, she fashions the equally otherly realms of night and dream into a universe apart, that is, into a new world with its own landscape, space, and time. To enter the nightworld is to enter an ideational dreamscape composed of stark geometric forms and of mental colors: "y el pincel invisible iba formando / de mentales, sin luz, siempre vistosas / colores las figuras" (ll. 281–83) [and the invisible brush was shaping likenesses in the mind's colors, without light yet beautiful still, *178*]. The Soul travels among ethereal abstractions that attain a vivid corpo*reality* as they are embodied in metaphors such as the pyramids, the ladder, the fountain, or the rose. Sor Juana's intellectual cosmos is neither a utopia nor a heaven or hell. Rather, it is the meeting place of heterogeneous bodies of knowledge. As such, Jacqueline Nanfito maintains, the *Sueño*'s space creates its own time outside time:

> Through the system of interreferences by which allusions are made simultaneously to past, present and future, . . . through the harmonious and poetic fusion of diachronic and synchronic aspects of time operative on all levels of reality, Sor Juana succeeds in transcending time and in creating one of the most solemn and affecting images landscape has ever offered. (425)

While one need not expect linear temporality from a poem, Nanfito's observation underscores the manner in which the simultaneous, synchronic temporality of the nightworld liberates itself from the strict linear progressions from night to day and from sleeping to waking that frame the poem. Sor Juana creates this oneiric universe and obliquely signs it: with her "I" at the end of the poem, with the "floating self images" to which I have referred, and with sporadic personal deictics ("I mean," "my mind").[59] Like Cavendish, if far less ostentatiously, both literally and literarily Sor Juana functions as the demiurge of her created world.

Cavendish creates a matriarchal world led by a Blazing Empress. Sor Juana creates an ideational cosmos ruled by a Dark Empress that abounds in feminine refigurations and figurations. I have already mentioned Sor Juana's tendency in the *PS* to depict the Divinity in feminine forms. Often the forms, like "Sabia Poderosa Mano" (l. 670) [Powerful and Knowing Hand, *187*], are only grammatically feminine, but it is striking to find the Divinity and humankind portrayed as "señora / de las demás" (ll. 668–69) [mistress of all others]. To the recasting of the Divinity and humankind should be added the fact that in the nightworld Sor Juana places more emphasis on Nature, the "second productive cause" (l. 623, *186*), than on the "First Cause" (God; l. 408, *181*) as the active creator and ruler of the world. In line 421 [*181*], for example, "Nature" appears as the creator of humankind.[60] The Sun may bring the light of day, but Nature governs the world–judiciously and harmoniously: "que la Naturaleza siempre alterna / ya una, ya otra balanza, / . . . en el fiel infiel con que gobierna / la aparatosa máquina del mundo" (ll. 160–64) [Nature always alternates from one side of the balance to the other, in the stable unsettled way in which she governs the complicated machine of the world]. Sor Juana does not go so far as to identify Nature with the feminine in anything but grammatical terms, but she does invoke the quintessentially maternal figure of Thetis as mother of vegetable matter. Wife of the ocean and mother of the rivers, Thetis nurses the earth with her "fruitful maternal breasts" (l. 628, *187*). Like Nature, Thetis guarantees the orderly working of her kingdom (ll. 633–39, *187*). Maternal imagery related to nature also crops up outside the nightworld, in the early section on the falling asleep of the world. There we find references to nests, cradles, and breasts.[61] The leitmotif of maternity resurfaces in the section on Arethusa and Ceres. Distraught over the loss of her daughter–"del dolor su vida iba perdiendo" (ll. 729) [losing her life from grief, *189*]–Ceres epitomizes maternal love both here and in Sor Juana's source, Ovid (book 5, 153).

That it is the female stream, Arethusa, who conveys the news about Persephone to Ceres places the *PS* in the matrilineal series of texts utilizing this myth to recover the feminine. Arethusa's deed also explains to a degree the unusual (especially for Sor Juana) abundance of maternal imagery in the *PS*. For the poem, from its first lines onward, associates knowledge with the feminine. We remember the oil of Minerva as well as the female Prometheuses of the overture. Inside the nightworld, the poem characterizes the questing Soul as feminine at pivotal points. Having internalized the world and "toda convertida / a su inmaterial ser y esencia bella" (ll. 292–93) [fully converted into her immaterial being and lovely essence], the feminized Soul undertakes her quest; at the peak of the intuitive attempt at knowledge she becomes "Reina soberana" "de lo sublunar" (ll. 438–39) [the sovereign queen of this sublunary world, *182*]. Last, we recall that Sor Juana singles out both the female Arethusa and the rose to represent the unfathomable complexities of knowledge. Harss notes the allusions to female physiology, sexuality, fertility, and virginity bound up in Sor Juana's rose (124), traditional symbol of the ephemerality of women's beauty. Sor Juana retains the conventional associations of the rose but converts it into an icon of epistemological inquiry emphatically inflected as feminine.[62]

At this juncture I would like to call attention to a particularly significant matter: in addition to adumbrating the nightworld in feminine terms, Sor Juana develops an alternative set of textual practices for it–practices that recent theorizing equates with "feminine" forms of representation. I recognize the potential for anachronism and essentialism inherent in my assertion. I also recognize that, as a dreamworld, the central portion of Sor Juana's text warrants a different logic and textuality. Nevertheless, as I hope to show, the textual practices of the nightworld itself (in contrast to the other two segments of the text) bear a meaningful resemblance to the fluid feminine discourse posited by Luce Irigaray, among others.[63] Irigaray, it is well known, advocates an oppositional women's discourse. Her "speaking as woman" defies the phallic values promulgated by the patriarchy: property, production, order, form, unity, visibility, erection (86). It replaces their fixity with a decentered fluidity that "resists and explodes every firmly established form, figure, idea or concept" and that disrupts "every dichotomizing" (79). In "The 'Mechanics' of Fluids," Irigaray characterizes the female economy as "continuous, compressible, dilatable, viscous, conductible, diffusable" and "flowing, fluctuating. Blurring" (111).[64] When we import Irigaray's essentialist notions of the feminine such as these into the context of the seventeenth century, we recall how dramatic a turnabout has taken place in the interim. For the French theorist valorizes precisely those illogical or antilogical qualities that the querelle misogynists scorned in women. In an exemplary dialectic, the preeminently rational and lucid Sor Juana will succeed in "liquifying" her nightworld while still keeping linear logic in view.

The broad outlines of the nightworld follow a discernible linear path that moves from the intuitive to the neo-Aristotelian means of understanding the world. However, within that horizontal diegesis the poem refuses linearity. Like Arethusa's stream, it wanders about, "deteniendo en ambages su camino" (l. 715) [pausing at times for roundabout meanders, 189]. Long digressions permit the poem to explore what Franco calls "the byways of knowledge" (33),[65] to introduce the contents of the curio cabinet, and to develop metaphorical plots and subplots. The "matrix moments" of the poem compound the nonlinear aspects of its structure. In collapsing figurations and prefigurations of the whole poem into small parcels, they endow it with the musical structure of a baroque fugue. One such musical matrix moment, the "intermezzo" on the pyramids (ll. 340–424, 180–82), illustrates the various nonlinear properties of the poem. A digression of spectacular length and disposition, it subsumes not only the pyramids but also the figure of Icarus, the works of Homer, and the Tower of Babel. Each of the subplots of this matrix moment singularly, and the digression in toto, enunciates the poem's central dictum of transgressive intellectual daring. So imbricated is the digression that by its end the reader can easily have lost sight of the original point of departure (the Soul looking down at the universe from the heights).

The poem may at times feel chaotic, but it still possesses its own unshakable order. As we have seen, the nightworld bristles with symmetries; each piece has a function in its plays of repetitions and differences; Sor Juana makes serious statements in its nooks and crannies. Moreover, the very digression on the pyramids articulates this premeditated structure. The (seemingly purposeless) subsection on the poetry of Homer, the only poet explicitly mentioned in the *PS*, informs us that it would be easier to steal Zeus's thunderbolt or Hercules's club than to dislodge a single line from Homer's works (ll. 391–98, *181*). From this we can deduce that for Sor Juana, poetry has an ironclad structure and that beneath the riverlike meanderings of the nightworld's textuality—which, like the nightchorus, pauses more than it sings—lies an ineluctable order, the order of disorder.

The disordering space of the nightworld allows ambiguities and contradictions free rein. I have already discussed the ambiguity of certain elements that change valence from dark to light when they enter the nightworld; we have already seen the destabilizing of traditional imagery of light and dark that renders several aspects of the poem irremediably ambiguous. Now I would like to look at the contradictory nature of the chiaroscuro nightworld, whose most signal feature is that it neither resolves nor collapses (as in "border-crossing") dichotomies. Rather, as does mystical discourse, it lets opposites coexist. Phaethon, both model and pernicious example, constitutes but one of several instances of this phenomenon. The pyramids, once dark and now bathed in light, are the glories of Egypt (l. 379, *180*) *and* "bárbaros jeroglíficos de ciego error" (ll. 381–82) [barbaric hieroglyphs of purblind error, *181*]. They symbolize the sublime yearnings of the Soul *and* the sinful Tower of Babel. Human beings are wrought of contraries, being an "altiva bajeza" or haughty lowliness (l. 694, *188*). The ascensional eagle is conflated with the fallen Icarus (ll. 331–39, *179*). At the height of her ascent to intuitive knowledge, the Soul experiences the contradictory emotions of joy and perplexity, perplexity and arrogance (ll. 436–37, *182*). What I find fascinating in the foregoing chain of paradoxes is not only its connection with "speaking as woman" but also its connection to the baroque worldview. I began chapter 1 of my study with a discussion of the contradictory age of the baroque. We can now see that Sor Juana projects this aspect of the baroque onto the idiosyncratic landscape and textuality of the nightworld, allowing contraries unproblematically to coexist as a reflection of the world's irreducible multiplicity.[66]

The figure of Phaethon conjoins one final opposition essential to the textualization of the nightworld. Phaethon mounted the heavens but plunged to his death in the sea: Sor Juana designs the nightworld's overarching space, its heaven, in the image of Neptune's underworld, the sea. Where Góngora's *Soledad primera*, self-stated model of the *PS*, situates its Brave New World on land (its pilgrim emerges from the water onto firm ground), Sor Juana's quester journeys through an otherly space insistently identified with water and opposed to land. Alcione (or Almone),[67] construed as a sea siren, and the sleeping submarine world introduce the aquatic theme in the first section of the poem. From the first, then, the fluid water world seeps in through the cracks of the ordered world. The lighthouse of Alexandria (mirror of the sea), the tears of Icarus falling to his watery grave, and the repeated portrayal of the attempt at intuitive knowledge as a shipwreck (ll. 478–79, *183*; ll. 560–70, *185*) confirm the aquatic disposition of the nightworld.

In the *Neptuno alegórico* Sor Juana implies that she considered the sea to be a world unto itself: "And Pliny says that there are many different animals and trees in the sea; and that not only does it lack nothing that is found on land, but has even more excellent things" (4.397). The *Neptuno* also suggests that when Sor Juana seeks an "otherly" space, that space will be Neptune's realm. Harss believes that the aquatic imagery of the *PS* reflects the subconscious of the female dreamer (112). Whether or not we fully agree with him, two things are clear. First, Sor Juana, mindful of her nightworld's transgressive nature, takes recourse to an established model of alterity in creating a nocturnal world distinct from the diurnal one. Second, she marks her oceanic world as feminine. Not Neptune but Alcione/Almone (siren of the seas), Thetis (ocean/river), and Arethusa (stream) appear in the poem as rulers of the water.

The poem's aquatic images find their complement in the fluid textual practices of the nightworld. I have devoted considerable attention in this chapter to detailing the "flowing, fluctuating. *Blurring*" metamorphoses, metaphorical echoes, ambiguities, similitudes, and syncretisms of the *PS*. Therefore, to conclude my discussion of the nightworld's differential nature, I would now like to examine how the *PS* engages with the oppositions of *dark/water/disorder/fluidity* versus *sun/land/order/boundaries*. The two outer poles of the *PS* establish the dayworld as a rigidly ordered hierarchical space. The animal kingdoms have their King and Queen, the human kingdom its God, and the text an orderly progression in dramatizing the coming of sleep (through metonymies) and the defeat of the Night. Inside the fluid nightworld, order loses its sway. In textual terms, linearity cedes to digression, clarity to ambiguity, metonymy to metaphor, the phallogocentric to the "feminine." In thematic terms, attempts to achieve order fail like a rejected skin graft. First, the intuitive attempt at knowledge telescopes all being into a single unmanageable glance. Then the Soul proposes to climb rung by rung the rigidly ordered ladder of Scholasticism, with its ten categories and four operations. The poetic speaker ruminates at length on the composition of the ladder. In actual fact it remains unclear whether she has even ascended the first rung!

The reentry into the dayworld imposes definitive order on incipient chaos by routing the wild Soul ("lacking harmony" [l. 952], "lacking order" [l. 956]) and by reinstating the preeminence of the male God. Returning dominion to the "outer senses" (l. 973, *195*), the Sun restores the world's stability and surety. The ending of the poem, which I described earlier as a phallic assault on or rape of the female Soul, can now be seen as bringing the restitution of the phallogocentric world–with its "lines of brilliant light" (l. 947), its "judicious" (l. 969) and "clearer" light (l. 974), its "orderly distribution" (l. 970), its Manichean battle between the Sun and the Dark Empress, and–in more strictly poetic terms–its ostensible banishing of metamorphoses and multiple masks. If the Father/Sun/God is the "Eternal Author," then this is *His* poetics, the very image of the patriarchy's imperious differentiating mechanisms. However, as I have observed at several points, the poem quietly resists closure, clarity, and linearity to the end. The nightworld filters into the dayworld not only through Aurora but also in the (obviously nonlinear) cyclicality of the rebellious Empress and the ambiguity of the "I." "Llegó, en efecto, el Sol cerrando el giro" (l. 943) [The Sun appeared, the circle now complete, *194*]: the monolithic and monological Sun would place closure, but the poem fights for aperture.

There remains to be explored one final gambit by Sor Juana to make a distinctive mark on the world of knowledge, one final manifestation of the author's will to signature: her utilization in the *PS* of science. I begin with the scientific imagery of the *PS*, most of which has a mechanistic cast. Sor Juana repeatedly refers to machines and gadgets: the pebble held by the eagle as an alarm clock (l. 136, *175*), the "complicated machine of the world" governed by nature (l. 165), the elaborate description of the body as a machine or "human clock" (ll. 205–33, *176*), the magic lantern. The notably unpoetic nature of machines prompts one to wonder if this is a genuine poetry of science or merely science thinly transposed into verse. However, it is clear that machines stimulate Sor Juana's poetic creativity and that she employs mechanistic imagery to considerable poetic effect. The extraordinary syntactic freedom of her poetic language, for example, allows the poet verbally to simulate the well-regulated inner workings of a machine (see ll. 160–65, among other examples).

But why write of machines in the first place? The ingenuity of machines meshes with the *ingenio* or wit essential to baroque poetry. Their cachet as the *ne plus ultra* of modernity must have appealed to Sor Juana's imagination and desire for encyclopedic coverage as they did with Cavendish. For, together with machines, Sor Juana invokes another emblem of modernity, the recent science of optics. She alludes to it in the curved mirror of the Alexandrian lighthouse, the pyramids (ll. 355–60, *180*), and the magic lantern–"guardando de la docta perspectiva, / en sus ciertas mensuras" (ll. 879–80) [maintaining the distances required by the science of perspective, *193*]. Science in general attracted Sor Juana, who possessed her own technical instruments. Hence, the curio cabinet of the *PS* also contains references to less current scientific theories as well: atomism, Ptolemaic cosmology, and Galen's medical notions.

The question of exactly how current Sor Juana's scientific knowledge was is an extremely thorny one. Was she familiar, directly or indirectly, with the contributions of Descartes or even with the heliocentric universe? Does her mechanism bear any relationship whatsoever to Newtonian physics?

Distinguished scholars have taken diametrically opposed positions on these issues, particularly in terms of the nun's familiarity with Descartes.[68] Textual evidence in the *PS* inclines me to agree with the position adopted by José Gaos and Luis Harss: that for Sor Juana, in her "colonial echo chamber" (Harss, 17), "the world of science beckons with its promise of systematic knowledge, but she has only glimpses of it and no framework in which to make sense of it" (Harss, 115; also see Gaos, 59). At the same time, the concerns of the present chapter lead me to explore a related question: What did it mean for Sor Juana to write about science? On the one hand, I have just suggested that for Sor Juana, it meant satisfying the baroque propensity for novelty and at the same time satisfying her intellectual leanings, her encyclopedic inclinations, and her will to signature. As did Cavendish, Sor Juana could lay claim to *scientia* through science.

On the other hand, science was a far more dangerous pursuit in Sor Juana's context than it was in Cavendish's. Cavendish might have jumped in where other women had never tread, but in her context at least science did not imply heresy. Sor Juana, writing in the shadow of the Inquisition ("I want no trouble with the Holy Office" [*290*, 4.444]), proves herself in the "Respuesta" to be fully cognizant of the dangers of straying outside the bounds of orthodoxy. Catholic orthodoxy, as any religious knew and as the case of Galileo had amply demonstrated with regard to science, exercised a monopoly over knowledge–a monopoly that in the short and the long runs science effectively challenged. Therefore, to practice science was to proceed with great caution. We will never know exactly what or how much Sor Juana knew about the subject, for she is likely to have hidden much from view. Even if she had read the Cartesian works of her friend, Sigüenza y Góngora, or exchanged information with him, she would not necessarily have incorporated the New Science into her writings. Bénassy-Berling rightfully views Sor Juana's knowledge of science as a terra incognita for modern scholars and the Mexican nun's silences as potentially significant (126–27; 116). For the most part, what Sor Juana does say about the subject is unreproachable or, as we will see, if not unreproachable, so intricately wrought as to be practically invisible. Hence, the Ptolemaic cosmology of the *PS*, its mechanism (to a degree sanctioned by Scholasticism),[69] its atomism, and so on. Along the same lines, Paz contends that Sor Juana received or filtered her modernity through the acceptable figure of Athanasius Kircher, practitioner of Jesuit syncretism who melded the very old and the very new into an indissociable whole (175–77).

Within this protocol of caution, and from the margins outside the institutions of knowledge, Sor Juana nonetheless takes a faintly perceptible but radical scientific stand of her own.[70] At various points the *PS* appears to advocate an empirical attitude toward the acquisition of knowledge. In other words, the *PS* dimly favors the senses and experimentation as vehicles to knowledge. The balanced mechanisms of Nature as it judiciously governs the "complicated machine of the world," and the "well-regulated movement" (l. 209, *176*) of the human body, suggest the attractions of Nature as an alternative epistemology—as a self-sufficient, harmonious model readily available to empirical investigation. Nature's phenomena, the stream and the rose, function as laboratories for learning. The Soul resorts to the method proven by scientific experimentation to cure herself from the blinding light. Sor Juana describes the method as "–recurso natural, innata ciencia / que confirmada ya de la experiencia, / maestro quizá mudo, / retórico ejemplar" (ll. 516–19) [natural procedure, this inborn wisdom, which, with confirmation by experience, a silent teacher perhaps, but exemplary persuader, *184*] and "empírica atención, examinada / en la bruta experiencia, / por menos peligrosa" (ll. 533–35) [empirical attention tested first in experiments performed on animals, where the danger is not so great, *184*]. An empiricism such as that which Sor Juana appears to be espousing here "challenged belief that knowledge could only come from the authorities, not the individual" (León, 25) and thus challenged the abstract doctrinaire philosophies propagated by the current rulers of the City of Knowledge, the church and the university. Consequently, Sor Juana exercises great prudence in expounding the virtues of this "silent teacher." She draws on the resources of syncretism to domesticate and neutralize her assertions. Effecting a poetic alchemy of heterogeneous scientific methodologies, the author amalgamates "empirical attention" with the accepted medical practices of Galen, with the "unknown sympathies or antipathies" (*184*, ll. 527–28) of Renaissance Neoplatonism and homeopathy, and with "Apollonian science" (*184*, l. 537). Given that Apollo links science or knowledge and poetry, Sor Juana's exposition of empiricism protectively reroutes itself into a poetics of similitude![71]

Sor Juana's empiricism may have affronted the City of Knowledge, but it favored the female autodidact. According to what Sor Juana says in the "Respuesta" of the time that she was forbidden to read, the world was her laboratory: "For, although I did not study from books, I did from everything God has created, all of it being my letters, and all this universal chain of being my book. I saw nothing without reflecting on it; I heard nothing without wondering at it—not even the tiniest, most material thing" (*224*, 458). She goes on in the "Respuesta" to cite several insights gleaned from direct observation. Similarly, in Sonnet #152 ("Green allurement of our human life" [*101*]) Sor Juana concludes: "que yo, más cuerda en la fortuna mía, / tengo en entrambas manos ambos ojos / y solamente lo que toco veo" [I, wiser in my fortune, have my eyes in my hands, and see only what I touch]. We can hear Cavendish's "Dialogue Between Melancholy and Mirth" and rejection of institutionalized science in Sor Juana's words. And from their blended voices we can deduce the value of empiricism for those barred from institutionalized knowledge, the reason why they embrace it: culture may exclude them, but nature is available to all as an ever-present source from which the individual can construct her or his own culture.[72]

IV.

CONCLUSIONS (PARTICULAR AND GENERAL)

We have just heard Sor Juana make a subdued case for empiricism in the "Respuesta" and the *PS*. At the same time, the abstract ideational world of the *PS* gestures toward empiricism's opposite, Cartesian pure thought.[73] The two tendencies, though contradictory, both speak to what I find most modern and willful in the *Primero sueño*–its categorical skepticism. Standing at the end of an era or episteme and encompassing it all in her mental glance, Sor Juana has arrived at a position akin to Descartes's categorical doubt. I say "akin to" because, as Francisco López Cámara has convincingly argued, Cartesianism manifested itself in the New World during the seventeenth century not through strict adherence to his method but in a spirit of skepticism (110). López Cámara contends that seventeenth-century Mexican intellectuals, on the cusp of modernity, were more apt to look back critically at no longer viable modes of thought than to look forward and to embrace new systems of thought in their totality (129). Much of what we have seen of Sor Juana confirms López Cámara's contentions. In her "colonial echo chamber" (be it the convent or Mexico), she receives unsystematic fragments of modernity and, as an autodidact, puzzles through the world and received ideas on her own terms.[74] The subject to which I turn in conclusion is how and to what effect Sor Juana performs a critique of prevailing epistemologies from her marginal position outside institutional frameworks.

Small corners of the *PS* may hint at empiricism as an alternative epistemology, but Sor Juana devotes almost all of the poem's central portion to the failure of the Soul's attempts to achieve knowledge through Platonic or neo-Aristotelian means.[75] The question immediately arises: Do we attribute the Soul's failures to its/her own inadequacies or to the insufficiencies of the systems themselves? I am convinced that, for obvious reasons, Sor Juana equivocates on this matter.[76] For one part, she eventually identifies the Soul with her "I," and in the passage describing the ladder of Scholasticism very exceptionally refers to "mi entendimiento" (l. 618) [my mind, *186*]. Sor Juana endows the "I" or intellectual Soul with strong emotions, showing her to be aghast at her own failures and a coward. Moreover, from the overture on the poet lays the groundwork for the Soul's inevitable failure by accentuating her hubris. All of the above tactics personify the Soul and safely personalize its defeat, leading José Gaos in his now classic article on the *PS* to conclude that "the poet's intention is unmistakable, indisputably patent: to give expression to the most important experience of her life: the failure of the yearning to know which had governed her whole existence–her own, Juana de Asbaje's" (67).

Alternatively, the Soul remains almost entirely generic, and its failures thus general and impersonal. And while she personalizes the quest, Sor Juana still exposes the defects inherent in each method. The failure of the intuitive attempt owes equally to the hubris of the Soul and to the unseizable enormity of the universe–its "immense assemblage," "unencompassable mass," "profusion of objects" (ll. 445, 446, 451, *182*). Aided by divine intervention, Theodidactus took in the entire world; Sor Juana finds her early modern world too complex to be subsumed into archetypes. The *PS* launches a far more trenchant and direct attack on Scholasticism. A thinly veiled irony underwrites Sor Juana's portrayal of the abstract, nonempirical nature of Scholasticism: its "artfully constructed categories" (l. 581), "mentales fantasías / donde la materia se desdeña / el discurso abstraído" (ll. 585–87) [purely mental fantasies of abstract thought, eschewing embodiment in matter, *185*].[77] Even Méndez Plancarte, usually so eager to depict Sor Juana as a model nun, reproaches her lack of "rigor" in terming the categories "mental fantasies." Clearly, Sor Juana is here paying the obligatory attention to what she calls "doctrine" (l. 600, *186*), and doing so none too wholeheartedly. (In the same section of the poem she also pays a token tribute to the doctrine of Communion [ll. 696–703, *188*].) That the cowardly poetic speaker, as I stated earlier, appears not to have mounted the all too formidable ladder and that Sor Juana writes herself into the critical portion of the Scholastic section with the phrase "my mind" (ll. 617–18, *186*) indicates that she once again scapegoats her unworthy "I"–now in an effort to avoid being accused of holding heretical opinions.

Viewed at close range and in its personal dimensions, the *PS* nuances, equivocates, and purposefully stammers. Viewed from farther afar and in its broad outlines, the *PS* makes a bold statement of epochal, almost epic, proportions on the state of knowledge in her times. At first, the *PS* invokes the episteme of a world organized by similitude. It conjures up the vision of an orderly balanced world, of the world as a well-regulated machine comprised of interlocking parts. The philosophical inquiries of the nightworld then attempt to filter that world through the grids of prevailing epistemologies. At each point, the grids prove insufficient. Quoting Faulkner's extraordinary hallmark of modernism, *Absalom, Absalom!*, I would say that they "just do not explain" (80). And when in the *PS* they fail to explain, the world reverts to a primal chaos. At the end of the attempt at intuitive explanation the blinded eyes of the Soul can only take in:

> de un concepto confuso
> el informe embrión que, mal formado,
> inordinado *caos* retrataba
> de confusas especies que abrazaba
> –sin orden avenidas,
> sin orden separadas,
> que cuanto más se implican combinadas
> tanto más se disuelven desunidas,
> de *diversidad* llenas– (ll. 548–56; italics mine)

[a rudimentary embryo of muddled discourse, one so shapeless that from the confusion of species it embraced it formed a picture of disordered *chaos*–associating species in no order, dissociating them in none, so that the more they mix and intermingle, the more they come apart in disarray from sheer *diversity*] (*185*)

Sor Juana paints a stunning picture here of the dissolution of the Neoplatonic worldview of similitudes. Further, under the optics of failure, the heretofore well-regulated machine becomes incomprehensibly complex: the defeated Intellect is overwhelmed by "la inmensa muchedumbre / de tanta maquinosa pesadumbre" (ll. 470–71) [by the immense agglomeration of a congeries so weighty, *183*]. A very similar movement takes place in the Soul's second attempt at knowledge. After the scary vision of primal chaos, the Soul seeks the strictest, most rigorous order, and finds it in (Scholastic, Aristotelian, Catholic) doctrine. As overwhelmed as before, at the end of the second attempt the Soul asks: "¿cómo en tan espantosa / máquina inmensa discurrir pudiera . . . ?" (ll. 771–72) [how can she hope to function in the face of so astounding and immense a machine?; *190*]. By this point, the machine has evolved from a symbol of the well-ordered world into one of the unknowable complexity of the universe.

No, they just do not explain. Not even Sor Juana's almost inaudible and conditional reference to a God who upholds the immense machine ("cuyo terrible incomportable peso / –si ya en su centro mismo no estribara–," its burden terrible, unendurable–were it not upheld at its very center [ll. 772–73, *190*])[78] rescues the world from its no longer comprehensible complexity or doctrine from the nun's critique. Subtending the artificial complacency of her own and her culture's syncretic endgames, Sor Juana has shown the sense- and order-endowing grids of her time to be insufficient, the world too unruly and complex to fit their patterns. Poised at the end of an era and, in the *PS*, at the edge of the world, Sor Juana bears witness to the crisis of its epistemologies. As they crumble, as the Law dissolves and fails to be replaced, the world threatens to dissolve into an existential chaos.[79]

Looking back over the various facets of this chapter, and indeed of this book, I would venture to say that in the *Primero sueño* Sor Juana bears witness not only to the breakdown of epistemologies but also to the early modern condition itself as I have understood and conveyed it in the foregoing pages. The poem nostalgically invokes a vision of order in a now fragmented world. It strives to defend that order in the face of encroaching disorder. It em-bod- ies the shifting grounds of the early/modern period that have figured so prominently in each chapter of this book–its ambiguities, tensions, contradic- tions, and instabilities. It stands at a watershed point: glancing backward with a critical eye and forward to catch flashes of a new economy no longer bound by theology, an economy glimmering with potential but not yet entirely formed. The *Primero sueño* also orchestrates the early modern condition as it pertains to the women I have discussed here. These women–like Sor Juana's female Prometheuses, the Soul and the "I"–attempt transgressively to wrest knowledge, the word, and the world from the patriarchy. They seek illumina- tion but also sanction. They profess an overt and a muted feminism. *Sirtes tocando de imposibles* /Brushing the shoals of impossible things: they cross boundaries onto dangerous reefs or domains of knowledge, they come up against walls of "imposibles," they dare to grasp what they desire despite the odds. They strategize, compromise, equivocate, and sometimes succeed. But often, as were the Soul and Sor Juana herself, they are chided or routed. They suffer from the opprobrium, internalizing it. Like the birdwomen of the *PS*, they are immortalized as freaks and left bearing burdens of guilt and shame.

Last, the improbable conjunction across geography, ideologies, and individualities of Sor Juana Inés de la Cruz and Margaret Lucas Cavendish underscores certain of the commonalities between seventeenth-century women writers that I have endeavored to bring to light in this study. United in their autodidacticism, will to signature, encyclopedic tendencies, fascination with science, feminist inclinations, and attempts to create new female worlds, the two authors are also composites of the other writers I have examined. Both Cavendish and Sor Juana emerge as acute scanners of the aspects of patriarchal culture (such as cross-dressing, the convent, the strong female protagonist) that lend themselves to an early modern feminism, and outspoken critics of the aspects of misogynistic culture (such as education and the negative factions of the *querelle des femmes*) that thwart it. Both can be willful self-namers who trade on their sex and uniqueness. Both contrive a bold literary signature for themselves through an extravagant style and radical theoretical platforms. Both venture into print, cutting a considerable figure in masculinist realms and in the public domain. Both avail themselves of conservative ideologies to advance their modernity. Musing and melancholy comprise both women's "scene of writing" in the literary and literal senses. Similarly and perhaps most emblematic of all, both women play out the early modern woman writer's drama from rooms of their own. Sor Juana retreats to the convent in order to pursue her scholarly vocation; Cavendish inters herself in Welbeck, "inclosing myself like an anchoret, wearing a frize gown, tied with a cord about my waste" (*Memoirs*, 233). Both writers imply that only by removing oneself from the world through encloisterment of one sort or another can the woman realize her potential. Not unlike their sixteenth-century female predecessors, Sor Juana and Cavendish retreat into book-lined cells, where each is protected by patriarchal structures (the church, marriage). In an advancement from the previous century, the walls of their cells sporadically give way and become permeable as Cavendish, Sor Juana, and others publish their works, infringing on masculinist discourse, and voicing their polemical views.

Not all seventeenth-century women writers enjoyed the conditional immunity of rooms (be they convents, estates, or salons) of their own. But almost all of those whom this study has examined either advocated or occupied them. Even Erauso shrank back into obscurity, changing her name. These women remained Promethean islands in the patriarchal landscape of the seventeenth century. They were pioneers, pilgrims, and harbingers of things to come. The eighteenth century would bring far more widespread educational opportunities for women; it would further unfasten cultural constructions of the female subject from the strict bounds of theology and the outlines of the *querelle des femmes*; it would open more doors for women from the cloistered rooms of their own into the outside world.[80] Until then, precariously straddling two eras, each of these real or de facto Tenth Muses had to contend with being an exception and exceptional, to being sui generis rather than a new genus.

Notes

Bibliography of Works Cited

Index

Notes

Introduction

1. See, for example, Georgina Sabat-Rivers, "Autobiografías: Santa Teresa y Sor Juana," in her *Sor Juana Inés de la Cruz y otros poetas barrocos de la colonia* (Barcelona: Promociones y Publicaciones Universitarias, 1992), and Electa Arenal and Amanda Powell, introduction to *The Answer/La Respuesta* (New York: Feminist Press, 1994), 21–22 et passim.

2. Here, and throughout the book, I cite Sor Juana's works from Alfonso Méndez Plancarte and Alberto G. Salceda's authoritative four-volume edition of her *Obras completas*. The numbers of her texts correspond to theirs (and have been widely adopted); I cite the volume number at the beginning of the discussion of each text or wherever I believe there might be confusion.

3. *La mística ciudad de Dios*, feeding into the controversy on the Immaculate Conception raging at the time, was condemned by Rome in 1680 but rescinded from the list of prohibited works by Carlos II. For a recent and modern treatment of María de Agreda, see Clark Colahan, *The Visions of Sor María de Agreda: Writing, Knowledge and Power* (Tucson and London: University of Arizona Press, 1994); on the controversies surrounding her works, see Fiscar Marison, *What the Universities of Europe, The Religious Orders and Learned Men Say of the "Ciudad de Dios"* (California: Academy Library Guild Press, 1914).

4. Méndez Plancarte, as he states, fails to pursue Sor Juana's reference to Agreda in the *Ejercicios de la Encarnación* (4.663); Colahan briefly notes certain correspondences between the two writing nuns (9). Marie-Cécile Bénassy-Berling, on the other hand, in her *Humanisme et Réligion chez Sor Juana Inés de la Cruz*, analyzes the connections between Sor Juana and Agreda. While reluctant to see a significant rapport between Agreda and Sor Juana, whom she portrays as opposing mysticism, Bénassy-Berling allows that the Mexican nun cites Agreda nontextually, that Sor Juana may have read her several years before writing the *Ejercicios*, and that she remains faithful to the structure but not the inspiration of *La mística ciudad de Dios* (269–70).

5. All references to Octavio Paz throughout the book, unless otherwise noted, are to his *Sor Juana*, the English translation of *Sor Juana Inés de la Cruz o las trampas de la fe*. I have critiqued Paz's discussions of Sor Juana's social and writerly female milieu in "Toward a Feminist Reading of Sor Juana Inés de la Cruz" (Merrim 1991, 21) and in "Sor Juana después de Paz: una restitución feminista," *Insula* 522 (May 1990): 20–22.

6. While recent years do show a slight increase in comparative work on Sor Juana (I call the reader's attention particularly to Georgina Sabat-Rivers's *Sor Juana Inés de la Cruz y otros poetas barrocos de la colonia*), remarkably few critics have attempted to link Sor Juana with writing women of her times outside the Hispanic environment. To my knowledge and dismay, for example, the present chapter contains the first detailed analysis of the "Respuesta" and the *querelle des femmes*.

7. J. R. Brink's anthology, exceptionally, does include an entire article on Sor Juana and on María de Zayas.

8. Nina Scott, in "'La gran turba de las que merecieron nombres': Sor Juana's Foremothers in 'La Respuesta a Sor Filotea,'" in *Coded Encounters: Writing, Gender, and Ethnicity in Colonial Latin America*, ed. Francisco Javier Cevallos-Candau et al. (Amherst: University of Massachusetts Press, 1994), traces the similarities between Sor Juana's text and that of Boccaccio (207). In their annotated translation of the "Respuesta" cited in n. 1, Arenal and Powell make a case for Sor Juana's possible knowledge of Christine de Pizan, in particular citing a passage from the Mexican text that bears a notable resemblance to *The Book of the City of Ladies* (124, 126). My sense is that the connections between Sor Juana and Christine may be quite apparent but not necessarily real. I believe that my analysis in this chapter supports the contention that due to the persistence of Boccaccio and of the *querelle des femmes* along the lines initiated by Christine, Sor Juana need not have had a direct familiarity with Christine to repeat her arguments. Gerda Lerner has noted, "Christine's culling the Bible for worthy heroines and examples set a precedent which would be followed for centuries, yet none of the women writing in the same vein ever cited her. Nor is there any evidence that they knew of her or her work" (145).

9. Of course, as chapter 4 discusses in detail, the "Respuesta" partakes of several conventions of religious women's writing. My point here is that it displays traits of secular women's writing as well.

10. Maclean provides extensive analyses of the *querelle* in seventeenth-century France, and Henderson and McManus and Woodbridge of the debate in England.

11. Maclean in his chapter 2, and Henderson and McManus in their chapter 1, divide *querelle* argumentation into the three categories.

12. The *querelle*'s critique of culture carries significant feminist implications. Lerner remarks that "the person engaging in reinterpretation considers herself fully authorized and capable" of challenging patriarchal authority (139); Kelly observes that "the early feminists, with no great educational credentials, were unremittingly critical of the authors—ancient, modern, even scriptural—at a time when the *auctores* were still *auctoritates* to many" (15) and that "their critique of culture was one of the major achievements of the early feminist opposition of misogyny" (19).

13. Other remarkable similarities between Sor Juana and De Gournay can be found in their autobiographical documents: Sor Juana's "Respuesta" and De Gournay's "Copie de la vie de la Damoiselle de Gournay, envoyée a Hinhenctum Anglois" (1616, reproduced by Elyane Dezon-Jones in her "Marie de Gournay: le je/u palimpseste," *L'Esprit Créateur* 23, no. 2 [1983]: 33–35). Both authors represent themselves as prodigies who mastered Latin with astonishing rapidity and thwarted their mothers' wishes in gaining a clandestine education, and as martyrs who suffered numerous obstacles in so doing. Christine de Pizan also mentions that in acquiring an education, she went against her mother's wishes (154). It would be interesting indeed to explore these coincidences: Do they derive solely from the women's exceptionality and from the obstacles their cultures placed in the way of women's education, or were they in any way topics of learned women's autobiographical writings?

14. I quote from the only English translation available of De Gournay's "Equality," that of Maja Bijvoet in Wilson and Warnke's anthology, *Women Writers of the Seventeenth Century*. Both of De Gournay's feminist tracts can be found in French in the recent edition by Milagros Palma cited in my bibliography.

15. I quote the lines of Saint Paul's Corinthians and Timothy from pp. 44 and 137, respectively, of the Norton Critical Edition of his works, *The Writings of St. Paul*, edited by Wayne A. Meeks.

16. De Gournay writes that Saint Paul mentions a woman as his "coadjutor in the service of God" and states that if the apostle "excludes women from the priesthood and forbids them to speak in the Church, he clearly does not do this out of contempt for women but rather out of fear that they would lead some men into temptation if they showed so publicly and openly the beauty and grace they have in greater measure than men, which would be inevitable when ministering and preaching" (*20*). Other points of contact between De Gournay and Fell include emphasis on Christ's favors to women, the example of Mary Magdalene, and the discussion of women who succeeded in saving their cities from siege.

17. Mary Astell, whom we meet in chap. 5, also took recourse to historicizing argument in explaining Saint Paul. That historicizing argument re-creating the context in Corinth was appropriate and necessary has been borne out by modern scholarship. See Constance F. Parvey's "Theology and Leadership of Women in the New Testament," in *Religion and Sexism: Images of Woman in the Jewish and Christian Traditions*, ed. Rosemary Radford Ruether (New York: Simon & Schuster, 1974), for a discussion of the theological and social context of Corinthians and other writings of Saint Paul. There one finds the important thesis, so consistent with the heuristics of Sor Juana and Fell, that "what Paul had understood as a kind of temporary status-quo ethics—in the context of the imminent end times—became translated two generations later into moral guidelines for keeping things as they are forever" (146).

18. Bearing out the arguments made by earlier writers in a fitting epilogue to their debates, many recent scholars have elucidated the apparent divide in Saint Paul's writings on women between innovation and conservatism. See, for example, Parvey's article cited in the previous note and William O. Walker Jr.'s "The 'Theology of Woman's Place' and the 'Paulinist' Tradition," *Semeia* 28 (1983): 101–12; both articles provide ample bibliography on the subject.

19. On Sor Juana's adherence to epistolary rhetoric and the rhetorical divisions of the "Respuesta," see Rosa Perelmuter's milestone article, "La estructura retórica de la *Respuesta a Sor Filotea*," *Hispanic Review* 51, no. 2 (1983): 147–58. There Perelmuter establishes incontrovertibly that the "Respuesta" divides into the *exordio* or salutation, the *narratio* or autobiographical section, the *prueba*, and the *peroratio*.

20. In Latin in the original: "Anus similiter in habitu sancto, bene docentes" (Titus 2:3; 4.462, *Obras completas* of Sor Juana).

21. These same theological stumbling blocks, the same war of opposing proof texts, would persist throughout the centuries to this day. As Parvey states: "These passages have not only had an impact on the later epistles within the New Testament but they have provided the shape for the fundamental religious and social attitudes toward women in both the Eastern and Western churches to the present day. These references have been used as proof texts for explaining why women should be prohibited from priestly and liturgical roles, and they still constitute a major justification for maintaining women in a subordinated role in the Church and in society at large" (125). The writings of Saint Paul fueled opposition to women in contexts other than the church. During the abolitionist and suffragette movements, for example, women like the Grimké sisters and Frances Willard, respectively, returned to his writings, still attempting two and three centuries later to neutralize them. On their readings of Saint Paul see Carolyn De Swarte Gifford, "American Women and the Bible: The Nature of Woman as a Hermeneutical Issue," in *Feminist Perspectives on Biblical Scholarship*, ed. Adela Yarbro Collins (Chico, Calif.: Scholars Press, 1985). The truly extraordinary irony of the whole trajectory is that recent scholars have disputed whether certain of

the offending texts were in fact written by Saint Paul himself, and thus whether they carry his weight and authority. On this matter see Walker's entire article; also Lerner (140) and Meeks.

22. All references to Maravall throughout the book unless otherwise noted are to his *Culture of the Baroque: Analysis of a Historical Structure*, the English translation of his *La cultura del barroco*. Here and elsewhere in this section of the chapter I quote Maravall on the crises of the seventeenth century for the pertinence of his focus to my own. Nevertheless, I draw equal sustenance for my framework from historians such as Theodore K. Rabb who support the widely diffused notion of the seventeenth century as characterized by crises that find their resolution by 1700. Rabb writes of this notion: "The term [crisis] has found its way into most new textbooks . . . and the current generation of students is apparently being taught that the 'crisis' can serve as an organizing principle no less powerful than 'Reformation' or 'Enlightenment'" (15). See the collection of essays *Crisis in Europe, 1560–1660*, ed. Trevor Aston (New York: Anchor, 1967), and Rabb's *The Struggle for Stability in Early Modern Europe* for presentations of the argument in a variety of spheres and for further bibliography on the subject.

23. Henderson and McManus, for example, question Woodbridge's assumptions of a direct correlation between society and literature, saying, "We cannot account for the prominence of the shrew stereotype in Renaissance England by tidy explanations of expanded female autonomy, for we simply do not have sufficient evidence that women as a group gained significant additional liberty" (51). They do, however, allow that the *Hic Mulier/Haec Vir* controversy arose from actual circumstances (52). The next chapter of the present study treats the phenomena of the "manly woman" and of cross-dressing more fully and theoretically.

24. I refer, of course, to the controversies unleashed by Joan Kelly's seminal and path-breaking article "Did Women Have a Renaissance?" (in her *Women, History and Theory: The Essays of Joan Kelly* [Chicago and London: University of Chicago Press, 1984]), especially regarding the transformations Kelly charts between the medieval and Renaissance periods. Even articles taking issue with Kelly on these grounds–such as Judith M. Bennett's "Medieval Women, Modern Women: Across the Great Divide" (in *Culture and History 1350–1600: Essays on English Communities, Identities and Writing*, ed. David Aers [Detroit: Wayne State University Press, 1992]) and David Herlihy's "Did Women have a Renaissance? A Reconsideration" (in *Medievalia et Humanistica: Studies in Medieval and Renaissance Culture* 13 [1985]: 1–16)–leave many of her basic economic and social assumptions intact.

25. Here we must move beyond Maravall's *Culture of the Baroque*: stunning and lamentable for its absence in his 1975 study is any substantive consideration of women as a group and/or as objects of the vast machine of repression and control he documents. Several of the essays in *Culture and Control in Counter-Reformation Spain* (ed. Anne J. Cruz and Mary Elizabeth Perry [Minneapolis and Oxford: University of Minnesota Press, 1992]) strive to compensate for this lack. Maravall himself does go on to discuss misogyny and crisis in his 1986 *La literatura picaresca desde la historia social (siglos XVI y XVII)*, but in any case it is debatable whether these discussions qualify him as a feminist historian.

26. I am reminded here of Alice A. Jardine's notion of gynesis (*Gynesis: Configurations of Woman and Modernity* [Ithaca and London: Cornell University Press, 1985]), which she defines in the following manner: "This other-than-themselves is almost always a 'space' of some kind (over which the narrative has lost control), and this space has been coded as *feminine*, as *woman*" (25; italics in original).

27. I agree entirely with Henderson and McManus's observation that the "rebellious and assertive behavior of the small percentage of women who engaged in these activities may have created widespread concern among men about the possibility of a general female rebellion against male dominance" (52).

28. *Hic Mulier, Haec Vir,* and many other treatises from the "woman controversy" in early modern England can be found in the Henderson and McManus anthology *Half Humankind.* However, they have excerpted the texts, and neither this quote nor the epigraph to this section of my chapter appears in the versions they present.

29. Almost needless to say, I am not maintaining that sixteenth-century patriarchs purported to place women on an equal footing with men. I am merely explicating a master narrative of a Renaissance moralist as a barometer of changes in symbolic positions regarding women. Women never ceased to be subordinated to men in the moralists' tracts; my point is that the Renaissance moralists operated on a principle of inclusion rather than exclusion and that their works characterized women as a desirable and necessary part of the social fabric rather than as a disruptive clinamen.

30. I call to mind here Paul Julian Smith's formulation in *Writing in the Margin: Spanish Literature of the Golden Age* (Oxford: Clarendon Press, 1987): "I suggest that Spain itself is the place of 'marginality,' the supplement to Europe (both excessive and essential) which at once conceals and reveals the criteria on which its exclusion is founded" (2). See his chap. 1 and the conclusion for an elaboration of this notion.

31. See *Historia y crítica de la literatura española,* 3/1: *Siglos de Oro: Barroco, Primer Suplemento,* ed. Aurora Egido (Barcelona: Editorial Crítica, 1992), 7, for a bibliography of critiques of Maravall. Notable among them is J. H. Elliott's review, "Concerto Barroco" (*New York Review of Books* 34, no. 6 [April 9, 1987]: 26–29). With his customary insight, Elliott registers reservations to the "monolithic uniformity" with which Maravall tends to endow the baroque period (27). Elliott is not convinced that Maravall, or anyone else, can present "a wholly persuasive interpretation of any phenomenon as diverse and complex as the European baroque" (27–28). Nevertheless, he praises Maravall's book as "an exceptionally brave, and sometimes brilliant, attempt to reintegrate the fragments into a meaningful pattern" (29).

32. Keller makes a similar argument, noting that two centuries after the *Malleus Maleficarum,* "at the moment in which modern science was being born, witches still embodied the fearful dangers of female sexual power" and that in "seventeenth-century England, the witch mania reached its apogee, and so, it might be argued, did fear of female sexuality" (60). Stallybrass, reading Bakhtin's *Rabelais and His World,* contrasts the grotesque body (one that emphasizes the body itself and the parts of the body "open to the outside world" [124]) with the closed classical body (one that emphasizes the head as the seat of reason). He states that seventeenth-century moralists differ from Erasmus "in the assumption that the woman's body, unlike the prince's, is *naturally* 'grotesque'" and that it "must be subjected to constant surveillance precisely because, as Bakhtin says of the grotesque body, it is 'unfinished, outgrows itself, transgresses its own limits'" (126). I return to the "grotesque body" and its relationship with misogyny in chap. 2.

33. I recall here the summary of Anderson and Zinsser, who conclude that in the seventeenth century, "Instead of breaking with tradition, descriptions of the female accumulated traditions: the classical, the religious, the literary, the customary, and the legal—all stated afresh in the secular language of the new age. Instead of being freed, women were ringed with yet more binding and seemingly incontrovertible versions of the traditional attitudes about their inferior nature, their proper function and role, and their subordinate relationship to men" (99). For a fascinating example of the manner

in which gender concerns wrote biology, see the discussion of William Harvey in the
last section of Laqueur's chap. 4.

34. In terms of the colonies of England and Spain, here I look briefly at Puritan
attitudes toward women in New England, a matter on which chap. 4 substantially
expands. On women and the Puritan world also see, for example, Pattie Cowell,
"Puritan Women Poets in America," and Cheryl Walker, "In the Margin: The Image of
Women in Early Puritan Poetry," both in *Puritan Poets and Poetics: Seventeenth-Century
American Poetry in Theory and Practice*, ed. Peter White (University Park and London:
Pennsylvania University Press, 1985). With regard to Mexico, it can be said that Spain,
desiring to control its colonies, not only projected its social and political structures
onto its satellites but further calicified them in that arena. Paz has written, "New Spain
was a society oriented toward opposing modernity, not achieving it" (259). On women
in colonial Mexico see Josefina Muriel, *Cultura femenina novohispana* (Mexico: UNAM,
1982), and Pilar Gonzalbo Aizpuru, *Las mujeres en la Nueva España: Educación y vida
cotidiana* (Mexico: El Colegio de México, 1987), wherein is stated, for example: "The
'good policy' that they attempted to impose on the Colony from its earliest years
involved hierarchical order and a general acceptance of the doctrinal and social principles on which specific norms of behavior rested" (253). Similarly, Asunción Lavrin
points out that Spain provided the social prescriptions for the colonies: "The intellectual source of this role definition was in Spain. Through a process of cultural transfer,
prescriptive literature and canons of behavior passed to Mexico and the rest of South
America" (1978, 25). My chap. 2 looks at the transfer of Spanish misogyny to the
colonies; the circumstances pressing on Sor Juana, as discussed throughout the book,
reflect the above contentions.

35. As does Timmermans but in greater detail, De Jean argues that the actions of
the *frondeuses* instigated a misogynist reaction, and further, that women continued in
their writings the political activity begun in the arena of the civil war (1991; see also
her essay, "Amazons and Literary Women: Female Culture During the Reign of the
Sun King," in *Sun King: The Ascendancy of French Culture During the Reign of Louis XIV*,
ed. David Lee Rubin [Washington, London, Toronto: Folger Books, 1992]).

36. Timmermans notes in this connection that under Louis XIV elite women
became an icon of culture and of French cultural superiority, with no ramifications for
social structures: "The society women [*mondaines*] celebrated for their cultivation or
their written works illustrate the superiority of Louis XIV's century over previous periods, and that of the French nation over others. The royal-national ideology found its
justification in this glorification, without the least threat to the social structure" (338).
With regard to social structures, one should certainly take into account Carolyn C.
Lougee's argument in her *Le Paradis des Femmes: Women, Salons, and Social Stratification
in Seventeenth-Century France* that defenses of women (as is often the case) were actually about something else—being defenses of the social mobility that salon culture represented and promoted.

37. Chilton, in his introduction to the English version of the *Heptaméron*, puts forth
the idea that Marguerite de Navarre was not the only author contributing to the work.
He maintains that several individuals may have contributed stories but that Marguerite
probably contributed some stories, edited others, and added the storytelling framework in which they are embedded (10).

38. The many and significant connections between Marguerite and Zayas require
a separate study. Summarizing, let me first say that in his "María de Zayas, An
Outstanding Woman Short-Story Writer of Seventeenth-Century Spain" (*University of*

Colorado Studies 13 [1929]: 1–56), Edwin B. Place identifies the *Heptaméron* as the source of several of Zayas's tales. Moreover, certain distinctive features, departures from the *Decameron*, appear in both works: the polyphonic construction of the texts, with their male and female narrators, each of whom boasts his or her own particular voice and assumes a different ideological position; an elaborate framework story, in which it is claimed that the embedded tales are true and told with a simple style in order to reach a wide public; the presence in the frame story of a main character (Parlemente in Marguerite, Lisis in Zayas) thought to represent the author and her views; and so on.

39. Henderson, Lerner, Hilda Smith, Wiesner, and Wilson and Warnke all discuss the phenomenon of seventeenth-century women publishing defenses of their own sex as a key advance of the century.

40. The "Respuesta" was first published posthumously in 1700 in Sor Juana's *Fama y obras póstumas*. Prior to that, as Paz notes, "it must have circulated in manuscript among her friends and admirers" (425).

41. I refer the reader to Wilson and Warnke's outstanding introduction to their *Women Writers of the Seventeenth Century*. Though relatively brief, it contains the best synoptic and pan-European discussion of women writers that I have encountered in the course of my investigations.

42. The constellation of issues and consequences resulting from their place in the public domain can productively equate even writers as notably divergent as Sor Juana and Aphra Behn. Although I have not found a place for Behn in this book, her work displays several of the issues that ensuing pages bring out, especially the tendency to multiple self-imaging, discussions of gender and fame, the longing for a past golden age and for a utopian community for women. One who wishes to pursue this comparison will profit from consulting *Rereading Aphra Behn: History, Theory and Criticism*, ed. Heidi Hutner (Charlottesville and London: University Press of Virginia, 1993), and particularly the contributions of Catherine Gallagher ("Who Was that Masked Woman? The Prostitute and the Playwright in the Comedies of Aphra Behn") and Judith Kegan Gardiner ("Liberty, Equality, Fraternity: Utopian Longings in Behn's Lyric Poetry").

43. On Teresa de Cartagena, see n. 72 to chap. 5.

44. I bear in mind Leah S. Marcus's query: "At what point does the early modern become the modern, and assuming pronounced elements of continuity between one and the other, how are scholars to define the relation between the two?" (42).

45. Why seventeenth-century women writers constructed the previous era as a golden age for women is a matter on which I can only speculate. Clearly, the assumption of a better world for women situated in the past suited their reformist (i.e., not radical) ideological platforms. Additionally, one might consider that what was most present to them from the recent past was not its social reality but its programmatic writings with their promise of education and their lists of illustrious women, as well as the historical consciousness of its outstanding women rulers (Isabel, Elizabeth). As Kelly remarks, because most early modern learned women were from the upper classes and led sheltered lives, they were more inclined to reflect on texts than on events from the past, such as the burning of witches (27).

46. I borrow the phrase "conservative romance" from Kelly (27), who refers to a different but related phenomenon. Kelly writes: "In the historical transition from feudal to bourgeois society, most of the early feminists of the *querelle* continued to appeal to, and carried on a conservative romance with, female representatives of the old order."

Chapter One: From Anomaly to Icon

1. I refer to Américo Castro's study of the conflictive relationships between the three groups that until the fifteenth century had coexisted peaceably in Spain: Christians, Muslims, and Jews. Beginning with the unification of Spain under Ferdinand and Isabel, the Christians predominated. Over the course of the subsequent two centuries, and particularly in the hegemonic climate of the seventeenth century, they subjected the other two groups to conversion, persecution, and exile. See Américo Castro, *De la edad conflictiva: Crisis de la cultura española en el siglo XVII* (Madrid: Taurus, 1976), and John Lynch, *Spain Under the Hapsburgs*, 2 vols. (Oxford: Basil Blackwell, 1981).

2. My chapter, which in essence focuses the indistinction of the categories of anomaly and icon, trades on Marjorie Garber's notion of border-crossing or category crisis. In *Vested Interests* Garber writes, "By 'category crisis' I mean a failure of definitional distinction, a borderline that becomes permeable, that permits of border crossings from one (apparently distinct) category to another: black/white, Jew/Christian, noble/bourgeois, master/servant, master/slave" (1993, 16). In her foreword to the English translation of Erauso's alleged memoirs, Garber adds to the preceding that in border-crossings "what seems like a binary opposition, a clear choice between opposites that define cultural boundaries, is revealed to be not only a construct but–more disturbingly–a construct that no longer works to contain and delimit meaning" (1996, xiv). My chapter and its notes will make it clear that although I find the above constructs tremendously pertinent to the baroque and illuminating of the two baroque authors the chapter treats, I do not fully subscribe to Garber's analysis of Erauso.

3. Corners of this study have appeared in *Review* 43 (1990): 37–41, and in *Y diversa de mí misma entre vuestras plumas ando: Homenaje internacional a Sor Juana Inés de la Cruz*, ed. Sara Poot Herrera (Mexico: El Colegio de México, 1993): 355–56. An earlier version of the complete study, "Catalina de Erauso: From Anomaly to Icon," was published in *Coded Encounters: Writing, Gender, and Ethnicity in Colonial Latin America*, ed. Francisco Javier Cevallos-Candau, Jeffrey A. Cole, Nina M. Scott, and Nicomedes Suárez-Araúz (Amherst: University of Massachusetts Press, 1994). The present chapter represents an extensively revised version of the *Coded Encounters* article, incorporating my more recent thoughts as well as the considerable amount of new material that has appeared on the subjects treated here since the first writing of the article in 1990. In compiling and conceptualizing the material for the original study (a much harder matter than at present, since Vallbona's indispensable 1992 edition of the *Vida* reprints the materials on Erauso previously scattered in obscure sources), I profited from the generous aid of several colleagues. Rima de Vallbona shared her excellent materials and ideas; Eduardo Forastieri-Braschi gave useful feedback; Luis Fernández Cifuentes, Enrique Pupo-Walker, and Mercedes Vaquero kindly obtained texts for me. Responses to the initial version of the paper, presented at the Five College Symposium, "Reflections of Social Reality: Writings in Colonial Latin America," in April of 1990, especially of Amanda Powell and Roslyn M. Frank, were of great help. I am particularly grateful to Antonio Carreño, a true colleague, for his interest and bibliographical suggestions. Given the relative paucity of critical material on Erauso, most of the notions put forth in this chapter are, as it were, home-grown: I have profited, as will be noted, from ideas generated in my seminars by (now former) graduate students at Brown University: María Dolores Reyero-Fernández, Teresa Langle de Paz, and Sylvia Santaballa.

4. As stated in the previous note, Rima de Vallbona gathers in her edition of the *Vida* almost all of the texts and material pertaining to Erauso, including the *relaciones*; she also provides full bibliographical references for them. For the reader's convenience, I quote this material from Vallbona's edition. With regard to the *relaciones*, Vallbona maintains in chaps. 1 and 2 of her dissertation (only a very small portion of which made its way into her edition of the *Vida*) that the *relaciones* were rhetorically embellished and sensationalizing synopses of Erauso's *Vida*. The similarities in information and even in language between the *relaciones* and the *Vida*, as well as the fact that at least one of the Spanish broadsides was issued from the same publishing house in which the original of the *Vida* was deposited, all support Vallbona's argument. Why the *relaciones* (the first of which, as I note in the text of my chapter, duplicates the tone and material of the *Vida*) were published, and the *Vida* perhaps not, is an interesting issue to ponder.

5. Though Erauso has remained a legend and a folk heroine for the Basques and the Mexicans, until recently the *Vida* had hardly been studied as a literary text. What published work there was on Erauso until the early 1990s was almost entirely of a historical nature, or were fictional adaptations of her life (see the bibliography in Vallbona's edition of the *Vida*). In devising a strategy for this chapter I have wrestled with the issue of analyzing what is most likely an (at least in part) apocryphal text. I should note that the studies appended to the 1996 English translation of the *Vida*, by Garber and Stepto, fail to contend with the (I believe significant) question of the work's authorship. Garber does not mention it; Stepto does (xxiv), but does not problematize it.

6. All page citations from the *Vida* correspond to Vallbona's edition. Although a readily available edition of the text (*Historia de la monja alférez escrita por ella misma*, ed. Jesús Munárriz [Madrid: Hiperión, 1986]) modernizes the orthography and may make for easier reading, I cite from Vallbona's edition because it is more faithful to the manuscript.

7. Erauso states that certain things happened to her in the court that she leaves out of her narrative because they are *leves* or light, which suggests that, taking little interest in what is *leve*, the text concentrates on weighty and dramatic matters (Vallbona, 119).

8. I am grateful to María Dolores Reyero-Fernández for pointing out some of the connections with the soldier's autobiography. See Vallbona (1981, 65, 185) for further discussion of the subject, including her observations that strict adherence to the truth was not necessarily expected of soldiers' autobiographies–which might explain some of the inaccuracies of the *Vida* if it were Erauso's own text.

9. Ferrer, in exile in Paris, utilized a transcription of the manuscript made by copyists in the employment of Juan Bautista Muñoz and lent to Ferrer by Francisco Bauzá. See the introduction to Fitzmaurice-Kelly's translation for more details (xxv–xxvi).

10. On this crucial issue, Vallbona notes that Erauso was from an upper-class Basque family and thus a monolingual one, that the convent in which Erauso lived was also Basque, and that most of her contact in the New World was with Basques. These facts, writes Vallbona, lead us to assume that Erauso had a limited knowledge of Spanish and/or that there are interferences of Basque in her Spanish (1992, 8). Vallbona also imparts Roslyn M. Frank's fascinating observation that it is not unusual for a Basque woman in monologue with herself to refer to herself in the masculine (35).

11. Aside from the arguments developed in the chapter, let me suggest some other possible reasons for Erauso's reward. (There may well be others.) First, her fellow

Basques might have intervened in Erauso's favor. The Basques were particularly influential in the New World: see the "Anonymous Description of Peru (1600–1615)" in Irving A. Leonard's *Colonial Travelers in Latin America* (New York: Knopf, 1972), 101, and Bartolomé Arzáns de Orsúa y Vela, *Tales of Potosí*, ed. R. C. Padden, trans. Frances M. López-Morillas (Providence: Brown University Press, 1975), xxvi–xxviii. Second, the chauvinistic attitude toward Spain that Erauso displays at the end of the *Vida* as well as in the *Tercera relación*, and to which attest the witnesses to the robbery in France (who claim that Erauso defended the king from the insults of Frenchmen; see Vallbona 1992, appendix 2), may also have curried her favor. Similarly, and third, a colonialist mentality, such as that which rewarded the dispassionately cruel renegade Hernán Cortés, might have found Erauso's crimes far less objectionable than they might appear to be. Michele Stepto makes a convincing case for Erauso as "the perfect colonialist" (xli); what I call in the chapter Erauso's "conquistador's reward" of an *encomienda* also aligns her with other "heroes" of the conquest whose behavior at once betrayed morality and, to paraphrase my epigraph, naturalized the combination of "honor" and "insult" to one's "country."

12. It is conceivable that the authors of these testimonials were also engaged in what we would now call a cover-up: covering their own backs for not having recognized Erauso as a woman and for allowing her to remain in their ranks.

13. In her unpublished master's thesis, "Catalina de Erauso en el lugar del *no sé qué*" (Brown University, 1993), Teresa Langle de Paz convincingly divides the several documents that take Erauso as their subject into "official" and "unofficial" stories; I draw on her characterization here.

14. On pp. 184–87 of the earlier version of this chapter published in *Coded Encounters* that I cite above, I broach the question of whether female cross-dressing was a social reality and whether the social reality gave rise to the literary motif, thus making female cross-dressing less of an anomaly than it would appear. I conclude that despite the fact that female cross-dressing was a significant phenomenon elsewhere (see, for example, Diane Dugaw, *Warrior Women and Popular Balladry, 1650–1850* [Cambridge: Cambridge University Press, 1989]), in all likelihood it was less so in Spain. Given the tendency of the patriarchy, discussed in my introduction with regard to the *Hic Mulier* pamphlet, to overreact to women in any numbers wearing men's clothing, Erauso's positive official reception further suggests the rarity of (at least publicly known cases of) women dressing as men. However, that it was working-class women who most often surreptitiously adopted male dress, for economic gain, might explain part of Erauso's enormous appeal for the masses.

15. Luis Vives reproduces this biblical injunction against cross-dressing in his influential *Instrucción de la mujer cristiana* [Instruction of the Christian Woman] in 1524–28, addressing it to women and prefacing it with the remarks: "One thing remains for me to say and I think there was no need to say it, and it is that a woman not dress as a man or wear any male clothing" (53–54).

16. Many authors, including Dugaw (152), Warner (46–47), and Bravo-Villasante (101–3), as well as McKendrick, substantiate this point at length. The positive affect of *manliness*–a word that, according to McKendrick, generally refers in golden age theater to a "woman's capacity for resolute action" (53)–clearly helps to explain the prevalence in literary works of this seemingly transgressive theme.

17. Perry also argues, supporting my later point on Erauso's legal acuity, that Catalina used two strategies to save herself from legal punishment: she won the protection of ecclesiastical law by telling the bishop in Guamanga that she was a virgin,

and she played into the legal system's special protection for "weak" women by presenting herself as a female. The law, Perry states, then made a hero out of a woman who chose to be a man—and of a "manly woman" who "participated in the making of her own myth" (135). Perry's argument on Erauso matches several points of the present chapter and its earlier version—written, I would note, before Perry's *Gender and Disorder* was published.

18. As its title indicates, a major contention of Laqueur's study is that in the one-sex model sex is as equally "made" or constructed as gender has always been, i.e., they are both sociological rather than ontological categories. He states, for example: "I want to propose . . . that in these pre-Enlightenment texts, and even some later ones, *sex*, or the body, must be understood as the epiphenomenon, while *gender*, what we would take to be a cultural category, was primary or 'real'" (8).

19. Stephen Greenblatt writes in *Shakespearean Negotiations* of the "embodied transvestism" of a hermaphrodite who was said to have sprung male genitalia as she jumped over a ditch: "There has been no transformation from woman into man—Marie was always in some sense Marin, whose true gender was concealed by his anomalous genital structure—but the *myth of such mobility* is preserved in the very form of the account that denies its anatomical possibility" (1988, 82; italics mine).

20. On the resurrection of women into men, see Ian Maclean, *The Renaissance Notion of Women: A Study in the Fortunes of Scholasticism and Medical Science in European Intellectual Life*, Cambridge Monographs on the History of Medicine (Cambridge and New York: Cambridge University Press, 1980), 14. With respect to the potential backsliding of male spectators into females, see Heise's fascinating article, which works the one-sex model into seventeenth-century theater—a rich line of investigation that warrants further study. For example, Heise writes of the British prohibition of female actors: "The assumption seems to be that when the male is confronted with unconcealed, un-covered femininity, he reacts, not by asserting his difference but by imitating and adjusting to the female. There is, then, *something fundamentally unstable about the male self*, which can only keep from lapsing into the identity of its sexual other by depriving her of a full expression of what is specifically her own" (369; italics mine).

21. Despite the positive potential bound up in early modern constructions of sexuality that my discussion brings out, I do not wish it to be construed as a glorification of the early modern period as an ideal site of free-flowing boundaries—for such, as we know, was hardly the case. Margaret Hunt's afterword to *Queering the Renaissance* (ed. Jonathan Goldberg [Durham and London: Duke University Press, 1994], 373) presents this argument and firm caveats to it.

22. According to the extant portraits of Erauso, verbal and pictorial, she did, however, possess several characteristics associated with the masculine; physically, she was indeed a "manly woman." Male clothing completed the statement.

23. On the treatment of lesbianism in early modern Spain, see Perry (123–25). Legally regulated in varying ways, lesbianism was to a large degree "culturally invisible" (Garber 1993, 71). However, see Valerie Traub's interesting "The (In)Significance of 'Lesbian' Desire in Early Modern England," in *Queering the Renaissance*, which editor Goldberg describes as delivering "possibilities for a number of kinds of lesbianism across a range of sites—differentiated by nationality, literary genres, disciplinary domains" (3) and which also discusses the proscription of tribadism.

24. Urban VIII (1568–1644) ascended to the papacy in 1623 and was a protector of the arts and literature, writing poetry himself (Vallbona 1992, 122). Although he sanctioned Erauso, he denied an appeal in 1624 by Mary Ward that he support her

order of unenclosed nun-educators against attacks from the English Jesuits and secular clergy. Ward's order was suppressed in 1631 (see King 1991, 111–13).

25. Erauso, it would appear, was no tribade (at least not on the receiving end). Perry observes, "Catalina may have broken every rule for women, but she preserved the most important one–virginity" (134).

26. On transvestite nuns also see Warner (151–52) and Garber (1993, 213–14).

27. It is interesting to note in this connection, as does Warner (151), that one of Joan of Arc's female voices, Saint Margaret of Antioch, was a transvestite saint.

28. Rosales's text appears in the nineteenth-century *Historia general del reino de Chile* (Valparaíso: Mercurio, 1877–78), and can be found, with an interesting commentary, in José Toribio Medina, *Biblioteca Hispano-Chilena: 1523–1817*, vol. 1, as well as in Vallbona's edition of the *Vida* (179–83). I cite from Vallbona.

29. There is much to say about other radical metamorphoses of Erauso's persona, especially about her Romantic revival in the nineteenth century by figures such as José María Heredia, Thomas De Quincey, and Ricardo Palma. Ferrer's preface to his (the first) edition of the *Vida* (*Historia de la monja Alférez, doña Catalina de Erauso, escrita por ella misma* [Paris: Julio Didot, 1829]), with its discussion of nature's "aberrations" and of the need for women's education, holds particular interest. I leave this task to another writing, or writer.

30. In her foreword to the new English translation of the *Vida* (1996), Garber applies the terms from her *Vested Interests* to the cross-dressing Erauso: essentially the notions of category crisis (see n. 2 above) and the "transvestite effect" ("The appearance of a transvestite figure in a text, I suggest . . . was almost invariably a sign of category crisis *elsewhere*: not, or not only, in the realms of gender and sexuality, but also, and equally importantly, in registers like politics, economics, history, and literary genre" [1996, xv]). Applied to Erauso, these constructs yield the following conclusion: "Tensions between Old and New World, between Indians and 'Spaniards,' between purebreds and 'half-breeds,' and between the merchant class and the nobility put under increasing pressure by the *encomienda* system of settlement and fealty could be said to have 'produced' a triumphant story of transvestite transgression–or, at least, to have produced a sympathetic audience for such a tale" (1996, xvi). While I agree that tensions of the times may have produced a sympathetic audience for the tale, I am not compelled by Garber's analysis. Tensions certainly abounded in the New World, but they redound rather lightly into the picaresque, theatricalized *Vida*, and I suspect that Garber is overreading references to them. Moreover, I believe that if in political terms Garber overhistoricizes the *Vida*'s resonances, in gender terms she underhistoricizes them–purposefully but perhaps unnecessarily. She begins her essay by saying, "How can we assess the erotic, social, and political effects of cross-dressing at a remove of almost four centuries, in the context of a culture very different from our own, and as described in a Spanish-language text?" (1996, vii). The query raises respectable issues, but they need not lead to an overexoticizing of the seventeenth-century Spanish context such as we find in Garber's conclusion: "In this engrossing and elegantly translated memoir the reader is afforded a glimpse into a world almost unimaginably alien and estranging" (1996, xxiii). Having, at least apparently, done little research into the gender ideologies of Erauso's context (the examples she cites are largely British and American), Garber reads opacity where it may not exist; her position may reflect her own positionality. In sum, I would suggest that in providing a (welcome) exception to my discussion in the introduction of the scant due that scholars from other fields pay to the Hispanic field, Garber may lamentably be reinforcing it.

31. I also find it difficult to accept Garber's application of "border-crossing" to Erauso. She contends that Erauso was rewarded not to reinstate categories but precisely because she confounded them. According to Garber, Erauso "confounds the 'forbidden mixtures' of gender, sexuality, class, and nation to emerge as a sign of Spain's–and Catholicism's–primacy in a changing and mysterious world. No wonder the king was willing to grant her a pension, and the Pope a dispensation" (1996, xviii). That the intransigently conservative, evangelizing, patriarchal, official Spain of the times should exalt "forbidden mixtures" strikes me as quite implausible. See, too, Angeline Goreau's review of *The Lieutenant Nun* in the *New York Times* (March 17, 1996, sec. 7, p. 29), where, for example, she states: "I cannot agree with the contention that this story reflects a 'blurring of the boundaries' that can be extrapolated to describe Spanish society as a whole. What seems remarkable, rather, is the degree to which Erauso's male persona conforms to the most cliched version of honor-besotted, trigger-happy machismo."

32. According to renowned late-sixteenth-century Spanish preacher Alonso de Cabrera (quoted by Mariscal, 92), "singularity" and "taking novelty out into public view" are properties of heretics–which would place yet another edge of effrontery on Erauso's person and story.

33. In "Le monstre, expression de l'insécurité dans la littérature et les spectacles de la Renaissance anglaise" (in *Monstres et Prodiges Au Temps de la Renaissance*, ed. M. T. Jones-Davies [Paris: Centre de Recherches sur la Renaissance, 1980]), M. T. Jones-Davies similarly presents literary monsters in Elizabethan England as a sign of the insecurity of the times and as a catharsis for it.

34. In his *Marvelous Possessions: The Wonder of the New World* (Chicago: University of Chicago Press, 1991), Stephen Greenblatt writes: "The perception in Descartes or Spinoza that wonder precedes recognitions of good and evil, like the perception in Aristotle or Albertus Magnus that it precedes knowledge, conferred upon the marvelous a striking indeterminacy and made it . . . the object of a range of sharply differing uses" (24). The value-neutral quality of wonder, preceding categorization, that Greenblatt elucidates speaks to the argument that I make in the chapter regarding the destabilizing of categories induced by wonder-eliciting monsters in conjunction with the esthetic of the bizarre.

35. Similarly, Teresa Langle de Paz (in the thesis cited in n. 13 above, 41) makes a case for the *relaciones* as a hybrid of official regulation and popular taste resistant to it.

36. I word this statement and my discussion of the presence of literary models in the *Vida* carefully. In chap. 3 of her dissertation and on pp. 8–9 of her edition, Vallbona identifies four "macrosequences" of a literary aspect in the text (picaresque, chronicle, adventures of *capa y espada*, popular and folkloric themes) that follow one after the other. What Vallbona sees as the contrivances and systematic nature of the macrosequences supports her view that "extrapolations of a markedly novelesque nature were interposed into the original text" (1981, 15). The features she notes are certainly present in the *Vida*. However, given the understated and essentially spontaneous tone of the text, as well as my continued uncertainty as to its author, I am only comfortable with stating that the text is highly emplotted, rather than overtly encoded, and that it plays up the points of convergence between Erauso's life and the literary modalities.

37. Vallbona (14) provides a table of the anachronisms and errors in the *Vida*.

38. Vallbona devotes her entire chap. 3 and several pages of the introduction to her edition to critical opinions on the authenticity of the manuscript on which the *Vida* is based. Rather than recapitulate the whole tangled critical history of the text, I note two

points from her discussion particularly relevant to mine. First, the theory espoused by Menéndez y Pelayo and Serrano y Sanz according to which Cándido María Trigueros, a known imitator of seventeenth-century texts and the transcriber of the *Vida* from the original, forged the text has effectively been disproved by Fitzmaurice-Kelly; it is therefore unlikely that the text is entirely apocryphal. Second, with Vallbona I find convincing the argument put forth by Diego Barros Arana in "La Monja Alférez–Algunas observaciones críticas sobre su historia–Noticias desconocidas acerca de su muerte," *Revista de Santiago* 1 (1872): 225–34. Barros Arana states that "the book attributed to the lieutenant nun and published under her name was not written by her but by one of the numerous persons . . . to whom Doña Catalina told her adventures in orderly form" and contends that Erauso's fame would have motivated a practiced author to write her life, "giving the appearance, however, of having been written by herself" (excerpted in Vallbona 1992, 6).

39. According to this scenario, among the various connections well worth exploring between the *Vida*, the *Infortunios*, and modern testimonial literature, the most obviously significant would be that in all three cases a more educated author transcribes and in all likelihood edits the oral tale of a less educated person whose life held literary and/or historical value. The fact that the lives of both Alonso Ramírez and Catalina de Erauso evoked picaresque literature would have motivated both authors. My thanks to Sylvia Santaballa for suggesting the relationship with testimonial literature.

40. See Merrim (1991). As I demonstrate in that article, Sor Juana also builds the split between the daring creative "monster" woman (in Gilbert and Gubar's terms) and the passive "angel" into other of her plays and, most revealingly, into her eucharistic drama, *El Divino Narciso*.

41. Ann Rosalind Jones describes a crucial aspect of this phenomenon (to which I return in chap. 4) in terms of the sixteenth century, noting, "Defenses of women, dedicated to noblewomen in court circles in Italy and France, celebrated learned and literary heroines. The rise of cities produced civic loyalties that were exploited by enterprising publishers in Venice and Lyon, for example, who advertised women's texts as evidence of the cultural superiority of their towns" (1990, 30).

42. In their introduction to *The Answer/La Respuesta* (New York: Feminist Press, 1994) Electa Arenal and Amanda Powell make the following pertinent observation: Sor Juana's "status as a rara avis (rare bird), while setting her apart from others of her sex and class in the public regard, made possible the physical and psychic space in which she thought and wrote. Respect for exceptionality was in part a reflection of the profound seventeenth-century interest in unusual natural phenomena that viewed artistic talent and intellectual drive in females as fascinating abnormalities. Sor Juana learned to exploit the fact that she was catalogued as a prodigy; she both defended and derided the hyperbolic terms of praise her exceptionality merited" (2). I should also note that Peruvian poet Juan del Valle y Caviedes wrote a letter to Sor Juana in which he compared the nun to Erauso for the reasons Arenal and Powell list (see Johnson 1993, 81, 101).

43. The last stanza of the poem reads: [supposing that you, the addressee of the poem, had managed to find the Phoenix–that is, her] "por modo de privilegio / de inventor, quiero que nadie / pueda, sin vuestra licencia, / a otra cosa compararme." Méndez Plancarte's notes to the poem (1.441) suggest that he accords primacy to my second, and more telling, reading of the stanza: that Sor Juana wishes to be compared *only* to the phoenix.

44. In his 1966 novel *El lugar sin límites* (Mexico: Joaquín Mortiz), Donoso presents a male transvestite, La Manuela, who with a flamboyant flamenco dance creates a space in which s/he can shed her abhorred identity as a male and definitively–if temporarily–assume her desired identity as a female. This carnivalesque space of inversion constitutes La Manuela's empowerment, her freedom from biological sex, her "limitless space."

45. Eleanor Commo McLaughlin, in "Equality of Souls, Inequality of Sexes: Women in Medieval Theology" (in *Religion and Sexism: Images of Women in the Jewish and Christian Traditions*, ed. Rosemary R. Ruether [New York: Simon & Schuster, 1974]), explicates Saint Thomas's notion of the creation of males and females, and states that for the author of the *Summa Theologica* "the female, although possessing a rational soul, was created solely with respect to her sexuality, her body, as an aid in reproduction for the preservation of the species" (217). McLaughlin maintains that the "finality of the female as a mere instrumentality, an aid to reproduction, is the only explanation Thomas can offer for the existence of a 'second sex'" (217). As she does with other problematic male views, Sor Juana would appear in Romance #48 to be recuperating Saint Thomas's conception for her own purposes.

46. Although to my knowledge Sor Juana never overtly mentions the one-sex model, it is unlikely that she had not come upon it in her readings. She had direct knowledge of Galen and Aristotle; she was a great reader of compendia and thus perhaps of the widely circulated treatise of Huarte de San Juan (a literary as well as scientific text). In any case, in a sense the church doctrine of the baptismal equality of souls, together with the Neoplatonic notion that souls have no sex that we saw in Romance #19, stood in for the one-sex model, being another deep-structure (even, conceivably, another backreading of the sexual deep-structure) that authorized and legitimated the sexual permutability her poems evince.

47. José Pascual Buxó makes the suggestive point that Sor Juana was working within the tradition of literary academies "which find in the royal and viceregal palaces a field enhanced by the constant competition–regarding merit, knowledge, talent, and adulation–in which the gentlemen and ladies of the court were so intensely engaged" ("Sor Juana Inés de la Cruz: amor y cortesanía," *Colonial Latin American Review* 4, no. 2 [1995]: 90). Sor Juana undoubtedly experienced such academies in the court before becoming a nun; I believe that she continued, in the theater of her mind, to partake of their competitive atmosphere even after becoming a nun.

48. Spain became the stronghold of Sor Juana's fame, as Paz submits (chap. 27), in part due to the efforts of her patroness, the Countess de Paredes–who was aware of Sor Juana's precarious situation in Mexico. The many panegyrics to Sor Juana included in the second edition of her *Obras* (Seville, 1692) thus speak not only to her fame but also to her need of defense in Mexico.

49. To flesh out the final period of Sor Juana's life, see part 4 of Paz, *Sor Juana*, and more recently, José Pascual Buxó, "Sor Juana: Monstruo de su laberinto," and Elías Trabulse, "La *Rosa de Alexandría*: ¿Una querella secreta de sor Juana?," both in *Y diversa de mí misma entre vuestras plumas ando: Homenaje internacional a Sor Juana Inés de la Cruz*, ed. Sara Poot Herrera (Mexico: El Colegio de México, 1993).

Notes to Chapter Two: Women on Love, Part I

1. I refer the reader, for example, to Electa Arenal and Stacey Schlau's *Untold Sisters: Hispanic Nuns in Their Own Works*, Clark Colahan's *The Visions of Sor María de*

Agreda: Writing, Knowledge and Power (Tucson and London: University of Arizona Press, 1994), Ana Navarro, ed., *Antología poética de escritoras de los siglos XVI y XVII*, and to Ruth El Saffar's *Rapture Encaged* and the Olivares and Boyce anthology discussed in this chapter.

2. As El Saffar states in her "In Praise of What Is Left Unsaid: Thoughts on Women and Lack in *Don Quijote*" (*MLN* 103, no. 2 [1988]: 205–22), she draws on Walter Ong's notion from his "Transformations of the Word and Alienation," in *Interfaces of the Word* (Ithaca: Cornell University Press, 1977), that in the sixteenth and seventeenth centuries the "identification with the all-powerful mother is broken through a complex con-junction of historical and technological forces" (El Saffar, 211–12).

3. I discussed *Hic Mulier* in the second section of the introduction. On fear of effeminacy in England see chap. 7, "Civilian Impotence, Civic Imprudence," of Linda Woodbridge's *Women and the English Renaissance* in which she states, for example: "Many writers viewed as effeminate the new city men who lived by wit and as outra-geously aggressive the new city women who showed any signs of assertiveness" (169).

4. El Saffar generally substantiates her assertions with examples from *La Celestina*, the picaresque novel and, especially, *Don Quijote*. I bring in Calderón's play as further literary testimony to the validity of her theories. Also see Coppélia Kahn's influential "The Absent Mother in *King Lear*," in *Rewriting the Renaissance: The Discourse of Sexual Difference in Early Modern Europe*, ed. Margaret W. Ferguson et al. (Chicago and London: University of Chicago Press, 1986), for an analysis of the maternal subtext in Shakespeare's play along the lines espoused by El Saffar.

5. Katharine M. Rogers's early but benchmark survey, *The Troublesome Helpmate: A History of Misogyny in Literature* (Seattle and London: University of Washington Press, 1966), takes this Freudian explanation of misogyny and misogynist discourse as its main theoretical premise.

6. See the introduction by Peter Stallybrass and Allon White to their *Politics and Poetics of Transgression* (New York and Ithaca: Cornell University Press, 1986). There they discuss how the "top" excludes the "bottom" of society, which nevertheless forms part of the "top's" being and which returns as "a primary eroticized constituent of its own fantasy life." "It is for this reason," the authors write, "that what is *socially* periph-eral is so frequently *symbolically* central (like long hair in the 1960s). The low-Other is despised and denied at the level of political organization and social being whilst it is instrumentally constitutive of the shared imaginary repertoires of the dominant cul-ture" (5–6).

7. This is the main point of Julie Greer Johnson's 1993 *Satire in Colonial Spanish America: Turning the New World Upside Down* from which I draw the bulk of my argu-ments on satirical discourse in Latin America.

8. Oñate (91–94) discusses two late-sixteenth-century Spanish profeminist tracts, by Juan de Espinosa and Cristóbal de Acosta, whose existence is unusual and whose sincerity–since they are addressed to their female patrons–is questionable. Amezúa, in his introduction to the *Novelas amorosas* of Zayas (xxii), mentions a little-known defense of women by Antonio Alvarez from 1637, *Memorial en defensa de las mujeres de España y de los vestidos y adornos que usan*, that I have not been able to consult.

9. The full-length works of colonial theater in Latin America, according to Julie Greer Johnson (1983, 130), presented a different case. There, in deference to another set of official needs, female characters were generally laudable and derived from an ide-alized portrait of Spanish women. The rebellious *mujer varonil*, Ana, of Sor Juana's *Los*

empeños de una casa, then, would be the exception rather than the rule in the nun's milieu and more the rule than the exception in the Spanish context.

10. Dawn Smith concludes her introduction to the volume, saying, "Although the essays in this collection range widely in their treatment of the subject of women in the Spanish *comedia*, one theme clearly dominates: women are perceived as an essentially subversive force. Yet while, on the one hand, their presence is unsettling, even disruptive, they are also cast in the role of restorative angels, the repository of the enduring values of the hierarchical status quo" (26). However, the works of Luis Vélez de Guevara–another example of the attempt to eke some new and sensational possibilities out of a tired tradition that we see in Zayas and her literary coterie–do exceptionally allow the *mujer varonil* to remain unregenerate. See B. B. Ashcom, "Concerning 'La mujer en hábito de hombre' in the Comedia" (57–58).

11. Once again, and as ever, one has to factor in the large and elusive possibility that when authors speak of gender, they may well be speaking of something else, and genuinely so. That is, a woman's rebellion in a literary work may represent rebellion in general and thus represent the author's counterhegemonic impulses.

12. Two poles of the debate can be seen in Kelly versus Rougement and Jeanroy. Kelly (in "Did Women Have a Renaissance," and "Early Feminist Theory and the *Querelle des Femmes*," both in her *Women, History, and Theory* [Chicago and London: University of Chicago Press, 1984]) argues that courtly love reflected women's superior position in the landed economy of the feudal state; following Jeanroy (*Anthologies des Troubadours* [Paris: Renaissance du livre, 1927]), Rougement maintains that "Provençal poetry and the notion of love which informs its themes, far from being accounted for by conditions prevailing at the time, seem to have been in flat contradiction to them" (76).

13. Bloch's book contains many stimulating formulations, especially his claim that the asceticism of the early Christian period, "synonymous with the deprecation of the feminine, was, in the High Middle Ages, simply transformed into an idealization both of women and of love" (10, also see chap. 4). His actual working out of the issue on literary grounds, based on matters of speech and silence shared by the two discourses, has proved less useful to me.

14. See, for example, Otis Green, vol. 1, chap. 6, and Paul Julian Smith, *Quevedo on Parnassus: Allusive Context and Literary Theory in the Love-Lyric* (London: Modern Humanities Research Association, 1987), 7.

15. Claudio Guillén trenchantly notes in his *Literature as System: Essays Toward the Theory of Literary History* (Princeton: Princeton University Press, 1971): "A genre endures . . . insofar as it continues to be a problem-solving model, a standing invitation to the matching of matter and form" (386); on sedimentation, Frederick Jameson writes in *The Political Unconscious: Narrative as a Socially Symbolic Act* (Ithaca: Cornell University Press, 1981): "The ideology of the form itself, thus sedimented, persists into the later, more complex structure as a generic message which coexists–either as a contradiction or, on the other hand, as a mediatory or harmonizing mechanism–with elements from later stages" (141).

16. For other contributions, see the works cited in n. 1 to this chapter, and Oñate and Nelken; also consult the introduction to *María de Zayas: Dynamics of Discourse*, which details works in progress on golden age women writers. Teresa Scott Soufas's *Dramas of Distinction: A Study of Plays by Golden Age Women* (Lexington: University Press of Kentucky, 1997) and her *Women's Acts: Plays by Women Dramatists of Spain's*

Golden Age (Lexington: University Press of Kentucky, 1997), published after the writing of this book, are welcome additions to the field.

17. On the attractions of the pastoral for women, see Elizabeth Rhodes's excellent "Skirting the Men: Gender Roles in Sixteenth-Century Pastoral Books," *Journal of Hispanic Philology* 11, no. 2 (winter 1987): 131–49.

18. Paz makes this claim on p. 399 of *Sor Juana Inés de la Cruz o las trampas de la fe* (only in the Spanish original, not in the English version). Olivares and Boyce intelligently counter it with a list of other women who had written similar works (48); also see the poems by Marcia Belisarda included in the anthology. Particularly important for our concerns, the organizing theme of Zayas's sixth "Desengaño," and especially (as we will see) the satirical poem that concludes the section, treats the double standard of men in a fashion extremely similar to Sor Juana's Redondilla #92, "Hombres necios . . ."

19. I take my cue from Jones: "These poets demonstrated that a relatively privileged feminine subject, although always already caught up in the politics of gender ideology and the grip of dominant signifying systems, could nonetheless be mobile within these systems. To read women writers–the rare few who prevailed among the violent gender hierarchies of early modern Europe–is to recognize how variously they negotiated their subordination to men's social power and the masculine orders of language" (1990, 9–10).

20. I borrow the phrase from Sheila Fisher and Janet E. Halley's introduction to *Seeking the Woman in Late Medieval and Renaissance Writings* (Knoxville: University of Tennessee Press, 1989), 11.

21. Paz does discuss at length Sor Juana's love poems to women. However, he places little emphasis on what I consider to be the crucial issue of reason versus passion. In fact, he asks, "Could one be a *feminist* in the seventeenth century" (303). Frederick Luciani, on the other hand, provides a fine discussion of reason in courtly poetry and in Sor Juana's love poetry (92–101), but does not view the matter in terms of women's issues. All of Sor Juana's poetry in this chapter, except where noted, can be found in vol. 1 (*Lírica personal*) of Méndez Plancarte's edition.

22. The first chapter of Luciani's dissertation provides a fuller exposition of critical positions on Sor Juana's love poetry; Ramón Xirau, in *Genio y figura de sor Juana Inés de la Cruz* (Buenos Aires: Editorial Universitaria de Buenos Aires, 1967), also summarizes the biographical questions to which it has given rise. Paz presents his view of Sor Juana's melancholic temperament on pp. 216–17 of his *Sor Juana.*

23. Sor Juana describes love in similar terms in the "No es tal, Sí es tal" [No it isn't, yes it is] interlude of *Los empeños de una casa* (act 2, scene 5).

24. The *liras* have a similar cast as the *endechas* but are more heterogeneous.

25. I refer to the Scholastic *cuestiones de amor* or *questions d'amour.* I treat this subject and the poems of "encontradas correspondencias" more fully in the next chapter.

26. Georgina Sabat-Rivers states that "we do not know the chronology of Sor Juana's sonnets" and that "their order of publication in the early editions does not seem to be significant except for some occasional thematic grouping" (1995, 119). She also reminds us of what we must keep constantly in mind: that the titles of the poems are written not by Sor Juana but by the editors of the first editions.

27. Luciani also cites this sonnet as an example of a *servidor* poem (72 ff.). The reader will find in his second chapter a more exhaustive exposition of the phases of courtly love in Sor Juana's poetry.

28. As the discussion of these stages of the courtly process demonstrates, they do not correspond to metrical forms. That is, Sor Juana does not necessarily utilize a given metrical form to express a given phase of courtly love–which but augments the complexity of her love poetry.

29. Terry finds contradictory the fact that in Romance #4 the poetic speaker denigrates Silvio's willed or elective love while in Décima #104 she praises the same type of love. The contradiction can appear less blatant when one realizes that the speaker's point in Romance #4 is to defend *her own* willed love, her decision to love Fabio and not Silvio. I am more comfortable with Terry's later suggestion that the love poems perhaps "revolve around a limited number of central ideas which they debate from different, though related, points of view" (302), for much of what appears to be contradictory in the nun's love poetry may well be ascribed to the fact that she details different kinds of love and different phases in the courtly love process.

30. Terry's article has greatly helped to crystallize my thinking on divine love in Sor Juana's poetry. For example, he states that there are "tensions involved in achieving divine love, and these come from the weakness of human nature, and particularly from the tendency of the attitudes of human love to intervene" (310).

31. Here I definitively part ways with George H. Tavard in his *Juana Inés de la Cruz and the Theology of Beauty: The First Mexican Theology* (Notre Dame and London: Notre Dame University Press, 1991). While usefully signaling the Neoplatonic nature of *ideal* love according to Sor Juana, Tavard entirely ignores the marked conflictive aspects of love in her conception. He refers, for example, to her "delicate celebrations of human love," and states that "even when they complain of absence–the beloved being removed by distance or by death–these poems always celebrate joy given and received. Therefore Juana has no difficulty passing from human to divine love, for she follows only one paradigm" (205). I have shown that the praxis of love in Sor Juana's poetry is such that her poetic narrators experience great difficulty in passing from human to divine love. The poet may have only paradigm for love in the sense of an ideal model, but in her personal lyric that model is achieved only in the poems of loving friendship from one woman to another.

32. Sonnet #172, "On a reasonable reflection which allays the pain of a passion," is the only exception that I have found. Here, in a moment of lucidity, the poetic voice recognizes that she, who has suffered most extremely in love, is therefore also the most fortunate. The poem has a double, somewhat ambiguous, thrust: its subject is the good fortune of having suffered for love, but its focus is the moment of rationality that mitigates the pain.

33. The same theme, of the language of tears or *hereos*, appears in Sonnet #164, "In which she allays misgivings with the rhetoric of tears."

34. Georgina Sabat-Rivers notes that the radical originality of Sonnet #165 lies in the fact that "the mind can accomplish anything," and that the last lines of the poem displace the activity of love to the mind. See her excellent synthetic essay, "Sor Juana Inés de la Cruz," in *Historia de la literatura hispanoamericana: Epoca colonial*, ed. Luis Iñigo Madrigal (Madrid: Cátedra, 1982), 281.

35. Following his (in my opinion, myopic) biographical agenda, Paz tends to attribute the role of absence and imagination in Sor Juana's poetry to her isolation in the convent. For example: "Jealousy, absence, death: different names of solitude. Alone–and because she is always alone–she invents these situations; in turn, the inventions help her to unburden herself and come to know herself: the life of her

imagination is also a means of introspection" (285). That the theme of solitude may well serve a variety of purposes for the female author can be seen in the following observation by Ann Rosalind Jones: "In the case of a woman poet, the absence of the male beloved fulfilled a social as well as a rhetorical requirement: it guaranteed the speaker's purity" (1990, 35).

36. Paz underscores the role of Neoplatonic tradition in authorizing Sor Juana's statements: "Without strict Platonic dualism [the separation of soul and body], her sentiments and those of María Luisa would have become aberrations" (216). Significantly enough, as will be discussed in chap. 3, we find a justification of lesbian love remarkably similar to Sor Juana's in the sixth "Desengaño" ("Love for the Sake of Conquest") of Zayas. As both examples indicate, the conjunction of commonplaces from Neoplatonic and Christian clearly provided a topical early modern defense of homosexual love.

37. It is interesting to note, with Bénassy-Berling (246), that beyond the case of one *villancico* attributable to Sor Juana, the poet fails to call the Virgin *divine*. She reserves this adjective for Lysi!

38. For a discussion of the poems in a male voice along these lines, see Ester Gimbernat de González, "Speaking Through the Voices of Love: Interpretation as Emancipation," in *Feminist Perspectives on Sor Juana Inés de la Cruz*, ed. Stephanie Merrim (Detroit: Wayne State University Press, 1991).

39. Paz also provides such a view, if a slightly less human one, when he writes: "Those poems were simultaneously courtly poems and homages of gratitude, palatial adulation and declarations of a Platonic infatuation" (214). Nina M. Scott, for her part, adds a productive dimension to the debate in contending that it is far more important to appreciate the importance of María Luisa's contribution to Sor Juana's professional life than it is to resolve the nature of their personal relationship. Had María Luisa not published the *Inundación castálida*, what might we today know of the nun? See Scott (1993, 167–69).

40. Sor Juana writes: "¡Oh siglo desdichado y desvalido / en que todo lo hallamos ya servido, / pues que no hay voz, equívoco ni frase / que por común no pase / y digan los censores: / ¿Eso? ¡Ya lo pensaron los mayores!" [Oh unhappy and impoverished century, in which we find that everything has been used up, for there is no word or conceit or phrase which is not commonplace, and of which the censors do not say, Oh that? Our elders already thought it up!]. See Frederick Luciani, "El amor desfigurado: El ovillejo de Sor Juana Inés de la Cruz," *Texto crítico* 34–35 (1986): 11–48, and "The Burlesque Sonnets of Sor Juana Inés de la Cruz," *Hispanic Journal* 8, no. 1 (fall 1986): 85–95. In the latter article, Luciani notes Sor Juana's "keen awareness of the permutations that can be realized by the writer who works with topoi that are over-familiar, time-worn" (91) and states that we can hear in her poems "the sound of literary clichés being exploded" (93). Also see poem 21 by Catalina Ramírez de Guzmán in the Olivares and Boyce anthology ("Retrato de la autora, habiéndosele pedido un galán suyo"), very akin to Sor Juana's Ovillejo #214 in its disarticulation of Petrarchan topics.

41. For discussions of the distinctive nature of the *barroco de Indias* along these lines see Jaime Concha, "La literatura colonial hispano-americana: Problemas e hipótesis" (*Neohelicon* 4, no. 12 [1976]: 31–50), Roberto González Echevarría, "Colonial Lyric," in *The Cambridge History of Latin American Literature*, vol. 1, ed. Roberto González Echevarría and Enrique Pupo-Walker (Cambridge, Eng.: Cambridge University Press, 1996), and Kathleen Ross, *The Baroque Narrative of Carlos de Sigüenza y Góngora: A New*

World Paradise. Ross, for example, locates the distinctiveness of Mexican baroque historiography in its special intertextuality: "The American nature of this baroque prose rests not in its use of conceits, digressions, and other standard tropes, but in the manipulation of previous histories of the conquest through the employment of language borrowed from literature. The polyphony of narrative voices in the prose, its fluid and changeable character, and an obsession with the reinterpretation of American history put a stamp of difference on the criollo historiography of the *barroco de Indias*" (45–46).

42. I allude to Thomas M. Greene's category of "Eclectic or Exploitative" imitation–"a very simple type of imitation" "by no means to be despised" (39)–which depends on *contaminatio*: "We might call this type eclectic or exploitative since it essentially treats all traditions as stockpiles to be drawn upon ostensibly at random. History becomes a vast container whose contents can be disarranged endlessly without suffering damage" (39).

43. I refer the reader to Otis Green's brief but suggestive discussion of "Will and Reason: the Scholastic and the Platonic positions" (1964, 171–72). On Thomistic thought in Sor Juana, one can consult Constance M. Montross, *Virtue or Vice? Sor Juana's Use of Thomistic Thought* (Washington, D.C.: University Press of America, 1981), and Josefina Muriel, *Cultura femenina novohispana* (Mexico: UNAM, 1982), 236–55.

44. On Cartesianism as a galvanizing force for late-seventeenth-century British women, see Hilda M. Smith, *Reason's Disciples: Seventeenth-Century English Feminists*. Although, as I have said, amorous complaint was a common topic in Hispanic women's poetry, I have not found any poet who utilizes it as a springboard for the defense of women's reason against *querelle* claims as does Sor Juana.

45. It did not behoove Sor Juana to proceed into the models of imitation that Greene terms "Heuristic" or "Dialectical"–models that call attention to the *difference* between the present and the past, present text and intertext. Male authors following these protocols strongly combat the past; it befitted women writers like Sor Juana to keep their subversions clandestine, to seem to respect etiologies, to mask difference, and thus subtly and subterraneanly to make the past function transitively.

46. On Sor Juana and music, see Paz ("The Reflection, the Echo," *Sor Juana*, part 4, chap. 16); Lavista; Ricardo Miranda ("Sor Juana y la música: Una lectura más"); Aurelio Tello ("Sor Juana, la música y sus músicos")–all three in *Memoria del Coloquio Internacional, Sor Juana Inés de la Cruz y el pensamiento hispano* (Morelos: Instituto Mexiquense de Cultura, 1995). Also see Electa Arenal, "Where Woman Is Creator of the Wor(l)d," in my 1991 edited collection.

47. Here and throughout the book I cite the *Desengaños amorosos* not from the Amezúa edition but from the more recent, better annotated edition of Alicia Yllera.

48. Although Zayas could have culled the topics of the *querelle* from other sources, her uncanny proximity to Christine de Pizan in technique (lists of illustrious women) and substance (Pizan takes as her main point men's slander of women, harks back to an earlier more perfect age, argues that men deny women an education out of fear, claims the equality of souls, defends women's constancy and denounces that of males, and so on) strongly suggests direct knowledge of the French author's work. That Zayas read the *Heptaméron*–no translation of which into Spanish appears to have existed at the time–in French is most likely; if Zayas knew French and had researched her female precursors, it is plausible that she had read Pizan.

49. Listing its proponents, Chevalier states that the reading of *La Celestina* as a moralistic work "perhaps prevailed in Golden Age Spain" (154), yet goes on to note

the qualms that the work incited. One particularly astute seventeenth-century commentator, Francisco Ortiz, observed that while an intelligent reader could perceive the philosophical *sententiae* of the work, an ignorant reader would be struck only by Calixto's immoral subterfuges (Chevalier, 162). Whether, as they in all likelihood should have, Zayas's works incited similar mixed reactions, we do not know. In chap. 4 of the same work, Chevalier also details the reception of *Lazarillo de Tormes* as a work of sheer diversion, neglecting the scandalous immorality of its final adulterous triangle.

50. I refer to, and build my discussion from, Peter N. Dunn's fine study, *Castillo Solórzano and the Decline of the Spanish Novel*.

51. Susan C. Griswold opened up the issue of the perspectivism of Zayas's novellas (which, I should repeat, replicate the pattern of Marguérite de Navarre's *Heptaméron*) in her 1980 article; H. Patsy Boyer developed it into the notion of "male" and "female" tales in her introduction to the translation of the *Novelas amorosas* and her "Toward a Baroque Reading of 'El verdugo de su esposa,'" in *María de Zayas: The Dynamics of Discourse*, ed. Amy R. Williamsen and Judith A. Whitenack (Madison and Teaneck, N.J.: Fairleigh Dickinson University Press; Cranbury, N.J., and London: Associated University Presses, 1995), as has Amy R. Williamsen in her "Challenging the Code: Honor in María de Zayas" in the same collection.

52. Even as she plays to a readership that conceivably includes misogynist males and attempts to neutralize their hostility, Zayas herself strives to undercut the inconsistencies her text occasions—among several ways, by drawing morals that exculpate her less than admirable female protagonists, by creating patently flawed male narrators, by having a male narrator (as in the case of "Judge Thyself," which may reference the story of Catalina de Erauso) turn around and tell a feminist story.

53. Thomas Hanrahan, in *La mujer en la novela picaresca*, vol. 1 (Madrid: Porrúa Turranzas, 1967), and Edward H. Friedman, in *The Antiheroine's Voice: Narrative Discourse and Transformations of the Picaresque* (Columbia: University of Missouri Press, 1987), present similar lines of argumentation.

54. On Ana Caro, in addition to Luna's introduction to her edition of *El Conde Partinuplés*, Ordóñez and the two works by Teresa Soufas cited in n. 16 above, see particularly Amy R. Williamsen, "Re-Writing in the Margins: Caro's *Valor, agravio y mujer* as Challenge to Dominant Discourse," *Bulletin of the Comediantes* 44, no. 1 (summer 1992): 21–30; Ruth Lundelius, "Ana Caro: Spanish Poet and Dramatist," in *Women Writers of the Seventeenth Century*, ed. Katharina M. Wilson and Frank J. Warnke; Teresa Soufas, "Ana Caro's Re-Evaluation of the *mujer varonil* and Her Theatrics in *Valor, agravio y mujer*," in Stoll and Smith.

55. Page numbers refer to Serrano y Sanz's edition of *Valor* and to Luna's of *Conde*.

56. The friendship between Caro and Zayas has often been remarked but has not been probed on literary grounds. I should also note that María de Zayas wrote a fascinating comedia, *La traición en la amistad* [Betrayal in Friendship] (now available in Soufas's anthology, *Women's Acts*). Rather than pushing the *mujer varonil* of male-authored comedias and other of their features to the limits of parody, Zayas works within an emphatically female economy similar to that of her novellas. She centers her play not primordially on romance but on female friendship and its betrayal, and on a picaresque female heroine censored by other women for her promiscuity. The matriarchal world of Caro's *El Conde Partinuplés* bears strong resemblance to that of Zayas's play, but adheres more closely to the conventional structures and plots of golden age drama.

57. Sor Juana's *Los empeños de una casa*, for example, appears quite tame in comparison with Caro's comedias. Through Ana, the rebellious deus ex machina of the play, and Leonor's misogynist father (48–49), Sor Juana opens up the theme of a woman's right to choose her spouse, but ultimately abdicates it. In Caro's plays, women not only act on but achieve their desires. For a rare comparison of Sor Juana's play to María de Zayas's, see Constance Wilkins, "Subversion through Comedy?: Two Plays by Sor Juana Inés de la Cruz and María de Zayas," in Stoll and Smith.

58. On p. 202 of *Valor* we find a clear evocation of Tirso de Molina's *El burlador de Sevilla*. Don Juan cries: "Todo fué burla, ¡por Dios!" [By God, it was all a trick!], and Estela (whose name means trail, wake–in the wake of a tradition?) replies: "Si acaso quedó burlada, / burla sería, don Juan" [If she was tricked, it was quite a trick, don Juan]. See the article by Teresa de Soufas cited above for a discussion of the play's intention to reform men and for a pessimistic conclusion regarding its efficacy.

59. Ordóñez principally argues that Zayas and Caro weave into their texts a self-consciousness of themselves as female makers of texts. While some aspects of her allegorical readings may be problematic, Ordóñez's point further bolsters my assertions regarding the two women's shared project to write and to market themselves as women authors.

60. Tomillo asks Ribete about new developments in Madrid, and Ribete answers: "Ya es todo muy viejo allá; / Sólo en esto de poetas / Hay notable novedad / Por innumerables, tanto, / Que aun quieren poetizar / Las mujeres, y se atreven / A hacer comedias ya" [Everything there is very dull; the only real novelty are poets. They're innumerable–even women want to poetize, and now they have the nerve to write plays]. When Tomillo exclaims at women's audacity, Ribete replies with a list of women authors past and present and comments: "Lustre soberano dan / Disculpando la osadía / De su nueva vanidad" (193) [They shed splendid light, which makes up for the boldness of their new vanity].

61. As Amezúa details (D., xxi) and as the reader can easily surmise, Zayas's style is far from as simple as it announces itself to be: hers is literally a rhetorical posture.

62. Other works on women's social reality in golden age Spain include P. W. Bomli; Marcellin Defourneaux, *La vida cotidiana en la España del siglo de oro* (Barcelona: Argos Vergaria, 1983); José Deleito y Piñuela, *La mujer, la casa y la moda (en la España del rey poeta)* (Madrid: Espasa-Calpe, 1946); Ludwig Pfandl, *Cultura y costumbres del pueblo español de los siglos XVI y XVII*; *Spanish Women in the Golden Age: Images and Realities*, ed. Magdalena S. Sánchez and Alain Saint-Saëns (Westport, Conn., and London: Greenwood Press, 1996). They are all, except the last work, rather sketchy and repetitive of one another; to my knowledge, Melveena McKendrick's first chapter remains the most synthetic, authoritative, and intelligent study of the subject. On the social reality of women in colonial Mexico, I refer the reader particularly to Josefina Muriel, *Cultura femenina novohispana*, cited above in n. 43, to Asunción Lavrin's fine "In Search of the Colonial Woman in Mexico: The Seventeenth and Eighteenth Centuries," and to the articles by Lavrin and Schons in my 1991 edited collection.

63. According to the bibliography appended to Yllera's introduction to the *Desengaños amorosos*, some eleven editions of Zayas's work were issued in the eighteenth century (73); Amezúa notes: "Unusually for the seventeenth century, which was so poor in novels, those of doña María enjoyed particular favor, and the presses of the largest Spanish cities vied with each other to publish them" (N., xxxi). As explanation for their popularity and as a final comment on the degree to which Zayas's novellas

were (mis)taken as moralistic, in the eighteenth century the Spanish Academy of History refused to print "Las tertulias murcianas" of Clara Jara de Soto, claiming that although her work was similar to Zayas's, it lacked the "clear moral ends," "interesting or instructive episodes," and the "entertaining variety" of its stated model (Nelken, 154–55). One nevertheless cannot help wondering if in the eighteenth century Zayas's feminist message, more akin to the interests of the state, had not finally become "readable" in its own right.

Notes to Chapter Three: Women on Love, Part II

1. I borrow the phrase from Nancy K. Miller (1980, 156) and from Hélène Cixous, who writes: "But somewhere else? There will be some elsewhere where the other will no longer be condemned to death. But has there ever been any elsewhere, is there any? While it is not yet 'here,' it is there by now–in this place that disrupts social order, where desire makes fiction exist" (*The Newly Born Woman*, trans. Betsy Wing [Minneapolis: University of Minnesota Press, 1986], 97).

2. Though its focus and arguments are different from mine, Paul B. Dixon's "Balance, Pyramids, Crowns, and the Geometry of Sor Juana Inés de la Cruz" (*Hispania* 67, no. 4 [December 1984]: 560–66) contains an interesting discussion of the significance of geometry for Sor Juana and her works.

3. Gerda Lerner writes of Hildegard of Bingen, a twelfth-century nun, that her "theology breaks sharply with the dichotomized categories of the scholastics and with the patriarchal hierarchies embedded in their thought. Hildegard's visions fuse male and female elements, the physical and the spiritual, the rational-practical and the mystical aspects of existence. It is no accident that the illuminations of her visions abound in circles, curves and waves, in *mandala*-like designs, which avoid any concept of hierarchy in favor of wholeness, foundedness and integration" (63). Margaret Lucas Cavendish's *Poems and Fancies* also abound in circles. As does Sor Juana, Cavendish alludes to Nicolas of Cusa's (1401?–64?) trope of God as a circumference whose center is ubiquitous (41). Given these convergences, the notion of an early circle-based feminist theology is well worth exploring.

4. Alfonso Méndez Plancarte terms the "ironic symmetries" poems "questions of love or discretion," and identifies them with a tradition begun by Ausonius and continued by such writers as Boscán, Mendoza, Lope de Vega, and Calderón. Georgina Sabat-Rivers also outlines the tradition from which Sor Juana's poems emerged on p. 281 of "Sor Juana Inés de la Cruz," in *Historia de la literatura hispanoamericana*, vol. 1, ed. Iñigo Madrigal (Madrid: Cátedra, 1982). See John Lough, *An Introduction to Seventeenth-Century France* (London, New York, Toronto: Longmans, Green and Co., 1954), 138–40, for a discussion of the "questions d'amour" or "questions galantes" in France at the time. On pp. 164–65 of *La Princesse de Clèves* (*33–34*), the characters debate a question of this nature: whether it is worse for a woman to be present or absent at a ball given by her lover. *LPDC* itself gave rise to the first public debate of a "question galante" when in April of 1678 the *Mercure Galante* asked its readers' opinions as to whether the Princesse should have confessed to her husband (see Laugaa, 20–40).

5. Lira #213 ("Which expresses feelingly the pain a loving wife suffers at her husband's death") displays another contradiction to the series, and another outcome. As I stated in the last chapter, it is the only tribute to mutual love in Sor Juana's repertoire. Here the poetic speaker has married not Silvio but Fabio, and mourns the end of their happy marriage.

6. I should note that the "ironic symmetries" poems that in Méndez Plancarte's edition bear the numbers 166–68, though published as a unit in the *Inundación castáli-da* and with the same titles, followed a different order there: 166–168–167 (poems 3, 4, 5, in *Inundación*). See Georgina Sabat's edition of the *Inundación* (pp. 91–92).

7. Although Kaps makes a strong case for the baroque nature of *LPDC* in her book (65–79), I present my own observations here.

8. Bray remarks, for example, that throughout the latter part of the century the discourse of love would continue to avail itself of the artificial style of *préciosité* espoused by the *précieuses* among others–that is, verbal conceits, vague terms, extravagant metaphors, periphrases, antitheses, the personification of abstractions, and so on (see part 2, chap. 6 of his book: "Préciosité et classicisme").

9. I will cite from the readily available edition of *La Princesse de Clèves* by Bernard Pingaud. His edition contains the short novels, *La Princesse de Montpensier* and *La Comtesse de Tende*, which I discuss. The English translation of *LPDC* from which I cite, by Terence Cave, also contains the short novels. I refer the reader to Cave's fine introduction to the translation for a balanced and current treatment of the question of the authorship of the three texts. There Cave notes, among other matters establishing Mme de Lafayette's predominant role in them, a feminine grammatical form from *LPDC*, which may well entail her "signature" of that text (xxi). Let me also take this opportunity to thank my colleague in French studies at Brown University, Professor Lewis Seifert, for sharing his impressive knowledge of French seventeenth-century literature with me. His generosity, guidance, and patience have been invaluable.

10. On p. 62 of his *Mme de la Fayette par elle-même*, Pingaud discerns an inwardness and tendency to self-critique and *desengaño* in the French aristocracy of the times similar to that noted by J. H. Elliott in "Self-Perception and Decline in Early Seventeenth-Century Spain" (in *Spain and Its World*) with regard to the Spanish aristocracy.

11. Beasley cites the central maxim of Mme de Villedieu's *Les désordres de l'amour* (1675), so similar to the lines I quote from Mme de Lafayette: "Love is the motivating force behind all the passions of the soul . . . If one carefully examines the secret motives of the revolutions that happen in monarchies, one will always find it guilty or an accomplice in all of them" (171).

12. I refer here to the privatizating and feminizing of history through fiction and memoirs mentioned in the introduction as the subject of Beasley's and De Jean's books. Along these lines it is worth noting that Lafayette described *LPDC* as a memoir and that she presumably ended her career writing the *Mémoires de la cour de France pour les années 1688–89*.

13. *Le triomphe de l'indifférence*, a true philippic against love and a justification of a life without men, came to light in the eighteenth century and was at first, though not now, thought to have been written by Mme de Lafayette due to its similarities to her views. See De Jean (1984, 898–99, 910 n. 25) for a discussion and description of the anonymous text, selections from which appear in Pingaud's edition of *LPDC*.

14. Lougee writes: "One does not find in feminist literature a celebration of the relationship between mother and child or indeed any sense of the woman's membership in her maiden or married family." She quotes Michel de Pure's contention that "the *Précieuse* is not the daughter of her father or her mother; she has neither. . . . The *Précieuse* is formed in the salon" (Lougee, 22).

15. On the *précieuses'* positions on love and marriage see, for example, Allentuch, Beasley, Bray, De Jean (1984; 1991), Lougee, and Dorothy Backer, *Precious Women: A Feminist Phenomenon in the Age of Louis XIV* (New York: Basic Books, 1974).

16. Chabanes, a study in many respects for the Prince de Clèves, does at most other moments exercise notable prudence and self-restraint. Perhaps the only moral act in *La Princesse de Montpensier* viewed positively comes when Chabanes pretends that it was he, and not Guise, with whom the Princesse had arranged the secret tryst, thus manifesting supreme self-control. The narrator praises his "générosité sans example" (69) [unparalleled generosity of spirit, *183*].

17. At the end of chap. 2 I stated that we have no substantial evidence of rebellion against the patriarchy on the part of Spanish women. Yet in her article, "Women Against Wedlock: The Reluctant Brides of Golden Age Drama" (in *Women in Hispanic Literature: Icons and Fallen Idols*, ed. Beth Miller [Berkeley, Los Angeles, London: University of California Press, 1983]), Melveena McKendrick asserts that a "number of women in Spain at the time" rebelled against marriage, forsaking it (142). Though conceivably to forsake marriage, among other reasons, women did withdraw to the convent, I would note that marriage allowed seventeenth-century Spanish women more freedom than they would have otherwise. Married women were at greater liberty to visit, to receive guests, to attend theatrical performances, to move around the city (albeit with chaperons).

18. Once again I am indebted to my colleague Antonio Carreño, who scouted the Spanish field for other examples of texts with convent endings.

19. The (unnamed) editor of the volume of the *Biblioteca de autores españoles* in which Contreras's novel can be found is not at all clear on the date of publication. See p. xxx of the volume for this confusing explanation.

20. I suspect that in Spanish golden age literature exile to the "Indies" (for male characters) fulfills something of this same textual function as retreat to the convent (principally, but not exclusively, for female characters). At least in Cervantes's "El celoso extremeño" the correlation is clear: at the end of the text Leonora takes herself to a convent and her would-be lover Loaysa to the Indies (whence Leonora's husband had just returned at the beginning of the tale).

21. In this tale from Zayas's *Novelas amorosas*, don Fadrique tries to prevent his innocent young wife, Gracia, from having sexual relations with other men by not initiating her into marital relations; his plans backfire and he returns from a trip to find her all the wiser and himself all the more foolish. The moral of the tale particularly captures the resemblance to Cervantes's "El celoso extremeño": "In the end, no matter how don Fadrique tried to prevent the catastrophe he'd been forewarned about . . . he fell into the very situation he feared, and it was a foolish woman who ruined his honor" (*153*, 216). Like Leonora, Gracia ends up in a convent—but happy and free and reunited with her mother. Very clear here is Zayas's refiguration of the convent found in Cervantes.

22. Leonora has in effect become the double of her husband's former controlling self. For example, she believes that she can control Loaysa by making him take an oath that once he is inside her house, he will do no more than sing and play: "Then if he has sworn . . . we've got him. How wise I was to make him swear!" (*169*, 124).

23. In her "To Read the Bride: Elision and Silence in Cervantes's *The Jealous Extremaduran*" (*Novel: A Forum in Fiction* 22, no. 3 [spring 1989]: 326–37), Emilia Navarro makes an argument regarding Leonora and the convent that, while using similar terms to mine, directly opposes my reading. Navarro sees Leonora, after Loaysa's entrance into the house, emerging as a full presence in possession of her own code and, in refusing to cede to his seduction, as contravening generic patterns that posit the function of the young bride as that of cuckolding the old husband. Leonora's resulting

silence, her withdrawal to the "elsewhere" (337) of the convent, and the narrator's final puzzlement regarding her silence, in Navarro's view, represent the breakdown of old literary patterns and Leonora's "functioning according to another code" (337)–still unarticulated and based on silence because "her speech cannot, will not, be understood" (336). Although I find this feminist reading intriguing, I also find it hard to equate with certain aspects of Cervantes's text. For example, the fact that Leonora moves from one established code (the young bride as cuckolder) into another (virtuous young woman, loyal wife), the immediate retreat of Leonora after the dalliance with Loaysa into conventional patterns of the loyal wife, her *refusal* of freedom, and especially the explicit equation of the convent with Carrizales's house. I am also left with the question of why–in this text where Carrizales overtly refutes the male code of honor–Leonora's alleged code must be left unexpressed.

24. On the mythological references of "El celoso extremeño," see Peter N. Dunn, "Las *Novelas ejemplares*," in *Suma cervantina*, ed. J. B. Avalle-Arce and E. C. Riley (London: Támesis, 1973), 100–105.

25. Two notes are in order here. First, to maintain the moral decorum of the tale as well as its two levels, Loaysa is represented ambiguously: as a devil and an angel, as Leonora's perdition and her salvation. Second, there exists a manuscript version of "El celoso extremeño" in which Leonora does not, it is strongly suggested, resist Loaysa's advances. For a summary of the critical interpretations of Cervantes's changes to the text see A. F. Lambert, "The Two Versions of Cervantes' *El celoso extremeño*: Ideology and Criticism," *Bulletin of Hispanic Studies* 57 (1980): 219–31. Whatever the reasons for Cervantes's change of the dénouement (critics generally accord in attributing it to moral considerations), the published version places Leonora's "culpability" not on the plane of conjugal fidelity but on the more interesting and characteristically Cervantine plane of the betrayal of potential freedom. In other words, the Leonora of the published version has betrayed not conventional morality but Cervantine morality. Moreover, the change also redounds onto the convent of the ending: were Leonora conventionally guilty, her retreat to the convent would appear as a just punishment, devoid of irony or of negative implications regarding Leonora's insufficient development as an individual. I would therefore suggest that in addition (as Lambert argues) to enhancing Carrizales's anagnorisis, the changes to the published version endow the character of Leonora (and her *lack* of anagnorisis) with greater pathos and originality, establishing her more fully as a counterpoint to Carrizales.

26. Moreover, many British women autobiographers of the seventeenth century (including Margaret Lucas Cavendish) professed their aversion to the married state; Sor Juana was hardly alone. See Cynthia Pomerleau, "The Emergence of Women's Autobiography in England," in *Women's Autobiography: Essays in Criticism*, ed. Estelle C. Jelinek (Bloomington and London: Indiana University Press, 1980).

27. Comte described the irreligious nature of *LPDC* to Anatole France in the following manner: "What has always struck me on reading this eminent work of the feminine spirit is the complete absence of any supernatural consideration; the name of God is not even pronounced, and yet the evolution of a human life, and moreover the life of a woman in a decisive crisis, takes place without anything appearing as either strange or illogical to us" (Laugaa, 197–98).

28. I borrow the phrase "irreligious redefinition" from Sandra M. Gilbert, who uses it to describe the rewriting of Bunyan's *Pilgrim's Progress* found in Brontë's *Jane Eyre*. See Sandra M. Gilbert and Susan Gubar, *The Madwoman in the Attic* (New Haven and London: Yale University Press, 1979), 370.

29. Kate Lilley also discusses Astell in her essay on Cavendish's *Blazing World*, saying: "Astell's vision is not of a closed order, but a flexible, separatist retreat, which acknowledges, and makes integral, responsibilities in the world at large" (113) and "the immaterial but profoundly gratifying spiritual, social and intellectual pleasures promised to the inhabitants of Astell's seminary as a second Eden are also offered as partly reproducible outside the walls of the retreat" (116).

30. I have read the play in the microfilm, *English Books 1641–1700* (Ann Arbor: University Microfilms), 502:11. Excerpts from *The Convent of Pleasure*, including the extensive descriptions of the projected convent, can be found in Moira Ferguson, *First Feminists: British Women Writers 1578–1799* (Bloomington and London: Indiana University Press, 1985), 86–90.

31. Sophie Tomlinson brings forth the fascinating detail that in some copies of Cavendish's 1668 *Plays*, "the final two scenes after the revelation of the Princess as a man are headed with a pasted-in slip reading 'Written by my Lord Duke,' but with no indication, as with similar instances elsewhere in Cavendish's texts, of where 'my Lord Duke's' ends" (156). Tomlinson goes on to suggest that there are "two ways of construing this textual anomaly: either Cavendish lost interest after the disclosure of the Princess as a man and left the writing of the play to her husband, or she did write the two final scenes, which poke fun at Puritan prurience and older women's sexual desires, but suspected they would be thought unseemly coming from a woman" (156). I am not sure that Tomlinson's explanations exhaust the possibilities: in accordance with the arguments that I develop in this chapter, might it not also be that Cavendish intended to write "otherwise" but retreated at the last minute, perhaps at her husband's prompting?

32. DuPlessis writes: "Soon after she accepts the man in the love plot, the female hero becomes a heroine, and the story ends" (8).

33. On the female bildungsroman of the nineteenth and twentieth centuries, the reader can consult, among others: DuPlessis; "A Dialogue of Self and Soul: Plain Jane's Progress," chap. 10 of Gilbert and Gubar's *The Madwoman in the Attic*, cited in n. 28 above; *The Voyage In: Fictions of Female Development*, ed. Elizabeth Abel, Marianne Hirsch, and Elizabeth Langland (Hanover and London: University Presses of New England, 1983); Annis Pratt, *Archetypal Patterns in Women's Fiction* (Bloomington: Indiana University Press, 1981).

34. To my knowledge, no critic has treated the framework story of Zayas's novellas as a female bildungsroman. Ruth El Saffar, however, focuses specifically and fruitfully (if in other terms) on the framework story in her 1995 essay, "Ana/Lysis and Zayas: Reflections on Courtship and Literary Women in the *Novelas amorosas y ejemplares*." As the reader will see, El Saffar's work on Zayas has stimulated my thinking on various points.

35. El Saffar sees the framework story as a "courtly love romance featuring the rivalry between Lisis and Lisarda and Don Juan and Don Diego" (1995, 193). The tales themselves, in her view, are embedded within that romance, "serving simultaneously as distractions, deferrals, and amplifications" (1995, 193).

36. Making a case for Lisis as a persona of Zayas herself, El Saffar discusses the ambiguity of the *Novelas* and concludes that "the tensions among the principal characters in the frame tale cry out for a resolution that nothing in the structure of the work admits" (1995, 197). I very much agree with her observations regarding the tensions in the work, but at the end of my chapter will explain them somewhat differently.

37. The "I" can be found on pp. 120, 258, 335, 404, 510 of the *Desengaños*.

38. Several tales have characters who are also actors in the novellas listening to stories told to them by others.

39. Margaret R. Greer, in "The M(Other) Plot: Houses of God, Man and Mother in María de Zayas" (in *María de Zayas: Dynamics of Discourse*, ed. Amy R. Williamsen and Judith A. Whitenack [Madison and Teaneck, N.J.: Fairleigh Dickinson University Press; Cranbury, N.J., and London: Associated University Presses, 1995]), sees the convent as "substitute mother-love," "an emotional safe haven in which the substitute female family is reconstituted" (109).

40. Enrique experiences a change of heart and becomes a monk, as do a couple of other male characters (Juan in the third *desengaño*, Ladislao in the ninth).

41. Elizabeth J. Ordóñez observes that in Zayas's works we find pairs of women entering the convent together, which underscores "the emergence of female bonding or matrilineal alternatives to patriarchal coding in text and social context" (8).

42. See, for example, the moral of Lisis's tale on p. 503 (*398*).

43. Poems in the *Desengaños* also associate Tantalus with jealousy and infidelity; see, for example, pp. 146, 316 (*61, 223*).

44. From the *Novelas* to the *Desengaños*, the male-dominated triangles have certainly taken a turn for the worse. In the *Novelas'* "Al fin se paga todo" [Just Deserts] the wife kills the brother of her husband who has had designs on her; in its "El jardín engañoso" [The Magic Garden] brother kills brother out of jealousy.

45. Sandra Foa states in her *Feminismo y forma narrativa: Estudio del tema y las técnicas de María de Zayas y Sotomayor* (Valencia: Ediciones Albatros, 1979): "The enormous success, during those years, of Spanish novelists in France, among them María de Zayas, leads us to suspect that Madame de Lafayette read Zayas" (93). She registers the similarities of the two authors in general terms: "Both have a very similar and negative view of the world, of love, and of marriage" (93). Foa ends on a cautionary note: "I do not want to overemphasize the resemblance between these two works. I merely wish to point out that the French work, written by a woman during a period of tensions and intrigues, is closer in tone and subject to María de Zayas's work than that of her Spanish contemporaries" (94). In the introduction to her edition of the *Desengaños*, citing Foa, Yllera also discusses the resemblance between the two authors: "Only one other seventeenth-century woman writer would express such profound disillusionment and a such great lack of confidence in love . . . : Mme de La Fayette in *La princesse de Clèves*" (47). Also see Yllera (84–85) for a list of seventeenth-century translations of Zayas's works into French.

46. While critics, as just noted, have considered the resemblance between the *Desengaños* and *LPDC* in general terms, I do not believe that anyone has brought out these specific points of contact. Another such point of contact is the exemplarity of Lisis revealed in the last words of the *Desengaños* ("no woman excels her"), which evokes the last words of *LPDC* ("Her life, which was quite short, left inimitable examples of virtue"). Of particular import is the fact that in the third *desengaño* Camila performs an *aveu* similar to that of the Princesse, an *aveu* that Lisis describes in terms that might well predict the situation in *LPDC*: "Furthermore, I can't imagine any woman in the world so foolish as to dare tell her husband that some gallant is making advances to her. Why, that would cause all kinds of problems, and the worst would be to arouse jealousy in a man previously free of it who could no longer live sure of his wife. The best thing about love is the sense of mutual trust and confidence" (*110*, 196). This and similar avowals are discussed by other characters on pp. 201 and 219 (*115, 132*) as well. One might therefore profitably examine the possibility that the *Desengaños*, and not (as

has been discredited) Mme de Villedieu's *Les désordres de l'amour*, suggested this key incident–whose literary provenance has given rise to so much discussion–to Mme de Lafayette.

47. See chap. 5 ("Feminist Thought and Society: *Honnêteté* and the *Salons*") of Ian MacLean's book for a discussion of the model of the "honnête femme" as developed in essays and literature of seventeenth-century France.

48. See Beasley's fascinating discussion of Coulommiers's history in her book (225–26). Beasley concludes that "Lafayette is evoking not only a place of solitude but also, and more importantly, a milieu with specific affinities to female historical initiative" and that "she makes it possible for the princess to be viewed as one of the heroic women who actually inhabited Coulommiers" (226).

49. Vigée makes a similar argument for the Princesse's internalization of Nemours in the *refus*, but views the action negatively.

50. The motivations of duty and *repos* are further reinforced in the last pages of the text when the narrator states: "Duty seemed to her a powerful reason for not marrying M. de Nemours, her peace of mind [*repos*] an insurmountable one" (*153*, 312).

51. Herrmann notes the "masculine" nature of the Princesse and the "feminine" nature of her husband: "If Madame de Clèves is a 'gentleman' [*honnête homme*], it may just as accurately be said that her husband is a 'lady' [*honnête femme*]. Each of these two beings transcends his or her sex, containing within themselves the virtues of the other" (38).

52. Laugaa presents representative samples from the three-hundred-year reception history of the novel, including substantial selections from Valincour (42–115). For a reading of Valincour's reactions to *LPDC*, see the section of Beasley's chap. 5 entitled, "Against Critical Norms: Lafayette's Rescripted Notion of Plausibility."

53. Haig also writes: "*Repos* is the very antithesis of commitment" (143).

54. The observation is Miller's (1988, 38), but its elaboration is mine.

55. De Jean maintains that Lafayette developed a "woman's language" for her heroine: "When dealing with the princess, readers must read between the lines: they must interpret (verbalize) the unsaid and even the unsayable, for the language of Lafayette's heroine is a language of lack, of silence, of repression, of gaps" (1984, 889). De Jean analyzes Valincour's critique of the elliptical style of *LPDC* on p. 890 of her article.

56. On Lafayette's rewriting of the historical personage of Nemours, see Allentuch (189–90) and especially Brody (112–14). In her chap. 5, Beasley also provides a trenchant discussion of Nemours's possibly unfaithful nature as read by the Princesse.

57. Unlike the King, who scoffed at the prophecy that he would die in a duel, both the Prince and the Princesse de Clèves operate within something of a "prophetic" mode, jumping to conclusions from uncertain evidence.

58. Kaps contends that *LPDC* gains from being read as a baroque text along these lines. To see the novel as baroque rather than classical (fixed, harmonious, orderly), she maintains, gives "a fuller, clearer picture of the world view which pervades the novel–where unity remains tentative, and where illusion, mutability, and paradox play dominant roles" (82).

59. Nancy K. Miller (1980, xi et passim) categorizes eighteenth-century French and English male-authored novels of women's development as euphoric (ending with the heroine's integration into society) or dysphoric (the heroine is not integrated into society and dies at the end). Obviously, in the texts I have considered, only the Princesse dies at the end; I use "dysphoric" for its opposition to "euphoric" and for the

manner in which it bears out Margaret L. King's statement that "when Renaissance women confronted the predicament in which women found themselves, their solution was not to change society, irreparably dominated by male concerns, but to escape it" (1991, 237).

Notes to Chapter Four: Auto-Machia

1. I will not, however, be considering all of Sor Juana's first-person poetry as self-representational. Specifically, I discount much of the love poetry examined in chap. 2, so ruled by courtly convention as to seriously undermine its self-representational nature. Moreover—except in the case of the poems of loving female friendship and the religious poems—the disjunction between the love theme of most of the poems and Sor Juana's status as a celibate nun, the lack of autobiographical details, and the multiplicity of postures that the poetic subjects assume, would (as noted in chap. 1) appear purposefully to attenuate the connection between the "I" of the writer and the "I" of the poems. This chapter will, nevertheless, examine the issues and texts of Sor Juana's love poetry that feed into the more manifestly self-representational works, noting at various points the significant continuity between the two genres.

2. On Sor Juana and Anne Bradstreet, see Owen Aldridge, "The Tenth Muse of America: Anne Bradstreet or Sor Juana Inés de la Cruz," in *Proceedings of the Xth Congress of the International Comparative Literature Association*, vol. 3, ed. Ana Balakian (New York: Garland, 1985), 177–88, and Nina M. Scott, "The Tenth Muse," *Américas* 30, no. 2 (1978): 13–20. Both contain many worthwhile observations but are largely introductory in nature.

3. Given the importance that, as we see later in the chapter, Bradstreet attaches to male figures, the fact that the poet perhaps changes voice after the death of her father acquires added significance. Stanford, however, identifies the change in Bradstreet's poetry with the death of her mother in 1643, with criticism she may have received in that year, and with the move from Ipswich to rural Andover. See the introduction to part 2, "The Andover Poems," in Stanford's book for more on the matter. I should also note that Bradstreet added to the second edition of her poetry, published in 1678: "The Author to Her Book," the elegies to her father and mother, "Contemplations," and "The Flesh and the Spirit." The elegies to Elizabeth, Anne, and Simon Bradstreet, which I discuss in the chapter, among several other poems, were included posthumously in the 1678 edition. Bradstreet's spiritual autobiography, "To My Dear Children," and "Upon the Burning of Our House," along with other personal writings found in her notebooks, were published for the first time in John Harvard Ellis's 1867 edition of all the extant works of Bradstreet. Except where noted, I cite from Jeanine Hensley's modernized edition, *The Works of Anne Bradstreet*, which contains all of the above works. On the editions of Bradstreet's poetry, see Elizabeth Wade White, "The Tenth Muse—A Tercentenary Appraisal of Anne Bradstreet," in *Critical Essays on Anne Bradstreet*, ed. Pattie Cowell and Ann Stanford (Boston: G. K. Hall, 1983).

4. Of the imperative to self-scrutiny Perry Miller observes that the "true saint, though under guidance of the spirit, applies himself the more intently, the more assiduously, to probing every recess of his being, to leaving no place unexplored in which sin might hide, to unmasking every disguise which nature puts on in its frantic effort to pretend holiness without actually surrendering its lusts" (56). Miller also comments that "if ever a theology tortured its votaries it was that taught by New England divines" (56).

5. Pettit, for example, states: "In this realm no other system of spirituality so concerned itself with problems of fear, doubt, and despair. None has so closely described the struggles of the interior life" (viii). See also Morgan (1963, 69–70); Martin (57).

6. I refer to Louis Althusser's formulation of subjectivity, that is, to his familiar notion that ideology interpellates individuals as subjects; I appeal particularly to Schweitzer's lucid explanation of this notion. "Every culture," she writes, "provides its members with 'organizing fictions' or 'ideologies' that define their relations to other people and the world around them, and that teach them the discourse and social codes upon which cultural meanings and a sense of self are based. This social and historical construction of selfhood is called *subjectivity*, the ongoing ideological process of recruiting individuals and transforming them into subjects who are shaped by, and maintain the set of values held by, the group or class in power" (1991, 7). In a religious context, redeemed subjectivity finds its definition in this significant, if seemingly confounding, statement by Althusser, in which the Subject=God: "*a subject through the Subject and subjected to the Subject*" ("Ideology and the State," in *Lenin and Philosophy and Other Essays* [New York: Monthly Review Press, 1971], 179; italics in original). In accordance with my larger argument we can say, with Peter Stallybrass, that if ideology interpellates individuals as subjects, here the subject is tentatively interpellated as an individual ("Shakespeare, the Individual, and the Text," in *Cultural Studies*, ed. Lawrence Grossberg, Cary Nelson, and Paula A. Triechler [New York and London: Routledge, 1992], 593). Let me also clarify that throughout the chapter, I subscribe to the by now fairly conventional distinctions between the terms *subjectivity, subjectivism,* and *subject position.* Subjectivity refers to the social or religious construction of the individual, as just defined; subjectivism refers to the individuality or interiority of the individual; subject position refers to the voices and stances a writer assumes in self-representation.

7. Walter Hughes notes in "'Meat Out of the Eater': Panic and Desire in American Puritan Poetry" (in *Engendering Men: The Question of Male Feminist Criticism,* ed. Joseph A. Boone and Michael Cadden [New York and London: Routledge, 1990]) that fear of self-erasure created in poet Edward Taylor a "poetics of panic": "He fears the volatility of desire and is at times repulsed by the prospect of its physical embodiment, but most of all he seems to fear that a union between himself and God will annihilate rather than elevate him" (118–19).

8. Kenneth R. Ball reads Bradstreet's letter as an archetypal statement of humility (30); Wendy Martin, in the third chapter of her book, discusses Bradstreet's personal writings in terms of preparationism and its emphasis on humility.

9. Shea writes: "The Religious experiences of Anne Bradstreet lack even the staple of Puritan autobiography–a description of the emergence of grace in its various signs and stages–and instead appears to substitute a kind of rudimentary apologetics" (116).

10. Stanford aptly notes that Bradstreet "relied on revelation through the scriptures and observation and experience of nature–i.e. faith and reason–to uphold her conclusions" to the theological doubts expressed in the letter (1974, 91).

11. I refer here, of course, to Borges's essay of the same title, "De la nadería de la personalidad," first published in *Inquisiciones* (Buenos Aires: Proa, 1925).

12. Cheryl Walker sums up the critical debate on Bradstreet's rebelliousness on p. 14 of her book, citing the positions of Stanford, Martin, and Watts. Walker concludes, as do I, that "Bradstreet's doubts are very much in keeping with those expressed in perfectly conventional Puritan self-examinations" (14).

13. More words have been spent on this issue than I can possibly summarize here.

I refer the reader to Raymond F. Dolle's *Anne Bradstreet: A Reference Guide* (Boston: G. K. Hall, 1990) for an amply annotated bibliography of critical treatments of Bradstreet.

14. Patricia Caldwell quotes Dickinson's title in the context of her discussion of the third elegy. Caldwell eloquently states: "Brevity and compression are the expressive strategy here, and the flickering, halting rhythm, the absence of an 'I,' and the silent spaces in the poem all suggest a speaker withdrawn or withdrawing, not unlike Emily Dickinson's speaker in 'After great pain, a formal feeling comes'" (23).

15. Randall R. Mawer also discusses the relationship between the first and second stanzas (212), the ambiguity of the last line of the first stanza (212), and the contrast in the third stanza between nature's and God's ways (213).

16. See Nina M. Scott's 1988 article (429–30) for a discussion of the authenticity of the "Autodefensa." I should note that it is not known whether the letter was sent. I cite the "Autodefensa" from the English translation found in the appendix to Paz's book.

17. Nina M. Scott (1988, 431) insightfully demonstrates that an important aspect of Sor Juana's self-defense in the "Autodefensa" involves the issue of the public versus the private sphere. While acknowledging that public study is considered unseemly for women, Sor Juana makes it clear that she has, inoffensively, performed her studies in private. Josefina Ludmer also addresses the private/public split in her essay on the "Respuesta," "Tricks of the Weak," claiming the private as the woman's sphere. I return to the matter of the public versus the private as arenas for women's education and agency in chap. 5.

18. Let me make it quite clear that I am not arguing for a causal relationship between the "Autodefensa" or the events to which it refers and all of Sor Juana's self-representations. Such a connection may exist, but the lack of dates for so many of Sor Juana's poems makes it impossible to determine exactly when and how the characteristic profile of her self-representational persona emerged.

19. The foregoing discussion of *Los empeños de una casa* and the "Autodefensa" adds to my previous analysis of the play in "*Mores geometricae*: The 'Womanscript' in the Theater of Sor Juana Inés de la Cruz" (1991). There I contend that in the comedia Sor Juana creates angel (Leonor) and monster (Ana) female protagonists who are overtly polarized but covertly equated as the two halves of a divided self. In an exemplary enactment of her competing self-representations, Sor Juana "signs" Leonor by writing the details of her own life into the character, but at the same time endows Ana with the traits of an assertive, prideful, creative woman unmistakably akin to those of the author. Given the argument of the present chapter, I would suggest the possibility that in *Los empeños* Sor Juana performs an additional act of doubling and dividing her "I." She may be seen to have relegated the dark, nonservile, and in all likelihood more authentic persona of the "Autodefensa" to the figure of the antiheroine–of Ana. In the public self-defense that is *Los empeños de una casa*, the spectral presence of Sor Juana's assertive and perhaps more true "I" hovers over the constructed and exculpatory figure of Leonor.

20. Bénassy-Berling notes that Sor Juana refers more infrequently than one might expect to Saint Teresa and also suggests that, in accordance with the image of Teresa promoted in New Spain, the Mexican nun may have known her more as a reformer than as a mystic (114–15, 224). While the degree to which Sor Juana herself sympathized with Teresa cannot be determined, that she considered her forebear's discourse capable of provoking sympathy in the reader might well explain the Mexican nun's

recourse to Teresian topics and locutions.

21. I refer to Gérard Genette's broad notion of the "architexte" as put forth in his *Introduction à l'architexte* (Paris: Seuil, 1979), 87–88.

22. Alison Weber made this statement with regard to Teresa in a paper read at an Northeastern Modern Languages Association conference on April 4, 1987, entitled "St. Augustine and St. Teresa: Plotting a Confession." In chap. 9 of her *Vida*, Teresa herself associates her conversion with the reading of Augustine's *Confessions*.

23. I recognize the enormity of this matter: it permeates the entire text and raises the issue of Saint Teresa's idiosyncratic and affective style. I do not purport to do it justice but only to lay the bases for contrast of Teresa with Saint Augustine and Sor Juana. On Teresa's style see, for example, Víctor García de la Concha, *El arte literario de Santa Teresa* (Barcelona: Ariel, 1978).

24. On Teresa's need to defend herself, see, for example, Weber's discussion of the Carmelite nun's precarious position as a woman and as an ecstatic in chap. 1 of her book.

25. As I explain in the third section of the present chapter, drawing on Curtius, humility topics also derive in part from devotional formulae and thus pertain to religious rhetoric.

26. Paz relates "Finjamos" to Lope's "A mis soledades voy," saying: "The same convention rules both poems: a knowledge that is immemorial, born of experience and not of books, expressed in fluid and sententious quatrains characterized by a certain artlessness" (298). As moral poems the two texts may present certain similarities, but as acts of self-representation they diverge notably. For one thing, the speaker of Lope's poem would appear to find his thoughts good company ("A mis soledades voy, / de mis soledades vengo, / porque para andar conmigo / me bastan mis pensamientos," To my solitudes I go, from my solitudes I come, for as company my thoughts alone suffice), where the speaker of Sor Juana's poem emphatically and significantly does not. For another, Lope's speaker eschews self-analysis, using interiority as a platform for pronouncements of a social and philosophical nature. Lope's poem revolves more around the present state of Spain than the state of the self.

27. Of "Finjamos" Alan S. Trueblood notes that the "very cleverness" of the poem, "with its depreciation of learning and extolling of pious ignorance, strikes one as the dutiful recitation of a lesson memorized. The poem opened the 1689 edition; one wonders if it was not placed first disingenuously, for purposes of edification" (14).

28. Pfandl's methodology in *Sor Juana Inés de la Cruz: La Décima Musa de México*, such as it is, makes his claims that Sor Juana's melancholy derives from a neurotic and narcissistic tendency to brood, and from a desire to be a man all too easy to deflate. The German author displays no knowledge of the literary conventions that might bear on her self-representations. Instead, as is well known, he construes the texts as transparent and unmediated depictions of her psychology, which he proceeds to explain in a vulgar, quasi-psychoanalytic manner.

29. The civil war of self-representations to which I refer may also correspond in part to the *semi*-private nature of the "Respuesta," addressed to Sor Filotea but tacitly intended for circulation. Where Sor Juana asserts herself in the private "Autodefensa" and negates herself in Leonor's speech and her poems for publication, in this semi-private document she does both.

30. Sor Juana refers to the Spanish nun no less than three times in the "Respuesta." One can easily read these mentions as signals of a strategic alliance with Teresa's *Vida*.

31. In the reprimand to Sor Juana attached to the published *Carta Atenagórica*, Sor

Filotea (Manuel Fernández de Santa Cruz, bishop of Puebla) writes: "My judgment is not so stern a censor as to disapprove of verse, an endowment for which you have found yourself so highly acclaimed; after all, Saint Teresa, Saint Gregory of Nazianzus, and other saints have sanctified this skill by their example. But I could wish that, as you imitate them in meter, you might do so as well in choice of subject" (*200*, 4.695).

32. As does Teresa (see Weber, 51), Sor Juana here makes clever use of the technique of prolepsis, that is, confessing something one can afford to concede in order not to concede another more vital point. The full prolepsistic statement from the "Respuesta" reads: "Though I readily confess that I am base and vile, I am not aware that anyone has seen an unseemly ditty by me" (*239*, 470).

33. I refer here to Luce Irigaray's notion of mimicry in *This Sex Which Is Not One*: "One must assume the feminine role deliberately. Which means already to convert a form of subordination into an affirmation, and thus to begin to thwart it." And "to play with mimesis is thus, for a woman, to try to recover the place of her exploitation by discourse, without allowing herself to be simply reduced to it" (176). According to this construct, Saint Teresa's "rhetoric of femininity" could also be considered mimicry, Sor Juana's a baroque and personal "stylization" (in Bakhtinian terms) of Teresa's "language"–and perhaps all use of humility topics by women authors have something of mimicry to them. For a more general discussion of Sor Juana's mimicry, see Franco (29–30).

34. In my article entitled "Narciso *desdoblado*: Narcissistic Stratagems in *El Divino Narciso* and the *Respuesta a Sor Filotea de la Cruz*" (*Bulletin of Hispanic Studies* 64 (1987): 111–17), I made a very similar argument regarding the manner in which the "I" of the "Respuesta" is emptied of self and filled with the desire for knowledge. Obviously, I still stand by that argument, but can now see more clearly its roots in Saint Teresa and Saint Augustine. I have discussed the connection with Teresa in the present chapter; the kinship between Sor Juana and Saint Augustine, with his ever-inquisitive mind and unquenchable thirst for knowledge, is also worthy of examination. Statements such as the following by Augustine–"My mind is on fire to solve this very intricate enigma. Do not shut the door, Lord my God, Good Father, through Christ I beg you, do not shut the door on my longing to understand these things which are both familiar and obscure" (236)–echo in the passion for knowledge Sor Juana expresses in the "Respuesta." I believe that the genuine intellectual curiosity that motivated the patristic origins of Scholasticism explains the personal attraction it held for Sor Juana.

35. Sor Juana's final penitential documents (esp. documents #409, #410, #411, #413 in vol. 4), with their formulaic but now unmitigated self-nihilations–such as "The most unworthy and thankless creature of all those that your Omnipotence has reared" (#410) and "I, the worst [woman] in the world" (#413)–at once represent the abdication of this subject position and its confirmation. On the one hand, they deny her selfhood any substance; on the other, they lay bare the discursive foundations of her subjectivity in religious rhetoric and thus contain both the origins and the terminus of her self-representations.

36. Caldwell notes that since Thomas Dudley was both poet and her father, Bradstreet "conflates precursor and muse into a 'doubly potent' masculine figure" (8). The poet herself calls him "father, guide, instructor too, / To whom I ought whatever I could do" ("To the Memory of My Dear and Ever Honoured Father," 201). When we also take into consideration Dudley's powerful political position and authority, we can see why Bradstreet's conceivable anxieties of authorship would crystallize around him and motivate not only this, but yet another exceedingly humble poem to her father

("To Her Father with Some Verses," 231).

37. In this prologue, which may also have inspired Sor Juana's twisted use of the imagery of the book as child that I discuss later in the chapter, Cervantes terms himself not the father but the stepfather of his character, Don Quijote. As does Sor Juana in her "Prólogo," he refuses to ask the reader to pardon his stepson's flaws. Yet Cervantes has reasons other than humility for reviling his creation. What more, he asks, could his wit cultivate "but the story of a dry, shriveled, and capricious child, full of a variety of thoughts never imagined by anyone else" (Porqueras Mayo, 72), since his so-called child was born in jail with him?

38. For bibliography on women and the Puritans, see n. 34 to the introduction.

39. How interesting that we hear in Woodbridge's words echoes of Sor Juana's own self-domestication, as expressed, for example, in the "Prólogo's" description of her works as written "en el corto espacio / que ferian al ocio las / precisiones de mi esta-do" [in the short space allowed to idleness by the demands of my status].

40. Jean Franco's stimulating discussion of Sor Juana's celebrity (23–24) supports the contention that the nun served as a symbol of the New World. Franco observes that "both religious and secular authorities saw political advantage in her celebrity" (23) either as a New World Saint Teresa in the eyes of the church or as a "secular symbol . . . by patrons who were anxious to exhibit the spiritual wealth of the New World" (24).

41. Amanda Porterfield comments that Bradstreet's feelings of indebtedness to her father, "which dominated her elegy to him, replicate the feelings of indebtedness to God that often dominated Puritan worship of God" (*Female Piety in Puritan New England* [New York: Oxford University Press, 1992], 174). Bradstreet's extolling of her father as God the Father exemplifies the fluid exchange between religious and earthly relationships upon which, according to Porterfield, Puritan humanism and its rhetoric were based. I add that on an even larger scale, it reflects the rigid social hierarchies of the Puritan world, which drew their sustenance—and unquestioning subordination of women—from the equation of man (*him*self, not humankind) with God.

42. Elizabeth Wade White (and others following her) has noted, however, that the Greeks honored thyme as an emblem of vitality and courage and that parsley was used in garlands paying tribute to the virtuous dead (241).

43. Several feminist-oriented critics have made concerted attempts to explain away Bradstreet's humility. Jane Donahue Eberwein, in her "'No Rhet'ric We Expect': Argumentation in Bradstreet's 'The Prologue'" (in *Critical Essays*, ed. Cowell and Stanford), reads the poem as "consistently ironic" (218). Eileen Margerum argues in "Anne Bradstreet's Public Poetry and the Tradition of Humility" (*Early American Literature* 18, no. 2 [1982]: 152–60) that the poet's apologies in several works "reveal her self-assurance rather than self-doubt" (153). Timothy Street refocuses the poet's figurations of her broken Muse into "empowering strategies that authorize Bradstreet to use a discourse that uses 'the feminine' only as an object" ("Gender, Genre, and Subjectivity in Anne Bradstreet's Early Elegies," *Early American Literature* 23, no. 2 [1988]: 153). Paula Kopacz, in "'To Finish What's Begun': Anne Bradstreet's Last Words" (*Early American Literature* 23, no. 2 [1988]: 175–87), summarizes the critical reception of Bradstreet's works and places the above-cited attempts in perspective. She observes that "it was predictable that early feminist critics would find Bradstreet rebelling both openly and covertly against her male-dominated culture" (176) and comments that such critics either deconstruct or understand ironically as expressions of rebellion the poet's use of conventions (177). I add that other more recent critical inquiries, such as Caldwell's and Schweitzer's (whose 1988 article takes direct issue

with Margerum's), rather than trying to snuff out several of the possible dimensions of Bradstreet's humility, have emphasized the poet's marginality and anxiety of authorship. My readings find theirs more well rounded and convincing.

44. I refer the reader to Schweitzer's 1988 article, "Anne Bradstreet Wrestles with the Renaissance," for a fuller reading of the poem along these very lines.

45. Bradstreet's Muse makes a final appearance in "Contemplations," where she declares herself inadequate to the task of praising her Creator. As the speaker lifts her "humble eyes" to the skies, her Muse is "mazed," and the speaker laments her "imbecility." Even the grasshoppers and crickets can raise their voices to their Maker; she, however, finds herself "mute." The correlation between Bradstreet's former Muse, unable to praise male figures, and that of "Contemplations," rendered mute before the Creator, again suggests that the humility and the self-abasement through hyperbolic praise of another of the early poems derive from religious discourse.

46. Another fascinating and germane case to explore along these lines of instability is the *Memoirs* of Margaret Lucas Cavendish, Duchess of Newcastle, considered a true precursor of modern autobiography for their penetrating self-analyses. I examine this and other texts by Cavendish, as well as her unstable gender attitudes, in chap. 5.

47. Various critics have commented on the strain of violence in Bradstreet's Quaternions and her equation of men with violence. Josephine Piercy believes that Bradstreet's early poetry "is the sublimation of the spirit of the rebellious woman who writes it during the period of her greatest trial" (*Anne Bradstreet* [New York: Twayne, 1965], 26). White states that there "is not a sin of the flesh or spirit that is not described, often with revolting detail, in her account of the ambitions, conquests, cruelties, and licentious self-indulgences of the monarchs of antiquity" (237). Robert D. Arner, in "The Structure of Anne Bradstreet's *Tenth Muse*" (in *Discoveries and Considerations: Essays on Early American Literature and Aesthetics*, ed. Calvin Israel [Albany: State University of New York Press, 1976]), notes that "The Four Monarchies" "functions to balance the easy surrender to masculine virtues in the first section, for insofar as it is mostly an extended criticism of kings and political institutions men have invented, it suggests a questioning of the political acumen and simple human wisdom of a succession of male potentates" (48). See also Paula Kopacz, "'Men can doe best, and Women know it well': Anne Bradstreet and Feminist Aesthetics" (*Kentucky Philological Review* 2 [1987]: 26).

48. Schweitzer (1988) matches Bradstreet's apocalyptic ending with an interesting, if also somewhat apocalyptic, reading of the poem; see pp. 306–7.

Notes to Chapter Five: The New Prometheus

1. Harss calls the *PS* "personal" and "confessional" in the deeper sense of a "spiritual autobiography" (21). He also calls it a "penitential poem: a humbling of pride in the constant admission of ignorance, and a prudent retreat at each point where speculation seems to be venturing too far" (97).

2. Here, and in the penultimate section of the chapter, I make a case for the gendered, feminine identity of the Soul. However, working with Sor Juana's own purposeful ambiguity, I will at different points in the chapter consider the Soul and her quest as generic, as gendered, and as both.

3. The theme of metamorphosis and the similarities between Ovid's portrayal of the various figures and that of Sor Juana make his poem the principal source for this section of the *PS*. On the other hand, that the Spanish literature of the times often used the owl as a code word for prostitutes or witches adds to the resonance and magni-

tude of Nyctimene's transgression.

4. I owe this observation to Sabat-Rivers (1991, 48). Her treatment of the opening figures of the *PS* and those of Harss, Franco, and Electa Arenal ("Where Woman Is Creator of the Wor(l)d" in my edited collection, *Feminist Perspectives on Sor Juana Inés de la Cruz*) are crucial to our full understanding of the overture. Franco, in fact, sees the negative figures of the overture as representing "a poetics based on transgression of the sacred," which will later be reversed in the "ethical humanist poetics" represented by Arethusa (34).

5. I refer to Eco's lines from scene 10: ". . . también alguna vez Narciso / enmudecer me hizo, / porque Su Sér Divino publicaba, / y mi voz reprendiéndome atajaba" (3.64) [once Narcissus also struck me mute because I spoke of his Divine Being, and he cut off my voice in punishment]. Both Eco and the weaving, storytelling Minyades thus fall into the lineage of Philomela—whose tongue was cut out so that she could not divulge Tereus's crime but who wove her story into a tapestry.

6. On Narciso and Eco as rhetorical figures, see my article, "Narciso *desdoblado*: Narcissistic Stratagems in *El Divino Narciso* and the *Respuesta a Sor Filotea de la Cruz*," *Bulletin of Hispanic Studies* 64, no. 2 (April 1978): 111–17.

7. On the importance of signature for women's writing see Miller, *Subject to Change*, and De Jean, *Tender Geographies*.

8. I draw my information on medieval women's education largely from King (1991), Kristeller, Sonnet, Stock, Lerner, and particularly from Ferrante.

9. Erasmus was a guest in the household of Sir Thomas More in 1509. There, as Erasmus's writings attest, he was impressed by the ideas on education More carried out in his own family. Vives, strongly influenced by Erasmus, arrived in 1523 in England, where he taught Mary Tudor, daughter of King Henry VIII and Queen Catherine of Aragon. He dedicated his work on the education of Christian women to the queen and clearly had her daughter's education in mind when writing it.

10. I draw my information on Renaissance learned women largely from Bomli, King (1980; 1991), Jordan, Lerner, McKendrick, Sonnet, and Stock. King (1991) provides extensive bibliography on the subject.

11. I draw my information on Protestant Reformation education largely from Hill's introduction to Astell, Barbour's introduction to Makin, King (1981), Lerner, Hilda Smith, Sonnet, Stock. See Davis (1975, chap. 3, "The City and Religious Change") for a useful discussion of the less than apparent drawbacks of the Protestant Reformation for women in France.

12. Bridget Hill, in her introduction to Astell, states: "Certainly from the 1530s onward there are cases of Protestants lamenting the passing of nunneries as useful places of education for women" (27). Hill discusses Thomas Becon, John Aubrey, Thomas Fuller, and Richard Allestree (27–28) as, among others, having made comments to this effect.

13. I draw my information on women's education in the seventeenth century from the sources cited with regard to the Reformation; from Gonzalbo Aizpuru, Henderson and McManus, Labalme, Maclean, McKendrick, Maravall (*Picaresca*), Pfandl (1929), and Vigil; from the seventeenth-century essayists themselves.

14. Among the many who have noted the seventeenth-century decline in the education of upper-class women in similar terms, King makes the following germane pronouncement: "The tradition of female humanism that began in the generation after Petrarch with the Paduan widow Maddalena Scovegni had died everywhere in Europe by the seventeenth century. Its place was taken by the study of dancing, drawing, and

needlework, and perhaps French and Italian. A few women were known for their remarkable learning in the difficult subjects that made up the humanist and more advanced curricula of science, philosophy and theology: Anna Maria van Schurman in the Netherlands and Sor Juana Inés de la Cruz in Mexico in New Spain" (1991, 211).

15. The sorry state of affairs also prompted the lines by Anne Finch, countess of Winchilsea (1661–1720), that Virginia Woolf made famous in *A Room of One's Own*: "How we are fallen! fallen by mistaken rules / And Education's more than Nature's fools; / Debarred from all improvements of the mind, / And to be dull, expected and designed"; and "They tell us we mistake our sex and way; / Good breeding, fashion, dancing, dressing, play, / Are the accomplishments we shou'd desire; / To write, or read, or think, or to enquire, / Would cloud our beauty, and exhaust our time, / And interrupt the conquests of our prime, / Whilst the dull manage of a servile house / Is held by some our utmost art and use" (quoted by Woolf on p. 62; a more extensive selection of Finch's works can be found in *By a Woman Writt: Literature From Six Centuries By and About Women*, ed. Joan Goulianos [Indianapolis and New York: Bobbs-Merrill, 1973], 71–85).

16. Hilda Smith writes: "These early feminists developed a central tenet that later women would have to rediscover to create an ideology to attack female subordination. In some ways their demands were limited, and they gave too much attention to education and too little to political or economic issues, but the questions they emphasized were the most relevant and practical for themselves and for their age" (207). The abuses of marriage, I should note, also came increasingly under attack, as can be seen in Cavendish's *The Convent of Pleasure* and Astell's *Reflections Upon Marriage*.

17. Several critics have described, in their examinations of one or the other text, certain of the interrelations between the four authors. As far as I know, however, no one has discussed the collective picture in detail or its implications.

18. The line in Astell to which I specifically refer concerns the fact that both Makin and Astell (versus Schurman) understand the learning of languages as a means rather than an end for young women. Makin gives her opinion that "in the Educating of Gentlewomen, greater care ought to be had to know things, than to get words" (34); Astell asserts, "It is not intended that she should spend her hours in learning *words* but *things*, and therefore no more Languages than are necessary to acquaint her with useful Authors" (152–53; italics in original).

19. Anglo-Saxon scholar Elizabeth Elstob, Daniel Defoe, and George Wheler all acknowledge their debt to Astell's "Proposal" (see Hill, 29; Hilda Smith, 115, 137).

20. Other advances from the humanist position found in Makin and Astell derive at least in part from the fact that Makin is advertising her own school and Astell seeking support for hers. Thus, both essayists support an education *outside* the home, one that might conceivably extend to middle- as well as upper-class women who can pay tuition. As noted in chap. 3, Astell also makes particular provision for unmarried women, whom her school would prepare for a career in the outside world.

21. As the earlier mentions of William Wotten and Clement Barksdale indicate, both men and women were writing in similar terms about women's education in the seventeenth century; for reasons of space and pertinence I have limited myself here to women essayists and the male writers directly related to them. Undoubtedly, the existence of a favorable male discourse on the subject would have prompted, facilitated, and legitimated the efforts of women writers.

22. One cannot ignore the strong possibility that Poullain's radical treatise owes more to his love of logic than to his love of women. Following on the medieval tradi-

tion of defending women as an exercise in logic, and in the footsteps of humanist Henrich Cornelius Agrippa von Nettesheim (whose *A Treatise of the Nobilitie and excellencye of woman kynde* bears notable resemblances to Poullain's), Poullain may well be rising to the purely intellectual challenge of exerting Cartesian logic on this most entrenched subject. Nevertheless, as was the case with other possibly "sham" feminist discourses, Poullain's was read and it impacted the contemporary scene (Lougee, 18). For an account of Agrippa along lines perhaps pertinent to Poullain, see Woodbridge, chap. 2 ("The Early Tudor Controversy").

23. As Electa Arenal and Amanda Powell note in their bilingual edition of the "Respuesta," *The Answer/La Respuesta* (New York: Feminist Press, 1994), "The *Answer* is a point-by-point retort to the bishop of Puebla, yet few have considered the *Answer* in this light. Much of what Sor Juana says and how she says it was determined by her reaction to his letter" (27). This, and Sor Juana's recourse to sixteenth-century tracts, makes particular sense given the fact that Lavrin notes, "Not a single work on feminine education was printed in colonial Mexico" (25).

24. Given the similarities in their positions, it is hardly inconceivable that here and elsewhere in her discussions of women's education Sor Juana has Vives in mind. In addition to what we have already seen of Vives's views, he recommends specifically that girls be taught by other females, preferably by one that is "aged, of pure life, held in high regard, calm of temperament, and very skilled in doctrine" (26).

25. Education at the local "Amiga" schools for girls, such as that attended by Sor Juana, usually ended for girls at age ten (Gonzalbo Aizpuru, 339). The first public and free "Amiga" school was founded in Mexico only in 1755 by the nuns of the Compañía de María, who employed in the education of females the curriculum that the Jesuits had long employed with males (Gonzalbo Aizpuru, 325–26).

26. Rosa Perelmuter summarizes this debate in her *Noche intelectual: La oscuridad idiomática en el* Primero sueño (Mexico: UNAM, 1982), 10–11.

27. For an important analysis of Sor Juana's treatment of Phaethon and Icarus, see Sabat-Rivers (1976, 86–96, 145–47).

28. In her suggestive discussion of Arethusa as emblematizing an ethical humanist poetics as over/against the transgressive poetics of the overture, Franco says that Arethusa "introduces a feminine form of creative redemption" (36).

29. On the absence or refiguring of Christian iconology in the *PS*, see Harss (23, 96), Paz (373), and Sabat-Rivers (1991, 150).

30. In the *Neptuno*, Sor Juana notes that classical authors have variously named Isis and that one writer has identified her with Venus, among others (4.365). Sor Juana's revisionary genealogy of Isis, in effect, renders all of the female mythological personages goddesses of wisdom!

31. Alliteration of A's predominates in the *PS*, but often alternates with or appears in conjunction with an alliteration of E's. From examples such as the one given in the body of my text I deduce that where the A's generally betoken positive ascencional daring, the E's can sound a cautionary or negative note (e.g., "y entre ellos, la engañosa encantadora / Alcione . . . ," and among them, the deceiving enchantress Halcyon [ll. 93–94]).

32. Interestingly enough, Bell states that some accounts make Aurora the mother of Phaethon by Aries and that in works of art Aurora (like Phaethon) most often appears winged or in a chariot (182).

33. Hence the title of Kathleen Jones's biography of Cavendish, *A Glorious Fame*. On Cavendish and fame, also see Jean Gagen, "Honor and Fame in the Works of the

Duchess of Newcastle," *Studies in Philology* 56 (1959): 519–38. Gagen maintains that "Margaret Cavendish alone of all the women writers of her day espoused writing as a career with the avowed intent of winning fame in accordance with the ideals of Renaissance humanism" (520).

34. Cavendish's fourteen published works included plays, poetry, fantasies, biography, autobiography, letters, "orations," and works on experimental and physical science (see Hilda Smith, 76). I will be focusing my discussion on two of her works in particular for the diversity of themes that they present and for their pertinence to the works of Sor Juana: her first work, *Poems and Fancies* (1653; I quote from a facsimile edition of the original), and *The Description of a New World Called the Blazing World* (1666; I quote from a modernized edition). I will also quote several times from the Duchess's autobiography, her *Memoirs* (1667), published in a modern edition together with *The Life of the (1st) Duke of Newcastle* and under that title.

35. I cannot refrain from making the unliterary observation that Cavendish's writings suggest her to have been what psychoanalysis considers a narcissist: a person with an unformed, unstable, unbounded picture of himself or herself, always in search of an identity. Todd states, "The Duchess seems in search of a sign for herself" (61). This would help us understand her contradictory self-images and her hypersensitivity to others' images of her.

36. In a passage of her *Memoirs*, Cavendish confesses that she does not speak much "because I am addicted to contemplation," yet admits that "when I am writing, sad and faind stories, or serious humours or melancholy passions, I am forced many times to express them with the tongue before I can write them with the pen" (205). On melancholy as a construct pertaining exclusively to men, see Juliana Schiesari, *The Gendering of Melancholia* (Ithaca and London: Cornell University Press, 1992), and the bibliography she presents on p. 4.

37. I draw my information here principally from the introduction by Nina Rattner Gelbart to the modern English translation of Fontenelle's work, *Conversations on the Plurality of Worlds*, from which I cite. I should note that Fontenelle's was only one of several such works packaging abstruse subjects for women and that Aphra Behn, in the preface to her translation, found it condescending to women (*A Discovery of New Worlds* [London: William Canning, 1688]).

38. On the hidden agenda of Cavendish's attraction to science see Grant (192), Jones (118), and Todd (66).

39. No doubt two current trends of the times, reason and metaphysical "wit" or "fancy," attract Cavendish and short-circuit in her works. In one section of *P&F*, Cavendish engages in an extravagant "similizing" that she justifies along contemporary poetic lines, saying, "So I intreat those that cannot find out the Conceit of my Fancies, to ask a Poet where the Conceit lies, before they Censure; and not to accuse my Book for Non-sense" (122). The heady dose of wit in her works undermines their claims to science but demonstrates Cavendish's propensity for incongruous hybrids and her desire to make an unforgettable mark on the various discourses of the times.

40. Grant (115 et passim), Gagen (529), Lilley (1992, 127–28), Sarasohn (306), all discuss aspects of Cavendish's theories of nature.

41. Lilley goes so far as to claim that Cavendish, aspiring to nature rather than culture, purposely misspelled and wrote ungrammatically. In proof, Lilley (*BW*, xxxiii) invokes lines from the second book of *The World's Olio* (1655) precisely to that effect but too prolix to quote here. At the very least, these lines establish Cavendish's awareness of her deviation from the norm; at most, they constitute yet another of the

author's self-justifying theories.

42. During the seventeenth century a "cabbala" (or Kabbala) could refer to any particularly enlightening philosophy (Sarasohn, 307).

43. I treat Cavendish's obsession with creating new utopian worlds in gender terms but am cognizant of the fact that it also conceivably responds to the political circumstances in the war-torn England of her times. Two poems from *P&F*, "Of an Island" and "The Ruine of the Island," in particular bring out Cavendish's political motivation; *BW* can be seen as defending absolute monarchy as well as the absolute Empress.

44. Descriptions in "Assaulted and Pursued Chastity" of cannibalism, sacrifices of human beings whose hearts are then offered to the king, a sun god and multitude of other gods, the natives' astonishment at the visitors' beards, and so on clearly recall the conquerers' accounts of Aztec Mexico. That the imperial city of the Blazing World "appeared in form like several islands; for rivers did run betwixt every street" (131) carries the Mexican influence into Cavendish's novel.

45. Almost needless to say, even the allegedly "real" Duchess who writes the preface to *BW* is a textual persona, a literary creation.

46. McGuire states that in her nonfiction Cavendish "repeatedly affirmed traditional ideas about women's inherent limitations; yet in her fictional works she created escapist visions of heroic female scholars and warriors" (193).

47. Hilda Smith makes the important point that Cavendish, like other women, was reinventing the wheel in that she came to her positions on gender on her own, "with little guidance from either her contemporaries or past writings" (13). Critics have tried to explain Cavendish's inconsistencies (especially in terms of Cavendish's monarchist platform), to explain them away, or to systematize them. Some, as would I, simply let them stand: Todd states that "any summary of the Duchess's thoughts on women is a succession of 'yets'" (65); McGuire asserts that Cavendish is "more interested in exploring all facets of an idea than in formulating manifestos" (193). In addition to the discussions of the subject in Gagen, Lilley (*BW*), McGuire, Sarasohn, Smith, Todd, Woolf, and Meyer, I refer the reader to Catherine Gallagher's controversial article, "Embracing the Absolute: The Politics of the Female Subject in Seventeenth-Century England," *Genders* 1 (1988): 24–39.

48. McGuire has the following to say about Cavendish's unipersonal feminism: "A recognizable pattern does emerge from her thoughts on women, a pattern which can be characterized as a tension between her conviction that women are inferior beings incapable of significant achievement and her fierce personal desire to achieve in ways that transcended the feminine properties of her day" (193).

49. Of course, Christine de Pizan had several centuries earlier written her less personal but still utopian feminist *Book of the City of Ladies*.

50. Du Bartas exercised a certain influence on Cavendish (Grant, 113) as well as on Bradstreet.

51. Of the lack of revelation in the *PS*, Paz says: "In Sor Juana's poem not only is there no demiurge, there is no revelation. *First Dream* is the first example of an attitude–the solitary soul confronting the universe–that later, beginning with romanticism, would be the spiritual axis of Western poetry" (367). Manuel Durán (109) specifically notes the difference between Dante's and Cicero's pilgrims and the failure of the Soul in the *PS* but, like Paz, fails to make any connection with gender. With regard to gender, the possibility also arises that María de Agreda's *La mística ciudad de Dios* served Sor Juana as a model for the *PS* as it did for the "Ejercicios devotos." In both Agreda's and Sor Juana's texts, as I observed in the introduction, God reveals to the Virgin Mary the mysteries of the universe

as a prelude to the Incarnation of the Word. While not closing off that possible influence, I would note that the secular, mortal questing Soul of the *PS* bears a greater resemblance to Theodidactus than to the Mary (who, although she is a woman, is one who must perforce receive revelation) of either text. I would also note that, perhaps expectedly, Cavendish wrote a dream poem of the "Theodidactus" sort in which her first-person speaker *does* receive divine revelation–a vision of the Divinity and of the whole cosmos. See "The Motion of Thoughts" in *P&F*, 40–41.

52. For Pfandl's extensive remarks on Sor Juana's autodidacticism, see the section entitled "El afán de cavilar" (112–51) in *Sor Juana Inés de la Cruz: La Décima Musa de México*. There, among other things, Pfandl associates her intellectual bent with a psychoneurotic personality and repressed sexuality.

53. On the state of Mexican universities at the time, see, among others: Bénassy-Berling (part 1, chap. 3), León (chap. 2), López Cámara, Leonard (*Baroque Times in Old Mexico*).

54. One could also include the ill-fated *Carta Atenagórica* in this list of hyperscholarly works and group it with the *Neptuno alegórico* as another attempt to show her extensive erudition around a single subject. Obviously, when Sor Juana's attempts to storm the City of Knowledge also infringed on the City of God, the most dire consequences ensued.

55. Paz maintains (156–57), supporting his contention with pointed proof, that although Sor Juana cites many sources she in fact draws most of her information from a single secondhand source that she fails to cite, Baltasar de Vitoria's *Teatro de los dioses de la gentilidad*. Sor Juana's reliance on manuals and encyclopedic secondhand sources is the downside of her autodidacticism, product of the unavailability of primary sources and her lack of knowledge of Greek or Hebrew. The nun's alleged plagiarism of Vitoria in the *Neptuno alegórico* is particularly telling of the autodidact's awareness of her condition. It speaks to Sor Juana's desire, no matter what, to display her (perhaps insufficient) erudition; in view of Paz's contentions, it can be said that the *Neptuno* is the place where her autodidacticism and her will to signature come into conflict and clash.

56. It is not by chance or even by my critical design that the *PS* meshes so well with Serres's notion of the encyclopedia. Serres has in mind, as one of his encyclopedic models, Lucretius's syncretic scientific poem, *De Rerum Naturum*–a work that Georgina Sabat-Rivers (1976, 16) has identified as a possible source for the *PS*. Moreover, as his emphasis on Hermes (Trismegistus) reveals, Serres can be considered a latter-day hermetic syncretist.

57. On Sor Juana and syncretic traditions see in particular Paz, Harss, Durán, and Elías Trabulse, *El Hermetismo y Sor Juana Inés de la Cruz* (Mexico: Litografía Regina de los Angeles, 1980).

58. On Sigüenza y Góngora's syncretism and the influences on his thinking, see López Cámara and D. A. Brading, *The First America: The Spanish Monarchy, Creole Patriots, and the Liberal State 1492–1867* (Cambridge, Eng.: Cambridge University Press, 1991), chap. 17.

59. On the deictics of the *PS*, see Rosa Perelmuter, "La situación enunciativa del *Primero sueño*," *Revista Canadiense de Estudios Hispánicos* 11 (1986): 185–91.

60. Sor Juana here reinflects but does not entirely contravene the Scholastic world picture. As Trueblood notes, the first productive cause is God, the second is Nature, "entrusted by God as His vice-gerent with overseeing the functioning of the universe" (186). The nun-writer refers specifically to Nature as Scholasticism's second cause and

further magnifies that entity in Loa #385 (3.484), having Nature say: "It is I who bestows being on the World, who carefully makes sure that the species live and individuals die."

61. Harss quite reasonably views these images as references to the "specifically female anatomy of the sleeper" (77).

62. My discussion of the rose and of the female figures of the nightworld draws on Sabat-Rivers, "A Feminist Rereading of Sor Juana's *Dream*" (1991).

63. For an interesting discussion of fluidity and the feminine in terms of literary theory, see Ruth Salvaggio, "Theory and Space, Space and Women," *Tulsa Studies in Women's Literature* 7, no. 72 (fall 1988): 261–82.

64. Irigaray's depiction of the fluid female economy dovetails at more than one point with the notion of the "encyclopedia" to which I have been subscribing. For example, "it allows itself to be easily traversed by flow by virtue of its conductivity to currents coming from other fluids or exerting pressure through the walls of a solid" (111).

65. See pp. 31–38 of Franco's book for an excellent discussion of digression in the *PS*. In this connection, Trueblood observes the "lack of proportion between the tenuous narrative thread recounting the experience of the dreaming mind and the weight of rhetoric and erudition that it sustains." He comments that "Sor Juana denies herself no opportunity to string along this thread excurses which begin as illustrative similes but turn into what even to a contemporaneous reader must have appeared as digressions, at times proliferating into sub-digressions" (22).

66. Sor Juana's sources and influences may provide the justification for specific instances of contradictions. For example, the dual nature of the pyramids may derive from what Harss describes as "Kircher's emblem of Egyptian philosophy: a pyramid of light inverted on a pyramid of darkness" (102) or the contradictory nature of man from Scholasticism (Paz, 376). Nevertheless, when taken together these local explanations speak to Sor Juana's overarching penchant for contradiction in the nightworld.

67. Not seeing any connection between Almone, who appeared in the original editions of the *PS*, and the context of the poem, Vossler and Méndez Plancarte replaced Almone with Alcione (despite the fact that she has equally little to do with the context of the section). Recent scholarship has tended to restore Almone, having discovered descriptions of her that exactly fit the *PS*. See Andrés Sánchez Robayna, *Para leer "Primero sueño" de Sor Juana Inés de la Cruz* (Mexico: Fondo de Cultura Económica, 1991), 95, 165. I thank Georgina Sabat-Rivers for bringing this matter to my attention.

68. Ermilio Abreu Gómez appears to have sparked the debate with his contention that the *PS* refers to the third rule of Descartes's *Discourse on Method* (see n. 33 in his 1940 edition of Sor Juana's *Poesías*). Most scholars (including Gaos and Paz) roundly deny any direct reference to Descartes in the *PS*. López Cámara, however, firmly establishes Sigüenza y Góngora's familiarity with Descartes, which raises the unresolvable issue of Sor Juana's familiarity with the new scientific method that I address in the body of my chapter.

69. Mechanism certainly predated Newtonian physics, and the notion of the world as a machine was a Scholastic commonplace (Harss, 88). Yet, as Harss remarks, there may be in these references "at least faint echoes of the New Science which (as Francis Bacon in his *Novum Organum*, 1620) was applying the 'mechanical' arts to scientific experiment" (88).

70. That Sor Juana subtly advocates empiricism as a viable method for acquiring knowledge is, in large part, the thesis of Tonia León's 1989 dissertation on the *PS* and

seventeenth-century scientific thought. Hers is the most substantive treatment of this important issue that I have found. She writes, "While both Scholasticism and Platonism are rejected as unsatisfactory for this purpose [of acquiring knowledge], the poem quietly insinuates that a combination of empirical and theoretical methods offers an approach to the natural world which will be fruitful" (v). Although I find the reading of the poem's ending that for León naturally ensues from such a position (i.e., that it represents a positive awakening of the senses to empiricism) rather too categorical, I have gleaned many useful insights, among other things, about the critique of prevailing epistemologies and empiricism in the *PS* (noted in my text and in these notes) from León's study. León's suggestion of the "other voice" of the *PS* that advocates empiricism is particularly tantalizing: "It is in the margins, in the parenthetic remarks, in the pauses, the asides, the descents, in the descriptions and observations of the lyric voice rather than in the narration of the *Alma*'s trials that one can read about the laws of nature and how information about these laws can be acquired. These remarks stand as a counterpoint both in tone and attitude to the main narration. They are quiet and calm, affirmative and knowledgeable" (234–35).

71. Harss (111) and León (chap. 5, esp. pp. 234–43) provide detailed readings of this passage and its many allusions.

72. Josefina Ludmer writes of the "Respuesta" in her "Tricks of the Weak": "It is always possible to claim a space from which one can practice what is forbidden in others; it is always possible to annex other fields and establish other territorialities" (93). Ludmer's insight well applies to Sor Juana's and Cavendish's annexation of knowledge to nature. That women throughout the ages have performed similar maneuvers with regard to knowledge, even within the most confining patriarchal ideologies, is illustrated by Teresa de Cartagena (dates unknown). In her *Admiración Operum Dey*, the first known Spanish defense of women's literacy by a woman, this orthodox fifteenth-century Spanish nun opens up a space for women's learning while remaining entirely within the medieval Christian construction of the female subject. Appealing to something resembling Holy Ignorance, she seizes on a space outside the City of Knowledge—the innate teachings of God—as the fount of true knowledge and declares it her source. See pp. 127–29 of *Arboleda de los enfermos y Admiraçión Operum Dey*. I thank Clara Castro-Ponce for pointing me to the connections between Sor Juana and Teresa de Cartagena.

73. León (243 et passim), López Cámara (124–27), and Arenal (130) all note the perhaps Cartesian predominance of the mind over the senses in the *PS*. Paul Dixon, in "Balance, Pyramids, Crowns, and the Geometry of Sor Juana Inés de la Cruz" (*Hispania* 67, no. 4 [December 1984]: 565), sees an alternation between "pure reason" and "perception" in the *PS*.

74. León sees in the *PS* an "attempt to clear the intellectual slate by examining everything for and by oneself: received information, one's own ideas and concepts and the information transmitted by the senses" (229).

75. Trueblood remarks that nearly half of the poem, "everything subsequent to the account of the soul's thwarted attempt at intuitive universal understanding, is given over to its ensuing cogitations as it ponders the pros and cons of undertaking a second flight" (21). One might equally say that nearly half the poem is devoted to pondering the failure of these methods.

76. León unequivocally attributes the Soul's failure to the insufficiencies of the system: "The inability of the *Alma* to see the pattern of the Universe as laid out by the Scholastics and other traditional philosophies has been read as mankind's total failure

to acquire knowledge. However, the cause of this problem resides within the prescribed world view itself rather than with the viewer. It is the old world picture which has failed to correspond to the information, the view, the data that the *Alma* is taking in" (159).

77. Harss (55) and León (202–4) discuss Sor Juana's critique of Scholasticism in this passage. As León notes (249), the nun had also taken the sterility of Scholastic reasoning to task in her Romance #2 ("Finjamos que soy feliz . . . ").

78. Harss observes: "The world's 'Central Support' (hastily invoked, but, seemingly with scant hope of deriving any comfort from it) is Sor Juana's abstract, almost absent God" (125).

79. I am reminded here of George Bataille's existential discussion in *Death and Sensuality: A Study of Eroticism and the Taboo* (New York: Walker and Co., 1962) of the ways in which order threatens to cede to disorder when the lines of human structures are transgressed.

80. It is not by chance or without deeper import that in *A Room of One's Own* and in early modernity Woolf rescues, as it were, Cavendish from oblivion. Cavendish–who did have a room of her own but nevertheless was barred from institutional learning, who exemplifies a woman "at war with her lot" (73)–duplicates the very scenario that Woolf experienced in her own life and that she dramatizes in her essay. Woolf imagines a Mary Carmichael still subject to the prohibitions of the patriarchally controlled City of Knowledge: "And as I watched her lengthening out for the test, I saw, but hoped that she did not see, the bishops and the deans, the doctors and the professors, the patriarchs and the pedagogues all at her shouting warning and advice. You can't do this and you shan't do that! Fellows and scholars only allowed on the grass! Ladies not admitted without a letter of introduction!" (97). The implicit, but very real, connections between the circumstances of the early modern learned ladies that I have portrayed in this chapter and those of early modernity's still-struggling woman writer portrayed by Woolf painfully equate the two eras and add a poignant coda to the investigations of this book. Well worth exploring are the parallels in terms of women's history and literature between the early modern era and early twentieth-century modernity.

Bibliography of Works Cited

Albistur, Maïté, and Daniel Armogath. *Histoire du féminisme français: du moyen âge à nos jours*. Paris: Des Femmes, 1977.

Allentuch, Harriet Ray. "The Will to Refuse in the *Princesse de Clèves*." *University of Toronto Quarterly* 44 (spring 1975): 185–98.

Altman, Leslie. "Christine de Pisan: First Professional Woman of Letters (1364–1430?)." In *Female Scholars: A Tradition of Learned Women Before 1800*, ed. J. R. Brink. Montreal: Eden Press Women's Publications, 1980.

Anderson, Bonnie S., and Judith P. Zinsser. *A History of Their Own: Women in Europe from Prehistory to the Present*. Vol. 2. New York: Harper & Row, 1988.

Anson, John. "The Female Transvestite in Early Monasticism: The Origin and Development of a Motif." *Viator* 5 (1975): 1–32.

Arenal, Electa. "This life within me won't keep still." In *Reinventing the Americas: Comparative Studies of the Literature of the United States and Spanish America*, ed. Bell Gale Chevigny and Gari Laguardia. New York and London: Cambridge University Press, 1986.

Arenal, Electa, and Stacey Schlau. *Untold Sisters: Hispanic Nuns in Their Own Works*. Albuquerque: University of New Mexico Press, 1989.

Ashcom, B. B. "Concerning 'La mujer en hábito de hombre' in the Comedia." *Hispanic Review* 28 (1960): 43–62.

Astell, Mary. *The First English Feminist: Reflections upon Marriage and Other Writings by Mary Astell*. Ed. and introduction by Bridget Hill. New York: St. Martin's Press, 1986.

Augustine, Saint. *Confessions*. Trans. Henry Chadwick. Oxford and New York: Oxford University Press, 1992.

Bakhtin, Mikhail M. *The Dialogic Imagination*. Trans. Caryl Emerson and Michael Holquist. Ed. Michael Holquist. Austin: University of Texas Press, 1981.

Ball, Kenneth R. "Puritan Humility in Anne Bradstreet's Poetry." *Cithara* 13 (1973): 29–41.

Barker-Benfield, Ben. "Anne Hutchinson and the Puritan Attitude Toward Women." *Feminist Studies* 1, no. 2 (1972): 65–96.

Barrionuevo, Jerónimo de. *Avisos (1654–1658)*. Biblioteca de Autores Españoles. Vol. 221. Madrid: Atlas, 1968.

Beasley, Faith E. *Revising Memory: Women's Fiction and Memoirs in Seventeenth-Century France*. New Brunswick and London: Rutgers University Press, 1990.

Beauvoir, Simone de. *The Second Sex*. New York: Random House, 1974.

Bell, Robert E. *Women of Classical Mythology: A Biographical Dictionary*. New York and Oxford: Oxford University Press, 1991.

Bellini, Giuseppe. *L'Opera Letteraria di Sor Juana Inés de la Cruz*. Milano and Varese: Is'tituo Editoriale Cisalpino, 1964.

Bénassy-Berling, Marie-Cécile. *Humanisme et religion chez Sor Juana Inés de la Cruz: La femme et la culture au XVIIe siècle*. Paris: Editions Hispaniques, Publications de la Sorbonne, 1982.

Bénichou, Paul. *Morales du grand siècle*. Paris: Gallimard, 1948.

Bercovitch, Sacvan. *The Puritan Origins of the American Self.* New Haven and London: Yale University Press, 1975.

Beverley, John R. "On the Concept of the Spanish Literary Baroque." In *Culture and Control in Counter-Reformation Spain,* ed. Anne J. Cruz and Mary Elizabeth Perry. Minneapolis and Oxford: University of Minnesota Press, 1992.

Blanco Aguinaga, Carlos. "Dos sonetos del siglo XVI: Amor-Locura en Quevedo y Sor Juana." *MLN* 77 (1962): 145–62.

Bloch, R. Howard. *Medieval Misogyny and the Invention of Western Romantic Love.* Chicago and London: University of Chicago Press, 1991.

Bomli, P. W. *La Femme Dans L'Espagne du Siècle d'Or.* The Hague: Martinus Nijhoff, 1950.

Borges, Jorge Luis. *Discusión.* Buenos Aires: Emecé, 1947.

——. *A Personal Anthology.* Ed. Anthony Kerrigan. New York: Grove Press, 1967.

——. *El informe de Brodie.* Buenos Aires: Emecé, 1970.

Bradstreet, Anne. *The Tenth Muse (1650).* Ed. Josephine K. Piercy. Gainesville: Scholars' Facsimiles & Reprints, 1965.

——. *The Works of Anne Bradstreet.* Ed. Jeannine Hensley. Cambridge, Mass.: Belknap Press of Harvard University Press, 1967.

Braudy, Leo. *The Frenzy of Renown: Fame and Its History.* New York and Oxford: Oxford University Press, 1986.

Bravo-Villasante, Carmen. *La mujer vestida de hombre en el teatro español (Siglos XVI–XVII).* Madrid: Revista de Occidente, 1955.

Bray, René. *La Préciosité et les Précieux.* Paris: Editions Albin Michel, 1948.

Brink, J. R., ed. *Female Scholars: A Tradition of Learned Women Before 1800.* Montreal: Eden Press Women's Publications, 1980.

Brody, Jules. "*La Princesse de Clèves* and the Myth of Courtly Love." *University of Toronto Quarterly* 38, no. 2 (January 1969): 105–35.

Brown, Gary J. "Rhetoric as Structure in the Siglo de Oro Love Sonnet." *Hispanófila* 65, no. 2 (January 1979): 9–39.

Brownlee, Marina S. "Postmodernism and the Baroque in María de Zayas." In *Cultural Authority in Golden Age Spain,* ed. Marina S. Brownlee and Hans Ulrich Gumbrecht. Baltimore and London: Johns Hopkins University Press, 1995.

Burckhardt, Jacob. *The Civilisation of the Renaissance in Italy.* Trans. S. G. C. Middlemore. London: Allen & Unwin; New York: Macmillan, 1928.

Calderón de la Barca, Pedro. *El mayor encanto amor.* In *Comedias de don Pedro Calderón de la Barca,* ed. Juan Eugenio Hartzenbusch. Biblioteca de Autores Españoles. Vol. 7. Madrid: Rivadeneyra, 1848.

——. *El José de las Mujeres.* In *Obras completas.* Vol. 1, ed. Angel Valbuena Briones. Madrid: Aguilar, 1959.

——. *La dama duende.* In *Obras completas.* Vol. 2, ed. Angel Valbuena Briones. Madrid: Aguilar, 1960.

Caldwell, Patricia. "Why Our First Poet Was a Woman: Bradstreet and the Birth of an American Poetic Voice." *Prospects* 13 (1988): 1–35.

Caro Mallén de Soto, Ana. *Valor, agravio y mujer.* In *Apuntes para una biblioteca de escritoras españolas, Primera parte,* ed. Manuel Serrano y Sanz. Biblioteca de Autores Españoles. Vol. 268. Madrid: Atlas, 1975.

——. *El Conde Partinuplés.* Ed. and introduction by Lola Luna. Kassell: Edition Reichenberger, 1993.

Cartagena, Teresa de. *Arboleda de los enfermos y Admiración Operum Dey.* Ed. Lewis Joseph Hutton. Madrid: Anejos del Boletín de la Real Academia Española, Anejo XVI, 1967.

Casa, Frank, and Michael D. McGaha. *Editing the Comedia.* Ann Arbor: Michigan Romance Studies, 1985.

Castillo Solórzano, Alonso. *La Garduña de Sevilla y anzuelo de las bolsas.* Madrid: Ediciones de "La Lectura," 1922.

Cavendish, Margaret Lucas (Duchess of Newcastle). *The Convent of Pleasure.* In *Playes written by the thrice noble, illustrious and excellent princesse, the Lady Marchioness Newcastle.* London: Printed by A. Warren for John Martyn, James Allestry and Tho. Dicas, 1662.

———. *The Life of the (1st) Duke of Newcastle & Other Writings by Margaret, Duchess.* Ed. Ernest Thys. London and Toronto: J. M. Dent & Sons; New York: Dutton, n.d. (Contains *Memoirs of the Duchess.*)

———. *Poems and Fancies.* Facsimile ed. of original, published in 1653. Yorkshire: Scholar Press Limited, 1972.

———. "Preface to Reader" from *The World's Olio.* In *By a Woman Writt: Literature from Six Centuries By and About Women,* ed. Joan Goulianos. Indianapolis and New York: Bobbs-Merrill, 1973.

———. "To the Two Most Famous Universities of England." In *First Feminists: British Women Writers 1578–1799,* ed. Moira Ferguson. Bloomington: Indiana University Press, 1985.

———. *The Description of a New World Called the Blazing World and Other Writings.* Ed. Kate Lilley. New York: New York University Press, 1992.

Cervantes Saavedra, Miguel de. *Exemplary Stories.* Trans. C. A. Jones. London: Penguin, 1972.

———. *Novelas ejemplares.* Ed. Harry Sieber. Madrid: Cátedra, 1980.

Céspedes y Meneses, Gonzalo de. *El español Gerardo, y desengaño del amor lascivo.* Biblioteca de Autores Españoles. Vol. 18. Madrid: Casa Editorial Hernando, 1925.

Chevalier, Maxime. *Lectura y lectores en la España del siglo XVI y XVII.* Madrid: Ediciones Turner, 1976.

Chodorow, Nancy J. *Feminism and Psychoanalytic Theory.* New Haven and London: Yale University Press, 1989.

Cixous, Hélène. "The Laugh of the Medusa." Trans. Keith Cohen and Paula Cohen. *Signs* 1 (summer 1976): 875–93.

Contreras, Jerónimo de. *Selva de aventuras.* Biblioteca de Autores Españoles. Vol. 3. Madrid: Casa Editorial Hernando, 1920.

Cruz, Anne J. "Sexual Enclosure, Textual Escape: The *Pícara* as Prostitute in the Spanish Female Picaresque Novel." In *Seeking the Woman in Late Medieval and Renaissance Writings: Essays in Feminist Contextual Criticism,* ed. Sheila Fisher and Janet E. Halley. Knoxville: University of Tennessee Press, 1989.

Curtius, Ernst Robert. *European Literature and the Latin Middle Ages.* Trans. Willard R. Trask. Princeton: Bollingen Series, Princeton University Press, 1973.

Davis, Natalie Zemon. *Society and Culture in Early Modern France.* Stanford: Stanford University Press, 1975.

Davis, Natalie Zemon, and Arlette Farge, eds. *A History of Women in the West: Renaissance and Enlightenment Paradoxes.* Cambridge, Mass., and London: Harvard University Press, 1993.

De Jean, Joan. "Editor's Preface: The Female Tradition." *L'Esprit Créateur* 23, no. 2 (1983): 3–8.

——. "Lafayette's Ellipses: The Privilege of Anonymity." *PMLA* 99 (1984): 884–902.

——. *Tender Geographies: Women and the Origins of the Novel in France.* New York: Columbia University Press, 1991.

Dekker, Rudolf M., and Lotte C. van de Pol. *The Tradition of Female Transvestism in Early Modern Europe.* New York: St. Martin's Press, 1989.

Delany, Paul. *British Autobiography in the Seventeenth Century.* London: Routledge & Kegan Paul, 1969.

Dunn, Peter N. *Castillo Solórzano and the Decline of the Spanish Novel.* Oxford: Basil Blackwell, 1952.

DuPlessis, Rachel Blau. *Writing Beyond the Ending: Narrative Strategies of Twentieth-Century Women Writers.* Bloomington: Indiana University Press, 1985.

Durán, Manuel. "Hermetic Traditions in Sor Juana's *Primero sueño.*" *University of Dayton Review* 16, no. 2 (spring 1983): 107–15.

Edkins, Carol. "Quest for Community: Spiritual Autobiographies of Eighteenth-Century Quaker and Puritan Women in America." In *Women's Autobiography: Essays in Criticism,* ed. Estelle C. Jelinek. Bloomington and London: Indiana University Press, 1980.

Egido, Aurora. "Los prólogos teresianos y la 'Santa Ignorancia.'" In *Congreso internacional teresiano.* Vol. 2, ed. Teofanes Egido Martínez, Víctor García de la Concha, and Olegario González de Cardenal. Salamanca: Universidad de Salamanca, 1983.

El Saffar, Ruth Anthony. "Literary Reflections on the 'New Man': Changes in Consciousness in Early Modern Europe." *Revista de Estudios Hispánicos* 23, no. 2 (May 1988): 1–23.

——. "Breaking Silences: Reflections on Spanish Women Writing." *Romance Languages Annual* 2 (1990): 1–8.

——. *Rapture Encaged: The Suppression of the Feminine in Western Culture.* London and New York: Routledge, 1994.

——. "Ana/Lysis and Zayas: Reflections on Courtship and Literary Women in the *Novelas amorosas y ejemplares.*" In *María de Zayas: The Dynamics of Discourse,* ed. Amy R. Williamsen and Judith A. Whitenack. Madison and Teaneck, N.J.: Fairleigh Dickinson University Press; Cranbury, N.J., and London: Associated University Presses, 1995.

Elliott, J. H. *Spain and Its World 1500–1700: Selected Essays.* New Haven and London: Yale University Press, 1989.

Erasmus, Desiderius. *The Colloquies of Erasmus.* Trans. Craig R. Thompson. Chicago and London: University of Chicago Press, 1965.

Erauso, Catalina de. "Petition of Catalina de Erauso to the Spanish Crown, 1625." Trans. Stephanie Merrim. *Review* 43 (July-December 1990): 37.

——. *Lieutenant Nun: Memoir of a Basque Transvestite in the New World, Catalina de Erauso.* Trans. Michele Stepto and Gabriel Stepto. Introduction by Michele Stepto. Foreword by Marjorie Garber. Boston: Beacon Press, 1996.

Faulkner, William. *Absalom, Absalom!* New York: Vintage Books, 1990.

Fell, Margaret. *Women's Speaking Justified (1667).* Introduction by David J. Latt. Los Angeles: Augustan Reprint Society, no. 194, 1979.

Ferguson, Margaret W., with Maureen Quilligan and Nancy J. Vickers. Introduction to

Rewriting the Renaissance: The Discourses of Sexual Difference in Early Modern Europe. Ed. Margaret W. Ferguson with Maureen Quilligan and Nancy J. Vickers. Chicago and London: University of Chicago Press, 1986.

Ferrante, Joan M. "The Education of Women in the Middle Ages in Theory, Fact, and Fantasy." In *Beyond Their Sex: Learned Women of the European Past,* ed. Patricia H. Labalme. New York and London: New York University Press, 1980.

Ferrer, Joaquín María de, ed. *Historia de la monja alférez.* Prologue by José María de Heredia. Madrid: Tipografía Renovación, 1918.

Fitzmaurice, James. "Fancy and the Family: Self-Characterizations of Margaret Cavendish." *Huntington Library Quarterly* 53, no. 3 (summer 1990): 198–209.

Fitzmaurice-Kelly, James. *The Nun Ensign* and *La monja alférez, A Play in the Original Spanish by Juan Pérez de Montalbán.* London: T. Fisher Unwin, 1908.

Foa, Sandra. "María de Zayas: Visión conflictiva y renuncia del mundo." *Cuadernos Hispanoamericanos* 331 (January 1978): 128–35.

Fontenelle, Bernard le Bovier de. *Conversations on the Plurality of Worlds.* Trans. H. A. Hargreaves. Introduction by Nina Rattner Gelbart. Berkeley, Los Angeles, and Oxford: University of California Press, 1990.

Foucault, Michel. *The Order of Things: An Archaeology of the Human Sciences.* New York: Vintage, 1973.

———. *The History of Sexuality.* Trans. Robert Hurley. Vol. 1. New York: Vintage Books, 1990.

Franco, Jean. *Plotting Women: Gender and Representation in Mexico.* New York: Columbia University Press, 1989.

Friedman, Susan Stanford. "Creativity and the Childbirth Metaphor: Gender Difference in Literary Discourse." *Feminist Studies* 13, no. 1 (1987): 49–82.

Gallagher, Catherine. "Who Was that Masked Woman? The Prostitute and the Playwright in the Comedies of Aphra Behn." In *Rereading Aphra Behn: History, Theory, and Criticism,* ed. Heidi Hutner. Charlottesville and London: University Press of Virginia, 1993.

Gaos, José. "El sueño de un sueño." *Historia Mexicana* 11 (July-September 1960): 54–71.

Garber, Marjorie. *Vested Interests: Cross-Dressing and Cultural Anxiety.* New York: Harper Perennial, 1993.

García Pinto, Magdalena. *Women Writers of Latin America: Intimate Histories.* Trans. Trudy Balch and Magdalena García Pinto. Austin: University of Texas Press, 1991.

Gibson, Wendy. *Women in Seventeenth-Century France.* New York: St. Martin's Press, 1989.

Gonzalbo Aizpuro, Pilar. *Historia de la educación en la época colonial: La educación de los criollos y la vida urbana.* Mexico: El Colegio de México, 1990.

González Echevarría, Roberto. "El 'monstruo de una especie y otra': *La vida es sueño.*" *Co-Textes* 3 (1982): 27–58.

Gournay, Marie le Jars de. "The Equality of Men and Women" and "The Ladies' Grievance." In *Women Writers of the Seventeenth Century,* ed. Katharina M. Wilson and Frank J. Warnke. Athens, Ga., and London: University of Georgia Press, 1989.

———. *Egalité des Hommes et des Femmes, 1622.* Preface by Milagros Palma. Paris: Côté femmes éditions, 1989.

Gracián y Morales, Baltasar. *El Político.* Ed. E. Correa Calderón. Madrid: Anaya, 1961.

——. *El Criticón*. Ed. Santos Alonso. Madrid: Cátedra, 1980.

Grant, Douglas. *Margaret the First: A Biography of Margaret Cavendish, Duchess of Newcastle*. Toronto: University of Toronto Press, 1957.

Green, Otis. *Spain and the Western Tradition: The Castilian Mind in Literature from El Cid to Calderón*. Vol. 1. Madison: Wisconsin University Press, 1963. (Vol. 2, 1964.)

Greenblatt, Stephen. *Shakespearean Negotiations: The Circulation of Social Energy in Renaissance England*. Berkeley and Los Angeles: University of California Press, 1988.

Greene, Thomas M. *The Light in Troy: Imitation and Discovery in Renaissance Poetry*. New Haven and London: Yale University Press, 1982.

Griswold, Susan C. "Topoi and Rhetorical Distance: The 'Feminism' of María de Zayas." *Revista de Estudios Hispánicos* 14 (1980): 97–116.

Grossi, Verónica. "El triunfo del poder femenino desde el margen de un poema: Otra lectura del *Primero Sueño* de Sor Juana Inés de la Cruz." *Mester* 20 (fall 1991): 27–40.

Haig, Stirling. *Madame de Lafayette*. New York: Twayne Publishers, 1970.

Harss, Luis. *Sor Juana's Dream*. New York: Lumen Books, 1986.

Heilbrun, Carolyn. *Hamlet's Mother and Other Women*. New York: Columbia University Press, 1990.

Heiple, Daniel. "Profeminist Reactions to Huarte's Misogyny in Lope de Vega's *La prueba de los ingenios* and María de Zayas's *Novelas amorosas y ejemplares*." In *The Perception of Women in Spanish Theater of the Golden Age*, ed. Anita K. Stoll and Dawn L. Smith. Lewisburg: Bucknell University Press; London and Toronto: Associated University Presses, 1991.

Heise, Ursula K. "Transvestism and the Stage Controversy in Spain and England, 1580–1680." *Theatre Journal* 44 (1992): 357–74.

Henderson, Katherine Usher, and Barbara F. McManus. *Half Humankind: Contexts and Texts of the Controversy about Women in England, 1540–1640*. Urbana and Chicago: University of Illinois Press, 1985.

Herrmann, Claudine. *The Tongue Snatchers*. Trans. Nancy Kline. Lincoln and London: University of Nebraska Press, 1989.

Hill, Bridget, ed. *The First English Feminist: Reflections Upon Marriage and Other Writings by Mary Astell*. New York: St. Martin's Press, 1986.

Hirsch, Marianne. "A Mother's Discourse: Incorporation and Repetition in *La Princesse de Clèves*." *Yale French Studies* 62 (1981): 67–87.

Huarte de San Juan, Juan. *Examen de ingenios para las ciencias*. Ed. Guillermo Serés. Madrid: Cátedra, 1989.

Ilsley, Marjorie Henry. *A Daughter of the Renaissance: Marie le Jars de Gournay, Her Life and Works*. The Hague: Mouton, 1963.

Ingarden, Roman. *The Literary Work of Art*. Trans. George G. Grabowicz. Evanston, Ill.: Northwestern University Press, 1973.

Irigaray, Luce. *This Sex Which Is Not One*. Trans. Catherine Porter and Carolyn Burke. Ithaca: Cornell University Press, 1985.

Irwin, Joyce L. "Anna Maria van Schurman: The Star of Utrecht (1607–1678)." In *Female Scholars: A Tradition of Learned Women Before 1800*, ed. J. R. Brink. Montreal: Eden Press, 1980.

Johnson, Julie Greer. *Women in Colonial Spanish American Literature: Literary Images*. Westport, Conn., and London: Greenwood Press, 1983.

——. *Satire in Colonial Spanish America: Turning the New World Upside Down*. Austin: University of Texas Press, 1993.

Jones, Ann Rosalind. "Surprising Fame: Renaissance Gender Ideologies and Women's Lyric." In *The Poetics of Gender*, ed. Nancy K. Miller, 74–93. New York: Columbia University Press, 1986.

——. *The Currency of Eros: Women's Love Lyric in Europe, 1540–1620*. Bloomington and Indianapolis: Indiana University Press, 1990.

Jones, Kathleen. *A Glorious Fame: The Life of Margaret Cavendish, Duchess of Newcastle, 1623–1673*. London: Bloomsbury, 1988.

Jordan, Constance. *Renaissance Feminism: Literary Texts and Political Models*. Ithaca: Cornell University Press, 1990.

Juana Inés de la Cruz, Sor. *Fama y obras póstumas*. Ed. Juan Ignacio Castorena y Ursúa. Madrid: Imprenta de Manuel Ruiz de Murga, 1700.

——. *Obras completas*. Ed. Alfonso Méndez Plancarte and Alberto G. Salceda (vol. 4). 4 vols. Mexico: Fondo de Cultura Económica, 1951–57. Vol. 1: Lírica personal; vol. 2: Villancicos y Letras Sacras; vol. 3: Autos y Loas; vol. 4: Comedias, Sainetes y Prosa.

——. *Inundación castálida*. Ed. Georgina Sabat de Rivers. Madrid: Clásicos Castalia, 1982.

——. *Carta de Sor Juana Inés de la Cruz a su confesor: Autodefensa espiritual*. Ed. Aureliano Tapia Méndez. Mexico: Impresora Monterrey, 1986.

Kaminsky, Amy Katz. "Dress and Redress: Clothing in the *Desengaños amorosos* of María de Zayas y Sotomayor." *Romanic Review* 79, no. 2 (March 1988): 377–91.

Kamuf, Peggy. *Fictions of Feminine Desire: Disclosures of Heloise*. Lincoln and London: University of Nebraska Press, 1982.

Kaps, Helen Karen. *Moral Perspective in* La Princesse de Clèves. Eugene, Oreg.: University of Oregon Books, 1968.

Keller, Evelyn Fox. *Reflections on Gender and Science*. New Haven and London: Yale University Press, 1985.

Kelly, Joan. "Early Feminist Theory and the *Querelle des Femmes*, 1400–1789." *Signs* 8, no. 1 (1982): 4–28.

King, Margaret L. "Book-Lined Cells: Women and Humanism in the Early Italian Renaissance." In *Beyond Their Sex: Learned Women of the European Past*, ed. Patricia H. Labalme. New York and London: New York University Press, 1980.

——. *Women of the Renaissance*. Chicago and London: University of Chicago Press, 1991.

Koehler, Lyle. *A Search for Power: The "Weaker Sex" in Seventeenth-Century New England*. Urbana, Chicago, and London: University of Illinois Press, 1980.

Kors, Alan C., and Edward Peters. *Witchcraft in Europe 1100–1700: A Documentary History*. Philadelphia: University of Pennsylvania Press, 1972.

Kristeller, Paul Oskar. "Learned Women of Early Modern Italy: Humanists and University Scholars." In *Beyond Their Sex: Learned Women of the European Past*, ed. Patricia H. Labalme. New York and London: New York University Press, 1980.

Labalme, Patricia H. "Women's Roles in Early Modern Venice: An Exceptional Case." In *Beyond Their Sex: Learned Women of the European Past*, ed. Patricia H. Labalme. New York and London: New York University Press, 1980.

Lafayette, Madame de. *Correspondance de Mme de La Fayette*. Vols. 1 and 2, ed. André Beunier. Paris: Gallimard, 1942.

——. *La Princesse de Clèves et autres romans.* Ed. Bernard Pingaud. Paris: Gallimard, 1972.

——. *The Princesse de Clèves, The Princesse de Montpensier, The Comtesse de Tende.* Trans. and introduction by Terence Cave. Oxford: Oxford University Press, 1992.

Laqueur, Thomas. *Making Sex: Body and Gender from the Greeks to Freud.* Cambridge, Mass., and London: Harvard University Press, 1990.

La Rochefoucauld, François VI, duc de. *Les Maximes de La Rouchefoucauld.* Ed. J.-F. Thénard. Paris: E. Flammarion, 1905.

Laugaa, Maurice. *Lectures de Mme de Lafayette.* Paris: Librairie Armand Colin, 1971.

Lavista, Mario. "Sor Juana *musicus.*" In *Memoria del Coloquio Internacional, Sor Juana Inés de la Cruz y el pensamiento novohispano.* Morelos: Instituto Mexiquense de Cultura, 1995.

Lavrin, Asunción. "In Search of the Colonial Woman in Mexico: The Seventeenth and Eighteenth Centuries." In *Latin American Women: Historical Perspectives.* Ed. Asunción Lavrin. Westport, Conn.: Greenwood Press, 1978.

Lawrence, D. H. *Fantasia of the Unconscious.* New York: Albert & Charles Boni, 1930.

León, Fray Luis de. *La perfecta casada.* In *Obras completas castellanas de Fray Luis de León.* Prologue by Félix García. 4th ed. Madrid: Biblioteca de Autores Cristianos, 1967.

León, Tonia. "Sor Juana Inés de la Cruz's *Primero Sueño*: A Lyric Expression of Seventeenth-Century Scientific Thought." Ph.D. diss., New York University, 1989.

Leonard, Irving A. *Baroque Times in Old Mexico.* Ann Arbor: Michigan University Press, 1959.

Lerner, Gerda. *The Creation of a Feminist Consciousness: From the Middle Ages to Eighteen-Seventy.* New York and Oxford: Oxford University Press, 1993.

Levisi, Margarita. *Autobiografías del siglo de oro.* Madrid: Sociedad General Española de Librería, 1984.

——. "Golden Age Autobiography: The Soldiers." In *Autobiography in Early Modern Spain,* ed. Nicholas Spadaccini and Jenaro Talens. Minneapolis: Prisma Institute, 1988.

Lewis, C. S. *The Allegory of Love: A Study in Medieval Tradition.* London: Oxford University Press, 1938.

Lezama Lima, José. *La expresión americana.* Santiago: Editorial Universitaria, 1969.

Lilley, Kate. "Blazing Worlds: Seventeenth-Century Women's Utopian Writing." In *Women, Texts and Histories 1575–1760,* ed. Clare Brant and Diane Purkiss. London and New York: Routledge, 1992.

López Cámara, Francisco. "El cartesianismo en Sor Juana y Sigüenza y Góngora." *Filosofía y letras* 20, no. 39 (1950): 107–31.

Lougee, Carolyn C. *Le Paradis des Femmes: Women, Salons, and Social Stratification in Seventeenth-Century France.* Princeton: Princeton University Press, 1976.

Luciani, Frederick. "The Courtly Love Tradition in the Poetry of Sor Juana Inés de la Cruz." Ph.D. diss., Yale University, 1982.

Ludmer, Josefina. "Tricks of the Weak." In *Feminist Perspectives on Sor Juana Inés de la Cruz,* ed. Stephanie Merrim. Detroit: Wayne State University Press, 1991.

Maclean, Ian. *Woman Triumphant: Feminism in French Literature 1610–1652.* Oxford: Clarendon Press, 1977.

Makin, Bathsua. *An Essay to Revive the antient Education of Gentlewomen.* Ed and introduction by Paula L. Barbour. Los Angeles: Augustine Reprint Society, no. 202, 1980.

Maravall, José Antonio. *La cultura del barroco.* Barcelona: Editorial Ariel, [1975] 1983.

——. *Culture of the Baroque: Analysis of a Historical Structure.* Trans. Terry Cochran. Minneapolis: University of Minneapolis Press, 1986.

——. *La literatura picaresca desde la historia social (siglos XVI y XVII).* Madrid: Taurus, 1986.

Marcus, Leah S. "Renaissance/Early Modern Studies." In *Redrawing the Boundaries: The Transformation of English and American Literary Studies,* ed. Stephen Greenblatt and Giles Gunn. New York: Modern Language Association of America, 1992.

Mariscal, George. *Contradictory Subjects: Quevedo, Cervantes, and Seventeenth-Century Spanish Culture.* Ithaca and London: Cornell University Press, 1991.

Martín, Luis. *Daughters of the Conquistadores: Women of the Viceroyalty of Peru.* Albuquerque: University of New Mexico Press, 1983.

Martin, Wendy. *An American Triptych: Anne Bradstreet, Emily Dickinson, Adrienne Rich.* Chapel Hill and London: University of North Carolina Press, 1984.

Mawer, Randall R. "'Farewel Dear Babe': Bradstreet's Elegy for Elizabeth." In *Critical Essays on Anne Bradstreet,* ed. Pattie Cowell and Ann Stanford. Boston: G. K. Hall, 1983.

McGaha, Michael D. "The Sources and Feminism of Lope's *Las mujeres sin hombres.*" In *The Perception of Women in Spanish Theater of the Golden Age,* ed. Anita K. Stoll and Dawn L. Smith. Lewisburg: Bucknell University Press; London and Toronto: Associated University Presses, 1991.

McGuire, Anne. "Margaret Cavendish, Duchess of Newcastle, on the Nature and Status of Women." *International Journal of Women's Studies* 1, no. 2 (1978): 193–206.

McKendrick, Melveena. *Women and Society in the Spanish Drama of the Golden Age: A Study of the* Mujer Varonil. London: Cambridge University Press, 1974.

Meeks, Wayne A., ed. *The Writings of St. Paul.* New York and London: W. W. Norton, 1972.

Merchant, Carolyn. *The Death of Nature: Women, Ecology, and the Scientific Revolution.* San Francisco: Harper & Row, [1980] 1989.

Merrim, Stephanie. "Toward a Feminist Reading of Sor Juana Inés de la Cruz" and "*Mores Geometricae*: The 'Womanscript' in the Theater of Sor Juana Inés de la Cruz." In *Feminist Perspectives on Sor Juana Inés de la Cruz,* ed. Stephanie Merrim. Detroit: Wayne State University Press, 1991.

Meyer, Gerald Dennis. *The Scientific Lady in England 1650–1760.* Berkeley and Los Angeles: University of California Press, 1955.

Miller, Nancy K. *The Heroine's Text: Readings in the French and English Novel, 1722–1782.* New York, Columbia University Press, 1980.

——. *Subject to Change: Reading Feminist Writing.* New York: Columbia University Press, 1988.

Miller, Perry. *The New England Mind: The Seventeenth Century.* Boston: Beacon Press [1939], 1961.

Millet, Kate. *Sexual Politics.* New York: Doubleday, 1970.

Morgan, Edmund S. *Visible Saints: The History of a Puritan Idea.* New York: New York University Press, 1963.

——. *The Puritan Family: Religion and Domestic Relations in Seventeenth-Century New England.* New York: Harper & Row, [1940], 1966.

Mullaney, Steven. "Strange Things, Gross Terms, Curious Customs: The Rehearsal of Cultures in the Late Renaissance." *Representations* 3 (1983): 40–67.

Myers, Kathleen A. "Sor Juana's *Respuesta*: Rewriting the *Vitae*." *Revista canadiense de estudios hispánicos* 14, no. 3 (1990): 459–71.

Nanfito, Jacqueline C. "*El sueño*: The Baroque Imagination and the Dreamscape." MLN 106, no. 2 (March 1991): 423–31.

Navarre, Marguerite de. *The Heptameron*. Ed. and trans. Paul A. Chilton. London: Penguin, 1984.

Navarro, Ana, ed. *Antología poética de escritoras de los siglos XVI y XVII*. Madrid: Castalia, 1989.

Nelken, Margarita. *Las escritoras españolas*. Barcelona: Editorial Labor, 1930.

Olivares, Julián, and Elizabeth S. Boyce, eds. *Tras el espejo la musa escribe: Lírica femenina de los Siglos de Oro*. Madrid: Siglo XXI, 1993.

Oñate, María del Pilar. *El feminismo en la literatura española*. Madrid: Espasa-Calpe, 1938.

Ordóñez, Elizabeth J. "Woman and Her Text in the Works of María de Zayas and Ana Caro." *Revista de Estudios Hispánicos* 19, no. 1 (January 1985): 3–16.

Ovid. *The Metamorphoses*. Trans. Horace Gregory. New York and London: Penguin, 1960.

Park, Katharine, and Lorraine J. Daston. "Unnatural Conceptions: The Study of Monsters in 16th and 17th Century France and England." *Past and Present* 92 (1981): 20–54.

Paun de García, Susan. "Zayas as Writer: Hell Hath No Fury." In *María de Zayas: The Dynamics of Discourse*, ed. Amy R. Williamsen and Judith A. Whitenack. Madison and Teaneck, N.J.: Fairleigh Dickinson University Press; Cranbury, N.J., and London: Associated University Presses, 1995.

Paz, Octavio. "Homenaje a Sor Juana Inés de la Cruz en su Tercer Centenario." *Sur* 206 (December 1951): 29–40.

———. "Manierismo, barroquismo, criollismo." *Revista Canadiense de Estudios Hispánicos* 1 (1976): 3–15.

———. *Sor Juana Inés de la Cruz o las trampas de la fe*. Barcelona: Seix Barral, 1982.

———. *Sor Juana, or, The Traps of Faith*. Trans. Margaret Sayers Peden. Cambridge, Mass., and London: Harvard University Press, 1988.

Perry, Mary Elizabeth. *Gender and Disorder in Early Modern Seville*. Princeton: Princeton University Press, 1990.

Pérez-Erdelyi, Mireya. *La pícara y la dama: La imagen de las mujeres en las novelas picaresco-cortesanas de María de Zayas y Sotomayor y Alonso del Castillo Solórzano*. Miami: Ediciones Universal, 1979.

Pettit, Norman. *The Heart Prepared: Grace and Conversion in Puritan Spiritual Life*. New Haven and London: Yale University Press, 1966.

Pfandl, Ludwig. *Cultura y costumbres del pueblo español de los siglos XVI y XVII. Introducción al siglo de oro*. Barcelona: Araluce, 1929.

———. *Sor Juana Inés de la Cruz: La Décima Musa de México*. Ed. Francisco de la Maza. Trans. Juan Antonio Ortega y Medina. Mexico: UNAM, 1963.

Pingaud, Bernard. *Mme de la Fayette par elle-même*. Paris: Seuil, 1959.

Pizan, Christine de. *The Book of the City of Ladies*. Ed. and trans. Early Jeffrey Richards. New York: Persea Books, 1982.

Porqueras Mayo, Alberto. *El prólogo en el manierismo y barroco españoles*. Madrid: Consejo Superior de Investigaciones Científicas, 1968.

Poullain de La Barre, François. *The Woman as Good as the Man; Or, the Equality of Both Sexes.* Trans. A. L. [*sic*]. Ed. and introduction by Gerald M. MacLean. Detroit: Wayne State University Press, 1988.

Quevedo y Villegas, Francisco de. *La fortuna con seso y la hora de todos.* In *Obras completas.* Vol. 1, ed. Felicidad Buendía. Madrid: Aguilar, 1966.

——*Obras completas.* Vol. 2, ed. Felicidad Buendía. Madrid: Aguilar, 1967.

Rabb, Theodore K. *The Struggle for Stability in Early Modern Europe.* New York: Oxford University Press, 1975.

Rama, Angel. *La ciudad letrada.* Hanover, N.H.: Ediciones del Norte, 1984.

Randel, Mary Gaylord. "Proper Language and Language as Property: The Personal Poetics of Lope's *Rimas.*" *MLN* 101 (March 1986): 220–46.

Reed, Helen H. "Fortune's Monster and the Monarchy in *Las relaciones de Antonio Pérez.*" In *Autobiography in Early Modern Spain,* ed. Nicholas Spadaccini and Jenaro Talens. Minneapolis: Prisma Institute, 1988.

Richelieu, Armand Jean du Plessis, Duc de. *Testamente Politique.* Ed. Louis André. Paris: Robert Laffont, 1947.

Rivers, Elias L. "Nature, Art and Science in Spanish Poetry of the Renaissance." *Bulletin of Hispanic Studies* 44 (1967): 255–66.

Robles, Antonio de. *Diario de sucesos notables (1665–1703).* Vol. 3, ed. Antonio Castro Leal. Mexico: Porrúa, 1946.

Rose, Mary Beth, ed. *Women in the Middle Ages and the Renaissance: Literary and Historical Perspectives.* Syracuse: Syracuse University Press, 1986.

Ross, Kathleen. *The Baroque Narrative of Carlos de Sigüenza y Góngora: A New World Paradise.* New York: Cambridge University Press, 1993.

Rougement, Denis de. *Love in the Western World.* Trans. Montgomery Belgion. New York: Pantheon, [1940], 1956.

Rousset, Jean. *La Littérature de l'Age Baroque en France: Circé et le Paon.* Paris: José Corti, 1954.

Sabat-Rivers, Georgina. *El "Sueño" de Sor Juana Inés de la Cruz: Tradiciones literarias y originalidad.* London: Tamesis, 1976.

——. "El *Neptuno* de Sor Juana: Fiesta barroca y programa político." *University of Dayton Review* 16, no. 2 (spring 1983): 63–73.

——. "A Feminist Rereading of Sor Juana's *Dream.*" In *Feminist Perspectives on Sor Juana Inés de la Cruz,* ed. Stephanie Merrim. Detroit: Wayne State University Press, 1991.

——. *Estudios de Literatura Hispanoamericana: Sor Juana Inés de la Cruz y otros poetas barrocos de la colonia.* Barcelona: Promociones y Publicaciones Universitarias, 1992.

——. "Love in Some of Sor Juana's Sonnets." *Colonial Latin American Review* 4, no. 2 (1995): 101–23.

Sarasohn, Lisa T. "A Science Turned Upside Down: Feminism and the Natural Philosophy of Margaret Cavendish." *Huntington Library Quarterly* 47, no. 4 (autumn 1984): 289–307.

Sarduy, Severo. *Barroco.* Buenos Aires: Sudamericana, 1974.

Schurman, Anna Maria van. *The Learned Maid; or Whether a Maid may be a Scholar? A Logick Exercise.* Trans. Clement Barksdale. London: John Redmayne, 1659.

Schweitzer, Ivy. "Anne Bradstreet Wrestles with the Renaissance." *Early American Literature* 23, no. 3 (1988): 291–312.

——. *The Work of Self-Representation: Lyric Poetry in Colonial New England.* Chapel Hill and London: University of North Carolina Press, 1991.

Scott, Nina. "Sor Juana Inés de la Cruz: 'Let Your Women Keep Silence in the Churches . . .'" *Women's Studies International Forum* 8, no. 5 (1985): 511–19.

——. "If you are not pleased to favor me, put me out of your mind . . . ": Gender and Authority in Sor Juana Inés de la Cruz." *Women's Studies International Forum* 11, no. 5 (1988): 429–38.

——. "Ser mujer, ni estar ausente, no es de amarte impedimento": Los poemas de Sor Juana a la condesa de Paredes." In *Y diversa de mí misma entre vuestras plumas ando: Homenaje internacional a Sor Juana Inés de la Cruz,* ed. Sara Poot Herrera. Mexico: El Colegio de México, 1993.

Serrano y Sanz, Manuel. *Apuntes para una biblioteca de escritoras españolas, Primera parte.* Biblioteca de Autores Españoles. Vol. 268. Madrid: Atlas, 1975.

Serres, Michel. *Hermes: Literature, Science, Philosophy,* ed. Josué Harari and David. F. Bell. Baltimore and London: Johns Hopkins University Press, 1982.

Shea, Daniel. *Spiritual Autobiography in Early America.* Princeton: Princeton University Press, 1968.

Smith, Barbara Herrnstein. *Poetic Closure.* Chicago: University of Chicago Press, 1968.

Smith, Hilda L. *Reason's Disciples: Seventeenth-Century English Feminists.* Urbana and Chicago: University of Illinois Press, 1982.

Smith, Sidonie. *A Poetics of Woman's Autobiography: Marginality and the Fictions of Self-Representation.* Bloomington and Indianapolis: Indiana University Press, 1987.

Sonnet, Martine. "A Daughter to Educate." In *A History of Women in the West: Renaissance and Enlightenment Paradoxes,* ed. Natalie Zemon Davis and Arlette Farge. Cambridge, Mass., and London: Harvard University Press, 1993.

Soufas, Teresa Scott. *Melancholy and the Secular Mind in Spanish Golden Age Literature.* Columbia and London: University of Missouri Press, 1990.

Spacks, Patricia Meyer. "Selves in Hiding." In *Women's Autobiography: Essays in Criticism,* ed. Estelle C. Jelinek. Bloomington and London: Indiana University Press, 1980.

Stallybrass, Peter. "Patriarchal Territories: The Body Enclosed." In *Rewriting the Renaissance: The Discourses of Sexual Difference in Early Modern Europe,* ed. Margaret W. Ferguson with Maureen Quilligan and Nancy J. Vickers. Chicago and London: University of Chicago Press, 1986.

Stanford, Anne. *Anne Bradstreet: The Worldly Puritan: An Introduction to Her Poetry.* New York: Burt Franklin & Co., 1974.

——. "Anne Bradstreet: Dogmatist and Rebel." In *Critical Essays on Anne Bradstreet,* ed. Pattie Cowell and Ann Stanford. Boston: G. K. Hall, 1983.

Stanton, Domna C. "The Ideal of 'Repos' in Seventeenth-Century French Literature." *L'Esprit Créateur* 15 (1975): 79–104.

——. "Woman as Object and Subject of Exchange: Marie de Gournay's *Le Proumenoir* (1594)." *L'Esprit Créateur* 23, no. 2 (1983): 9–25.

Stepto, Michele. Introduction to *Lieutenant Nun: Memoir of a Basque Transvestite in the New World.* Trans. Michele Stepto and Gabriel Stepto. Boston: Beacon Press, 1996.

Stimpson, Catharine R. Foreword to *Rewriting the Renaissance: The Discourses of Sexual Difference in Early Modern Europe,* ed. Margaret W. Ferguson with Maureen Quilligan and Nancy J. Vickers. Chicago and London: University of Chicago Press, 1986.

Stock, Phyllis. *Better Than Rubies: A History of Women's Education.* New York: G. P. Putnam's Sons, 1978.

Stoll, Anita K., and Dawn L. Smith, eds. *The Perception of Women in Spanish Theater of the Golden Age*. Lewisburg: Bucknell University Press; London and Toronto: Associated University Presses, 1991.

Teresa de Jesús, Saint. *Camino de perfección* and *Vida de Santa Teresa de Jesús*. In *Obras completas*, ed. Luis Santullano. Madrid: M. Aguilar, 1932.

——. *The Life of Teresa of Jesus*. Trans. E. Allison Peers. New York: Image Books, 1960.

——. *Libro de las Fundaciones*. Ed. Víctor García de la Concha. Madrid: Espasa Calpe, 1982.

Terry, Arthur. "Human and Divine Love in the Poetry of Sor Juana Inés de la Cruz." In *Studies in Spanish Literature of the Golden Age Presented to Edward M. Wilson*, ed. R. O. Jones. London: Tamesis, 1973.

Timmermans, Linda. *L'accès des femmes à la culture, 1598–1715*. Paris: Honoré Champion, 1993.

Todd, Janet. *The Sign of Angelica: Women, Writing and Fiction, 1660–1800*. New York: Columbia University Press, 1989.

Todorov, Tzvetan. *Symbolisme et Interprétation*. Paris: Seuil, 1978.

Tomlinson, Sophie. "'My Brain the Stage': Margaret Cavendish and the Fantasy of Female Performance." In *Women, Texts and Histories 1575–1760*, ed. Clare Brant and Diane Purkiss. London and New York: Routledge, 1992.

Torgovnick, Marianna. *Closure in the Novel*. Princeton: Princeton University Press, 1981.

Toribio Medina, José. *Biblioteca Hispano-Chilena: 1523–1817*. Vol. 1. Amsterdam: N. Israel, [1879–99], 1965.

Treasure, G. R. R. *Seventeenth-Century France*. London: Rivingtons, 1966.

Trueblood, Alan S. *A Sor Juana Anthology*. Cambridge, Mass., and London: Harvard University Press, 1988.

Val, Joaquín del. "La novela española en el siglo XVII." In *Historia general de las literaturas hispánicas*. Vol. 3, ed. Guillermo Díaz-Plaja. Barcelona: Barna, 1953.

Vallbona, Rima de. "Vida histórica y ficción en *Vida i sucesos de la Monja Alférez*." Ph.D. diss., Middlebury College, 1981.

Vallbona, Rima de, ed. *Vida i sucesos de la Monja Alférez. Autobiografía atribuida a Doña Catalina de Erauso*. Tempe: Arizona State University Center for Latin American Studies, 1992.

Vega y Carpio, Lope Félix de. *La vengadora de las mujeres*. In *Obras escogidas*. Vol. 1, ed. Federico Carlos Sainz de Robles. Madrid: Aguilar, 1952.

——. *Arte nuevo de hacer comedias / La discreta enamorada*. 3d ed. Madrid: Espasa-Calpe, 1967.

——. *Poesía selecta*. Ed. Antonio Carreño. Madrid: Cátedra, 1984.

Vigée, Claude. "*La Princesse de Clèves* et la tradition du refus." *Critique* 159–60 (1960): 723–54.

Vigil, Mariló. *La vida de las mujeres en los siglox XVI y XVII*. Madrid: Siglo XXI, 1986.

Vives, Juan Luis. *Instrucción de la mujer cristiana*. Trans. Juan Justiniano. Madrid: Signo, 1936.

Walker, Cheryl. *The Nightingale's Burden: Women Poets and American Culture Before 1900*. Bloomington: Indiana University Press, 1982.

Warner, Marina. *Joan of Arc: The Image of Female Heroism*. New York: Knopf, 1981.

Watts, Emily Stipes. "The posy UNITY: Anne Bradstreet's Search for Order." In *Puritan Influences in American Literature*, ed. Emory Elliott. Urbana and London: University of Illinois Press, 1979.

Weber, Alison. *Teresa of Avila and the Rhetoric of Femininity.* Princeton: Princeton University Press, 1990.

Welles, Marcia. "María de Zayas y Sotomayor and Her *Novela cortesana:* A Re-evaluation." *Bulletin of Hispanic Studies* 55 (1978): 301–10.

White, Elizabeth Wade. *Anne Bradstreet: The Tenth Muse.* New York: Oxford University Press, 1971.

Wiesner, Merry. "Women's Defense of Their Public Role." In *Women in the Middle Ages and the Renaissance: Literary and Historical Perspectives,* ed. Mary Beth Rose. Syracuse: Syracuse University Press, 1986.

Williams, Raymond. *Marxism and Literature.* Oxford: Oxford University Press, 1977.

Wilson, Katharina M., and Frank J. Warnke. Introduction to *Women Writers of the Seventeenth Century.* Athens, Ga., and London: University of Georgia Press, 1989.

Woodbridge, Linda. *Women and the English Renaissance: Literature and the Nature of Womankind, 1540–1620.* Urbana and Chicago: University of Illinois Press, 1984.

Woolf, Virginia. *A Room of One's Own.* New York and Burlingame: Harcourt, Brace & World, 1957.

Zayas y Sotomayor, María de. *Novelas amorosas y ejemplares.* Ed. and prologue by Agustín G. de Amezúa y Mayo. Madrid: Aldus, 1948.

——. *Desengaños amorosos.* Ed. and prologue by Agustín G. de Amezúa y Mayo. Madrid: Aldus, 1950.

——. *Desengaños amorosos.* Ed. and introduction by Alicia Yllera. Madrid: Cátedra, 1983.

——. *The Enchantments of Love: Amorous and Exemplary Novels.* Trans. and introduction by H. Patsy Boyer. Berkeley, Los Angeles, and Oxford: University of California Press, 1990.

——. *The Disenchantments of Love.* Trans. and introduction by H. Patsy Boyer. Albany: State University of New York Press, 1997.

Index